lonely planet

KT-147-785

Los Angeles

Andrea Schulte-Peevers

David Peevers

LONELY PLANET PUBLICATIONS
Melbourne · Oakland · London · Paris

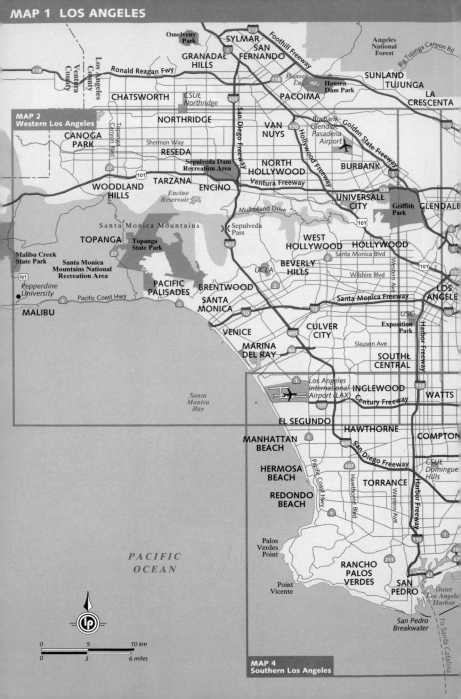

MAP 1 LOS ANGELES

Los Angeles
2nd edition – August 1999
First Published – April 1996

Published by
Lonely Planet Publications Pty Ltd A.C.N. 005 607 983
192 Burwood Rd, Hawthorn, Victoria 3122, Australia

Lonely Planet Offices
Australia PO Box 617, Hawthorn, Victoria 3122
USA 150 Linden St, Oakland, CA 94607
UK 10a Spring Place, London NW5 3BH
France 1 rue du Dahomey, 75011 Paris

Photographs
Air Combat USA, Chas W Beam (Los Angeles Public Library Photo
Collection), Jim Corwin, Lee Foster, David R Frazier, Rick Gerharter,
David Peevers, Andrea Schulte-Peevers, Nathan Trujillo, Nik Wheeler

Some of the images in this guide are available for licensing from
Lonely Planet Images.
email: lpi@lonelyplanet.com.au

Front cover photograph
'The Muralists,' 1989; mural by Richard Wyatt (Nik Wheeler)

ISBN 0 86442 551 1

text & maps © Lonely Planet 1999
photos © photographers as indicated 1999

Printed by Colorcraft Ltd, Hong Kong

All rights reserved. No part of this publication may be reproduced,
stored in a retrieval system or transmitted in any form by any means,
electronic, mechanical, photocopying, recording or otherwise, except
brief extracts for the purpose of review, without the written permission of the publisher and copyright owner.

**Although the authors
and Lonely Planet try
to make the informa-
tion as accurate as
possible, we accept
no responsibility for
any loss, injury or
inconvenience
sustained by anyone
using this book.**

Contents

2   Contents

The Authors

Andrea Schulte-Peevers

Andrea is a Los Angeles-based writer, editor and translator who owes her love for languages and travel to her mother, who began lugging her off to foreign lands when she was just a toddler. She got her high-school education in Germany, and then left for London and stints as an au-pair, market researcher and foreign-language correspondent. In the late 1980s, Andrea swapped gloomy England for Southern California and the hallowed halls of UCLA. She hit the job market armed with a degree in English literature and chartered a course in travel journalism. Assignments have taken her to all continents but Antarctica, and she's still dreaming about exploring the Himalayas. Andrea's assignments for Lonely Planet have included the *Germany*, *Berlin* and *California & Nevada* guides.

David Peevers

David holds advanced degrees in eclectic theoretics, the science that posits if anything can happen, it will – except absolutely differently. He has driven spikes on the railroad, written musicals for children, guided on whitewater rivers and sailed schooners throughout the Caribbean. David has lugged cameras up every medieval tower in Germany, been a publisher of art, and written and photographed for magazines, governments and colleges worldwide. He flies high-performance aircraft to relax and was recently surprised – while in Australia – to learn he is absolutely typical of Lonely Planet authors, whom he refers to as 'the species.' David has also contributed to Lonely Planet's *Germany*, *Berlin* and *California & Nevada* guides.

FROM THE AUTHORS

Writing a guide to a megacity like Los Angeles is like writing a book about a small country, and we couldn't have done it without the following people, all of whom we would like to thank profoundly for their help, encouragement and insight.

Carol Martinez and Stacey Litz of the LACVB for their unstinting support and good dinners, and for getting us in touch with all the right people; their colleague Marcus Bastida for opening the doors to LA's seamier sides; Jack Kyser of the LA Economic Development Council for sharing economic and culinary insights; Peter Kwong and Pedro Chan for taking us behind the scenes of Chinatown; Kathleen Spaglione of the Laguna Beach Visitors Bureau, Julien Foreman of the Catalina Island Visitors Bureau, Ann-Marie Rogers of the Santa Barbara Visitors Bureau; and Connie Baker at the Big Bear Lake Visitors Center for helping us with our research.

Special thanks to our fellow authors: Marisa Gierlich for sharing her firsthand knowledge of bars and restaurants in the South Bay; Scott McNeely for use of his research and information on Las Vegas;

and John Gottberg, who wrote the first edition of the *Los Angeles* guide.

Heaps of thanks also go to the many folks at the LP USA office, especially Eric Kettunen for his enthusiasm and insistence on making this the kind of book LA truly needs and deserves; Kate Hoffman for having an open ear and a big heart, and for sticking up for us in times of need; Suki Gear for her patience and good humor, and for making us look good on paper; Paige R Penland for sharing her knowledge of East LA and for writing the sidebars on car culture and body modifications; plus everyone else who worked hard to make this book a reality.

This Book

The first edition of *Los Angeles* was written by John Gottberg.

FROM THE PUBLISHER

In Lonely Planet's US office, this sparkly second edition of *Los Angeles* was edited by Suki Gear, with much help from Paige R Penland and guidance from senior editor Kate Hoffman. Proofreading was done by Suki, Tom Downs, Andrew Nystrom and Wade Fox. Design and layout were executed by Rini Keagy and Wendy Yanagihara, with guidance from Scott Summers and Margaret Livingston. The cover was designed by Rini, with assistance from Hugh D'Andrade. The index was created by Ken DellaPenta.

Maps were painstakingly created by Dion Good, with help from Bart Wright, Tim Lohnes, Kimra McAfee, Kimberley Moses, Guphy, Jenny King, Monica Lepe, Mary Hagemann and Tracey Croom. Alex Guilbert and Amy Dennis oversaw their efforts. Illustrations were drawn by Hayden Foell, Hugh D'Andrade, John Fadeff and Jim Swanson.

THANKS
Many thanks to the travelers who used the last edition and wrote to us with helpful hints, advice and interesting anecdotes. Your names appear in the back of this book.

Foreword

ABOUT LONELY PLANET GUIDEBOOKS

The story begins with a classic travel adventure: Tony and Maureen Wheeler's 1972 journey across Europe and Asia to Australia. Useful information about the overland trail did not exist at that time, so Tony and Maureen published the first Lonely Planet guidebook to meet a growing need.

From a kitchen table, then from a tiny office in Melbourne (Australia), Lonely Planet has become the largest independent travel publisher in the world, an international company with offices in Melbourne, Oakland (USA), London (UK) and Paris (France).

Today Lonely Planet guidebooks cover the globe. There is an ever-growing list of books, and there's information in a variety of forms and media. Some things haven't changed. The main aim is still to help make it possible for adventurous travelers to get out there – to explore and better understand the world.

At Lonely Planet we believe travelers can make a positive contribution to the countries they visit – if they respect their host communities and spend their money wisely. Since 1986 a percentage of the income from each book has been donated to aid projects and human-rights campaigns.

Updates Lonely Planet thoroughly updates each guidebook as often as possible. This usually means there are around two years between editions, although for more unusual or more stable destinations the gap can be longer. Check the imprint page (following the color map at the beginning of the book) for publication dates.

Between editions, up-to-date information is available in two free newsletters – the paper *Planet Talk* and email *Comet* (to subscribe, contact any Lonely Planet office) – and on our website at www.lonelyplanet.com. The *Upgrades* section of the website covers a number of important and volatile destinations and is regularly updated by Lonely Planet authors. *Scoop* covers news and current affairs relevant to travelers. And, lastly, the *Thorn Tree* bulletin board and *Postcards* section of the site carry unverified, but fascinating, reports from travelers.

Correspondence The process of creating new editions begins with the letters, postcards and emails received from travelers. This correspondence often includes suggestions, criticisms and comments about the current editions. Interesting excerpts are immediately passed on via newsletters and the website, and everything goes to our authors to be verified when they're researching on the road. We're keen to get more feedback from organizations or individuals who represent communities visited by travelers.

Lonely Planet gathers information for everyone who's curious about the planet – and especially for those who explore it firsthand. Through guidebooks, phrasebooks, activity guides, maps, literature, newsletters, image library, TV series and website, we act as an information exchange for a worldwide community of travelers.

Research Authors aim to gather sufficient practical information to enable travelers to make informed choices and to make the mechanics of a journey run smoothly. They also research historical and cultural background to help enrich the travel experience and allow travelers to understand and respond appropriately to cultural and environmental issues.

Authors don't stay in every hotel because that would mean spending a couple of months in each medium-size city and, no, they don't eat at every restaurant because that would mean stretching belts beyond capacity. They do visit hotels and restaurants to check standards and prices, but feedback based on readers' direct experiences can be very helpful.

Many of our authors work undercover; others aren't so secretive. None of them accept freebies in exchange for positive write ups. And none of our guidebooks contain any advertising.

Production Authors submit their raw manuscripts and maps to offices in Australia, the USA, the UK or France. Editors and cartographers – all experienced travelers themselves – then begin the process of assembling the pieces. When the book finally hits the shops, some things are already out of date, we start getting feedback from readers and the process begins again....

WARNING & REQUEST

Things change – prices go up, schedules change, good places go bad and bad places go bankrupt – nothing stays the same. So, if you find things better or worse, recently opened or long since closed, please tell us and help make the next edition even more accurate and useful. We genuinely value all the feedback we receive. Julie Young coordinates a well-traveled team that reads and acknowledges every letter, postcard and email and ensures that every morsel of information finds its way to the appropriate authors, editors and cartographers for verification.

Everyone who writes to us will find their name in the next edition of the appropriate guidebook. They will also receive the latest issue of *Planet Talk*, our quarterly printed newsletter, or *Comet*, our monthly email newsletter. Subscriptions to both newsletters are free. The very best contributions will be rewarded with a free guidebook.

Excerpts from your correspondence may appear in new editions of Lonely Planet guidebooks, the Lonely Planet website, *Planet Talk* or *Comet*, so please let us know if you *don't* want your letter published or your name acknowledged.

Send all correspondence to the Lonely Planet office closest to you:

Australia: PO Box 617, Hawthorn, Victoria 3122
USA: 150 Linden St, Oakland, CA 94607
UK: 10A Spring Place, London NW5 3BH
France: 1 rue du Dahomey, 75011 Paris

Or email us at: talk2us@lonelyplanet.com.au

For news, views and updates, see our website: www.lonelyplanet.com

HOW TO USE A LONELY PLANET GUIDEBOOK

The best way to use a Lonely Planet guidebook is any way you choose. At Lonely Planet, we believe the most memorable travel experiences are often those that are unexpected, and the finest discoveries are those you make yourself. Guidebooks are not intended to be used as if they provided a detailed set of infallible instructions!

Contents All Lonely Planet guidebooks follow the same format. The Facts about the Country chapters or sections give background information ranging from history to weather. Facts for the Visitor gives practical information on issues like visas and health. Getting There & Away gives a brief starting point for researching travel to and from the destination. Getting Around gives an overview of the transport options available when you arrive.

The peculiar demands of each destination determine how subsequent chapters are broken up, but some things remain constant. We always start with background, then proceed to sights, places to stay, places to eat, entertainment, getting there and away, and getting around information – in that order.

Heading Hierarchy Lonely Planet headings are used in a strict hierarchical structure that can be visualized as a set of Russian dolls. Each heading (and its following text) is encompassed by any preceding heading that is higher on the hierarchical ladder.

Entry Points We do not assume guidebooks will be read from beginning to end, but that people will dip into them. The traditional entry points are the list of contents and the index. In addition, however, some books have a complete list of maps and an index map illustrating map coverage.

There may also be a color map that shows highlights. These highlights are dealt with in greater detail later in the book, along with planning questions and suggested itineraries. Each chapter covering a geographical region usually begins with a locator map and another list of highlights. Once you find something of interest in a list of highlights, turn to the index.

Maps Maps play a crucial role in Lonely Planet guidebooks and include a huge amount of information. A legend is printed on the back page. We seek to have complete consistency between maps and text, and to have every important place in the text captured on a map. Map key numbers usually start in the top left corner.

> Although inclusion in a guidebook usually implies a recommendation, we cannot list every good place. Exclusion does not necessarily imply criticism. In fact, there are a number of reasons why we might exclude a place – sometimes it is simply inappropriate to encourage an influx of travelers.

Introduction

Overwhelming. Intimidating. Frightening. Or even, Where *is* it? No other city on earth is so talked about, yet so misunderstood. Los Angeles is feared for its natural disasters, dreaded for its crime and violence, disparaged for its jammed freeways and poor air quality and scorned for what some call a plastic personality. Many visitors don't even bother spending time here, preferring to quickly head off to more human-scale destinations like Santa Barbara, San Francisco and the natural wonders of the Southwest. But because you bought this book, you're obviously not one of them. Congratulations! You're about to discover one of the world's most fascinating cities.

Here's the deal: LA is not an easy place to grasp. It doesn't feel like any city you've ever known. It's vast and amorphous, with no clearly defined center. But the key to understanding – and appreciating – the place is to throw out the notion that it's a city. In fact, it's a conglomeration of 88 independent

cities, some of them with quite distinct identities (Santa Monica, Pasadena and Long Beach among them), many others merely nondescript sprawls, blending anonymously into the urban maelstrom.

LA is sometimes called the 'Big Orange' (a moniker intended to counter New York's 'Big Apple'). But we like to think of it as the 'Big Onion,' a city where you continually peel away the layers – one by one – until you arrive at your own feeling of what it's all about. There are things about LA that will make you weep. Other layers will make you feel excited about the prospects for humankind.

Best known, perhaps, is Creative LA, the epicenter of the world's movie and media industries. Then there's Global LA, a cutting-edge experiment in how the nations of the world might one day live in relative harmony. Consider Historical LA, where monuments and buildings allow us to trace the city's evolution from Native American tribal ground to Spanish mission settlement, Wild

DAVID PEEVERS

West outpost to 20th-century megalopolis. Natural LA, a place where you can surf in the morning, hike in midday and ski at night: It's no dream.

But the most important facet is perhaps Innovative LA. This is where the latest technology – from animation to satellites to medical equipment – is dreamed up. Trends are born here, ideas that swim out of LA's stream of consciousness and make their way around the world. Surfing, shopping malls, drive-through culture, step aerobics and hip-hop music all conquered the globe from here.

What makes us personally fall in love with LA again and again is its wealth of human experience, an endless menu of intriguing flavors and textures. Any time the mood strikes, we can explore a different culture, food, music – or even a historical period – simply by driving a few miles across town. We can savor authentic chow mein in Chinatown, top-notch sushi in Little Tokyo, matzo soup in the Fairfax District, California cuisine in Beverly Hills or burritos in East LA. Dancing? Do we don zoot suits and do the jitterbug or go for salsa and merengue, or perhaps just good old-fashioned rock & roll? We can see Pacific Islanders perform in their tradi-tional costumes one weekend, jam with jazz greats on Central Ave on another, or wave at celebrities participating in the Hollywood Christmas Parade. Impressionist paintings at the Getty Center, indigenous pottery at the Southwest Museum, black sculptures at the California African American Museum, Latino murals in East LA…the choices are endless. 'Boredom' does not appear in the Los Angeles lexicon.

Getting to know LA as a visitor means exploring it bit by bit, layer by layer, neighborhood by neighborhood. Don't expect to pack in a visit to the Getty Center, a beachside lunch in Santa Monica, shopping in Beverly Hills and strolling the Hollywood Walk of Fame all in one day. Sure, it can be done, but you will be exhausted and fed up. Instead, restrict your visit to certain neighborhoods that interest you. Use this book for some pretrip research, and then budget at least one full day in each area. Changing your accommodations every other day is a good idea, as it will minimize long drives.

As you peel away layer after layer, Los Angeles will reveal itself to you in all its mesmerizing and seductive complexity, offering you a rewarding and memorable experience.

Facts about Los Angeles

HISTORY

The earliest residents of the Los Angeles area were the Gabrieleño Indians and the Chumash Indians, who arrived in this desert region between 5000 and 6000 BC. The Gabrieleño, who lived inland, were hunters and gatherers whose staple food was the acorn, finely ground and made into bread or porridge. They were also fine weavers who wove root fibers into watertight baskets. The Chumash, on the coast, built 25-foot boats that carried them to offshore islands.

Rain was too scarce and inconsistent for permanent agriculture. The Gabrieleño swapped their seeds and skins to the Chumash for fish and soapstone pots. In religious matters both tribes were animistic, placing special importance in the powers of such birds as the eagle and crow, and on the porpoise, which was considered a sort of guardian spirit. Earthquakes were blamed on the restlessness of seven giants who held the world on their shoulders. Warfare was rare and horses were unknown before the Spanish arrived.

The first European known to have laid eyes upon the Los Angeles basin was Portuguese sailor Juan Rodríguez Cabrillo, who sailed the coast in 1542. He observed a brown haze over the landscape – no doubt from campfires at the Gabrieleño village of Yangna, located near modern Downtown LA. Cabrillo named Santa Monica Bay, from which he looked, Bahia de los Fumos, or 'Bay of Smokes.'

The Mission Era

The Spanish had been in Mexico for more than two centuries before they finally undertook exploring the northern wilderness they called Alta (Upper) California. In 1769, California governor Don Gaspar de Portolá and Franciscan Father Junípero Serra led an expedition from San Diego north to Monterey, looking all the while for likely sites on which to build missions so they could Christianize the heathen natives.

Father Junípero Serra

Follow-up expeditions established 21 California missions along El Camino Real, 'The King's Highway,' under the direction of Father Serra. There were two in greater Los Angeles: the Mission San Gabriel Archangel, built in 1771, and the Mission San Fernando Rey de España, founded in 1797. (Restorations can still be visited.) The Gabrieleño who gathered at these missions and built their communities around them had no previous concept of heaven or hell, but they began trading hard labor for supposed salvation. In the process, the Gabrieleño were exposed to a variety of diseases, from measles to syphilis, that decimated the tribes.

In 1781, the missions embarked on a plan to create separate agricultural communities to produce food and support their expansion. Forty-four *pobladores*, or settlers, were assigned from San Gabriel to establish a new town near the village of Yangna, on the banks of a cottonwood-lined stream about 9 miles southwest of the mission. The town they established, El Pueblo de Nuestro Señora la Reina de los Angeles del Río Porciúncula (The Town of Our Lady the Queen of the Angels of the Porciúncula River), was named after a saint whose feast day had recently been celebrated.

The racially diverse pobladores (most were mestizos of mixed Spanish, Indian and African blood) had a daunting task. Half of them were children, and their townsite lacked both a harbor and a navigable river. What's more, the Anza Trail – an overland supply route to Mexico blazed in 1774 by Juan Bautista de Anza – had been severed at the Colorado River (a few days' ride east of the pueblo) by hostile Yuma Indians. There would be no supplementary goods coming by land and only rare shipments by sea.

But Los Angeles, as the pueblo became known, grew into a thriving farming community. Taking full advantage of long sunny days and sufficient water, the settlers developed orange and olive groves, vineyards, wheatfields, and herds of cattle, sheep and horses. It was fortunate the community had achieved such self-sufficiency: during the Mexican War of Independence (1810-21) Alta California was virtually cut adrift from the mother country to the south, and Los Angeles and other pueblos were entirely on their own.

Ranchos
By the early 19th century California was already well known to the foreign merchant seamen who navigated up and down its seacoast. Until Mexican independence, foreign trade was officially banned by the Spanish, but the lure of imported luxuries in so remote a location was irresistible. *Contrabandistas* traded where and when they pleased, anchoring in secluded coves, paying bribes when necessary and thumbing their noses at the weak territorial administration.

Initially sea otters were the primary draw; a single adult pelt earned $300 worth of tea, silks, spices and ceramics in China. New England whalers also worked this coast, harvesting the great mammals as they migrated north from Baja California. But cattle provided the primary products. Tallow (for soap and candles) and hides (for shoes) were exported to the East Coast of the USA in exchange for such manufactured goods as cloth, footwear, tools and cutlery.

Upon Mexican independence in 1821, many of that new nation's citizens looked to California to satisfy their thirst for private land. By the mid-1830s, the missions had been secularized, with a series of governors doling out hundreds of free land grants. This process gave birth to the rancho system. The *rancheros*, as the new landowners were called, prospered and quickly became the social, cultural and political fulcrums of California. Their lands, which averaged 16,000 acres in size, were largely given over to livestock to supply the hide-and-tallow trade.

Enterprising *Californios* often sold 75,000 or more hides a year, for an average price of $2 apiece. Although some made fortunes – they paid no taxes and footed no public-works projects – California rancheros were largely illiterate and lived in nonpermanent dwellings. They had no schools and their homes generally lacked wooden floors, windows or running water.

Immigrants from the USA became the merchant class. Joseph Chapman, a blond Boston millwright-cum-pirate, became the first Yankee, or *Yanqui*, Angeleno in 1818; he was known as El Inglés or 'The Englishman.' Others followed slowly; by the mid-1830s there were still only 29 US citizens residing in Los Angeles. But these few bought entire shiploads of imported goods from seafarers, and in exchange delivered full cargoes of 40,000 hides. In setting up a system of credit for rancheros, they established California's first banking system.

An overland route to the States was established by the colorful and well-traveled fur trapper Jedediah Smith, who arrived at the San Gabriel mission from across the Sierra Nevada in 1826. Kit Carson, a legend of the American West, helped forge the Santa Fé Trail to Los Angeles in 1832. But most Easterners didn't know much about California until 1840, when the publication of Richard Henry Dana's *Two Years Before the Mast* gave an account of his mid-1830s experience in the coastal hide-and-tallow trade. 'In the hands of an enterprising people, what a country this might be,' Dana wrote of Los Angeles, which had a population of just over 1200.

As a River, It's a Washout

All rivers have a history and find their destiny in the sea. But few have had to suffer the ignominious fate of the 58-mile-long Los Angeles River. The lush appearance of this limpid, tree-lined stream in 1829 caused the great fur trader Kit Carson to pronounce the Los Angeles area 'truly a paradise on earth.' For more than 3000 years – until the Spanish set up a pueblo near what is now Downtown LA – the wetlands formed by the river were the exclusive domain of the Shoshone Indians.

What the Indians could have told the Spanish – if they'd been asked – was that this river had an unpredictable and even freakish nature. Throughout the city's infancy, the river made itself repeatedly felt and feared. Whenever the rains came to the local mountains, the river jumped its banks, flooding fields and homes. And in the fierce winter of 1824-25, it actually changed course altogether, heading south and emptying into the sea at San Pedro instead of Santa Monica Bay.

In 1914 rains swelled the river to the point where its flow equaled that of the mighty Colorado River. Heavy flooding and more course changes continued until 1934, when the entire LA County area was deluged by four days of torrential rains, resulting in millions of dollars of damage and the loss of 113 lives. LA declared war on the river and called in the Army Corps of Engineers.

In 1938 the Corps canalized the river; 10,000 workers applied 3 million barrels of concrete by hand, resulting in what you see today. The vegetation of the river survives only along short stretches of remaining natural riverbed, which accounts for only 17% of its entire length. The rest of the riverbed is a concrete sluiceway – the brunt of many cruel jokes and the sight of epic Schwarzenegger truck crashes – that leads the river to its current outlet in Long Beach.

Still, in winter months when the rains come, Angelenos eye the only real river they've got a little nervously, and perhaps wistfully ponder how yet another Los Angeles landmark came to an inglorious concrete ending.

Bear Flag Republic & Statehood

While the average American wasn't well acquainted with California until the 1840s, the federal government had shown interest in this new land since the early '30s. Impressed by its potential wealth, and imbued with the doctrine of Manifest Destiny to extend the US border from coast to coast, President Andrew Jackson sent an emissary to offer the financially strapped Mexican government $500,000 for California. Though American settlers were by then showing up by the hundreds, especially in Northern California, Jackson's emissary was tersely rejected. A political stew was brewing.

In 1836, Texas seceded from Mexico and declared itself an independent republic.

When the US in turn annexed Texas in 1845, Mexico broke off diplomatic relations and ordered all foreigners without proper papers deported from California. Outraged Northern California settlers revolted, captured the nearest Mexican official and, supported by a company of US soldiers led by Captain John C Frémont, declared California's independence in June 1846 by raising their 'Bear Flag' over the town of Sonoma.

The Bear Flag Republic existed for all of one month. (The banner lives on, however, as the California state flag.) War had broken out in Texas in May after Mexican and US patrols clashed over disputed territory. That gave the US all the justification it needed to invade Mexico. By July, US naval units occupied every port on the California coast, including the capital, Monterey. On August 13, troops led by Frémont and Commodore Robert F Stockton overtook Los Angeles without a shot being fired. Final opposition was squelched the following January after a skirmish at Paso de Bartolo on the San Gabriel River.

US troops captured Mexico City in September 1847, putting an end to the war. As a part of the 1848 Treaty of Guadalupe Hidalgo, the US paid $15 million for all Mexican territories west of the Rio Grande and north of the Gila River (in Arizona), including California.

Only two years later, California was admitted as the 31st of the United States. The primary reason behind this accelerated recognition was gold, which suddenly appeared in quantity enough to provide full monetary support for US coinage.

Small quantities of the precious metal were first unearthed near the San Fernando mission in 1842. Digging some wild onions, Mexican rancher Francisco López was astounded to find a sparkling nugget snarled in the roots. About 3000 ounces, worth about $53,000, was recovered before the deposits were gone late the following year.

That discovery was nothing compared to what happened in Northern California a few years later. James Marshall's discovery on the American River in January 1848 led to the greatest gold rush the world has seen before or since. The sudden onslaught of tens of thousands of argonauts in the north (80,000 in 1849 alone) had an undeniable impact on LA as well. Southern California's rancheros were called upon to feed the miners, and they quickly discovered that the new wealth of the mining camps could earn them 10 times the money they were getting from the hide-and-tallow traders. In no time, the landowners were richer than the miners themselves.

With California statehood, Los Angeles was incorporated (on April 4, 1850) and made the seat of broad Los Angeles County. It was an unruly city of dirt streets and adobe homes, of saloons, brothels and gambling houses that thrived on the fast buck. But by 1854, Northern California's gold rush had peaked and the state was thrust into a depression. While unemployed miners swarmed to LA and other cities, banks and businesses that had harnessed their futures to miners' fortunes closed their doors.

Making matters worse for the rancheros was the land commission sent west by Congress in 1851. Everyone who had received a land grant two decades earlier was now forced to prove its legitimacy with documents and witnesses. By 1857 some 800 cases had been reviewed by tribunal, 500 in favor of the original, pre-rancho landowners. Many ranchos now passed into the hands of the US government. Landowners that endured the tribunal were again tested by declining cattle prices and a brutal three-year drought (1862-65). Many Californios were bankrupted, their ranchos mortgaged, subdivided, fenced and planted by the new Angelenos.

Hatred of Anglo domination spread quickly through the Latino community, provoked in part by an 1855 state edict, known as the 'Greaser Law,' which levied a $20-per-month tax on foreign nationals. Many of the newly poor Mexicans resorted to highway robbery, both of Wells, Fargo & Co stagecoaches (holdups averaged twice a month for 14 years) and – beginning in the 1870s – railroads.

From Small Town to Big City

When the first transcontinental railroad, the Central Pacific (later renamed the Southern Pacific), was completed in 1869, San Francisco was far and away California's metropolitan center. Los Angeles' parched climate, its distance from both fresh water and mining resources, and its vulnerability to major earthquakes left it much smaller than such central coast towns as Santa Barbara and San Luis Obispo. LA's isolation made it unattractive to the San Francisco power brokers who owned the Central Pacific. But a bit of wheeling and dealing brought a spur line to LA in 1876, via the San Joaquin Valley. In 1885, the Atchison, Topeka & Santa Fe Railroad directly linked Los Angeles across the Arizona desert to the East Coast.

The orange industry helped lure people to Southern California with images such as this, from Bradford Bros, Inc.

Coincidental with the arrival of the railroad was the establishment of an orange-growing industry in Southern California. Around 1874, three Brazilian navel (seedless) orange trees were shipped from the federal Department of Agriculture to Eliza and Luther Tibbetts, botanists in Riverside, a town east of Los Angeles. So successful were these trees, which produce their fruit in winter, that a second crop of summer-produced Valencia oranges was established in what is now Orange County. By 1889 more than 13,000 acres in six counties were planted with orange trees, dramatically improving the previously woebegone local economy.

Unlike many fruits, oranges easily survive long-distance rail shipping. As California oranges found their way onto New York grocery shelves, coupled with a hard-sell chamber of commerce advertising campaign, Easterners heeded the advice of crusading magazine and newspaper editor Horace Greeley to 'Go West, young man.'

Los Angeles' population jumped from 2300 in 1860 to 11,000 in 1880, and to more than 50,000 in 1890. It reached 100,000 in 1900.

Never mind that there was no natural harbor, or that the supply of fresh water was inadequate to support even a small town. Sharp minds and willing spirits would overcome these obstacles. The first of these needs was addressed by the construction of a harbor at San Pedro, 23 miles south of City Hall. Work began in 1899 and the first wharf opened in 1914, the year the Panama Canal was completed. Suddenly 8000 miles closer to the Atlantic seaboard by virtue of this new passageway, San Pedro became the busiest harbor on the West Coast.

But bringing drinkable water to the growing city required a much more complex solution. The sporadic flow of the Los Angeles River (as the Río Porciúncula was now known) may have been adequate for the original pueblo, but even when supplemented by scattered artesian wells, the local water supply wasn't nearly sufficient.

Stretching the City's Limits

The enormity and the seemingly illogical shape of the City of Los Angeles is in large part a result of the city's quest for water.

The San Fernando Valley was annexed shortly after the turn of the 20th century, just as William Mulholland was proposing plans for diverting Owens River water over 250 miles of desert to Southern California. Mulholland's choice site for storing the water was the Valley. He knew that engulfing such a large territory would broaden the city's tax base, which was needed to help pay for the costly building of the aqueduct.

Other towns were incorporated for more or less the same reason: LA wasn't about to share its hard-earned water without getting anything in return. In many cases, nearby towns were faced with an ultimatum: they could succumb to the growth of Los Angeles or die of thirst.

In 1904, city water bureau superintendent William Mulholland visited the Owens Valley, on the southeastern slopes of the Sierra Nevada (233 miles northeast of LA) and returned with a startling plan. Voters gave him the $24.5 million he needed to build an aqueduct that would carry melted snow from the mountains to the city, and by November 1913, Owens River water was spilling into the San Fernando Valley. Its flow has been increased from 26 million gallons daily when it opened to 525 million gallons. The system remains controversial, especially to Owens Valley ranchers and to environmentalists, but it supplies more than 75% of the city's water. Most of the rest, as well as Southern California's electricity, comes from dams on the Colorado River, 300 miles east.

Zoom to the Present

LA's population soared to 1 million by 1920, 2 million by 1930. The discovery of oil was largely responsible for that exponential growth. Though the presence of bubbling tar had much earlier called attention to an abundance of crude oil, it wasn't until 1892, when Edward Doheny drilled a well near Downtown LA, that a sophisticated and highly profitable regional oil industry took off. Local refineries were constructed and storage methods were developed. Meanwhile, the introduction of the automobile generated a growing need for fuel; enormous profits awaited those who could pump their oil fast enough. New strikes were still being made at Santa Fe Springs and Signal Hill in the early 1920s. The demand for exporting much of that oil also caused a boom in shipping and related harbor industries.

During WWI, the Lockheed brothers and Donald Douglas – making note of Los Angeles' ideal test-flight weather and its capacity to house large work forces – established aircraft manufacturing plants in the area. Two decades later, with another world war brewing, the aviation industry employed enough people to help lift LA out of the Great Depression. By the end of WWII, billions of federal dollars had been poured into Southern California military contracts, and thousands of families had moved to the region to work at the plants. Through the Cold War years, increased dependence on federal spending led some critics to call Los Angeles a 'Federal City.'

A new real estate boom, capitalizing on the influx of aviation employees, brought about whole new suburbs south of Los Angeles. Lakewood, just north of Long Beach, is the classic example: the entire city was developed almost overnight to house employees of McDonnell-Douglas. It is said that in a single hour of one day in 1946, 107 new tract houses were sold there.

During the war and the years immediately following, the railroads drew thousands of black maintenance workers from Texas and Louisiana to Los Angeles. Still more arrived when it became apparent that a vibrant black community was developing in South Central LA. What had been just a small colony before the war grew into one of the nation's great black cultural centers by 1950.

But it is the film industry that has symbolized 20th-century Los Angeles. In modern

LA, it's known simply as 'The Industry.' Independent producers were attracted here beginning in 1908 for numerous reasons. Southern California's sunny climate allowed indoor scenes to be shot outdoors – an essential given the unsophisticated photo technology of the day. Any location, from ocean to desert to alpine forest, could be realized nearby. What's more, the proximity of the Mexican border enabled filmmakers to rush their equipment to safety when challenged by the collection agents of patent holders like Thomas Edison.

Studios were constructed in Culver City and Universal City, but the capital of filmdom was the LA suburb of Hollywood. Soon moviegoers were succumbing to the romance of Southern California as portrayed in silent films. Organ music accompanied one-reel comedies and westerns that made stars of Charlie Chaplin and Tom Mix. And directors like DW Griffith and Cecil B De Mille became luminaries in their own right. 'Talkies' soon eclipsed the silent films, and color cinematography made the movies seem even more real. In addition, fashion fads flowed from popular movies, soon shaping styles around the world.

Ever since studios first found their home in Los Angeles, the city has raced to live up to the hype created by the film industry. That vision helped attract two new breeds of immigrant: the eccentric artisan – from writers and musicians to painters and architects – and the fashionable hedonist, those drawn by the broad sandy beaches and the temptations of Hollywood.

But all the while, trouble was brewing in the city. Policy-makers had turned a blind eye to growing ethnic friction for decades, including a week-long spell of urban warfare between Anglo sailors and Latino teenagers in 1943, known as the Zoot Suit Riots. In the 1960s, South Central LA was faced with increasing tension as the quality of life there continued to decline. The unrest came to a boil in August 1965 in one of the nation's worst race riots: The primarily black neighborhood of Watts exploded with six days of burning and looting. Thirty-four people died in the riots, and more than a thousand were wounded.

South Central Los Angeles, populated mainly by blacks and Latinos, saw subsequent riots in 1979 and 1992. The latter, a direct result of the notorious Rodney King

The WWII Battle of LA

Los Angeles old-timers can tell you that less than three months after the Japanese attack on Pearl Harbor, a mysterious battle took place in the skies over Los Angeles.

On February 23, 1942, a Japanese submarine surfaced near Santa Barbara and shot several rounds into a beachside oil field. The entire West Coast tensed up in anticipation of further attacks. They didn't have to wait long.

Just two nights later, at 7 pm, warning came of a possible attack. By midnight, radar screens picked up an unidentified flying object approaching Los Angeles. Three hours later, an object resembling a balloon of some sort was sighted over Santa Monica. Antiaircraft guns opened fire. Tracers lit up the sky. Reportedly some 1400 rounds were fired skyward, but no bombs fell in retaliation. Whoever – whatever – it was that 'attacked' Los Angeles that night disappeared into thin air. At the war's end, Japanese military spokesmen denied having had anything to do with it.

Oddly, the submarine attack that precipitated this paranoia may not have had any military purpose. Legend has it that the submarine's commander, Kozo Nishino, had sworn revenge on the oil field 10 years earlier when his oil tanker visited Southern California. Apparently he accidentally sat on a prickly pear cactus and some locals rudely laughed at him.

beating and trial, cost 51 lives and $1 billion in property damage. Oddly, much of the violence in 1992 was directed at Korean shopkeepers in fringe neighborhoods and in Koreatown, perhaps reflecting resentment over the apparent ease with which these newcomers had established successful businesses in poor black neighborhoods.

Certainly the riots were a consequence of pent-up frustrations over unequal opportunities in jobs, education, housing and welfare as well as questionable treatment by the Los Angeles Police Department and court system. But in reality, much of the damage done was also perpetrated by greedy looters who saw the unrest as an ideal time to go 'shopping' for free televisions and appliances. (Television footage of these events bears out this truth.) Strangely, the city's police force – normally efficient – was seen almost nowhere. (For more on the riots, see The Los Angeles Riots: 1992 & 1965 in Things to See & Do.)

Whether LA can ever attain racial harmony depends largely on whether the city can integrate its diverse social and ethnic communities. The rich walled enclaves of Beverly Hills are a world apart from the poverty of South Central and East Los Angeles. More than 80 different languages and dialects are spoken in the homes of the city's schoolchildren. In a more perfect world, modern Los Angeles would certainly be a polyglot melting pot. As it exists now, it's more a carbolic stew of racial and class resentments.

A strand of hope lies in the city's unified response to natural disasters. Major earthquakes in the San Fernando Valley in 1971 and 1994 were devastating indeed, but they brought out the best in Angelenos: looting was at a minimum, goodwill at a maximum. The same heartfelt response is often the result when fires, floods and mudslides periodically ravage the area.

GEOGRAPHY & GEOLOGY

Los Angeles County encompasses geographical extremes from subtropical desert and 74 miles of seacoast to a pair of offshore islands and at least one peak above 10,000 feet. But the most notable aspect of LA's geography is that it straddles one of the world's major earthquake fault zones. The great San Andreas Fault runs northwest to southeast within 33 miles of Downtown LA at its nearest point. More than three dozen lesser faults also crisscross the metropolitan area like tremulous cracks on an eggshell.

Since the mid-1850s, when a pair of massive quakes (estimated at more than 7.0 on the Richter scale) shattered the young town, no tremors of equal strength have struck Los Angeles itself. But the city lives in fear and awe of Mother Nature's power. Earthquakes rated above 6.0 have wreaked death and destruction in LA five times this century – with epicenters near Long Beach in 1933, in the San Fernando Valley in 1971 (Sylmar) and 1994 (Northridge), and two in 1992 in the Big Bear region. Angelenos live in fearful knowledge that 'The Big One' may strike any moment.

CLIMATE

One of LA's greatest assets is its temperate Mediterranean climate, a prime reason why so many people are drawn here. Most of the county is protected from extremes of temperature and humidity by the mountain ranges to its north and east. August and September are the hottest months, January and February the coolest and wettest.

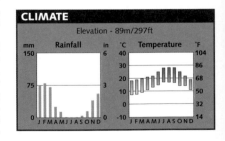

Temperatures

The highest temperature ever recorded was 110°F in 1955 and the lowest was 27.9°F in 1949. The average Los Angeles temperature, though, is around 70°F (21°C), with summer highs usually in the mid 80s to low 90s and winter lows typically in the mid 50s to low 60s.

How high the mercury climbs depends very much on location, with temperatures rising the farther you get away from the ocean. Offshore breezes keep beach communities 10°F to 15°F cooler than areas farther inland or in the San Fernando Valley, which is the hottest area during summer. Coastal fog also contributes to the cooling effect, though it usually burns off by noon. Evenings tend to be cool throughout the city, even at the peak of summer. In fall and winter especially, daily temperature variations can be extreme; temperature drops from daytime highs of 100°F to nighttime lows of 50°F are not uncommon.

Elevation is another climate-determining factor. Most winters, the thermometer falls far enough below freezing to support ski resorts in the San Gabriel Mountains, often without the use of artificial snowmaking equipment. Driving into the mountains in those months may mean leaving the valley floor in a T-shirt and putting on snow chains an hour later.

Sunshine

Those who keep track of such things say downtown Los Angeles gets 186 days of sunshine a year; the beaches get 137. Morning fog and clouds are typical along the coast, especially in summer. They normally burn off by late morning, giving the rest of the day over to sunny skies.

Rainfall

LA's average annual rainfall is 14.68 inches, which falls almost exclusively between November and April. While not the rule, periods of heavy rain sometimes occur in January and February.

Winds

Because of LA's hot, dry summers, winds are feared primarily for the fire danger they create. From August to November, the Santa Ana winds occasionally rush into Los Angeles from the high desert to the east, racing down canyons (where they are heated by compression) as fast as 70 mph. The Santa Anas are usually accompanied by clear skies and warm weather – and perhaps something more intangible in the air. Raymond

Chandler wrote that Santa Anas were a time when 'meek little wives feel the edge of the carving knife and study their husbands' necks.'

The chaparral-covered slopes of the Santa Monica and San Gabriel Mountains and the Laguna Hills are susceptible to wildfires at these times. In 1993, more than a thousand homes in Malibu, Laguna Beach and Altadena (near Pasadena) were destroyed and 240 sq miles of private and national forest land burned by brush fires. Complicating matters are the winter rains, which guarantee severe mudslides on slopes that have been denuded by summer fires.

ECOLOGY & ENVIRONMENT
Smog

For decades, one of LA's biggest environmental problems has been smog, a composite term of 'smoke' and 'fog.' In 1996, federal air pollution standards were exceeded on 115 days at one or more locations in the LA County area, most commonly in the eastern San Gabriel Valley. In general, the air is cleanest in the coastal area, where offshore breezes provide some relief.

Auto exhaust and industrial emissions are the chief culprits in generating such pollutants as carbon monoxide, nitrogen oxides, and particulate matter (PM). The greatest health hazard though – especially for people with respiratory problems – is the invisible gas ozone, which forms when sunshine causes nitrogen oxides and organic gases to react. The concentration of pollutants varies

A typical summer day in LA

throughout the year as weather conditions shift. While carbon monoxide and PM levels are highest in fall and winter, ozone levels reach their peak during sun-intensive summer days. Summer also brings the greatest number of inversion days, when a warm air layer traps the noxious fumes.

Cars and factories were first identified as the main sources of air pollution in the late 1940s, which was also when the first air quality regulatory body formed. Since the mid-1970s, the South Coast Air Quality Management District (SCAQMD) has been in charge of regulating emissions from cars and factories and enforcing federal, state and local air pollution laws. A far-reaching clean-up plan, adopted in 1989, has already produced tangible improvements: while there were 120 Stage 1 pollution alerts in 1979, the number dropped to just seven incidents in 1996. Despite such remarkable progress, LA's air quality still leaves much to be desired. The SCAQMD has a toll-free, taped information service with hourly updates of air pollution levels in the LA area (☎ 800-242-4022). If you want to speak with a person, call ☎ 800-242-4666.

Water

Supply The aqueduct built by William Mulholland and Fred Eaton in 1908 – together with a newer one completed in 1970 – still delivers 75% of LA's water supply today (also see the boxed text Water for LA). A further 10% is being coaxed from the Colorado River and brought here via a third 300-mile aqueduct. Only the remaining 15% comes from natural local aquifers, which are replenishable underground beds that store rain and runoff. The largest such catchment is the San Fernando Valley Groundwater Basin, which holds the equivalent of a two-year water supply for a million people.

Most of the used water eventually ends up in Santa Monica Bay, usually after treatment in sewage plants. Only water headed for the ocean via storm drains is not treated at all, which makes swimming in the bay after major rains a health hazard. About 100 million gallons a day are reclaimed at two major plants and used for landscaping, maintaining local golf courses and cooling power plants.

From 1987 to 1993, California experienced one of its worst droughts in history, with precipitation ranging between 61% and 90% below normal. As a result, the state has made revolutionary progress in cutting back on water use. Water suppliers signed a conservation agreement with environmental groups, requiring water utilities to adopt 16 'best management practices' for conservation, including offering rebates on low-flush toilets and providing free water audits to those who implement the practices with the most force. Furthermore, the Department of Water Resources set up a water bank that bought surplus water and sold it to those with shortages.

Quality It's always safe to drink water from the tap or from public fountains, though most people seem to prefer the taste and quality of bottled or filtered water.

The ocean water quality of Santa Monica Bay has seen dramatic improvement, making swimming and surfing at most beaches much safer today than a mere decade ago. Thanks to efforts led in part by the Santa Monica-based advocacy group Heal the Bay, tougher laws and regulations are now in force. For example, the extension of the discharge pipe of the Chevron plant in El Segundo, the diversion of dry-weather runoff from storm drains, and a reduction of sludge discharge all have contributed to healthier conditions.

Heal the Bay issues a monthly Beach Report Card, which evaluates ocean water quality based on a grading system from A+ to F. The report is available by calling Heal the Bay at ☎ 800-432-5229 or by visiting its website at www.healthebay.org/healthebay.

GOVERNMENT & POLITICS

The city of Los Angeles is governed by a mayor (the executive branch) and a 15-member city council (the legislative branch), each of whom is elected by the people for a four-year term. Other elective offices are those of the controller and of the city attorney. On July 1, 1993, Republican Richard

Water for LA

The growth of semi-arid Los Angeles into a megalopolis is inextricably linked to water. When the city's population surged to 200,000 people in the early 20th century, ground-water levels were insufficient to meet the city's needs, let alone sustain further growth. It was apparent that water had to be imported. Fred Eaton, a former LA mayor, and William Mulholland, the city water bureau superintendent, knew just how and where to get it: by aqueduct from the Owens River Valley,

at the foot of the Eastern Sierras, some 250 miles northeast.

The fact that Owens Valley itself was settled by farmers who needed the water for irrigation purposes didn't bother either the men or the federal government, which actively supported the city in acquiring land and securing water rights in the valley area.

Work on Mulholland's aqueduct began in 1908. An amazing feat of engineering – crossing barren desert floor as well as rugged mountain terrain for 233 miles – it opened to great fanfare on November 5, 1913. An extension to the Mono Basin in 1940 lengthened the aqueduct by 105 miles. The Owens Valley, though, would never be the same. With most of Owens Lake drained, the once-fertile valley became barren, causing farms to close and businesses to go bust. A bitter feud between valley residents and the city ensued; some foes even used dynamite to sabotage the aqueduct. Formal arbitration in 1929 ended with LA making a few concessions. It's against the backdrop of these 'water wars' that Roman Polanski's Academy Award-winning *Chinatown* is set.

To this day, LA's Department of Water and Power owns 307,000 acres in the Inyo and Mono Counties, and resentment towards the thirsty giant to the south persists.

Riordan – a lawyer, entrepreneur and self-made millionaire – succeeded five-term mayor Tom Bradley, a Democrat. Riordan was reelected in 1997. One of the mayor's chief responsibilities is creating an annual budget, which is then submitted for approval by the city council. The mayor also approves or vetoes ordinances, appoints city officials and commissioners and plays host to foreign and domestic dignitaries.

The city council keeps itself busy enacting ordinances, levying taxes, authorizing public improvements, ordering elections and adopting traffic regulations, among other responsibilities. Public council meetings take place Tuesday, Wednesday and Friday at 10 am in the Council Chamber of City Hall. Currently, the council reflects the rainbow of diversity that is characteristic of LA and includes black, Latino, Asian, white and gay members. Day-to-day administrative duties are distributed among 36 departments and bureaus, including the Department of Water and Power and the Housing Authority, which are controlled by boards appointed by the mayor.

LA County, comprising 88 independent cities including Los Angeles, is governed by the Board of Supervisors. Also elected to four-year terms, its five members have vast executive and legislative powers over LA County. This process results in a jurisdictional nightmare of some 700 separate government units, including various police and fire departments, which all compete for tax revenues.

ECONOMY

Los Angeles did not get off to a good start in the 1990s, as it was plagued by high unemployment, an eroding tax base, draconian spending cuts and budget problems.

One factor precipitating the crisis was a sharp drop in federal spending on defense, previously one of LA's main industries, following the end of the Cold War. Sharp federal spending cuts beginning in the late 1980s resulted in a loss of more than 180,000 jobs between 1988 and 1995. Further losses came from a veritable exodus of companies tired of dealing with an impermeable fabric of red tape, strict environmental laws and high taxes. Many resettled in business-friendlier pastures in Arizona and states farther east. And it certainly didn't help that one plight after another descended on the city: drought, riots, floods, earthquakes, fires. What next, everyone wondered? Godzilla?

Major economic restructuring, coupled with the end of the recession, finally resulted in a tangible rebound for LA in recent years. An interesting statistic comparing the gross product ranking of LA County and California with that of major nations places California at number seven, just ahead of China and Brazil; LA County comes in 21st position, still ahead of Sweden and Austria. However, unemployment figures, stubbornly remaining at around 7.5% and far above national average, reflect that LA hasn't yet hit full stride.

LA enjoys a relatively diversified economic base. Here, as in most industrialized nations, the service industry is by far the largest sector, providing about 32% of all jobs (most of them in the business and professional management fields). Manufacturing takes second place with 17% or 646,000 workers, lagging slightly behind the Chicago metropolitan area. In third position is retail, which tallies in at 15%, with the remainder split among smaller sectors such as transportation, communication, public utilities, finance, insurance and real estate.

Another reliable source of income is, not surprisingly, the tourism industry. In 1996, more than 23 million overnight visitors infused about $10.5 billion into the local economy and provided employment for 253,000 people.

Another sector flourishing dramatically is the motion picture industry, largely because of increased demand in the US and abroad as well as new and enhanced technologies. Between 1990 and 1996, employment in the film industry skyrocketed from 143,300 to 224,300, and 'The Industry' generated more than $26 billion in revenue. And the future continues to be bright for the film industry, with demand expected to grow a further 7% by 2001.

Most businesses in LA are small to medium in size (1 to 99 employees). Almost 98% of the 350,000 businesses fall into this category, while only 309 companies count more than 1000 employees. The top three regional employers are Boeing (28,000), Bank of America (26,500) and Hughes Electronics (26,000). Walt Disney employs 18,000 people.

POPULATION & PEOPLE

There's much confusion about how many people live in LA, largely because there's confusion about what constitutes LA in the first place. The largest unit, and the one most frequently cited by economists, is the so-called LA Five-County area. Counting 15.8 million inhabitants, it comprises the counties of Los Angeles, Orange, San Bernardino, Riverside and Ventura, which themselves are divided into 178 separate cities.

The most useful figure, though, is the one applied to LA County, which consists of 88 incorporated cities, including Santa Monica, Beverly Hills and West Hollywood. The smallest city is Vernon with just 80 inhabitants, while the largest is the city of Los Angeles proper, home to 3.68 million people. The total population of LA County is 9.4 million. For all intents and purposes, we use LA County figures in this book, unless mentioned otherwise.

A common misconception is that the LA population decreased following a series of natural disasters in the early 1990s. While it is true that thousands of people left the area, a far larger number elected to migrate *to* LA, accounting for a net gain of nearly half a million people between 1990 and 1996.

The ethnic makeup of LA County is considerably diverse, with Latinos accounting for 4 million (42%), whites for 3.29 million (35%), Asians and Pacific Islanders for 1.13 million (12%), blacks for 963,000 (10%) and Native Americans for 27,300 (less than 1%). LA's ethnic composition is changing rapidly, with Latinos as the fastest-growing group (up by 4% since 1990); the sharpest drop is in the population of whites (down by 6% since 1990). In fact, nearly half of the Spanish-speaking population of California lives in LA County, especially in East Los Angeles and surrounding communities. Blacks predominate in South Central, mainly south of the Santa Monica (10) Fwy between the 405 and 110 Fwys to Long Beach.

LA children celebrate their heritage.

DAVID PEEVERS

Traditional Asian communities – Chinatown and Little Tokyo – can be found just a few blocks north and east of City Hall, respectively. Farther east of Downtown, Monterey Park has become a largely Chinese enclave, while an area near the border with Orange County has been designated 'Little Saigon' for its concentration of Vietnamese residents. The recent influx of Koreans is most visible around Vermont Ave and Olympic Blvd, where several blocks of strip malls house Korean businesses. Long Beach is the home of approximately 40,000 Cambodians, the largest Cambodian community in the USA.

ARTS

No city in America can claim the artistic versatility that Los Angeles has. And since the beginning of the 20th century, no other city can claim the cultural influence – both high and low – that LA exerts worldwide.

Film

Los Angeles culture is unique in that the city's primary artform, film, is also a major export. It's a medium with a powerful presence in the lives of not only Americans, but of people throughout the world. Consequently, images of Los Angeles are distributed far beyond the city's limits, ultimately reflecting back on the city itself. Few people can come to Los Angeles without some cinematic reference to the place, and many who have settled here make every effort to live up to the hype.

The movie industry is hardly unaware of the relationship between cinema and the city of Los Angeles. With ever-increasing regularity, films feature the city not only as a setting but as a topic – and in some cases, almost as a character.

Drama Perhaps the greatest film about Los Angeles is *Chinatown* (1974). Directed by Roman Polanski and starring Jack Nicholson and Faye Dunaway, this is the story of LA's early-20th-century water wars. Robert Towne's brilliant screenplay deftly deals with the shrewd deceptions that helped make Los Angeles what it is today.

Blade Runner (1982) is a sci-fi thriller directed by Ridley Scott and starring Harrison Ford, Rutger Hauer and Sean Young. The film projects modern Los Angeles far into the 21st century, with newer buildings reaching farther into the sky – icy fortresses contrasting starkly with chaotic, neglected streets. A multilingual pidgin (including Spanish and Japanese) is quite convincingly the street language, and LA's water problems are ironically solved by a moist, greenhouse-effect climate.

John Singleton's *Boyz 'N the Hood* (1991), starring Cuba Gooding, Jr, offers a major reality check: maybe this is what it's really like to come of age as a black teen in today's inner city. Meanwhile, Lawrence Kasdan's *Grand Canyon* (1991), starring Danny Glover and Kevin Kline, presents a glimmer of hope as black and white families cope with the sobering realities of racial tensions in modern LA. *Falling Down* (1992) offers a much more cynical treatment of racial issues in Los Angeles. It stars Michael Douglas as a frustrated white man who goes on an angry rampage through the city's ethnic neighborhoods.

Robert Altman's *Short Cuts* (1993) poignantly weaves together several stories by Raymond Carver to show a sadly depraved Los Angeles. Populated by characters of all walks of life, played by the likes of Lily Tomlin, Andie MacDowell, Tim Robbins and Robert Downey, Jr, this film leaves no aspect of LA culture unexamined.

Hollywood on Hollywood The film industry itself is a popular subject in the movies. Stories about regular people who come to Hollywood and struggle to make it big are especially popular. *A Star is Born*, first made in 1937 by director David O Selznick, stars Janet Gaynor as a woman who rises to stardom at the same time her movie-star husband (Fredric March) declines in popularity. Obviously, this story has a timeless appeal: it was remade in '54 with Judy Garland, and again in 1976 with Barbra Streisand.

The '50s produced a pair of major critiques of The Industry. Billy Wilder's *Sunset Boulevard* (1950), starring Gloria Swanson and William Holden, is a fascinating study of the way in which Hollywood discards its aging stars. The Paramount lot and Schwab's Drugstore (no longer there) are two of its many local settings. Vincent Minelli's *The Bad and the Beautiful* (1952) takes a good, hard look at the filmmaking business, with Lana Turner recalling the exploits of an aggressive, egotistic film producer, played by Kirk Douglas.

A much more contemporary comment on Hollywood is Robert Altman's *The Player*, released in 1992. Starring Tim Robbins and Fred Ward, this is a classic satire on the movie-making machinery, featuring dozens of cameos by the very actors and actresses being spoofed.

Crime With so many hardboiled detective novels coming out of Los Angeles, it's only natural that a distinct style of film adaptations followed. Movie trailers simply called them thrillers – but the French, taking note of the original new style, called it *noir* and the name stuck. You can discover the dark side of 'Los Angleez' from the '40s to the present through many noir classics available on videocassette.

See if you can keep up with the rapid-fire, racy patter of Fred MacMurray and Barbara Stanwyck in Billy Wilder's *Double Indemnity* (1944). Based on James M Cain's short novel, this film ironically features Edward G Robinson as the honest good guy. And if you really enjoy tense, snappy dialogue, check out Humphrey Bogart and Lauren Bacall in *The Big Sleep*. Both of these films make free use of Los Angeles as a dark, foreboding backdrop.

The original *Dragnet* movie – released in 1954, directed by and starring Jack Webb – is basically a big screen pilot for the long-running television show. But in following the daily doings of Sergeant Joe Friday of the LAPD, you will get some sense of the criminal aspect of 1950s Los Angeles and a tour of various locations throughout LA as a bonus. You might miss the cynicism and irony of more hardboiled noir classics, though.

Kim Basinger plays the sultry Lynn Bracken in *LA Confidential*.

Recent crime films set in Los Angeles include *The Grifters* (1991), starring John Cusack as a slick con-man living in the Bryson Hotel on Wilshire Blvd, and *Devil in a Blue Dress* (1995), starring Denzel Washington as reluctant South Central detective Easy Rawlins.

The films of Hollywood's latest auteur, Quentin Tarantino, are self-consciously influenced by noir classics, westerns, and Hong Kong thrillers, and prominently feature modern-day Los Angeles. *True Romance* (1993), written by Tarantino, stars Christian Slater as a naive and unbelievably lucky fugitive who deflects his trouble toward greedy film tycoons. *Pulp Fiction* (1994), written and directed by Tarantino, is a humorous and ironic view of LA from the bottom up. In very Chandleresque fashion, Tarantino creates a surreal Los Angeles through convincing original dialogue. For all of its action, the film is quite realistically stuck much of the time in cars cruising LA's streets.

But the most recent contender for 'Best LA Movie' this side of *Chinatown* would have to be the visceral and brilliant *LA Confidential* (1997), starring Kevin Spacey, Kim Basinger and the wonderfully slimy Danny DeVito. 'Hard-hitting' doesn't begin to describe the violent world of deals, sexual betrayal and double-crossing that drive both good and bad cops to hubristic destinies – and deaths – in the LA of the crime-ridden '50s. Basinger won the Academy Award for her supporting role as a sensitive prostitute. But it's a lesson in film acting to watch Russell Crowe – playing a victimized and manipulated brute cop – as he destroys entire *buildings* in pursuit of something finer within himself. Tarantino, take note.

Comedy The flip-side of noir must be comedy, which allows for equally suitable presentations of Los Angeles. Who would deny that the LA lifestyle can be downright silly?

Perhaps the most outrageously sardonic comment on LA is Tony Richardson's *The Loved One* (1965). With a screen adaptation by Terry Southern and Christopher Isherwood, which takes great liberties with the Evelyn Waugh novel, this film is certain to delight and disgust you. It features such stars as Sir John Gielgud (who hangs himself from a swimming pool diving board) and Liberace (appearing as a huckstering mortician).

A pair of Paul Mazursky films capture different aspects of Los Angeles in ironic fashion: *Down and Out in Beverly Hills* (1985) is an eccentric comedy featuring Nick Nolte as a homeless man who cons his way to become a permanent family member of a wealthy Beverly Hills couple (played by Richard Dreyfuss and Bette Midler). And *Scenes from a Mall* is just that – the movie is shot almost entirely in a shopping mall. Woody Allen and Bette Midler go through much of the modern-day LA experience while trying to shop.

In *LA Story* (1991), comedian Steve Martin parodies the city that he calls home. Just about every aspect of LA life – from enemas to earthquakes to cappuccino – gets the irreverent Martin treatment.

Music

Throughout the 20th century, Los Angeles has been a mecca for musical talent, whether native or imported.

European Composers Several important early-20th-century composers joined LA's community of exiled European artists – like Bertolt Brecht and Thomas Mann – in the '30s and '40s. Their ranks included Otto Klemperer, who later became music director of the LA Philharmonic, Kurt Weill and Arnold Schoenberg, who arrived in 1936, took a professorship at UCLA and composed his *Fourth Quartet*. Igor Stravinsky settled in Hollywood in 1940 and as an Angeleno wrote his *Symphony in C* and the opera *Rake's Progress*.

Jazz Jazz began to flourish in LA in the 1920s when horn player Kid Ory became conductor of a recording orchestra made up entirely of black musicians. Throughout the 1920s, jazz was played throughout town and eventually merged with swing and, under the leadership of Benny Goodman, became part of Big Band music.

In the 1940s jazz arrived in a big way, especially on Central Avenue, the main commercial strip of the African American community. Other major venues were the Swanee Inn on Westwood Blvd and the Hi-De-Ho just west of Downtown. It was while holding a nightly gig in Hollywood that Charlie Parker was offered a seven-month engagement in Camarillo State Hospital's drug rehab ward. Looking back on that experience, he later recorded 'Relaxing at Camarillo' for LA's Dial label. Many great jazzmen were born in Los Angeles, Dexter Gordon, Charles Mingus and Art Pepper among them.

In the '50s, West Coast Jazz was born with artists such as Pepper, Buddy Collette, Gerry Mulligan, Chet Baker and Shelly Manne performing under LA's relaxing influence. At clubs such as Shelly's Manne-Hole in Hollywood and the Lighthouse at Hermosa Beach, they created a soothing, harmonically sophisticated style of jazz that took the edge off the East Coast-oriented bop scene. Jazz fell into a slump in the '60s, as other styles like rhythm & blues and soul became more popular and musicians sought more fertile ground in Europe, leaving only underground avant-garde artists to hold the torch in LA. The scene picked up again in the 1980s and today jazz is as popular as ever, evidenced by the hugely popular Playboy Jazz Festival (see Special Events in Facts for the Visitor) and by the proliferation of public jazz concert series and music played in restaurants and nightclubs.

Rhythm & Blues From the '40s through the '60s, South Central was home to a number of outstanding nightclubs presenting blues, R&B, jazz and soul. Watts churned out vocal groups in the doo-wop tradition, including the Penguins, who first recorded 'Earth Angel' for Doo-Tone records. A juke joint crawl in the mid-'50s would likely have included sets played by T-Bone Walker, Amos Milburn or Charles Brown.

At the hub of a thriving Watts musical scene, Johnny Otis brought many forms of music to the public's attention with his popular Johnny Otis Orchestra – featuring Little Esther Phillips – and his record label, DIG. Starting in the early '60s, Sam Cooke performed hit after hit and ran his SAR record label, attracting soul and gospel talent from around the country to Los Angeles.

Rock & Roll Though rock & roll was from its beginning recorded in LA, the first home-grown talent to make it big in the '50s was Richie Valens, whose 'La Bamba' was a rockified traditional Mexican folk song. In the early '60s, LA's beaches and suburbs were treated to a highly popular style of rock & roll called surf music. Dick Dale and his Del-Tones, the Beach Boys, and Jan and Dean were all local talent. In the mid-'60s, a group of UCLA students – among them the 'lizard king,' Jim Morrison – formed the Doors, who grooved on the Sunset Strip for half a decade.

LA has produced two of rock's most original writers and performers. With his band, the Mothers of Invention, Frank Zappa began his indescribable career with the album *Freak Out* in the mid-'60s. With a voice rusted by bottom-shelf bourbon and filterless cigarettes, Tom Waits has brought the world music built on sounds dragged out from a tin pan alley junkyard, influenced by the varied likes of Louis Armstrong, Kurt Weill and Charles Bukowski.

Perhaps the definitive LA rock band is X. Though not strictly punk, X's combination – the vocals of Exene Cervenka and John Doe over the rockabilly guitar licks of Billy Zoom – created an original, decidedly Angeleno sound that simply blew the doors off the local punk scene. For a more pronounced punk sound, Black Flag led the way with the rants of singer Henry Rollins.

In the mid-'80s, Los Lobos emerged from East LA with a Mexican-influenced rock sound that crossed racial boundaries around the country. Out of Downey came Dave and Phil Alvin and the Blasters, which led the rockabilly revival. Also bred locally, the Red Hot Chili Peppers exploded on the national scene in the late '80s with a highly charged, funk-punk sound.

Rap & Hip-Hop The area stretching from South Central LA down to Long Beach is the local rap hotbed. Seminal rappers Eazy E, Ice Cube and Dr Dre all got their start in the group NWA, the band that put Compton and West Coast rap on the map. Dr Dre went on to found Death Row Records with Suge Knight, launching such popular artists as 2Pac Shakur and Snoop Doggy Dog. Eazy-E, NWA's driving force, went on to found Ruthless Records, which launched acts including Kid Frost (one of the first well-known Latino rappers) and Grammy-Award-winning Bone Thugs-n-Harmony. Cypress Hill, a uniquely successful crossover hip-hop outfit, emerged from the LA scene, as have popular rappers such as Coolio, Brandy and Usher.

Today known as hip-hop, Southern California's vibrant youth subculture has come a long way since local radio station KDAY became America's first commercial rap station. What began a decade ago as a grassroots art form has become one of the city's most popular cultural exports, from baggy jeans to billion-dollar movie deals.

Literature

LA has been a temporary home to many illustrious 20th-century writers, among them William Faulkner, F Scott Fitzgerald and Aldous Huxley. During WWII, German writers Bertolt Brecht and Thomas Mann resided in LA, exiled from their war-torn homeland. While much of the local writing talent seems to be harnessed to the film industry – even Faulkner and Fitzgerald were in LA primarily to make a living writing screenplays – Los Angeles provides an immense wealth of irresistible material to writers. Bookworms will find that novels about the city make for fascinating reading.

LA Novels LA has been a favorite subject of novelists since the 1920s. Many have regarded LA in political terms, often viewing it unfavorably as the ultimate capitalist city. Classics in this vein include Upton Sinclair's *Oil!* (1927), a work of muckraking historical fiction with socialist overtones.

Nathanael West's *The Day of the Locust* (1939) is one of the best – and most cynical – novels about Hollywood ever written. Every paragraph seems to place one little observation upon another, which strangely (for this city that so steadfastly insists on revising itself) still hold true a half century later. Two other novels that make sharply critical observations about the early years of Hollywood are F Scott Fitzgerald's final work, *The Last Tycoon* (1940), and Budd Schulberg's *What Makes Sammy Run?* (1941). Evelyn Waugh's *The Loved One* (1948), on the other hand, takes a satirical look at the funeral trade in Hollywood.

John Fante's *Ask the Dust* (1939) is a tour of Depression-era Los Angeles. The fame and fortune fantasies of struggling writer Arturo Bandini jar violently against the grim reality of LA's dusty Downtown streets, where 'the smell of gasoline makes the sight of palm trees seem sad.' Aldous Huxley's novel *After Many a Summer Dies the Swan* (1939) is a fine and ironic work based on the life of publisher William Randolph Hearst (as was Orson Welles' film *Citizen Kane*).

More recent examples of LA fiction include several books published in 1970: Terry Southern's *Blue Movie* concerns the decadent side of Hollywood; Joan Didion's *Play*

It as It Lays looks at Angelenos with a dry, not-too-kind wit; *Post Office*, by poet-novelist Charles Bukowski, captures the down-and-out side of Downtown (Bukowski himself worked at Downtown's Terminal Annex); and *Chicano*, by Richard Vasquez, takes a dramatic look at the Latino barrio of East LA.

The mid-'80s brought the startling revelations of Bret Easton Ellis' *Less Than Zero*, about the twisted lives of wealthy Beverly Hills teenagers. Covering quite a different terrain, Richard Rayner's *Los Angeles Without a Map* (1988) is about a British man who gets lost in his Hollywood fantasies.

An easy-reading collection of works by 18 writers – Fitzgerald, West and Chandler, as well as Sam Shepard, Martin Amis and Henry Miller – is *Los Angeles Stories* (1991), edited by John Miller.

Crime For all the literary attention placed on the city, it is crime fiction – traditionally called 'pulp fiction' for the cheap, pulpy paper formerly used by paperback publishers – that really captures Los Angeles. The city has such a short, dense history, with fortunes shifting so dramatically and the inflated hype of the American dream contrasting so sharply with the ever-present specter of desperate, downtrodden hangers-on, that pulp fiction has struck a natural, resounding chord with the American public – as has its big-screen manifestation, film noir.

The undisputed king of the LA pulps is Raymond Chandler, who wrote several books from the '30s to the '50s featuring the struggling private investigator Philip Marlowe. Chandler's works are filled with troubled characters riding the tide of evil

Literary Potshots

Many literary giants of the early 20th century came to Hollywood at one time or another, offering up their talents to the studio gods. Unfortunately, few left feeling they'd raised Hollywood's standards for screenwriting, and even fewer enjoyed the experience. F Scott Fitzgerald never left, but not necessarily by choice: a notorious drunk, he died in Hollywood of a heart attack at the age of 44. Nathanael West was killed in a car crash at 36. Whether in parting or not, they all managed to fire off a salvo or two about the screen trade.

Nelson Algren (on working with director Otto Preminger) 'If I took *him* seriously, I couldn't take *myself* seriously.'

Raymond Chandler 'If my books had been any worse, I would not have been invited to Hollywood. If they had been any better, I would not have come.'

Graham Greene 'If there was any truth in the original, it had been carefully altered. If anything had been left unchanged, it was because it was untrue.'

Ernest Hemingway 'Take your manuscript and pitch it across. No, on second thought…first let them toss the money over. Then you throw it over, pick up the money, and get the hell out of there.'

Evelyn Waugh 'Each book purchased for motion pictures has some individual quality, good or bad, that has made it remarkable. It is the work of a great array of highly paid and incompatible writers to distinguish this quality, separate it, and obliterate it.'

Nathanael West 'There's no fooling here. All the writers sit in cells in a row, and the minute a typewriter stops, someone pokes his head in the door to see if you are thinking.'

Raymond Chandler: the king of pulp fiction

forces that seem to govern the metropolis – before they sink to the bottom. If you start with Chandler's best-known work, *The Big Sleep* (1939), chances are you'll want to read all of the others, too – among them *The Lady in the Lake* and *The Long Goodbye*.

Another LA pulp writer is James M Cain, who continues to enjoy a popularity that rivals Chandler's. Cain's books – including *The Postman Always Rings Twice* (1934), *Mildred Pierce* (1941) and *Double Indemnity* (1943) – are tense concoctions mixing sex and crime, always with a pervading sense of the enormous opportunities waiting to be seized in Los Angeles.

In Steve Fisher's *I Wake Up Screaming* (1941), inside Hollywood dope serves as backdrop to the tale of a blonde beauty, on the brink of stardom, who suddenly turns up dead. When this one was made into a movie, sensitive filmmakers took out the Hollywood dirt and set the story in New York. But crime and the movies turned out to be a popular combination. *The Woman Chaser* (1960), by Charles Willeford, is about a sleazy and successful used car salesman who gives up his business and dives headlong into writing, producing and directing a motion picture – sticking at all costs to his own artistic vision.

The Grifters (1963) is by novelist Jim Thompson, who has been described as a sort of bastard child of Chandler and Hammett. Strange as that sounds, Thompson is even weirder. *The Grifters* is about a slick young con-man who preys on the suckers of LA, and his oddly possessive mother who won't leave him alone. Since the '50s, Ross MacDonald has continued to mine the Chandler vein, with Los Angeles figuring prominently in novels such as *The Moving Target* and *The Barbarous Coast*.

In recent years, crime fiction set in LA has enjoyed an enormous resurgence. In 1990 Elmore Leonard came out with *Get Shorty*, about a Florida loan shark who comes to Southern California to collect a large sum of money from a Hollywood producer. Instead – or perhaps inevitably – he gets mixed up in the film business.

Walter Mosley's Easy Rawlins novels, set in Watts, have been hugely popular. (Bill Clinton counts himself among Mosley's loyal fans.) *Devil in a Blue Dress, A Red Death, White Butterfly, Black Betty* and *A Little Yellow Dog* place hero Rawlins in a series of situations – always with historically accurate contexts – that test his desire to remain an honest citizen.

James Ellroy's acclaimed quartet of LA police novels, *The Black Dahlia, The Big Nowhere, LA Confidential* and *White Jazz*, are a dizzying time trip through decades of LA's corruption-filled history. After you've read those, check out *Hollywood Nocturnes*, in which Ellroy vividly captures Hollywood at its raciest in the hyper-delusional, over-sexed story of hip-talking accordion player Dick Contino.

Theater

After New York, LA is the country's second most influential and important city for live theater. It's a lively scene, fueled by the fact that LA is home to one quarter of the nation's professional actors. In the 1960s, a major contribution to the theater scene came in the form of the Music Center, adjacent to the Civic Center downtown, which houses two of LA's most important stages. These are the 2100-seat Ahmanson Theater,

NIK WHEELER

A Hollywood fixture since 1930

which attracts touring Broadway productions, and the 750-seat Mark Taper Forum, which often presents experimental works. Century City's 1829-seat Shubert Theater also hosts major musicals. Other famous theaters include the Pantages in Hollywood and the Pasadena Playhouse.

In recent decades, small independent theaters, the equivalent of off-Broadway and off-off Broadway stages, have flourished as well, concentrated in West Hollywood, Hollywood and North Hollywood. Many of them are housed in converted structures such as warehouses, retail stores and even a natural forest. Under the Equity Waiver Program, theaters of 99 seats or fewer are allowed to pay nonequity (nonunion) rates to their actors, often resulting in professional actors working alongside amateurs.

Architecture

Despite the city's relative youth, Los Angeles' building styles have gone through a seemingly continual evolution. The Mission style was popular in the late 19th century. In the early 20th, it was the California bungalow, the paradigm of which is the 8000-sq-foot Gamble House in Pasadena. Frank Lloyd Wright was commissioned to build several homes in LA between 1917 and 1923; the Millard House in Pasadena and the Ennis-Brown House near Griffith Park offer some of his finest work. The designs of Irving Gill and of Austrians RM Schindler and Richard Neutra, who introduced the International style to LA, are also highly acclaimed.

Downtown Los Angeles still features some of the city's finest buildings. Among them are the 1893 Bradbury Building, a Victorian treasure, and the 1939 Union Passenger Terminal, a fine example of Mission Revival. Parts of Hollywood in particular seem to stand as monuments to the fantastic Art Deco style so popular in the 1920s and '30s. For details on some of the finest in LA architecture, see the Los Angeles Architecture chapter.

Painting & Sculpture

The first art schools in Los Angeles date to the 1880s and include the LA School of Art and Design, founded by Louisa Garden MacLeod, and the college of fine arts at the University of Southern California. A decade or so later, the young city saw an influx of painters migrating to sunnier climes from the East Coast and also from San Francisco. Many settled around the Arroyo Seco in Pasadena as well as in Topanga Canyon, Laguna Beach (Orange County) and Avalon on Catalina Island. Known as the 'Eucalyptus School,' these painters specialized in pleasant Impressionist-style landscapes with natural and pastel color palettes.

The seeds of Modernism were laid in 1916. Rex Slinkard and Stanton Macdonald-Wright founded the Modern Art Society, whose members were largely artists returning to LA from the East Coast or Europe, where they had picked up Cubism, Expressionism and Fauvism. The Otis Art Institute, another important college that survives, also dates roughly to this time. Major Modernists from the '20s to the '40s included Jackson Pollock, Charles White, Man Ray, Eugene Berman, Albert King and Oskar Fischinger. While many were thematically inspired by the California landscape and sunlight initially, by the '40s and '50s, attention turned

Murals & the Impact of Public Art

Nothing bridges social gaps like the visual arts. Surrounded by speakers of more than 80 languages – many living in poverty and unable to afford museum visits, performances or movies – LA-area artists are taking steps to ensure their messages are heard by those residents who need it most.

The Social & Public Art Resource Center (SPARC), 685 Venice Blvd in Venice, is one such group dedicating itself to the production, exhibition and preservation of multiethnic art projects, notably the city's more than 1000 murals. SPARC describes its ultimate goals as recognizing 'the importance of an artist's culture as a basic source for the art-making process... and to encourage a diversity of expression that will manifest itself in works that rise from within communities, rather than works that are imposed upon them.'

Founded in 1976 by three women artists, SPARC has provided countless opportunities for established artists and youth apprentices to embellish their neighborhoods. Some spectacular projects include the *Great Wall of Los Angeles*, a half-mile mural along the Tujunga Wash in the San Fernando Valley, showing the history of ethnic Californians from prehistoric times to the 1950s. It was painted over six summers from 1974-79 by about 400 children and teenagers under the leadership of Judith Baca.

In 1988 the *Great Walls Unlimited: Neighborhood Pride* program was conceived, which, cosponsored by LA's Cultural Affairs Department, has resulted in some 70 murals, mostly in East LA and South Central but also in Koreatown, Long Beach and parts of the San Fernando Valley. SPARC headquarters in a former jail in Venice also contains a Mural Resource and Education Center and an art gallery.

SPARC and the Mural Conservancy of Los Angeles (MCLA) run docent-led bus tours of LA's 'street gallery,' showcasing the works of particular muralists or neighborhoods, about a dozen times per year. Tours cost $25, $20 for students and seniors. Areas visited most often include East LA, Downtown, South Central, Hollywood and Venice. Most tours introduce at least one of the featured artists. Call ☎ 310-822-9560 for a schedule of upcoming tours.

to the materialism, consumerism and technological progress that characterized the era.

The trend continued through the '60s when LA experienced a major art boom, with a slew of new galleries and museums opening and painters migrating to the city from all over the world. Among them flourished a gaggle of avant-garde artists including Edward Kienholz, Robert Irwin and John Mason, whose works were pioneered by the Ferus Gallery. Other major artists were David Hockney, who had come here from England, Richard Diebenkorn and Ed Ruscha. The '70s saw an emergence of art by ethnic artists, notably the Latino group 'Los Four' (Frank Romero, Beto de la Rocha, Gilbert Lujan and Carlos Almaraz), which

focused on public art and gave the city many colorful murals and extravagant sculptures. Women artists were always underrepresented, although muralist Judith Baca has certainly left her mark all over the city.

LA still has a lively art scene, with many museums and private galleries concentrated in Beverly Hills, West Hollywood and Santa Monica. The main publication keeping tabs on all current exhibits is *Artscene*, a free monthly that lists dozens of galleries.

RELIGION

Los Angeles may have a reputation as a secular Babylon, a soulless Sodom and Gomorra, but the fact is that religion in all its diversity has always thrived here, especially in the first half of the 20th century. LA gave birth to a number of churches – some might be more suitably called cults – including the Church of the Nazarene in 1908, Aimee Semple McPherson's International Church of the Foursquare Gospel in 1923, the Church of Scientology in 1958 and the Metropolitan Community Churches (catering to gays and lesbians). Evangelist Billy Graham launched his national career here during the Los Angeles crusade of 1949. And a disillusionment with traditional faiths and an interest in spirituality in recent decades also generated the New Age movement, which has spread from LA across the country and beyond.

Though Protestant evangelism, brought here by early migrants from the Midwest, dominated in LA until the middle of the 20th century, increased immigration from all over the world has led to immense religious diversification. These days more than 600 distinct religious groupings can be identified in the LA area, making it more diverse than London and New York. Christianity dominates, with more than 2.5 million Catholics alone. Large Protestant faiths in LA include Methodist, Presbyterian, Episcopalian, Lutheran, Church of Christ, Reform and Baptist. Evangelical and Pentecostal Christians and Mormons are among the fast-growing congregations. Forty percent of all Buddhists living in the US reside in the LA area, and there are more Jews here (about half a million) than in Tel Aviv.

LANGUAGE

English is LA's primary and 'official' language, though Spanish is almost as widely spoken. There are entire neighborhoods

Koreatown signs

where foreign languages dominate. Koreatown, for instance, has many store signs in Korean letters only; signs also appear in local languages in Chinatown and of course sections of East LA where Mexican-Americans dominate. Spanish is the first language of some 80% of those whose native tongue is not English. Other large linguistic niches are Vietnamese, Hmong and Cantonese.

In 1981, bilingual education was introduced, requiring schools in districts with many non-English-speaking children to provide teaching in those children's native language. This law was repealed by public ballot in 1998 and immediately became a source of controversy.

Los Angeles Architecture

Architecture in LA is as multifaceted as the city's image. In a place where anything goes, the buildings too have pushed creative boundaries, reflecting the different lifestyles, incomes and tastes of its heterogeneous population.

A major turning point in LA history – and its architecture – came in the early 20th century. Until then, the city had produced very little in the way of innovation, preferring to emulate styles developed and popularized on the East Coast. After 1850, the simple adobe and mud constructions of the early Spanish and Mexican settlers had gradually been replaced by structures made from wood and brick. Styles such as Greek Revival, Italianate, Eastlake, Queen Anne and Colonial Revival began to proliferate, making the city look very much like a sunbelt Minnesota.

After 1900, as LA experienced exponential growth, the new stream of humankind entering the city also brought with it young and eager architects ready to cut their teeth and build with new styles and materials. Space was abundant and land was cheap. One of the dominant forms developed early on was the bungalow, an outgrowth of the Arts and Crafts movement (also known as Craftsman) and inspired by buildings from the Far East.

Bottom: The Craftsman-style Gamble House in Pasadena

In many ways, Craftsman laid the foundation for the Modernist style that was to follow. One of its basic tenets was to adapt the form of the building to its natural environment. Frank Lloyd Wright gave the impetus

DAVID PEEVERS

DAVID PEEVERS

Left: After 14 years of planning, the 110-acre Getty Center opened in 1998.

with his Hollyhock House and also drew a slew of other architects to LA, including Austrians Rudolph Schindler and Richard Neutra. In true LA fashion, other forms such as Art Deco, Streamline Moderne and Mission Revival flourished simultaneously. The Modernist style prevailed.

After WWII, an ambitious building program covered the suburbs with miles of tract housing – cheap digs for the growing city. But LA's Downtown changed noticeably only in the 1960s and '70s when the city repealed the 150-foot height limit (enforced because of the earthquake danger). At that point new technology made it possible to build tall structures capable of withstanding major tremors. Looking at Downtown today, it's hard to imagine that clusters of high-rises didn't take shape until the early '80s.

New architects have since begun moving away from stark Modernist features. Led by Frank Gehry, they have experimented with fragmentation and unconventional building materials such as corrugated iron sheeting, wire mesh and fiberglass. Though influential, not all these architects have proven successful. But as the billion-dollar Getty Center (designed by Richard Meier) illustrates, a nearly bottomless budget often begets the grandest designs.

ARCHITECTS

The following are some of the most important people associated with Los Angeles architecture; their work can be seen in various parts of the city.

Frank Lloyd Wright (1867-1959)

Frank Lloyd Wright is considered one of the most prolific and influential architects in the USA. Wright came to LA in 1917 to work on the Hollyhock House (see Hollywood in the Things to See & Do chapter), built in a style he called California Romanza, which incorporated pre-Columbian elements. Inspired by a set of building blocks he played with as a child, Wright also created 'textile block' houses, made from blocks of prefab concrete. He worked feverishly and constantly until his death at 92, dedicated to architecture – which he poetically defined as 'music frozen in time.'

Lloyd Wright (1890-1978)

Frank's eldest son, Lloyd, began his career as a landscape architect for the Boston-based firm of Olmsted & Olmsted in 1911, eventually coming to California and joining the firm of Irving Gill. After stints as a set and airplane designer, Lloyd began collaborating with his father on the Hollyhock House. Although he was a prolific architect in his own right, his work has largely been overshadowed by his father's.

Greene & Greene

The brothers Charles (1868-1957) and Henry (1870-1954) Greene were educated at the Massachusetts Institute of Technology and arrived in LA in 1893, when the Arts and Crafts movement (also known as Craftsman) was beginning to take hold. They earned their place in architectural history for their invention of the Craftsman bungalow, hugely popular in the early 20th century. Overhanging eaves, terraces and sleeping porches functioned as transitions between – and extensions of – the house and its natural setting.

Rudolph Schindler (1888-1953)

Right: Schindler's Oliver House in Silver Lake, built in 1933

DAVID PEEVERS

A great admirer of Frank Lloyd Wright, the Austrian-born Schindler took a job with an architectural firm in Chicago, where Wright's firm was located, hoping that one day he would meet his idol and perhaps work for him. Schindler's dream came true when he became a Wright associate and moved to LA in 1920 to work on the Hollyhock House. Though inspired by Wright, Schindler also created his own more Modernist and radical designs, evident in his own home at 833 Kings Rd in West Hollywood (see the Things to See & Do chapter). Some of its elements went on to become staples of Southern California architecture, such as sliding doors, concrete-slab flooring and rooms opening onto a central courtyard.

Richard Neutra (1892-1970)

In his mid-20s, Richard Neutra confessed to his diary that he was anxious to leave his native Vienna, Austria, to find a place 'where one does not have to fear the winter, where one does not have to slave, but finds time to think and more importantly, to be a free spirit.' In 1924 Neutra found such a place in LA. Working tirelessly and frantically, he is considered one of the most influential Modernists, obsessed with the concept he called 'bio-realism': achieving organic harmony between the spatial needs of humans and the natural environment. Neutra made ample use of windows and terraces, glass, lightweight steel and other materials suited to the Southern California climate.

Frank Gehry (born 1929)

Frank O Gehry is regarded as one of the most outstanding contemporary LA architects. He often uses unconventional materials such as plastic sheering and wire-mesh screens in his designs, which still seem to integrate into their respective environments. He was the recipient of several honorary doctorate degrees and countless awards, including the prestigious Pritzker Prize for Architecture (1989). His designs in LA include the Santa Monica Place shopping mall (1981), the Cabrillo Maritime Museum (1981), the Temporary Contemporary Museum (1983) and Loyola Law School (1984). He is also the architect of the future Walt Disney Concert Hall (see Downtown in the Things to See & Do chapter).

Richard Meier (born 1934)

Meier is another architect who, like Gehry, has managed to perfect and transcend the Modernist visions of early-20th-century architects such as Schindler and Neutra. Until now, his pinnacle of achievement has been the Getty Center, a commission he received after an illustrious career. For the Getty, he departed from his signature gleaming, white-paneled facades, using travertine marble instead. Meier also designed the Museum of Television and Radio in Beverly Hills.

Bottom left: Part of the Neutra Colony in Silver Lake

Bottom right: Meier's Museum of Television and Radio

DAVID PEEVERS

DAVID PEEVERS

RICK GERHARTER

Top: Details of Frank Lloyd Wright's Ennis-Brown House

STYLES
Victorian

Better known as Queen Anne/Eastlake style in California, Victorian architecture was popular in the late 19th to early 20th century. Mostly residential, it consists of frilly multistory homes accented by gables, turrets, mansard roofs, wrap-around porches, heavy detailing and ornamentation, and painted facades in a variety of textures. Few examples survive in LA, but Carroll Ave in Echo Park has a whole cluster of them (see Downtown in Things to See & Do).

Mission Revival

With its simpler classical lines, Spanish Colonial architecture – as the Mission style is also called – was a reaction to the more elaborate Queen Anne style and a nostalgic hearkening back to the early days of California missions. Hallmarks are arched doors and windows, solid walls and red-tile roofs (used mostly for public buildings but also for residences). The style's heyday lasted from 1890 to 1915.

Craftsman

This residential bungalow was popular with the middle classes from 1905 to 1930. The Craftsman style was an outgrowth of the Southern California Arts and Crafts movement, based in the Arroyo Seco in Pasadena. Its most skilled practitioners were architects Charles and Henry Greene; many of their homes survive throughout Pasadena (see Tour II). Houses are distinguished by a boxy shape topped by a low-pitched gabled roof, often with exposed rafters. Boulders often constitute the foundations, lower wall sections and chimneys. Many houses have multiple porches and terraces.

Revivals

In the 1920s, it was very popular to copy earlier styles, often blending them together and thus creating an architectural hodgepodge that was surprisingly aesthetic. No style was safe, including Neoclassical, Baroque, Tudor, Pueblo and French Norman; exotic elements were even borrowed from Mayan, Aztec and Egyptian architecture. You will find examples throughout Los Angeles, including the houses of worship on the Wilshire Corridor (see Tour IV later in the chapter) and several buildings Downtown (Tour I).

Art Deco

Art Deco was a favorite style in the 1920s and '30, especially for public and office buildings. The style is characterized by vertical lines and symmetry that create a soaring effect, often mitigated by a stepped pattern toward the top. Ornamentation is heavy, especially above doors and windows, and may consist of floral motifs, sunbursts or zigzags. Excellent examples in LA are the Eastern Columbia building in Downtown and the Wiltern Theater and former Bullocks Wilshire department store, both on Wilshire in the Koreatown area (detailed in the Things to See & Do chapter).

Left: The Wiltern Theater, inside the Zigzag Moderne Pellissier Building

ANDREA SCHULTE-PEEVERS

Streamline Moderne

Related to Art Deco, Streamline Moderne sought to incorporate the machine aesthetic, in particular the aerodynamic aspects of airplanes and ocean liners. Horizontal bands of smallish, circular windows – like ship portholes – and smooth curved facades were typical elements, as were simulated railings and the use of aluminum and stainless steel. Look for this style in the Coca-Cola Bottling Plant in Downtown and in the Crossroads of the World building on Sunset Blvd in Hollywood.

Modernist

Also called the International Style Modern, this style was initiated in Europe (mostly Germany) by Bauhaus architect Walter Gropius, Mies van der Rohe and Le Corbusier. In LA, Rudolph Schindler and Richard Neutra, both of whom had come to Southern California from their native Austria, were its early practitioners. They sowed the seeds for much of the architecture that's still with us today, both in its residential and 'corporate' forms. Characteristics include a boxlike shape, open floor plans, flat roofs, plain and unadorned facades and interior walls, and the abundant use of glass. Examples of Schindler's and especially Neutra's architecture concentrate in Silver Lake (Tour III). Also of interest is Schindler's private home in West Hollywood.

Tour I – The Glamour Years: Downtown Architecture & History

Central Library, 630 W 5th St

The Central Library was designed by Bertram Goodhue in 1922. Goodhue, inspired by the discovery of King Tut's tomb the same year, incorporated many Egyptian motifs into the building. Note the sphinxes on either side of the 5th St entrance and the gilded pyramidal tower. Not to be missed is the 2nd-floor rotunda with its gigantic 48-light chandelier, at that time one for each state in the Union. The lavish 1933 mural offers snapshots of LA history, such as the founding of the missions and the advent of the railroads. The adjacent Children's Room features a mural and also a beautifully painted wood-beamed ceiling.

Right: Central Library's lavish interior

DAVID PEEVERS

Library Tower, 633 W 5th St

The tallest building in LA has 73 floors and juts 1017 feet into the air. Designed by Henry Cobb, an architect from the New York firm of IM Pei, the Library Tower was attacked by an alien spaceship in the 1996 movie *Independence Day*. Take a peek into the lobby; the walls are adorned with several angel murals.

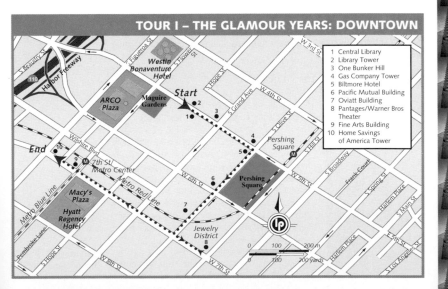

TOUR I – THE GLAMOUR YEARS: DOWNTOWN

1 Central Library
2 Library Tower
3 One Bunker Hill
4 Gas Company Tower
5 Biltmore Hotel
6 Pacific Mutual Building
7 Oviatt Building
8 Pantages/Warner Bros Theater
9 Fine Arts Building
10 Home Savings of America Tower

DAVID PEEVERS

DAVID PEEVERS

One Bunker Hill, 601 W 5th St

This 12-story Art Deco Moderne office tower with classical elements dates to 1931 (Allison & Allison) and is a composition of limestone and terra-cotta. The reliefs above the entrance recall the building's former occupant, the Southern California Edison company, and depict energy, light and power. More than a dozen types of marble were used in the monumental 40-foot lobby. The mural was painted by Hugo Ballin, a set designer for Cecil B De Mille.

Gas Company Tower, 555 W 5th St

If you've seen the movie *Speed*, you might recognize this modern office tower squatting on the northeast corner of Pershing Square (1991; Richard Keating). Its monotonous blue-glass facade is broken up on the top floors by an oval wedge (allegedly in the shape of a gas flame). The lobby is reached via two flights of escalators. Through a glass wall you can glimpse the 35,000-sq-foot mural *Dusk* by Frank Stella on the adjacent building. Integrated into the lobby floor are rows of inverted fountains, which continue outside beyond the glass wall and are allowed to spurt forth from the ground.

Top left: Library Tower, One Bunker Hill and Gas Company Tower

Top right: First Business Bank (One Bunker Hill)

Biltmore Hotel, 515 S Olive St

DAVID PEEVERS

Dominating the Olive St side of Pershing Square is one of LA's grandest and oldest hotels. Designed by the team that also created New York's Waldorf Astoria, it has hosted presidents, the 1960 Democratic National Convention and eight Academy Awards ceremonies. The hotel's sumptuous interior boasts carved and gilded ceilings, marble floors, grand staircases and palatial ballrooms in styles ranging from Renaissance to Baroque to Neoclassical. The Pershing Square entrance leads to a chapel-like side lobby with a carved and painted wooden ceiling. The double staircase with an ornamental railing leads to the Rendezvous Court, modeled after the court of Spain's Queen Isabella.

Left: Built in 1923, the Biltmore Hotel is still in operation.

Pacific Mutual Building, 523 W 6th St

An impressive Beaux Arts structure from 1922 (Dodd & Richards), the Pacific Mutual Building boasts a facade that faintly resembles a Greek temple. There's a suggestion of fluted Corinthian columns that visually support the three-story arched entrance topped by terra-cotta sculptures. The lobby's vaulted ceiling and its marble floors, walls and staircase are worth a look, too.

Oviatt Building, 617 S Olive St

Dating to 1928, the Oviatt is an Art Deco gem conceived by the mildly eccentric James Oviatt, owner of the men's clothing store previously on the premises. (The building now houses a restaurant.) Oviatt fell in love with Art Deco on a visit to Paris and subsequently had carpets, draperies and fixtures shipped over from France, including the purportedly largest shipment of etched decorative glass by René Lalique ever sent. Note the bronze doors and carved wooden interiors of the elevators. Oviatt's own digs were a huge, two-story penthouse, complete with pool, roof garden and tennis court.

Right: Pacific Mutual Building

Bottom left: Detail from the Oviatt Building

Bottom right: Oviatt Building lobby and Cicada Restaurant

DAVID PEEVERS

DAVID PEEVERS

DAVID PEEVERS

Pantages/Warner Bros Theater, 401-421 W 7th St

This movie palace, built in 1920, features a rounded-corner tower and a white terra-cotta facade clad with floral decorations and fluted columns. Though it now has been remodeled into a jewelry mart, parts of the auditorium – including the Baroque ceiling, the balcony seats and the proscenium – can still be seen.

Fine Arts Building, 811 W 7th St

This 12-story 1927 Walker & Eisen structure is a visual feast inside and out. The facade features a plethora of floral and animal ornamentation, and sculptures perched above arcaded windows on the 2nd and 3rd floor. The cathedral-like lobby, though, is especially striking. Built in Spanish Renaissance style, it has a galleried mezzanine from which large sculptures representing the arts gaze down. It's all topped by a flat-beamed and painted wooden ceiling and anchored by a delightful fountain. Flanking rows of glass alcoves are used for changing art exhibits.

Los Angeles Conservancy Tours

The Los Angeles Conservancy is a nonprofit organization with a mission to preserve and raise awareness of the historical buildings in LA. Trained docents conduct a series of entertaining and informative themed walking tours through the Downtown area. Except where noted, tours meet at 10 am, last up to 2½ hours and cost $5 to $8. Reservations are required; call ☎ 213-623-2489.

Art Deco (every Saturday) – Spotlights various landmarks built in this jazzy, geometric style en vogue in the 1920s and '30s

Biltmore Hotel (2nd Saturday at 11 am) – One-hour behind-the-scenes tour of this glamorous hotel, including the health club, kitchen and presidential suite

Broadway Theaters (every Saturday) – Takes you inside the Orpheum and other theaters (also see Historic Core Walking Tour in Things to See & Do)

Little Tokyo (1st Saturday) – Teaches the history of this Japanese enclave and visits the interiors of a church and a temple

Marble Masterpieces (2nd Saturday) – Explores the use of marble in lobbies of office buildings and hotels

Palaces of Finance (3rd Saturday) – Visits LA's old financial district along Spring St

Union Station (3rd Saturday) – Tours the last great railway station built in the US (1939), including a visit to the legendary Fred Harvey restaurant

Terra Cotta (1st Saturday) – Tours many Downtown facades that are richly decorated with this molded clay, which translates as 'burnt earth'

Mecca for Merchants (4th Saturday) – Travels along 7th St, LA's top shopping area in the first 30 years of the 20th century

Pershing Square (every Saturday) – Visits the square's landmarks and relates its history

Angelino Heights (1st Saturday) – Tours LA's first suburb, with its late-19th-century Victorian homes, including visits inside two of them

Home Savings of America Tower, 660 S Figueroa St

Rising above the Metro Rail station at 7th and Figueroa Sts is this remarkable structure, designed by Tim Vreeland. Travertine and green marble cover the base of the tower, while two floral glass murals rise to a height of 40 feet. Take the elevator to the 1st-floor sky lobby, decked out in polished marble in natural and burgundy tones and crowned by a mural of a romanticized portrayal of LA.

DAVID PEEVERS

Right: Gamble House Interior

Tour II – Craftsman & Beyond in Pasadena

The area along the eastern flank of the alluvial gulch known as Arroyo Seco teems with excellent examples of Craftsman bungalows built in the early 20th century. Prime practitioners of this architectural style, Charles and Henry Greene designed many of the homes.

Gamble House, 4 Westmoreland Place

The Gamble House is a 1908 Greene & Greene design considered the world's best example of Craftsman bungalow architecture. It features terraces, bedroom porches for outdoor sleeping and overhanging eaves to keep out the sun. A designated National Historic Landmark, it is now a study center maintained by the USC School of Architecture. Original furnishings, also designed by the brothers, share attention with the rare and

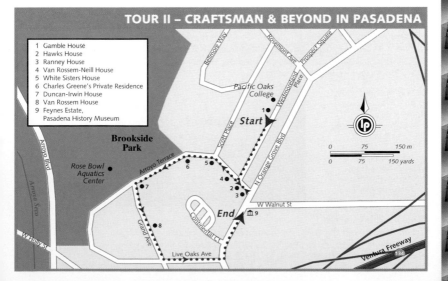

TOUR II – CRAFTSMAN & BEYOND IN PASADENA

1 Gamble House
2 Hawks House
3 Ranney House
4 Van Rossem-Neill House
5 White Sisters House
6 Charles Greene's Private Residence
7 Duncan-Irwin House
8 Van Rossem House
9 Feynes Estate,
   Pasadena History Museum

Brookside Park

Rose Bowl Aquatics Center

Pacific Oaks College

Start

End

0   75   150 m
0   75   150 yards

Ventura Freeway

DAVID PEEVERS

dark woods – teak, maple, oak, redwood – all hand-polished to a satin finish, and the leaded art glass, especially in the front door. The Gamble House starred as the home of mad scientist Doc Brown (Christopher Lloyd) in the three *Back to the Future* movies. Guided one-hour tours (☎ 626-793-3334) depart roughly every 20 minutes noon to 3 pm, Thursday to Sunday except major holidays. Tours are $5, $4 for seniors, $3 for students, free for children.

Top: Former Charles Greene residence

Bottom: The Gamble House was originally the home of an heir to the Procter and Gamble riches.

Other Greene & Greene Homes

Tranquil Arroyo Terrace has the highest concentration of homes by the brothers, including **Charles' private residence** at 368 Arroyo Terrace, begun in 1902 but altered and enlarged numerous times.
Other examples include the following:

Hawks House (1906)
    408 Arroyo Terrace
Ranney House (1907)
    440 Arroyo Terrace
Van Rossem-Neill House (1903-6)
    400 Arroyo Terrace
White Sisters House (1903) 370 Arroyo Terrace (built for Charles' sister-in-law)

ANDREA SCHULTE-PEEVERS

More structures are on Grand Ave, around the corner from Arroyo Terrace, including the large **Duncan-Irwin House** (1900-6) with a beautiful facade at 240 Grand Ave, and the **Van Rossem House** (1904) at 210 Grand Ave.

ANDREA SCHULTE-PEEVERS

Top: Feynes Estate in Pasadena

Feynes Estate, 470 W Walnut St

This beautiful 18-room mansion is home of the Pasadena Historical Society (☎ 626-577-1660). Built in 1907 by Robert Farquhar in the Beaux Arts style, it was once owned by the Finnish consul, which explains the small display of Finnish folk art in the former garden sauna. The main house contains a local history museum with antique furnishings, paintings and Oriental rugs adorning the main floor and archival photos in the basement. Guided tours are offered at 1, 2 and 3 pm Thursday to Sunday (closed holidays) and cost $4, $3 for seniors and students, free for children.

Tour III – Modernist Visions in Silver Lake

Silver Lake – especially the streets framing the Silver Lake reservoir – has a great concentration of milestone residential architecture, allowing for a quick survey of LA's best-known Modernists, Richard Neutra and Rudolph Schindler. Except for the Neutra homes, which date primarily to the 1950s and '60s, most were built during the 1920s and '30s. Many have dramatic reservoir views. All are private homes, so please do not disturb the residents. Note that this is not a walking tour, as the homes are spread across several miles.

Richard Neutra Private Residence, 2300 E Silver Lake Blvd

Having spent his early LA years living in Schindler's house on Kings Rd, Neutra was able to create his own residential vision in 1933 thanks to a $3000 grant by Dutch patron CH Van der Leeuw. The Silver Lake Reservoir is visible from the upper floor, where he placed the private quarters, including living room, sleeping porches and roof deck. His studio and guest quarters are on the lower floor. The house burned down in 1963 and was re-created by Neutra's son Dion. It is now owned by Cal Poly Pomona's School of Environmental Design and may be viewed by appointment only (☎ 909-869-2667). Neutra's ashes are buried beneath a eucalyptus tree in the garden.

Neutra Colony

The full extent of Neutra's architectural vision shines through in a convenient cluster of private homes built just south of his own in the area where Silver Lake Blvd intersects with Earl St and Cove Ave. They include the following:

DAVID PEEVERS

Yew House (1957)
　2226 Silver Lake Blvd
Kambara House (1960)
　2232 Silver Lake Blvd
Inadomi House (1960)
　2238 Silver Lake Blvd
Sokol House (1948)
　2242 Silver Lake Blvd
Treweek House (1948)
　2250 Silver Lake Blvd
Reunion House (1949)
　2240 Earl St
O'Hara House (1961)
　2210 Neutra Place
Akai House (1961)
　2200 Neutra Place

Left: A Modernist home in the Neutra Colony

TOUR III – MODERNIST VISIONS IN SILVER LAKE

1　Richard Neutra Private Residence
2　Neutra Colony:
　　Yew House, Kambara House,
　　Inadomi House, Sokol House,
　　Treweek House, Reunion House,
　　O'Hara House, Akai House
3　Walker House
4　Droste House
5　Oliver House
6　Silvertop House
7　Lovell House
8　Ennis-Brown House

Roosevelt Municipal Golf Course

Griffith Park

Vermont Canyon Rd

Commonwealth

Greendower Ave

Dower

LOS FELIZ

Los Feliz Blvd

Ambrose Ave

Finley Ave

Clarissa Ave

Franklin Blvd

N Vermont Ave

Hillhurst Ave

Russell Ave

Melbourne Ave

Kingswell Ave

Prospect Ave

Rodney Drive

Hollywood Blvd

Barnsdall Art Park

Clayton Ave

W Sunset Blvd

Sunset Drive

W Sunset Blvd

Fountain Ave

Lexington Ave

N Hoover Ave

Santa Monica Blvd

Waverly Drive

Rowena Ave

Rowena Reservoir

Griffith Park Blvd

St George's Rd

Hyperion Ave

SILVER LAKE

Michaeltorena St

Descanso Drive

Ivanhoe Reservoir

Riverside Drive

Rowena Ave

Glendale Blvd

Fletcher Drive

Armstrong Ave

Kenilworth Ave

Neutra Place

Silver Lake Reservoir

Effie St

Griffith Park Blvd

Landa St

Golden Gate Ave

Cove Ave

Earl St

Baxter St

Edgecliff Drive

Tommy Lasorda Field of Dreams

600 m
300

300　600 yards

Kenilworth Ave

Rudolph Schindler designed several houses on this quiet street. The mint-colored Walker House (1936), whose dramatic garden side is unfortunately not visible from the street, is at 2100 Kenilworth Ave. What is visible are the sliding front doors and two-door garage. Atop a slope at 2025 Kenilworth Ave is the slightly crumbling Droste House (1940), painted in the same color.

Micheltorena St

Schindler's Oliver House (1933), 2236 Micheltorena St, has a modest street side exterior that belies the gabled roofline facing the garden and the wooden rooftop sundeck. One of the most remarkable buildings is expressionist John Lautner's Silvertop House (1957), at 2128 Micheltorena St, which features angular and round forms, a cantilevered driveway and a pool.

Lovell House, 4616 Dundee Drive

Bottom left and right:
Ennis-Brown House

The Lovell House was the structure that catapulted Richard Neutra to architectural stardom. Built in 1929, it is quintessential International Style, featuring modern-age materials such as a light-weight steel frame that took only 40 hours to erect. Its open, free-flowing floor plan and suspended balconies are typical of Neutra's vision. This house was most recently featured in *LA Confidential*.

Ennis-Brown House, 2607 Glendower Ave

Not far from the Lovell House is this 1924 Frank Lloyd Wright structure on a hillside overlooking the city. It is the last of his four 'textile block' houses and has a somber, almost foreboding, monumental exterior. Some two dozen forms of prefab concrete blocks, held together with steel spikes, were used in the construction. The main living area is on the upper floor, reached via a marble staircase. Besides offering great views, the living room also has a fireplace topped by a glass mosaic. Tours of the Ennis-Brown House (☎ 323-660-0607), by reservation only, take place the second Saturday of every odd month and cost $10, $5 for students and seniors.

RICK GERHARTER

DAVID PEEVERS

ANDREA SCHULTE-PEEVERS

Tour IV –
Wilshire Corridor
Churches & Temples

Wilshire Blvd between Western Ave and Hoover St has the greatest concentration of religious structures in LA. Most date back to the 1920s, when Wilshire was being developed as a fashionable thoroughfare, and the buildings' size and elaborate features indicate the pre-Depression era of prosperity. These days, most are supported and maintained by Korean immigrant congregations. Stylistically, these churches are a theatrical hodgepodge of various styles borrowed from different time periods and places around the world. It's not unusual to find soaring Gothic arches paired with a Byzantine dome and a Romanesque rose window. While purists might scorn this seemingly incongruous blending, in most cases architects managed to come up with aesthetically pleasing and functional creations.

Christ Church,
635 S Manhattan Place
at Wilshire Blvd

Originally a synagogue, the Renaissance Revival-style Christ Church was built by Russell & Alpaugh in 1924 and is now a nondenominational congregation. It sports a triple-arched entranceway topped by a row of arched bays separated by carved medallions.

Top left: First Congregational Church

Bottom left: Christ Church

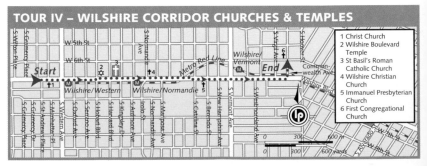

TOUR IV – WILSHIRE CORRIDOR CHURCHES & TEMPLES

1 Christ Church
2 Wilshire Boulevard Temple
3 St Basil's Roman Catholic Church
4 Wilshire Christian Church
5 Immanuel Presbyterian Church
6 First Congregational Church

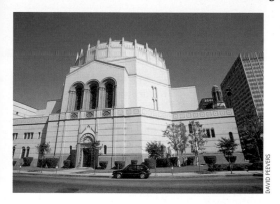

Top: Wilshire
Boulevard Temple

Wilshire Boulevard Temple, 3663 Wilshire Blvd at Hobart

This dignified synagogue houses the largest and oldest Jewish Reform synagogue in LA, with a congregation of more than 2400 families. A short staircase leads to a Romanesque three-arched portal, topped by a rose window and lorded over by an enormous dome. Inspired by a synagogue in Florence, Italy, it was designed by a team of architects that included Abram M Edelman, the son of the temple's first rabbi. The sanctuary is a breathtaking symphony of black marble, gilded altar fixtures, stained-glass windows, hardwood doors, wainscoting and bronze chandeliers – and above it all a soaring cupola. Of particular note is the frieze mural that wraps around the entire interior. Donated by the movie-mogul Warner brothers and painted by Hugo Ballin, it depicts 3000 years of Jewish history, culminating with an eerie foreshadowing of the Holocaust. The history of LA Jews is shown in an exhibit in the foyer. The sanctuary itself is closed, but you may find someone kind enough to let you inside. The entrance is on the east side via the parking lot.

Judson Studios: A Legacy of Stained Glass

Those with an interest in LA churches are likely to come across superb stained-glass windows of near supernatural luster and transparency. These windows may well be the product of the Judson Studios (☎ 323-255-0131), a small workshop hidden away in a rambling villa at 200 S Ave 66, which has been in the same family for five generations.

The vast majority of the Judsons' work is for churches, though they've also created a football-field-size vaulted ceiling for the Tropicana Hotel in Las Vegas from their diminutive digs. Here in LA, examples of their work include the rotunda of the Natural History Museum in Exposition Park and the windows of St James Episcopal Church on Wilshire Blvd. The latter features the work of three generations of Judsons, each employing a different style. Look for the Craftsman window (1926) in the north elevation, the Neo-Gothic one (1952) in the south elevation and the contemporary Gothic (1995) in the clerestory. Karen Judson demystifies the stained-glass-making process during entertaining tours of the studios offered on the third Thursday of each month at 2 pm ($5). There's also a gallery, open between September and June, from 10 am to 4 pm Tuesday to Friday and from noon on Saturday (free admission).

DAVID PEEVERS

St Basil's Roman Catholic Church, Wilshire Blvd at Kingsley Drive

Top: The Picasso-influenced St Basil's Roman Catholic Church

St Basil's, designed in 1974, is one of the rare modern churches on Wilshire Blvd. A fairly typical example of 1970s aesthetics, its exterior is reminiscent of Pablo Picasso at the height of his Cubist period. Unadorned concrete columns seem to support each other at odd angles and are intersected by floor-to-ceiling abstract stained-glass windows. Sculptures inside the church depict the Stations of the Cross.

DAVID PEEVERS

Wilshire Christian Church, Wilshire Blvd at Normandie Ave

The work of Robert Orr (1923), this is an extravagant, frilly pile of reinforced concrete inspired by the hugely popular Northern Italian Romanesque style. This church features an octagonal campanile with a red-tile roof and a French rose window.

Immanuel Presbyterian Church, 3300 Wilshire Blvd

This church dates from 1927, and with its very prominent tower of 200 feet, stylistically emulates the 15th-century French Gothic cathedrals. Inside, the ceiling of its vaulted nave is decorated with colored stencil drawings. The church's floors are done in tile, and there are plenty of carved-wood fixtures, including the pulpit.

First Congregational Church, Commonwealth Ave at W 6th St

One block north of Wilshire Blvd, this church was built by Allison & Allison in 1932 and was inspired by the late Gothic Magdalen College at Oxford, England. It's built in the shape of a cross and sports a central tower ringed by small turrets. Below a rose window is the arched portal, whose cast-bronze door shows scenes from the New Testament. The church's multiple organs have a total of almost 11,900 pipes; recitals take place regularly. Founded in 1867, this church is also home to LA's oldest Protestant congregation.

Left: Wilshire Christian Church

Bottom: Immanuel Presbyterian Church

DAVID PEEVERS

Top: Another architectural gem, the Frank Gehry House

DAVID PEEVERS

Tour V – LA on the Cutting Edge

Frank Gehry and Richard Meier are two of the architects that have made their mark in LA in the '80s and '90s. Both have taken on large and small-scale commercial and residential commissions that have stretched the frontier of LA architecture.

The Getty Center, 1200 Getty Center Drive

The most remarkable work of architecture in recent LA history is the hilltop Getty Center (1998; Map 2). Its fortresslike appearance from vantage points below vanishes the moment you find yourself face to face with the complex. Architect Richard Meier has made perfect use of the hill's natural shape, placing buildings along the outline of a ridge. Openness is the connecting element between each of the structures, as they all lead to courtyards and terraces and are angled and spaced to provide different views of the city and the mountains at every turn. Designing no

Bottom: Meier carefully chose every shape and angle on the Getty Center.

DAVID PEEVERS

building over two stories tall, Meier built additional subterranean floors connected by corridors.

The museum consists of five sequential pavilions entered from a central courtyard accented by an elongated fountain. Also accessible from here are the circular garden, a cafe and other facilities. Sensuously curved buildings are juxtaposed with geometric ones. Add the California sunshine to the mix and you get a most remarkable alchemy of light and shadow. It's an effect further enhanced by the stone used in the Getty's construction: cream-colored, cleft-cut, textured and fossilized travertine marble. Reflecting the sunlight in the early morning, the marble literally seems to absorb the rays in the afternoon before radiating a golden warmth.

Chiat/Day Building, 340 Main St, Venice

The West Coast headquarters of this international advertising agency (Map 12) was designed by Frank Gehry and may already be familiar to some. It's a standout primarily for the gigantic pair of binoculars that constitutes its entrance, which Gehry developed in collaboration with artists Claes Oldenburg and Coosje van Bruggen. Besides providing access to the parking garage, the binoculars also contain several conference rooms; each cylinder is topped by a skylight.

RICK GERHARTER

Top: At three stories tall, the Chiat/Day Building is hard to miss.

DAVID PEEVERS

Santa Monica Place

Shopping malls don't elicit praise for their designs, but this 1981 Frank Gehry creation, at the southern end of the Third Street Promenade (Map 12), deserves kudos. Not only does it offer a compact and upscale shopping experience, you can do it all in a light-flooded modern monument to commerce. Gehry has miraculously managed to give the tight space an airy feel, through the use of glass and by wrapping the three-tiered mall around a sectioned and angled atrium. Color and public art produce an ambience that's both whimsical and sophisticated.

Bottom: Santa Monica Place is often used in Hollywood shoots, including scenes in *Terminator II* and *Beverly Hills 90210*.

Facts for the Visitor

WHEN TO GO

Any time of year can be a good time to visit Los Angeles, but the best months are usually April to June and September and October. The beaches are liveliest in summer when college students are on break, but hotel prices rise accordingly. During shoulder seasons, tourist crowds are smaller, prices are lower, and most attractions are still open and operating. The winter months, while somewhat cooler and rainier, can still offer beautiful days. Many points of interest may be closed, however, and others will certainly have shorter hours and fewer days of operation.

WHAT TO BRING

Generally speaking, Los Angeles is a casual city that makes few fashion demands unless you want to join the see-and-be-seen crowd, in which case there are enormous fashion demands. The average visitor can pack light most times of the year. Cotton is the best fabric to carry. Except in winter, plan on shorts and T-shirts during the day, long pants or skirts and shirts or blouses for the evening. A few upscale restaurants require men to wear a jacket, but not necessarily a shirt and tie. In fall, winter and early spring, you will need a light overcoat for after dark. Bring sturdy, broken-in walking shoes and pack open-toed sandals or thongs for the beach. You will need sunglasses and sunscreen even on overcast days.

ORIENTATION

Covering 464 sq miles, the city of Los Angeles is vast indeed. Yet its meandering boundaries, which extend 50 miles from San Fernando to San Pedro, 25 miles from Pacific Palisades to Highland Park, comprise only a fraction of 4083-sq-mile LA County. There are 88 incorporated cities within the county, many of them independent (such as Santa Monica, Beverly Hills, West Hollywood and Culver City) but surrounded by the city of LA. This book covers attractions, lodgings, restaurants, etc within the boundaries of LA County; some popular destinations beyond the county are covered in the Excursions chapter.

LA County occupies a broad coastal plain, bordered on its west and south by the Pacific Ocean, on its north by the San Gabriel Mountains, and on its east by smaller ranges that run to the Mojave Desert. The Santa Monica Mountains separate Hollywood and Beverly Hills from the San Fernando Valley to the north; neighboring Orange County, home of Disneyland and Laguna Beach, extends along the coast to the southeast.

Getting around Los Angeles need not be hard if you have a car and a basic understanding of LA's network of freeways. Eight of them tangle like knotty vines near the Downtown core, each changing in name. (See the Major Freeways boxed text in Getting Around.) Maps are essential at all times when driving.

The Shoestring Corridor

The City of Los Angeles *does* have boundaries, but if you were to trace the city's limits, you'd end up with an indescribable shape. The patchwork look is the result of decades of expansion, during which Los Angeles absorbed the smaller surrounding towns.

The most interesting aspect of the shape of Los Angeles is the long narrow strip known as the Shoestring Corridor, which was annexed by the city in 1906. Sixteen miles long, but just half a mile wide, this strip connects central LA to the city's harbor in San Pedro, slicing through the cities of Gardena, Carson, Torrance and Lomita. On any clearly demarcated map, it appears that the City of Angels has the tail of a devil.

Some communities of visitor interest aren't on the freeway system at all, and must be reached via city streets. Principal among these are Beverly Hills and West Hollywood, located west of Downtown but north of the Santa Monica Fwy.

MAPS

In most cases, the maps in this book are comprehensive enough for you to navigate within particular neighborhoods without getting lost. Handout maps, such as those available at hotels, car-rental agencies and tourist offices, may be insufficient if you plan on spending any length of time exploring the nooks and crannies of LA County. To cover the entire area, you most likely need several maps. Single maps showing all of the county provide only an overview and are not useful for serious navigating.

The driver's bible is the annually updated, fully indexed *Thomas Guide* ($17.95), which has more than 180 pages of detailed city maps. Call ☎ 800-899-6277 to order, or visit any local bookstore. For something less pricey (or free to members) but sufficiently detailed, you can get maps from the Automobile Association of Southern California (also see Useful Organizations, later in this chapter).

TOURIST OFFICES
Local Tourist Offices

Maps, brochures, lodging information and tickets to theme parks and other attractions are available through the Los Angeles Convention and Visitors Bureau. The Downtown office (Map 5; ☎ 213-689-8822, fax 213-624-1992), 685 S Figueroa St, Los Angeles, CA 90017, is open weekdays 8 am to 5 pm, Saturday from 8:30 am. The Hollywood Visitor Information Center (Map 9; ☎ 213-689-8822), in the early-20th-century Janes House at 6541 Hollywood Blvd, is open daily except Sunday from 9 am to 5 pm. The LACVB also maintains a 24-hour multilingual events hotline at ☎ 213-689-8822.

Many of the independent cities within the county either maintain their own tourist offices or provide information through their chambers of commerce (which tend to have an interest in promoting their members first, and therefore aren't necessarily objective). Contact any of these agencies for specific information about lodgings or attractions in that particular city only:

Anaheim/Orange County
(☎ 714-999-8999)
800 W Katella Blvd, Anaheim, CA 92802

Beverly Hills Visitors Bureau
(☎ 310-271-8174,
www.itlnet.com/beverlyhillscc)
239 S Beverly Drive,
Beverly Hills, CA 90212

Catalina Island Chamber of Commerce
(☎ 310-510-1520, www.catalina.com)
1 Green Pier, Avalon,
Santa Catalina Island, CA 90704

Hollywood Chamber of Commerce
(☎ 323-469-8311)
7018 Hollywood Blvd, Hollywood, CA 90028

Hermosa Beach Chamber of Commerce
(☎ 310-376-0951)
323 Pier Ave, Hermosa Beach, CA 90254

Long Beach Convention & Visitors Bureau
(☎ 562-436-3645, www.golongbeach.org)
1 World Trade Center, suite 300,
Long Beach, CA 90831

Malibu Chamber of Commerce
(☎ 310-456-9025)
23805 Stuart Ranch Rd, Malibu, CA 90263

Marina del Rey Chamber of Commerce
(☎ 310-821-0555, www.llitlnet.com/marina)
4111 Via Marina, Marina del Rey, CA 90292

Pasadena Convention & Visitors Bureau
(☎ 626-795-9311, www.pasadenavisitor.org)
171 S Los Robles Ave, Pasadena, CA 91101

San Pedro Chamber of Commerce
(☎ 310-832-7272, www.sanpedrochamber.com)
390 W 7th St, San Pedro, CA 90731

Santa Monica Convention & Visitors Bureau
(☎ 310-319-6263, www.santamonica.com)
520 Broadway, suite 250
Santa Monica, CA 90401 and
(☎ 310-393-7593) 1400 Ocean Blvd,
Santa Monica, CA 90401

Venice Chamber of Commerce
(☎ 310-396-7016, www.venice.net)
583 Venice Blvd, Venice, CA 90291

West Hollywood Convention & Visitors Bureau
(☎ 310-289-2525)
8687 Melrose Ave, M-26,
West Hollywood, CA 90069

Tourist Offices Abroad

The USA does not have a well-developed tourist office system. Contact your local US diplomatic office concerning information from the United States Travel & Tourism Administration (USTTA). Information on California tourism can be obtained by mail from the California Division of Tourism (☎ 916-322-1396, 800-862-2543), 801 K St, suite 1600, Sacramento, CA 95814.

Request local information by calling or writing to the tourist agencies listed above. You may be asked to send a postage-paid envelope (or international reply coupons if writing from abroad) for them to return brochures and pamphlets to you.

DOCUMENTS
Passport

Most foreign visitors to the United States are required to possess a passport and many also need a valid US visa (see the following section). Canadians must have proper proof of Canadian citizenship, such as a citizenship card with photo ID or a passport, provided they enter the US from the Western Hemi-sphere – with the exception of Cuba – and plan to stay 90 days or less.

Although most visitors to the US ultimately have no problem entering the country, immigration and customs officials at Los Angeles International Airport (LAX) are not famous for their people skills. They may try to intimidate you by firing off a barrage of questions concerning the length of your stay, whether you have relatives in the US, where you will be staying or traveling to, how much money you're carrying, and so on. Be prepared to show your return flight ticket; try to remain as calm as possible and answer all questions politely. Be aware that until you have passed through the last formality, you have few rights.

If you feel you've been harassed by an immigration officer (sexist comments have been among the unpleasantries experienced by the female part of this author team), demand to speak with a supervisor immediately. Supervisors are generally better qualified; you can state your complaint to them directly or they will give you a complaint form to fill out. Normally this is all you need

HIV & Entering the USA

Anyone entering the USA who isn't a US citizen is subject to the authority of the Immigration and Naturalization Service (INS). The INS can keep people from entering or staying in the USA by excluding or deporting them; this is especially relevant to travelers with HIV (human immunodeficiency virus). Though being HIV-positive is not grounds for deportation, it is a 'ground of exclusion,' and the INS can invoke it to refuse admission.

Although the INS doesn't test people for HIV, it may try to exclude anyone who answers Yes to this question on the nonimmigrant visa application form: 'Have you ever been afflicted with a communicable disease of public health significance?' INS officials may also stop people if they seem sick, are carrying AIDS/HIV medicine or, sadly, if the officer happens to think the person 'looks gay,' though sexual orientation is not legally a ground of exclusion.

It's imperative that visitors know and assert their rights. Immigrants and visitors who may face exclusion should discuss their rights and options with a trained immigration advocate before applying for a visa. For legal immigration information and referrals to immigration advocates, contact the National Immigration Project of the National Lawyers Guild (☎ 617-227-9727), 14 Beacon St, suite 506, Boston, MA 02108; or the Immigrant HIV Assistance Project, Bar Association of San Francisco (☎ 415-782-8995), 465 California St, suite 1100, San Francisco, CA 94104.

to do, but as a further step you can call the US Immigration Service at ☎ 310-215-2101. If you feel like you're being treated inappropriately by a US Customs agent, again ask to speak with a supervisor or call the US Customs offices at ☎ 310-215-2414 (or 2415).

Visas

A reciprocal visa-waiver program applies to citizens of certain countries who may enter the USA for stays of 90 days or less without needing to obtain a visa. Currently these countries are Andorra, Argentina, Australia, Austria, Belgium, Brunei, Denmark, Finland, France, Germany, Iceland, Ireland, Italy, Japan, Liechtenstein, Luxembourg, Monaco, The Netherlands, New Zealand, Norway, San Marino, Slovenia, Spain, Sweden, Switzerland and the UK. Under this program you must have the following: a roundtrip ticket on an airline that is participating in the visa-waiver program, proof of financial solvency and a signed form waiving the right to a hearing of deportation; you will also not be allowed to extend your stay beyond the 90 days. Consult with your travel agent or contact the airlines directly for more information.

All other travelers will need to obtain a visa from a US consulate or embassy, a process that can be done by mail in most countries. Your passport should be valid for at least six months longer than your intended stay in the USA. You'll need to submit a recent photograph, 1½ inches square (37mm x 37mm), with the application. Documents of financial stability and/or guarantees from a US resident are sometimes required, particularly for citizens of developing countries.

Visa applicants may be required to 'demonstrate binding obligations' that will ensure their return back home. Because of this requirement, those planning to travel through other countries before arriving in the USA are generally better off applying for their US visa before they leave their home country, rather than while on the road.

The most common visa is a Non-Immigrant Visitor's Visa, B1 for business purposes, B2 for tourism or visiting friends and relatives. A visitor's visa is good for one or five years with multiple entries, and it specifically prohibits taking paid employment in the USA.

The validity period for US visitor's visas generally depends on what country you're from. The length of time you'll be allowed to stay in the country is ultimately determined by US immigration authorities at the port of entry.

If you're coming to the USA to work, you will need a different type of visa, and the company or institution you'll be going to should make the arrangements. Allow six months in advance of your planned arrival for processing the application.

Visa Extensions If you want, need or hope to stay in the USA longer than the date stamped on your passport, apply for an extension *before* the stamped date. Because immigration officers usually assume you already are or will be working illegally, come prepared with concrete evidence that you've been traveling extensively and will continue to be a model tourist rather than sticking to one place and joining the 9-to-5 brigade. A wad of traveler's checks looks much better than a solid and unmoving bank account. It's also a good idea to bring a US citizen with you to vouch for your character.

Extensions are handled by the US Government's Justice Department's Immigration & Naturalization Service (☎ 213-526-7647), 300 N Los Angeles St, open weekdays 6 am to 3 pm, Thursday to 1 pm. Information over the telephone is dispensed from 7 am to 5:30 pm weekdays.

Travel Insurance

No matter how long or where you're traveling, be sure to purchase travel insurance. It may seem an extravagant expense at first, but it's nowhere near the cost of a medical emergency in the USA.

Ideally, coverage should not only include medical expenses and luggage theft or loss, but also cover you in case of cancellations or delays in your travel arrangements. The best policies are those that also extend to the worst possible scenario, such as an accident that requires hospitalization and return flight home. Check your medical policy at home; some may already provide worldwide coverage, in which case you only need to protect yourself against other problems.

Ask both your insurer and your ticket-issuing agency to explain the finer points, especially what supporting documentation is required in case you need to file a claim. STA Travel and Council Travel offer travel insurance options at reasonable prices. Within the USA, Access America (☎ 800-284-8300) and Travel Guard (☎ 800-826-1300) are both quite reasonable and reliable insurers. Make sure you have a separate record of all your ticket details – or better still, a photocopy of them. Also make a copy of your policy, in case the original is lost.

Buy travel insurance as early as possible. For instance, if you buy it the week before you leave, you may find that you're not covered for flight delays caused by strikes or other industrial action that may have been in force before you took out the insurance.

Driver's License & Permits

Bring your driver's license if you intend to drive a car. If you're a foreign visitor, an International Driving Permit is useful though not mandatory. Local traffic police are more likely to accept it as valid identification than an unfamiliar document from another country. This permit is usually available for a small fee from your national automobile association and valid for one year. Make sure to also bring your valid national license, as you will need to present it along with the international one. A driver's license is also a useful form of identification when seeking access to bars, shows or other age-restricted facilities.

Hostel Card

A couple of hostels in Los Angeles are part of Hostelling International/American Youth Hostel (HI/AYH), which is affiliated with the International Youth Hostel Federation (IYHF). If you don't already have one, you can purchase membership on the spot when checking in.

Student & Youth Cards

If you're a student, bring along an International Student Identification Card (ISIC), a plastic ID-style card with your photograph. Available at your university or at student-oriented travel agencies, the ISIC card often entitles you to discounts on transportation (including airlines and local public transport), and on admission to museums and sights as well as meals at university cafeterias. If you're a US student, carry your school or university's ID card.

Seniors' Cards

People over the age of 65 (sometimes 60 or 62) usually qualify for the same discounts as students (see above). All you need is an ID with a photograph and proof of age, should you be carded. The best card to carry is the AARP membership card, available to those over 55 for an annual fee of $8 (see Senior Travelers later in this chapter).

Photocopies

The hassle of losing your passport or other vital documents can be considerably reduced if you have a record of their numbers and issue dates, or even better, photocopies of the relevant data pages. Also add the serial numbers of your traveler's checks (cross them off as you cash them) and photocopies of your credit cards, airline ticket and other travel documents. Keep all this emergency material separate from your passport, checks and cash, and leave extra copies at home. If you lose your passport, get a statement from the police immediately and contact your nearest consulate.

EMBASSIES & CONSULATES
US Embassies & Consulates

US diplomatic offices abroad include the following:

Australia
   (☎ 2-6270-5000)
   21 Moonah Place, Yarralumla ACT 2600
   (☎ 2-9373-9200) Level 59 MLC Center,
   19-29 Martin Place, Sydney NSW 2000
   (☎ 3-9526-5900)
   553 St Kilda Rd, Melbourne, Victoria

Canada
   (☎ 613-238-5335)
   100 Wellington St
   Ottawa, Ontario K1P 5T1

(☎ 604-685-1930)
1095 W Pender St, Vancouver, BC V6E 2M6
(☎ 514-398-9695)
1155 rue St-Alexandre, Montreal, Quebec

France
(☎ 01 42 96 12 02)
2 rue Saint Florentin, 75001 Paris

Germany
(☎ 2-28-33-91)
Deichmanns Aue 29, 53179 Bonn

Ireland
(☎ 1-687-122)
42 Elgin Rd, Ballsbridge, Dublin)

Japan
(☎ 3-224-5000)
1-10-5 Akasaka Chome, Minato-ku, Tokyo

Mexico
(☎ 5-211-0042)
Paseo de la Reforma 305, 06500 Mexico City

The Netherlands
(☎ 70-310-9209)
Lange Voorhout 102, 2514 EJ The Hague
(☎ 20-310-9209)
Museumplein 19, 1071 DJ Amsterdam

New Zealand
(☎ 4-722-068)
29 Fitzherbert Terrace, Thorndon, Wellington

United Kingdom
(☎ 0171-499-9000)
5 Upper Grosvenor St, London W1
(☎ 31-556-8315)
3 Regent Terrace, Edinburgh EH7 5BW
(☎ 232-328-239)
Queens House, Belfast BT1 6EQ

Consulates in Los Angeles

Most foreign embassies in the United States are located in Washington, DC, but a lot of countries, including the following, have consular offices in Los Angeles. For addresses and telephone numbers of other consulates, please consult the Yellow Pages under Consulates & Other Foreign Government Representatives.

Australia
(☎ 310-229-4800, fax 310-277-2258)
2049 Century Park E, 19th fl,
Los Angeles, CA 90067

Canada
(☎ 213-346-2700, fax 213-346-2767)
550 S Hope St, 9th fl, Los Angeles, CA 90071

DAVID R FRAZIER

The Blessing of the Animals (Leo Politi) – in the Mexican consulate courtesy of El Pueblo de Los Angeles Historical Monument

France
(☎ 310-235-3200, fax 310-479-4813)
10990 Wilshire Blvd, suite 300,
Los Angeles, CA 90024

Germany
(☎ 323-930-2703, fax 323-930-2805)
6222 Wilshire Blvd, suite 500,
Los Angeles, CA 90048

Japan
(☎ 213-617-6700, fax 213-617-6727)
350 S Grand Ave, suite 1700,
Los Angeles, CA 90071

Mexico
(☎ 213-351-6800, fax 213-389-9249)
2401 W 6th St, Los Angeles, CA 90057

New Zealand
(☎ 310-207-1605, fax 310-207-3605)
12400 Wilshire Blvd, suite 1150,
Los Angeles, CA 90025

United Kingdom
(☎ 310-477-3322, fax 310-575-1450)
11766 Wilshire Blvd, suite 400,
Los Angeles, CA 90025

CUSTOMS

US Customs allows each person over the age of 21 to bring 1 liter of liquor and 200 cigarettes duty-free into the USA. US citizens are allowed to import, duty-free, $400 worth of gifts from abroad, and non-US citizens are allowed to bring in $100 worth.

Should you be lucky enough to carry more than $10,000 in US or foreign cash, traveler's checks, money orders or the like, you need to declare the excess amount. There is no legal restriction on the amount that may be imported, but undeclared sums in excess of $10,000 may be subject to confiscation. Under no circumstances should you attempt to import non-prescription narcotic drugs, including marijuana, unless you have a hankering to try out American prisons.

If you arrive directly at LAX from overseas, you will undergo customs and immigration formalities there. If your flight makes an intermediate stop at another US port, even if you did not change flights, you will go through customs and immigration at that first point of entry into the USA.

At LAX, after clearing immigration, hand the customs form (which you filled in on the plane) to a customs official. Even if you have nothing to declare, you may be directed to follow the red line to an inspector, who will x-ray and perhaps hand-search your entire luggage. Occasionally, the 'dog detectives' employed by the Drug Enforcement Agency may sniff you and your luggage for narcotics or illegal foodstuff. Luckier travelers are sent along the green line and spared this procedure.

California is an important agricultural state, so most food products – especially fresh, dried and canned meat, fruit, vegetables and plants – may not be brought into Los Angeles, thus preventing the spread of pests, fungi and other diseases. You should avoid bringing any such food items. If you suddenly remember that pineapple in your backpack, leave it on the plane or chuck it in the trash before you reach customs. There's the threat of potential fines and jail time if you break this law, though in reality the items in question are more likely to be simply confiscated (the fate of a wonderful Westphalian ham we once brought back from Germany). Bakery items and cured cheeses *are* admissible.

If you drive into California across the border from Mexico or the neighboring states of Oregon, Nevada or Arizona, you may have to stop for a quick inspection and questioning by officials of the state Department of Food and Agriculture.

If you want to bring your dog, be sure to carry certificates stating that it is free of diseases communicable to humans and has been vaccinated against rabies.

MONEY
Currency

The US dollar is divided into 100 cents (¢). Coins come in denominations of 1¢ (penny), 5¢ (nickel), 10¢ (dime), 25¢ (quarter) and the seldom-seen 50¢ (half dollar). Quarters are the most commonly used coins in vending machines and parking meters, so it's handy to have a stash of them; they're available in $10 rolls at all banks. Notes, commonly called bills, come in $1, $2, $5, $10, $20, $50 and $100 denominations – $2 bills are rare but perfectly legal. There is also a $1 coin, which the government has tried (unsuccessfully) to bring into mass circulation; you might get them as change from ticket and stamp machines. Be aware that $1 coins look similar to quarters.

Exchange Rates

At press time, exchange rates were:

country	unit		dollars
Australia	A$1	=	$0.64
Canada	C$1	=	$0.66
France	FF1	=	$0.17
Germany	DM1	=	$0.56
Hong Kong	HK$10	=	$1.30
Japan	Y121	=	$1.00
New Zealand	NZ$1	=	$0.53
UK	UK£1	=	$1.62
euro	€ 1	=	$1.07

Exchanging Money

Most major currencies and leading brands of traveler's checks are easily exchanged in Los Angeles. Banks usually offer the best rates and are typically open Monday to Thursday 10 am to 5 pm, Friday to 6 pm, and Saturday to 1 pm. LAX has currency-exchange offices in all terminals, but exchange rates are not great; you may want to change your money into dollars or traveler's checks while in your home country.

There are literally hundreds of banks around Los Angeles, the most prevalent being Bank of America, First Federal and Union Bank. Among the foreign-exchange brokers, one of the most dependable is Thomas Cook (☎ 800-287-7362 – for all branches), with locations in Beverly Hills at 452 N Bedford St and 9461 Wilshire Blvd, and in West Hollywood at 8901 Santa Monica Blvd. Another agency is American Express, with locations at 8493 W 3rd St (Map 10; ☎ 310-659-1682) near the Beverly Center mall, in Downtown at 901 W 7th St (☎ 213-627-4800) and also 801 S Grand Ave (☎ 213-624-0111), and in Santa Monica at 1250 4th St (Map 12; ☎ 310-395-9588).

Cash

Though carrying cash is more risky, it's a good idea to travel with some ($50 or so) for the convenience. Cash is useful for tipping and for small purchases at convenience stores or vending machines. However, any cash you lose is gone forever, and very few travel insurers will come to your rescue. We suggest you limit your cash to about $300.

Traveler's Checks

Traveler's checks offer greater protection from theft or loss and can be used as cash in many places. American Express and Thomas Cook are widely accepted and have efficient replacement policies.

Keeping a record of the check numbers and the checks you have used is vital when it comes to replacing lost checks. Keep this record separate from the checks themselves.

Be sure to buy traveler's checks in US dollars. Restaurants, hotels and most stores accept US-dollar traveler's checks as if they were cash, so you'll rarely have to use a bank or pay an exchange fee.

Take most of the checks in large denominations. It's only toward the end of a stay that you may want to change a smaller check to make sure you aren't left with too much local currency.

ATMs

Automatic teller machines are perhaps the best, safest and most convenient way of obtaining cash. For a nominal service charge (usually $1 or $2), you can withdraw cash from an ATM using a bank card linked to your personal checking account. Credit card withdrawals usually have a 2% fee with a $2 minimum. Practically all banks have these 24-hour machines. The Plus and Cirrus systems are the most prevalent networks in LA.

Foreign visitors should note that the exchange rate with an ATM is usually the best available, though high service fees may cancel out that advantage. Check the fees and availability of services with your home bank before you leave. When using an ATM, it's best to pick one in a crowded area, as the risk of being robbed is as real here as anywhere else in the world. Avoid using ATMs at night.

More and more businesses, from gas stations to grocery stores, also offer the ATM option. To make a purchase or withdraw cash, you simply slide your card through and then key in your PIN (personal identification number). Always keep handy the phone number for reporting lost or stolen cards.

Credit Cards

Major credit cards are accepted at most hotels, restaurants, gas stations, shops, car-rental agencies, grocery stores, ticket vendors, movie theaters and other places. And in fact, certain transactions will be impossible to perform without that little piece of plastic. You'll need a credit card whenever you want to book theater tickets by phone, rent a car or guarantee a room reservation.

Even if you loathe credit cards, it's a good idea to carry one for emergencies. Having a Visa or MasterCard in your deck is helpful, as others (Discover, JCB, Diners Club, etc) are not as widely accepted.

Carry copies of your credit card numbers separately from the cards. If you lose your credit cards or they get stolen, contact the company immediately at these numbers:

American Express	☎ 800-528-4800
Diners Club	☎ 800-234-6377
Discover	☎ 800-347-2683
MasterCard	☎ 800-826-2181
Visa	☎ 800-336-8472

Security

Be cautious – but not paranoid – about carrying money. Use the safe at your hotel or hostel for your valuables and excess cash. Don't display large amounts of cash in public. A money belt worn under your clothes is a good place to carry excess currency when you're on the move or otherwise unable to stash it in a safe. Avoid carrying your wallet in a back pocket of your pants. This is a prime target for pickpockets, as are handbags and the outside pockets of day packs and fanny packs (bum bags).

Costs

Naturally, spending lots of money in LA is not hard, but it's a bit harder to spend little. The secret to staying within budget is to cut costs where you can, such as with accommodation and food. Hostels usually charge about $15 per bunk, and no-frills motel rooms cost as little as $35 per double. Rates tend to be slightly higher during the summer months and around all holidays. Luxury hotels may set you back $200 and up per room, though lower weekend rates are often available.

Dining out *can* be enjoyable and even exotic in Los Angeles, without being a strain on your wallet. You can find good restaurant meals for $10 – or even half that for some lunch specials. Los Angeles does take pride in its contemporary cuisine, so if you would like to experience the latest chichi restaurant, you can expect to pay $40 and up per person. Overall, you can cut costs by having no or few alcoholic drinks. Those on a tight budget may get by cheapest by simply purchasing food at supermarkets.

Public transportation is inexpensive (25¢ to $1.85, depending on the system) but not always a viable option for getting around Los Angeles. Renting a car is fairly reasonable, and gasoline costs a fraction of what it does in Europe and in most of the world. Parking costs, however, can add up. (For more information on operating a car, see the Getting Around chapter.)

If you're very economical, you can expect to survive in LA on $40 a day per person. If you can afford to spend twice that, you'll start living quite comfortably.

Tipping

Service gratuities are not really optional in the US. Wait staff in restaurants and bars, hotel room attendants, valet car parkers, bellhops and others are paid minimum wages (currently $5.25/hour) and rely upon making a reasonable living through tips. Service has to be absolutely *appalling* before you should consider not tipping (in which case a complaint to the manager is warranted).

In sit-down restaurants, 15% is considered mandatory; consider leaving 20% for superior service. (To figure an appropriate tip easily, just double the sales tax.) Leave cash tips on the table; otherwise add the tip to the amount on the credit card slip. Bartenders and cocktail servers also get 15%, left in change as you pay for drinks. Don't tip at fast-food, takeout or buffet-style restaurants where you serve yourself.

In hotels, unless you're in and out the next day, give your room attendant $1 per person per day (left on the pillow each day). Fancy hotels may have concierges; they get nothing for just answering a question, but $5 or more for special services such as securing tickets to sold-out shows.

Taxi drivers expect about 10%, so if you have an $18 fare it's adequate to let the cabbie keep the change from a $20. One or two dollars is a sufficient tip for parking valets, unless posted signs call for more.

Baggage carriers (skycaps in airports, porters in hotels) get $1 for the first bag and 50¢ for each additional bag. In the budget hotels, tips are not expected.

Special Deals

The US is probably the most promotion-oriented society on earth, and LA is no exception. Though the bargaining common in many other countries is not widespread, you can often work angles to cut costs. For example, at hotels in the off-season, casually and respectfully mentioning a competitor's rate may prompt a manager to lower the quoted price. Artisans may consider a negotiated price for large purchases. Discount coupons are widely available – check circulars in Sunday papers, at supermarkets, tourist offices or chambers of commerce.

Taxes

Unlike many countries of the world, including neighboring Canada, the USA has no value-added tax. Each state, instead, sets its own tax: most have sales tax, many have state income taxes, some – including California – have both.

Occasionally, the tax is included in the advertised price (some examples are plane tickets, gasoline, drinks in a bar and admission tickets for museums or theaters). Restaurant meals and drinks, accommodations and most other purchases are taxed, and this is added to the advertised cost. Unless otherwise stated, prices given in this book don't reflect local taxes.

In LA, the state sales tax of 7.25%, and an additional county sales tax of 1% (for a total of 8.25%), applies to all restaurant bills as well as most shopping. It does *not* apply to grocery shopping, except for certain taxable items such as alcoholic beverages.

A 'transient occupancy tax' is added to room rates at all hotels, motels and even hostels. Because this is a tax levied by individual cities, it varies, ranging from 11.85% in Pasadena, 12% in Santa Monica, 13% in West Hollywood to 14% in Los Angeles and Beverly Hills. Services such as manicures, haircuts and taxi rides, are not taxed.

POST & COMMUNICATIONS
Postal Rates

Postage rates increase every few years. At the time of writing, rates for 1st-class mail within the USA are 33¢ for letters up to 1oz (22¢ for each additional ounce) and 20¢ for postcards.

International airmail rates (except to Canada and Mexico) are 60¢ for a half-ounce letter, $1 for a 1oz letter and 40¢ for each additional half ounce. The international postcard rate is 50¢. Letters to Canada are 46¢ for a half-ounce letter, 52¢ for a 1oz letter and 40¢ for a postcard. Letters to Mexico are 40¢ for a half-ounce letter, 46¢ for a 1oz letter and 35¢ for a postcard. Aerogrammes are 50¢.

The cost for parcels airmailed anywhere within the USA is $3.20 for 2 pounds or less, increasing by $1 per pound up to $6 for 5 pounds. For heavier items, the rates differ according to the distance mailed. Books, periodicals and computer disks can be sent by a cheaper 4th-class rate.

Sending Mail

Generally, postage stamps are available at post offices only, though occasionally they're also sold at supermarkets. Be aware that stamp-dispensing machines that are commonly found in convenience stores can be a rip-off, charging you more than face value and sometimes not returning change.

If you have the correct postage, you can drop your mail into any blue mailbox. However, if you need to weigh your mail or are sending a package 16oz or larger, you must bring it to a post office. There are dozens – if not hundreds – of post office branches throughout LA. Most have restricted opening hours, usually weekdays 9 am to 5 pm, to noon on Saturday. The main post office (Map 5; ☎ 213-617-4543) is the Terminal Annex next to Downtown's Union Station at 900 N Alameda St. Other handy post offices are at 325 N Maple Drive in Beverly Hills (Map 11; ☎ 800-275-8777), 1248 5th St in Santa Monica (Map 12; ☎ 310-576-2626), and 967 E Colorado Blvd in Pasadena (☎ 626-405-0879). If none of these are close by, check the phone book or call ☎ 800-275-8777.

Letters sent within Los Angeles usually take one day for delivery; delivery time for intrastate and interstate mail depends on the distance and remoteness of the addressee and can be anything from one day to a week. Mail sent to major cities overseas usually takes about four to seven days, though this varies from country to country. For guaranteed fast delivery, most people rely on more costly private carrier services such as FedEx and UPS (United Postal Service).

Receiving Mail

You can have mail sent to you care of 'General Delivery' at any post office that has its own five-digit zip (postal) code. Select a convenient post office, ask them for the correct address and pick-up times. Mail is usually held for 10 days before it's returned to the sender. Ask your correspondents to write 'hold for arrival' on their letters. Mail should be addressed like this:

    Lucy Chang
    c/o General Delivery
    Los Angeles, CA 90025

If you have an American Express Card or traveler's checks, you may have mail sent to any American Express office (for addresses, see Exchanging Money earlier in this chapter or check the phone book). The service is free if you present your card or checks upon pick-up. The sender should make sure that the words 'Client's Mail' appear somewhere on the envelope. American Express will hold mail for 30 days but won't accept registered post or parcels.

Telephone

All phone numbers within the USA consist of a three-digit area code followed by a seven-digit local number. If you call locally, just dial the seven-digit number. If you are calling outside your area code, dial 1 + the three-digit area code + the seven-digit number. If you're calling from abroad, the country code for the USA is 1.

For directory assistance within the LA area, dial ☎ 411. For directory assistance outside of LA, dial 1 + the three-digit area code of the place you want to call + 555-1212. For example, to obtain directory assistance for San Francisco, dial ☎ 1-415-555-1212.

Beware: The costs for this service are outrageous and may go up in the near future.

Area Codes Thanks to a growing population and new technology such as fax machines, computer modems, cellular phones and pagers, LA has been running out of phone numbers and has had to subdivide existing area codes. This process has created an incredibly complicated and confusing patchwork. After a new area code is introduced, the old one may still be used for another six months. Further additions are apparently under discussion.

Downtown LA	☎ 213
Hollywood	☎ 323
Beverly Hills	☎ 310
West LA	☎ 310
Santa Monica	☎ 310
South Bay	☎ 310
Pasadena	☎ 626
San Fernando Valley	☎ 818
Long Beach	☎ 562
Northern Orange County	☎ 714
Southern Orange County	☎ 949
Santa Barbara	☎ 805
Riverside	☎ 909
San Diego	☎ 619

The 800 and 888 area codes are designated for toll-free numbers within the US and sometimes Canada as well. For directory assistance on a toll-free number, dial ☎ 800-555-1212 (no charge). Numbers beginning with 900 – phone sex, horoscopes, jokes, etc – charge premium rates.

Many businesses use letters instead of numbers for their telephone number in an attempt to make it snappy and memorable. Sometimes it works, but sometimes it's difficult to read the letters on the phone (1 – none; 2 – ABC; 3 – DEF; 4 – GHI; 5 – JKL; 6 – MNO; 7 – PRS; 8 – TUV; 9 – WXY).

Pay Phones Calls within LA cost a minimum of 35¢, and rates go up with distance (for example, calls from Santa Monica to Hollywood cost 55¢ and are limited to three minutes). Long-distance rates vary depending on the destination and which telephone company you use – call the operator (☎ 0) for rate information. Be sure to decline the operator's offer to put your call through, however, because operator-assisted calls are exorbitant compared to direct-dial calls.

Making international calls with cash from pay phones can be expensive and frustrating, because phones are only equipped to accept quarters. You will be required to deposit sufficient coins to pay for the first three minutes. Some pay phones allow the use of credits cards, but be sure to read the small print about rates before punching in your number. You'll save money if the person you're calling is willing to call you back. Simply place a brief call to provide the direct number listed on the pay phone.

Hotel Phones If you're staying at an expensive hotel, it's best to resist making calls from your room. Most hotels add a service charge of 50¢ to $1.50 per call even for local and toll-free calls, and have especially hefty surcharges for long-distance calls. Just as with pay phones, it may be cheaper to have the person call you back at the hotel. Ironically, the cheaper the hotel, the more likely it is to levy no surcharges at all; sometimes local calls are even free.

International Calls For a direct international call, dial 011 + the country code + the area code and phone number. (To find the country code, check a local phone book or call the operator.) International rates depend on the time of day, the destination and the telephone company you use. The lowest international rates available are for calls made from phones in private homes. So if you're staying with someone, find out how much the call will cost and reimburse them.

Prepaid Calling Cards A new long-distance alternative is prepaid calling cards, which allow purchasers to pay in advance, with access through an 800 number. In amounts of $5, $10, $20 and $50, these cards are available from Western Union, some markets, convenience stores and tourist offices. They may be used from any phone by dialing the 800 number followed by the card code (both listed on the card itself) and then, at a prompt, the number you are calling. The company's computer keeps track of how much value you have left. These cards are often a good deal and are definitely a superior alternative to using coins at pay phones. Be cautious of people watching you dial in the card code – thieves memorize numbers and use them to make costly calls.

Fax
Shops that specialize in office services are the best and most reasonably priced locations from which to send and receive facsimiles. You'll find Mail Boxes Etc and the 24-hour Kinko's franchises throughout the Los Angeles area. Prices tend to be much higher at hotel business-service centers, which may charge as much as $1.50 per page within the US and up to $10 per page overseas. (Some hotels don't charge for receiving faxes, however.)

Email & Internet Access
If you set up an email account with a free Internet access service such as 'Hotmail' (www.hotmail.com), you can access your email from any computer with a Web connection. Otherwise, check with the provider of your account for local access numbers within LA. If you have your own laptop computer, modem and cable, you should be able to connect to the Internet via phone lines in hotels and private homes.

Other locations for getting on-line include public libraries and cybercafes (see the boxed text Where to Log On).

WEBSITES
The World Wide Web is a rich resource for travelers. You can research your trip, hunt down bargain air fares, book hotels, check on weather conditions or chat with locals and other travelers about the best places to visit (or avoid!).

There's no better place to start your Web explorations than the Lonely Planet website (www.lonelyplanet.com). Here you'll find succinct summaries on traveling to most places on earth, postcards from other travelers and the Thorn Tree bulletin board, where you can ask questions before you go or dispense advice when you get back. You can also find travel news and updates to many of Lonely Planet's most popular guidebooks, and the subWWWay section links you to the most useful travel resources elsewhere on the Web.

Web resources abound for Los Angeles. Many of the following are useful in planning and researching your trip; others are just for fun.

General Interest

@LA

www.at-la.com

This has got to be the Godzilla of websites: well-organized and comprehensive, it has links to more than 26,000 sites, sorted in 24 categories and countless sub-categories. Everything from arts/humanities to tourism is covered. The recipient of multiple awards, this site is searchable and also offered in a faster low graphics version.

Official City of Los Angeles Site

www.ci.la.ca.us

This comprehensive site covers everything from city news to the city council agenda to city-sponsored events. There are links to the Los Angeles Police Department, libraries, museums, events and more.

Yahoo Los Angeles

www.yahoo.com/Regional/U_S_States/California/Metropolitan_Areas/Los_Angeles_Metro/

Yahoo's local site provides oodles of links to useful sites in such categories as education, health, travel and transport, events, entertainment as well as the Yellow Pages.

Where to Log On

A multimedia megalopolis, Los Angeles won't hinder anyone wishing to use that fine new friend of travelers, the Internet. If carrying your own laptop and modem is an option, one of the easiest ways to log on or use email is from your hotel room. When making reservations, make sure your room is equipped with a phone line. (This generally won't be a problem, especially with hotels catering to business travelers.) When traveling without such hardware, another simple way to connect is to swing by any public library branch, all of which are equipped for Web browsing, accessing chat groups and sending and retrieving email. You may have to become a library member or produce somebody else's library card to gain access to the computers.

Cybercafes exist throughout LA, though for some reason they are more prevalent in coastal communities. In Santa Monica, the *World Cafe* (Map 12; ☎ 310-392-1661), 2820 Main St, has six terminals with high-speed fiber-optic connections available from 6 to 11 pm nightly except Monday. It also offers free classes, usually on Wednesday. Near Third Street Promenade, the *Interactive Cafe* (Map 12; ☎ 310-395-5009), 215 Broadway, has several terminals as well as a great range of international magazines. It's popular with European visitors.

In Venice is one of LA's oldest cybercafes, *Cyber Java* (Map 12; ☎ 310-581-1300), 1029 Abbot Kinney Blvd. A cross between a cafe and a computer lab, it has a helpful and knowledgeable staff and enough gadgets to give you an office away from the office. Besides Macs and PCs with fast Internet lines and word processing programs, there's a scanner and printers as well as a fax and copy machine. Internet access is $2.25 for 15 minutes; $9 buys an hour. Classes are held regularly. It's open until 11 pm, and yes, it has coffee too. There's a second 24-hour branch at 7080 Hollywood Blvd at La Brea Blvd in Hollywood (☎ 323-466-5600).

In Long Beach you'll find *Megabyte Coffeehouse*, 4135 E Anaheim St, which also has introductory workshops for $15 and advanced classes for $45. It's open every day until at least midnight.

Publications

Los Angeles Times

www.latimes.com

The on-line version of the daily newspaper has international and local news as well as the latest headlines.

www.latimes.com/HOME/DESTLa

This is an excellent guide for visitors with information on nightlife, shopping, beaches, hiking and sights in addition to a humorous on-line version of Steve Harvey's *LA Times* column, 'Only in LA.'

www.calendarlive.com

For up-to-date news on what's on in LA, this exhaustive listing is hard to beat. There are links to hotels, museums, festivals, books, activities and more; many of them are reviewed by an *LA Times* staffer. Best of all, the site is searchable.

LA Weekly

www.laweekly.com

LA's main entertainment weekly has a fairly good on-line version with access to a back-issue archive.

Downtown News

www.downtownnews.com

The *Downtown News* is an excellent weekly newspaper focused exclusively on developments and events in Downtown LA. The site also has tours, descriptions of landmarks, shopping tips, a restaurant guide and lots more.

Transportation

Metropolitan Transit Authority

www.mta.org

This huge website has information on all MTA public transport options, including the Blue Line and Green Line light-rail lines, the Red Line subway and buses.

Big Blue Bus

pen.ci.santa-monica.ca.us/bus

This is the website of the Santa Monica-based Big Blue Bus company with information on routes, schedules, fares, points of interest as well as maps.

Amtrak

www.amtrak.com

Amtrak's well-designed website has schedules, fares and special offers; on-line reservations are possible as well.

Greyhound Bus Lines

www.greyhound.com

The national bus service has an interactive site to check fares and schedules, as well as information on package deals and passes.

BOOKS

Most books are published in different editions by different publishers in different countries. As a result, one book might be a hardcover rarity in one country while it's readily available in paperback in another. Fortunately, bookstores and libraries can search by title or author, so your local bookstore or library is the best place to find out if the following recommendations are available.

Lonely Planet

Lonely Planet publishes several other titles that visitors to LA might find useful. For detailed information on destinations beyond the scope of this book, check out the comprehensive *California & Nevada* guide. LP also publishes Pisces diving & snorkeling guides, including *Southern California* by Darren Douglas. All are available at bookstores or may be ordered from the Lonely Planet website at www.lonelyplanet.com.

Guidebooks

There's a slew of specialized LA guides worth considering. One of the best and most intelligently researched and written is *Discover Los Angeles* (1997) by Letitia Burns O'Connor and published by the J Paul Getty Trust. The author provides thorough descriptions of major sights and destinations throughout LA County and supplements them with essays about cultural topics such as music, literature and theater. She also adds insightful passages about the various neighborhoods.

The *Museum Companion to Los Angeles* (1996) by Borislav Stanic tells you all about the city's museums – large and small – with their hours, parking information and other details. *Off the Beaten Path in Southern California* by Kathy Strong is full of ideas for short getaways and explorations of lesser-known areas in Southern California.

For a different look at LA, consider the excellent *LA Bizarro* (1997) by scenesters Anthony R Lovett and Matt Maranian, who unearthed some truly weird nooks and crannies in LA and introduce them in amusingly written essays. A good source for gay and lesbian travelers is Andrew Collins' *Gay Guide to Los Angeles and Southern California*, with lots of snappily written detailed information on hotels, bars, restaurants and more.

Other guides to consider are *LA Times* columnist John McKinney's series of hiking guides, including the *Day Hiker's Guide to Southern California* (1998) and *Walking Los Angeles: Adventures on the Urban Edge* (1998). Also good reads are *Places to Go with Children in Southern California* (1992) by Stephanie Kegan, and *Away for the Weekend: Southern California* (1993) by Michele and Tom Grimm.

History & Politics

One of the best and most comprehensive sources for just about anything you ever wanted to know about LA is *Los Angeles A to Z* (1997), a heavy encyclopedia meticulously researched and written by Leonard and Dale Pitt and published by the University of California. The 600-page tome covers it all, from AAA to Zuma County Beach, followed by several appendices.

For LA history, check out *Southern California Country: An Island Upon the Land* (1946) by Carey McWilliams; *City-Makers* by Remi Nadeau (1948); *Los Angeles: The Enormous Village, 1781-1981* (1981) by John D Weaver; *Ethnic LA* (1990) by Zena Pearlstone; and a pair of books by State Librarian of California Kevin Starr, *Inventing the Dream* (1985) and *Material Dreams* (1990). Also worth considering is *A Short History of Los Angeles* by Gordon DeMarco.

General

A good introduction to LA's architecture is *Architecture in Los Angeles* (1985) by David Gebhard and Robert Winter. For a more social view of the city's architecture, check out *City of Quartz: Excavating the Future in Los Angeles* (1990) by Mike Davis, and *Los Angeles: The Architecture of Four Ecologies* (1971) by Rainer Banham.

For books relating to the film industry, look for any of the following: *Hollywood: The Pioneers* (1979) by Kevin Brownlow and John Kobal, *Adventures in the Screen Trade* (1985) by William Goldman, *City of Nets: A Portrait of Hollywood in the 1940s* (1986) by Otto Friedrich, *Behind the Scenes* (1989) by Rudy Behlmer, or *The Devil's Candy* (1991) by Julie Salamon.

If you're on a mission to tour the seamy side of Tinseltown, take a look at Kenneth Anger's *Hollywood Babylon* (1975) or read Richard Alleman's *The Moviegoer's Guide to Hollywood* (1985).

For the morbidly interested, *Death in Paradise: An Illustrated History of the LA County Department of Coroner* (1998), by Tony Blanche and Brad Schreiber, documents the behind-the-scenes crime-solving heroics performed by coroners in some of the most celebrated cases, including the 1871 Chinese Massacre and the 1994 Simpson/Goldman murders.

Biographies

Bookstores are usually overflowing with biographies and autobiographies of Hollywood legends past and present. The following provide background to Hollywood and The Industry: *My Autobiography* (1964) by Charles Chaplin, *Norma Jean: The Life of Marilyn Monroe* (1969) by Fred Lawrence Guiles, *Hollywood's Master Showman: The Legendary Sid Grauman* (1983) by Charles Beardsley, *Hollywood Days, Hollywood Nights* (1988) by Ben Stein, and *Goldwyn* (1989) by A Scott Berg.

NEWSPAPERS & MAGAZINES
Los Angeles Times

The *Los Angeles Times* (25¢ daily, $1.50 Sunday) is the third-largest daily newspaper in the US (after the *Wall Street Journal* and the *New York Daily News*). Its daily circulation is 1.1 million; the Sunday edition is 1.4 million. The newspaper was founded in 1881 and later purchased by Harrison Gray Otis, then a conservative voice in the burgeoning city. More than 20 Pulitzer Prizes have been

RICK GERHARTER

awarded to individual writers and for team coverage, including reports on the 1992 Rodney King riots and the 1994 Northridge earthquake. The Sunday edition includes an expanded Calendar section, an excellent source for finding out about cultural events during your stay.

Other Newspapers

Over the last decade, the *LA Times* has managed to squash almost all local competition, starting with the demise of the Hearst Corporation's *Herald-Examiner* in 1989. These days, its principal (if outclassed) competition comes from the *Daily News*, based in the San Fernando Valley, and the *Orange County Register*.

Some of the smaller cities within LA County manage to support their own local papers, including the *Long Beach Press-Telegram*, the *Pasadena Star News* and the *Los Angeles Sentinel*, which serves the African American community. The oldest community newspaper, the Santa Monica *Outlook*, founded in 1875, succumbed in early 1998.

There are also small, advertisement-driven, local community newspapers that are often distributed free. Also free is the *LA Weekly*, issued on Thursdays and available from bookstores, video stores, restaurants and convenience stores. It is required reading for the latest on cutting-edge scenes, trends and events, from mainstream to downright bizarre. Other freebie event rags include the *New Times*, *Showtime* and *The Argonaut*.

International newspapers and those from major US cities are widely available in large bookstores, such as Borders and Barnes & Noble. Major newsstands – particularly prevalent in Santa Monica, West Hollywood and Hollywood – are another good source to try.

Magazines

In recent years, the monthly *Los Angeles Magazine* has undergone frequent turnover of ownership and editorial staff but seems to have finally hit its stride again, especially after it incorporated its main competition, *Buzz*, in mid-1998. This high-brow glossy magazine tries hard to capture the constantly evolving LA *zeitgeist*. Features can be anything from gushy to cynical in tone and cover the spectrum from fluff to investigative, the celebrities to the homeless. Its extensive restaurant listings and reviews are digested with gusto by locals. To keep up with the show-biz scene, consult 'the trades': *Variety* and the *Hollywood Reporter*.

RADIO & TV

Greater Los Angeles has 14 television stations and 34 radio stations, a substantial number of them serving the metropolis' thriving non-English-speaking populations.

The major network affiliates are KCBS, Channel 2; KNBC, Channel 4; KABC, Channel 7; and KTTV (Fox), Channel 11. Independent stations are KTLA, Channel 5; and KCOP, Channel 13. KCET, Channel 28, is affiliated with the Public Broadcasting System. The Spanish-language KMEX, Channel 34, is a Univision affiliate.

Of course, in this day of satellite communications, you can pick up CNN for 24-hour international news, MTV for nonstop rock videos, and dozens of other stations.

For radio, check into KNX 1070 AM or KFWB 980 AM for all-day news and traffic. For music stations, you might try one of the following:

frequency	station	type of music
88.1	KLON	jazz and blues
88.5	KCSN	country
89.9	KCRW	public radio
91.5	KUSC	classical
93.9	KZLA	country
94.7	KTWV	New Age
95.5	KLOS	rock
98.7	STAR	alternative pop
101.1	KRTH	classic rock
101.9	KSCA	Mexican regional
102.7	KIIS	top 40
104.3	KBIG	adult contemporary
105.1	KKGO	classical
105.9	KPWR	hip-hop
106.7	KROQ	alternative rock

PHOTOGRAPHY & VIDEO
Film & Equipment
Print film is widely available at supermarkets and discount drugstores. In general, buy film for the purpose you intend to use it. For general-purpose shooting – for either prints or slides – 100 ASA film is just about the most useful and versatile; it gives you good color and enough speed to capture most situations on film. If you plan to shoot in dark areas or in brightly lit night scenes without a tripod, switch to 400 ASA.

The best and most widely available films are made by Fuji and Kodak. Fuji Velvia and Kodak Elite are easy to process and provide good slide images. Try to stay away from Kodachrome: it's difficult to process quickly and generates lots of headaches if not handled properly. For print film, you can't beat Kodak Gold, though Fuji is comparable and Agfa is coming along.

Film can be damaged by excessive heat, so avoid leaving your camera and film in the car or placing them on the dashboard while driving.

Best Shots in LA

LA offers a plethora of terrific images. The following list suggests places where you are likely to bag some real 'grabbers.'

Garden and architectural scenics
Huntington Gardens in Pasadena; Getty Museum on the Westside.

Portraits of 'The LA Scene' (trends, tattoos, etc)
Melrose Ave; Sunset Strip at night; the Third Street Promenade in Santa Monica; Venice Boardwalk any time of day or year.

Overviews of the city, ocean and mountains
Griffith Park Observatory or Yamashiro Castle in Hollywood (city); Palisades Park in Santa Monica (ocean); LA Convention Center (city with mountains in the background when the smog behaves).

Definitive shots of the Hollywood sign
Top of Beachwood Drive, off Franklin in Hollywood; Griffith Park Observatory. (Note: The sign is trademarked and copyrighted by the Hollywood Chamber of Commerce, which loves to sue for commercial use of its 'real estate.')

Beaches, babes, dudes and waves
Best beach: Santa Monica. Best babes and dudes: Hermosa Beach and Zuma Beach. Waves and surfers: Manhattan Beach (especially around the Pier), Malibu and Zuma Beach.

'Ethnic LA'
First rule: Be cool. There are definite no-go zones and you'd best respect the locals when you whip out your expensive zoom lenses. Riotous Latino life unfurls safely in Downtown along Broadway; great murals are found in East LA and South Central; Chinatown and Little Tokyo are easily accessible, and the people – once you've gained trust and respect – are normally happy to pose.

Historic architecture
Downtown LA; downtown Long Beach; central Hollywood; Wilshire Blvd in Mid-City.

It's worth carrying a spare battery for your camera to avoid disappointment when your camera dies in the middle of nowhere. If you're buying a new camera for your trip, do so several weeks before you leave and practice using it.

Drugstores are a good place to get your film processed cheaply. If you drop the film off by noon, you can usually pick it up the next day. A roll of 100 ASA 35 mm color film with 24 exposures will cost about $6 to be processed. Many venues offer double sets of prints for much less than double the cost. However, one-hour processing services charge up to $11 per 24-exposure roll.

For professional processing and electronic imaging, highly recommended is A&I and its imaging component, A&I Digital. A&I is in Hollywood at 933 N Highland Ave (☎ 323-856-5255) and in Santa Monica at 1550 17th St (Map 12; ☎ 310-264-2622).

For general photo and camera needs, check out the following: Without question the finest camera and film house on the West Coast is the legendary Samy's Camera (Map 10; ☎ 323-938-2420), 200 S La Brea in Hollywood. In Westwood the biggest and best is Bel-Air Camera (Map 11; ☎ 310-208-5150), 10925 Kinross Ave. For good, neighborly service, go to Boulevard Camera (Map 12; ☎ 310-451-0707), at 1201 Wilshire Blvd in Santa Monica.

If your Nikons or Hasselblads take a nosedive just when you're heading out to shoot Pamela Anderson at home, go directly to Camera Service Center (Map 2; ☎ 310-397-0072), 4355 Sepulveda Blvd in Culver City. And right next door, at 4353 Sepulveda, you'll find Cary Photo Lab (☎ 310-398-2484) for excellent B&W work.

Video Systems

Overseas visitors videotaping highlights of their trip should remember that the US uses the National Television System Committee (NTSC) color TV standard, which, unless converted, is not compatible with other standards (PAL or SECAM) used in Africa, Europe, Asia and Australia. Be sure to bring blank tapes that are compatible with your camcorder.

Airport Security

All flight passengers have to pass their luggage through x-ray machines. In general, airport x-ray technology isn't supposed to jeopardize lower-speed film (under 1600 ASA). Recently, however, some new high-powered machines designed to inspect *checked* luggage have been installed at major airports around the world. These machines are capable of conducting high-energy scans that destroy unprocessed film. To be on the safe side, it's best to carry film and loaded cameras in your hand-luggage and ask airport security people to inspect them manually. Pack all your film into a clear plastic bag that you can quickly whip out of your luggage. This not only saves time at the inspection points but also helps minimize confrontations with security staff.

TIME

California is in Pacific Time Zone, which is Greenwich Mean Time minus eight hours. Therefore, when it is noon in Los Angeles, it is 8 pm in London, 9 am in Honolulu, 3 pm in New York, 4 am (the next day) in Singapore and 6 am (the next day) in Sydney or Auckland.

Daylight saving time is in effect from the last Sunday in April to the last Sunday in October. Clocks are set ahead one hour in the spring ('spring forward'), and set back one hour in the fall ('fall back'), meaning that sunset is an hour later during the long days of summer.

ELECTRICITY

Electric current in the US is 110V and outlets are suited for flat two-prong or three-prong (two flat, one round) plugs. If your appliance is made for another electrical system, you will need a transformer or adapter; if you didn't bring one, check drugstores, hardware or consumer-electronics stores such as Radio Shack (for several locations, see the Yellow Pages).

WEIGHTS & MEASURES

When it comes to measurement, LA is no different from the rest of the United States, which clings stubbornly to the Imperial system. Distances are in inches, feet, yards and miles. Three feet equal 1 yard (.914 meters); 1760 yards or 5280 feet equal 1 mile. There are 1.6 kilometers in 1 mile.

Dry weights are in ounces (oz), pounds (lb) and tons (16oz are 1 pound; 2000lb are 1 ton). There are 454 grams in 1 pound.

Liquid measures differ from dry measures in that 1 pint equals 16 fluid oz; 2 pints equal 1 quart, 4 quarts equal a US gallon – or 3.8 liters. (Gasoline is dispensed by the US gallon.)

Temperature is given in degrees Fahrenheit, whereby 32° is the freezing point (0° Celsius).

For information at a glance, see the conversion chart on the inside back cover of this book.

LAUNDRY

Most hostel-style accommodations and many midpriced motels offer laundry facilities at coin-op rates. Larger hotels, however, charge exorbitant prices for one-day service. (How does $2 for a pair of underpants sound?) In such cases, you may want to do your own wash in your bathroom, or deliver your load to a laundry that will charge you as much per pound as the hotel charged for washing those skivvies. No matter where you're staying, you're never far from a coin-operated laundry. If you haven't already spotted one while driving around, ask your hotel for the nearest laundromat.

TOILETS

Foreign visitors should know that the puritanical prudeness, so prevalent in the US, even extends to this most basic human need. Toilets are never called 'toilets' but a slew of euphemisms, including restroom, bathroom, powder room, washroom, men's and ladies' rooms, and little boys' and little girls' rooms.

Public toilets are basically nonexistent, so you have to be assertive and creative in finding facilities. Shopping malls and department stores, hotel lobbies, museums and other public places are your best bets. Ducking into a bar is an OK alternative, though keep in mind that you have to be over 21 to even enter and may be carded at

the entrance. Casual restaurants such as diners and cafes are usually an option, though fancy ones (where you have to pass the host or hostess) may refuse you. Many of the beaches, such as Zuma, Santa Monica, Venice and Manhattan Beach, have decent facilities.

Except in emergencies, don't even bother with places posting signs like 'No public restroom' or 'No public facilities.' Though ubiquitous, gas-station toilets tend to be fairly gross and you often have to ask the cashier for the key.

HEALTH

Los Angeles is a typical first-world destination when it comes to health. The only foreign visitors who may be required to have immunizations are those coming from areas with a history of cholera and yellow fever.

Health Insurance

Health care is outstanding in LA, but it's also very expensive, and without insurance even minor health concerns can easily bust your entire travel budget. Unless your health plan at home provides worldwide coverage, definitely take out travel health insurance. Without evidence of insurance, hospitals may refuse care in all but life-threatening emergencies and refer you instead to LA County/USC Medical Center (Map 3; ☎ 323-226-2622), a public facility at 1200 N State St in East LA where you may have to endure agonizingly long waits while people suffering from gunshot, traffic or stab wounds are attended to before you.

Wide varieties of policies are available and your travel agent should have recommendations. International student travel policies handled by STA Travel and other organizations are usually a good value. Some highly regarded insurers are Access America (☎ 800-284-8300) and Travel Guard (☎ 800-826-1300). Some policies specifically exclude 'dangerous activities' such as scuba diving, motorcycling and even trekking. If these activities are on your agenda, search for policies that include them.

While you may find a policy that pays doctors or hospitals directly, be aware that many private doctors and clinics in LA will demand payment at the time of service, especially if you're not a local resident. Unless you need acute treatment, it's best to call around and choose one willing to accept your insurance. No matter what the circumstances, be sure to keep all receipts and documentation. Some policies ask you to call back (reverse charges) to a center in your home country for an immediate assessment of your problem. Also check whether the policy covers ambulance fees or an emergency flight home.

Medical Services

Should you require emergency treatment, call ☎ 911 and request an ambulance. Or have someone take you to the emergency room (ER) at a major hospital such as the Hollywood Presbyterian Hospital (Map 9; ☎ 323-660-5350), 1300 N Vermont Ave near Barnsdall Park; the Cedars-Sinai Medical Center (Map 10; ☎ 310-855-5000), 8700 Beverly Blvd near Beverly Hills and West Hollywood; or the UCLA Medical Center (Map 11; ☎ 310-825-9111), 10833 LeConte Ave in Westwood. Have your insurance card ready for display.

For outpatient treatment of non-life-threatening ailments – such as a sprained ankle, a bladder infection or a serious flu – ask someone you know to recommend a doctor or check under Clinics in the Yellow Pages.

If you don't have insurance or have a plan with a high deductible, you can keep costs down by going to a state-subsidized clinic catering to low-income people. These are usually well-equipped and staffed with nurse practitioners (highly qualified nurses), volunteer doctors or doctors in residency. Often you can get an appointment on the same day. Fees are sliding-scale, assessed on your ability to pay.

Venice Family Clinic (Map 12; ☎ 310-392-8630), 604 Rose Ave in Venice, is among the best for general health concerns. The Women's Clinic (Map 11; ☎ 310-203-8899), 9911 Pico Blvd, suite 500 in Century City, provides gynecological care, and is a good place to go – for both women and men – when suspecting venereal disease. The Los

Angeles Free Clinic has two branches, one (Map 9; ☎ 323-462-4158) at 6043 Hollywood Blvd in Hollywood, and another (Map 10; ☎ 323-653-1990) at 8405 Beverly Blvd near the Beverly Center mall.

Nonprescription medications, as well as condoms, can be purchased in drugstores throughout LA. Condoms are also commonly available from vending machines in public restrooms at universities, bars and night clubs and in some restaurants and hotels. Prescription drugs are filled at every pharmacy. After hours, try one of the large drugstore chains, such as Sav-On or Rite Aid, whose on-premise pharmacies stay open 24 hours.

Precautions

While LA water is safe to drink, it does not taste great, and most people prefer bottled water. The sun presents far greater health risks. Unless you're aiming for the complexion of a lobster or you are foolish enough to ignore skin-cancer warnings, cover every exposed body part with high-SPF (sun protection factor) sunscreen whenever outdoors – and not just when lying by the pool or going to the beach. Days often start out cool and overcast only to turn gloriously sunny by lunchtime, so carry a small tube of sunscreen with you.

Coastal communities aside, summers can get unbearably hot in LA, making heat exhaustion a common problem. It's easily avoided by drinking lots of liquids, preferably plain water. To cut costs, you might consider carrying a water bottle with you and refilling it at water fountains or in restrooms.

WOMEN TRAVELERS

Women often face different situations when traveling than men do. In general, women are safe alone in most parts of LA, though it's always good to be aware of your surroundings. Avoid walking alone at night, except when in touristy areas such as Third Street Promenade in Santa Monica or Universal City Walk.

Try to avoid the 'bad' or unsafe neighborhoods or districts any time of day. If you must go into or through these areas, use a private

DAVID PEEVERS

vehicle (car or taxi). If you are unsure which areas are considered unsafe, ask at your hotel or telephone a tourist office for advice. Tourist maps can sometimes be deceiving, compressing areas that are not tourist attractions and making the distances look shorter than they are. As with anywhere else, it's more dangerous to walk at night, though crimes can occur even in the daytime.

Given strict US anti-sexual-harassment laws, getting hassled by men is a much rarer occurrence here than in other parts of the world. However, some men may interpret a woman drinking alone in a bar as a bid for male company, whether you intend it that way or not. If you don't want the company, most men will respect a firm but polite 'no thank you.' If someone continues to harass you, protesting loudly will often make the offender slink away with embarrassment – or will at least draw attention to your predicament. If you are assaulted, call the police (☎ 911) or the 24-hour Rape and Battering Hotline (☎ 310-392-8381) operated by the Los Angeles Commission on Assaults Against Women. The Santa Monica-UCLA Medical Center at 1250 16th St in Santa Monica has a dedicated 24-hour Rape Treatment Center (Map 12; ☎ 310-319-4000).

To deal with potential dangers, some women protect themselves with a whistle, mace, pepper spray or self-defense training. It's hugely ironic that while getting a gun in LA involves little more than buying one at a gun store, the legal purchase and carrying of mace requires you to have a special license issued only after attending a four-hour workshop. If you're interested in such a license, ask at any police station about sessions offered in the neighborhood.

Organizations

To find out about local happenings, drop by the Sisterhood Bookstore (Map 11; ☎ 310-477-7300), 1351 Westwood Blvd, and look at their bulletin board. While you're there take a look at their travel section, which offers many books geared towards women travelers. They also carry *The Women's Yellow Pages*, an excellent resource.

The YWCA has several locations in Los Angeles at 2501 W Vernon Ave (☎ 213-295-4288) and in Santa Monica at 2019 14th St (☎ 310-452-3881).

Planned Parenthood (☎ 800-328-2826) has 10 clinics in the Los Angeles area, providing gynecological care, birth control, and testing for pregnancy and sexually transmitted diseases. The Women Helping Women Services talkline (☎ 213-655-3807) provides counseling.

GAY & LESBIAN TRAVELERS

As the cosmopolitan capital of California, it's no surprise that LA boasts a high concentration of the state's gay population. Outdone in sheer number only by San Francisco's Castro district, West Hollywood is by far the gayest community in LA with countless restaurants, bars, clubs, cinemas and shops owned by, and largely catering to, a homosexual audience. The beach cities of Santa Monica and Venice also have established gay and lesbian communities, as do Silver Lake, North Hollywood and Studio City. Long Beach has a fairly large homosexual contingent as well.

Tolerance of homosexuality is generally high in LA, and the sight of homosexual couples holding hands or kissing is not uncommon, especially – of course – in gay communities.

Resources & Information

A Different Light Bookstore (Map 10; ☎ 310-854-6601), 8853 Santa Monica Blvd,

West Hollywood, is the area's number-one gay bookstore and is also a fine place to go to start learning your way around. You can browse the stacks daily until midnight. Nearby is Unicorn Bookstore (☎ 310-652-6253), 8940 Santa Monica Blvd, with a smaller selection. The Sisterhood Bookstore (Map 11; 310-477-7300), 1351 Westwood Blvd, Westwood, has books, music, jewelry and crafts by women for women, though it does not cater exclusively to lesbians. In Pasadena, Page One: Books by and for Women (☎ 626-796-8418), 1200 E Walnut St, has plenty of lesbian fiction and nonfiction.

Gay and lesbian magazines are excellent sources for catching up on the latest trends, hot dance clubs, health & fitness centers and restaurants. You'll find stacks of these free periodicals by the entrances to gay-friendly establishments. The market is hugely competitive and many magazines disappear into thin air faster than moths in a flame.

Among the most established are *Frontiers Magazine* and *Edge*, both of which provide full coverage of events, the bar and restaurant scene, as well as news and entertainment features. Others to look out for are *In Los Angeles* and *Front Magazine*. All are published bi-weekly. Among lesbian publications, the *Lesbian News* has demonstrated the greatest longevity (since 1975); another source is the monthly *LA Girl Guide*. At some outlets you may also find the very useful *Gay & Lesbian Yellow Pages*, chock-full with gay-friendly businesses and organizations from AIDS/HIV to woodworking. It's free and is published annually.

Useful publications for sale include *The Women's Traveller* with listings for lesbians and *Damron's Address Book* for men, both published by Damron Company (☎ 415-255-0404, 800-462-6654), PO Box 422458, San Francisco, CA 94142-2458. *Ferrari's Places for Women and Places for Men* is another good source. Also available is the *Gay Guide to Los Angeles & Southern California* by Andrew Collins.

Organizations

The LA Gay & Lesbian Center (☎ 323-993-7400, www.gay-lesbian-center.org), 1625 N Schrader Blvd in West Hollywood, is a one-stop service and health agency. Besides operating several clinics, it also offers legal services, a packed schedule of activities and a youth center. Most services are free or low cost.

For AIDS- and HIV-related questions, contact the AIDS Hotline of Southern California (☎ 800-922-2437), the National AIDS/HIV Hotline (☎ 800-342-2437) or the AIDS Healthcare Foundation (☎ 800-243-2101). AIDS Project Los Angeles (APLA; ☎ 323-993-1600) has offices at 1313 N Vine St in Hollywood.

If you've been harassed, threatened or assaulted, you can report the incident to the Gay & Lesbian Alliance Against Defamation (GLADD; ☎ 800-429-6334), the Anti-Violence Project (☎ 323-993-7673) or City of West Hollywood – Gay Bashing Complaints (☎ 323-848-6470). The ACLU – Gay & Lesbian Rights Chapter (☎ 323-977-9500) is an advocate group with offices at 1616 Beverly Blvd.

Other organizations include the Gay & Lesbian National Hotline (☎ 888-843-4564, www.glnh.org); the Gay, Lesbian & Bi Center (☎ 310-379-2850) at 2009-A Artesia Blvd in Redondo Beach; the Lambda Legal Defense & Education Fund (☎ 323-937-2728, www.lambdalegal.org) at 6030 Wilshire Blvd, suite 200; and the National Gay/Lesbian Task Force (☎ 202-332-6483) in Washington, DC.

DISABLED TRAVELERS

Public buildings (including hotels, restaurants, theaters and museums) are required by law to be wheelchair accessible and to have special restroom facilities. Public transportation services (buses, trains and taxis) must be made accessible to all, including those in wheelchairs.

Getting around Los Angeles on public transport while confined to a wheelchair is possible but requires some planning. The Metropolitan Transportation Authority and other public transport agencies, such as the Big Blue Bus company of Santa Monica, operate a fleet of wheelchair-accessible buses. For schedule information, call (☎ 213-626-4455, or TDD ☎ 800-252-9040). The Paratransit Referral Service Info Line (☎ 800-431-7882) gladly refers mobility-impaired people to door-to-door transportation services in LA County. For information about traveling to and from Los Angeles International Airport, contact Travelers Aid (☎ 310-646-2270), or visit one of their many booths at the airport (the largest is in the Tom Bradley Terminal). Car rental companies can supply hand-controlled vehicles at a day or two's notice, and taxi services can provide vans to accommodate wheelchairs.

Larger private and chain hotels (see the Places to Stay chapter for listings) have suites for disabled guests. Telephone companies are required to provide relay operators for the hearing impaired; call ☎ 800-735-2922 (voice) or TDD/TTY at ☎ 800-735-2929. Many banks now provide ATM instructions in Braille, and you will find audible crossing signals (such as the famed 'cuckoo-crossings' in Santa Monica) as well as dropped curbs at busier roadway intersections.

All major airlines, Greyhound buses and Amtrak trains allow service animals to accompany passengers, and frequently sell two-for-one packages when attendants of seriously disabled passengers are required. Airlines will also provide assistance for connecting, boarding and deplaning the flight – just ask when making your reservation. (Note: Airlines must accept wheelchairs as checked baggage and have an onboard chair available, though some advance notice may be required on smaller aircraft.)

Organizations

A central clearinghouse for information, referrals and tips about accessibility and service availability is the LA County Commission on Disabilities (☎ 213-974-1053 or TDD at ☎ 213-974-1707). Other useful numbers include the Center for the Partially Sighted (☎ 310-458-3501), which provides counseling, equipment and health information programs; the 24-hour Crisis Line for the Handicapped (☎ 800-426-4263), which offers volunteer counseling, support, information and referrals; and the Greater LA Council on Deafness (GLAD; ☎ 213-478-8000 voice and TDD) for counseling, interpretation, information and referrals.

SENIOR TRAVELERS

Although the age at which one qualifies for benefits varies with the attraction, people of 50 years and up can expect to receive cut rates and benefits. Make sure to inquire whether your hotel, restaurant or other establishment offers such discounts. Local seniors centers (see the Yellow Pages) can usually help with recommendations, or the County of Los Angeles Area Agency on Aging (☎ 213-738-4004) can send you its Senior Center Directory, which might refer you to helpful people.

Elderhostel (☎ 877-426-8056), 75 Federal St, Boston, MA 02110, organizes programs in most US cities, including Los Angeles, which feature college level courses of study in addition to pleasant accommodations. Grand Circle Travel (☎ 617-350-7500), 347 Congress St, Boston, MA 02210, offers senior travelers escorted tours and travel information. It also provides a free booklet entitled *Going Abroad: 101 Tips for Mature Travelers* that will prove useful in planning for domestic travel as well.

It is certainly worth contacting the American Association of Retired Persons (☎ 202-434-2277), 601 E St NW, Washington, DC 20049 – a flash of its membership card (available at just $8 a year to US residents over 55) is often enough to bypass any '65 and up' limits for senior rates.

LOS ANGELES FOR CHILDREN

Traveling successfully with young children requires planning and effort. Don't try to overdo things; even for adults, packing too much into the time available can cause problems. And make sure the activities include the kids as well – balance that day at the Getty Center with a visit to the zoo or the beach. Include the kids in the trip planning; if they've helped to work out where you are going, they will be much more interested when they get there. LP's *Travel with Children* by Maureen Wheeler is a good source of information for this kind of thing. For area-specific information, also consider

Places to Go with Children in Southern California (1992) by Stephanie Kegan.

Most car-rental firms have children's safety seats for hire at a nominal cost, but be sure to book them in advance. The same goes for highchairs and cots (cribs); they're common in many restaurants and hotels, but in limited numbers. The choice of baby food, infant formulas, soy and cow's milk, disposable nappies (diapers) and the like is great in LA supermarkets. Diaper changing stations can be found in many public restrooms in malls, department stores and in family-oriented restaurants.

It's perfectly fine to bring your kids, even toddlers, along to casual restaurants (though not to many of the upscale ones), cafes and daytime events.

Most of the larger hotels offer a baby-sitting service, and others may be able to help you arrange one. Alternatively, there are a number of agencies you can contact. Be sure to ask whether your sitter is licensed and bonded, what the person charges per hour, whether there's a minimum fee and whether the sitter charges extra for meals and transportation. Established agencies you might try include the Baby Sitters Guild (☎ 323-658-8792), Best Babysitters Service (☎ 323-857-0023), Family Care Agency (☎ 310-550-8936) and Baby Sitters Agency of Santa Monica (☎ 310-306-5437).

Activities

It's easy to keep kids entertained in LA, given the myriad choices for outdoor explorations along the beaches, in the mountains and even in the urban core. Amusement parks such as Disneyland, Knott's Berry Farm, Universal Studios and Six Flags Magic Mountain are of course hugely popular among the kids, but – exhilarating as they may be – they're also very expensive and exhausting for everyone in the family. This book contains plenty of ideas for fun things to do, including but not limited to what's listed here. For ideas about what to do outdoors, see the Activities section in the Things to See & Do chapter.

Here is a short list of destinations with references to those sections of the Things to See & Do chapter containing more detailed information.

Aquarium of the Pacific
  (Coastal Communities – Long Beach)
California Science Center
  (Downtown – Exposition Park)
Carole & Barry Kaye Museum of Miniature Art
  (Mid-City – Miracle Mile)
Children's Museum (Downtown)
Gene Autry Western Heritage Museum
  (Griffith Park)
Griffith Observatory & Planetarium (Hollywood)
Kidspace (Pasadena)
Los Angeles Zoo (Griffith Park)
Museum of Flying
  (Coastal Communities – Santa Monica)
Natural History Museum of LA County
  (Downtown – Exposition Park)
Page Museum at La Brea Discoveries & La Brea
  Tarpits (Mid-City – Miracle Mile)
UCLA Center for Ocean Discoveries
  (Coastal Communities – Santa Monica)

Galleries

LA has a few galleries dedicated to children. They include the excellent Every Picture Tells a Story (Map 10; ☎ 323-932-6070), 7525 Beverly Blvd, which has lots of original art by children's-book illustrators. Storyopolis (Map 10; ☎ 310-358-2500), 116 N Robertson Blvd, is similar but also has a book and toy section, as well as children's activities such as storytelling and craft workshops.

Children's Book World (☎ 310-559-2665), 10580½ W Pico Blvd in west LA, offers free storytelling sessions for children ages three to eight every Saturday. At Color on Clay (☎ 213-896-0078), 404 S Figueroa St, No 312, kids choose a ceramic object (plates, mugs, etc) and paint it, letting their imagination go as wild as they want. The object is then fired in a kiln and may be picked up three days later or mailed to you.

Theater

Since 1963, Bob Baker Marionette Theater (Map 5; ☎ 213-250-9995), 1345 W 1st St in Downtown, has enthralled kids ages two to 12 with its adorable singing and dancing marionettes and stuffed animals that interact with their young audiences seated on a carpet. It's pure magic. Shows are weekdays at 10:30 am and weekends at 2:30 pm, no show on Monday. Tickets cost $10. There's free parking next to the theater.

In Santa Monica, the Puppet and Magic Center (☎ 310-656-0483), 1255 2nd St, is a 40-seat theater with regularly scheduled performances as well as puppet workshops and a puppet museum. Shows are $3.50 to $6; the workshop is $3.

Other theaters that occasionally stage shows for children include the Santa Monica Playhouse, the Coronet Theater and Will Geer Theatricum Botanicum (for details on these, check out the Entertainment chapter). Also check the Calendar section of the *LA Times*.

USEFUL ORGANIZATIONS
Headquarters of the Automobile Association of Southern California (Map 5; ☎ 213-741-3111), a subdivision of the American Automobile Association (AAA), are in a Spanish colonial mansion at 2601 S Figueroa St, and there are several other offices throughout the metropolitan area. The 'auto club' provides its members and those of affiliated clubs with motoring information for the LA region including maps, accommodation suggestions and helpful travel planners. It also provides members with emergency road services and towing (☎ 800-400-4222).

Hostelling International (HI), the new name of the International Youth Hostel Federation (IYHF), has its local office beside the Santa Monica hostel, at 1434 2nd St, Santa Monica CA 90401 (☎ 310-393-9913). Members (for $25 per year) can take advantage of some of the lowest bed rates available by bringing their membership cards and easy spirits to any of HI's six Southern California hostels.

LIBRARIES
City Libraries
The Downtown Central Library (Map 5; ☎ 213-228-7000), 630 W 5th St, in a historic building designed by Bertram Goodhue, is the repository of 2.1 million books and half a million historical photographs. Restoration after a fire in 1986 resulted in a 1993 reopening with an additional wing that doubled the library space. The collection is supplemented with plenty of art and an active calendar of readings, lectures, storytelling sessions for kids and art exhibits.

Library hours are Monday and Thursday through Saturday 10 am to 5:30 pm, Tuesday and Wednesday noon to 8 pm, and Sunday 1 to 5 pm. Free guided tours are held weekdays at 12:30 pm, Saturday at 11 am and 2 pm, and Sunday at 2 pm.

Here are some of the highlights:

1st Floor/Old Wing This is where the information desk, check-in and check-out counters and main copy machine sections are located; also here are a cafe, the Photography Gallery and the Popular Library with recently published books.

2nd Floor/Old Wing This houses the Children's Reading Room in a beautifully muralled section off the 64-foot-tall Lodwrick M Cook Rotunda, with a painted dome, an impressive chandelier representing the solar system and the card catalogue drawers from the old library. Music and arts & recreation departments are here as well. Also note the pair of sphinxes made from marble with bronze headdresses and wings in the alcove opposite the children's reading room.

2nd Floor/New Wing Walk to the eight-story atrium (four floors above ground, four below) named after former LA mayor Tom Bradley who died suddenly in September 1998. The whimsical chandeliers floating from the glass ceiling are made of fiberglass, aluminum and foam and represent the three categories of information available in the library: the natural world, the human-made world and the spiritual world.

Go to Lower Level 1 for books on business and economics. Lower Level 2 focuses on science and technology, while Lower Level 3 houses the social science, philosophy and religion sections. Lower Level 4 has books on history and a historic photo collection.

Other excellent public libraries are the **Beverly Hills Library** (☎ 310-288-2220), at 444 N Rexford Drive, which has 225,000 volumes and specializations in local history and fine arts; the **Santa Monica Library** (Map 12; ☎ 310-458-8600), 1343 6th St, with 405,000 books, including major collections in art, business, fiction and history; and the **Glendale Central Library** (☎ 818-548-2020), 222 E Harvard St, a repository of 400,000 tomes with focal points on business and California and local history.

University Libraries

The **University of California at Los Angeles** (UCLA; Map 11; ☎ 310-825-4321), on Westwood Blvd in Westwood, has a vast library containing 6.6 million volumes spread over 10 departments in separate buildings. Of greatest general interest is the Research Library (☎ 310-825-4732, reference 310-825-1323), though there are also specialized libraries on the arts, bio-medical, engineering and math sciences, geology, law, management, music and physics. UCLA also operates the historic William Andrews Clark Library in the West Adams district (see Things to See & Do for details).

The **University of Southern California** (USC; Map 6; ☎ 213-740-6050), just north of Exposition Park, has a network of 17 libraries with a total of 2.8 million books, 3 million photographs, and electronic databases. USC's collections in architecture, cinema, international and public affairs, American literature, regional history, marine science, philosophy, Latin American studies and Korean studies are particularly noteworthy. The main repository is the Doheny Memorial Library (☎ 213-740-4039).

Other university libraries in LA County include the James Lemont Fogg Library (☎ 626-396-2233; 70,000 volumes) of the **Art Center College of Design** in Pasadena at 1700 Lida St; the **Caltech** Library System (Map 16; ☎ 626-395-6405; 567,000 volumes) at 1201 E California St also in Pasadena; the **Cal State Northridge** Oviatt Library (☎ 818-677-2285; 1.1 million volumes), 18111 Nordhoff St; and the **Cal State Los Angeles** John F Kennedy Memorial Library (☎ 213-343-4927; 1 million volumes), 5151 State University Drive.

CULTURAL CENTERS

The French Alliance Française de LA (☎ 310-652-0306) is at 215 S La Cienega Blvd in Beverly Hills. The German Goethe Institute (Map 10; ☎ 323-525-3388) is at 5750 Wilshire Blvd, suite 100, in the Miracle Mile district.

DANGERS & ANNOYANCES

Much has been written about crime in Los Angeles, though overall figures have gone down in recent years. If you take ordinary precautions, chances are you won't be victimized.

It is perhaps too obvious to state that you should avoid 'bad' neighborhoods, especially after dark. The streets of Hollywood yield dangers from drug addicts and crazed people, and should be avoided after nightfall; ditto for Venice. Much of South Central LA and East LA are plagued with interracial gang activity, so be informed of the dangers before wandering into those areas, even before the sun goes down. Exercise a bit of extra caution in Silver Lake, parts of Downtown and West Hollywood. Safer

areas at night are Santa Monica, Beverly Hills, Westwood, Marina del Rey, Redondo Beach, Hermosa Beach, Manhattan Beach and Pasadena.

In general, be aware of your surroundings and who may be watching you. Avoid walking on dimly lit streets at night, particularly when alone. Walk purposefully. Avoid unnecessary displays of money or jewelry. Divide money and credit cards to avoid losing everything. Always aim to use ATM machines in well-trafficked areas and keep your eyes open constantly.

Depending as much as Los Angeles does upon the automobile, it should come as little surprise that car thefts and even car jackings are more common here than in other areas of the country. Always lock your car and put valuables out of sight, even if leaving the car for just a moment. Never leave anything of value – cameras, video cameras, purses, etc – in the back seat: you may return to your car to find all the windows broken. Rent a car with a lockable trunk, but don't leave valuables behind when you park. Keep your windows closed and your doors locked if anyone approaches your vehicle. If your car is bumped from behind in a remote area, don't stop until reaching a well-lit, busy area or service station. Gangs who orchestrate freeway 'accidents' and then sue are not uncommon. However, freeway shootings, a plague in the early '90s, have been almost completely curtailed.

Thefts are rare in major hotels with good security, but they are not uncommon in other accommodations, especially cheap motels. Keep your room locked when you're gone, and take advantage of the office safe for jewelry or documents you may not be carrying with you. Never leave money or cameras in view in restaurants or bars. Beware of pickpockets and petty thieves in crowds. Keep tight hold of your purse or wear your money and passport in a secure place on your person. If you are unlucky enough to have something stolen, report it immediately to your hotel's front desk or to the nearest police station (see Emergency for more information).

Street people and panhandlers abound in certain parts of town such as Downtown and Santa Monica, which is known for its liberal attitude toward the homeless. Nearly all of the panhandlers are harmless. It's your judgment call whether it's appropriate to offer them money or anything else.

EMERGENCY

In case of emergency, dial ☎ 911 and request assistance from the police, fire department, ambulance or paramedics. Some other crisis contacts include:

AIDS Hot Line	☎ 800-342-2437
Alcohol & Drug Referral Hotline	☎ 800-252-6465
Crisis Response Unit	☎ 800-833-3376
Poison Information Center	☎ 800-777-6476
Rape & Battering Hotline	☎ 310-392-8381
Suicide Prevention Hotline	☎ 800-333-4444

Local telephone directories have a First Aid & Survival Guide, which includes advice on surviving an earthquake and a list of steps in performing CPR.

If you have something stolen, report it to the police – you'll need a police report to make a claim if you have a travel insurance policy. If your credit cards, cash cards, or traveler's checks have been stolen, notify your bank or the relevant company as soon as possible. For refunds for lost or stolen traveler's checks (not credit cards) call American Express (☎ 800-221-7282), MasterCard (☎ 800-223-9920), Thomas Cook (☎ 800-223-7373) or Visa (☎ 800-227-6811). For lost American Express Cards call ☎ 800-528-4800. To report other lost or stolen credit cards, check the local Yellow Pages under Credit Cards.

Foreign visitors who lose their passport should contact their consulate in Los Angeles; a list of consulate phone numbers are listed earlier in this chapter, as well in the Yellow Pages under Consulates. Consulates usually prefer to issue you a temporary 'get you home' passport and will also suggest you apply for a replacement when you get back. Having a photocopy of the

Shake, Rattle & Roll: Earthquakes in LA

Being caught in an earthquake is perhaps what travelers to LA fear most. In fact, earthquakes occur in greater number than most visitors realize – dozens a week. Most are of a magnitude that makes them detectable only by sensitive seismological instruments. Occasionally, a tremor of 4.5 or 5.0 on the Richter scale may give you a start and rattle a few glasses; it will pass in a moment, leaving only heart palpitations.

Many Angelenos are prepared with an emergency kit for major earthquakes. Ideally, it includes a first-aid kit, portable radio, flashlights and extra batteries, blankets, essential medications, three days' worth of food and three gallons of water per person.

Look on the inside front cover of any telephone directory for more details, or call the Earthquake Preparedness Hotline (☎ 818-908-2671).

In the extremely unlikely event that you're in Los Angeles during a major earthquake – such as the January 1994 Northridge trembler – the LA Fire Department recommends you do the following:

Mother Nature's aftermath (1994)

- If you are indoors, stay indoors. Immediately take cover under a desk or table, or under a doorway. Stay clear of windows, mirrors, or anything in danger of falling, such as bookshelves or file cabinets. Don't use the elevators. If you're in a shopping mall or large public building, expect the alarm or sprinkler systems to come on.
- If you are outdoors, get into an open area away from buildings, trees and power lines. If you are driving, pull over to the side of the road away from bridges, overpasses and power lines. Stay inside the car until the shaking stops.
- If you are on a sidewalk near buildings, duck into a doorway to protect yourself from falling bricks, glass and debris.
- Prepare for aftershocks.
- Afterward, check first for personal injuries, then for fire hazards (such as gas leaks or electrical-line damage) and spilled chemicals or medicines. As the city water supply may become polluted, you should boil any tap water before drinking it until notified otherwise. Use the telephone only if absolutely necessary. Turn on the radio and listen for bulletins.

important pages of your passport will make replacement that much easier.

LEGAL MATTERS

If you are stopped by the police for a traffic offense, you'll usually be given a ticket stating the amount of the fine, which you have 30 days to pay. There is usually no point in getting into a discussion, which may only make your predicament worse and even get you in jail for a brief period. (Also see the Car & Motorcycle section in the Getting Around chapter for automobile-related concerns.) Nude sunbathing, or going topless in the case of women, is against the law on LA beaches and you may be fined – and will certainly draw a huge crowd! – for indecent exposure.

It's generally forbidden to have an open container of an alcoholic beverage in public, regardless of whether you're in a car, on the beach, in a park or on the sidewalk. The drinking age is 21 and is strictly enforced. If you look even close to 21, you will likely be asked to show your ID (identification with your photograph on it) to prove your age, whether in a bar, restaurant, liquor store or supermarket. You could incur stiff fines, jail time and penalties if caught driving under the influence of alcohol. Drug use also generates zero tolerance among police officers and can get you into serious trouble with the law.

If you are arrested, you are allowed to remain silent. There is no legal obligation to speak to a police officer if you don't wish, but never walk away from one until given permission. Anyone who is arrested is legally allowed (and given) the right to make one phone call. If you don't have a lawyer or family member to help you, call your consulate. The police will give you the number upon request.

BUSINESS HOURS

Regular business hours are 9 am to 5 pm, but there are certainly no hard and fast rules. Many retail shops stay open Monday through Saturday from 9 am to 6 pm, but most actually stay open a lot longer. Mall shops don't usually close until 8 or 9 pm weekdays and 6 or 7 pm weekends. Finding 24-hour supermarkets, convenience stores and gas stations is generally easy anywhere in Los Angeles.

Post offices are open from 9 am to 5 pm weekdays, and some branches are also open to noon on Saturday. Banks are usually open from either 9 or 10 am to 5 or 6 pm weekdays; a few are also open to 1 or 2 pm on Saturday. Check with individual branches for precise hours.

PUBLIC HOLIDAYS

California observes most US national holidays. On these days, all government offices (including post offices) and banks will be closed. Some individual businesses, museums and restaurants may close as well, particularly on Thanksgiving, Christmas and New Year's Day. Many holidays are observed on the nearest Monday.

New Year's Day	January 1
Martin Luther King, Jr, Day	3rd Monday in January
Presidents' Day	3rd Monday in February
Easter	A Sunday in late March or April
Memorial Day	Last Monday in May
Independence Day (aka 4th of July)	July 4
Labor Day	1st Monday in September
Columbus Day	2nd Monday in October
Veterans' Day	November 11
Thanksgiving Day	4th Thursday in November
Christmas Day	December 25

SPECIAL EVENTS

Los Angeles has a packed calendar of special events, with many festivities celebrating the traditions and culture of a particular ethnic group. Dates for most events shift slightly from year to year, so for specifics call the number listed with each entry below or the Los Angeles Convention & Visitors Bureau events hotline at ☎ 213-689-8822. Details are also published in the *Los Angeles Times* and *LA Weekly*. An admission fee applies to all events listed in this section that are not designated as free.

King Kong at the Tournament of Roses Parade

January

Tournament of Roses Parade (☎ 818-419-7673), January 1 – A cavalcade of marching bands, grinning celebrities and enormous flower-coated floats, proceeding along Pasadena's Colorado Blvd every New Year's Day. Floats are available for post-parade viewing at Victory Park, also in Pasadena.

Rose Bowl Game (☎ 818-449-1400) – A football game, matching college champions from the Midwest (Big 10) and West Coast (Pac-10); takes place after the Tournament of Roses Parade.

Martin Luther King Celebration & Parade (☎ 800-945-2589 or 310-570-6816), late January – A free parade, musical entertainment, food stalls and more at Baldwin Hills Crenshaw Mall and King Park.

February

Chinese New Year (☎ 213-617-0396), usually late January/early February – Free festivities feature fireworks, paper dragons, carnival rides and other traditional revels in the heart of Chinatown.

Los Angeles Bach Festival (☎ 213-385-1345), dates vary – Founded by John Smallman in 1934, this is one of the oldest such classical music festivals in the USA. Tickets are $11 to $16; the festival takes place at First Congregational Church, 540 S Commonwealth Ave.

Nissan Open Golf Tournament (☎ 800-752-6736), last week of February – Major golf tournament taking place at Riviera Country Club in Pacific Palisades.

March

LA Marathon & Bike Tour (☎ 310-444-5544), first Sunday in March – This 26-mile race begins at Figueroa and 6th Sts in Downtown and proceeds through Chinatown, Hollywood and Echo Park. Racers must register in advance. Free to watch.

Spring Festival of Flowers (☎ 818-952-4401), mid-March to mid-April – Model landscapes and bulb plantings at Descanso Gardens in La Cañada Flintridge.

April

Toyota Grand Prix of Long Beach (☎ 800-752-9524), early to mid-April – A week-long auto-racing spectacle drawing world-class drivers.

Blessing of the Animals (☎ 213-628-1274), Saturday before Easter – People from all parts of Southern California bring their pets to Downtown LA's Olvera St to be blessed in a colorful parade.

Thai New Year Festival (Songkran) (☎ 818-780-4200), weekend close to April 13 – Traditional, free festivities with Thai classical dance and music, food and merchandise at Wat Thai Temple, at 8225 Coldwater Canyon in North Hollywood.

Ringing in the Chinese New Year

Los Angeles Times Festival of Books (☎ 800-528-4637, ext 72665), usually third weekend in April – Free fair with author readings and discussions, storytelling, children's activities, food booths and more; takes place on UCLA campus in Westwood.

Fiesta Broadway (☎ 310-914-0015), last Sunday in April – Huge Cinco de Mayo street fair celebration with entertainment from renowned Latino singers along historic Broadway in Downtown; free admission.

May

Pacific Islander Festival (☎ 310-401-7202), first weekend in May – Filled with music, dance, food, arts and crafts celebrating the indigenous cultures and arts of Pacific islands such as Hawaii, Fiji and Tahiti. Admission is free; takes place at Ken Malloy Harbor Regional Park, 25820 S Vermont Ave.

Cinco de Mayo Celebration (☎ 213-624-3660), early May – Mexicans and Anglos alike celebrate the Mexican victory over the French at the Battle of Puebla (1862) with traditional foods, dances and mariachis; free festivities abound in the Pueblo area around Olvera St in Downtown.

Venice Art Walk (☎ 310-392-9255), mid-May – Private studio tour of Venice-based artists along with tasting of gourmet dishes from several local restaurants.

Topanga Banjo Fiddle Contest (☎ 818-382-4819), mid-May – Intended to cherish and preserve bluegrass music, more than 100 contestants participate in fiddle, banjo, guitar, mandolin, singing and band categories. Entertainment is provided by professional string bands; held at Paramount Ranch, Cornell Rd near Agoura in the Santa Monica Mountains.

UCLA Jazz & Reggae Festival (☎ 310-825-9912), Memorial Day weekend – International jazz artists perform on Sunday, reggae artists on Monday. There's an international marketplace with arts, crafts and food for sale. Admission is free; the festival takes place on the UCLA Intramural Field.

June

Cajun & Zydeco Festival (☎ 562-427-3713), first weekend in June – Cajun and zydeco music and home-cooked Cajun and Creole food. Dance instructors teach the two-step, Harlem shuffle and other dances. It's held at the Rainbow Lagoon behind the convention center in Long Beach.

Playboy Jazz Festival (☎ 310-449-4070), second weekend in June – Two-day festival with top performers of traditional, fusion, big band, experimental, Latin, Dixieland, bop and blues; takes place at the Hollywood Bowl, 2301 N Highland Ave, Hollywood.

Great American Irish Fair & Music Festival (☎ 818-503-2511), second weekend in June – More than a dozen entertainment areas with bagpipe bands, Irish step dancing, a medieval village, old-timey crafts stalls, and Irish food and drink. Admission is $15; held at Santa Anita Park Racetrack, 285 W Huntington Drive, Arcadia.

Mariachi USA Festival (☎ 213-848-7717), third weekend in June – Big fiesta celebrating the finest mariachi music and ballet folklorico, with a big fireworks finale; held at the Hollywood Bowl, 2301 N Highland Ave, Hollywood.

Los Angeles Gay & Lesbian Pride Celebration (☎ 323-860-0701), late June – The largest such celebration west of the Mississippi with live entertainment, 250 vendors and food stalls throughout West Hollywood.

July

Lotus Festival (☎ 213-485-1310), usually first weekend after July 4th – The largest lotus bed outside China, in Echo Park Lake, is the setting for this Asian Pacific celebration, with entertainment, dragon-boat races, food, a flower show and an art exhibit. Admission is free. Echo Park Lake is between Park Ave and Glendale Blvd.

Echo Park hosts the Lotus Festival.

DAVID PEEVERS

Malibu Art Festival (☎ 310-456-9025), last weekend in July – More than 150 exhibitors displaying paintings and sculptures, jewelry, photography, textiles and crafts, with free live entertainment. The festival is held at 23545 Civic Center Way between Cross Creek and Webb Way in Malibu.

Tennis Open Tournament LA (☎ 310-824-1010), late July – International tennis tournament draws top players to the Tennis Center courts on the UCLA campus in Westwood.

August

Central Avenue Jazz Festival (☎ 213-485-2437), first August weekend – Festival brings back the golden days of historic Central Ave, once a hub of the jazz scene. There are free live performances by jazz musicians as well as jam sessions; held between 42nd and 43rd St on Central Ave.

Nisei Week Japanese Festival (☎ 213-687-7193), early to mid-August – A free Japanese festival in Little Tokyo, with a parade, karaoke, kimono-clad dancers and crafts demonstrations.

African Marketplace and Cultural Faire (☎ 323-734-1164), mid- to late August – A free celebration of the diversity of African culture, with more than 350 crafts booths and lots of entertainment and music; held at Rancho Cienega Park, 5001 Rodeo Blvd.

September

Long Beach Blues Festival (☎ 562-436-7794), Labor Day weekend – This is the largest such festival west of Chicago, with big-name acts and blues-related merchandise. Admission is $30; held at California State University at Long Beach, at Pacific Coast Highway (1) and Atherton.

Los Angeles County Fair (☎ 909-623-3111), begins second Thursday after Labor Day – Huge fair that runs for 18 days and offers carnival rides, prizes, livestock exhibits and live country entertainment. The fair is held at the LA County Fairgrounds in Pomona.

Oktoberfest (☎ 310-327-4384), early September to late October – The largest Southern California Oktoberfest, with beer, sausages, oompah bands and silly contests. Admission is $5; held at Alpine Village, 833 W Torrance Blvd, Torrance.

Mexican Independence Festival (☎ 213-624-3660), weekend closest to September 16 – A free weekend celebration with top performers and celebrities from Mexico; held all along Olvera St in Downtown.

Simon Rodia Watts Towers Jazz Festival (☎ 213-485-1795), late September – Free jazz, gospel and blues festival surrounding the Watts Towers at 1727 E 107th St.

Simon Rodia Watts Towers Day of the Drum Festival (☎ 213-847-4646), late September – Free festival that attracts drummers from around the world.

Thai Cultural Day (☎ 310-827-2910), usually second Sunday in September – Parade, traditional dances, costume contests, food demos, storytelling and Thai boxing; held at Barnsdall Art Park, 4800 Hollywood Blvd, Hollywood.

Festival of Philippine Arts & Culture (☎ 213-389-3050), mid-September – Free festivities include dance and music performances, film, theater and food; held at Cabrillo Beach in San Pedro.

Koreatown Multi-Cultural Festival (☎ 323-730-1495), mid-September – Free festival featuring drill teams, marching bands, traditional dances, tae kwon do and parades; held at Ardmore Park.

DAVID PEEVERS

Halloween – West Hollywood style

Catalina Island Country Music Festival (☎ 619-458-9586), late September – Two-day festival celebrating the sounds of country music in the gorgeous circular Art Deco ballroom of the Casino building.

October

South Bay Greek Festival (☎ 310-540-2434), early October – Free festival with music, dancing, Greek crafts and food; held at St Katherine Greek Orthodox Church, 722 Knob Hill in Redondo Beach.

Scandinavian Festival (☎ 323-661 4273), early October – Folk dancing, food, arts and crafts, and Nordic costumes. Admission is $4; the festival is held at the MGM Plaza, 2425 Colorado Ave in Santa Monica.

Halloween Party, October 31 – Free rambunctious street fair with eccentric, and occasionally X-rated, costumes all along Santa Monica Blvd in West Hollywood.

November

Día de los Muertos (☎ 213-624-3660), November 2 – Mexican Day of the Dead celebrates the return of the dead to earth for one day each year. There are also a candlelight procession, decorated altars and skull-shaped candy. Admission is free; held on Olvera St in Downtown.

Doo Dah Parade (☎ 818-449-3689), Saturday after Thanksgiving – Free wacky parody of the traditional Rose Parade, with such staple marchers as a precision briefcase drill team, a roving volleyball game and the West Hollywood Cheerleaders. (Beware of artificial seagulls 'anointing' unsuspecting onlookers!) Held all along Colorado Blvd in Pasadena.

Hollywood Christmas Parade (☎ 323-469-2337), late November or early December – Free parade featuring celebrities from film and TV ringing in the season by waving at bystanders from flashy floats. There are also horse riders, classic cars and marching bands; held along Hollywood Blvd in Hollywood.

December

Holiday Festival of Lights (☎ 323-913-4688), throughout December – Largest lighting display in Southern California, in Griffith Park.

Christmas Boat Parade (☎ 310-821-7614), mid-December – Many beautifully decorated and twinkling yachts illuminate the harbor in Marina del Rey; admission is free. The best viewing is from Burton Chase Park.

Craft Arts of Día de los Muertos

Las Posadas (☎ 213-968-8492), daily on the eight days before Christmas – Free candlelight processions that relive Mary and Joseph's journey to Bethlehem and honor the Christ child in colorful Latino fashion, followed by piñata-breaking for kids; held on Olvera St and surrounding streets.

DOING BUSINESS

Los Angeles is the largest business, financial and industrial center on the West Coast and is currently experiencing a boom, which attracts talented workers from the country's more moribund areas. The city has become ever more progressive in beating the business drum and now has a host of advocacy and outreach programs designed to make doing business here well-oiled and successful. The following is only a brief outline of partnerships and resource centers to help you understand local practices and find the help you need to get down to business.

The Los Angeles Economic Development Corporation (LAEDC) (Map 5; ☎ 213-622-4300, www.laedc.org), 515 S Flower St, 32nd floor in Downtown LA. Good for an overview of doing business in Los Angeles. For basic questions, it also has a First Stop Resource Center at ☎ 800-752-3228. The LAEDC is basically connected with every business advocacy group in Southern California and furnishes myriad publications and referrals to resources. It also publishes a yearly Business Resource Guide that lists virtually all agencies involved in finance, manufacturing and import/export.

US Small Business Association (SBA) (☎ 818-552-3210, hotline ☎ 800-827-5722), 330 N Brand in Glendale. The SBA can give you referrals to any type of agency you may need to contact.

Los Angeles Chamber of Commerce (☎ 213-580-7500, www.lachamber.org), 350 S Bixel St. It can quickly provide you with publications or referrals that will get you up and running in LA.

Los Angeles Business Council (☎ 310-475-4574), 10850 Wilshire Blvd in Westwood. A mainstay of business for 68 years, it helps with regional and local referrals and services.

To find out what's happening at street level, pick up a copy of the *Los Angeles Business Journal*, sold at bookstores, newsstands and some convenience markets. Another useful resource is Pacific Bell's *Business to Business Yellow Pages* (available at libraries), which lists businesses and agencies by category.

For translation or interpreting services, call International Conference Systems (☎ 310-642-2900, 800-237-6306), 5777 W Century Blvd, suite 1000, in Century City; or Berlitz (☎ 310-260-7100, 800-367-4336), 525 Broadway in Santa Monica.

WORK

If you're not a US citizen or legal resident (with a green card), there's a lot of red tape involved in getting work in the US, and rather severe penalties (a heavy fine for your employer, deportation for yourself) if you're caught working illegally. If you have particular skills, as well as a sponsoring employer or close relative living in the US, you have a reasonable chance of getting a special working visa from an American embassy before you leave your own country.

The type of visa varies depending on how long you're staying and the type of work you plan to do. Generally, you need either a J-1 visa, which you can obtain by joining a visitor-exchange program, or a H-2B visa, which you get when being sponsored by a US employer. The former is issued mostly to students for work in summer camps; the latter is not easy to obtain because the employer has to prove that no US citizen or permanent resident is available to do the job. If you lack connections, it's unlikely you'll be granted a working visa.

Information on legal student employment opportunities is best obtained from a university, in your own country or in the USA.

Getting There & Away

AIR

If you're flying into Los Angeles, you'll most likely land at Los Angeles International Airport (LAX), 17 miles southwest of Downtown LA. Smaller regional airports, handling mostly shorter-distance domestic travel, are Burbank-Glendale-Pasadena Airport (☎ 818-840-8847), 14 miles northwest of Downtown, and Long Beach Airport (☎ 310-421-8293), 22 miles south.

Outside of LA County are John Wayne-Orange County Airport in Newport Beach (☎ 714-252-5006), 40 miles southeast; and Ontario International Airport in San Bernardino County (☎ 909-983-8282), 40 miles east. The Getting Around chapter has details on how to travel to and from LA County airports.

Los Angeles International Airport (LAX; Map 2)

LAX (☎ 310-646-5252, www.quickaid.com/airports/lax/) handles all overseas and most domestic flights in and out of the city and is the fourth-busiest airport in the world (behind Chicago O'Hare, Atlanta Hartsfield and Dallas-Fort Worth). Some 60 million passengers, a quarter of them international, pass through LAX's eight terminals each year. All but one terminal are situated around a two-level, central traffic loop that also provides access to short-term parking garages. Each of the terminals has cafeterias, snack bars, cocktail lounges, newsstands, gift shops, baggage carts ($1.50), nurseries and storage lockers. Ticketing and check-in are on the upper (departure) level of each terminal, while baggage claim areas are on the lower (arrival) level.

Some 80 passenger carriers and 20 cargo carriers serve LAX. The hub for most international airlines is the Tom Bradley International Terminal (TBIT), named after LA's first African American mayor. Airlines based here include Air France, Alitalia, British Airways, China Airlines, Qantas, Korean Airlines and Mexicana. KLM, Air Canada, Air New Zealand and Virgin Atlantic are now based in Terminal 2 (T2), while Lufthansa is in T6 and Swissair in T5. Among major US airlines, United is in T7, Continental in T6, Delta in T5, American in T4, TWA in T3 and Southwest Airlines and USAir in T1.

Getting Around LAX To travel between terminals, board the free Shuttle A beneath the LAX Shuttle sign on islands outside each terminal on the lower level. Hotel courtesy shuttles stop here as well. A free minibus equipped with a wheelchair lift for the disabled can be ordered by calling ☎ 310-646-6402. (For details on public transportation, taxis, door-to-door shuttles and other means of transport, see the Getting Around chapter.)

WARNING

The information in this chapter is particularly vulnerable to change. Prices for international travel are volatile, routes are introduced and canceled, schedules change, special deals come and go, and rules and visa requirements are amended. Airlines and governments seem to take a perverse pleasure in making price structures and regulations as complicated as possible. In addition, the travel industry is highly competitive and there are many hidden costs and benefits.

The upshot of this is that you should get quotes and advice from as many airlines and travel agents as possible, and make sure you understand how a fare (and any ticket you may buy) works before you part with your hard-earned cash. The details given in this chapter should be regarded as pointers and are not a substitute for your own careful, up-to-date research.

Air Travel Glossary

Baggage Allowance This will be written on your ticket and usually includes one 44lb (20kg) item to go in the hold, plus one item of hand luggage.

Bucket Shops These are unbonded travel agencies specializing in discounted airline tickets.

Bumped Just because you have a confirmed seat doesn't mean you're going to get on the plane (see Overbooking).

Cancellation Penalties If you have to cancel or change a ticket you purchased at a discounted rate, there are often heavy penalties involved; insurance can sometimes be taken out against these penalties. Some airlines impose penalties on regular full-fare tickets as well, particularly against 'no-show' passengers.

Check-In Airlines ask you to check in a certain time ahead of the flight departure (usually one to two hours on international flights). If you fail to check in on time and the flight is over-booked, the airline can cancel your booking and give your seat to somebody else.

Confirmation Having a ticket written out with the flight and date you want doesn't mean you have a seat until the agent has checked with the airline that your status is 'OK' or confirmed. Meanwhile you could just be 'on request.'

Courier Fares Businesses often need to send urgent documents or freight securely and quickly. Courier companies hire people to accompany the package through customs and, in return, offer a discount ticket that is sometimes a phenomenal bargain. In effect, what the companies do is ship their freight as your luggage on regular commercial flights. This is a legitimate operation, but there are two shortcomings – the short turnaround time of the ticket (usually not longer than a month) and the limitation on your luggage allowance. You may have to surrender all your allowance and take only carry-on luggage.

ITX An ITX, or 'independent inclusive tour excursion,' is often available on tickets to popular holiday destinations. Officially it's a package deal combined with hotel accommodation, but many agents will sell you one of these for the flight only and give you phony hotel vouchers in the unlikely event that you're challenged at the airport.

Lost Tickets If you lose your airline ticket, an airline will usually treat it like a traveler's check and, after inquiries, issue you another one. Legally, however, an airline is entitled to treat it like cash; and if you lose it, then it's gone forever. Take good care of your tickets.

MCO An MCO, or 'miscellaneous charge order,' is a voucher that looks like an airline ticket but carries no destination or date. It can be exchanged through any International Association of Travel Agents (IATA) airline for a ticket on a specific flight. It's a useful alternative to an onward ticket in those countries that demand one, and is more flexible than an ordinary ticket if you're unsure of your route.

Air Travel Glossary

No-Shows No-shows are passengers who fail to show up for their flight. Full-fare passengers who fail to turn up are sometimes entitled to travel on a later flight. The rest are penalized (see Cancellation Penalties).

On Request This is an unconfirmed booking for a flight.

Onward Tickets An entry requirement for many countries is that you have a ticket out of the country. If you're unsure of what your next move may be, the easiest solution is to buy the cheapest onward ticket you can find to a neighboring country or a ticket from a reliable airline that can later be refunded if you do not use it.

Open Jaw Tickets These are return tickets on which you fly out to one place but return from another. If available, these can save you backtracking to your arrival point.

Overbooking Airlines hate to fly with empty seats and since every flight has some passengers who fail to show up, airlines often book more passengers than they have seats. Usually excess passengers make up for the no-shows, but occasionally somebody gets bumped. Guess who it is most likely to be? The passengers who check in late.

Point-to-Point Tickets These are discount tickets that can be bought on some routes in return for passengers waiving their rights to a stopover.

Reconfirmation At least 72 hours prior to departure time of an onward or return flight, you must contact the airline and 'reconfirm' that you intend to be on the flight. If you don't do this, the airline can delete your name from the passenger list and you could lose your seat.

Restrictions Discounted tickets often have various restrictions on them – such as advance payment, minimum and maximum periods you must be away (eg, a minimum of two weeks or a maximum of one year), and penalties for changing the tickets.

Round-the-World Tickets RTW tickets give you a limited period (usually a year) in which to circumnavigate the globe. You can go anywhere the carrying airlines go, as long as you don't backtrack. The number of stopovers or total number of separate flights is decided before you set off, and they usually cost a bit more than a basic return flight.

Stand-By This is a discounted ticket on which you only fly if there is a seat free at the last moment. Stand-by fares are usually available only on domestic routes.

Travel Periods Ticket prices vary with the time of year. There is a low (off-peak) season and a high (peak) season, and often a low-shoulder season and a high-shoulder season as well. Usually the fare depends on your outward flight – if you depart in the high season and return in the low season, you pay the high-season fare.

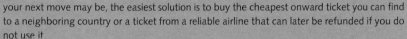

LEE FOSTER

Meet the Jetsons at The Encounter restaurant and bar, above LAX.

Information & Services QuickAid touch-screen computer monitors, located in all terminals, provide free information about ground transportation, costs and other subjects. Some volunteer-staffed Travelers Aid (☎ 310-646-2270) information booths operate 6 am to 9 pm daily on the arrival level of each terminal.

The central information booth and postal center are in the TBIT. There are no banks, but ATMs are in T1, T4, T5 and T7 and in the TBIT; there are foreign exchange offices in all terminals.

Free courtesy phones for information about the airport, ground transportation and accommodations are found in all terminals, as are credit card phones and TDD telephones for the hearing-impaired (near the Travelers Aid booths). The TDD telephone number for information is ☎ 310-417-0439; California Relay Service for the Deaf is at ☎ 800-342-5833.

Other useful numbers include the Lost & Found at ☎ 310-417-0440, the Airport Police at ☎ 310-646-7911 and Customs & Immigration at ☎ 310-215-2414. For an information booklet about the airport, contact the Public Affairs Bureau at ☎ 310-646-5252.

Luggage Lockers & Storage Lockers are in the boarding areas of all terminals. Larger luggage can be stored in the baggage storage areas in T1, T3, T7 and in the TBIT, which also has a luggage repair station.

Medical Emergencies On the departure level of the TBIT is a first-aid station (☎ 310-215-6000), open 7 am to 11 pm daily. For more serious problems, care is available at Centinela Hospital (☎ 310-215-6020), 9601 Sepulveda Blvd, just outside the airport complex.

Smoking Suppress the urge – a guy named 'Nosmo King' has left his card all over the airport. You are still allowed to smoke outside, however.

Burbank-Glendale-Pasadena Airport (Map 17)

The Burbank Airport (☎ 818-840-8847, 800-835-9287, www.bur.com), 2627 Hollywood Way, is about 14 miles northwest of Downtown LA. It's small, easily accessed and an excellent alternative to LAX for certain domestic flights. Burbank has two terminals, with American, America West and Southwest Airlines based at Terminal A, and United and Alaska Airlines based at Terminal B.

About 6000 passengers arrive here daily from domestic destinations ranging from

Albuquerque to Wichita. The airport is well connected to public transportation and is served by Amtrak and Metrolink trains as well as free local shuttles to Downtown Burbank with connections beyond.

The USA & Canada

Los Angeles is a major hub in North American air traffic, so there should be little trouble finding a flight or connection to just about anywhere on the continent. The *Los Angeles Times* produces a weekly travel section in which you'll find any number of travel agents' ads. Local offices of Council Travel and STA Travel generally have competitive fares. STA Travel has offices at 920 Westwood Blvd in Westwood (Map 11; ☎ 310-824-1574) and at 411 Santa Monica Blvd in Santa Monica (Map 12; ☎ 310-394-5126). Council Travel is at 10904 Lindbrook Drive in Westwood (Map 11; ☎ 310-208-3551). For more branches, check the Yellow Pages.

In Canada, Travel CUTS (☎ 888-838-2887, 416-977-2185 in Toronto) is a chain of budget travel agencies with offices in all major cities. The *Toronto Globe and Mail* and *Vancou er Sun* carry travel agents' ads.

Regional airlines are also a good bet, as they tend to fly routes more often than their globe-trotting competitors. Southwest Airlines (☎ 800-435-9792) covers the western USA extensively and often has special rates undercutting major airlines. United Airlines is also better than average and offers a wide range of destinations. Research is, of course, key to finding the flight that's best for you.

Fares Fares change as often as the winds, but nearly all of the best fares come with an 'advance order' stipulation, which means you must purchase them seven to 21 days in advance to get the bargain rate. 'Companion fares' are also increasingly common, letting two people travel for the price of one. Roundtrip fares to the East Coast typically go for around $400 (give or take $100). Roundtrip tickets to Chicago hover at around $250, slightly less to Denver or Dallas; and if you feel like darting up to San Francisco to catch the sunset, you'll pay around $100.

Continental flights outside the USA likewise vary depending upon the frequency of flights, the time of year, the distance traveled and the whim of the industry. Some average roundtrip fares for Canada are Vancouver ($270), Edmonton ($330), Toronto ($400), and Montreal and Quebec City ($450). Again, these fares are rough guidelines of

Major Airlines

The following airlines serve LAX and offer toll-free telephone numbers.

US-Based Airlines

Alaska Airlines	☎ 800-426-0333
Aloha Airlines	☎ 800-367-5250
American Airlines	☎ 800-433-7300
America West	☎ 800-235-9292
Continental Airlines	☎ 800-525-0280
Delta Air Lines	☎ 800-221-1212
Hawaiian Airlines	☎ 800-367-5320
Northwest Airlines	☎ 800-225-2525
Reno Air	☎ 800-736-6247
Southwest Airlines	☎ 800-435-9792
Trans World Airlines	☎ 800-221-2000
United Airlines	☎ 800-241-6522
USAir	☎ 800-428-4322

International Airlines

Aer Lingus	☎ 800-223-6537
Aeroméxico	☎ 800-237-6639
Air Canada	☎ 800-776-3000
Air France	☎ 800-237-2747
Air New Zealand	☎ 800-262-1234
American Airlines	☎ 800-433-7300
British Airways	☎ 800-247-9297
Cathay Pacific	☎ 800-233-2742
KLM	☎ 800-374-7747
Japan Airlines	☎ 800-525-3663
LTU International Airways	☎ 800-888-0200
Lufthansa Airlines	☎ 800-645-3880
Mexicana Airlines	☎ 800-531-7921
Qantas	☎ 800-227-4500
Singapore Airlines	☎ 800-742-3333
Varig Brazilian Airlines	☎ 800-468-2744
Virgin Atlantic	☎ 800-862-8621

what to expect. Call a travel agent or check the newspapers for specifics.

Other Countries

If you're flying to Los Angeles from abroad, the plane ticket will probably be the most expensive item in your budget, and buying it can be intimidating. It is always worth putting aside a few hours to research the current state of the market. Start early: Some of the cheapest tickets must be bought months in advance, and some popular flights sell out early. Ask other travelers for recommendations, look at the ads in newspapers and magazines, consult reference books and watch for special offers. Then, phone several travel agents for bargains. Find out the fare, the route, how long the ticket is valid and any restrictions that may apply.

Cheap tickets are available in two distinct categories: official and unofficial. Official ones have a variety of names, including advance-purchase tickets, advance-purchase excursion (Apex) fares, super-Apex and simply budget fares. Unofficial discount tickets are released by the airlines through selected travel agents, and it's worth shopping around to find them. If you call the airlines directly, they may not quote you the cheapest fares available, except when there's an airfare war on between competing airlines. In most cases, roundtrip tickets are cheaper than two one-way tickets.

If you are flying to Los Angeles from Europe, Australia or Southeast Asia, you may find the cheapest flights are advertised by obscure agencies whose names haven't yet reached the telephone directory. Many such firms are honest and solvent, but there are a few rogues who will take your money and disappear to reopen elsewhere a month later under a new name. If you feel suspicious about a firm, don't give them all the money at once – leave a deposit of 20% or so and pay the balance when you get the ticket. If they insist on cash in advance, go somewhere else or be prepared to take a big risk. Once you have the ticket, call the airline to confirm that you are actually booked on the flight.

You may decide to pay more than the rock-bottom fare for the security of a better-known travel agent. Reliable firms such as STA Travel and Council Travel, with offices worldwide, and Flight Centre in Australia are not going to disappear overnight, leaving you clutching a receipt for a nonexistent ticket.

Once you have a ticket, make a photocopy or at least write down its number, the flight number and other relevant details, and keep the information somewhere separate from the ticket. If the ticket is lost or stolen, this will help you get a replacement.

Visit USA Passes These are coupons good for flights within the USA that non-US citizens buy in their home countries. They're usually an excellent deal and offer substantial savings over tickets purchased within the USA. Typically, the minimum number of coupons is three or four and the maximum is eight or 10, and they must be purchased in conjunction with an international airline ticket anywhere outside the USA except in Canada and Mexico.

Coupons cost anywhere from $100 to $160, depending on how many you buy. Delta, American and Continental all have good programs; call these and other airlines for information. Many airlines require you to plan your itinerary in advance and to complete your flights within 60 days of arrival, but rules vary among individual airlines. A few airlines may allow you to use coupons on standby, in which case call the airline a day or two before the flight and make a 'standby reservation.' Such a reservation gives you priority over all other travelers who just appear and hope to get on the flight the same day.

Round-the-World Tickets Airline RTW tickets are often real bargains and can work out to be no more expensive, sometimes cheaper, than an ordinary return ticket. RTW prices start at about $1300 (UK£850, A$1800). These tickets are for 'short' routes such as Los Angeles-New York-London-Bangkok-Honolulu-Los Angeles. As soon as you start adding stops that are south of the equator, fares can go as high as $2000 or $3000.

All the major airlines offer RTW tickets in conjunction with other international airlines and permit you to fly anywhere on their route systems as long as you do not backtrack. You may have to book the first sector in advance; cancellation penalties apply. Tickets are usually valid from 90 days up to a year. If you're planning to include Los Angeles on your itinerary, be aware that most airlines restrict the number of sectors that can be flown within the USA and Canada to four, and some airlines black out a few heavily traveled routes (such as Honolulu to Tokyo). Your best bet is to find a travel agent that advertises or specializes in RTW tickets.

Circle Pacific Tickets These tickets allow you to swing through Los Angeles as part of an itinerary to a variety of destinations around the Pacific Rim – Australia, New Zealand, North America and Asia. You may use a combination of airlines as long as you keep traveling in the same circular direction. Fares, generally about 15% cheaper than RTW tickets, include four stopovers, with the option of adding additional stops at $50 each. There's a 14-day advance purchase requirement, a 25% cancellation penalty and a maximum stay of six months.

Circle Pacific routes essentially have the same fares: $2449 when purchased in the USA, A$3500 in Australia and C$3309 in Canada.

Europe Many airlines, including British Airways, United Airlines and Virgin Atlantic, have nonstop services between London and Los Angeles. From continental Europe, KLM flies from Amsterdam, Air France from Paris, Swissair from Zurich, Lufthansa from Frankfurt, and Iberia from Madrid. An excellent, little-known option is a direct, nonstop flight to LA from Düsseldorf, near the Dutch border in Germany, which is offered by LTU International Airways (a German leisure airline). Its

flights are competitively priced and operate weekly, though from spring to fall only. Many other international and US airlines arrive in LA via a stop in a gateway city (usually Chicago or Miami) and continue on to connecting domestic flights. The direct flight takes about 11 hours westbound (London to Los Angeles), and nine or 10 hours eastbound depending on the prevailing winds.

Fares vary with the season, with peak periods during the summer months (June to September) and around Christmas. Midweek flights are sometimes cheaper than those departing Friday and Saturday. The cheapest fares are generally available in London, though other major continental gateways – Frankfurt, Amsterdam, Paris – also have competitive rates. A straightforward economy roundtrip ticket is around $800. Apex tickets, which usually must be purchased 21 days in advance and involve cancellation penalties, start at $500.

Most major cities have publications favored by advertisers offering discounted tickets, such as *Time Out*, the *E ening Standard* and *TNT* in London. STA Travel, Council Travel and Trailfinders are reliable agents for cheap tickets (especially for students and anyone under 30), with offices throughout the world, including the ones in these major European cities:

STA Travel
  (☎ 0171-361-6161)
  86 Old Brompton Rd, London SW7, UK
  (☎ 069-43-01-91)
  Bergerstrasse 118, 60316 Frankfurt, Germany
Council Travel
  (☎ 0171-437-7767)
  28 A Poland St, London W1, UK
  (☎ 0211-36-30-30)
  Graf-Adolph-Strasse 18,
  42112 Düsseldorf, Germany
  (☎ 089-39-50-22)
  Adalbertstrasse 32, 80799 Munich, Germany
  (☎ 01-44-41-89-80)
  1 Place de l'Odéon, 75006 Paris, France
Trailfinders
  (☎ 0171-937-5400)
  194 Kensington High St, London W8 7RG, UK

Australia & New Zealand Both Air New Zealand and Qantas fly directly to Los Angeles. United Airlines has nonstop flights to Sydney and Auckland. Trips to LA from Auckland take 12 to 13 hours and from Sydney 13½ to 14½ hours. Some typical Apex roundtrip fares range from A$1400 to A$1800 from the Australian east coast and from NZ$1800 to NZ$2000 from New Zealand.

Check the Saturday travel sections of the *Sydney Morning Herald* and Melbourne's *Age* newspaper for ads offering cheap fares, or try the following agencies:

STA Travel
   (☎ 03-9660-2868) Level 4, Union Bldg,
   RMIT, Melbourne, Vic 3000
   (☎ 02-9411-6888) Shop 17, 3-9 Spring St,
   Chatswood, Sydney, NSW 2067
   (☎ 03-9349-2411)
   222 Faraday St, Carlton, Vic 3053
   (☎ 09-380-2302) 1st floor, New Guild Bldg,
   University of Western Australia,
   Crawley, Perth, WA 6009
   (☎ 09-307-0555) 2nd floor, Student Union
   Bldg, Princes St, Auckland University,
   Auckland
Flight Centre
   (☎ 03-9650-2899) Bourke Street Flight Centre
   19 Bourke St, Melbourne, Vic 3000
   (☎ 02-9235-0166) Martin Place Flight Centre
   Shop 5, State Bank Centre, 52 Martin Place,
   Sydney, NSW 2000
   (☎ 09-325-9222) City Flight Centre Shop 25,
   Cinema City Arcade, Perth, WA 6000
   (☎ 09-309-6171) Auckland Flight Centre
   Shop 3A, National Bank Towers,
   205-225 Queen St, Auckland

Asia Los Angeles has a huge network of business links with Asia, so there are many flights to and from Asian capitals. Hong Kong is the discount plane ticket capital of the region, but its bucket shops can be unreliable; ask the advice of other travelers before buying a ticket. STA Travel, which is dependable, has branches in Hong Kong, Tokyo, Singapore, Bangkok and Kuala Lumpur. Many flights to LA go via Honolulu, Hawaii.

United Airlines has three flights a day to Honolulu from Tokyo with connections to Los Angeles. Northwest and Japan Airlines also have daily flights to LA from Tokyo. Other airlines include Air China, Cathay Pacific, Korean Airlines, Malaysian Airlines, Philippine Airlines, Singapore Airlines, China Airlines and EVA Airways, as well as American Airlines.

Latin America Roundtrip flights from Mexico City average around $300; the fares continue to rise the farther south you go. Most flights from Central and South America to destinations in the USA go via Los Angeles, Miami or Houston. Continental Airlines has flights to LA from approximately 20 cities in Mexico and Central America, including San José, Guatemala City, Cancún and Mérida.

Departure Taxes
Airport departure taxes are normally included in the cost of tickets bought in the USA, though they may not be included with tickets purchased abroad. There's a $6 airport departure tax charged to all passengers bound for any foreign destinations. However, this fee, as well as a $6.50 North American Free Trade Agreement (NAFTA) tax charged to passengers entering the USA from a foreign country, are hidden taxes added to the purchase price of your ticket.

BUS
USbus
The San Fernando Valley-based USbus (☎ 818-721-6000, TheUsbus@att.net in the USA; ☎ 01892-532060, amaduk@attmail .com in the UK) covers the country on a flexipass system primarily geared toward young, independent travelers (those under 18 must be accompanied by an adult). USbuses travel in the daytime along nine predetermined routes, picking up and dropping off at HI-accredited youth hostels or other budget accommodations. You may travel on as many routes as you wish.

Los Angeles is the gateway for five routes headed for such destinations as San Diego,

San Francisco, Seattle, Las Vegas, Flagstaff (near the Grand Canyon) and Yosemite National Park. All sectors must be pre-booked (a sector is a journey from one stop to the next), though standby seats are occasionally available.

Summer 1999 flexipass fares were $199 for five days of travel within a 15-day period, $299 for 10 days of travel during a 25-day period, $399 for 15 days in a 40-day period, $639 for 30 days in a 60-day period and $799 for 45 days in a 90-day period.

The Ant

'Ant' stands for Adventure Network for Travelers (☎ 800-336-6049 within North America, 415-399-0880 in all other locales, anttrips@theant.com, www.theant.com), a San Francisco-based company that operates a hop-on, hop-off service similar to the USbus but limited to California, Nevada and Arizona.

Both of their loop routes pass through Los Angeles. The Northern Loop ($239) travels via Las Vegas, Death Valley, Lake Tahoe, Yosemite and San Francisco; Southern Loop ($199) hits include San Diego, Mexicali (Mexico), Phoenix, Grand Canyon, Bryce and Zion National Parks and Las Vegas. Both loops combined are $329. There's also the Coastal Cruiser shuttle bus between LA and San Francisco ($89 one way, $169 roundtrip).

You have six months in which to complete the loop(s). If you don't want to do an entire loop, you can also buy individual segments. Each night, the Ant stops at inexpensive hostels, motels or campgrounds (your guide can make free reservations).

Greyhound Bus Lines

Greyhound (☎ 800-231-2222) is the only nationwide bus company, serving Los Angeles from cities all over North America. Buses are air-conditioned and decently maintained, though travel companions may occasionally smell a bit unpleasant. Dealing with Greyhound on the telephone is often an investment in time and patience, *especially* once you get through to an operator.

The 24-hour main LA terminal (Map 5; ☎ 213-629-8421) is at 1716 E 7th St at Alameda St in Downtown. The area is a bit rough, but the station itself is safe enough inside. Other LA-area Greyhound stations are at 1409 N Vine St, Hollywood (Map 9; ☎ 323-466-6384); on 4th St between Colorado Blvd and Broadway in Santa Monica (Map 12; no phone); and 464 W 3rd St in Long Beach (Map 15; ☎ 562-432-7780).

Greyhound's prices are very reasonable, though bargain airfares can occasionally match or undercut its fares on long-distance routes (for example, to San Francisco). On some shorter routes, it may be cheaper to rent a car than ride the bus, especially if you have a group of two or more people.

The trip to San Diego costs $13/$22 one way/roundtrip; buses depart from Downtown LA at least once an hour and the journey takes from 2¼ to 3¾ hours, depending on the number of stops en route. Service to Santa Barbara is $13/24, with about a dozen buses a day making the trip in two to three hours. San Francisco is served almost hourly, with trips costing $36/69 and taking anything from eight to 12 hours.

Fourteen-day advance-purchase tickets to any destination in the USA are $89 each way, and those bought at least 21 days in advance are $79. Greyhound's unlimited travel pass, called the Ameripass, is available for seven, 15 or 30 days. In 1998, rates were $199/299/409, respectively.

Green Tortoise

Another alternative for West Coast travelers is a throwback to Ken Kesey's Merry Pranksters of the late '60s and the nearest thing in America to the 'Magic Bus.' When you hit the road with San Francisco-based Green Tortoise Adventure Travel (☎ 415-956-7500, 800-867-8647 from outside of the Bay Area), 494 Broadway, your journey may be more memorable than your destination.

Green Tortoise operates like a mobile commune. You travel in converted sleeper coaches outfitted with mattresses on raised platforms and bunk beds; there are couches, tables, kitchen appliances and stereos but no restrooms (the bus will make stops 'as necessary'). Note that smoking and alcohol are not allowed on the bus. Weekly service up and down the West Coast between Seattle and Los Angeles costs $79 each way.

TRAIN
Amtrak
America's national rail system, Amtrak (☎ 800-872-7245, www.amtrak.com), operates up and down the California coast and all over the USA. In Los Angeles, it arrives and departs from Union Station (Map 5; ☎ 213-624-0171), at 800 N Alameda St in Downtown LA.

Interstate trains stopping in LA are the *Coast Starlight*, going daily between LA and Seattle with stops including San Luis Obispo, Sacramento, Klamath Falls and Portland; the *Southwest Chief*, with daily departures to Chicago via Flagstaff, Albuquerque and Kansas City; and the *Sunset Limited*, with service thrice weekly to Orlando via Tucson, El Paso, Houston, New Orleans and Jacksonville.

Service within Southern California along the *San Diegan* route between San Luis Obispo and San Diego is quite good and efficient. Getting to points in Northern California is more complicated. San Francisco is reached either by traveling on the *Coast Starlight* and changing to an Amtrak motor coach in Emeryville or by taking the motor coach to Bakersfield and boarding the *San Joaquin* route. These trains stop in Oakland, where a motor coach will shuttle you to San Francisco.

Fares & Passes Basic fares between LA and San Diego are $23 each way and the trip takes three hours. Fares to San Francisco range from $46 to $77 one way and from $92 to $154 roundtrip, depending on availability and day of travel; the journey takes roughly 12 hours. Trips to/from Santa Barbara cost $18 each way (2½ hours). To be on the safe side, book in advance, especially during summer and around major holidays.

The best overall value is the Explore America Pass, available to US visitors and North Americans alike, which permits three

stops within 45 days of travel. This pass divides the country into three zones, with travel in one zone (western, central or eastern) costing $228 in peak season, $198 off-season; two adjacent zones are $318/258; all zones are $378/318. You must book your itinerary in advance, however, specifying travel dates and destinations.

Non-US citizens also have the option of the USA Rail Pass, which must be purchased from a travel agent outside the USA or from an Amtrak office within the country (you must show a foreign passport). The pass allows you to get on and off wherever you wish within its lifespan. 'Custom class' seats and sleeping accommodations cost extra. Prices vary from high to low season:

duration	route	high/low season
15 days	National	$425/285
	West Coast	$315/195
	East Coast	$250/205
30 days	National	$535/375
	West Coast	$310/260
	East Coast	$395/255

Metrolink
Metrolink is Southern California's commuter train network. Trains shuttle between Downtown LA and various points north, south and east of the city. See the Getting Around chapter for more information.

CAR & MOTORCYCLE
If you're driving a car or riding a motorcycle into Los Angeles, there are several routes by which you might enter the metropolitan area.

From San Francisco and Northern California, the fastest route to LA (about six hours) is via Interstate 5 (or I-5), a heavily traveled freeway through the San Joaquin Valley, which is miserably hot in the summer and boring always. I-5 enters LA County at the 4183-foot Tejon Pass ('The Grapevine'); it is known as the Golden State Fwy through Burbank to Downtown, the Santa Ana Fwy through Anaheim to Irvine, and then the San Diego Fwy as it hits the coast at Capistrano Beach and continues to the Mexican border.

The alternative to I-5 from San Francisco, taking about eight hours, is US 101 (or the 101 Fwy), a somewhat curvier and far more picturesque freeway that follows the inland edge of the Coast Ranges south from San Jose to San Luis Obispo, staying close to the coast through Santa Barbara. The 101 Fwy enters LA as the Ventura Fwy, becoming the Hollywood Fwy and ending where it joins I-5 in Downtown.

By far the most scenic – and slowest – route is via the Pacific Coast Hwy (also known as PCH, or simply Hwy 1), which takes at least 10 hours. This road clings to the cliffs of the Big Sur coast between the Monterey Peninsula and San Luis Obispo, where it joins the 101 Fwy. While the views are spectacular, curve-riddled PCH is subject to fog, landslides and other travel hazards.

From San Diego and other points south, I-5 is the obvious route. At Irvine, the 405 (San Diego) Fwy branches off I-5 and takes a westerly route to Long Beach and Santa Monica, avoiding Downtown LA entirely and rejoining I-5 near San Fernando. This route can be a time-saver if you're headed to the Westside.

If you're coming into LA from Las Vegas or the Grand Canyon, you'll want to take I-15 to the 10 Fwy; these meet near Ontario. The 10 Fwy is the main east-west artery through LA and leads on to Downtown and Santa Monica.

On freeways, speed limits are normally 65 miles per hour (104 km per hour) in LA County and occasionally 70 mph (112 kph) on the open road. Most drivers push their speed 5 to 10 mph higher than the posted limits. If you go faster than that, expect to be pulled over by the ever-vigilant officers of the California Highway Patrol.

If you're planning an extended road trip, you might want to join the American Automobile Association (AAA). For more information, see Useful Organizations in the Facts for the Visitor chapter.

HITCHHIKING

Hitching is never entirely safe anywhere in the world, and we definitely do not recommend it. Travelers undeterred by the potential risk should be aware that on the whole, hitchhiking is uncommon in modern-day America and hitchers are generally viewed with suspicion. Few motorists are willing to stop for a thumb. Use extreme caution, both when hitchhiking and picking up hitchhikers.

At the risk of sounding sexist, women should never hitchhike alone or even with another woman. Drivers are often reluctant to pick up lone men, so a man and a woman together have the best chance of getting a ride and of being safe. You can hitchhike on roads and highways; on freeways you must stand at the on-ramp. The best method for hitching a ride might be to ask someone

---

Where the Freeways Begin

LA's first freeway was the Arroyo Seco Parkway, which opened to traffic in 1940. You can drive the Arroyo Seco today, although it is now just a small stretch of the 110 Fwy connecting Downtown to Pasadena. You'll notice a distinct difference between the Arroyo Seco and the modern postwar freeways. Just 6 miles long and modeled after Robert Moses' parkway system in New York, its sharp turns whip through Elysian Park and wind around Raymond Hill. Even without heavy traffic, you'll have to hit your brakes frequently.

A year after the opening of the Arroyo Seco, the Los Angeles Regional Planning Commission issued a report entitled *A Master Plan for Highways*, which included an ambitious 'Parkway Plan' for the network of freeways that was built during the following two decades. The report suggested that innocuous-sounding parkways would further distribute the region's population, thus paving the way for more growth. It also proclaimed that a well-maintained system of roads would assure that 'the people of the region will not readily abandon the flexible mobility of the individually owned motor car.'

pulling into a gas station; this also allows you to check out the person (and vice versa). Be prepared for more refusals than offers.

BOAT

Although LA has a major port, ocean travel is not a common way for visitors to arrive. Several cruise lines do operate out of San Pedro Harbor, which is connected by the Harbor (110) Fwy to Downtown LA.

Some trans-Pacific freighters run to and from Australia, New Zealand and the South Pacific. Contact Freighter World Cruises (☎ 626-449-3106), 180 S Lake Ave, suite 335, Pasadena, CA 91101, for information.

ORGANIZED TOURS

LA is the gateway to exploring the great sights of California and the national parks of the Southwest. While it's easy to rent a car and travel to the Grand Canyon or Yosemite by yourself, group travel is often preferable, especially to the young, the cost-conscious and those traveling alone.

LV International Tours (☎ 800-456-3050) has a repertory of about a dozen trips, including a four-day foray taking in Las Vegas, the Grand Canyon, Bryce Canyon and Zion National Parks. Tours cost $299 in summer and $259 in winter. The four-day Las Vegas-only tour is $169 to $199.

For a less conventional approach to touring, try the Missing Link (☎ 800-209-8586).

Founded in 1997, this company runs tours to main Southwest attractions that may include camping on Native American land in the Grand Canyon, hikes through spectacular scenery and add-on adventure activities. Head guides are biologists and outdoor specialists. At the moment, a handful of tours depart from LA, including the three, four and five-day Grand Canyon/Las Vegas ($180/220/235) tours and one-week 'Best of the West' journeys that add Zion and Bryce Canyon National Parks, Lake Powell and the Colorado River to the basic itinerary ($350). At press time, a 10-day trip to the southern tip of the Baja California peninsula was in the planning stages. Prices include camping or hostel stays, transportation, some meals and guided tours. Missing Link also operates a $35 shuttle service between LA and Las Vegas.

The one-week Coyote Trail tour offered by Road Runner USA (☎ 800-873-5872), which leads small group tours all over the world, takes in roughly the same destinations and costs $499 October to April, $50 to $90 more in the summer months. Its 10-day 'California Cooler' tour includes Lake Havasu, the Grand Canyon, Las Vegas, Yosemite National Park, San Francisco and California's Pacific Coast, and costs $549 to $689. For details on all the tours, ask for a free brochure. It also has an office in England (☎ 892-51-27-00), 64 Mt Pleasant Ave, Tunbridge Wells, Kent TN1 1QY.

Getting Around

Los Angeles is an enormous metropolis with many forms of public transportation. The Metropolitan Transportation Authority (MTA) oversees an extensive system that includes buses, light-rail trains and a fledgling subway. Still, the automobile remains by far the area's most popular mode of transportation. Before rushing headlong into the bumper-to-bumper melee, though, you ought to consider all of your transportation options.

TO/FROM THE AIRPORTS
Los Angeles International Airport (LAX; Map 2)

Shuttle The best way to get away from LAX, short of renting a car, is via private mini-shuttle vans, which stop outside each terminal under the signs marked 'Shuttle.' These are a compromise of time and expense between costly taxis and less convenient and slower public transportation. Your choice of shuttle service will depend upon your destination; Inquire at the ground transportation desk near each baggage claim and then confirm the destination with the driver.

Most shuttles operate 24 hours a day and provide door-to-door service, dropping you off at your accommodation. You may have to wait your turn along the route, because they're doing the same for up to a half-dozen other passengers. You'll pay according to how far you're traveling, usually $10 to $20, or at least half the cost of a taxi. All American Shuttle (☎ 310-641-4090, 800-585-2529), Prime Time (☎ 800-262-7433) and Super Shuttle (☎ 310-450-2377, 800-258-3826) are some of the companies that serve the LA and Orange County areas.

Bus The budget-conscious approach is to take the free 24-hour Shuttle C bus, which stops outside each terminal every 10 to 20 minutes, to the LAX Transit Center at 96th St and Vicksburg Ave (Map 2). Here you can connect to public buses that will take you anywhere in the greater Los Angeles area. For more information, see Bus, later in this chapter, or call the MTA at ☎ 800-266-6883 (within LA County only).

Taxi Outside each terminal are curbside taxi dispatchers who will summon a cab for you. Average fares are $25 to Santa Monica, $35 to Downtown or Hollywood and up to $80 to Anaheim (Disneyland). A $2.50 airport surcharge will be tacked onto your fare, and there may be additional fees for excess luggage. Taxis are the fastest and most convenient way to travel; with two or three people to share the expense, they can also be relatively inexpensive.

Train LAX is not directly served by trains. The closest station, a 10-minute bus trip away, is Aviation, on the Metro Green Line. Take the free Shuttle G bus that stops on the lower (arrival) airport level beneath the LAX Shuttle signs. The light-rail Green Line runs south to Redondo Beach and then east to Norwalk. On an eastbound train, you can transfer at the Rosa Parks (Imperial/Wilmington) station to the Metro Blue Line, which will take you north to Downtown LA or south to Long Beach. The fare is just $1.35.

Car If you don't already have a rental-car reservation, you can make a booking from courtesy phones in the arrival areas. Rental offices are outside the airport, with each company operating free shuttles, which circle the arrival areas continuously. Stand outside the terminal and flag down the vehicle of the company with which you made your reservation. For details on renting a car, see Car Rental, later in this chapter.

Other Airports

If you're flying into or out of another airport serving Southern California – Burbank (☎ 818-840-8847), Long Beach (☎ 310-421-8293), John Wayne-Orange County (☎ 714-252-5006) or Ontario (☎ 909-983-8282) – you'll find many of the same transportation options available at LAX, including a wide choice of shuttle services. The Metro Rail, however, does not serve any airport other than LAX.

BUS

Only 10% of the LA County population relies upon public transportation to get them around the city each day. A network of 208 separate bus routes spans the metropolis.

Metropolitan Transportation Authority (MTA)

For full information on all MTA bus routes – including maps, timetables and passes – the MTA (☎ 800-266-6883 within LA County, www.mta.net) has several customer centers throughout LA. In Downtown, go to Level C of ARCO Plaza, 515 S Flower St, open 7:30 am to 3:30 pm (Map 5); in Hollywood, there's one at 6249 Hollywood Blvd, open 10 am to 6 pm; the one in the Miracle Mile district in Mid-City is at 5301 Wilshire Blvd and is open 9 am to 5 pm (Map 10); in the

---

MTA Bus Routes

Here are a few of the more commonly used MTA routes from Downtown LA. Most services run from 5 am to 2 am at intervals of every 15 minutes or so.

No 1 – Hollywood Blvd
No 2 – Sunset Blvd
No 4 – Santa Monica Blvd (24 hours)
No 10 – Melrose Ave
No 20 – Wilshire Blvd (24 hours)
No 22 – to Santa Monica via Wilshire Blvd
No 27 – to Beverly Hills (nonstop)
No 33 – to Venice Beach
No 60 – to Long Beach
No 79 – to Huntington Library,
    Art Collection and Botanical Gardens
No 96 – to Burbank Studios
No 436 – to Venice Beach (express)
No 439 – to LAX and South Bay (express)
No 446 – to San Pedro (express)
No 456 – to Long Beach (express)
No 460 – to Disneyland (express)

San Fernando Valley, go to 14435 Sherman Way, No 107, in Van Nuys, between 10 am and 6 pm. The MTA Downtown headquarters at Union Station is at the Transit Center-East Portal and is open 6 am to 6:30 pm. All MTA offices are closed on weekends.

Fares The regular base fare is $1.35 for unlimited travel on a single bus or rail line in one direction (exact change is required). Transfers are 25¢ each use. Between 9 pm and 5 am the fare is 75¢. Freeway Express buses cost $1.85 to $3.85, depending on the route and distance. Weekly passes are $11 for unlimited travel throughout the network and are issued from Sunday to Saturday. Monthly passes, good for travel during any calendar month, are $42. Semi-monthly passes – valid either for the first or second half of the month – are $21. All passes are sold only at MTA customer centers.

Big Blue Bus

Santa Monica's Big Blue Bus (☎ 310-451-5444) is what everyone wishes public transportation throughout LA was like: clean, efficient and responsive to customer needs. Its fleet serves much of the Westside, including Westwood, Pacific Palisades and LAX, as well as Santa Monica and Venice. There's even a special service to the Getty Center (bus No 14). The fare is only 50¢ and transfers to another Blue Bus are free (those to an MTA or Culver City bus are 25¢). The fastest and most comfortable way to get to Downtown LA from Santa Monica is via express bus No 10 ($1.25). All buses run 5:30 am to midnight Monday to Saturday, from 6:30 am Sunday.

Culver City Bus

The Culver City Bus (☎ 310-253-6500) provides service throughout Culver City and the Westside, including LAX. Buses run 5:30 am to 11 pm weekdays, 6 am to 11 pm weekends. Fare is 60¢. Transfers to the Big Blue Bus or MTA buses are 25¢.

Downtown Area Short Hop (DASH)

Downtown Los Angeles is also served by a minibus system – DASH – which is a great way to see the city and spare yourself the hassle and expense of parking. These buses run constantly, at intervals of six to 15 minutes, between the most interesting areas of Downtown 6:30 am to 6:30 pm weekdays and 10 am to 5 pm Saturday. Each trip costs 25¢; transfers to another DASH are free. Six separate routes, three of them meeting at City Hall, extend from Chinatown in the north to Exposition Park in the south, and from the Financial District and Central Library in the west to Little Tokyo and the

Big Red Cars

CHAS W. BEAM, COURTESY LOS ANGELES
PUBLIC LIBRARY PHOTO COLLECTION

Long before LA's freeways were built – even before William Mulholland brought water to the Los Angeles Basin – the many corners of this far-reaching, seemingly unplanned metropolis were connected by a complex network of electric railways. By 1901 these 'Big Red Cars' were consolidated under Henry E Huntington's Pacific Electric Railway. Today, these old rail cars are romanticized by train buffs and old-timers who fondly recall riding them. Youngsters are often amazed that a complete light-rail network existed in LA: It seems so antithetical to the Auto-topia of today. Huntington also owned a streetcar system called the Yellow Cars, which operated in Downtown LA. When he got bored with his trains in 1910, Huntington sold his empire to the Southern Pacific Railroad.

At their peak, the Red Cars covered over 1100 miles of track stretching as far east as San Bernardino, west to the Pacific Ocean, north to San Fernando and south to Huntington Beach. Trains traveled at speeds of up to 50 mph on private rights-of-way, outside the ever-increasing automotive traffic.

In the early days, aggressive real estate developers supplied Pacific Electric with a surplus of passengers by hyping Los Angeles as a haven of health. Dozens of housing subdivisions along the Pacific Electric tracks were developed, with blocks and blocks of quaint imitation-Craftsman bungalows. Midwesterners and Easterners, lured by the sun and the availability of land, moved to Southern California by the millions.

Ultimately, automobiles spelled the doom of fixed-rail transit in Los Angeles. Not only did cars intrude on the trains' rights-of-way; public funds shifted toward the building of more roads while trains fell into a state of neglect. Beginning in the late 1930s, Red Car lines were discontinued at a steady rate. When the last of the Red Cars ended its final run (from Downtown to Long Beach) in April of 1961, all the trains had either been junked or sold to the Argentine capital, Buenos Aires.

The total shift from fixed-rail transit to car-oriented transit has in recent years prompted theories of a conspiracy on the part of the auto and oil industries. In the 1930s, a group of large corporations, including Firestone Tire and General Motors, set up a surrogate company called National City Lines to buy up and destroy public rail systems throughout the USA. A federal court found them guilty of anti-trust violations in 1949 and imposed a moderate fine.

The unveiling of the ruse came too late for the Red Cars. By the middle of the 20th century, people preferred the speed and convenience of cars, laying the groundwork for the traffic congestion that still victimizes LA today. With that situation getting worse, nostalgia for the Red Cars and a call for a new network are once again being voiced.

Arts District in the east. Call ☎ 808-2273 (no area code required within LA County) for more information. Maps are available from this number, at tourist offices or on DASH buses.

TRAIN

Long without a viable urban rail system, Los Angeles in recent years has been taking steps toward remedying that deficiency.

Metro Rail

Metro Rail refers to the network of three light-rail lines that provide connections between Downtown and the communities of Hollywood, Long Beach, Redondo Beach and Norwalk. Overall, these trains offer a clean and inexpensive way to travel and, provided they stop near your points of embarkation and disembarkation, are faster than the freeways. One-way tickets go for $1.35 and are dispensed by coin-operated machines. For Metro Rail information, call ☎ 800-266-6883 within LA County or check www.mta.net.

Blue Line Metro Rail's 22-mile Blue Line operates between Downtown LA's Metro Center station at 7th and Flower Sts and Long Beach (terminating downtown near the convention center) from 5 am to 10 pm (northbound) and 11:20 pm (southbound) daily. Trains travel at intervals of six to 20 minutes. The Red and Blue Lines meet at the Metro Center station. The Blue Line connects with the Green Line at the Imperial/Wilmington stop.

Red Line The Red Line runs underground from Union Station through Downtown to MacArthur Park and Western Ave. The newest segment, to central Hollywood, is scheduled to open in May 1999. The next leg, to North Hollywood in the San Fernando Valley, is under construction and scheduled for completion in 2000 (don't hold your breath). Red Line trains run every five to 10 minutes between 5 am and 11:15 pm daily.

Green Line The 20-mile Green Line runs west from Norwalk parallel to the 105 Fwy. It

The Surfer Line

Drive past LAX on the 405 Freeway – whether en route to the airport or elsewhere – and you'll likely get stuck in a crawling cavalcade of cars. Such congestion is bound to get even worse if plans to expand LAX are realized. So why doesn't LA do what most sensible metropolises around the world are doing and provide a viable public transportation option? Nah – not LA. Rather than providing easy, inexpensive and direct access to LAX, this city has a rail line that is famous for *not* going to LAX – the Green Line.

Making a beeline for the airport as it travels from its eastern terminus in Norwalk toward the ocean, the Green Line suddenly jerks south – a mere stone's throw from the airport boundary – and heads straight for Redondo Beach. The mind boggles, especially since the Green Line intersects with the Blue Line serving Downtown and Long Beach (both major hotel and convention areas), and thus could easily have whisked business travelers and other visitors straight to the airport, without traffic jams. Getting to the terminals now requires getting off at the Aviation station, dragging your luggage to a bus stop and taking a 10-minute ride – surely doable, but a lot less convenient.

Ironically, it was LAX authorities themselves who opposed the Green Line being routed to the airport directly, allegedly because it would interfere with airline safety (why don't other airports around the world have that problem?). Rumor has it that the prospect of diminished returns from its parking-lot concessions, costing $7 and more per day, stood in the way of logic and environmental consciousness. In the end, the Green Line, which cost a billion dollars to build, is a shining example of the mismanagement and shortsightedness that bogs down the city and has driven the Metropolitan Transportation Authority into bankruptcy.

connects with the Blue Line at the Imperial/
Wilmington stop, then curves south, bypass-
ing LAX (see The Surfer Line boxed text)
and terminating at Marine Ave in Redondo
Beach. There's a free shuttle bus between
LAX and the Aviation station (a 10-minute
ride). Trains operate 4:30 am to 11:30 pm
daily at intervals of six to 20 minutes.

Metrolink

Metrolink (☎ 800-371-5465) is a 404-mile
system of six commuter train lines operated by the Southern California Regional
Rail Authority, connecting Downtown LA's
Union Station with the four counties surrounding Los Angeles – Orange, Riverside,
San Bernardino and Ventura – as well as
San Diego. Lines in operation are the Ventura County Line (eight trips each weekday), the Santa Clarita Line (10), the San
Bernardino Line (12), the Riverside Line
(seven) and the Orange County Line (five).
A sixth line, the Inland Empire Line, connects San Bernardino and Riverside with
Orange County (four). Most trains run during peak commute hours; some lines offer
restricted Saturday service.

You can purchase tickets from vending
machines on station platforms or from the
ticket window at Union Station. Amtrak
tickets are not valid on Metrolink, and vice
versa. Fares are zone-based (for example,
Downtown LA to Oxnard at the Ventura
County line is $8.75 one way; Downtown to
San Bernardino is $7.75). Transfer to the
Red Line is free. There's a 25% discount for
off-peak travel.

CAR & MOTORCYCLE

By far the best way to get around LA is by
car or motorcycle. The city sprawls across
such a huge geographical area that you'll
likely spend some time behind the wheel –
unless time is no factor, or you're focusing
your visit on one particular neighborhood,
or money is extremely tight. Don't let horror
stories about LA freeways (all 1000 miles'
worth) scare you off. Even if the pretzel-
shaped interchanges and access ramps seem
daunting at first, while traffic can jam up for
miles behind any fender-bender, the city's

celebrated freeways are by far the fastest
and easiest way to get around the city.

In Los Angeles, there is one car for every
1.8 residents, a statistic that includes children
and other nondrivers. But despite the sheer
volume of traffic, the city is not hard to get
around, especially if you stick as much as possible to major arteries such as Santa Monica
and Wilshire Blvds. Street signs are large, easy
to read, and are usually posted far enough
ahead of major intersections that you know
which lane you want to be in. It's wise to
map out your route before you start driving,
however, and to avoid rush 'hour' – roughly
speaking, from 7 to 10 am and 3 to 7 pm.

It will help to memorize LA's major freeways (see the Major Freeways boxed text)
by name as well as by number. If you get lost,
don't fret: There are emergency call boxes
every mile or so, and frequent on-ramps and
off-ramps where you can exit the freeway
and pull into the nearest gas station to ask
directions.

Driving Conduct & Special Rules

Many Angelenos banish manners from their
cars and turn into maniacs, speed freaks and
crazies who cherish cutting you off, riding
your bumper or not letting you change
lanes. In these situations, it's best to stay as
calm as possible and not be provoked, especially if you don't know your way around.

Speed limits, unless posted otherwise, are
35 miles per hour (56 km per hour) on city
streets and 65 mph (104 kph) on freeways.
Most drivers exceed these limits by a few
miles per hour, however. Keep in mind that
tickets can also be given for driving too
slowly as well as driving hazardously fast.
Watch for school zones, which can be as slow
as 15 mph during school hours – these limits
are strictly enforced. Ne er pass a schoolbus
when its rear red lights are flashing: Children
are getting off the bus at these times. And as
in any large city, you'll encounter ambu-
lances with their sirens wailing. Should you
see or hear one of these coming, do everything you safely can to steer over to the right
curb and halt, allowing it to pass.

Seatbelts – and motorcycle helmets – must
be worn at all times. It's illegal for anybody

in the car (not just the driver) to consume alcohol while driving. Any open containers of booze must be stashed in the trunk. Keep your driver's license, registration papers and insurance information with you, in case you get stopped by the police.

LA drivers live and die by their *Thomas Guides*, voluminous, spiral-bound books of street maps with detailed indexes that pinpoint every address in LA County. Equally important to the average Angeleno are 'eye-in-the-sky' traffic reports, carried on the AM stations KNX 1070 and KFWB 980 every six minutes. Airborne pilots report freeway jam-ups as they occur and suggest alternate routes.

A few hints for first-time US drivers: Unless a sign indicates otherwise, you can turn right at a red light, as long as you don't impede intersecting traffic – which has the right of way. At intersections with four-way stop signs, cars proceed in the order in which they arrived. If two cars arrive simultaneously, the one on the right has the right of way. This can be an iffy situation as opinions may differ over who arrived first: Better to be safe than sorry.

On freeways, you may pass slower cars on either the left or the right side; if two cars are trying to get into the same central lane, the one farther right has priority. The far-left lane is often separated by two double yellow lines, meaning it's a 'diamond lane' and reserved for car pools of two, three or more passengers – make sure to check how many passengers are required to use each particular diamond lane. Fines for driving without the minimum number of people are prohibitively stiff (up to $271).

Parking
Parking is one of the biggest bugaboos for LA drivers. Metered parking often costs 25¢ per 15 minutes and may be limited to one hour. Be aware of colored curbs, as parking patrols issue tickets relentlessly:

Major Freeways

Angelenos live and die by their freeways. Most freeways are known both by their number and their name, which can get confusing. In general, those going east-west have even numbers and those running north-south have uneven numbers. There are emergency call boxes with free phones placed every half mile.

The following are LA's major freeways:

I-5 – Golden State Fwy	From Downtown northwest to Bakersfield
I-5 – Santa Ana Fwy	From Downtown southeast to Irvine
I-10 – San Bernardino Fwy	From Downtown east to San Bernardino
I-10 – Santa Monica Fwy	From Downtown west to Santa Monica
Hwy 60 – Pomona Fwy	From I-5 Downtown east to I-10 at Beaumont
US 101 – Hollywood Fwy	From I-5 and I-10 Downtown northwest to Hwy 170 in North Hollywood
US 101 – Ventura Fwy	From Hwy 134 in North Hollywood west to Ventura
I-110 – Harbor Fwy	From I-101 Downtown south to San Pedro
I-110 – Pasadena Fwy	From I-101 Downtown north to Pasadena
I-210 – Foothill Fwy	From I-5 in Sylmar east to I-10 in Pomona
I-405 – San Diego Fwy	From I-5 in San Fernando southeast to I-5 at Irvine
I-605 – San Gabriel River Fwy	From I-210 in Duarte south to I-405 in Long Beach
I-710 – Long Beach Fwy	From I-10 in Alhambra south to Long Beach

■ no parking

☐ loading zone

☐ loading zone

■ 20-minute limit

■ disabled parking

You may pay as much as $30 for simply being 30 seconds late in returning to your vehicle. Always study signposts for restrictions. Parking on residential streets – especially those near nightlife areas – is often reserved for residents. Be sure to keep your vehicle off the road during street cleaning hours – usually early on a weekday morning – which are posted as well. And of course, don't block driveways or park too closely to fire hydrants or bus stops.

Naturally, it's safest to put your car in a parking garage, though this may cost you a bundle. To cut costs, look for city-run public garages, more prevalent in independent cities like Santa Monica, Beverly Hills and West Hollywood. These usually offer two hours of free parking and low rates thereafter. Parking in business districts such as Century City or Downtown can cost as much as an insane $3.50 for each 20-minute period. In Downtown, this can easily be avoided by choosing a lot on the area's perimeter, which may charge just $3 all day.

Parking at motels and cheaper hotels is usually free, while fancier ones charge anywhere from $5 to $20 a day in addition to the room rate. Valet parking at nicer restaurants and hotels is ubiquitous and can be both a convenience and a scam. In areas where there is basically no public parking at all (Melrose Ave, for example), the valets are a welcome sight. But in places such as the Yamashiro restaurant in Hollywood, where you watch the attendant drive your car a few feet to the restaurant's parking lot and then charge you $3.50 for the 'favor,' it can be infuriating.

Car Rental

If you're going to rent a car, the best place to do so may be at the airport upon your arrival. Although agencies are located throughout the LA area, you may find that your bargaining power goes farthest at LAX, where the competition is greatest. Costs are highest in summer and during major holiday periods and lowest on weekends, when business travel is down.

You will need a credit card and a driver's license in order to rent a car. Rental rates for midsize cars range from $25 to $45 per day, $120 to $200 per week, more in heavy tourist seasons; larger or luxury cars are considerably more expensive. Unless you won't be driving much, get a deal that gives you unlimited mileage. Most rental agencies require that drivers be at least 21 years old; drivers under 25 normally must pay a surcharge of $5 to $15 per day. Rates do not include the 8.25% sales tax…or insurance.

Most North American travelers have credit cards that provide collision insurance if the card is used to pay for the car rental. If you are an overseas visitor, check with your credit card company to see if this option is available to you (your home auto insurance will not cover you in the US). Otherwise, you'll have to pay about $9 to $11 a day for a loss-damage waiver (covering any damage to the rental agency's car) and again for a liability insurance supplement (covering personal injury as well as damage to the other car). That's sometimes more than $20 a day over and above the rental cost. It is optional, but considering your liability if you *do* have an accident, buying insurance is highly advisable.

Gasoline in the US is quite inexpensive by foreign standards. Although prices fluctuate, expect to pay around $1.20 per US gallon (3.8 liters) for basic unleaded. Be sure to return your rental car with the same amount of gas you drove away with, or you'll be charged double for fuel.

Be aware that rental cars are often a target for theft. Never leave your luggage or other valuables in a parked vehicle, especially not in plain sight. Very small cars sometimes have no trunk cover, so everything you're carrying is open to view. This is not a good idea for visitors toting all their worldly possessions.

No agency will allow you to take its car into Mexico, and some may even have limits on which other US states you may drive to.

Major car-rental agencies with offices at LAX and elsewhere include the following:

Alamo	☎ 800-327-9633
Avis	☎ 800-831-2847
Budget	☎ 800-527-0700
Enterprise	☎ 800-736-8222
Hertz	☎ 800-654-3131
National	☎ 800-227-7368
Thrifty	☎ 800-367-2277

Some independent agencies that may have lower rates include the following:

Avon (☎ 310-277-4455)
  1100 S Beverly Drive in Beverly Hills
Midway (☎ 800-366-0643)
  1901 Ocean Ave in Santa Monica,
  and (☎ 800-643-9294)
  4900 W Century Blvd near LAX

Rapid (☎ 323-467-7368)
  6848 W Sunset Blvd in Hollywood
Rent-A-Wreck (☎ 310-478-0676)
  12333 W Pico Blvd in west LA

If money is no object, you can rent everything from a Rolls Royce to a Porsche and beyond at Beverly Hills Rent-A-Car (☎ 800-479-5996), Exotic Car Rental (☎ 800-385-8888), Rent A Classic Convertible (☎ 310-280-0260) or Sunbelt Sports Car Rental (☎ 310-410-2025).

Limousine Rental

If you're a budding movie star, want to make a grand entrance at a party, or just enjoy tooling around town behind tinted windows, you might consider renting a chauffeur-driven limo. Rates start at $45 per hour for a six-passenger stretch limo (from $75 for limos seating 10). There's usually a three-hour minimum, and tax and tip are not included. Check the Yellow Pages or try Diva

Coping with Traffic

It should come as no surprise that, in terms of volume, Los Angeles has the worst traffic in the USA. If you're entering Los Angeles by car, you may want to time your arrival away from heaviest commuter hours (roughly 7 to 10 am, 3 to 7 pm on weekdays). Weekend travel is generally a lot smoother, except between 5 and 8 pm. Unfortunately, there's no guarantee that you'll avoid tie-ups, which are usually the result of an accident up the road and can occur any time, easily doubling your travel time. On freeways, having at least two (sometimes three) people riding in a car entitles you to drive in the speedier 'diamond' (carpool) lane. *Never* drive in this lane without the minimum number of people in the car; the fines are horrendous.

Except for short distances, surface streets are usually a poor alternative to freeways. The city – stoplights and all – is just too large to traverse quickly. Some important parts of town, notably Beverly Hills and West Hollywood, are not served by any freeway, however. Reasonably fast roads traveling north-south are La Brea Ave and La Cienega Blvd; avoid Fairfax Ave. Olympic Blvd is the best east-west route, though Santa Monica Blvd can be OK as well; Wilshire Blvd is comparatively slow. The most scenic road is Sunset Blvd, though with its dangerous curves and high speeds, it's not always the safest to negotiate.

Accidents Do Happen

Accidents do happen – especially in such an auto-dependent city as LA. It's important that a visitor knows the appropriate protocol when involved in a 'fender-bender.'

- DON'T TRY TO DRIVE AWAY! Remain at the scene of the accident; otherwise you may spend some time in the local jail.
- Call the police (and an ambulance, if needed) immediately, and give the operator as much specific information as possible (your location, if there are any injuries involved, etc). The emergency phone number is ☎ 911.
- Get the other driver's name, address, driver's license number, license plate number and insurance information. Be prepared to provide any documentation you have, such as your passport, international driver's license and insurance documents.
- Tell your story to the police carefully. Refrain from answering any questions until you feel comfortable doing so (with a lawyer present, if need be). That's your right under the law. The only insurance information you need to reveal is the name of your insurance carrier and your policy number.
- Always comply with an alcohol breathalyzer test. If you opt not to take the test, you'll almost certainly find yourself with an automatic suspension of your driving privileges.
- If you're driving a rental car, call the rental company promptly.

Limousine (☎ 310-278-3482), Fox Limousine (☎ 213-641-9626), Limos for Less (☎ 800-689-8005) or Pacific Limousine (☎ 310-649-5466).

Motorcycle Rental

The Southern California climate is biker-friendly, though LA city traffic is not. Still, if you've always wanted to experience that *Easy Rider* feeling, hopping on a Harley 'Hog' and driving along Route 66 and up the Pacific Coast Hwy may be the way to go. Among the companies worth trying are Eagle Rider Motorcycle Rental (☎ 800-501-8687), 20917 Western Ave in Torrance, and Rent a Custom Harley-Davidson (☎ 888-434-4473), 4161 Lincoln Blvd in Marina del Rey, which has multilingual staff and provides helmets, leather jackets and basic liability insurance.

Both have a range of models from which to choose, including the Bad Boy and the Heritage Softtail Classic. Most rentals go for $75 to $150 a day. Bartels' Harley-Davidson (☎ 310-823-1112), 4141 Lincoln Blvd, has officially licensed T-shirts, motor clothes and accessories. Make sure you get a helmet for

yourself and any passenger: Helmets are required by law in California, and the law is strictly enforced.

Car Purchase

If you're spending several months in LA, a used vehicle is worth considering, though purchasing one can be quite a hassle. If you go this route, it helps to have experience working on cars. Otherwise, spend $50 to have a mechanic check the car for defects before you buy (stay away from vendors who refuse to let you do this). You can check the official value of a used car by looking it up in the *Blue Book*, a listing of cars by make, model and year issued, and the average resale price (available at bookstores and libraries).

Although used-car dealers can simplify the process, purchasing a car from a private individual is usually cheaper. Check the classified ads in the *LA Times* as well as the various free weeklies, and pick up a copy of the *Recycler* to find a good deal. If you purchase a car from an individual, you must have the car's emissions smog-tested at a garage and get a certificate that verifies the vehicle meets state standards (cars sold by dealers have already been tested).

You must also purchase an auto insurance policy, which can be rather costly. Rates depend on a variety of factors such as your age, the make and year of the car, whether it has airbags or security devices, and where you live. The annual premium for a 1991 Honda Civic with a purchase price of $1500, for example, would be about $500 for liability insurance only (the required minimum) and about $700 for full coverage (including theft and collision insurance).

To register your car, take the smog certificate and proof of insurance, along with the ownership title and bill of sale, to any office of the Department of Motor Vehicles (DMV). Make an appointment (addresses and phone numbers are available at www.dmv.ca.gov), or plan on spending several hours waiting in line. Expect to pay between 7% and 12% of the cost of the car for the registration. If you buy from a dealer, you can usually skip the DMV: The paperwork is done for you and the registration bill follows in the mail.

As your departure from the USA approaches, you must set aside time to sell the car. Rather than sell it to a used-car dealer for a pittance, take out an ad in a local newspaper or in the *Recycler* (☎ 323-660-8900) and wait for calls. (The *Recycler* is a weekly newspaper with classified ads for secondhand items. There's no charge for noncommercial ads.)

TAXI

Unlike New York, Chicago and other big cities, you can't just thrust your arm out and expect to hail a taxi in LA. Except for those lined up outside airports, train stations, bus stations and major hotels, cabbies respond to phone calls rather than hand waves. Fares are metered; you pay $2 at flag fall, $1.80 per mile. Occasionally there are additional charges for luggage (50¢ per piece) and passengers in excess of three (75¢ per person).

Checker	☎ 800-300-5007
Independent	☎ 800-521-8294
United Independent	☎ 800-822-8294
Yellow Cab	☎ 800-200-1085

BICYCLE

Cyclists are entitled to their share of any city street in Los Angeles. Freeways, on the other hand, are reserved for automobiles and motorcycles. Be aware that the number of cyclists on LA streets is relatively small, and riding aggressively is likely to antagonize already jangled motorists. Wear a helmet; it just makes sense. For details on recreational biking, see Activities in the Things to See & Do chapter.

Bicycles & Public Transport

If you're looking to use your bike *and* public transportation, you're in for a challenge. Bicycles are not allowed on any buses in the county. You may take them on Metro Rail trains during nonpeak times (*not* between 6 to 9 am and 3 to 7 pm) as long you have a permit. Permits are issued free at any of MTA's customer centers (see the Metropolitan Transportation Authority section earlier in the chapter). Metrolink trains allow bikes aboard at no charge any time, without permits.

WALKING

Tell an Angeleno, 'I'll just walk,' and they're bound to try talking you out of it. In Los Angeles, dispersion is the rule of city planning and all but a few strips were developed with motorists, rather than pedestrians, in mind. If you hate to see all those sidewalks going to waste, sections of Downtown, Santa Monica, Beverly Hills and central Hollywood are areas where 'hoofing it' will prove worthwhile – but you'll probably have to drive there first.

We have included several walking tours in the Things to See & Do and Los Angeles Architecture chapters.

ORGANIZED TOURS

Most Los Angeles-area tour companies operate year-round, with stepped-up schedules during the peak visitor periods of summer and the Christmas holidays. You can book directly with the tour operators, through your hotel front desk or with any tourist office. Discounted tours are available at hostels.

Bus

There are many companies offering essentially the same kind of tours at roughly the same prices. The city tour provides an overview, covering everything from Downtown LA to Hollywood, Beverly Hills and some stars' homes. Lasting an entire day, the tour costs around $40. Theme park tours going to Universal Studios, Disneyland, Knott's Berry Farm and Six Flags Magic Mountain are priced between $60 and $75, admission included. Children's discounts are available.

Some of the larger tour companies are Starline Tours of Hollywood (☎ 323-463-3333), LA Tours (☎ 323-962-6793) and GuideLine Tours (☎ 213-465-3004, 800-604-8433). EuroPacific Tours (☎ 800-303-3005) has a city and stars' homes tour and an LA by Night tour, each costing $42 and lasting 4½ hours. Trolleywood Tours (☎ 323-469-8184) offers fun and fact-filled one-hour tours of Hollywood aboard a cute trolley ($16), and two-hour tours of about 60 Beverly Hills celebrities' homes in a van ($29).

Air

Many companies offer tours of LA by helicopter. One of the oldest is HeliUSA (☎ 310-641-9494), which has flights over Hollywood, Downtown, Griffith Park and Beverly Hills by night for $99. Flights in combination with a three-course dinner cost

Hollywood Is Dead! Long Live Hollywood!

Murder and maniacs, sex and suicide, drugs and deviants. Sound like the ingredients of your average Hollywood movie? Perhaps, but they're also the focus of a not-so-average Hollywood tour. Courtesy of Grave Line Tours (☎ 323-469-4149), and at a cost of $44 per 'body,' comes a rather unique exploration of the dark – and dead – side of Tinseltown. In the course of 2½ hours, up to six 'mourners' at a time are whisked around Los Angeles, where they visit some 80 sites where the rich and famous met the Grim Reaper, often under less than glamorous circumstances.

Grave Line Tours is the brainchild of Greg Smith, an ex-mortician from Kansas with a twisted sense of humor and a bizarre penchant for the hereafter. His gossipy journey through movieland morbidity covers lurid scandals, mysterious murders and spooky incidents from the silent-movie era to OJ Simpson. You hear titillating 'tales from the crypt' about Hollywood legends Marilyn Monroe, Gary Cooper, Humphrey Bogart, Jayne Mansfield and many others.

You will see it all while traveling in a roomy 1971 silver Cadillac hearse, while a taped commentary (sometimes accompanied by theme music from films of the dead stars) plays along. Occasionally the guide may treat you to his own brand of gallows humor: 'Did you know that Judy Garland was one of three stars to die on a toilet?' he asked his incredulous passengers on our tour. (The others, if you must know, were Elvis and Lenny Bruce.)

$119. Torrance-based Bravo Helicopters (☎ 800-773-5946) has a short ride over the South Bay and LA Harbor costing $90 and a long flight cruise that takes in Downtown, Hollywood, Beverly Hills and the beaches for $170. Another option is HeliNet (☎ 818-902-0229), which has 20-minute flights over Universal Studios, Downtown, Hollywood and Beverly Hills for $85; add 30 minutes and $54 and you also see the stars' Malibu Colony and Malibu Canyon as well as the San Fernando Valley.

The old-fashioned way to travel is aboard a biplane, offered by Bi-Plane Adventures (☎ 818-834-5957), based in Pacoima in eastern LA County. The $99 tour flies over the San Gabriel Mountains with views of the Mojave Desert; the $149 tour also includes the major city landmarks; the $189 tour extends to the coast.

Boat

Easily the favorite ocean trip for LA visitors and residents alike is a roundtrip day cruise to Santa Catalina Island. Boats depart daily for the Mediterranean-flavored town of Avalon from several mainland harbors, including Long Beach and San Pedro, and Newport Beach and Dana Point in Orange County (see Santa Catalina Island in the Excursions chapter).

Other tour boats take visitors whale watching, harbor sightseeing or dinner cruising, including Hornblower Dining Yachts (☎ 310-301-9900), 13755 Fiji Way, Marina del Rey; Shoreline Village Cruises (☎ 562-495-5884), 401 Shoreline Village Drive, Long Beach; Spirit Cruises (☎ 310-548-8080), Berth 77, Ports O'Call, San Pedro; and 22nd Street Sportfishing (☎ 310-521-0222), 141 W 22nd St, San Pedro.

Things to See & Do

Los Angeles is a vast place with enough to keep you busy for a few years. Places of interest, museums, sights and other diversions are described in this chapter by neighborhood. Recreational activities are at the end.

Downtown

Perennial doubters and incorrigible cynics will never believe it, but LA does have a center. Yes, there is a *there* there. The place of work for tens of thousands of commuters, it's here where powerful international banks and corporations are headquartered, their skyscrapers rising against the backdrop of the San Gabriel Mountains. Few areas of LA have as much to offer per square mile as Downtown. It is rich in history (this is, after all, the birthplace of the city), wonderful architecture, exciting restaurants, superior cultural institutions and countless smaller surprises. In fact, it is possible to 'travel around the world' in just a day as you make your way from ethnic enclaves like Chinatown and Little Tokyo to the Mexican marketplaces of Olvera St and Broadway and back to the 21st-century America of the financial district.

The future looks bright for Downtown as major redevelopments are taking place or are planned. New attractions, such as the expanded Japanese American National Museum and the Colburn School of Performing Arts, have galvanized the community. And the stimulus to Downtown will only increase with the opening of new venues like the Staples Center sports arena, the cutting-edge Walt Disney Concert Hall and even the new Downtown cathedral.

Orient yourself at the Civic Center, America's second-largest complex of government buildings (next to Washington, DC). Northeast of here, across the 101 Fwy, are El Pueblo de Los Angeles and Chinatown. Southeast is Little Tokyo; southwest is the main business district. Farther south are the Garment District, the convention center, and, past the 10 Fwy, Exposition Park.

Getting around Downtown is easy; most places of interest are quickly reached by walking. For the foot-weary, there's a great

Highlights

Coming up with a list of the best things to do in LA is no easy endeavor, thanks to the limitless spectrum of experiences, locations and sights the city has to offer. What follows is a list of things we like to do and that we think our readers will enjoy as well. Some of these will seem obvious, others may be surprising, but all of them will make for special memories:

- Browsing, dining and strolling along Santa Monica's Third Street Promenade
- Dining with a view of city lights (Yamashiro Castle in Hollywood is a good spot)
- Discovering the world at the California Science Center
- Driving along Sunset Blvd from Downtown to the Pacific Ocean
- Hiking in the Santa Monica Mountains
- Soaking up local color at Downtown's Grand Central Market
- Spending the day at Universal Studios Hollywood
- Strolling the beach from Santa Monica Pier to Venice Boardwalk
- Sunning, swimming and surfing at Zuma, Santa Monica or Manhattan Beach
- Taking a picnic to a concert at the Hollywood Bowl
- Touring the Huntington Library, Art Collection & Botanical Gardens
- Visiting the Getty Center

public transport system in the form of mini-buses called DASH, which operate at five to 10-minute intervals and cost just 25¢ per ride. If you arrive by car, park in a cheap lot on the periphery rather than in the extor-tionary lots in the center.

FINANCIAL DISTRICT WALKING TOUR

LA's modern business and financial district extends 7 blocks south from the Civic Center to 8th St and from the 110 Fwy, 6 blocks east to Hill St. Much of the area is atop historic Bunker Hill, which a century ago was LA's most fashionable residential neighborhood, flecked with stately Victorian mansions. In the 1920s an influx of transients made this chic enclave deteriorate into a slum. After WWII, it took the city almost 20 years to decide on restoring or razing. But in the end, the demand for progress accounted for the forest of glass and concrete buildings now occupying the hill. Grand Ave bisects the two main complexes: the Wells Fargo Center to the west and California Plaza to the east. Also here are large condominium complexes and the futuristic Westin Bonaventure Hotel, whose quintet of cylindrical glass towers is instantly recognizable to moviegoers (think *Terminator* and *In the Line of Fire*).

Central Library

Our tour begins at the LA public library system's Central Library (1922; ☎ 213-228-7000), 630 W 5th St, which is chockablock with more than 2.5 million books and histor-ical photographs, and full of art and archi-tectural detail. (Also see Libraries in the Facts for the Visitor chapter as well as the Los Angeles Architecture chapter.)

In 1986, a pair of devastating fires de-stroyed or damaged more than a million books. But in 1993 – and some $214 mil-lion later – Central Library reopened,

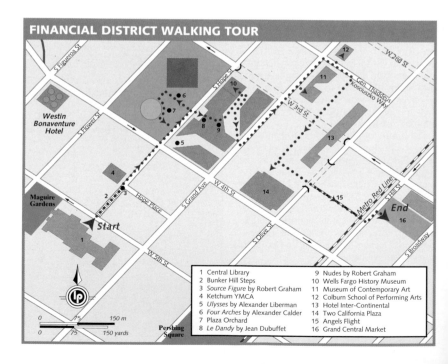

FINANCIAL DISTRICT WALKING TOUR

Westin Bonaventure Hotel

Maguire Gardens

Start

End

Pershing Square

1 Central Library	9 *Nudes* by Robert Graham
2 Bunker Hill Steps	10 Wells Fargo History Museum
3 *Source Figure* by Robert Graham	11 Museum of Contemporary Art
4 Ketchum YMCA	12 Colburn School of Performing Arts
5 *Ulysses* by Alexander Liberman	13 Hotel Inter-Continental
6 *Four Arches* by Alexander Calder	14 Two California Plaza
7 Plaza Orchard	15 Angels Flight
8 *Le Dandy* by Jean Dubuffet	16 Grand Central Market

boasting a new eight-story glass-roofed atrium and the stylish **Maguire Gardens**. This tranquil 1½-acre park has cypress, olive and other trees that shade the sinuous walkways, where benches offer a respite. Highlights are the three pools and adjoining steps bisecting the park. Called *Spine*, they were created by artist Jud Fine in 1993 and incorporate animal figures intended to show the evolution of life. Symbols carved into the risers of the steps paralleling the pools trace the development of communication.

Free guided library tours run weekdays at 12:30 pm, Saturday at 11 am and 2 pm and Sunday at 2 pm. Library hours are Monday and Thursday through Saturday from 10 am to 5:30 pm, Tuesday and Wednesday noon to 8 pm, Sunday 1 to 5 pm.

Bunker Hill Steps

Opposite the library's 5th St exit are the Bunker Hill Steps, LA's retort to Rome's Spanish Steps. The steps lead up from the Library Tower, LA's tallest building; they deliver you to a fountain and idealized female nude by Robert Graham called *Source Figure*. Just beyond, on your left, is the **Ketchum YMCA**, where Downtown suits work off stress. Terraces with outdoor cafes invite a quick bite or drink. Walk up the steps and continue straight (north) on Hope St.

Hope St

The freeform sculpture on your right, outside the Mellon Bank Center, is Alexander Liberman's *Ulysses* (1988). Farther on, the red sculpture outside the ARCO world headquarters (not to be confused with ARCO Plaza, a few blocks west) is Alexander Calder's *Four Arches* (1974). Also take a stroll to the Plaza Orchard, a small park atop the ARCO garage, where three waterfalls plunge into a lower-level pool. Cross the street and enter the Wells Fargo Court; note Jean Dubuffet's cartoonish sculpture *Le Dandy* (1982) in the window by the entrance. The escalator whisks you to a glassy atrium accented by a gardenlike landscape and more nudes by Robert Graham. Turn left and exit through the door to get to the Wells Fargo History Museum.

Wells Fargo History Museum

This small museum (☎ 213-253-7166), in the Wells Fargo Center at 333 S Grand Ave, is often overlooked. Established in the wake of the great California gold rush of the late 1840s, the Wells Fargo Co grew to be synonymous with the maturation of the American West through its banking and stagecoach operations. This museum relives that era with such artifacts as an original stagecoach and a 2lb gold nugget. Hours are weekdays 9 am to 5 pm, and admission is free. Exit the museum, turn right, walk to Grand Ave, turn left and head toward the pyramid rooftop of the Museum of Contemporary Art.

Museum of Contemporary Art (MOCA)

On the east side of Grand Ave, at 250 Grand, is Downtown's most touted museum, the Museum of Contemporary Art (☎ 213-626-6222 for recorded information). Known locally as MOCA, the building is a work of art in itself. Japanese architect Arata Isozaki combined cubes, pyramids and barrel vault shapes with glass, aluminum and red sandstone to create a unique structure that suits its purpose perfectly. Inside is a maze of galleries that are filled with paintings, sculptures and photographs from the 1940s to the present.

On view are important traveling exhibits as well as works from MOCA's permanent collection, considered one of the world's most important of the period. Styles represented include Abstract Expressionism, Pop Art, Minimalism and conceptual art by such artists as Robert Rauschenberg, Mark Rothko, Jackson Pollock, Willem de Kooning, Andy Warhol and Alberto Giacometti. There's also a great gift shop. MOCA hours are 11 am to 5 pm, closed Monday; admission is $6 ($4 for students and seniors). On Thursday, hours are extended to 8 pm, and admission is free after 5 pm. Tickets are also good for same-day admission to MOCA's sister museum, the Geffen Temporary Contemporary (see the Little Tokyo section, later in this chapter).

Exit the Museum of Contemporary Art at the northeast side and cross the small

General Thaddeus Kosciuszko Way to the Colburn School of Performing Arts.

Colburn School of Performing Arts

The idiosyncratic structure with the oversized zinc-clad roof just north of MOCA, at 200 S Grand Ave, is home to the Colburn School of Performing Arts (☎ 213-621-2200). Often called the 'Julliard of the West,' the building incorporates a chamber music hall where students perform. Walk southwest past MOCA (it's now on your right) and the Hotel Inter-Continental to get to **Two California Plaza**, with its sunken watercourt, the site of summer lunchtime concerts. On the southeastern side is Angels Flight.

Angels Flight

A newly resurrected city landmark, Angels Flight bills itself as 'the shortest railway in the world': the antique funicular takes about one minute to cover the steep incline between California Plaza and Hill St. Originally opened in 1901, Angels Flight was mothballed in the '60s to make room for Bunker Hill's growth. Nineties nostalgia breathed new life into the little trains, which resumed their rattling in 1996. Angels Flight operates daily between 6:30 am and 10 pm; rides cost 25¢ each way.

From the Angels Flight Hill St station, cross the street and walk up Hill St to the west entrance of the **Grand Central Market**,

Angels Flight: the 1-block railway

a terrific place for delicious, inexpensive snacks. For details, see the next section, Historic Core Walking Tour, and the Places to Eat chapter.

HISTORIC CORE WALKING TOUR

Pershing Square and the area southeast form LA's historic Downtown core. Once elegant and bustling commercial arteries, the district's streets are now lined with aging shops, movie theaters and warehouses in need of renovation. But people looking past the decay and grime will find strikingly beautiful architecture dating back to glamorous periods in city history – the birth of motion pictures and the pre-Depression roaring '20s. Still a vibrant neighborhood, it's now a commercial center of Latinos. This tour can be combined with Tour I of the Los Angeles Architecture chapter.

Pershing Square

Our tour starts at LA's oldest public park (1886), framed by 5th, 6th, Olive and Hill Sts. Pershing Square got a $14 million facelift in 1994, intended to create a revitalized nexus for the Downtown community, but the park remains sadly underutilized. Devoid of viable performance spaces and other infrastructure, it attracts few people, though in all fairness the park has come a long way from the 'grime and crime' scene it was.

The park is anchored by a 120-foot purple tower and has water attractions and plenty of public art – a stylized earthquake fault line and historical ceramic postcards embedded in concrete benches. The phalanx of imposing structures surrounding the square is covered on Tour I of the Los Angeles Architecture chapter. Now walk south on Hill St or Olive St to 8th St, turn left and head over to Broadway.

Broadway

A vibrant Latino retail hub, Broadway – especially between 3rd and 9th Sts – is the busiest commercial street west of Chicago. To visitors, the street may at first seem a confusing cacophony of sounds, smells and garish storefronts. Mariachi music blares, shop windows hawk billowy party gowns, and

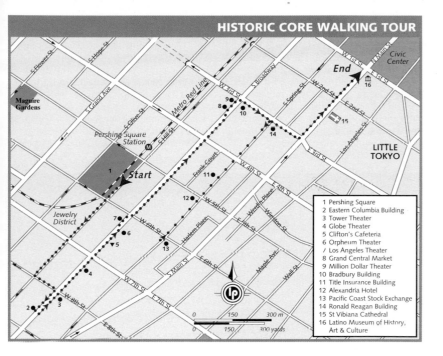

HISTORIC CORE WALKING TOUR

1 Pershing Square
2 Eastern Columbia Building
3 Tower Theater
4 Globe Theater
5 Clifton's Cafeteria
6 Orpheum Theater
7 Los Angeles Theater
8 Grand Central Market
9 Million Dollar Theater
10 Bradbury Building
11 Title Insurance Building
12 Alexandria Hotel
13 Pacific Coast Stock Exchange
14 Ronald Reagan Building
15 St Vibiana Cathedral
16 Latino Museum of History,
   Art & Culture

huge signs advertise everything 'cut-rate.' But Broadway's main attraction is its great density of historic buildings – especially its 11 movie palaces built between 1913 and 1931 – that recently won this area National Register Historic District status. In the early days of filmmaking, Broadway played host to stars including Mary Pickford, Douglas Fairbanks and Charlie Chaplin as they leapt from limousines to attend lavish premieres.

Architecturally, the theaters are a marvelous hodgepodge of styles, from Spanish Gothic to French Baroque. Their dramatic facades and flamboyant interiors were inspired by European churches, palaces and castles. Sadly, many have been allowed to crumble or – worse yet – to become bargain shopping arcades. A few lucky theaters now show Spanish-language movies. Most of the buildings can only be seen from the outside – unless you're on an LA Conservancy tour (see the related boxed text in the Los

Angeles Architecture chapter). For superb images of the lavish interiors, check out the excellent coffee-table book called *The Last Remaining Seats*, photographed by Robert Berger and Anne Conser and available from Navigator Press in Pasadena.

Turn right on Broadway and walk to the **Eastern Columbia Building** (1927), magnificent in its turquoise terra-cotta mantle, at 849 Broadway. A premier example of the Art Deco Zigzag Moderne style, it was originally home to two clothing stores, Columbia and Eastern Outfitting. Look for the gilded sunburst pattern above the entrance and for the clock faces on the soaring tower.

Retrace your steps and continue north on Broadway. The **Tower Theater** (1927) at the corner of 8th St was the first theater built expressly for showing 'talkies.' This was the project on which Charles Lee, who would become LA's premier theater designer during the '30s and '40s, cut his teeth. Its primarily

Baroque elements are drawn from a variety of European structures, including the Paris Opera House. The tower's top was lowered after a 1971 earthquake. The splendid interior is now used as a movie location. On the next block, at 744 Broadway, was the **Globe Theater** (1913), originally a Beaux Arts design and the first Broadway theater to show feature-length films. Sadly it has been converted into a swap meet/flea market, though some of the upper galleries remain.

Interrupt your movie theater tour and step inside **Clifton's Cafeteria** (☎ 213-627-1673), a venerable Downtown eatery at 648 S Broadway. Clifton's was founded in 1931 by a Salvation Army captain who doled out free grub to starving Angelenos during the Great Depression. 'Grub' is still what is served here, but the ultra-campy setting is what warrants a closer look. Sprawling over several open levels, Clifton's is an enchanted forest with fake trees, squirrels and deer.

What's Free

Museums (Always Free)
Cabrillo Marine Aquarium (San Pedro)
California African American Museum (Exposition Park)
California Science Center (Exposition Park)
The Center – Civil Rights Museum (Watts)
Fort MacArthur Military Museum (San Pedro)
Frederick's of Hollywood Lingerie Museum (Hollywood)
Getty Center (Westside)
Hollywood Exhibit at Roosevelt Hotel (Hollywood)
Local History Museums: Manhattan Beach, Hermosa Beach, Redondo Beach
Los Angeles Contemporary Exhibits (Hollywood)
Malibu Lagoon Museum (Malibu)
Marine Studies Lab & Aquarium (Manhattan Beach)
Museum in Black (Leimert Park)
Museum of African American Art (Leimert Park)
Travel Town Museum & Train Rides (Griffith Park)
USC Fisher Gallery (Downtown)
Wells Fargo History Museum (Downtown)

Museums (Occasionally Free)
Geffen Contemporary (Downtown) – Thursday 5 to 8 pm
George C Page Museum of La Brea Discoveries (Mid-City) – 1st Tuesday of the month
Heritage Square Museum (Mt Washington & Highland Park) – Friday 10 am to 3 pm
Huntington Library, Art Collection & Botanical Gardens (Pasadena) –
   1st Thursday of the month
Japanese American Museum (Downtown) – 3rd Friday of the month
Long Beach Museum of Art – Friday 5 to 8 pm
Museum of Modern Art (Downtown) – Thursday 5 to 8 pm
South Coast Botanical Gardens (Palos Verdes Peninsula) – 3rd Tuesday of the month

Tours
Art Center College of Design campus (Pasadena)
Caltech campus (Pasadena)
Judson Studios (Highland Park; see the Los Angeles Architecture chapter)

For some spiritual sustenance, make a visit to Clifton's small chapel.

Just beyond, at 630 Broadway, is the old **Orpheum Theater** (1925), a spectacular French Renaissance building, which is still fully functional, including its Wurlitzer organ. The 90-foot-high auditorium has a gold-leaf coffered ceiling and wrought-iron chandeliers. The **Los Angeles Theater** (1931), 615 Broadway, is a Lee design on the north side of Broadway and was the last (and grandest) movie palace built here. Seating more than 2000 in its French Baroque setting, the theater featured opulent details such as a vaulted, coffered ceiling, a lavish central staircase leading to a crystal fountain and Corinthian columns. Opening with the premiere of Chaplin's *City Lights*, it went dark in 1994.

Walk 3 blocks north on Broadway to the **Grand Central Market**. This bustling food bazaar has been in business since 1917 and is

KCET Studios (Silver Lake)
Los Angeles Times (Downtown)
Music Center of LA County (Downtown)
Olvera St walking tour (Downtown)
Pacific Design Center (West Hollywood)
UCLA campus (Westside)
USC campus (Downtown)

Historic Sights
Avila Adobe – Olvera St (Downtown)
Brand Park's Doctor's House (Glendale)
Camera Obscura (Santa Monica)
Cemeteries: Forest Lawn (Hollywood Hills and Glendale); Hollywood Memorial Cemetery, Westwood Cemetery
Clark Library (South Central)
El Alisal/Lummis House (Mt Washington & Highland Park)
El Molino Viejo (Pasadena)
Greystone Park (Beverly Hills)
Griffith Park Observatory (Griffith Park)
Mann's Chinese Theater forecourt (Hollywood)
Old Plaza Firehouse (Downtown)
Self-Realization Fellowship Lake Shrine (Pacific Palisades)
Will Rogers' home (Pacific Palisades)
Wrigley Mansion (Pasadena)

Entertainment & Activities
Coffeehouse poetry readings, concerts, etc (see the Entertainment chapter)
Coronet Theater – Monday nights (see the Entertainment chapter)
Mice Improv Comedy All-Stars – Saturday nights (see the Entertainment chapter)
Nightclubs – some nights there are no cover charges (see the Entertainment chapter)
Sierra Club hikes (see Guided Hikes)
Swing-dancing lessons at the Derby (see the Entertainment chapter)
Wine tastings at San Antonio Winery (Downtown)

crammed with stalls selling herbs, spices, cheeses and candy, plus nearly every vegetable, fruit and animal that grows – all at rock-bottom prices. Numerous food stalls provide delicious sustenance and character galore. (For dining suggestions, see the Places to Eat chapter.)

Next door, a less lavish theater than the previous ones, but with easy access, is the **Million Dollar Theater** (1918) at 307 Broadway, one of the oldest large movie palaces in this country. Note the squiggly, heavily ornamented facade and the coffered ceiling, both in the Spanish Churrigueresque style. The theater was taken over by a Spanish-language evangelical church in 1992.

Across the street is one of LA's architectural highlights, the elegant **Bradbury Building** (1893; ☎ 213-626-1893), 304 Broadway. Now an office building, it was featured in the movie *Blade Runner*. Its modest exterior accentuates the visual splendor of the interior. Behind heavy oak doors, a five-story galleried atrium is flooded by daylight streaming through a tent-shaped glass roof. The black filigree of the cast-iron banisters is offset by walls of tawny glazed bricks and red marble staircases. A pair of manually operated open-caged elevators takes employees, unhurriedly, to their offices.

The Bradbury was the final project of mining millionaire turned real estate developer Lewis Bradbury. According to legend, the architect George Wyman – a mere draftsman – accepted the commission after

DAVID PEEVERS

Inside the Bradbury Building

communicating with his dead brother via a Ouija board. For inspiration, Wyman drew upon a 1887 novel by Edward Bellamy, *Looking Backward*, about a utopian civilization in the year 2000. The building was Wyman's only success, and Bradbury died a few months before its completion. The lobby is generally open weekdays 9 am to 6 pm, to 5 pm on weekends. You're free to step inside, though security guards may prevent you from walking up the stairs or taking the elevator. From the Bradbury Building, head southeast on 3rd St to Spring St.

Spring St

In the 1920s, Spring St was *the* center of finance, wearing with pride the title 'Wall Street of the West.' By the '60s, though, as the new financial district began springing up around Bunker Hill, it had deteriorated and become one of Downtown's less savory streets. Recently declared a Historic District by the city, efforts to bring new life to this artery are underway.

As you hit Spring St, right in front of you at 300 Spring St is the **Ronald Reagan Building**, whose lobby features a large-scale, feverishly colorful mural by Carlos Almaraz and Elsa Flores called 'California Dreamscape.' (Legend has it that the building was originally to be called the Reagan State Office Building before someone realized that its abbreviation would read, 'Reagan SOB.')

Many of the buildings from Spring St's heyday still survive. Architecture fans may want to detour west along Spring St, in particular noting the lovely lobby of the Art Deco **Title Insurance Building** (1928) at 433 Spring St and the **Alexandria Hotel** (1906) on the southwest corner of 5th St, noteworthy for its interior palm court. Also see the gray, monumental **Pacific Coast Stock Exchange** (1930) at 618 Spring St, with its fluted pilasters. These buildings and many more are covered on the LA Conservancy Palaces of Finance tour.

Retrace your steps north on Spring St to the Ronald Reagan Building and turn right on 3rd St. Walk 1 block to Main St and turn left. Travel north on Main St until you see the condemned **St Vibiana Cathedral** on your right. One block farther is the Latino Museum of History, Art & Culture.

Latino Museum of History, Art & Culture

The tour concludes at this small museum (☎ 213-626-7600), 112 S Main St, which was finally born in May 1998 after a 15-year gestation period. Its mission is to present the aesthetic sensibilities of Latin American artists and to celebrate their historical and artistic contributions. In a former Bank of America building, this small space is still a work in progress as renovation depends on funds. The main facade, featuring a stylized bas-relief of pedestrians, was still under construction long after gates opened for the inaugural showing. Future exhibits are set to include photographs of LA during the '40s and the '80s and a retrospective of Los Cuatro, four artists of the East LA School of Painting. Hours are 10 am to 4 pm (closed Sunday and Wednesday). Call ahead to confirm its hours, or check the listings in city magazines.

CIVIC CENTER (MAP 5)

Extending 8 blocks east to west from San Pedro to Figueroa Sts, the Civic Center contains the most important of LA's city, county, state and federal office buildings, including courthouses and the main police station. This is where the infamous OJ Simpson murder trial took place in 1995 (at the US Federal Courthouse Building, 312 N Spring St), and where law-enforcement officers coordinated anti-riot activities in 1992 (at the LAPD headquarters at Parker Center, 150 N Los Angeles St).

City Hall

Anyone who grew up watching television in the '50s and '60s can tell you about Los Angeles City Hall, 200 N Spring St. It was, after all, the 'Daily Planet' building where *Superman* leapt into the sky and was also featured as Los Angeles' main police station in *Dragnet*.

Built in 1928 in a jumble of styles including Art Deco, Byzantine and Romanesque, the 28-story building (Downtown's tallest

Purple People Greeters

The Downtown Center District of Los Angeles is an affiliation of property owners and merchants who realized that to many people 'going Downtown' meant a highly unsavory if not outright dangerous experience. To battle this image they hired a small army of mostly young people to patrol the streets on foot, by bike or in cars. The 'Purple People Greeters' intercede when things get iffy, call the LAPD when things get *real* rough, and simply provide tourists with directions and suggestions about the clubs, restaurants and sights of Downtown.

It's easy to spot these welcoming folks: Traveling in pairs like Mormon missionaries, they all wear purple T-shirts with 'District Safety' or 'Downtown Guide' emblazoned on the back. You can also visit them at their Service Center (☎ 213-624-2425) at 801 S Hill St.

DAVID PEEVERS

until 1966) has recently gone the way of many of LA's aging stars by having a $235 million face-lift. Its most distinctive feature is the sleek tower capped with a stepped pyramid. Inside, marble columns and a colorful ceramic-tile dome add stateliness to the City Hall rotunda. Eclectic artworks – including a Shinto shrine from Japan and a giant holographic portrait of former mayor Tom Bradley – serve notice that LA is no ordinary city.

Tours are suspended during renovation, which will bring it up to par with earthquake and other safety codes and will continue well into the new millennium.

Children's Museum

North across Temple St from City Hall is the Los Angeles Children's Museum (☎ 213-687-8800), in an aging facility at 310 N Main St. Among the 15 exhibits is 'Club Eco,' which playfully teaches about environmental issues such as recycling, and 'Take Care of Yourself,' which addresses health and safety. There are also television, recording and animation studios (after all, this *is* LA) and a city bus (youngsters can take the driver's seat) on re-created city streets.

Besides showing kids a good time, the museum also tries to give parents and children a better appreciation of how and where learning takes place. There's been talk about renovating this museum in 1999; rumors are also circulating that this facility may close altogether and move to Griffith Park. Check to see if it's still open before you go. Hours are 10 am to 5 pm on weekends year-round. From late June to early September, it is also open weekdays 11:30 am to 5 pm. Admission is $5; free for children under two.

Los Angeles Times

Western North America's largest daily newspaper (☎ 213-237-5757) is catty-corner from City Hall in a subdued Art Deco 10-story building at 202 W 1st St. Free 35-minute tours, offered weekdays at 11:15 am, introduce visitors (10 years and older) to the inner workings of this giant of the print-media world. The entrance is at 145 S Spring St; there's free parking in the garage at 213 S Spring St. You can also arrange to go on a one-hour tour of the *Times'* Olympic Plant printing facility, 2000 E 8th St, whose pressroom is twice the length of a football field.

Tours, by reservation only, run Tuesday and Thursday at 10 am and 1:15 pm.

The Music Center

The complex of three theaters known collectively as the Music Center of Los Angeles County (☎ 213-972-7211), 135 N Grand Ave, dominates the northwestern end of the Civic Center mall between 1st and Temple Sts. The sculpture surrounding a lusty fountain is by Jacques Lipschitz. Also note the whimsical bronze door designed by Robert Graham.

With 3200 seats, the **Dorothy Chandler Pavilion** is the largest of the three theaters and is also the oldest, dating to 1964. Besides being the main venue of the Los Angeles Philharmonic, the Los Angeles Opera and the Los Angeles Master Chorale, it also alternates with the Shrine Auditorium as the host of the Academy Awards. At the 2084-seat **Ahmanson Theater** you're likely to see a visiting Broadway musical, while the 742-seat **Mark Taper Forum** presents a wide variety of theater productions, from avant-garde drama to literary satire.

Free one-hour guided tours (☎ 213-972-7483) of all facilities depart from the main entrance of the Dorothy Chandler Pavilion. From May to October, tours run Tuesday, Thursday, Friday and Saturday between 10 am and 1:30 pm. The rest of the year, they run Tuesday to Thursday and Saturday; the last tour on Saturday is at noon. Reservations are not required.

Walt Disney Concert Hall

By the time you're reading this, ground should have been broken for a fourth theater to be located just south of the Music Center on 1st St. Conceived as the future home of the Los Angeles Philharmonic, this daring structure was designed by renowned – and controversial – Frank Gehry and will seat almost 2400. With a projected cost of $250 million, finance has hampered construction. But recent cash infusions from corporations and donors seem to have given the 'green light' for Disney Hall. Its design features include a central orchestra platform wrapped by tiered audience seating and a canopied, sail-like hardwood ceiling.

Clusters of billowing sails in blends of limestone and stainless steel continue the maritime theme. Two small outdoor amphitheaters will also be part of the complex, all scheduled to open in 2001.

New Catholic Cathedral

Another major Downtown project soon to be underway is the New Catholic Cathedral, the mother church of the archdiocese headed by Cardinal Roger Mahoney. Designed by Spanish architect José Rafael Moneo, the massive church complex will be located on Temple St between Grand Ave and Hill St, and will sport Mission-style colonnades, gardens, the cardinal's private residence and a conference center. Set to open in 2000, it will replace the old Cathedral of St Vibiana (1876) on Main St, which was damaged beyond repair in the 1994 earthquake.

EL PUEBLO HISTORIC PARK (MAP 5)

This 44-acre state historic park northeast of the Civic Center commemorates the site where the city was founded in 1781 and preserves many of its earliest buildings. (It was declared a state historic park in 1953.) A visitors' center (☎ 213-628-1274 for tour information, ☎ 213-680-2525 for general information) is lodged in the Sepulveda House, 622 N Main St, entered from Olvera St. It houses exhibits and shows a free film of LA history, shown Monday through Saturday at 11 am and 2 pm. Volunteers lead two-hour guided walking tours describing 27 historic buildings; tours leave hourly between 10 am and 1 pm, Tuesday through Saturday. Reservations are required. Fiestas and celebrations, including Mardi Gras, the Blessing of the Animals, Cinco de Mayo and Las Posadas, take place in the pueblo throughout the year.

Olvera St

The park's main visitor attraction is Olvera St, a narrow, block-long passageway. Known as Wine St in the 18th century, it was renamed in 1877 to honor the first LA County judge. By the early 20th century, Olvera St

had devolved into a slum, with many of its buildings empty and crumbling. A visit from civic champion Christine Sterling in 1926 turned things around. Putting her power behind rescuing this historic lane, she solicited help and money from her famous friends, such as *LA Times* publisher Harry Chandler; prison laborers were hauled in to grade and pave the street.

Olvera St reopened in 1930 as an open-air Mexican marketplace and has been a tourist attraction ever since. Shops, restaurants and the stalls of vendors selling hand-woven clothing, leather belts and bags, handmade candles and piñatas line the brick alley. Shops are open daily 10 am to 6 pm, later in summer.

Olvera St boasts LA's oldest extant building, the **Avila Adobe** (1808). It was built by Don Francisco, a wealthy ranchero who came to LA from Sinaloa in the late 18th century and became its mayor in 1810. Restored to their original appearance, the furnished rooms can be toured for free. Christine Sterling herself, affectionately nicknamed the 'Mother of Olvera St,' lived here until her death in 1963. Avila Adobe is usually open Tuesday through Saturday 10 am to 3 pm.

DAVID PEEVERS

Olvera St marketplace

The 1887 **Sepulveda House** (☎ 213-628-1274), 622 N Main St, whose back entrance extends to Olvera St, contains the visitors' center. A two-story Eastlake Victorian built during the boom of the 1880s, it's an architectural hybrid of Mexican and American traditions. Its 2nd floor was originally a boarding house, then contained a puppet theater before becoming a USO canteen during WWII. The house was restored in the 1980s. Another Olvera St structure is the **Pelanconi House** (1855), LA's first brick building, once occupied by a winery.

Old Plaza & Around

Olvera St spills into the Old Plaza, the central square of the original pueblo. Statues of Felipe de Neve, who led the first group of settlers, and Spanish King Carlos III, who ruled at that time, are here along with an ornate bandstand and Australian Moreton Bay fig trees.

West of the plaza is the **Church of Our Lady the Queen of the Angels** (☎ 213-629-3101), at 535 N Main St, originally built of adobe by Franciscan monks and native laborers between 1818 and 1822. Rebuilt in the 1860s, it still serves a largely Spanish-speaking congregation.

The area south of the plaza boasts various other early structures, including the 1858 **Masonic Hall** (☎ 213-626-4933), 416 N Main St, a two-story Italian Renaissance building with period furnishings. The 1870 **Pico House**, 430 N Main St, was once an elegant hotel built by Pio Pico, the last Mexican governor of California. The adjacent Italianate **Merced Theater**, 422 N Main St, dates from the same time. In 1884 the city's first fire station, the **Old Plaza Firehouse** (☎ 213-625-3741), 134 Paseo de la Plaza, was built. It went through incarnations as a saloon, boarding house and stores and is now a museum of 19th-century fire-fighting equipment and photographs. The museum is open Tuesday to Saturday 10 am to 3 pm; admission is free.

Union Station

Southeast of El Pueblo is Union Station (1939; ☎ 213-683-6875), 800 N Alameda St, the last of the great railroad stations in the US. It harmoniously blends Spanish Mission style with Streamline Moderne elements and features a 135-foot clock tower, a marble-floored waiting room and massive original chandeliers dangling above clunky leather armchairs. The station is often used as a movie location; you may have seen it in *Bugsy*, *The Way We Were* or *Union Station*.

The beautiful, double-domed building north of the station is the **Terminal Annex**, LA's central post office. This is where Charles Bukowski worked for years, inspiring the novel *Post Office* in 1971.

CHINATOWN (MAP 5)

Chinatown covers the 16-sq-block area north of El Pueblo along Broadway and Hill St between Sunset Blvd and Bernard St. Chinese have been a presence in Los Angeles since the 1850 census recorded two male house servants – Ah Fou and Ah Luce. Their population grew quickly in the late 19th century as more Chinese were imported as railroad workers. Called 'coolie slaves,' many also toiled as cooks, servants, ranch hands or farm help. Discrimination was rampant and often turned violent, as evidenced by the Chinese Massacre of 1871, which left 19 Chinese men and boys dead. To add insult to injury, original Chinatown was demolished in the 1930s to make room for Union Station. Most of the Chinese population then moved a few blocks north to found present-day New Chinatown.

Fewer than 5% of LA's 200,000 Chinese Americans make their home here today; the majority live in suburban Monterey Park. Chinatown, however, is clearly still their social and cultural center. In February its streets become a feast for the senses as giant dragons, decorated floats and lion dancers take part in the spectacular Chinese New Year parade. On any day of the year you can enjoy fresh Cantonese or Sichuan delicacies at dozens of restaurants, or browse in shops whose offerings vary from cheap kitsch to exquisite silk clothing and art.

Other shops display a profusion of bizarre produce and culinary oddities such as dried sea cucumber, elk antlers and pickled ginseng. Huge assortments of boxed exotic teas are sold along with medicinal potions mixed by herbalists who follow ancient recipes. Peer into the meat and fish shops and you'll realize just how fresh the food can be in the local restaurants: many of the animals – including frogs – are sold alive. **Superior Poultry** (☎ 213-628-7645), 750 N Broadway, has been in business for more than half a century and is the last place in the entire city to sell live poultry. Customers make their selections from dozens of clucking chickens crammed in metal cages in the front room, which are then dispatched, plucked, drawn and cut up by a league of uniformed executioners in the back room.

The more touristy section of Chinatown is a plaza of gift shops and restaurants called **Gin Ling Way** on the eastern end of Broadway. Near the elaborately decorated entrance gate is a statue of Sun Yat Sen, the founder of Taiwan and regarded by many Chinese as the 'George Washington of China.' Just beyond – to the left – is a whimsical wishing well and a five-tiered pagoda housing the legendary Hop Louie restaurant. Also note the curvilinear rooflines, many featuring animal figures that protect the building from evil.

Just west of here, at 931 N Broadway, is the **Kong Chow Temple**, on the 2nd floor above the East West Federal Bank. To enter, ring the bell and someone will come to let you in. Kong Chow, which translates as 'old temple,' is more than 100 years old and filled with antiques. Chinese Buddhists are big on fortune telling – look for a wooden cup con-

taining 100 bamboo sticks engraved with Chinese numbers. Hold it in both hands and shake it at an angle until one stick pops out. If you want to find out what your fortune holds, ask the caretaker to look up the number in a booklet, where you'll find such enchanting messages as 'Keep your ideas about things and people to yourself.'

A museum of Chinese American history is in the early planning stages. Ask at El Pueblo's visitors' center for a walking-tour map of Chinatown ($1.50). On weekends, the Chinese Chamber of Commerce operates a combination tour/dim sum lunch for $18 (lunch at 12:30 pm, followed by the two-hour tour around Chinatown).

LITTLE TOKYO (MAP 5)

Immediately south of the Civic Center is Little Tokyo, roughly bounded by 1st and 4th Sts on the north and south, Alameda St on the east, and Los Angeles St on the west. This bustling neighborhood was first settled by early Japanese immigrants in the 1880s. During WWII, it was effectively decimated by the anti-Japanese hysteria that led to the forced internment of thousands of US-born Japanese. It took the community decades to recover. Today Little Tokyo – or 'J-Town' – is again the social, economic and cultural center for nearly a quarter million Japanese Americans. The LA Conservancy (☎ 213-623-2489) conducts its Little Tokyo walking tour on the first Saturday of the month ($5).

Japanese American National Museum

Start your exploration of Little Tokyo at the Japanese American National Museum (☎ 213-625-0414), 369 E 1st St. The museum originally opened in 1992 in the historic Nishi Hongwanji Buddhist temple (1925). In 1998, a new second building adjacent to the original opened, increasing exhibit space fivefold.

The new museum exhibits objects of work and worship, photographs and art that relate the history of Japanese emigration to, and life in, the United States during the past 130 years, including the painful chapter of the WWII camps. The interactive Legacy Center contains a database of concentration

Got ginseng?

DAVID PEEVERS

camp records, allowing visitors to scan lists for relatives and friends. Another section explains and encourages experimentation with origami – or paper-folding – techniques. Other exhibits highlight the history of particular Japanese communities. Hours are 11 am to 5 pm, to 8 pm on Thursday, closed Monday. Admission is $4, $3 for seniors over 62, students and children; admission is free on the third Friday of the month.

Geffen Contemporary

Affiliated with the Museum of Contemporary Art (MOCA), the Geffen Contemporary (☎ 213-626-6222) is an enormous redesigned loft at 152 N Central Ave, just behind the new Japanese American National Museum. Until it received a large cash infusion from the Geffen Foundation in 1995, the museum was called the Temporary Contemporary because it housed MOCA's collection while MOCA's permanent building was being erected. Geffen Contemporary was never intended to become a permanent facility – hence the original name – but MOCA hung on to the Frank Gehry-designed space because it was well-suited for large-scale installations. Hours are Tuesday to Sunday 11 am to 5 pm; admission is $6, $4 for seniors and students. On Thursday, hours are extended to 8 pm and admission is free after 5 pm. Tickets are also good for same-day admission to MOCA.

Elsewhere in Little Tokyo

Across 1st St from the Japanese American National Museum is the **Japanese Village Plaza** (☎ 213-620-8861), 335 E 2nd St, a winding block-long pedestrian mall designed to resemble a rural hamlet in Japan. It's lined with about 40 traditional shops and restaurants (see Places to Eat); a *yagura*, or medieval lookout tower, marks its 1st St entrance. Also note the haiku and tanka poems on wooden boards above a bench usually occupied by community elders. The plaza is also used to celebrate Buddha's birthday, the Cherry Blossom Festival and Tanabata, the Festival of Lovers.

The modern **Japanese American Cultural & Community Center** (☎ 213-628-2725),

244 S San Pedro St, is around another corner to the south. Within the center are a gallery, bookstore and library. Adjoining are the fan-shaped Japan American Theater (☎ 213-680-3700), where you might witness *kabuki, noh* or *bunraku* theater performances, and the beautifully landscaped James Irvine Garden, also called Seiryu-en, or 'the Garden of the Clear Stream.' Another block south, at the corner of Alameda and 3rd St is the huge **Yaohan Plaza**, which incorporates a department store, a food hall and several more restaurants.

Worth a quick look are the traditional Japanese garden on the 4th floor of the New Otani Hotel, 120 S Los Angeles St, and the Astronaut Ellison S Onizuka St, a pedestrian mall dedicated to the Japanese American space explorer who died in the space shuttle *Challenger* tragedy of 1986.

SOUTH PARK (MAP 5)

The South Park district is roughly bordered by the 110 Fwy and Hill Sts to the west and east, respectively, and 9th St and the 10 Fwy north and south. Anchored by the Convention Center, South Park is a neighborhood that's slowly being transformed from sleepy and run-down to vital and spiffed up. Developers hope that the new Staples Center, a major stadium currently under construction on Figueroa St, will bring much needed stimulus to the entire Downtown area. Most fans will have to either walk or shuttle to the stadium, and ideally they will patronize a whole new generation of restaurants, cafes and shops surrounding the stadium.

Grand Hope Park

Peaceful Grand Hope Park, south of 9th St between Grand and Hope Sts, was one of the earliest South Park beautification projects upon its completion in 1993. Designed by Lawrence Halprin, it features a clock tower, a decorative fountain, flower-festooned pergolas, a playground and coyote statues. Flanking its Grand Ave side is the Fashion Institute of Design and Merchandising (☎ 213-624-1200), 919 S Grand Ave, attended by 3000 students from 45 countries.

Museum of Neon Art (MONA)

A rocking Elvis and serene Mona Lisa are just two of the vibrant neon signs on view at the Museum of Neon Art (☎ 213-489-9918), 501 W Olympic Blvd on the park's southwest corner. The only permanent facility of its kind, the unusual museum showcases artists working in neon, electric and kinetic art. Works from the museum collection also grace some facades at Universal City Walk. Neon devotees may want to join MONA's nighttime bus tours of signs, movie marquees and public art offered monthly for $35 (reservations required). Museum hours are Wednesday to Saturday 11 am to 5 pm, Sunday from noon. Admission is $5 adults, $3.50 for seniors and students; free between 5 and 8 pm on the second Thursday of the month.

Los Angeles Convention Center

The Los Angeles Convention Center, on Figueroa St south of 11th St, is city-owned. It tripled in size to 810,000 sq feet with a controversial $500 million expansion completed in 1993. Timing couldn't have been worse as the recession and the wave of natural and human disasters that struck LA in the early '90s made potential convention-eers turn elsewhere. As late as 1996, the Convention Center ran a deficit of $19 million. City boosters hope that the improved economy has turned the tide and that the Center will now generate half a billion dollars in city revenues a year…a big maybe.

Staples Center

The Staples Center, under construction at the time of writing, will be a state-of-the-art basketball and ice-hockey arena located northeast of the Convention Center. The new home of the LA Lakers, LA Clippers and LA Kings (who will move here from the Great Western Forum) is scheduled to open in October 1999 at a projected cost of $300 million. Promised to supply the 'clearest sightlines,' the Staples Center will seat about 20,000 for basketball games and slightly fewer for hockey. Besides sports events, the owners plan on hosting live concerts and other programs year-round.

FASHION DISTRICT (MAP 5)

Also known as the Garment District, this 56-block area toward the southern end of Downtown (framed by Broadway and Wall Sts, and 7th St and Pico Blvd) is the heart of LA's clothing manufacturing and wholesale

The Story Behind the Garment Glitz

Clothing manufacturing has been an important industry in LA since the 1920s and now provides more jobs than the industry in New York City, making LA the country's leader. In 1996, the rag trade pumped $16.5 billion into the economy and kept more than 110,000 Angelenos on the payroll. It's estimated that there are at least another 25,000 undocumented workers, most of them illegal immigrants.

Despite its positive economic impact, the industry's image is anything but favorable. Sewing-machine operators – usually Latina and Asian women – often toil under inhuman conditions, crammed like cattle into sweatshops set up in crumbling warehouses with no air-conditioning and minimal sanitary facilities. Workers get paid on a piecework basis, often earning less than the legal minimum hourly wage of $5.25. They are hired and dismissed at will and have almost no rights. Only 1% dare belong to the garment workers union.

In 1995, a virtual slave house was uncovered in the city of El Monte in eastern LA County, where 72 Thai women had been kept imprisoned for seven years, forced to work 17-hour days at $2 an hour. The story made headlines around the world, generating vociferous demands for stringent regulations. Unfortunately, in the end these fizzled faster than last season's fashions.

center. For the dedicated bargain shopper, it's 'Fashion Nirvana.'

Strolling around here is more evocative of a Middle Eastern souk than the sterility of an American mall. Overstuffed racks of Technicolor swimsuits, flowery summer dresses and Tommy Hilfiger knockoffs spill from tiny storefronts onto the sidewalks. Piles of scarves, cotton socks and cheap T-shirts compete for space with men's blazers and leather belts slung over rails like dead snakes.

Negotiating the cacophonous alleys, you'll run into swarthy peddlers winking, clapping their hands, and doing whatever they can to catch your attention. But there are also more traditional shops, with changing rooms, where you can browse peacefully – although they're more expensive and not nearly as much fun. (See the Shopping chapter for further details on how and where to shop in the Fashion District.)

Flower Market

If you walked along the 700 block of Wall St and Maple Ave at noon, you'd never know that only a few hours earlier a mad hubbub had enlivened the quiet streets. During the wee hours the warehouses swarm with buyers, grasping bunches of blossoms and flitting from stall to stall like bees in heat. A intense mélange of scents – from tangy Hawaiian ginger to sweet roses and pungent lilies – wafts through the air. Buckets of snapdragons in profuse color and other posies are heaped onto waiting trucks that deliver this fragrant freight to flower shops throughout Southern California.

The LA market is the largest cut-flower market in the country, employing nearly 2000 people. Flower cultivation in the city originated in 1892 when Japanese-American farmers planted fields south of Downtown and in then rural Santa Monica. The flower market itself dates to 1913 and moved to its current location in 1923. It was originally off-limits to retail shoppers, but rules have recently been relaxed. The market is now open to the public 8 am to noon Monday, Wednesday and Friday, and 6 am to noon Tuesday, Thursday and Saturday. Admission is $2 weekdays, $1 on Saturday. To soak up the atmosphere and scarf down a hearty breakfast, drop in at the Flower Market Coffee Shop on Wall St.

Coca-Cola Bottling Plant

This 1937 plant is a perfect example of the Streamline Moderne style inspired by the sleek forms of ocean liners and airplanes. Located in an otherwise unattractive industrial section of Downtown at 1334 S Central Ave, the plant has a facade featuring design elements like a ship's bridge, porthole windows, ship doors and metal balconies. The corners of an adjacent office building sport two enormous Coke bottles.

ARTS DISTRICT (MAPS 3 & 5)

In the dilapidated industrial section on the eastern edge of Downtown, a lively loft arts district has sprung up. There are plenty of artists' studios and galleries, mostly filled with highly unusual and experimental art. The **Brewery Art Complex** is a self-contained artist colony at 2100 N Main St. Begun in the early 1980s, its studios now sprawl over many buildings in this former brewery. Artists work in many media, including sculpture, architecture, painting, photography and design. Studios are closed to the public except during the twice-annual free Brewery Art Walks (usually in spring and fall), though you can wander around to examine the large installations – usually works in progress – scattered throughout. The complex also contains two galleries, **SITE** (Seeking It Through Exhibitions; ☎ 213-221-9039) in Bldg A-9 and **LA Artcore** (☎ 213-276-9320) at 650A S Ave 21. LA Artcore's main branch is at 120 Judge Aiso St. The galleries are usually open Wednesday to Sunday noon to 4 pm; call to confirm the hours.

Another concentration of galleries and studios is around Traction Ave, just east of Little Tokyo. Here you will find the **Spanish Kitchen Studios and Gallery** (☎ 213-680-4237), 734 E 3rd St, run since 1992 by multimedia mavens Voychek Szaszor and Paul Oberman. These two produce and sponsor independent videos and films, which are screened during public events. Spanish Kitchen is usually open weekdays 11 am to 4 pm. Also here is the

Cirrus Gallery (☎ 213-680-3473), 542 S Alameda St, which combines a print workshop and gallery under one roof. Founded by Jean Milant in 1969, it has been in its current location since 1979 and represents contemporary California artists. Milant also publishes major artists such as Lita Albuquerque and John Baldessari. The gallery is open Tuesday to Saturday 10 am to 5 pm.

San Antonio Winery

Don't miss this one! You should definitely treat yourself to a wine tasting at the San Antonio Winery (☎ 213-223-1401), 737 Lamar St, the last remaining winery in the city. It takes a vivid imagination to realize that the barren industrial wasteland just north of the 101 Fwy and west of I-5 was once the germ cell of California's fecund wine industry. In the early 1830s, Frenchman Jean Louis Vignes was among the pioneers to bring the cherished grape to Los Angeles, then hardly more than a far-flung outpost on the country's edge. But as the California gold rush and railroad construction brought an influx of new immigrants – including many from Mediterranean Europe – the demand for wine skyrocketed and new vineyards popped up all across the state.

In 1917, the year when Italian immigrant Santo Cambianica founded San Antonio Winery, LA already had nearly 100 wineries. The fledgling business managed to tough out the Prohibition years by producing sacramental wine and by selling grapes to home wine-makers. By the '50s, it was one of California's largest wineries, producing mostly inexpensive table varieties. In the late '70s, San Antonio started making quality vintage wines, specializing in oaky chardonnays and full-bodied cabernet sauvignon. You will not find any of its vineyards beneath smoggy LA skies; they are all in Monterey, Napa and Sonoma Counties near San Francisco.

All wines may be tasted for free in the tasting room, where affable patriarch Steve Riboli, a descendant of Santo Cambianica, is usually at hand to answer questions. Self-guided tours behind the scenes are free as well, and there's a restaurant to help sop up the wine. Hours are 10 am to 6 pm, Sunday to Tuesday, to 7 pm Wednesday to Saturday.

EXPOSITION PARK AREA (MAP 6)

Exposition Park, which began as an agricultural fairground in 1872, covers the equivalent of 25 sq city blocks south of Exposition Blvd and west of Figueroa St. When this became a public park in the early 20th century, its master plan called for a cluster of museums that are still its main attraction. The **Aerospace Museum** in the northeast corner is currently under renovation but still displays some outdoor exhibits (mostly airplanes). A 1994 decision to upgrade the park is supposed to result in wide tree-shaded promenades and well-lighted paths.

Another park attraction is the **Rose Garden** from 1927, a groomed sprawl of 15,000 bushes, representing some 150 varieties of the noble blossom. It is a popular wedding spot and is open daily from 8:30 am to sunset from April to December; admission is free.

Exposition Park is directly served by DASH buses. The surrounding area, once one of LA's grandest residential districts, is marked by many Victorian, Queen Anne and Art Deco structures.

Natural History Museum of LA County

On the park's northwestern edge, at 900 Exposition Blvd, sits an imposing 1913 Spanish Renaissance-style structure, home to the Natural History Museum of LA County (☎ 213-763-3466, www.nhm.org).

San Antonio Winery

DAVID PEEVERS

The museum's vast collections chronicle the earth's 4.5-billion-year evolution and showcase the astonishing diversity of natural life. On the ground level, two huge habitat halls present **African and North American mammals**, but it's the dinosaurs that are the most reliable crowd-pleasers: a Tyrannosaurus rex and a triceratops are pitched in battle in the foyer.

For more in-depth study, visit the **Dinosaur Hall**, where pride of place goes to a rare and complete tyrannosaurus skull, a complete cast of a mamenchisaurus skeleton and models of an allosaurus and a carnotaurus. Also on this floor, the **Gem & Mineral Hall** dazzles with some 2000 specimens, including 300lbs of gold.

Several smaller galleries on the ground floor are dedicated to American history from the pre-Columbian era to 1914. A particular highlight is the **The Times Mirror Hall of Native American Cultures** with its collections of Navajo textiles, baskets from California and the Great Basin, beadwork from the Plains and a re-created pueblo cliff dwelling. For a thorough survey of 400 years of **California history**, head to the lower level.

The mezzanine level is home to the **Insect Zoo**, where a plethora of local and exotic creepy crawlies includes tarantulas, Madagascan hissing cockroaches, butterflies, scarab beetles and even a giant ant farm. Farther upstairs, you'll find the **Great Bird Hall** with 27 interactive learning stations and three imaginatively presented walk-through habitats. In the **Marine Life Hall** on the same floor, dioramas showcase California sea life from the intertidal to the deep-sea zones. Also here is the slimily preserved 14½-foot-long megamouth, one of the world's rarest sharks.

If you're traveling with young children, you might want to check out the **Discovery Gallery** on the ground floor, where assistants help select 'discovery boxes'; depending on their age, the children will find such things as stuffed animals, building blocks, a puzzle or an animal bone.

Museum hours are weekdays 9:30 am to 5 pm, weekends from 10 am. Admission is $8, $5.50 for seniors over 62 and students, $2 for children ages five to 12.

California Science Center

If your memory of school science makes you groan, then a visit to the California Science Center (☎ 213-724-3623) will make you realize that, gee, science *can* be fun. A $130 million reinvention of the former Museum of Science and Industry, the California Science Center, southeast of the Natural History Museum at 700 State Drive, opened to great fanfare in February 1998. It has quickly become one of LA's favorite family destinations. A hands-on, interactive, state-of-the-art facility, the museum couches educational experience in a playful environment that is also a visual treat. Complicated scientific principles are presented accessibly and often with a great sense of humor.

Admission is free, making the California Science Center one of LA's best bargains. Parking is $5 (enter from Figueroa and 39th Sts), though free street parking is often available. Hours are 10 am to 5 pm daily except major holidays. On weekday mornings the place is aswarm with schoolkids, so try to visit in the afternoon. For fortification, go to McDonald's or the Megabytes Cafe on the ground floor. Or you can take your snack to the lovely Rose Garden adjacent to the north exit. At the more grown-up Rose Garden Cafe on the 3rd floor, you can get your latte along with lovely views. Back on the ground floor is the ExploraStore, which stocks a huge assortment of educational and fun toys.

Science Plaza Whimsical public art graces the walkway to the Science Center. **The Pavers** consists of 74 paving stones inscribed with whimsical quotes, games, images and scientific riddles. The **California Gate** features two tall granite plates shaped in such a way that the negative space between them shows the outline of California. Connecting the Science Center with the IMAX Theater (see below) is an 88-foot-high cylindrical pavilion embellished by hundreds of shimmering spheres. These are suspended above a circular granite bench representing a cross-section of a DNA strand.

Science Court Three levels of exhibits wrap around this central, skylit courtyard.

Suspended from the 112-foot-high glass atrium is the **Hypar**, or Hyperbolic Paraboloid, a kinetic sculpture that slowly expands and contracts to form bizarre shapes. The Science Court even has a circuslike attraction, the **High Wire Bicycle**: Junior daredevils are strapped into a harness, then pedal along the thick cable 43 feet above the floor, counterbalanced by an enormous weight attached to the bicycle. The tilting ride is completely safe. Rides are $3 each.

Exhibits An escalator snakes up to the 2nd floor, where there are two main exhibition areas. Off to the left is **World of Life**, whose fundamental message is that all living beings – from amoebae to cacti to Homo sapiens – share the same basic needs, including reproduction, the intake and processing of energy, and the disposal of waste. You can compare the human heart to that of a mouse or an elephant, or hop on a red blood cell and take a computer fly-through of the circulatory system. Nearby, you'll meet Gertie, whose head slowly rises in the air, unraveling her intestines. Kids lo e seeing 'Gertie's Guts.' Interestingly, it's the live animal exhibits that really make the kids squeal. These include incubators where baby chicks hatch and a glass case where tadpoles turn into frogs.

The **Bodyworks** theater is the undisputed museum highlight. It stars a super-sized techno-doll named Tess who's billed as '50 feet of brains, beauty and biology.' Tess provides an even more revealing look at her insides than Gertie; cutaways show Tess' organs, bones, muscles and veins. Interacting

with her cartoon sidekick, Walt, via a video screen, Tess 'comes to life' in a 15-minute multimedia show intended to illustrate homeostasis (the body's ability to maintain internal balance even as external conditions change – such as during exercise). Small children may still have trouble understanding the science, but there's no doubt they will remember Tess.

Virtual reality games, high-tech simulators, laser animation and other such gadgetry await in the **Creative World** exhibit located on the 2nd and 3rd floors to the right of the escalator. The focus here is on human innovations in the fields of communication, transportation and structures. In the Communication area, you can send and receive video messages, participate in digital jam sessions or play virtual soccer or volleyball. The Structures gallery explains static principles of bridges and buildings. A highlight here is the **earthquake simulator**, which is fun for out-of-towners but gave the authors nasty flashbacks of the last big jolt. Finally, there's the Transportation gallery, where you get a close up look at a solar-powered car and learn what makes planes fly and boats sail.

IMAX Theater

Affiliated with and connected to the California Science Center is the IMAX Theater (☎ 213-744-2014), whose giant screen – 90 feet wide, seven stories high – and six-channel surround-sound system present awe-inspiring nature films. Movies are screened in both 2D and newly developed 3D format for which you don polarized, lightweight glasses. A 3D projector uses two 15,000-watt xenon bulbs, bright enough to be seen with the naked eye if they were on the moon. Movies are presented daily from 10 am to 9 pm. Tickets are $6.25, $4.25 for seniors, $3.75 for children. There's a $1 surcharge for 3D films.

California African American Museum

The state-owned California African American Museum (☎ 213-744-7432), in the park's northeastern corner at 600 State Drive, does an excellent job presenting the complex range of African and African American art

Defying death at the Science Court

and artifacts in an educational and pleasing environment. Items from the permanent collection are viewed on a rotating basis and may include fertility figures, ceremonial implements, funeral statues, masks and headdresses. The art of several African countries is here in creations of animal skins, raffia, wood, terra-cotta and ivory. The museum's fine arts collection includes works by painters of the 1920s Harlem Renaissance, when black American artists established a cultural identity in the various media. Special exhibits complement the permanent collection throughout the year. Museum hours are Tuesday to Sunday 10 am to 5 pm, closed on major holidays; admission is free.

Los Angeles Memorial Coliseum

The Los Angeles Memorial Coliseum (☎ 213-748-6131), south of the California Science Center at 3911 S Figueroa St, has played host not only to the 1932 and 1984 Summer Olympic Games, but also to the baseball World Series in 1959 and to Super Bowl I and VII. In 1960, Democratic presidential nominee John F Kennedy and his future VP, Lyndon B Johnson, gave their acceptance speeches here. Built in 1923 and enlarged in 1932, the monumental stadium seats 106,000 people. The headless bronze bodies of a female and a male nude – designed by LA artist Robert Graham for the 1984 Olympics – greet visitors approaching the characteristic Art Deco eastern entrance. Major damage during the 1994 earthquake resulted in thorough retrofitting. One-hour tours run Tuesday, Thursday and Saturday (except on event days) at 10:30 am, noon and 1:30 pm and cost $4 for adults, $2 for students, $1 for children (call ☎ 213-765-6347 for reservations). Enter through Gate 33a.

The adjacent **Los Angeles Memorial Sports Arena** (☎ 213-748-6136), at 3939 S Figueroa St, dates from 1959 and hosts rock concerts, ice shows, a circus and even the occasional rodeo.

University of Southern California (USC)

Founded in 1880, USC (☎ 213-740-5371, www.usc.edu) is one of the oldest private research universities in the American West. Its 155-acre campus, just north of Exposition Park, consists of the College of Letters, Arts and Sciences as well as 17 professional schools. In 1996 student enrollment was 28,100, including 4200 foreign students, mostly from Asian countries. USC is particularly noted for its School of Cinema-Television, the oldest (since 1929) and the highest ranked in the country. Distinguished alumni include directors George Lucas, Ron Howard and Robert Zemeckis. Other alumni include John Wayne, architect Frank Gehry, astronauts Neil Armstrong and Charles Bolden, Gulf War General Norman Schwarzkopf, and, of course, OJ Simpson. Free 50-minute campus walking tours are offered daily from 10 am to 3 pm; call ☎ 323-740-6605 for reservations.

Fisher Gallery The USC Fisher Gallery (☎ 213-740-4561), 823 Exposition Blvd, was founded in 1939 by Elizabeth Holmes Fisher. Its permanent collection includes Thomas Doughty's *Along the Mohawk* (1828) and other 19th-century American landscapes. Works by Thomas Gainsborough, Sir Joshua Reynolds, Benjamin West and other British artists are as much a part of the collection as paintings from the 19th-century French Barbizon School, including Rousseau's *The Lake in the Forest* and Corot's *Le Lac*. Several rooms are reserved for changing exhibitions showcasing the work of student artists, emerging local and national artists and contemporary international artists. The gallery is open Tuesday to Friday noon to 5 pm, Saturday 11 am to 3 pm; closed May through August. Admission is free.

Shrine Auditorium At the northeast corner of campus is the double-domed Shrine Auditorium (☎ 213-749-5123), 665 W Jefferson Blvd. When completed in Moorish style in 1926, it was the largest theater in the US, seating almost 6500. Its pipe organ is still the biggest of any theater in the world. Besides being the occasional home of the Grammy Awards, the American Music Awards and the Academy Awards, it is also the gathering place and headquarters of the Al-Malaikah

Temple, a subdivision of the Arabic Order of Nobles of the Mystic Shrine, who are also known as Shriners.

Historic Churches

Three corners of the intersection of Adams Blvd and Figueroa St are occupied by historical buildings, two of them churches. Despite its mission-like appearance, the structure in the southwest corner is actually just the headquarters of the Automobile Club of Southern California (☎ 213-741-3111), 2601 S Figueroa St.

Standing tall at a 45-degree angle to the northwest corner is Catholic **St Vincent De Paul** (1925; ☎ 213-749-8950), 621 W Adams Blvd. Its exterior is a fine example of Spanish Baroque and features a bell tower ringed by statues of the four Evangelists and a dome covered in kaleidoscopic tiles. Inside, it's worth paying particular attention to the Italian Renaissance-style stained-glass windows, the coffered and painted ceiling, the carved choir stalls and the gold-leafed main altar. St Vincent's has an active congregation, with masses held in either English or Spanish twice every day and seven times on Sunday. Visiting hours are 7 am to 4:30 pm daily.

A bit removed from the southeast corner, at 514 W Adams Blvd, you'll find **St John's Episcopal Church** (1925; ☎ 213-747-6285). (Enter by ringing the bell of the office to the left of the church.) The design of St John's was inspired by a Romanesque church in a village near Rome. Italian artisans crafted the elaborate exterior, including the depiction of the Evangelists around the rose window. Inside, St John's is a three-nave structure with narrow side aisles separated from the central nave by slender Corinthian columns. The wood-beamed, hand-painted ceiling is an exact replica from an 11th-century Tuscan church. Most eye-catching, though, are the patterned marble walls and mosaics of the chancel area, and the gold-drenched Lady Chapel to the right of the altar. If you look carefully, you may also find the tiny footprints in the tiled floor next to the last seat on the right of the 10th pew; these were supposedly left by a child of one of the masons

working on the church. From June to September, hours are 9 am to 3:30 pm weekdays, 9 am to noon weekends; closed Tuesday. The rest of year, it's open Monday and Thursday 9 am to 5 pm, Wednesday to 7 pm, Friday to 3 pm and weekends 9 am to noon. Admission here and at St Vincent's is free.

East LA

Driving into East LA – just beyond the LA River east of Downtown – feels a bit like crossing the border from San Diego into Tijuana. With more than 90% of its 1 million residents being Latino, this area is as close to a barrio as it gets within the USA. Mexican influx in the area began in the 1920s and today East LA's 15 sq miles have the largest concentration of Mexicans outside of Mexico. Until then, the area had been more heterogeneous, with large pockets of Jewish, Armenian and Russian populations.

Life in the barrio is tough but lively. People shop and mill about in the streets lined with bakeries, *tiendas* (convenience stores), botanicas selling herbal cures and toy shops. Brightly colored murals adorn many facades. But behind the color, life can look pretty grim. The district suffers from typical ghetto problems such as high unemployment, low income, high crime, poor schools and inferior infrastructure. One thing East LA has plenty of is cemeteries, a sad fact

Mariachis sing of love and revolution.

RICK GERHARTER

To Save & Protect

Guadalupe is beautiful, dark-skinned and wears an innocent smile and flowing robes. She's also the most powerful woman in East LA, a vast neighborhood that's almost entirely Latino. Revered and feared, Guadalupe stops robberies, invokes people to treat each other with respect, protects store owners and keeps taggers (graffiti artists) from defacing buildings. And

she's just about everywhere: you see her around every street corner, gracing stores, apartment buildings and churches.

Her full name is Virgen de Guadalupe and she's a strong spiritual symbol among Mexican Catholics living in neighborhoods where violence and destruction of property are as normal as the sunrise. Her image acts as a deterrent to criminals, perhaps more effectively than an entire battalion of cops. Shop owners especially have discovered that having a mural of the Virgen on their facade will keep business out of harm's way. Gang bangers and grandmothers cross themselves when walking by the paintings. One tough guy in an interview with the *LA Times* said: 'I don't really trip on her...but I respect her because she's the mother of God. She was pregnant through the spirit.' In a way it's nothing less than a miracle that it's not prison or even death that scares the bejesus out of these guys. It's a tiny woman in a robe.

that underscores the violence so prevalent in this gang-infested neighborhood.

Crisscrossed by four freeways, East LA's main artery is Cesar E Chavez Ave, formerly known as Brooklyn Ave, which is basically a continuation of Sunset Blvd. In general, East Los Angeles is not conducive to touristic visits. There's little to see here and, though unlikely, the risk of becoming the victim of a crime is greater here than almost anywhere else in LA (with the possible exception of Compton).

If you're interested in seeing what life in the barrio is like, come in the daytime. Communication may be easier if you speak at least a few words of Spanish, since not everyone here is bilingual.

Good streets to see are **Cesar E Chavez Ave, Mission Rd** and the neon-festooned **Whittier Blvd**, whose section between the 710 Fwy and Atlantic Blvd has been dubbed 'East LA's Sunset Strip' for its concentration of clubs, bars and restaurants. A darker moment in Whittier Blvd's history came on August 29, 1970, when an anti-Vietnam-War demonstration in Belvedere Park just north of here was interrupted by police, which resulted in severe rioting. In the melee, Ruben Salazar, a noted Latino journalist covering the incident for the *Los Angeles Times*, was killed by a gas pellet fired by a sheriff's deputy.

PLAZA DE LA RAZA (MAP 3)

Plaza de la Raza (☎ 323-223-2475), 3540 N Mission Rd at Valley Blvd, is a community arts center that in many ways is the cultural and artistic heart of this area. Spread over several buildings in 46-acre Lincoln Park, it was founded in 1970 by actress

Margo Levin and unionist Frank Lopez. Its primary mission is to provide free or inexpensive after-school classes in theater, dance and the fine arts to underprivileged children in this neighborhood. There's also a theater and a small gallery. Dance performances and festival events are often held here in front of the park's pond. The park itself, created in 1870, is notable for its 300 species of trees.

MARIACHI PLAZA (MAP 3)

Mariachis are traditional Mexican musicians who play an endless repertory of folkloric songs on trumpet and guitar. They are usually dressed in black ranchero suits and often wear broad sombreros. Every day in the afternoon, freelance mariachis congregate beneath wall-sized murals, suitably depicting a group of musicians, at the corner of Boyle Ave and 1st St, where they wait to be hired for restaurant performances or social gatherings.

SELF-HELP GRAPHICS GALLERY (MAP 3)

This community arts center (☎ 323-264-1259), 3802 Cesar E Chavez Ave, was founded in 1972 by Sister Karen Boccalero, a Franciscan nun with a strong belief in the healing powers of art. It's housed in a clunky building that would be nondescript were it not for its cheerful decoration of broken glass and pottery shards. Inside is a gallery with changing exhibits, as well as a shop. The center is renowned for its workshop where students learn how to make multihued silkscreen prints.

LA Street Gangs

Although gangs have been around in California since before the gold rush days – appearing wherever government was weak – modern criminal gangs as we know them are a late-20th-century phenomenon. Originally close-knit neighborhood affiliations banding together to escape the oppression of poverty, gangs today are true horrors: well-armed and financed, free of conscience and predatory.

With films like *Colors* and *Boyz 'N the Hood* bringing LA's inner-city struggle to a mainstream audience, gangs like the Crips and the Bloods have made headlines around the world. But black gangs are not the only players in LA's juvenile crime circuit. Latino gangs are, in fact, even more prevalent, and Asian, Pacific Islander and white gangs figure prominently in the mix. There are over 1100 street gangs in Los Angeles, with over 150,000 members, and only now are serious efforts being made to discourage pre-adolescents from joining gangs. Culture and recreation meccas, like the Peace & Justice Center at 1220 4th St, are providing creative outlets for disempowered kids by hosting poetry and theater workshops, musical jams and discussion groups. Still, the killing continues.

One gang-banger we interviewed was going to college because that's what his younger brother – murdered – had wanted most for himself. But it was hard on this macho guy to give up 'the life': you could see it in his eyes. In the barrio – as in the teachings of Mao – true power comes from the barrel of the gun.

There's no denying that LA gangs are as vicious as the media conveys. But greater Los Angeles is no war zone. A truce between the Bloods and the Crips has been in effect since 1992 – an encouraging precedent. And the only gang activity seen by the majority of Angelenos is the work of 'taggers,' graffiti-happy 'homeboys' with a penchant for vandalism – and, possibly, art. But areas to avoid are the poorest sections of South Central, East LA, Long Beach and Unglued. Still better advice is to follow basic travel safety precautions wherever you go: Drive with your doors locked, never display your valuables, and always keep your eyes open.

EL MERCADO (MAP 3)

If you only visit one place in East LA make it El Mercado, a wonderfully boisterous, sticky and colorful indoor market at 3425 E 1st St. Among stalls clamoring for your attention are those selling authentic tortilla-making machines and mariachi outfits for toddlers. At butcher shops you learn that no animal part is unfit for consumption. Tripe, beef tendon and pig snout are hawked next to ham, steak and *chorizo* (a spicy sausage that goes well with scrambled eggs). Fresh fish, shrimp and ceviche are here, as are handmade tamales and other delicacies. At a couple of lively restaurants upstairs you might be serenaded by mariachi musicians (see Places to Eat).

BREED SHUL (MAP 3)

It's hard to imagine that the East LA district of Boyle Heights was once almost 100% Jewish and had 27 active synagogues. The only one to survive as a building, though no longer as an active congregation, is the Breed Shul, 247 N Breed St (1 block west of Soto St). Until WWII it was the largest Orthodox shul west of Chicago. It was forced to close when there weren't any Jews left in Boyle Heights and has been empty and crumbling ever since. The brick facade, in Renaissance style, features leaf ornamentation and Jewish symbols around an arched entrance portal. Inside, there's stained glass, wood carvings and murals. Condemned by the city for earthquake damage, the building has an uncertain fate, and demolition may be inevitable unless someone steps forward to rescue it and give it a new purpose.

North Central/ Griffith Park

This section describes the various neighborhoods north of Downtown, bordered by Glendale and the San Gabriel Valley in the north, Pasadena to the east and Hollywood to the west. Highlights include some of LA's earliest suburban communities, the nation's largest city park and Dodger Stadium, home of the Major League baseball team.

ECHO PARK (MAP 5)

This community is named after the 26-acre Echo Park, at Glendale Blvd and Park Ave, which surrounds a nicely landscaped lake with paddleboats available for hire. The lake is blanketed by the largest lotus bed outside China and is the setting of the Lotus Festival, a celebration of Asian Pacific culture that takes place every July.

A few blocks east of the lake is **Angelino Heights**, LA's original commuter suburb, which grew on a hillside in the 1880s and was linked to Downtown by a trolley line. Its greatest appeal is its cluster of beautifully restored and lovingly maintained Victorian homes, especially in the 1300 block of Carroll Ave (there are a few more on Kellam Ave, 1 block north). All are private residences and can only be admired from the outside, though the interior of some may be viewed during the walking tours given monthly by the LA Conservancy (see the boxed text in the Los Angeles Architecture chapter).

Angelus Temple

Opposite the north end of Echo Park is the mammoth circular and domed Angelus Temple, the headquarters of the International Church of the Foursquare Gospel, founded by the eccentric and charismatic Aimee Semple McPherson (1890-1944) in 1923. The angelic-looking McPherson distinguished herself by recognizing the power of a new technology – the radio – to spread her faith and philosophy. Through her show-biz-style 'Sunshine Hour,' broadcast on a church-owned radio station (KFSG, still in operation today at 96.3 FM), she essentially pioneered the televangelism of today.

Though hugely popular, Sister Aimee was not without controversy. In 1926, she disappeared into the ocean in Santa Monica, only to 'resurface' four weeks later, claiming that she had been kidnapped. Rumor has it that she had really been holed up with a lover at a remote site. She was charged with conspiracy, though the district attorney eventually dropped the case. Mentally unstable for years, Sister Aimee went the way of so many flamboyant Hollywood stars: She overdosed on drugs. Her church, however, still has

Radio evangelist Aimee Semple McPherson employed show-biz techniques to spread the Lord's word.

about 17 million members worldwide. The Angelus Temple seats up to 5000 people and is impressive with stained-glass windows and a stage-like altar.

ELYSIAN PARK (MAP 5)

Just east of Echo Park is this neighborhood, whose focal point is Dodger Stadium and the park from which it derives its name. Created in 1886 as a recreational refuge, the Elysian Park has changed much over the years. Reshaped by a landslide in 1937, a large section was handed over to the LA Police Department, which still maintains its training academy here. In 1940 the Pasadena Freeway took another big chunk out, as did the construction of Dodger Stadium in 1959.

Dodger Stadium

On a chaparral-cloaked hilltop overlooking Downtown stands Dodger Stadium (☎ 323-224-1400), 1000 Elysian Park Ave. It's home to the Los Angeles Dodgers, one of Major League baseball's most popular and cosmopolitan teams, which moved to LA from Brooklyn in 1958. The stadium seats 56,000 and is widely regarded as one of the most magnificent ballparks in the USA. For more

information on the Dodgers, see Spectator Sports in the Entertainment chapter.

MT WASHINGTON & HIGHLAND PARK (MAP 3)

These two neighborhoods wrap around the Arroyo Seco, a gorge following a dry riverbed (the meaning of its Spanish name) that runs from the San Gabriel Mountains to the Los Angeles River. It was flooded with artists and architects in the early 20th century, but lost its idyllic setting to the Pasadena (110) Fwy in 1940. Several of its attractions still spotlight a pre-metropolitan LA.

Southwest Museum

Looking out over the Arroyo Seco from its perch atop Mt Washington, the Southwest Museum (☎ 323-221-2164), 234 Museum Drive, holds one of the most formidable collections of Native American art and artifacts in the US. It's also LA's oldest museum, founded in 1907 by Charles F Lummis (see El Alisal, below, and the boxed text Don Carlos' Crusade).

Built in Mission Revival style, it sports a distinctive seven-story tower and is reached via a steep driveway. Hours are 11 am to 5 pm daily except Monday. Admission is $5, $3 for seniors and students, $2 for children ages seven to 18.

Collections The Southwest Museum boasts an astonishing array of items from prehistoric, historic and contemporary days, with each of the four halls dedicated to a native North American culture: the Great Plains, the Northwest Coast, the Southwest and California. This division allows visitors to compare the widely differing traditions, rituals, clothing, crafts, religious ceremonies, and social and political organizations that developed in each of these areas. Notable items include moccasins, flaring feather headdresses, jewelry, work tools such as fleshers and knives, a Lakota teepee, dioramas of Indian scenes made in the 1930s, totem poles, winnowing trays and a replica of a sacred site with petroglyph carvings.

The museum also owns one of the largest basket collections in the USA (11,000 items), as well as some 7000 pieces of pottery and 6600 paintings, textiles, religious icons and decorative and folk art from Latin America. Because of crippling space restrictions, only 7% of the museum's extraordinary holdings are displayed at one time. A major draw for scholars from around the world is the Braun Research Library.

El Alisal

This house was built by Charles F Lummis, LA's first city librarian and a prolific writer and editor who was almost single-handedly responsible for the preservation of LA's original 18th-century missions at San Gabriel and San Fernando. Also called the Lummis House (☎ 323-222-0546), 200 E Ave 43 at Carlota Blvd, it was built by Charles Lummis himself between 1898 and 1910. Trying to capture the Western spirit in its construction, Lummis used granite boulders from the adjacent Arroyo Seco for walls, telephone poles for ceilings and iron railway rails as wall reinforcements. Today the Historical Society of Southern California is based here. Visiting hours are Friday to

Don Carlos' Crusade

By the mid-1880s, Los Angeles had proven itself a city capable of generating huge amounts of capital. Many men had made fortunes, and these same men, now the oligarchs of a large city, became suddenly aware that for all of its growth and potential, Los Angeles still didn't seem to have any culture.

That's when Charles Fletcher Lummis arrived. Suffering from malaria, Lummis (1859-1928) left his Cincinnati home in 1884 for the Southern California sun – and he walked the entire way! During his five-month, 3000-mile hike, he cabled installments of an illustrative travel series to the *LA Times*, and on reaching his destination he accepted a job as editor for the paper.

Lummis very quickly asserted himself as preacher of Southern California culture. As a writer of books and editor of a highly popular magazine called *Land of Sunshine*, he spread the notion that the California sun made life healthier and more productive. He also developed the dubious idea that California's mission heritage was an example of a new, more leisurely way of life – far more humane than life in East Coast cities. He urged Angelenos to build their city in the spirit of the missions and other Spanish models of civilization.

But in his enthusiasm for Spanish culture Lummis was a bit eccentric. He called himself 'Don Carlos' and dieted strictly on chili, tamales and refried beans. And though he'd originally come to Los Angeles for his health, in just four years he nearly worked, drank, ate and smoked himself to death, suffering a massive stroke before the age of 30. He recovered and then spent 15 years building his mansion, the highly original El Alisal (meaning 'sycamore'). The building still stands near the Southwest Museum, which he cofounded, and is a fascinating tribute to this unusual man's life. It now houses the headquarters of the Historical Society of Southern California.

Ironically, Lummis' gospel was distributed throughout the East and Midwest by real estate promoters – and the mass society and industrialism that resulted were the exact opposite of what he seemed to have in mind.

Sunday noon to 4 pm; admission is free, but donations are certainly appreciated.

Heritage Square Museum

Eight vintage Victorian buildings dating from 1865 to 1914 were rescued from the wrecking ball by the LA Cultural Heritage Board and moved to Heritage Square (☎ 626-449-0193), an open-air museum at 3800 Homer St, just off the Ave 43 exit of the Pasadena (110) Fwy. Some structures have already been restored; others are still awaiting their face-lifts. Highlights include the 1876 Perry House with its Italianate facade, and the Hale House, built in the Queen Anne/Eastlake style in 1885. The Longfellow Hastings Octagon House of 1893 is one of only three surviving octagonal houses, which were popular in the late 19th century. Another standout is the Lincoln Avenue Methodist Church from 1897. The museum ticket booth is housed in a former railroad depot (1887) of the Southern Pacific Railroad.

Museum hours are 10 am to 3 pm on Friday, when admission is free. On weekends, it's open 11:30 am to 4:30 pm. Admission is $5, $4 for seniors over 65 and teenagers to age 17, $2 for children ages seven to 12, free for children under seven. Buildings may be entered only during tours, which are offered on the hour between noon and 3 pm and are included in the admission price.

GRIFFITH PARK (MAP 8)

Spreading across a rugged mountainous area, Griffith Park is five times the size of New York's Central Park and is the nation's largest municipal park. California oak, wild sage and manzanita blanket much of its 4107 acres, with elevations ranging from 384 to 1625 feet (Mt Hollywood). The famous Hollywood sign is atop Mt Lee, on the northern border.

Griffith Park got its name from Colonel Griffith J Griffith, an immigrant from South Wales who'd made his millions in gold mining speculation. He donated more than 3000 acres to the city in 1896 on the condition 'It must be made a place of recreation and rest for the masses.' Upon his death in 1919, Griffith bequeathed additional moneys for the construction of an amphitheater and an

The switchblade fight in *Rebel Without a Cause* was filmed at Griffith Observatory.

observatory. (Note that Griffith wasn't all Mr Nice Guy: He spent two years in San Quentin prison for attempted murder of his wife.)

It's fair to assume that Griffith would be pleased with the results. Griffith Park remains a respite from urbanity and offers lots of outlets for recreation, education and entertainment. Within its boundaries are not just the theater and observatory he envisioned, but also a zoo, a major museum, golf courses, tennis courts, playgrounds, bridle paths and hiking trails.

Griffith Park is bounded by the Ventura (134) Fwy to the north, the Golden State (I-5) Fwy to the east, Los Feliz Blvd to the south and the Hollywood (101) Fwy to the west. Approaching from the south, the most direct route into the park is via Vermont Ave. You can also enter via Western or Canyon Aves. Get directly onto either Griffith Park Drive or Zoo Drive by taking the respective exit from I-5.

The park is open daily from 6 am to 10 pm, but roads and bridle and hiking trails close at sunset (except the one leading to the observatory). Outdoor activities are detailed in the Mountains and Activities sections later in this chapter.

Griffith Observatory & Planetarium

Narrow winding roads – or, for the physically adept, trails – lead up to the Griffith Observatory & Planetarium (☎ 323-664-1191, www.griffithobs.org), 2800 E Observatory Rd. Located on the southern slopes of

Mt Hollywood, facing the city, its bronze domes have been a local landmark since 1935. (You may recognize the setting from scenes in *Rebel Without a Cause*.) The view from here alone is worth making the trip. The entire Los Angeles basin, from the mountains to the east via the high-rises of Downtown to the gleaming Pacific in the distance, sprawls out below you. The view is particularly magnificent on a clear day and at night.

Hall of Science Highlights of this hands-on astronomy museum are 6-foot-diameter globes of earth and moon, several meteorites and a Mars rock, spacecraft and telescope models including a one-fifth-scale model of the Hubble Space Telescope, a Foucault Pendulum and a seismograph. Interactive computer games test your knowledge of astronomy. From mid-June to mid-September hours are 12:30 to 10 pm daily. The rest of the year, it's open weekdays 2 to 10 pm, weekends from 12:30 pm, closed Monday. Admission is free.

Telescopes These are in the observatory's two smaller domes. The east dome has a 12-inch Zeiss refracting telescope to view the moon and our solar system's planets. Viewing hours are 7 to 9:45 pm nightly, except Monday in winter and beginning at dusk in summer; admission is free. The west dome contains a solar telescope and is not accessible, though the images it produces can be viewed from the Hall of Science.

Planetarium The large central dome harbors the planetarium theater, with live multimedia presentations several times daily. Its 1964 Zeiss telescope weighs 1 ton and projects about 9000 stars. From mid-September to mid-June shows take place weekdays at 3 and 7:30 pm and weekends at 1:30, 3, 4:30 and 7:30 pm, closed Monday. The rest of the year, shows are presented daily at 1:30, 3 and 7:30 pm (also at 4:30 pm on weekends). Shows cost $4, $3 for seniors over 65, $2 for kids.

Greek Theater

Just within the park's southern boundary is the Greek Theater (☎ 323-665-1927), 2700 N Vermont Ave, which showcases popular musical talent as well as ballet and other dance performances from May to October in a natural, open-air amphitheater. Also built with funds left by Griffith, the Greek Theater opened in 1930 and offers seating to audiences of around 6000.

Los Angeles Zoo

The LA Zoo (☎ 323-644-6000), 5333 Zoo Drive, may not compete for superlatives with the renowned San Diego Zoo to the south, but the LA Zoo outshines in at least one area. In August 1998 the Chimpanzees of Mahale Mountains exhibit opened, where 13 chimps dwell in a new $5 million habitat, paid for by local voters. It's an exhibit – complete with waterfall and 'abandoned' buildings – that will make even the most impassioned animal lover feel that zoos might sometimes do valuable service. It's part of a $15 million Great Ape Forest expansion project that should see completion by 2001.

In the meantime you can still view more than 1200 mammals, birds, amphibians and reptiles on the zoo's 80 acres, where natural habitats are re-created. These are laid out according to the animals' continental origins: North and South America, Africa, Australia and Eurasia.

There is also an aquatic section, a reptile house, a big walk-through aviary and the Adventure Island children's zoo. The LA Zoo has also been instrumental in helping the world's population of California condors inch its way back from near extinction. Many other rare animals – skinks to mountain tapirs – have been successfully bred here. The zoo is open daily 10 am to 5 pm; admission is $8.25, $5.25 for seniors over 65, $3.25 for children two to 12.

Gene Autry Western Heritage Museum

Anyone interested in history of the American West should visit this wonderful museum (☎ 323-667-2000, www.autry-museum .org) on the eastern edge of Griffith Park at 4700 Western Heritage Way. Opened in 1988, it was financed with a $54 million donation from the Gene Autry Foundation and features 10 galleries that skillfully combine scholarship and showmanship.

Gene Autry (1907-1998) became a millionaire several times over as an actor and singer, earning him the title of 'The Singing Cowboy.' In the 1940s, Autry brought lasting change to the rodeo scene when he brought in entertainers in order to open up the sport to a wider audience. Autry also recorded nine gold records – including 'Rudolph, the Red-Nosed Reindeer' and 'Back in the Saddle Again.' He parlayed his earnings into three music publishing companies, four radio stations, a Palm Springs resort and a Major League baseball team, the California Angels.

The Western Heritage Museum also offers concerts, gallery talks, symposia, panel discussions, film screenings and storytelling sessions for children. Hours are 10 am to 5 pm Tuesday to Sunday. Admission is $7.50, $5 for seniors and students, $3.50 for children.

Collections Start your tour of the permanent galleries on the main level in the Spirit of Discovery gallery, which shows how the West was 'discovered' again and again by various peoples, from prehistoric tribes to Native Americans to missionaries. Then head to the basement for a look at the panoramic mural by Guy Deel. The first gallery on your right documents the harsh realities of overland transportation and life on the Western trails. Historically sensitive issues, such as the Trail of Tears (when 4000 Native Americans lost their lives after being forced from their land), are addressed as well.

Ensuing galleries deal with the clashes between conquerors and Native Americans, including General Custer's (in)famous 'Last Stand' at Little Bighorn, and explain the roles played by large groups of people that came to the West – many of them drawn by the California gold rush – including Europeans, Chinese, Mexicans, Mormons and Canadians. A huge carved mahogany saloon bar from 1880, gaming tables and cheating devices illustrate aspects of that era's free-wheeling social life. The flipside of that coin – a prevailing climate of violence and lawlessness – is given poignant emphasis in the Colt Collection. From here swagger over to the Spirit of the Cowboy Gallery, which sheds light on the lives of real cowboys of yore and today. Back upstairs, other rooms show how the West has been glorified and romanticized in fine art, movies, radio, TV and advertising.

Travel Town Museum

Railroad buffs will not want to miss this nostalgic museum on the northern edge of Griffith Park at 5200 W Zoo Drive. Travel Town (☎ 323-662-5874) is an outdoor transportation museum that specializes in pre-WWII railroad antiques. Some 16 steam and diesel locomotives (the oldest from 1864), 10 freight cars and cabooses, and nine passenger cars – including several sleepers – form part of the collection. Kids of any age may climb onto some of the locomotives and imagine themselves as engineers. There's also a warehouse-sized hall displaying historical fire engines and fire-fighting equipment as well as a huge model-train network, which a local hobby club operates Sundays from 11 am to 2:30 pm.

The best day to visit Travel Town is the first Sunday of every month, when volunteers run free rides on a caboose pulled by a diesel engine. Popular are the free docent-led tours of several luxurious, fully restored Union Pacific passenger cars offered on the first Saturday and first and third Sunday of the month. Trips on a miniature train run daily ($1.75 adults, $1.25 children). From April to September, hours are 10 am to 5 pm weekdays, to 6 pm weekends; it closes one hour earlier the rest of the year. Admission is free.

Los Angeles Live Steamers Located just east of the Travel Town Museum, the Live Steamers is a local club devoted to the preservation of locomotives through scale models. Free public rides are offered Sundays 10 am to 3 pm. Come early, as lines can get quite long.

Kid Stuff

Kids' attractions, centered in the park's southeast corner, include the **Griffith Park**

Southern Railroad (☎ 323-664-6788), a miniature train ride in operation since 1948, which makes a 1-mile loop past pony rides, through an old Western town and a Native American village. Rides operate 10 am to 4:30 pm weekdays, until 5 pm weekends, and cost $1.75 for adults, $1.25 for children. An old-fashioned 1926 **merry-go-round** (☎ 323-665-3051) operates nearby (11 am to 5 pm daily in summer, weekends only in winter). To get to this area, follow Crystal Springs Drive up the park's eastern flank.

Forest Lawn Memorial Park – Hollywood Hills

Just west of Griffith Park, at 6300 Forest Lawn Drive, is this 340-acre cemetery (☎ 323-254-7251), which boasts sculptures and artwork, plus a fine catalog of dead celebrities including Lucille Ball, Liberace, Bette Davis and Stan Laurel. (For background on Forest Lawn cemeteries, see the entry on the even more grandiose Glendale branch later in the chapter.) The **Court of Liberty** is a patriotic homage to America's founding fathers. From the center of the terraced court of Albert Speer-like proportions soars a statue of George Washington. Note the grave of Stan Laurel on your right as you walk toward a gigantic mosaic mural. Here, millions of minuscule tiles form a sentimental but nonetheless impressive depiction of the country's founding.

Behind follows the **Hall of Liberty** (open daily 10 am to 4:45 pm), which contains a replica of the Liberty Bell as well as a Mexican history museum. Just west of here is the **Lincoln Terrace** with a memorial statue of the president and a smaller mosaic with scenes from his life. The cemetery grounds are open daily 8 am to 6 pm; admission is free (unless you're planning to stay forever).

South Central

Gangs, drugs, poverty, high crime and driveby shootings are just a few of the negative images – not entirely undeservedly – associated with this district. Yet pockets of this area are surprisingly appealing, both culturally and historically. Early LA big wigs built grand mansions here, while culture and the arts – especially jazz music – thrived to the point where South Central invited comparison to New York's Harlem.

Most of the area's neighborhoods and commercial strips were hard hit by the 1992 riots, as they were by the Watts riots of 1965 (see the boxed text). While not a traditional tourist destination, South Central has a culture and history entirely its own; especially for those interested in LA's African American heritage, it should not be overlooked.

WEST ADAMS (MAP 2)

In the 1920s, the West Adams district, encompassing the area just south of the 10 Fwy between Crenshaw Blvd to the west and Vermont Ave to the east, was one of LA's best addresses. Hollywood movie stars like Fatty Arbuckle lived here, as did industrial magnates like the Doheny family. Although West Adams has long been supplanted by other fashionable communities farther west, many of its mansions, churches and other notable buildings from the early 20th century survive.

One of the finest examples is the **Doheny Mansion**, 8 Chester Place, a 20-acre parklike enclave between W 23rd St and W Adams Blvd. This mansion is a French Gothic chateau designed in 1900 by Theodore Eisen and Sumner Hunt. It is often the site of chamber music concerts organized by the Da Camara Society (☎ 310-440-1351).

William Andrews Clark Memorial Library

One of LA's best-kept secrets is this gem of a library (☎ 323-731-8529) at 2520 Cimarron St. Today an adjunct to UCLA, it was built in 1926 by noted architect Robert Farquhar for William Andrews Clark Jr, the son of a copper-mining millionaire. Clark Jr amassed an extraordinary book collection particularly focused on English history and literature of the 17th and 18th century, and the works of Oscar Wilde. While the written works are primarily of interest to scholars and researchers, everybody will be able to

The Los Angeles Riots: 1992 & 1965

April 29, 1992: 'Not Guilty.' The words cut through the stifling air of a hushed Simi Valley courtroom like a dagger through silk, their gravity still a notion unfathomed. More than a year earlier, Simi Valley – a quiet, heavily Caucasian desert community on the very north-western rim of LA County – had been the site where a cuadrilla of LAPD officers beat Rodney King. A resident had immortalized the drubbing on videotape, which showed the cops relentlessly kicking, beating and shouting at the African American as he crouched on the asphalt. The images were beamed across the globe *ad nauseam*.

'Not Guilty.' The verdict that acquitted the officers of all charges unleashed a torrent of fury that would consume the city for three days. Thousands of enraged residents of South Central began looting stores in their own community, setting buildings ablaze and assaulting innocent by-standers. Like wildfire, the rioting quickly enveloped other neighborhoods. Businesses and schools closed throughout the city and a dusk curfew was imposed, leaving frightened Angelenos huddled in their homes watching events unfold on television. A tearful Rodney King sobbed, 'Can't we all just get along?' – an appeal to the rioters that was as naive as it was futile. National Guardsmen, stationed on rooftops, patrolling the streets with machine guns and stationed with armored vehi-cles at places like Venice Beach, finally helped restore a semblance of order. The shocking toll: more than 50 dead, 4000 injured, 12,000 arrested and $1 billion in property damage.

The riots of 1992 were eerily reminiscent of the Watts Riots a generation earlier. Back in August 1965, it was a routine traffic stop that triggered an angry mob to explode with rage, determined to pay LA back for decades of oppression, injustice and discrimination. As the city began to lick its wounds six days later, then-Governor Pat Brown appointed a commission to study the causes of the riots. It found high unemployment in south LA (double that in the rest of the city), overcrowded and underfunded classrooms, and housing-discrimination laws that kept African Americans ghettoized and in sub-standard homes.

Almost 30 years later, people were once again asking 'Why?' Given that the Civil Rights Act of 1964 should have removed much of the institutional discrimination, Angelenos are split about the root causes of the '92 riots. Many recognize that forms of discrimination still exist, that treatment of whites and non-whites by the police and courts is different and that South Central's schools and infrastructure are inferior to those in wealthy Westside communities. However, many also suspect that the riots were not politically motivated at all but rather an expression of simple material greed. TV images of laughing hordes hauling everything from sneakers to VCRs from ravaged stores and triumphantly posing with their loot for the cameras have left many thinking that the 'riots' were little more than a free-for-all shopping spree. The police were nowhere to be seen (there was a fierce battle raging between the Police Commissioner and the City Council at the time) and teargas never made an appearance.

The initial spark of the riots was racial rage. What followed was merely an ugly – and offi-cially condoned – party. Perhaps the question to ask is: Has LA learned? Or will it burn again a generation from now?

appreciate the library's idyllic garden setting and sumptuous Italian Baroque interior.

The vestibule is a symphony in multihued, patterned marble, crowned by a painted ceil-ing depicting Apollo with his mother, Leto, and the Nine Muses. The grand music room was modeled after a chamber in the doge's palace in Venice, Italy; it is clad in oak walls and velvet drapery and features a Steinway grand piano, Persian carpet and a richly carved ceiling. The two book rooms are lined by two levels of bronze bookcases as well as alabaster chandeliers and trompe l'oeil decorations. Chamber music concerts and readings take place occasionally. The Clark Library is open to the public weekdays 9 am to 4:45 pm; free admission.

CENTRAL AVE (MAP 3)

The northern end of Central Ave, just south of Downtown, was the center of African American life from the 1920s until the 1960s, though not entirely by choice. Kept from moving to other neighborhoods by restrictive racial covenants, LA blacks essentially became ghettoized around the time of WWI. Another regulation – the Jim Crow restrictions – kept black actors and musicians out of the evolving movie industry. As a result, Central Ave became a center of jazz and other entertainment.

The **Dunbar Hotel** (☎ 323-234-7882), 4225 S Central Ave, which opened in 1928 as a hotel for black visitors, took on unofficial headquarters status. Every major black musician, including Lena Horne, Ella Fitzgerald, Count Basie and Duke Ellington, stayed in this hotel. Clubs such as the Parisian Room, Ivy's Chicken Shack and Club Alabam thrived until the start of the area's decline in the '50s. Clubs closed and the Dunbar started falling into decay, even facing the threat of demolition in 1988. Restored since, it's now a senior citizens' home. To get a sense of Central Ave's heyday, visit the small exhibition in the Dunbar lobby.

LEIMERT PARK (MAP 7)

The Leimert Park neighborhood is south of Martin Luther King Jr Blvd and east of Crenshaw Blvd in the Crenshaw district. It is a lovely area with quiet streets canopied by towering trees and lined by gorgeous single-family homes. Leimert Park was named after architect Walter Leimert, who conceived the space as a community for affluent whites. Ironically, it is now predominantly inhabited by affluent, professional African Americans and has in recent years witnessed a steep cultural revival, making it the hub of cutting-edge black arts. The action is centered in Leimert Village, a 2-block strip of Degnan Blvd between 43rd St and Leimert Plaza. At 4344 Degnan Blvd you'll find the World Stage performance gallery and, at 4327 Degnan Blvd, the Dance Collective (☎ 323-292-1538). Around the corner is Fifth Street Dick's jazz coffeehouse, 3347½ W 43rd Place, and around the corner again, at 4339 Leimert Blvd, is Babe & Ricky's 'house of blues.' Check the Entertainment chapter for details.

Museum in Black

This museum cum gallery (☎ 323-292-9528), 4331 Degnan Blvd, displays unusual masks, fertility and spiritual power figures, instruments, jewelry, beads and other artifacts, most imported from Africa. It is owned by the quirky Brian Breye, an outspoken community advocate who began his career as a dealer in oriental antiques. An avid collector over the past 30 years, he shops for his art in Mali, Nigeria, Ivory Coast and other African countries. Most of the pieces are for sale and are considered highly collectible. Ask to see the wonderfully cluttered back room where Breye has amassed an astonishing collection of 'Negro' memorabilia – cookie jars, salt and pepper shakers, books, dolls, photos, etc – attesting both to the humiliation and the accomplishments of American blacks over the past decades. Hours are usually weekdays noon to 6 pm; admission is free.

Museum of African-American Art

This small museum (☎ 323-294-7071), 4005 S Crenshaw Blvd, is housed on the 3rd floor of the Robinsons-May department store in the Baldwin Hills Crenshaw Plaza mall. Look for the works of Palmer Hayden, a leading painter of the Harlem Renaissance, as well as art by blacks from Africa, the Caribbean, South America and the US. Hours are 11 am to 6 pm Thursday to Saturday, noon to 5 pm Sunday. Admission is free.

CITY OF VERNON (MAP 3)

There's not much reason to go to industrial Vernon, about 2 miles southeast of Downtown. Its only redeeming value for the traveler is a highly unusual – some might even say macabre – landmark: the **Farmer John Pig Mural**, 3049 East Vernon Ave. The gigantic mural, which covers the exterior facade of a sausage factory, depicts a bucolic landscape inhabited by happy oinkers romping and frolicking about in the lush countryside, clearly oblivious to their future as pork rind. It's the work of Les Grimes, who, incidentally, died after falling from a scaffold while painting the mural.

WATTS (MAP 3)

Watts is about 7 miles due south of Downtown and is served by the Blue Line light railway to Long Beach. Trains have passed through Watts since 1902 when the Pacific Electric Company built a railway junction here. In those days, Watts was a multiethnic farming community of working-class Italian, German, Japanese, Chinese and Latino immigrants. Within a couple of decades, it became dominated by African Americans, largely because of racial covenants prohibiting them from settling in other neighborhoods. In the 1990s, the area's ethnic makeup changed again; now about half of the population is Latino.

Watts has been repeatedly in the headlines for its high crime rate and drug-related gang activity. Dark marks in its history are the six days of racially charged rioting in 1965 and the 1992 Rodney King riots (see boxed text). While the area is generally safe to travel through in the daytime, it's best avoided at night.

Watts Towers

One of the few reasons tourists venture into this part of South Central is to see the Watts Towers, 1765 E 107th St, now administered by the Cultural Affairs Department (☎ 323-847-4646). The life's work of Italian immigrant Simon Rodia, this curious and unique folk-art monument has the same whimsical and filigree aspects often associated with Spanish architect Antonio Gaudí. It's hard to fathom, though, that the towers are the product of a solitary and unskilled laborer, working with no architectural training and only simple tiling tools. In that sense, the towers are nothing less than a testament to human imagination, vision and perseverance.

In 1921, Rodia set out to 'make something big' – and then spent the next 33 years doing just that. Supporting his towers are slender columns containing steel reinforcement, which he tied with wire, wrapped with wire mesh and covered by hand with cement. Incorporated into the facade are glass, mirrors, sea shells, rocks, ceramic tile and pottery. Most of the glass comes from soda bottles, especially green 7-Up bottles. When, in 1954, he decided his work was finished, the sculpture consisted of several towers (the tallest standing almost 100 feet), a gazebo with a circular bench, three bird baths and other sections. The same year, he suddenly gave the land to a neighbor and moved to the San Francisco Bay Area, where he died 11 years later having never returned to LA. In the 1960s the towers were scheduled for an appointment with the wrecking ball. Luckily, neighbors banded together and the towers were saved. The riots left them unscathed, though the 1994 earthquake did

Watts Towers: Simon Rodia's masterpiece

not. The towers have been under restoration ever since, and tours have been suspended at least until 2001. In the meantime, they're still worth a visit; most details can still be appreciated through the fence.

Watts Towers Art Center

This community arts center (☎ 323-485-1795), adjacent to Rodia's structure at 1727 E 107th St, sponsors free art classes, dance and theater workshops, and other programs designed to involve the community and help locals express themselves artistically. Begun in 1970, it was funded entirely through a community campaign known as 'One Square Inch,' whereby each dollar donated 'bought' the donor a square inch. Within is an excellent permanent display of ethnic folk instruments, while a different gallery showcases changing exhibits of contemporary fine art by local and national artists, both emerging and established.

Watts Labor Community Action Center (WLCAC)

This 7-acre complex, simply known as The Center (☎ 323-563-5600), is at 10950 S Central Ave in the historic heart of Watts. It was built after the 1992 riots as a symbol of community pride and a place for locals to define themselves through art and cultural expression. Its other main goal is to attract Angelenos from other parts of the city, as well as tourists, to Watts and reverse the negative perceptions of the area.

Lording over the parking lot is **The Mother of Humanity**, a bronze sculpture by Nigel Binns, which blends physical features and spiritual symbols of all races in a tribute to woman. The northern edge of the complex features the **Mudtown Flats**, a row of facades intended to re-create Central Ave in its 1920s and '30s heyday. Off to the east is the Ted Watkins Center for Communication, a 35,000-sq-foot space containing a theater and the excellent **Civil Rights Museum**. A tour of the latter starts with a peek into the hull of a slave ship and continues with a walk down a virtual Mississippi Delta dirt road, complete with live crickets, wagons, trees and other props. It leads to the 'Countdown to Eternity,' an exhibit focused on telling the story of Martin Luther King Jr and the 1960s Civil Rights Movement through photographs and artifacts. The Center, which also sponsors concerts and other events, is open daily. Free tours are available, but call ahead.

Hollywood

CENTRAL HOLLYWOOD (MAP 9)

Visitors to Hollywood expecting a dreamworld of celluloid perfection, filled with beautiful and dazzling artistry, are in for a big bummer. Hollywood is all grit and grime, the entire entertainment industry is everywhere *but* here, and you're about as likely to bump into Tom Cruise or Michelle Pfeiffer in Hollywood as you are to be around for that 9.0 earthquake everybody talks about.

By the time the 1960s rolled around, the glamour of Hollywood was gone and the big stars and studios had moved on. What remains is Hollywood's storied past – its greatest asset – but you'll have to come to terms with some depressing realities to find it. Those who are blinded by their love for movie history will still find Hollywood's streets lined with many of the fabled haunts from its heyday. You can still root out the places where Sinatra crooned or where Bogie and Bacall pounded their martinis. And old movie palaces like the El Capitan and the Chinese Theater don't lose their

COURTESY LOS ANGELES PUBLIC LIBRARY PHOTO COLLECTION

Hollywood Hills in the 1920s

Hollywood Walk of Fame

RICK GERHARTER

Mann's Chinese Theater

DAVID PEEVERS

Re-created *Star Trek* set at the Hollywood Entertainment Museum

LEE FOSTER

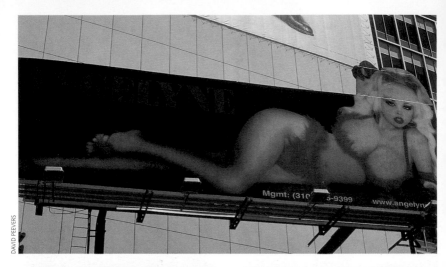

Celebrity wannabes – Angelyne, Dennis Woodruff and impersonators at Universal Studios

majesty just because it's now *Saving Private Ryan* and not *From Here to Eternity* up on their screens. And there's good reason to hope that a disastrous period for Hollywood is coming to an end worthy of a Gable and DeHavilland kiss.

At the end of the millennium, real change is enveloping Hollywood. The opening of the Metro Red Line subway station, which will whisk people between Downtown and Hollywood in minutes, is slated for May 1999. Two remodeled movie palaces, the El Capitan and the Egyptian, were recently reopened. A new museum, the Hollywood Historical Museum, should inaugurate in 1999.

But the most exciting and visible development will be the construction of a gigantic new center that will bring the Oscars – and all the show-biz glamour – back to Hollywood. The $385 million complex just east of Mann's Chinese Theater will incorporate not only a custom-designed theater for the Academy Awards, but also a 14-screen movie theater, hotel, ballroom, shops, restaurants, clubs and live broadcast studios. Developers and civic boosters are betting the farm that this project will fuel Hollywood's revitalization into the next century. Let's hope it won't become a soulless, commercial, theme-park environment like the

Ghost Expeditions: If the Spirit Moves You...

There was a chill in the air and a fearful sense of foreboding as the ancient gate creaked open and…all right, we're exaggerating. It was a usual balmy night in Hollywood – but it *was* midnight and the gate at the entrance to the Vogue Theater *did* creak a little as we met with kindred morbid souls and our guides to the beyond in search of the paranormal, a term that has enormous irony when applied to LA. The dead – like nearly everyone else in LA – are apparently uneasy.

We were entering the Vogue as guests of the International Society for Paranormal Research (ISPR) to hunt up the spooks in this 'very active' site of ghost activity. ISPR's director, Dr Montz, and his psychic sidekick, Daena Smoller, were taking us into realms where the rational never go. We were there to plumb the psychic depths and find if we were adepts ourselves or just hopeless realists.

Through musty tunnels beneath the theater's stage, in the claustrophobic room where a projectionist had died – and periodically reappears – we held onto dowsing rods and nosed around for psychic currents in the rooms, awaiting the ultimate: a sighting. Our rods were emphatically still, but those of others whirled like the blades of a helicopter. One woman swooned, saying, 'She's blowing on the back of my neck' – an allusion to the children who died in a schoolhouse fire on this very spot at the turn of the 20th century. We were missing something. Not a screech, not an unexplained stench, not so much as a raised hair on the back of the neck. But weird, anyway.

About 3 am, having this book to write and feeling cross-eyed with fatigue, we left our wide-eyed cohorts sniffing for the eternal. We headed home with apologies to these very nice people who had at least made our initial ghost hunt fun. And then…on the freeway our car went berserk: strange rattlings, the loss of gears, and we were suddenly filled with inexplicable feelings of dread. The next day we got word that our repairs would only amount to a cheap 28¢ part. What was it that Daena had told us? Ah, yes, 'The children's spirits in this theater like to play *little* tricks. And they *do* like to travel around, just like us.' Nah, it couldn't be.

If you too would like to participate in one of the ISPR 'ghost expeditions' throughout LA's haunts, call them at ☎ 323-644-8866 or 323-464-7827. Or take a trip to their website at www.hauntings.com.

Universal City Walk. But this is Hollywood, kid. No business, no show.

In the meantime, the **Janes House** (☎ 323-461-9520), 6541 Hollywood Blvd, houses a visitors' center where you can pick up information and pamphlets and book your tours. The building itself is a rare remnant of the mansions that once lined this street – then known as Prospect Ave – in the early part of the 20th century. Built in 1903 in turreted Queen Anne style, the Janes House was a longtime family-run school for Industry children.

Hollywood Sign

Visible from just about anywhere, this is Hollywood's, and indeed LA's, most recognizable landmark. Located on Mt Lee in Griffith Park, it was built in 1923 at a cost of $21,000 as an advertising gimmick for a real estate development called Hollywoodland. In 1932 a young actress named Peggy, despondent over her nonexistent career, jumped to her death from the letter H. Until 1939 a caretaker, living behind an L, maintained the sign. In 1945, the land was deeded to the city, which – recognizing the sign's promotional value – merely chopped off the last four letters. Each letter is 50 feet tall and made of sheet metal. The sign has always been a favorite with pranksters: the sign read 'Ollywood' during the Iran-Contra hearings and dope-heads once turned it into 'Hollyweed.' To prevent people from following Peggy's or the pranksters' examples, the city has made it illegal to hike to the sign. For good views of it, head to the Griffith Park Observatory or to the top of Beachwood Canyon Drive.

Paramount Pictures Studios

The only movie studio still in Hollywood proper is Paramount, 5555 Melrose Ave, whose wrought-iron gate has made movie history itself, notably in *Sunset Boulevard* (1950) when an aging diva (Gloria Swanson) drove onto the lot believing her career was about to be revived. The gate is at the corner of Bronson Ave and Marathon St and is not to be confused with the main gate on Melrose Ave. Two-hour walking tours of the historic lot run weekdays on the hour from 9 am to 2 pm and cost $15. Children under 10 are not admitted. Call ☎ 323-956-1777 for reservations.

Hollywood Memorial Park Cemetery

Just north of Paramount, bordering Santa Monica Blvd, is this fabulous cemetery stacked with the legendary dead. In the Cathedral Mausoleum in the park's southeast corner are the tombs of Rudolph Valentino, Peter Lorre and Peter Finch. Just north of here is a pond where you'll find the graves of Tyrone Power, who died during a dueling scene on a set in Madrid, and Jayne Mansfield, who lost her head – literally – in a car accident. Cecil B De Mille resides here in a white sarcophagus alongside his wife, and John Huston, whose last film was an adaptation of Joyce's *The Dead*, now rests after a life of genius and lust. Just west of the Cathedral Mausoleum is the reflecting pool with the tomb of Douglas Fairbanks. Farther east is the Jewish cemetery – Beth Olam – where notorious gangster Bugsy Siegel is buried in the southwest corner. The entrance to Hollywood Memorial Park is at 6000 Santa Monica Blvd between Gower St and Van Ness Blvd. Hours are 8 am to 5 pm daily.

HISTORIC HOLLYWOOD WALKING TOUR

Our tour takes in major sights in historic central Hollywood. It's set up as a 2½-mile loop starting from the shiny silver sculpture at the intersection of Hollywood Blvd and La Brea Ave, then heads east along Hollywood Blvd, south on Vine and back west on Sunset Blvd. If you're pressed for time, do the Hollywood Blvd section only. Also look out for the historic sign markers posted along Hollywood Blvd for information supplementing our tour.

Hollywood Walk of Fame

Big Bird, Bob Hope, Marilyn Monroe and Julio Iglesias are just a few of the celebrities being sought out, admired, photographed – and stepped on – day after day. Conceived by businessman Harry Sugarman as a tribute

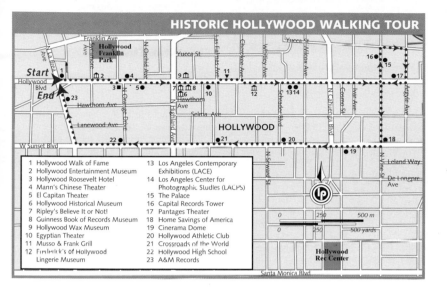

HISTORIC HOLLYWOOD WALKING TOUR

1   Hollywood Walk of Fame
2   Hollywood Entertainment Museum
3   Hollywood Roosevelt Hotel
4   Mann's Chinese Theater
5   El Capitan Theater
6   Hollywood Historical Museum
7   Ripley's Believe It or Not!
8   Guinness Book of Records Museum
9   Hollywood Wax Museum
10 Egyptian Theater
11 Musso & Frank Grill
12 Frederick's of Hollywood
      Lingerie Museum

13 Los Angeles Contemporary
      Exhibitions (LACE)
14 Los Angeles Center for
      Photographic Studies (LACPS)
15 The Palace
16 Capital Records Tower
17 Pantages Theater
18 Home Savings of America
19 Cinerama Dome
20 Hollywood Athletic Club
21 Crossroads of the World
22 Hollywood High School
23 A&M Records

to the artists and entertainers that put Hollywood on the map, the Walk of Fame has for decades faithfully fulfilled its other purpose – luring tourists to Tinseltown. Since Joanne Woodward received the first star in 1960, more than 2000 marble-and-bronze stars have impacted the sidewalks on Hollywood Blvd between La Brea and Gower St and along Vine St between Yucca St and Sunset Blvd. Each star has the celebrity's name engraved and an emblem identifying his or her artistic field – movies, TV, radio, recording or live theater. Induction ceremonies are held once or twice a month. Call the Hollywood Chamber of Commerce at ☎ 323-489-8311 for the schedule.

Hollywood Entertainment Museum

It took 12 years of debate, planning and fundraising – and only six months of construction – to bring to life the first Industry museum actually located in Hollywood. Just a few stars west of Mann's Chinese Theater, the Hollywood Entertainment Museum (☎ 323-465-7900), 7021 Hollywood Blvd, employs state-of-the-art technology to give

visitors a simplified yet fun look at the history and mystery of movie making – even if it doesn't capture the glitz and glamour of the art.

Visits start in the central rotunda lorded over by the Goddess of Entertainment, looking suspiciously like Oscar's cousin. This is the only section that may be explored without a guide, so take your time to admire the 12-x-12-foot model of '30s Hollywood incorporated into the elevated stage. Also here is an ominous metal device called a 'beauty calibrator,' used by make-up artists to determine imperfections in an actress's face.

A guide then takes you to the Foley Room where sound effects are created and the Editing Suite, which displays equipment from various periods. Then it's off to the Backlot, intended to give you an idea of the various departments you might find in a studio's real backlot, including the prop room, wardrobe department and art director's office. You'll see original items from movies including *Forrest Gump, The Addams Family* and *Star Trek.* Trekkies especially will love getting beamed up to the *USS Enterprise* via the Transporter Room. Sit in the captain's chair on this re-created set or zero in on *Star Trek* trivia on interactive screens. More down-to-earth is the place where everybody knows your name – the set of *Cheers* – next door.

Museum hours are 10 am to 6 pm, closed Monday. Admission is $7.50, $4.50 for seniors over 65 and students, $4 for children.

Hollywood Roosevelt Hotel

Rife with history, the Hollywood Roosevelt Hotel (☎ 323-466-7000), 7000 Hollywood Blvd, began attracting luminaries shortly after its 1927 opening. In 1929, Douglas Fairbanks hosted the first Academy Awards ceremony here, doling out what was then called the 'Merit Awards' to Janet Gaynor (best actress) and Emil Jannings (best actor). In the '30s, the hotel's Cineclub jazz lounge saw Errol Flynn, F Scott Fitzgerald and Salvador Dalí – the latter in town to make movie sets – quenching their thirst. The Cineclub is now called Cinegrill (see the Entertainment chapter).

For those who believe in such things, the hotel cleverly hones a reputation of being haunted. There are tall tales of calls made from a room without a phone, reflections of Marilyn Monroe in a mirror and Montgomery Clift's ghost slamming doors. More earthly are the Roosevelt's impressive lobby with its hand-painted ceiling and wrought-iron grill work, and the pool with its faded mural by David Hockney. One of the best historical exhibits about Hollywood is on the mezzanine level (no charge). Also see Places to Stay.

Mann's Chinese Theater

The most famous of Hollywood movie palaces, Mann's Chinese Theater (☎ 323-464-8111), 6925 Hollywood Blvd, was conceived in 1927 by movie mogul Sid Grauman. To see the temple-like interior you have to buy a ticket for the first-run films still being shown here. However, access to the famous forecourt, where more than 150 screen legends have left their mark, is free. Leaving one's foot or handprints in wet cement has been a special honor since Douglas Fairbanks, Mary Pickford and Norma Talmadge started the tradition, though some celebrities have chosen to immortalize other body parts such as their nose (Jimmy Durante) and legs (Betty Grable).

El Capitan Theater

The El Capitan (☎ 323-467-7674), at 6838 Hollywood Blvd, has an impressively ornate Spanish Colonial facade and a flamboyant East Indian-inspired interior. Built for live performances in 1926, it was converted to a movie house in the 1940s when it premiered *Citizen Kane*, voted best movie ever by the American Film Institute in 1998. Now owned by Disney, the El Capitan Theater recently underwent its second restoration and is now screening first-run films.

Hollywood Historical Museum

The historical Max Factor Building at 1666 Highland, previously occupied by the make-up magician's own museum (now integrated into the Hollywood Entertainment Museum), will be the site of the new Hollywood Historical Museum set to open in 1999. It will incorporate a new version of the fabled restaurant, Chasen's. Call the Hollywood Visitor Information Center, at ☎ 213-689-8822, for updates.

Ripley's Believe It or Not!

The rooftop T-rex of Ripley's Believe It or Not! (☎ 323-466-6335), 6780 Hollywood Blvd, beckons passers-by to examine its 300 exhibits of the weird and wild. An adventurer, reporter and collector, Robert Ripley traveled the world in search of curiosities, introducing them through his syndicated newspaper cartoons after 1918. Inside this amusing, if sensationalist, 'odditorium' are images of the giraffe-necked African woman, a two-headed goat, a six-legged cow and a man with a 4-foot crowbar stuck through his head. Also on display is a shrunken human head and a sculpture of Marilyn Monroe made from 264,000 discarded $1 bills. Hours are 10 am to 11 pm daily. Admission is $8.95, $5.95 for children, free for kids under four.

Guinness Book of Records Museum

Practically next door, at 6764 Hollywood Blvd, is the gaudy entrance to the Guinness

Book of Records Museum (☎ 323-462-8860), housed in a former movie theater. While some of the exhibits reflect general knowledge (the tallest mountain, biggest planet), others illustrate bizarre records such as the woman with the most tattoos and the most time spent asleep on a tight rope (185 days). Its hours are 10 am to midnight Sunday to Thursday, to 2 am Friday and Saturday. Admission is $7.95, $6.50 for seniors, $4.95 for children ages six to 12.

Hollywood Wax Museum

No celebrities around to snare your stare? Don't fret. The Hollywood Wax Museum (☎ 323-462-5991), across the street at 6767 Hollywood Blvd, features 220 celebrities frozen like deer in a headlight. You'll see passable waxen images of show biz greats such as Liz Taylor, Tom Cruise and (ooh... look!) Leonardo DiCaprio. American presidents, prominent athletes and even religious figures are also here. The icky Chamber of Horrors is good fun, as is the marvelously ironic 'monster gallery' inhabited by Hannibal Lecter, King Kong and...Mike Tyson! Hours and prices are the same as the Guinness Museum's. If you feel you must visit both, you can save with a combination ticket costing $14.95/11.95/8.95.

Egyptian Theater

Hollywood's oldest cinema is the 1100-seat Egyptian Theater at 6712 Hollywood Blvd, built in 1922. Inspired by the discovery of King Tut's tomb, its design incorporates faux-stone doors with hieroglyphs and sphinx heads. In its heyday, it even had live caged monkeys and usherettes clad in Cleopatra-style garb. The Egyptian was recently restored and is now home to the American Cinemathèque (☎ 323-466-3456), a nonprofit film organization. Public screenings include a daily film on the history of Hollywood, evening programs focusing on art and revival, as well as foreign films and documentaries (also see Entertainment).

Musso & Frank Grill

On the next block, at 6667 Hollywood Blvd, is the Musso & Frank Grill, a survivor and

The closest you may get to the stars:
Baywatch at the Hollywood Wax Museum

legend. The oldest restaurant in Hollywood, it's been in business since 1919 and numbered Hollywood darlings Mary Pickford and Douglas Fairbanks among its first guests. Literary lions such as William Faulkner and F Scott Fitzgerald followed in the '40s, and the restaurant is still a favorite Industry hangout today. (Decor and menu have changed little since those days of yore.) Also see the Places to Eat chapter.

Frederick's of Hollywood Lingerie Museum

Getting to Frederick's Lingerie Museum and Celebrity Lingerie Hall of Fame (☎ 323-466-8506), 6608 Hollywood Blvd, means navigating through a denser maze of bras, negligees, panties and garter belts than you'd find at a '60s Hollywood pool party. But you will eventually arrive in a smallish back room where you can admire such 'flimsies' as a tasseled bustier worn by Madonna, Joan Crawford's billowy underskirt and boxers once sported by Robert Redford. You will also get a not-so-serious look at the evolving shape of bra fashions. All this for free between 10 am and 6 pm Monday to Saturday, noon to 5 pm Sunday.

Los Angeles Contemporary Exhibitions (LACE)

LACE (☎ 323-957-1777), 6522 Hollywood Blvd, has nothing to do with Frederick's Lingerie. This is an artist-run shopfront gallery providing artists on the cutting edge of painting, sculpture, video, photography,

Famous Alumni

If you want to find out where your favorite celeb studied algebra and French, visit any of the following schools (except for Immaculate Heart and Harvard-Westlake, all are public schools):

Beverly Hills High
241 S Moreno Drive (Map 11)
Corbin Bernsen, Albert Brooks, Nicolas Cage, Richard Chamberlain, Jamie Lee Curtis, Richard Dreyfuss, Carrie Fisher, Lenny Kravitz, Swoosie Kurtz, Rob Reiner, Pauly Shore

Fairfax High
7850 Melrose Ave at Fairfax Ave (Map 10)
Slash of Guns N Roses

Glendale High
1440 E Broadway
John Wayne

Hollywood High
1521 N Highland Ave at Sunset Blvd (Map 9)
Carol Burnett, Linda Evans, Judy Garland, James Garner, Barbara Hershey, John Ritter, Jason Robards, Mickey Rooney, Charlene Tilton

Immaculate Heart High
5515 Franklin Ave (Map 9)
Tyra Banks, Natalie Cole, Mary Tyler Moore

Le Lycée Français
10361 W Pico Blvd (west LA)
Jodie Foster

Los Angeles High
4650 W Olympic Blvd (Mid-City)
Dustin Hoffman

Marshall High
3939 Tracy St (Silver Lake)
Leonardo DiCaprio

Narbonne High
24300 Western Ave (Harbor City)
Quentin Tarantino

Polytechnic High
1600 Atlantic Ave (Long Beach)
Snoop Doggy Dog

Redondo Union High
631 Vincent Park (Redondo Beach)
Demi Moore

Santa Monica High
601 Pico Blvd
Glenn Ford, Rob Lowe, Chris Penn, Sean Penn, Charlie Sheen

University High
11800 Texas Ave (Map 12)
Jeff Bridges, Randy Newman, Nancy Sinatra, Elizabeth Taylor, Tone Loc

Van Nuys High
5535 Cedros Ave
Marilyn Monroe, Robert Redford

Venice High
13000 Venice Blvd
Myrna Loy

Westlake School for Girls
(now Harvard-Westlake) 700 N Faring Rd
Candice Bergen, Debby Boone, Bridget Fonda, Tracy Nelson, Sally Ride, Tori Spelling, Shirley Temple

music and performance art a place to showcase their work. Primarily local and regional artists present largely conceptual and often site-specific works. Performance art and film screenings supplement the exhibit schedule, which changes about every two months. LACE is open noon to 5 pm weekends, to 6 pm Wednesday and Friday, to 8 pm Thursday; admission is free.

Next door, at 6518 Hollywood Blvd, is another avant-garde gallery, the **Los Angeles Center for Photographic Studies** (☎ 323-466-6232). Begun in 1974, LACPS is LA's only nonprofit gallery for evolving photography-based media, including videography, photography and cinematography. Hours are 11 am to 5 pm Wednesday to Saturday; admission is free.

Hollywood & Vine

The mystique of Hollywood's most fabled intersection had its origin in broadcasts of nearby radio stations, which always began with an enthusiastic 'Brought to you from Hollywood and Vine.' But don't look for landmarks here.

Walk a few steps north on Vine St to the famous **Capitol Records Tower**, 1750 N Vine St, designed to look like a stack of records. Across the street is the 1924 Art Deco **The Palace**, 1735 N Vine St, a dance and live music venue in its present incarnation, following stints as a stage theater, radio studio, variety theater and TV production studio (also see the Entertainment chapter).

A few yards east of the intersection is the **Pantages Theater** (☎ 323-468-1770), 6233 Hollywood Blvd, considered one of America's finest examples of Art Deco architecture. Its vaulted lobby holds statues of a movie director and an aviatrix, presumably in their only Hollywood coupling. Opened in 1930, the Pantages was bought by Howard Hughes in 1949 and hosted the Academy Awards throughout the 1950s and the Emmys in the '70s. A movie palace until 1977, it was converted into a live theater and now often hosts elaborate Broadway musicals and concerts (also see Entertainment).

Continue the tour by heading south on Vine St to Sunset Blvd. The northeast corner is occupied by the **Home Savings of America** standing in the former site of NBC's Radio City, demolished in 1964. The bank still honors its Hollywood roots by inscribing its marble facade with the names of the famous, and there's a tile mosaic depicting some of the legends. Take a peek inside the lavish lobby to see its murals, stained-glass windows and mosaics. Turn west (right) on Sunset.

Cinerama Dome

Looking like half of a giant golf ball, the Cinerama Dome (☎ 323-466-3401), 6360 Sunset Blvd at Ivar, opened in 1963, its geodesic dome a complete novelty and reflection of technological progress at the time. This cinema has a giant curved screen and a sound system capable of projecting God's voice (also see Entertainment).

Hollywood Athletic Club

Built in 1923 in Spanish-Mediterranean style, this beautiful building at the corner of Sunset Blvd and Seward (6525 Sunset) once boasted a pool, gym, fitness room and star-studded (no pun intended) male-only membership. Johnny Weissmuller and Buster Crabbe, both famous for playing Tarzan, as well as Rudolph Valentino, John Wayne and other hunks, were among those who swam laps and pumped iron here. The first Emmy broadcast came from here in 1949 (with TV in its infancy, there weren't that many awards). It's now a chic dance and pool hall with a fancy restaurant (see Entertainment).

Crossroads of the World

This incongruous cluster of buildings at 6671 Sunset Blvd was designed as one of LA's earliest shopping malls in 1936 by Robert Derrah, a noted Streamline Moderne architect who also designed the Coca-Cola Bottling Plant on Central Ave in Downtown. Derrah once again applied a nautical theme, here building the central structure in ship shape, its bow topped by a tower, which is crowned by a rotating globe. European-style cottages, many in mock-Tudor, flank this structure and now contain offices.

Hollywood High School

Hollywood High School, 1521 N Highland Ave at Sunset Blvd, has an impressive roster of alumni, but because of changing demographics it's no longer a celluloid breeding farm. The high school still looks impressive, especially the Science Building with its bas-relief by Bartolo Mako above the entrance.

A&M Records

Some of the greatest silent epics starring a bowler-hatted Charlie Chaplin, including *City Lights* (1931) and *The Great Dictator* (1940), were made in this mock-Tudor cluster, 1416 La Brea Ave at Sunset. The studio was founded by Chaplin himself in 1919. It was purchased by Herb Alpert and Jerry Moss (hence A&M) in 1966 and turned into a recording studio. Quincy Jones and Burt Bacharach are among those who recorded here. Continue north on La Brea Ave to get back to the start of the tour.

HOLLYWOOD HILLS (MAP 9)

Two to three generations ago, stars such as Ethel Barrymore and Gloria Swanson made their homes along the rugged ridges above Hollywood and in canyons such as Laurel, Nichols, Runyon and Beachwood. Today, the Hollywood Hills are getting a new infusion of life from young actors like Lou Diamond Phillips and Rebecca de Mornay. More stars live in Whitley Heights, a series of Italian villa-style houses built into the hillside above Franklin and Highland Aves by architect Hobart J Whitley.

Better known is the **Freeman House** (☎ 323-851-0671), 1962 Glencoe Way at Hillcrest Rd, designed by Frank Lloyd Wright in 1924. Tours of this experimental Mayan-influenced home run Saturday at 2 and 4 pm ($10, $5 students). Features include the first glass-to-glass corner windows and a textile-block construction technology that required laying 12,000 handmade concrete tiles.

Each summer, these homes echo with some of the world's finest live music wafting upwards from the **Hollywood Bowl** (☎ 323-850-2000), 2301 Highland Ave, an outdoor amphitheater that looks like a giant beehive in aerial photographs. It's the summer home of the LA Philharmonic Orchestra, and concerts often sell out (also see Entertainment). The Bowl opened in 1916 with a performance of *Julius Caesar* with a Who's Who cast including Douglas Fairbanks Sr and Tyrone Power. The first concerts were in 1922. The original concert shell was designed by Lloyd Wright, Frank's son, though the current one is by Frank Gehry.

Pioneering movie director Cecil B De Mille's original 1913 horse barn is now home to the nearby **Hollywood Studio Museum** (☎ 323-874-2276), at 2100 N Highland Ave. Originally located at Selma and Vine Sts, it was in this barn that De Mille shot *The Squaw Man* (1913), the first movie ever produced in Hollywood. The barn was moved to the Paramount Studios lot in 1927 and arrived at its present spot in 1985. Fully restored, it has exhibits on early filmmaking,

including costumes and a replica of Cecil B De Mille's office.

Nearby is the **John Anson Ford Theater** (☎ 323-466-1767), 2580 Cahuenga Blvd. Built in the 1930s, the Ford has a hillside backdrop of palms and cypress that gives it a particularly intimate feeling (also see the Entertainment chapter).

SILVER LAKE & LOS FELIZ (MAP 9)
Barnsdall Art Park

Occupying an olive-shrouded hill on Vermont Ave between Hollywood and Sunset Blvds (enter from Hollywood Blvd), Barnsdall Art Park is a city-owned cultural and arts center offering low-cost art classes to children and adults. Of minor interest to the visitor are the center's art galleries, which showcase contemporary works by students, faculty and community artists from throughout Southern California.

The park's main attraction, though, is the **Hollyhock House** (1921; ☎ 323-913-4157), Frank Lloyd Wright's first LA project. It was built for oil heiress Aline Barnsdall (1882-1946), a progressive and philanthropy-minded single mother dedicated to arts and theater as well as topics hugely controversial in the 1920s – birth control and socialism.

The original plan called for the creation of a cutting-edge theatrical community, which would include the main residence (the Hollyhock House) of Aline and her daughter Sugartops, plus two more homes and a director's house, actors' dormitory, motion picture

Frank Lloyd Wright's Hollyhock House

ANDREA SCHULTE-PEEVERS

theater and other structures. Only the three residences were ever built before Aline abandoned her plans and donated the complex to the city in 1927. The only structure still extant besides the Hollyhock House currently houses the Barnsdall Art Center. Though Wright designed the complex for the most part, construction was supervised by his son Lloyd Wright and his apprentice Rudolph Schindler, both of whom inserted their own signature marks.

The Hollyhock House was Wright's first attempt at integrating architecture with the Southern California environment, a style he later labeled 'California Romanza.' His dramatic interpretation extends the interior living space by juxtaposing each room with an equivalent outdoor space. He uses skylit walkways, glass doors, porches and colonnades to establish relationships between the two. Other elements are a central courtyard with a small amphitheater and rooftop terraces with great views of the Hollywood Hills and the city. Varying ceiling and floor levels serve as transitional elements between rooms. Stylized renditions of the hollyhock, Aline's favorite flower, are incorporated throughout.

Earthquakes and time have caused major structural and cosmetic damage, which is why the house will be under restoration over the next few years. One-hour tours will be offered at least through summer 1999 on Wednesday to Sunday at noon, 1, 2 and 3 pm and cost $2, $1 for seniors, free for children. If you're visiting after summer 1999, check with ☎ 323-913-4157 for tour availability.

KCET Studios

KCET (☎ 323-666-6500), the television channel that produces and provides access to public programming, has its headquarters and studio facilities at 4401 Sunset Blvd. Free tours of the small studio, which focuses on educational rather than entertainment aspects of television, are offered by appointment. Besides learning the history of the studio lot, built in 1920, you'll also get insight into what happens in a sound studio and other departments. In LA, KCET is received on Channel 28.

MELROSE AVE (MAP 10)

Until a few years ago, Melrose was LA's epicenter of coolness and *the* place for eccentric fashions spawned by the drug-induced creativity of its avant-garde designers. Unfortunately, the wheel of trendiness has moved on, taking some of Melrose's edge with it, as mainstream (the Gap) and even downscale shops have moved in. This is not to say that Melrose isn't fun anymore. The section between La Brea Blvd and Fairfax Ave, especially, still has fabled restaurants and unique boutiques just weird enough to confirm every LA cliché ever concocted.

Don't even bother showing up before noon on any day, and if you can, come on Saturday when you'll see magenta-and-lime-haired grunge rockers, skinhead motorcyclists, pierced-nosed headbangers and Armani-clad record execs dazzling wide-eyed tourists. Wild shop windows and freakishly colorful facades reflect the diversity of humankind. And it should be noted: for a stark contrast to the trendy frenzy that is Melrose, most residents on the surrounding side streets are Orthodox Jews.

Some stores of the 'Only in LA' variety continue to maintain a strong presence. **Condomania** (☎ 323-933-7865), 7306 Melrose Ave, has an amusing and extensive collection of sexual toys and anything you'll ever need to wrap 'Mr Pudgey.' Across the street at 7325 Melrose Ave, **Off the Wall** (☎ 323-930-1185) specializes in 'antiques and weird stuff' – and they're not kidding. Stepping into this chaotic mini-warehouse feels like entering a movie studio prop room: Depression-era radios balance next to cardboard armchairs. A life-sized plastic cow grazes near the original revolving-door entrance of the Brown Derby, a legendary LA restaurant. Though the place seems like a museum, everything is for sale.

The motto of **Wound & Wound** (☎ 323-653-6703), 7374 Melrose Ave, is 'We do not stop playing because we grow old; we grow old because we stop playing.' Take that to heart as you browse through an incredible assortment of wind-up toys and music boxes, antique to brand-new, guarded over by a stern but amiable proprietor.

Keep going till you get to 7574 Melrose Ave, a store whose innocent name, **Scents from Above**, may make you think of soaps, oils and aromatherapy. Well, they have those, but the sign 'Must be 18+' should tip you. Walk into the back room and you'll find edible underwear, blow-up dolls, X-rated videos, erotic lingerie and vibrators in all shapes and sizes (don't bring grandma).

For other Melrose stores, including those selling vintage fashions, club clothing and music, see the Shopping chapter.

WEST HOLLYWOOD (MAP 10)

West Hollywood is one of LA's hippest areas, teeming with nightclubs, restaurants and elegant hotels, many of them legends. The Pacific Design Center and numerous galleries add an artsy touch, and trendy shops cater to fashion slaves from all over the city. West Hollywood is also the heart of LA's gay and lesbian community, which makes up one third of the area's 36,000 residents. June's 'Christopher Street Pride Parade' attracts a quarter of a million people to Santa Monica Blvd, and the festivities on Halloween are not to be missed.

West Hollywood was incorporated as a city in 1984 as a result of an unlikely alliance between (mostly Jewish) senior citizens and the gay and lesbian population. Statistically, about one third of the residents are over the

Body Modifications

They say beauty is only skin deep, and many Angelenos can tell you from personal experience that, indeed, this is true. From full-body tattoos to collagen-injected lips, Los Angeles is America's body shop, ready and willing to provide whatever modifications you need to fit into the mold of your choice.

For a relatively subtle form of rebellion, try a piercing at one of LA's many studios. While a nose ring may be enough to shock your grandmother, there are plenty of other piercing options available, including eyebrows, nipples and, of course, genitalia. Piercing studios abound, but sensitive types may want to try Funny Farm (Map 9; ☎ 323-913-7043) at 4651 Melbourne Ave in Los Feliz/Hollywood.

If you feel you can't hit the beach without a little color, ink-wielding artists abound throughout the city – check out some of these tattoo studios for the best in tinted flesh. Celebrity entries include The Purple Panther (☎ 323-882-8165), 7560 W Sunset Blvd, where Dave Navarro of the Red Hot Chili Peppers was inked, and LA Tattoo (☎ 323-463-3919), 6700 Hollywood Blvd, which left its mark on Barbed Wire's post-apocalyptic bad girl, Pamela Anderson (Lee). Others to look into include Body Electric Tattoo (☎ 323-954-0408), 7274½ Melrose Ave; Art & Soul Tattoo, 2604 S Robertson Blvd; and Bert Grimms Tattooing (☎ 562-432-9304), 22 S Chestnut Place in Long Beach, LA County's first tattoo parlor (purportedly Bonnie Parker was once a client). Of course, if you spot some local color you really like, just ask the proud owner about the artist. Be sure to observe several artists' work, as well as the shop's overall cleanliness and professionalism, before committing to a tattoo. Even if you are on a budget, this is one area where you probably won't want to skimp.

age of 55; recent Russian Jewish immigrants account for another 12%.

West Hollywood's **Convention and Visitors' Bureau** (☎ 310-289-2525, 800-368-6020, fax 310-289-2529) is at 8687 Melrose Ave, suite M26, on the mezzanine level in the Pacific Design Center. Hours are 8:30 am to 5:30 pm weekdays.

Sunset Strip

On Sunset Blvd, wrote Henry Miller in 1945, a visitor will discover:

...eurythmic dancing, ballroom dancing, tap dancing, artistic photography, ordinary photography, lousy photography, electro-fever treatment, internal douche treatment, ultraviolet-ray treatment, elocution lessons, psychic readings, institutes of religion, astrological demonstrations, hands read, feet manicured, elbows massaged, faces lifted... flatulence dissipated, business improved, limousines rented, the future made clear, the war made comprehensible, octane made higher and butane lower...Chinese herbs are very good for you, and without a Coca-Cola life is unthinkable.

More than half a century has passed, and everything – and nothing – has changed. The characters are new, but the street scene is as eclectic as ever, swarming with dancers, photographers, and medical and spiritual charlatans. If anything is truly new, it's that the

If you get a tattoo and decide you don't like it, there's no reason to worry. Check the LA Yellow Pages or www.plastic-surgery.net for a referral to the laser surgeon nearest you. They'll clean that ink up in no time – for a price (and a little more pain).

Have you suspected that all those bronzed bods baking in the California sunshine are a little too good to be true? You're right. LA may be the only place on earth where women routinely write off breast enhancement on their taxes as a 'business expense.' You didn't think all those model/actresses were born that way, did you? Body sculpting isn't just for the famous in this town, although being rich certainly helps. Cosmetic surgeons performing liposuction, facial sculpting, buttock lifts and other services are waiting to transform *you* into the next Miss America – or, more likely, the next Ms May.

Men are not immune to that desire for perfection. LA's plastic surgeons offer a gamut of services to keep you looking like a decathlon athlete even if you never leave the tanning salon. Hair implants are only the beginning; tummy tucks, biceps enhancement and pectoral implants will surely attract the mate of your dreams. And, for the gift that keeps on giving, finish it all off with penile augmentation surgery, to 'gain length *and* thickness.' It's just the thing to go with your Prince Albert piercing.

It's no use wondering whether public health in Los Angeles would improve if more of the city's doctors were dedicated to healing the sick rather than beautifying the healthy, just as there's little point in musing that LA's art scene would rise to greater heights if more local geniuses painted on canvas instead of skin. Such weighty concerns inspire little pause for thought in the City of Angels. This is a place where the body is not a temple – it's an investment. Enjoy the scenery!

Paige R Penland

The fabulous West Hollywood cheerleaders

DAVID PEEVERS

fabled Strip – Sunset Blvd between Laurel Canyon Blvd and Doheny Drive – has become the billboard capital of the world. These enormous and imaginative vanity boards are one-of-a-kind placards for new movies, new recordings, wannabe stars, and recently, anti-smoking campaigns.

As you travel west on Sunset Blvd (coming from central Hollywood or Downtown), you know you've reached the Strip when you see an impressive Norman castle looming above the road to your right. This is the **Château Marmont Hotel**, 8221 Sunset Blvd, built in 1927 and best known as the place where comedian John Belushi died of a drug overdose. In years past, such luminaries as Greta Garbo and Howard Hughes (who is said to have used binoculars to watch bikini-clad swimmers from his suite) were regular guests.

The Places to Stay, Places to Eat and Entertainment chapters of this book have details on many of the establishments along the Sunset Strip. From a sightseeing standpoint, as you continue west, these are some of the places to keep an eye out for:

The Argyle, 8358 Sunset Blvd
A glorious monument to Art Deco, the Argyle (1931) is an elegant hotel that was formerly known as Sunset Towers and the St James' Club. Old-time Hollywood stars such as John Wayne and Errol Flynn rented rooms here; it's also a frequent movie location, featured in *Pretty Woman* and *The Player*. According to myth, Wayne once kept a cow in his 12th-floor penthouse.

Thunder Roadhouse, 8371 Sunset Blvd
Patrick Swayze and Mickey Rourke are rumored to have bought their Harley Davidsons at this cycle shop cum biker bar. Its owners include actors Dennis Hopper and Peter Fonda and country singer Dwight Yoakam.

Hyatt Hotel, 8401 Sunset Blvd
Ostensibly just another installment in this chain of contemporary luxury hotels, this facility was actually a favorite haunt of rock & rollers in the '70s. Dubbed 'Riot House,' the action here was wild indeed. Led Zeppelin once rented six floors and rode motorcycles in the hallways, according to Art Fein's *LA Musical History Tour*, which also reports that Jim Morrison was kicked out for hanging out of a window by his fingertips.

House of Blues, 8430 Sunset Blvd
This is part of the national chain in which Dan Aykroyd is a primary investor. If you can get in (your best strategy is to come for dinner and then stay), you're guaranteed a night of great music and celebrity watching.

Comedy Store, 8433 Sunset Blvd
There are three separate rooms to showcase both young and established stand-up talent. David Letterman, Robin Williams and Roseanne Barr (as she then called herself) were relative unknowns when they first appeared here. Originally the club was called Ciro's and was a famous and somewhat shady hangout in the '40s and '50s.

Mondrian Hotel, 8440 Sunset Blvd
Signage is apparently considered too garish for the Mondrian; look for the two giant door sculptures anchored in the driveway. Inside you'll find some of the finest in interior design, providing a perfect backdrop for all the city's beautiful who gather here. The air is even more refined in the Sky Bar on the top floor, currently the hottest ticket in town. It's so exclusive, newspapers have done stories on its doormen. Don't even think about getting in without being on 'the list.'

Sunset Marquis, 1200 N Alta Loma Rd
A half-block off the Strip, this is a designer hotel for rock stars such as Eric Clapton, Billy Joel and Bruce Springsteen, who can use the property's private recording studio and have a drink in its ground-floor bar.

Tower Records, 8801 Sunset Blvd
To bolster its claim as the world's largest record/compact disc store, Tower added an annex to market its complete stock. It's open daily until midnight.

Viper Room, 8852 Sunset Blvd
This is the notorious nightclub where young actor River Phoenix died of drug-related complications in 1993. Owned by actor Johnny Depp, it's a favorite hangout for musicians and other hyper show-biz types.

The next couple of blocks on the north side of Sunset read like a 'where's where' of LA rock history: **Whisky A Go Go** at 8901 Sunset Blvd; **The Roxy** at 9009 Sunset Blvd; the **Rainbow Bar & Grill** at 9015 Sunset Blvd; and the **Key Club**, the former Gazzarri's, at 9039 Sunset Blvd. The Doors, Jimi Hendrix, Bob Marley, Bruce Springsteen and Van Halen are among the many who have performed at these clubs. And if you're into Hollywood history, it was at the Rainbow (then the Villa Nova) that actress Marilyn Monroe and baseball star Joe DiMaggio met on a 'blind' date in 1953. For details on these clubs, see the Entertainment chapter.

To see where serious musicians buy their instruments, head to the **Guitar Center**, a giant store at 7425 Sunset Blvd (Map 9). Its walls are lined floor to ceiling with any guitar imaginable – acoustic, electric, bass, plastic – in all shapes, materials, colors and prices. In the basement is the vintage collection where prized treasures like Martin guitars cost up to $10,000. Upstairs are the drum and percussion departments. The staff is super friendly, even if all you want to do is browse.

Rock Walk of Fame

LA does not just have a Hollywood Walk of Fame and a Porno Walk of Fame (see below) but also a Rock Walk of Fame, right in the entrance of the Guitar Center store (Map 9). Immortalized in concrete are the hands of legends such as BB King, ZZ Top, Steely Dan, the Doobie Brothers and dozens more.

Porno Walk of Fame

The Porno Walk of Fame, right outside the Tomkat gay movie theater at 7734 Santa Monica Blvd, is not where you'll want to take your children. Even those who wouldn't touch a porn movie with a 10-inch pole know the names of such 'divas' and studs as Linda

Lovelace and Harry Reems of *Deep Throat* fame, or Marilyn Chambers from *Behind the Green Door*. Voyeuristic types expecting cement prints of performers' signature body parts will be disappointed. The only extremities immortalized in cement are the hands and feet of about a dozen hard-core legends.

The Design District

At the heart of a triangle framed by Santa Monica, Beverly and La Cienega Blvds is the Pacific Design Center (☎ 310-657-0800), 8687 Melrose Ave at San Vicente Blvd. This giant glass block, known to locals as the 'Blue Whale,' contains more than 200 showrooms in its 1.2 million sq feet of floor space. The public may browse the furnishings and accessories, but a better way to see the Design Center is on a free one-hour tour (offered weekdays at 10 am; call ahead). Exhibitions of cutting-edge design and architecture are shown in the Murray Feldman Gallery.

Surrounding streets - mainly Melrose Ave and Robertson and Beverly Blvds – are called the Avenues of Design because they contain some 300 additional design shops and showrooms. There are another three dozen art galleries in the vicinity, including the **Margo Leavin Gallery** (☎ 310-273-0603), 812 N Robertson Blvd, unmistakable for Claes Oldenburg's *Knife Slicing Through Wall* sculpture, which makes a statement in its facade.

The Schindler House

A must-see for Modernist-architecture fans is the Schindler House (☎ 323-651-1510), 835 N Kings Rd, 2 blocks north of Melrose Ave. Viennese immigrant architect Rudolph Schindler (1887-1953), a Frank Lloyd Wright disciple, built the house and studio in 1921 and lived here until he died in 1953. In the 1920s, it was a gathering place for intellectuals, including novelist Theodore Dreiser and composer John Cage. Schindler's house has Craftsman-style elements, such as large rooms and canopied outdoor sleeping areas, but the architect also provided prototypes for design elements that have since become staples of California architecture. The flat-roofed building is divided into stark studio-like rooms with concrete walls and flooring;

one side of each room has a glass front opening onto a courtyard with sliding doors. In 1925, Schindler shared the house with his associate Richard Neutra, also an Austrian architect.

Heavily altered after Schindler's death, the house was meticulously restored to its original state by the Friends of the Schindler House (FOSH). Since 1994 it has been jointly maintained by FOSH and the Austrian Museum of Applied Arts (MAK) and functions as a think tank for current issues in art and architecture through public lectures, performances, workshops, symposia and exhibitions. The MAK Center for Art & Architecture (Schindler House) is open 11 am to 6 pm Wednesday to Sunday. Admission is $5; free docent tours are offered on weekends only.

Mid-City

This section describes the area wedged between the Westside (discussed in the next section) and Downtown, north of the 10 Fwy but south of Hollywood. Its principal artery is Wilshire Blvd, which cuts east to west over a total length of 16 miles. Once a path followed by the Yangna Indians between their village in the Elysian Hills and the tar pits of Hancock Park, it was extended 16 miles from the city to the sea in the late 19th century and named for local entrepreneur H Gaylord Wilshire. En route, it passes through an eclectic variety of neighborhoods: Koreatown, Hancock Park, Miracle Mile, the Fairfax District, Beverly Hills, Westwood and Santa Monica, terminating at the Pacific Ocean.

MACARTHUR PARK AREA (MAP 5)

Located just over a mile west of Downtown, MacArthur Park (named for General Douglas MacArthur) is a likely location to begin a westbound exploration of the Mid-City district via Wilshire Blvd. The park itself has been a household name since Richard Harris released the ridiculously epic pop song of the same name some 25 years ago. Revitalized by the 1993 opening of a Metro Red Line terminal, this former swampland is now

at the heart of a largely Latino and Asian community. Come in the daytime to see 80 species of trees and shrubs, a dozen city-commissioned avant-garde sculptures and a small lake with paddleboats. On a sunny afternoon the park is one of LA's coolest spots for a picnic; though as with most inner-city parks, it's best avoided at night, as you may encounter drug traffic and its related violence.

Grier Musser Museum

The small Grier Musser Museum (☎ 213-413-1814), 403 Bonnie Brae St, is located on a once-fashionable street in one of the district's few surviving Queen Anne-style homes. On display is an eclectic collection of antiques, furniture, collectibles and curios. The museum has erratic hours, so call ahead. Posted hours are noon to 4 pm Wednesday to Friday, from 11 am Saturday. Admission is $5, $3 for students and seniors, $2.50 for children.

KOREATOWN (MAP 2)

Just west of MacArthur Park is the heart of Koreatown, an enclave dominated by about 70,000 immigrants from Korea and their offspring. It's a steadily growing community, both in number and physical borders, with expansion especially creeping north toward Hollywood. Very much a self-contained universe, streets sport store signs and billboards in Korean letters, restaurants serve Korean delicacies, and there are many Korean banks, churches, schools and other businesses. Many Koreans earn a living as small-business owners of clothing stores, grocery and convenience markets, and gas stations, not just in Koreatown but in other communities, notably in South Central. This has caused rivalry and resentment between African Americans and Koreans, which reached an apex during the 1992 riots, when more than 2000 Korean-owned businesses fell victim to the raging mob. Much healing and rebuilding has taken place since, and today sections of Koreatown boast spiffed-up sidewalks and fashionable new malls and grocery stores.

The Koreatown area contains dozens of gorgeous historic churches, some of which are described in detail in Tour IV of the Los Angeles Architecture chapter.

Wiltern Theater

This lovely Art Deco theater, inside a fabulous Zigzag Moderne high-rise called the Pellissier Building (1931), gets it name from its location – at the southeast corner of Wilshire Blvd and Western Blvd. It has the same turquoise facade as the Bullocks Wilshire, about a mile east. In 1982, its date with the wrecking ball already set, the Wiltern received a last-minute stay of execution from the LA Conservancy, then got a new lease on life from a preservation-minded developer who bought and restored it to original specifications.

Ambassador Hotel

Opened in 1922 and one of LA's earliest and grandest hotels, the Ambassador Hotel now sits abandoned in a lot at 3400 Wilshire Blvd after closing its doors in 1990. In its heyday, it could accommodate 3000 guests – many of LA's leading families, movie greats and presidents among them. The most fashionable boogied to big band music at the Coconut Grove nightclub. In 1968, the hotel gained notoriety when Sirhan Sirhan assassinated Robert Kennedy there. (RFK had just received the Democratic presidential nomination.) No buyer has been found and it looks as if another landmark will be allowed to crumble. Meanwhile, film crews use it for location shots.

Bullocks Wilshire Department Store

When the Bullocks Wilshire Department Store, 3050 Wilshire Blvd, opened in 1929, it was an overnight sensation. On opening day, hundreds of thousands of people crammed through the doors of what is often regarded as the first suburban department store in the USA. A prime example of 1920s Art Deco, it features terra-cotta walls clad with copper and a central tower jutting skyward from the five-floor base structure, which gives it the stature and appearance of a public building.

Boasting a large parking lot, Bullocks Wilshire was the first store to cater to customers arriving by car. For LA's poshest it became *the* place to shop and cap successful sprees with afternoon tea in the 5th-floor tearoom, a tradition that survived until the store closed in 1992. No longer located in a fashionable location, it was looted in that year's riots, causing its owners to abandon it shortly thereafter. Fortunately, this lovely landmark was rescued by Southwestern University in 1997. The building now functions as its School of Law library and administrative offices; interior decorations remain intact. According to a public affairs spokeswoman, public tours may be offered in the future. Call ☎ 323-738-6731 for information.

St Sophia Cathedral

St Sophia (☎ 323-737-2424), 1324 S Normandie Ave, has been called the most beautiful cathedral in the world; its opulence certainly made us feel like we were walking into a giant's treasure chest, spilling over with gold, crystal and jewels. The central place of worship for Southern California's Greek Orthodox population, this 850-seat church perfectly illustrates symbiosis of modern technology and ancient architecture. Completed in 1952, its Byzantine-style interior is devoid of supporting pillars, allowing an unobstructed view of the ornately carved, gilded altar screen. Every square inch of the sumptuous interior is swathed with expertly executed murals and illuminated by muted light streaming through radiant stained-glass windows. Crystal chandeliers from the former Czechoslovakia provide additional light sources.

St Sophia was the brainchild of Greek immigrant and movie theater mogul Charles P Skouros. Skouros almost single-handedly raised the money, then hired the best craftsmen and artists from the theater industry to build his vision. His goal was for the church 'to be so grand and so beautifully appointed that when our people come to pray, they will be uplifted and feel closer to God.' See for yourself if he succeeded. Open 10 am to 2 pm daily, except Thursday and Sunday when there's a service at 10 am; free admission.

MIRACLE MILE DISTRICT (MAP 10)

The stretch of Wilshire Blvd between La Brea and Fairfax Aves earned the epithet

'Miracle Mile' after a far-seeing entrepreneur, AW Ross, bought previously empty land beside the Rancho La Brea Tar Pits in 1920 and turned it into an important business and shopping district by the early 1930s. Many of Downtown LA's famous retailers opened branches here, but by the 1960s other areas, most notably the suburban shopping malls, put an end to the miracle. Today, the strip is also known as 'Museum Row.'

La Brea Tar Pits

We'll start by clearing up a common misconception: the La Brea Tar Pits are not filled with tar but with asphalt. While tar is a by-product of the destructive destilling of coal or peat, asphalt is the lowest grade of crude oil. This oil formed from marine plankton deposited in an ocean basin between 5 and 25 million years ago and gathered in a subterranean oil field. Over the past 40,000 years, this asphalt seeped to the surface, which accounts for the gooey slick filling the pits today. It was 1906 before scientists realized that the bubbling ooze had acted like flypaper, entrapping animal and plant life during the Pleistocene Ice Age, 40,000 to 10,000 years ago. The large Lake Pit outside the Page Museum at La Brea Discoveries (see below) graphically illustrates this process with fiberglass models of a mammoth family. Pit excavations have yielded more than 1 million fossilized skeleton parts, including those of long-extinct mammals such as saber-toothed cats, ground sloths, mammoths and mastodons, along with 200 different bird, reptile, insect, and plant species.

Excavations still take place – usually from July to mid-September – when visitors may observe the process from the Pit 91 Visitors Observation Station from 10 am to 4 pm Wednesday to Sunday; admission is free. For information, call ☎ 323-934-7243.

Page Museum at La Brea Discoveries

Tar pit discoveries are exhibited in the adjacent Page Museum at La Brea Discoveries (☎ 323-934-7243, www.tarpits.org), 5801 Wilshire Blvd, opened in 1977 and named after its founder, a local millionaire and philanthropist. The museum lets you study the fossilized skeletons of long-extinct mammals that once roamed the LA Basin. The fierce saber-toothed cat (incidentally the state fossil of California) was capable of killing much larger animals, including young mammoths, with its giant jaw and dagger-like fangs. Also here are a mastodon and a 15-foot imperial mammoth with tusks of royal proportions. Both are ancestors of today's elephants. The most prevalent animal, the dire wolf, is given its own 'Wall of Fame' – 404 mounted skulls. The least represented species is Homo sapiens; the only human remains found are those of a young woman believed to have been murdered about 9000 years ago.

Nearby is the glass-encased Paleontology Laboratory where scientists in white robes fuss over an astounding assortment of bones. New discoveries are carefully cleaned, identified, cataloged and stored. But the biggest crowds gather for the film starring everyone's favorite reptile: the dinosaurs. This is especially ironic because dinosaurs had long become extinct by the time the La Brea Tar Pits had formed; in any case, dinosaurs avoided LA altogether. But catering to the current dino-craze, the museum continually shows this film explaining the daily life of these giant lizards with surprisingly realistically recreated animals and natural environments.

Museum hours are 9:30 am to 5 pm Tuesday to Friday, open at 10 am Saturday and Sunday (also open Monday during the summer). Admission is $6, $3.50 for students or

I've fallen and I can't get up!

JIM CORWIN

seniors, $2 for children ages five to 12; free the first Tuesday of each month.

Los Angeles County Museum of Art (LACMA)

Just west of the tar pits in Hancock Park is LACMA (☎ 323-857-6000), 5905 Wilshire Blvd, considered one of the leading art museums in the US (and, indeed, the world) for its size and variety, not to mention the importance of its works. Several buildings surround a central courtyard. Largest is the four-level Ahmanson Building with a staggering permanent collection encompassing art, sculptures and decorative arts from Europe, Asia and America. Highlights of the latter include works by George Bellows, John Singer Sargent, Mary Cassat, Winslow Homer and Diego Rivera. But the collection is especially strong in Western art, from Italy's early Renaissance to modern masters like Picasso, Kandinsky, Rothko and David Hockney.

Also on display are 12 centuries of ancient and Islamic art with pieces from Egypt, Greece, Rome, Turkey and Iran. The museum's assemblage of Southeast Asian art encompasses stone and bronze sculpture, painting and decorative arts. Its Far Eastern section has works from as early as the Neolithic period (400 to 1800 BC) as well as items from the Imperial and Song dynasties and a replica of a Ming-period scholar's studio. A highlight of the Pavilion for Japanese Art is the collection of rare Shin'enkan temple paintings.

With more than 150,000 works, LACMA's collection is so huge that only 5% of its treasures can be exhibited at any one time. In addition, the museum mounts several special exhibits annually, drawn from its own collection, and also hosts high-caliber visiting shows (for example, Picasso, Van Gogh and Diego Rivera). The 500-seat Bing Center auditorium offers a film series, concerts and the museum store.

In late 1998, LACMA took over the space of a former May Co department store a few blocks west of the original museum at the corner of Fairfax Ave and Wilshire Blvd. Called LACMA West, the annex hosted a world-class traveling Van Gogh exhibit as its inaugural show. One floor is used by the Southwest Museum (see Mt Washington & Highland Park earlier in this chapter).

Museum hours are noon to 8 pm Monday, Tuesday and Thursday, to 9 pm Friday, 11 am to 8 pm weekends. Admission is $7, $5 for seniors over 62 and students, $1 for children ages six to 17.

Carole & Barry Kaye Museum of Miniature Art

Have you ever wished you could gather up all the most wonderful sights from your travels and assemble them in one spot? It's the kind of fantasy Carole Kaye turned into – sort of – reality with her Museum of Miniature Art (☎ 323-937-6464, www.museumofminiatures .com), 5900 Wilshire Blvd. About 750 artists and craftspeople have meticulously replicated some 350 palaces, houses, natural environs and more on a scale of 12:1.

Thankfully, the kitsch factor has been kept to a minimum, and most exhibits enchant with historical detail and superb craftsmanship. Among the most imposing miniatures are the 12-x-8-foot **Forum Romanum** consisting of 51 separate buildings, the 10½-foot-tall **Vatican** and France's **Fontainebleau Palace**, which took a team of artists 1½ years to finish. On the other end of the size spectrum are microminiatures such as a minuscule sculpture of Charlie Chaplin leaning on a walking stick made of a spider's web. Other highlights include the **Titanic** made from 75,000 toothpicks and a football field with players made from chewing-gum wrappers. Museum hours are from 10 am to 5 pm Tuesday to Saturday, from 11 am Sunday. Admission is $7.50, $6.50 for students up to 21 and seniors over 65, $3 for children.

Petersen Automotive Museum

LA's love affair with the automobile is celebrated at the Petersen Automotive Museum (☎ 323-930-2277, www.petersen.org), 6060 Wilshire Blvd, named after the publisher who provided the seed money for the $40 million facility. It is housed in a former department store that has been imaginatively converted into three floors of exhibition space.

Even non-car buffs will enjoy the ground-floor exhibit, which leads you through a mock streetscape of LA in the '20s and '30s while engagingly showing how LA's growth into a megacity is intricately tied to the evolution of the automobile. Several inventions, including gas stations, billboards, mini-malls, drive-in restaurants and movie theaters, were spawned as cars became the commonplace method of transport. Expansive galleries on the 2nd floor are devoted to rotating exhibits, which may feature cars owned by celebrities or those used in movies, vintage motorcycles, muscle cars or a fleet of Duesenbergs. The 3rd floor houses a 'discovery center,' which teaches kids science by way of the automobile. Museum hours are 10 am to 6 pm, closed Monday. Admission is $7, $5 for students and seniors, $3 for children ages five to 12.

FAIRFAX DISTRICT (MAP 10)
The spine of LA's principal Jewish neighborhood is Fairfax Ave – sometimes affectionately called 'Kosher Canyon' – between Santa Monica and Wilshire Blvds. Though many liberal Jews have scattered to the four winds within the metropolis, Orthodox and Hassidic Jews (who moved here from East LA's Boyle Heights as new Latino immigrants flooded into that area) maintain a strong presence. There are lots of Yeshivas (gender-segregated Orthodox day schools) as well as scores of delis, Kosher butchershops, antique furniture stores and other small businesses.

For visitors, the main point of interest is the **Farmers' Market** (☎ 323-933-9211), 6333 W 3rd St. Several of the 150-plus well-established vendors offer an international array of hot and cold foods as well as fresh produce and unique gift items. It's also a great place to grab a freshly baked pastry and a cup of coffee or fruit juice, and spend time people-watching (also see Places to Eat). A bit north of the Farmers' Market, **CBS Television City** (☎ 323-852-2624) is at 7800 Beverly Blvd. Offices of network executives dominate the structure, but a handful of game shows are produced here. Just south, toward Olympic Blvd, Fairfax Ave

becomes dominated by Ethiopian immigrants, numbering about 35,000. There are several excellent Ethiopian restaurants here (see Places to Eat).

Westside

Ask five people what they consider to be LA's 'Westside' and you'll get five different answers. Some will say it encompasses everything west of La Cienega Blvd; for others, the border is the 405 Fwy; some even include anything west of Downtown. In this book, we have defined Westside as the stretch of communities that separates the coastal communities (Santa Monica, Venice, Marina del Rey) from Hollywood. From north to south, Westside consists of Bel Air, Brentwood, Westwood, Beverly Hills and Culver City.

BEVERLY HILLS (MAP 11)
Everywhere in the world, the mere mention of Beverly Hills conjures an image of fame and wealth. TV and film have done their part in reinforcing this image. As TV's *Beverly Hillbillies*, Buddy Ebsen and Irene Ryan discovered the pleasures and pitfalls of mansion life. Julia Roberts learned the joys of a Rodeo Drive shopping spree and a suite at the Regent Beverly Wilshire in *Pretty Woman*. And Robin Leach's *Lifestyles of the Rich and Famous* probably spends more time in Beverly Hills than in any other location.

The reality of Beverly Hills is not so different from the myth. Stylish and sophisticated, this city-within-a-city is indeed a place where the rich and famous frolic. Rodeo Drive is lined with a veritable Who's Who of fashion designers' shops. Opulent manors face manicured grounds on palm-shaded avenues winding gently uphill on the north side of Santa Monica Blvd, while south of Wilshire Blvd are the more simple, but no less elegant, bungalows of the merely upper class.

Golden Triangle
An exploration of Beverly Hills should start in the 'Golden Triangle' district, bordered on the south by Wilshire Blvd, on the northwest

by Santa Monica Blvd and on the northeast by Cañon Drive. Rodeo Drive cuts through the heart of the Triangle, beginning at the front doors of the Regent Beverly Wilshire Hotel at 9500 Wilshire Blvd. Other streets to walk are Wilshire Blvd, Beverly Drive and Camden Drive. For further details, see Places to Stay, Places to Eat and Shopping.

Rodeo Drive

Connecting Santa Monica and Wilshire Blvds, Rodeo Drive is a 3-block artery of style that to many visitors represents the holy grail of fashion and ranks high on their list of must-sees. But unless you were born with a trust fund or feel like flagrantly maxing out your credit cards, you'll find little to do here other than sauntering down one side of the street and up the other. Lined up in a glimmering row are the Pradas, Guccis and Armanis of this world, precious bastions of good taste supplied by the fickle minds of 30-something designers halfway around the world.

Julia Roberts' humiliating experience in *Pretty Woman* may come to mind when you have to deal with waifish salesgirls with an attitude that belies their rather humble

Max out your credit cards on Rodeo Drive.

LEE FOSTER

station in life. Venturing inside one of these emporia will put you close to noble woods and polished marble arranged in Zen-like minimalism. Price tags will be hard to find, the unspoken maxim being 'if you have to ask, you can't afford it.' And instead of seeing a celebrity – who usually arrive after shop hours – you're more likely to be sidling up to T-shirted tourists from Dubuque or Tokyo.

With a few exceptions, the architecture along Rodeo Drive is rather plain. An exception is the **Anderton Court**, a Zigzag construction by Frank Lloyd Wright at 328 Rodeo Drive that is not considered one of his best. The Rodeo Collection, 421 N Rodeo Drive, a recessed multilevel shopping mall, is quite nice as well. Most people gravitate to Two Rodeo Drive, which resembles a Tuscan hillside village to all those unfamiliar with the real thing. Cynics claim it wasn't created to provide an aesthetic anchor to Rodeo Drive but rather to increase retail space, which goes for a bloated $300 per sq foot. The only truly classy structure here is the Regent Beverly Wilshire Hotel whose sumptuous Italian Renaissance facade exudes a more authentic variety of Old World charm (see Places to Stay).

Curious Homes

If you venture farther north on Rodeo Drive, beyond Santa Monica Blvd, you'll quickly come across the **O'Neill House** (1989) at 507 Rodeo Drive. A freeform Art Nouveau structure in the tradition of Catalan architect Antonio Gaudí, it has art glass windows, mosaic tilework, skylights and stucco finish.

A few blocks west of Rodeo Drive is the **Spadena House**, 516 N Walden Drive, which is appropriately nicknamed the 'Witch's House.' Built in 1921 as a silent-film set and office in Culver City, it was moved here in the 1930s. With its pitched, thatched roof and a moat crossed by a wooden bridge, the house indeed looks like something conjured up by the Brothers Grimm.

Beverly Hills Civic Center

At the northeastern edge of the Golden Triangle along Santa Monica Blvd east of Crescent Drive is the sprawling Civic Center, anchored by the statuesque **City Hall**, 455 N Rexford Drive, a 1932 Spanish Renaissance concoction. It features a classical base topped by an eight-story tower with a gilded cupola. (This rather phallic type of architecture is typical of many public buildings from that era.) Also of note is the terra-cotta-embellished **Beverly Hills Post Office** (1933), nearby at the southeast corner of Cañon Drive and Santa Monica Blvd. City Hall is framed by contemporary buildings connected by oval courtyards, the result of a 1980s expansion. Part of the complex is the **Beverly Hills Library** (☎ 310-288-2200), 444 N Rexford Drive, one of the few places of real substance in this status-conscious city.

Academy of Motion Picture Arts and Sciences

With headquarters at 8949 Wilshire Blvd (☎ 310-247-3900), this is the organization that brings you the annual Academy Awards. Started by Douglas Fairbanks in 1927, the academy staged its first ceremonies (then called the Merit Awards) at the Roosevelt Hotel in Hollywood in 1929. At that time, only three awards – for best actor, actress and film – were given out. According to Hollywood lore, the prized trophy – the Oscar – got its rather mundane name from academy librarian and later executive director, Margaret Herrick, who innocently mentioned its faint resemblance to her uncle Oscar.

Center for Motion Picture Study

The Academy of Motion Picture Arts and Sciences maintains a remarkable reservoir of film history, the Center for Motion Picture Study (☎ 310-247-3000) at 333 S La Cienega Blvd. It's housed in the former Beverly Hills Waterworks, another project instigated by Douglas Fairbanks in the 1920s. The academy salvaged the crumbling Italian Romanesque facility in the late 1980s, then spent three years and $6 million breathing new life into this beautiful structure. The building now houses a staggering archive of 6 million still photographs, 20,000 books, 60,000 scripts, 1400 periodicals, 17,000 posters, production files on nearly 100,000 movies, and biographic files on more than 80,000 filmmakers.

Add to that the private collections of John Huston, Alfred Hitchcock and Mary Pickford.

The heart of this research facility is the noncirculating Margaret Herrick Library, which is open to the public, but with very tight security. Besides signing in and out, you must lock up your belongings and leave a photo ID. The special collections may only be viewed by prior appointment. Hours are 10 am to 5:30 pm weekdays, except Wednesday; admission is free.

Virginia Robinson Gardens

Virginia Robinson was the wife of department store magnate Harry Robinson. Their estate at 1008 Elden Way is one of the oldest in Beverly Hills (1911) and was bequeathed to the city upon her death in 1977. Covering more than 6 acres, its gardens are a symphony of terraced hillsides, flower-festooned patios, brick stairs and shaded footpaths. Some 1000 plant varieties are harmoniously tossed together in a profusion of color. Besides magnolias, roses and kafir lilies, there are 50 types of camellias, including one named in honor of Virginia. The huge palm garden boasts the largest grove of king palms outside of Australia. The 6000-sq-foot mansion, where the Robinsons once threw lavish parties for the Hollywood elite, has been left in the state of opulence enjoyed by the couple. It's open for viewing on guided tours by reservation only (☎ 310-276-5367) and costs $6, $3 for seniors, students and children over five.

Greystone Park & Mansion

Popular with wedding parties and film producers, the Greystone Park & Mansion (☎ 310-550-4654), 905 Loma Vista Drive, provides a restorative respite from city life. Its gardens, manicured to perfection, are tranquil (no playing or picnicking allowed) and offer lovely views of Beverly Hills. The mansion was built in 1928 by tycoon Edward L Doheny for his only son; it is off-limits to the public. The mansion's name was inspired by the material used in its construction, a rather drab blend of Indiana limestone walls topped by a Welsh slate roof. The Dohenys sold the huge estate in the mid-'50s and it has since been used primarily as a film location. Scenes from such blockbusters as *The Bodyguard*, *The Witches of Eastwick*, *All of Me*, *Ghostbusters* and *Indecent Proposal* were shot here. The grounds and gardens are open daily 9 am to 6 pm; admission is free.

Museum of Television and Radio

Contrary to its name, the Museum of Television and Radio (MTR; ☎ 310-786-1000, www.mtr.org), 465 N Beverly Drive, is not a traditional showcase of artifacts and exhibits, but a humongous archive preserving original works of two of the 20th century's most important media. Encompassing 90,000 programs spanning 75 years, the entire collection is accessible to museum visitors through a computerized library. This is the place to come to view the 1958 pilot of the *Zorro* TV series, Frank Sinatra footage from 1962, or interviews with James Dean.

At easy-to-use touchscreen terminals, you select programs by searching the archive by actor or entertainer name, by show title or by subject category. You will be handed a printout and escorted to one of about 60 private viewing consoles, where you access your choices by punching in a three-digit number. You can view portions or all of a program, fast forward to a particular frame, or watch the same scene over and over. Except when people are waiting, there's no limit on your time at the console.

The MTR, which opened up in 1996, is housed in a stunning building by Getty Center architect, Richard Meier, bearing his trademark architectural elements: travertine marble, blonde wall coverings, a starkly white environment with soaring open spaces and natural light surging in through huge windows.

The MTR is open Wednesday to Sunday noon to 5 pm (Thursday to 8 pm). Admission is $6 adults, $4 for seniors and students, $3 for children under 13.

Beverly Hills Hotel

Featured on the cover of the Eagles' *Hotel California* album, the Beverly Hills Hotel (☎ 310-887-2887), 9641 Sunset Blvd, is as revered in LA as the countless Hollywood legends who have cavorted there. Affectionately known as the 'Pink Palace,' this swank hotel – with its inimitable Polo Lounge and discreet bungalows – has served as unofficial hobnobbing headquarters of the power elite since 1912. In the '20s, it was Chaplin, Swanson and Valentino holding court in this Disney-esque version of the Alamo. By the '40s, the Polo Lounge was the notorious post-chukker hangout of the lords of the polo crowd, including Darryl F Zanuck, Spencer Tracy and Will Rogers. Marlene Dietrich had her own 7-x-8-foot bed installed in Bungalow 11, and Howard Hughes, the billionaire recluse, went progressively off his nut during 30 years of delusional semi-residence here.

By the time the '50s rolled around, genuine royalty began rubbing shoulders with such Hollywood aristocracy as Frank Sinatra's 'Rat Pack,' who boozed and brawled away long nights. Elizabeth Taylor bedded six of her eight husbands here in various bungalows. While filming *Let's Make Lo e*, Yves Montand and Marilyn Monroe were probably doing just that; Marilyn is also reported to have 'bungalowed' both JFK and RFK here as well.

By the '70s, the Pink Palace had lost its luster and the stars went elsewhere to frolic. For years, the hotel was tossed back and forth among financial titans, only to become – on its 75th birthday – another vessel in the fleet of its current owner, the Sultan of Brunei. Having spent an alleged $176 million to acquire it, the Sultan sank another $100 million into its restoration. When she reopened in 1995, the grand dame had regained her blush, lurid wink and ability to seduce the power players back to her stage. Scripts are once again read, and deals cut, by the pool where young starlets stretch languidly in the hopes of 'discovery.' (Also see Places to Stay.)

Self-Guided Tour of the Stars' Homes

It's on the winding, tree-lined streets that climb the Santa Monica Mountain foothills where you'll find the lavish estates of Beverly Hills' famous denizens, from Douglas

Fairbanks to Warren Beatty. Many of the sprawling Spanish haciendas, stately Tudor mansions and French Provençal farmhouses were and are home to celebrities that have shaped Hollywood history. This is where they live, frolic – and die. The area is most comfortably explored on a guided bus tour. (See Organized Tours in the Getting Around chapter for more information.)

If you have a car, you can save some money by doing your own touring. Maps to the stars' homes are hawked for a few dollars in souvenir shops and by street vendors positioned along Sunset and Santa Monica Blvds. Addresses of living stars change with some frequency, though, and these maps may not always be up to date.

We've put together our own tour of the glamorous, the notorious, the frivolous and the ostentatious. As you drive the winding streets, don't expect to actually see somebody famous. In many cases, you won't even see the actual homes; their privacy is preserved by huge walls, dense canopies of trees and security patrols. In fact, you can pretty much tell how rich or famous – or both – a resident is by the amount of security features, which can include robotic cameras, armed guards and fierce dogs. In general, stars don't like tourists pulling up to their mansions, but legally there's little they can do as long as you remain on public grounds. Finally, it goes without saying (but here it is anyway) that under no circumstances should you disturb the residents. Our tour takes about 2½ hours.

Start at the intersection of Sunset Blvd and Benedict Canyon, both of them rich turf for the star struck. Head north on the canyon road, turn right onto Summit Drive and proceed to the top. It was **Mary Pickford** and **Douglas Fairbanks** who first brought glamour to Beverly Hills when they built their hilltop home, Pickfair, at 1143 Summit Drive by expanding a hunting lodge owned by Fairbanks. The house itself is gone, demolished by later owner Pia Zadora, but the generous grounds are still visible through the gate. Just below, at 1085 Summit Drive (corner of Cove), is the Spanish-style former home of **Charlie Chaplin**, which got the nickname

'Breakaway House' because things were always falling apart. Rumor has it that a chintzy Chaplin hired studio carpenters to build it in their spare time. Only the driveway is visible.

Head back downhill, continue north on Benedict Canyon, then turn left on Green Acres Drive, which culminates outside the extraordinary 48,000-sq-foot estate built by comedian **Harold Lloyd** at 1740 Green Acres Drive. Lloyd lived here for 40 years until his death in 1971, but almost nothing of the lavish mansion with its 44 rooms and 26 bathrooms can be seen from the street (nor can you see the grounds' waterfall, Olympic-size pool and nine-hole golf course). In fact, even as you approach the gate, a camera will eerily zoom around to follow your every move – just smile and wave.

Backtrack to Benedict Canyon, continue north to Cielo Drive and turn left, which takes you into a narrow side canyon. The densely canopied driveway at 10048 Cielo Drive leads to the house where followers of Satanist Charles Manson butchered actress **Sharon Tate** (highly pregnant with a child from husband, Roman Polanski) and four other victims on August 9, 1969. The story goes that Manson had ordered the killings because he wanted to scare record producer Terry Melcher into furthering his own singing career; Melcher had lived in the house prior to Tate and Polanski.

Just off Cielo Drive is Bella Drive, a steep unkempt road leading up to Falcon Lair, the fortress-like former residence of **Rudolph Valentino**. Unfortunately, its current residents managed to have the access road declared private, making it off-limits to the public. Head back down to 1579 Benedict Canyon, the house where 1950s 'Superman,' **George Reeves**, died in an apparent suicide in 1959, supposedly because he was despondent over his waning career.

Return south on Benedict Canyon, turn right on Lexington Rd, then right on Whittier Drive and left on Monovale Drive. The house at 144 Monovale Drive was the **Elvis Presley** LA residence from 1967 to 1975; you can glimpse parts of it through the fence. Farther on, Monovale Drive becomes Carolwood Drive with the comparatively modest house at 245 Carolwood Drive previously occupied by **Burt Reynolds** and **Loni Anderson** and Beatle **George Harrison** before that. More impressive are the two homes next door at 265 and 275 Carolwood Drive, whose merely rich – but not famous – owners have adorned their front lawns with several amazing modern sculptures, partly visible through the gate and over the wall. Turn around, then follow Carolwood Drive south to Sunset Blvd.

The house at 10100 Sunset is where bombshell **Jayne Mansfield** once resided. It was nicknamed the 'Pink Palace' (not to be confused with the Beverly Hills Hotel) because she had everything, down to the sinks, fireplace and swimming pool, painted pink and in the shape of a heart. Rumor has it that the crack in the heart carved into the driveway cement happened at the exact moment she was decapitated in a car accident. The villa's current owner is Engelbert Humperdinck. The impressive mansion behind the Pink Palace is called **Owlwood** and was at one time or other occupied by Marilyn Monroe, Sonny and Cher, and Tony Curtis.

Heading west on Sunset, turn left into Charing Cross Rd, and watch out for bunnies as you make your way past Hugh Hefner's **Playboy Mansion**, 10236 Charing Cross Rd, its driveway guarded by a Madonna sculpture. The mansion is big, but not as big as the

chateau of TV producer **Aaron Spelling,** at 594 N Mapleton Drive at Club View, next to Holmby Park (follow Charing Cross, then go left on Mapleton to the end). Spelling's otherworldly digs are commensurate with his extraordinary success, including credits like *Charlie's Angels, The Love Boat, Dynasty, Beverly Hills 90210* and *Melrose Place.* The partly visible cream-colored mansion allegedly has 123 rooms and at one time was inhabited (not counting domestics) only by Spelling and his wife, Candy, and their children, Randy and Tori – the latter known best for her role as Donna on TV's *Beverly Hills 90210.* While here, also note the house at 595 Mapleton Drive, an off-white seemingly windowless cube, which takes minimalism to its extreme.

Work your way back to Sunset Blvd, turn left, then head north (right) through the gates of swank Bel Air on Bel Air Rd. Turn right on St Pierre Rd and follow it up and back down the hill. On your right at 486 St Pierre Rd is the former estate of actor **Johnny Weissmuller** of *Tarzan* fame. To keep those muscles in shape, the actor had a swimming pool in the shape of a moat built into his forest-like estate, which can be glimpsed through the trees. Turn around, then turn right on St Cloud Lane. The house at 345 St Pierre, at the intersection, was where, in 1942, swashbuckler **Errol Flynn** allegedly raped a 17-year-old girl during a party. Even the

The Spelling compound

DAVID R FRAZIER

statutory rape charge didn't damage his reputation; it was revealed that the sex was apparently consensual and that he had been wearing nothing but his shoes and socks. Flynn's film *They Died with Their Boots On* was released shortly thereafter.

St Cloud veers off to the right; where it joins Bel Air Rd is the estate (invisible from the road) of former president and first lady **Ronald** and **Nancy Reagan,** at 668 Bel Air Rd, their first home after vacating the White House. The original address read 666 Bel Air Rd, but because that number is associated with the Sign of the Beast in the New Testament, a superstitious Nancy had it changed. Follow Bel Air Rd as it loops back onto Sunset Blvd, where you turn left.

Follow Sunset Blvd east, then turn right on Whittier Drive and left on Linden Drive. You're now in the Beverly 'Flats,' where mansions are more visible. The house immediately on your left at 810 Linden Drive was where gangster **Bugsy Siegel** was gunned down on June 20, 1947. Siegel is often given credit as the founder of modern Las Vegas because he saw its potential as a gambling resort and urged the mob to build the first hotel, the Flamingo. In 1991 his story was retold in the movie *Bugsy*.

Head back to Sunset, turn right, then left on Roxbury Drive, where **Jimmy Stewart** lived in the Tudor-style home at 921 Roxbury. Not far is the former home of comedienne **Lucille Ball**, star of the long-lived TV hit series *I Love Lucy*, at 1000 Roxbury.

Back on Sunset Blvd, continue east, then turn right onto Bedford Drive. The building at 730 Bedford was where Cheryl Crane, the daughter of **Lana Turner**, stabbed to death her mother's lover, gangster Johnny Stompanato, with a kitchen knife. She was acquitted on the grounds that it was justifiable homicide; Stompanato had repeatedly abused and beaten Turner. Two blocks south, at 512 Bedford Drive, is the equally notorious former home of 1920s actress **Clara Bow**, the 'It Girl' and apparent nymphomaniac who was said to have bedded the entire USC football team one night in 1927.

Continue east on Sunset Blvd, then turn right on Maple Drive. At 720 Maple is the former home of **George Burns** (the cigar-chomping comedian who died in 1996) and his beloved wife, Gracie Allen. The facade was featured in their joint TV show in the 1950s. Follow Maple south, then turn right on Elevado and left on Elm Drive, where a real 'Nightmare on Elm Street' occurred on August 20, 1989: two well-groomed young men named **Lyle** and **Eric Menendez** blew the heads off their parents, Jose and Kitty. Their extended shopping sprees after the deaths seemed suspicious, but in the end it was a confession to their psychiatrist (overheard by another patient who reported it to police) that got the two arrested. The ensuing trial revealed a pattern of sexual abuse on the part of the parents, but this didn't prevent the jury from sending the boys to jail for life. This concludes the tour. Sunset Blvd is just north, and Santa Monica Blvd is south of here.

BEL AIR & BRENTWOOD (MAPS 2 & 11)

The three most prestigious, expensive and star-studded communities in Los Angeles all start with the letter B. Next to Beverly Hills, Brentwood and Bel Air sprawl on the western and eastern sides of the 405 Fwy, respectively. Bel Air, founded in the 1920s by Alphonzo E Bell, is a purely residential neighborhood with a pretzel-shaped network of streets that can be confusing to non-residents. It is a favorite hideaway of stars whose sybaritic homes are generally out of sight behind security gates and heavy foliage. Heavy cream-colored gates off Sunset Blvd announce that you have arrived. Despite appearances, this is not a gated community, meaning you are free to drive and walk around, as long as you don't trespass onto private property.

Brentwood is comparatively low-key, accessible and less exclusive. Popular with young professionals, it also has its fair share of celebrities. Marilyn Monroe died in her house at 12305 5th Helena Drive on August 4, 1962, reportedly of a drug overdose. But it was the death of Nicole Simpson and Ron Goldman on June 12, 1994 – and the subsequent trials of former football great OJ

Simpson – that made Brentwood a household name. For months after the trials, Nicole's condominium home at 875 Bundy Drive (now 871), where the murders took place, and the Simpson estate at 360 Rockingham Ave, were besieged by tourists. Interest has since waned, and to further purge the area of such horrible memories, OJ's mansion was recently demolished by its new owner. Among Brentwood's most attractive streets is the stretch of San Vicente Blvd between Wilshire Blvd and the beach. Its wide, grassy median strip, lined by mature trees, is popular with joggers, while the area surrounding the intersection with Barrington Ave is its commercial and culinary heart.

The Getty Center

One of LA's newest attractions hunkers atop a hillside like an impregnable medieval fortress, but this monumental cluster of massive white edifices is oddly a very welcoming place – once you arrive within its vast courtyards.

The Getty Center (☎ 310-440-7300), 1200 Getty Center Drive, opened to the world in December 1998 after 14 years of planning and construction and a billion dollars in expenditure. This 110-acre 'campus' unites the art collections assembled by the oil magnate J Paul Getty – previously displayed at the Getty Villa in Malibu – with several Getty-sponsored institutes focused on conservation, art research and education.

On view in four two-story pavilions is the museum's permanent collection; a fifth one features changing exhibitions. While the skylit galleries on the upper floors of each building focus on paintings, the lower floors are given over to sculptures, illuminated manuscripts, drawings, European furniture, photos, glass, ceramics and other decorative arts.

Decorative arts were a particular passion of Getty himself, who acquired his first work of art in 1931 and became a serious collector a few years later. His accumulation of 18th-century French decorative arts ranks as one of the most prominent in the US, as does his antiquities collection. Paintings never interested Getty much, but since his death in 1976 (which added $700 million to the museum),

the Getty Trust has managed to expand the collection and acquire some impressive works, with a focus on pre 20th-century Europeans. This collection now includes masterpieces of the Italian Renaissance, 15th- to 17th-century Dutch works and French 18th- and 19th-century paintings. The string of heavy hitters represented extends from Fra Bartolommeo, Mantegna, Pontormo, Rubens, Van Dyck and Goya to the perennially crowd-pleasing French Impressionists Monet, Renoir, Degas and Cézanne as well as van Gogh.

What distinguishes the Getty from other museums is that its curators haven't assumed that visitors are art experts; they strive instead to educate and to make art accessible to all. Introductory panels near each gallery entrance are supplemented not just with labels identifying individual works but also with portable, laminated 'gallery cards,' which provide background on an artist, a period, an art form or a method. Each of the pavilions has an Art Access room with easy-to-use computer terminals for more in-depth study. Portable CD audioguides ($2) allow you to customize your own tour by punching in the number next to each object to hear analysis and commentary. Family Rooms with displays, hands-on activities and games make learning about art fun for children. And a daily program of gallery talks, lectures, films, concerts and other events is offered as well.

To many, even more impressive than the art itself is the Getty Center's architecture and design, which create an environment

The billion-dollar Getty Center

DAVID PEEVERS

that is both welcoming and uplifting. (For more details, see Tour V of the Los Angeles Architecture chapter.) There's a harmonious blend in which open spaces and low buildings placed around a central courtyard collaborate with fountains, exotic landscaping and the sun – which creates intricate interplay between light and shadow. And there are the sweeping views revealing new perspectives at every angle. On days when winds have dispersed the smog, the 360-degree views extend from a silvery sliver of ocean across the city sprawl to the often snow-capped San Gabriel Mountains and back to the Santa Monica Mountains, bringing into focus the juxtaposition of urbanity and nature that is LA. Even getting to the Getty is an experience. With parking structures banished to the bottom of the hill, driverless trams whisk visitors up to the campus.

The Getty is open Tuesday and Wednesday 11 am to 7 pm, Thursday and Friday to 9 pm, weekends 10 am to 6 pm. Admission is free, making this one of the best bargains in town. If you're driving, parking reservations are mandatory (call ☎ 310-440-7300) and there's a $5 charge. The Getty is served by MTA bus No 561 and the Big Blue Bus No 14; when arriving by public transportation, no reservation is needed and there's no charge at all aside from the bus ride.

Skirball Cultural Center

A cluster of galleries, performance spaces and exhibits, the Skirball Cultural Center (☎ 310-440-4500), 2701 N Sepulveda Blvd, takes visitors on a journey through the history of the Jewish people, showcasing their contributions to the world and to America, often with refreshing irreverence. Unlike most Jewish museums, the Skirball goes far beyond the events of the Holocaust; the simple yet powerful memorial to that time consists of half a dozen photographs of Jewish victims and a single burning lamp. With this dignified display, the museum seems to be saying, 'enough said.'

The $65 million center, which opened in 1996, was designed by noted architect Moshe Safdie and named after Jack Skirball, an ordained rabbi, producer of Hitchcock films

and real estate tycoon. The Stephen S Wise Temple (the largest Reform congregation with 4000 families), the University of Judaism and the Milken Jewish High School are nearby.

Judaica displayed at the Skirball is an outgrowth of the collection begun at Hebrew Union College in Cincinnati, Ohio, in 1875. Objects as old as 6000 years trace the evolution of Jews, their subjugation under the Egyptians, Romans and Nazis, the epoch of the Diaspora and the founding of Israel.

Themed galleries examine the history of Jewish holidays and rituals, the importance of synagogue life and the significance of the Torah and menorah. An eye-opening exhibit about Harry Truman expresses admiration for this US president who – against fierce opposition – fought for the establishment of Israel. The most charming exhibits deal with the arrival of European Jews in successive waves of immigration to America.

Interactive touchscreens and video displays add just the right touch of *tech*, and children should delight in the Discovery Center, where they become hobby archeologists and can dig into the past – literally – by unearthing ancient artifacts.

The Skirball Center is open daily noon to 5 pm, Sunday from 11 am. Admission is $8, $6 for seniors and students, free for children under 12. There is a free summer outdoor concert series on Thursday evenings as well as a packed schedule of lectures, concerts and performances (prices vary).

WESTWOOD (MAP 11)

Built on the site of Rancho San Jose de Buenos Aires, Westwood Village is today one of LA's biggest centers for first-run movies: The 1931 Spanish tower of Mann's **Village Theatre**, 961 Broxton Ave, and the 1937 Art Deco design of Mann's **Bruin Theatre**, 948 Broxton Ave, dominate the village. Its proximity to UCLA, as well as its inexpensive cafes and youth-oriented stores, make Westwood a favorite of students.

Armand Hammer Museum of Art and Cultural Center

At the foot of Westwood village is Armand Hammer Museum of Art and Cultural Center

(☎ 310-443-7000), 10899 Wilshire at Westwood Blvd. The museum opened just a couple of weeks before Hammer's death in 1990 and was drifting aimlessly in LA's cultural sea until UCLA took over its operations in 1994. Henry Hopkins, who had distinguished himself as director of the Museum of Modern Art in San Francisco in the '80s, became its director and, despite a comparatively weak collection, it has risen in stature ever since.

The late industrialist's $450 million collection of European and American Old Masters, Impressionist and post-Impressionist paintings forms the museum's basis. Drawings by French caricaturist Honoré Daumier are especially well-represented and are the largest such collection this side of the Atlantic. The museum also hosts special exhibitions, offers shows put together with works from the university's Grunwald Center for the Graphic Arts, and puts on a lively cultural program. Hours are 11 am to 7 pm Tuesday to Saturday (Thursday to 9 pm), to 5 pm Sunday. Admission is $4.50, $3 for seniors and students, free for those under 17; admission is free Thursday after 6 pm.

University of California at Los Angeles (UCLA)

Established in 1919, UCLA (☎ 310-825-4321, www.ucla.edu), 405 Hilgard Ave, moved to Westwood from Vermont Ave near Downtown in 1929 and now encompasses 235 buildings on a 419-acre campus in the foothills of the Santa Monica Mountains. In 1996, it had nearly 24,000 undergrads and 11,000 graduate students enrolled in more than 100 programs, including medicine, law, film and TV, and performing arts. Four Nobel Prize laureates and seven winners of National Medals of Science are included among its faculty. Research milestones include being the birthplace of the Internet in 1969. Alumni include Francis Ford Coppola, track and field athlete Jackie Joyner-Kersee and former LA mayor Tom Bradley. UCLA's Extension program attracts about 100,000 people to its 4500 courses each year, making it the largest metropolitan continuing-education school in the nation. Free student-guided campus tours are offered weekdays 10:30 am and 1:30 pm by reservation only (call ☎ 310-825-8764).

The campus grounds are beautifully landscaped and contain several architecturally interesting buildings, as well as museums and exhibit spaces. A self-guided tour might start in the center of the campus, located just beyond the terminus of Westwood Blvd. Here, in Westwood Plaza, you'll find the statue of the **Bruin Bear**, the UCLA mascot; the plaza is often the site of concerts or public gatherings. On the right is Ackermann Union with several restaurants, shops and the bookstore. To the left is **Pauley Pavilion**, the 13,000-seat arena for basketball and volleyball games. Farther west is the LA Tennis Center, built for the 1984 LA Olympics and now the site of the annual Los Angeles Open.

From Westwood Plaza, head east up Bruin Walk to a cluster of historic buildings flanking **Royce Quad**. These are UCLA's original structures, built in Italian Romanesque style. Powell Library, with its octagonal tower, is the main undergrad library. Directly across is the landmark Royce Hall, containing an auditorium with an antique pipe organ. Farther east are Kinsey Hall and Haines Hall.

Head down Janss Steps, located at the western end of Royce Quad, to get to the **Fowler Museum of Cultural History** (☎ 310-825-4361), exhibiting a world-class collection of art and artifacts from Latin America, Africa, Asia, and the Pacific. It's open Wednesday through Sunday noon to 5 pm, Thursday to 8 pm. Admission is $5, $3 for seniors and students. Just beyond the Fowler is the John Anderson Graduate School of Management, housed in a dramatic state-of-the-art structure completed in 1995.

East of here is the section referred to as North Campus, devoted largely to the arts and letters. Toward the area's eastern end, just beyond the University Research Library tower with its 3 million tomes, is the quiet and picturesque **Franklin D Murphy Sculpture Garden** with 70 works by Rodin, Moore, Calder and others. North of the garden are Macgowan Hall, which houses the school of Arts and Architecture, and Melnitz Hall, which houses the school of Theater, Film and TV. The UCLA Film and TV Archive in East Melnitz Hall houses a huge number of programs and footage surpassed only by the Library of Congress. To the left is the Dickson Art Center with the **New Wight Art Gallery**, which displays student works.

Work your way back south past **Schoenberg Hall**, which houses a collection of non-Western musical instruments, and to the southeastern periphery of the campus where you'll find the **Mildred E Mathias Botanical Garden** with its more than 4000 plant species. The cluster of buildings just east of the gardens constitutes UCLA's renowned Center for the Health Sciences. Wind your way through this labyrinth and you'll find yourself back on Westwood Blvd.

Westwood Memorial Park

This small, star-studded cemetery is a bit hard to find, hidden as it is behind Westwood's office stalagmites at 1218 Glendon Ave (from Wilshire Blvd, turn south onto Glendon Ave and look for the driveway immediately to your left). Here you'll find the crypt of Marilyn Monroe; Joe DiMaggio sent roses every week until 1982, and Hugh Hefner has allegedly reserved the adjacent box to be close to the ultimate Hollywood babe. Also here are Natalie Wood, John Cassavetes, Roy Orbison and Frank Zappa (in an unmarked grave) as well as Dominique Dunne of *Poltergeist* fame, strangled to death by her boyfriend at age 23 in 1982.

Writer Truman Capote lies in a space formerly occupied by Peter Lawford. Rumor has it that Capote's ashes were stolen from Joanne Carson's (former wife of Johnny Carson) home but ultimately returned. Meanwhile, Lawford's crypt had been vacated for defaulting on payments, so Carson bought it and had Capote interred there.

CENTURY CITY (MAP 11)

Adjoining Beverly Hills at its southwest corner is Century City, once the backlot of 20th Century Fox studios. As the Tom Petty song goes, 'Don't want to live in Century City,' and indeed not many people do. Highrise office buildings shoot skyward along Avenue of the Stars, which is the main

conduit of this important business and entertainment center.

Near the **Century City Shopping Center**, 10250 Little Santa Monica Blvd, is the **Shubert Theater**, 2020 Avenue of the Stars, one of LA's leading venues for Broadway productions. Actress Glenn Close had a highly successful run here in 1993 with *Sunset Boulevard*. It's part of the ABC Entertainment Center and Century Plaza Towers, a huge business-and-theater complex, built in 1975 by Minoru Yamasaki, the architect of New York City's World Trade Center. Yamasaki also designed the Century Plaza Hotel, across the street at 2025 Ave of the Stars.

At the foot of Century City, still clinging tenaciously to its original piece of real estate, you'll find the **20th Century Fox Film Corp**, 10201 W Pico Blvd. Tours are not offered by this studio, but if you peer through its front gate, you see a turn-of-the-19th-century New York street set. This studio was home to Marilyn Monroe, Shirley Temple, and many, many other stars.

Museum of Tolerance

The Museum of Tolerance (☎ 310-553-9036, www.wiesenthal.com), 9786 W Pico Blvd, uses the latest interactive technologies to make visitors confront their own closely held beliefs while teaching them about racism and bigotry. It's an enlightening, scary and painful experience. The 28,000-sq-foot exhibition has two main thematic sections: the **Tolerancenter**, focusing on racism and prejudice in America, and the **Holocaust section**, chronicling the history of the Holocaust as it pertains to Jews. The only way to experience this museum is on a 2½- to three-hour tour.

The tone is set up front, when you must choose from two doors leading to the Tolerancenter. One says 'Prejudiced,' the other 'Not Prejudiced.' Those choosing the latter will find it closed. The highlight of this section is the Point of View Diner, a re-created '50s American diner, where you'll be served with the message of personal responsibility. Sitting at individual video terminals, each person inputs their opinions about a staged newscast involving drunk driving or a hate speech. The results are tabulated instantly.

Next up is the Holocaust section, which first examines the roots of the rise of Nazi power in 1920s Germany. Then – as soft carpeting gives way to rough concrete – it's off to a concentration camp, including a 'gas chamber' where you're showered with film footage from actual camps. At the beginning, each visitor is given a photo passport of a child, which is fed into various terminals along the way to reveal his or her fate.

In the **Multimedia Learning Center,** on the 3rd floor, you can research a variety of Holocaust-related topics. Also here are such artifacts as letters by Anne Frank, a bunk bed from the Majdanek camp and Göring's dress uniform cap.

This museum, conceived and implemented by the adjacent Simon Wiesenthal Center, clearly and effectively communicates important messages. One might wish that it was a bit more inclusive in its historical portrayal, however, especially in the Holocaust section. Non-Jewish groups targeted by the Nazis aren't mentioned at all, and neither is the existence of German resistance groups. No attempt is made to put the 12 years of Nazi rule into the context of Germany's history of 1000+ years, leaving at least some of the visitors we talked to filled with predictable loathing for that country. This seems, in rather gasping irony, rather prejudicial.

To see for yourself, visit weekdays from 10 am, with the last tour starting at 4 pm. On Friday the last tour starts at 1 pm (3 pm April to October). On Sunday, the museum opens at 11 am; the last tour is at 5 pm. Admission is $8, $6 for seniors, $5 for students, $3 for children. Tours depart continuously throughout the day.

CULVER CITY (MAP 2)

Few people realize that, in the '30s and '40s, about half of the nation's movies were made in this rather nondescript pocket of LA County, about 6 miles southwest of Hollywood. Thanks to the initiative of real estate developer and Culver City founder, Harry Culver, movie studios began settling here as early as 1915. The largest studio was Metro-Goldwyn-Mayer (MGM), though there were also a number of others, attracting such moguls as Cecil B De Mille and Samuel Goldwyn, Orson Welles and David O Selznick.

Culver City Studios (☎ 310-836-5537), 9336 W Washington Blvd, is closed to the public. There's not much left to see, anyway, save the Southern facade of Selznick's offices and a few rental stages. At one time, however, this lot saw the production of some of the greatest movies in history, including *Gone With the Wind* and *Citizen Kane.* **Sony Pictures Entertainment** (☎ 310-280-8000), 10202 W Washington Blvd, has taken over the former MGM empire. (MGM recently traded its five lots for an office in Beverly Hills.) Tours of the lot, available by reservation only, include the imposing Thalberg Building, erected in Moderne style in 1939.

Abutting Culver City at its eastern edge is the **Kenneth Hahn State Recreation Area,** 4100 La Cienega Blvd, created as LA was sprucing up for the 1984 Summer Olympic Games. The 315-acre plot is planted with shrubs and trees from all over the world: 140 species in all, one for each nation that competed in those Olympics. Oil derricks once crowded this landscape, which now features hiking trails and two fishing ponds.

Museum of Jurassic Technology

At some point when perusing the dark labyrinths of the Museum of Jurassic Technology (MJT; ☎ 310-836-6131), 9341 Venice Blvd, you will begin to laugh helplessly; madness will begin to nibble at your mind. If this feeling persists, exit immediately – or risk becoming an exhibit yourself. The MJT is an assemblage of improbably weird and pedantic displays, seemingly compiled from combing the garage sales of a parallel – but niftily twisted – universe.

Right by the entrance is a small booth where the MJT's history and its spiritual and metaphysical goals are announced in the voice of God Almighty, while a crude video of some object like the Tower of Babel is encircled in smoke. You begin your tour and encounter a 'mouse sandwich,' once known as a cure for the croup; a sculpture of Pope John Paul II created by a failed violin teacher – in the eye of a needle; a NASA-like plotting map of bright pins on a darkened outline of the USA showing the location of 1937 trailer parks; and a sculpture of a child with a duck's head breathing into its mouth – a bit of medical 'quackery,' pardon the pun.

By now you are gasping, 'WHAT?!?' The MJT may or may not be an actual museum (some actually consider it an artwork). It may be a set designed by Borges to test theories for the stories he wrote, or a complete exercise in ironic near-hysteria by MJT curator David Wilson. It's all state-of-the-art display in its tiny housing, and sound systems gently massage and direct you as you helplessly meander. It's maddening, irksome, weird to a fault and howlingly funny even when you feel like Anthony Perkins is watching you through some knothole. There is nothing Jurassic about any of it, and you can find more technology in a bicycle shop. But one thing about the MJT is true above all else: it will stay in your mind for a long, long time. Museum hours are 2 to 8 pm Thursday, noon to 6 pm Friday to Sunday; admission is $4.

Coastal Communities

The Pacific Ocean is LA's greatest asset, and the communities along the coast are naturally among the most sought-after and expensive places to live. This chapter covers them all, from Malibu in the north to Long Beach near the Orange County line.

MALIBU & TOPANGA (MAP 2)

If Los Angeles is a 'city on the edge,' Malibu is even more so. Late summer wildfires regularly raze the chaparral-cloaked slopes of the Santa Monica Mountains, often taking with them homes in Topanga, Latigo and other canyons. In denuding the hillsides, the fires also pave the way for the even more damaging mudslides that follow heavy winter rains. Coastal homes seem to be most victimized by the slides, and it's not uncommon for Malibu commuters to find the Pacific Coast Hwy (1) to Santa Monica and LA closed.

Nevertheless, Malibu is a romantic destination for many visitors, even if its image as a mecca for hedonistic surfers and sun lovers is hard to find. Beachfront enclaves are often walled off from the outside world, leaving no public rights-of-way to the sand and surf on the other side. Malibu Pier fell victim to winter storms and is currently closed; apparently there's little willingness in this well-off community to restore the landmark.

A handful of state parks and state beaches offer the best access. Traveling from east to west over a stretch of about 25 miles, they include Las Tunas, Malibu Surfrider, Pt Dume, Zuma and Leo Carrillo (see the Beaches boxed text). **Pepperdine University** (☎ 310-456-4000) surely has one of the most beautiful campuses in the world, rising above a grassy slope at 24255 Pacific Coast Hwy with views of the Pacific and the mountains. Affiliated with the Church of Christ, it was founded in 1937 by George Pepperdine, who had made a fortune selling car supplies.

The rugged mountains that rise abruptly behind Malibu are encompassed by the Santa Monica Mountains National Recreation Area, 30401 Agoura Rd, Agoura Hills (☎ 818-597-1036). More than 150,000 acres of erratically forested hills with many miles of trails are under National Park Service administration. (For details, see Mountains later in this chapter.)

Adamson House

The history of Malibu and its development into a celebrity enclave is directly tied to the Rindge family, the last owners of the Spanish land grant called Malibu. When Frederick H Rindge acquired the land in 1892, it was remote and largely undeveloped. After his death, his widow, May, fought tooth and nail to prevent first the Southern Pacific Railroad from laying tracks across her land and then the state of California from building a highway.

The railroad was never built, but May's loss to the state in 1923 gave the world the Pacific Coast Highway. Around the same time, in order to replenish her finances, May also leased some land west of the Malibu Lagoon to movie stars, which resulted in the famed Malibu Colony. Still a walled enclave of ridiculously priced beachside homes, the Malibu Colony is naturally off-limits to the general public.

The Adamson House (☎ 310-456-8432), 23200 Pacific Coast Hwy, was built on a prime spot of coast along Malibu Creek for May's daughter, Rhoda Rindge Adamson, in 1928. It's a beautiful Spanish Colonial villa laced with Moorish elements in enchanting surroundings. The house itself, as well as fountains, the pool and bathhouse, is famous for being lavishly decorated with patterned glazed ceramic tiles, manufactured at the Malibu Potteries Tile Company, which was owned by the Rindges between 1926 and 1932. The only way to see the house is on a guided tour given Wednesday to Saturday at 11 am, noon, 1 and 2 pm; admission is $2, children $1.

Malibu Lagoon Museum

Adjacent to the Adamson House is this local history museum, which will tell you all about the history of Malibu, from its days as a Chumash Indian habitat to its period as Rancho Malibu, and the evolution of the Malibu Colony. The history of surfing is covered and there's also a display of Malibu Potteries tile. Hours are 11 am to 3 pm Wednesday to Saturday; admission is free.

J Paul Getty Museum

Long before the Getty Center opened, there was the original Getty Museum at 17985 Pacific Coast Hwy, housed in a reconstruction of the Roman Villa dei Papiri. Currently undergoing extensive remodeling, this museum is set to reopen as the Getty Villa in 2002 and will house Getty's collection of Greek and Roman sculptures.

Topanga Canyon

Perhaps the most intriguing drive from Malibu into the mountains is via Topanga Canyon. An alternative lifestyle community even before it was discovered by hippies in the '60s, Topanga still embraces a collection of homes that range from ramshackle to modern rustic. The emphasis today is on New Age philosophy, as exemplified by the music and cuisine at the Inn of the Seventh Ray (see Places to Eat).

Theatricum Botanicum, 1419 N Topanga Canyon Rd, serves the artistic community with a summer series of Shakespeare and other plays in an outdoor amphitheater. It was founded in 1953 as an artistic outlet by the actor Will Geer (best known as Grandpa Walton in the TV series), who, along with others, was blacklisted during the McCarthy era (also see the Entertainment chapter).

Topanga State Park, 20825 Entrada Rd, climbs the mountain ridge to the east of the park. A network of trails extends through its 9000 acres all the way to Will Rogers State Historic Park (also see Mountains later in this chapter).

PACIFIC PALISADES (MAP 2)

Pacific Palisades is an upscale community north of Santa Monica, rife with celebrities (including Arnold Schwarzenegger, Tom Cruise and Tracy Ullman) and common millionaires. They live ensconced in gorgeous Mediterranean-style villas nestled into five major canyons cutting through the Santa Monica Mountains all the way to the ocean.

This region was already a popular seaside resort for wealthy Angelenos in the late 19th century, but the colony of Pacific Palisades was founded in 1922 by a group of Methodists (led by Charles C Scott) to serve as a place of cultural, educational and religious edification. Founders purchased lots at $1000 each and settled on the mesa above Potrero Canyon. When the Depression hit, the group was forced to sell off land to private investors, and neighborhoods sprang up all around, many of them luring a sizable community of artists and writers in the 1920s to 1940s. Today, Pacific Palisades' pleasures are still largely natural, with easy access to rambling hiking trails offering sweeping vistas over the Santa Monica Bay.

Will Rogers State Historic Park

Part of the Santa Monica Mountains, this lovely park was named after Will Rogers (1875-1935), a much-revered cowboy, humorist and actor who also dispensed his acerbic commentary on the radio and in newspaper columns. In the late 1920s, Rogers traded Beverly Hills for this ranch estate, where he

Beaches

Beaches are one of LA County's greatest assets. An abundance of sunshine, a warm climate and lots of activities draw people to the shorefront year-round. Surfing, sailing, swimming, skating, bicycling, sunbathing, playing volleyball and basketball – or simply strolling through the sand – are all enjoyed by locals and visitors alike.

Water temperatures become tolerable by late spring and are highest (about 70°F) in August and September. In winter the Pacific becomes chilly, which doesn't stop surfers from hitting the swells in wetsuits. Most beaches provide showers and restrooms, lifeguards, snack stands and regular clean-up. With miles and miles of wide sandy shores to enjoy, the beaches rarely get packed with people. The most popular and populated beaches are those in Santa Monica, Venice and Manhattan Beach.

Hazards are few but shouldn't be ignored. Swimming is usually prohibited for three days after major storms due to dangerously high pollution levels from untreated runoff sweeping into the ocean through storm drains. Heal the Bay, a nonprofit environmental organization, issues monthly Beach Report Cards in which the ocean water quality at 60 LA beach locations is graded from A+ to F. Call ☎ 800-432-5229 or check its website at www.healthebay.org /healthebay for details.

Another element of danger is strong currents, often called riptides, which occur when different currents collide, dragging swimmers away from the shore. Be aware of white, frothy water and flat waves. People getting caught in riptides account for 85% of lifeguard rescues.

The following beaches, though by no means a complete list, are some of our favorites:

Leo Carrillo State Beach This beach (☎ 805-488-5223) is the northernmost in LA County, about 30 miles north of Santa Monica. It's popular with sunbathers who hang out in the section west of the Sequit Point dividing line, while surfers dominate the territory east of the point. There's also a nature trail, tide pools and caves carved into the cliffs.

El Pescador, El Matador & La Piedra Beaches These beaches, a few miles south of Leo Carrillo, are secluded hideaways and are popular with trendy Angelenos willing to make the drive up the coast. They're small and can get crowded, though limited parking provides built-in crowd control. To get to the sand, you must descend steep paths leading down from Pacific Coast Hwy (1). El Matador is the most scenic, with its eroded rock formations and natural arches. Rip currents are a danger here, making these beaches unsuitable for small children.

Zuma Beach County Park Zuma is one of LA's most beautiful beaches, a wide white sandy strip more than 2 miles long. It's especially popular with scantily clad, carousing teenagers. Swimming and body surfing are great here; the water is clean and the waves are large. There's a parking lot (for a fee) and free street parking, though look out for restrictions. Immediately to the south is the narrow **Westward Beach** (☎ 310-457-9891), a better choice for families. Even farther is **Point Dume Beach**, best reached by taking the trail from Westward Beach to the top of the bluff and descending the stairway on the other side; this takes you to a small cove that is LA's only (unofficial) nude beach.

Malibu Lagoon State Beach Also known as Surfrider Beach, Malibu Lagoon (☎ 310-456-9497) has some of the best surfing, with superb swells that make for extended rides. Even those not handy with the board enjoy the spectacle of watching dedicated dudes and dudettes riding the waves to shore. Unfortunately, the water quality here leaves much to be desired; after heavy rains the Heal the Bay score is regularly an F, the result of spillage from the algae-rich lagoon.

Will Rogers State Beach This beach (☎ 310-394-3266), 3 miles long and narrow, is quite a favorite with families. There are several playgrounds and the surf is not very strong here, which is why it's also good for surfing novices. At the foot of Chautauqua Blvd you can watch the athletically inclined bump, set and spike on the volleyball courts. Avoid the section at the mouth of Santa Monica Canyon (near San Vicente Blvd) where a storm drain discharges right into the sea.

Santa Monica & Venice State Beaches These are among LA's most popular beaches, offering something for everyone. There's a paved shoreline walk with separate lanes for bicyclers and skaters. Children's playgrounds abound and sanitary facilities are spaced only a few hundred yards apart. Snack bars and rental stations for boogie boards, skates and bikes are everywhere. The Santa Monica Pier is an attraction in itself (see the Santa Monica section). Beaches are reasonably clean, though relatively crowded. The nicest stretch is about half a mile south of the Santa Monica Pier. Parking in beach lots is pricey (about $8). You can also park inexpensively in Santa Monica's municipal lots, on 2nd and 4th Sts, and walk to the shore. Or you can hunt for street parking a few blocks inland, though spaces are scarce and the meters are monitored constantly.

South Bay Beaches The seaside is what characterizes the laid-back communities of Manhattan Beach, Hermosa Beach and Redondo Beach. Homes here literally fringe the sand. Surfers like the area near the pier in Manhattan, and the large waves make this stretch less suited for small children. Both Hermosa and Manhattan are beach-volleyball capitals. Hermosa is very much a party and pick-up beach with beer-swilling college kids spilling out of pubs that line the Strand and Pier Ave.

Redondo Beach is narrower and more family-friendly. A popular summer adventure is a visit to the *Seaside Lagoon* (☎ 310-318-0681), 200 Portofino Way, Kings Harbor in Redondo. This is a heated ocean-water swimming pool with a sandy bottom, in an environment that includes picnic tables, volleyball courts and areas for sunbathing. A renovation should be completed by the 1999 season. Hours are 10 am to 5:45 pm daily between Memorial Day and Labor Day. Admission is $3.50, $2.50 for children ages two to 17.

Long Beach With its more than 10 miles of shorefront, Long Beach is certainly no misnomer. Thanks to a breakwater 2 miles offshore, however, the water here is eerily flat with few waves, which is good for swimming and windsurfing, though obviously not for boogie boarding or surfing. Long Beach trains its own lifeguards, a tradition in force since 1919. The beach along Appian Way, on the north side of Naples Island, is a good place to come with small children. 'Horny Beach,' next to the Gondola Getaway pier at 5437 E Ocean Blvd, is the area's gathering spot for hormone-crazed teens.

lived until he died in a plane crash in Alaska in 1935. His wife, who survived him by eight years, deeded the estate to the state in 1944.

Today, visitors explore the chaparral-covered hills once wandered by Rogers and check out his private polo field where he was often joined by buddies Spencer Tracy and Walt Disney. (It is now a club hosting matches on weekends year-round.) Rogers' home (☎ 310-454-8212) is open to the public and still contains his personal furnishings. A short film about Rogers' life and career is shown at the visitors' center. Park hours are 8 am to sunset; the ranch house is open 10 am to 5 pm. Admission is free, but there's a $5 parking fee. The park entrance is west off Sunset Blvd and is marked by signs.

Self-Realization Fellowship Lake Shrine

Whatever negative feelings or stress you may have, they're likely to evaporate on a visit to the Self-Realization Fellowship Lake Shrine (☎ 310-454-4114), 17190 Sunset Blvd. The 10-acre site is a natural amphitheater of paradisiacal beauty and serenity. Stroll along the narrow paths, around a spring-fed lake, through the sunken gardens, past ponds, waterfalls and lush vegetation.

Founded in 1920 by Paramahansa Yogananda, a widely admired spiritual leader born and educated in India, the fellowship is dedicated to helping people of all races, creeds and cultures on their spiritual search. Sri Yogananda spent 30 years of his life in the US, opening the Lake Shrine to the public in 1950.

Highlights of the grounds are the Court of Religions, where each of the five principal religions is acknowledged with its symbol; the Windmill Chapel, a reproduction of a 16th-century Dutch windmill; the Golden Lotus Archway, topped by gilded copper lotus flowers; and the Gandhi World Peace Memorial where a portion of Mahatma Gandhi's ashes are interred in a stone sarcophagus. Towering atop the hillside is the New Temple, an octagonal edifice adorned with stained glass, tile and wood and again crowned by a gilded lotus. The grounds are open Tuesday to Saturday from 9 am to 4:30 pm, Sunday from 12:30 pm; admission and parking are both free.

SANTA MONICA (MAP 12)

Generations of people around the world have grown up thinking Santa Monica *is* California. Films, TV and popular music have given us the picture of endless summer along the Pacific beaches, where perfect bodies surf by the pier, Rollerblade and frolic beneath towering palm trees. But in recent years Santa Monica has outgrown its movie mythology and origins as a quaint seaside resort to become – quite simply – one of the most entertaining places in the LA area.

Santa Monica is among the safest places to visit in LA County, and most of its attractions are easily explorable on foot. Highlights are the pleasure pier, a pedestrianized promenade, a cliffside park overlooking the ocean and miles of beach. The air quality, shopping, dining and entertainment are better than almost anywhere in LA. For these reasons, many of the giants of entertainment – including Sony, MGM and MTV – have moved here in recent years. Some complain that this success has cost Santa Monica its small-town charm.

The Santa Monica **Visitors Bureau** (☎ 310-393-7593), in a little kiosk at 1400 Ocean Blvd, has brochures, maps and public transportation information. Hours are 10 am to 5 pm daily. To get around downtown Santa Monica, hop on the electric Tide Shuttle (25¢ per ride), which runs every 15 minutes between noon and 10 pm (to midnight on weekends).

Santa Monica Pier

Most likely you know the Santa Monica Pier, even if you've never been there in person. Just about any movie or TV program set in LA features at least one establishing shot of the pier's historic lighted arch. Behind it, a steep incline spans Pacific Coast Hwy and leads to the most lively and beloved pier in the entire county. It is not just favored for its great views of the beach and the Santa Monica skyline, but also for its many restaurants, night clubs and family entertainments. The pier was plagued with gang activity for

Fun in the sun: Pacific Park on the
Santa Monica Pier

many years, but pier planners successfully
eliminated this problem by locating a police
station right on the boardwalk itself.

Santa Monica Pier originally consisted of
two adjacent quays, which are joined together today: a municipal pier built in 1909
for fishing and strolling, and a pleasure pier
with amusements and food venues dating
from 1916. A remnant from that era is the
Hippodrome, home of a quaint **carousel** that
starred with Paul Newman and Robert Redford in the film classic *The Sting*. It's a lovely
old-fashioned affair, and its cheerfully hand-
painted horses endear it to children large
and small.

The pier's other main draw, the **Pacific
Park** (☎ 310-260-8744), opened in 1998 and
is basically a scaled-down Coney Island.
There's a small roller coaster and a full-size
Ferris wheel worth riding for the views
alone, plus a host of smaller kiddy rides and
arcade games. Admission to the park is free,
but rides cost $1 to $3; $15 buys a wristband
for unlimited rides on the day of issuance.
Hours seem to change often but generally
are Sunday to Thursday 10 am to 10 pm (to
5 pm in winter), weekends to midnight (2 pm
to midnight in winter).

Right beneath the Hippodrome is the
UCLA Ocean Discovery Center (☎ 310-393-
6149), a teaching facility dedicated to de-
mystifying the oceans to students of all ages.
Operated by UCLA's marine science department, the center's 4000 sq feet hold display
tanks showcasing local marine life and two
touch tanks where visitors can interact with

urchins, bat rays and baby sharks. A large
moon jellyfish tank teems with hundreds of
these diaphanous creatures swirling in an
amazing slow-motion ballet. Friendly young
volunteers stand by to answer questions.
Summer hours are 2 to 6 pm Tuesday to Friday, from 11 am Saturday, 11 am to 5 pm
Sunday. From Labor Day to Memorial Day,
it's open weekends only from 11 am to 5 pm.
Admission is $3, free for children under two.

On Thursday nights in summer, the pier
comes to life with the **Twilight Dance Series**,
free outdoor concerts featuring major local
and national talent such as Bo Diddley,
Queen Ida and LA's own Ozomatli. It often
seems as if all of LA turns out for what are
definitely some of the best free parties in
town, so come early if you want to stake out
some turf near the stage (concerts start at
7:30 pm).

Palisades Park

Palisades Park hugs the sandstone bluff that
parallels the ocean, separating the city from
the white sandy beach. Lorded over by
gracefully swaying Washington palm trees,
the park presents you with the vast sweep of
Santa Monica Bay. It's a great place to sit
quietly on a bench, but the park also attracts
flocks of joggers, strollers, sunset meditators,
lovers, tai chi practitioners and Russian
immigrants playing cards in the shade.

The park begins just north of the pier. This
is also where you'll find one of Santa Monica's oldest attractions, the **Camera Obscura**
inside the Senior Recreation Center, 1450
Ocean Ave. An early version of the single-
lens reflex camera, the Camera Obscura was
a sensation when it opened in 1899. Ask for
the key at the desk on your right, then head
up the stairway to discover a completely
dark room where a 5-foot circular image of
Ocean Ave is projected onto a table. This
effect, first described by Aristotle, is achieved
by bouncing sunlight from the outside off a
mirror and then down through a convex lens
that projects it on a surface. Hours are 9 am
to 4 pm weekdays, from 11 am on weekends;
admission is free.

As you stroll north from here, you'll notice several gun emplacements built to hold

DAVID PEEVERS

Palisades Park in Santa Monica

off any Japanese attacks during WWII. Farther north, where Santa Monica Blvd meets the park, is a commemorative plaque marking the western terminus of the Will Rogers Highway, also known as Route 66, the 'Main Street of America.' A couple of blocks north, right at Wilshire Blvd, is a statue of the city's namesake, Saint Monica, a minimalist rendition and absurdly phallic.

Third Street Promenade

Before its ambitious revamping in 1989, this walking mall was home to dusty shops, dilapidated facades and homeless people. The city spent a few million dollars and implemented some very strict anti-homeless laws. Today, pedestrian-only 3rd St between Broadway and Wilshire has turned into a permanent street party. Peruvian flutes mingle with bluegrass guitar and classical cellos in a parade of free street entertainment. Eccentric shops, restaurants and cafes with outdoor seating, and no fewer than 17 movie screens draw the crowds to one of the most happening places in the county. It's far and away the most successful entertainment destination in LA. (Also see the Places to Eat and Entertainment chapters.)

Angels Attic Museum

Toy trains travel along the ceiling, and tiny dolls inhabit crenelated castles and Tudor homes in this adorable little museum (☎ 310-394-8331) at 516 Colorado Ave. Housed in a two-story Victorian villa dating to 1895, the museum has a Noah's ark's worth of miniature animals plus a gallery of precious dolls.

The museum is open Thursday to Sunday from 12:30 to 4:30 pm. Admission is $6.50, $4 for seniors, $3.50 for children.

Bergamot Station

The 30 or so galleries berthed within the sprawling industrial grounds of Bergamot Station (☎ 310-453-7535), 2525 Michigan Ave, have been a nexus of the LA art scene since the complex's opening in 1994. Originally a stop on the Red Line dating to 1875 (see Big Red Cars in the Getting Around chapter), the area became an industrial site before being abandoned. It took the vision of an art dealer and a TV producer to look beyond the ramshackle corrugated tin buildings; they gave impetus to the architectural rebuilds that resulted in one of the most esteemed exhibit spaces in LA.

In addition to housing the Santa Monica Museum of Art (see below), Bergamot Station boasts established galleries like those of Sherry Frumkin and Shoshana Wayne. But it's also home to lesser-known galleries with specializations as diverse as handmade paper, traditional Japanese ukiyo-e art, contemporary photography and jewelry. Bergamot Station's future looks bright with the prestigious Mark Taper Forum theatrical group planning to build a 26,000-sq-foot theater in the complex; the theater should go a long way toward making Bergamot Station the multi-use community-oriented facility it wants to be.

The Shopping chapter has details on some of the galleries. Bergamot Station's own printed guide is also available at any of the galleries.

Santa Monica Museum of Art Beneath copious skylights placed in a corrugated tin roof, the Santa Monica Museum of Art (☎ 310-586-6488) was recently relocated from Main St to Bergamot Station. Museum coordinator Ashley Emenegger has arranged a saucy and irreverent home with energy levels reflecting her vision. You're liable to encounter any of the traditional art forms on display, including interactive video and photography. The museum often throws public parties during special events, such as the

World Artists For Tibet happening. The organization holds top ranking among California art cadres, and their Friday-night salon series is right at the edge of what is evolving on the local scene: You might encounter performance artists or get involved in discussions about surrealist cooking or the symbolic power of trees. Hours are 11 am to 6 pm Wednesday to Sunday; there's a suggested donation of $3.

Santa Monica College
One of LA County's premier educational facilities and among the finest of its kind in the nation is Santa Monica Community College (SMC; ☎ 310-450-5150), 1900 Pico Blvd. Sometimes referred to as 'Stanford-on-Pico,' this two-year college transfers more students to the University of California system (including UCLA and Berkeley) than any other community college in the state. Its list of alumni includes Arnold Schwarzenegger (who studied English here), Dustin Hoffman, astronaut Buzz Aldrin and actress Linda Gray. The Santa Monica Track Club, which has produced 27 Olympic-medal winners and launched the careers of Carl Lewis and other athletes, is based at the college.

Popular destinations are the **Photography Gallery,** the **Art Gallery,** the **Community Theater** and the outdoor pool. The state-of-the-art **Planetarium** (☎ 310-452-9223) pulls in big crowds for its weekly Night Sky Shows, where mysteries from quarks to quasars are explained in three dimensions by a Digistar projection system, the only one on the West Coast. The shows are followed by lectures given by scientists from JPL, Cal Tech and other eminent research facilities. Tickets are $4 per show or $7 for both.

Museum of Flying
You don't have to be an airplane aficionado to enjoy the excellent Museum of Flying (☎ 310-392-8822), 2772 Donald Douglas Loop North, right at the Santa Monica Municipal Airport, which is entered from Ocean Park Blvd. Housed in an enormous hangar are three floors of exhibits with such legends of flight as the Mitsubishi Zero, the P-51 Mustang, WWI Fokker's and a replica of the

Voyager, the first aircraft to make a nonstop flight around the world. Other aircraft dangle midair in eerie quiet and aeronautic elegance. There are interactive 'Build a Plane' displays, a flight simulator for kids and models of futuristic spacecraft that will have the young ones speculating about their future on Mars. On the tarmac is a well-maintained fleet of military planes from WWII. (The entire museum is somewhat of a showcase for militarism due to Southern California's role in producing warrior aircraft.) Museum hours are from 10 am to 5 pm Wednesday to Sunday. Admission is $7, $5 for seniors, $3 for children.

VENICE (MAP 12)
A hundred years ago the stretch of coastline where Venice Beach lies today was nothing but dreary swampland – just the sort of place that developer Abbot Kinney was looking for.

After acquiring substantial wealth as heir to the family cigarette fortune, New Jersey-born Kinney set out to bring culture to Los Angeles in the days before filmdom. His goal was to build a model community that would be a regional center for art, music, theater and lectures. Kinney had the marshes drained and dug a 16-mile network of canals. He brought a dozen gondoliers from Europe to pole through his artificial paradise, which attracted scores of new residents and merchants, and had a spectacular grand opening celebration on July 4, 1905. Even back then, the LA public was more interested in entertainment than edification, so Kinney

Venetian sand sculptor

converted his 'Venice of America' into a beachfront amusement park, complete with a Ferris wheel, a hydrogen-filled balloon and 'The Rapids' (a sort of precursor to Disney's 'Thunder Mountain' water ride).

Hollywood soon superseded Venice in popularity, however, and Venice soon disintegrated into a haven of speak-easies and gambling halls during Prohibition. In 1925, five years after Kinney's death, Venice residents asked to be annexed to the city of Los Angeles, which paved over most of the canals. Today, 3 miles of canals survive, though there is talk of doing away with those as well. South of Venice Blvd and east of Pacific Ave, along wee Dell Ave, you'll find an enclave of cozy bungalows and four arched Venetian bridges.

Kinney may have been a little kooky, but he unwittingly set the trend for the Venice of the future. Throughout the 20th century, the community attracted whatever was the counterculture of its decade, be it Lawrence Lipton and Stuart Perkoff of the '50s Beat generation, the hippies of the '60s (Jim Morrison and the Doors were among those who lived here), the New Agers of the '70s and '80s, or the Rollerblading, image-obsessed babes and dudes of the '90s. In many ways, much more than Beverly Hills and certainly more than Hollywood, Venice generates the image of the free-wheeling, laid-back, slightly crazed but creative and cutting-edge city that many people expect LA to be.

Ocean Front Walk

The chief attraction of modern Venice is its Ocean Front Walk, also called the Venice Boardwalk (even though it is completely paved). Extending from Marine St in the north to the **Venice Pier** at the border of Marina del Rey to the south, this 1½-mile stretch must be explored by foot or, as many do, by bicycle or in-line skates.

Come to Venice Beach any time of day, but for full effect, come on a warm Saturday or Sunday afternoon. Permanent shops and cafes are on the east side of the beachwalk, while ambulatory vendors hawk their wares next to the sand; the human circus flows in between.

DAVID PEEVERS

Muscle Beach boys

No words can do this crazy scene justice. You'll encounter jugglers and acrobats, tarot readers and Mad Hatter headwear vendors, jug-band musicians and political types circulating petitions to decriminalize marijuana. You'll watch bikini-clad women watching body builders watching themselves flex at **Muscle Beach**, just around the corner from two of California's most famous indoor gyms: Gold's Gym at 360 Hampton Drive, and World Gym at 812 Main St (see Activities later in the chapter). A few steps away are the basketball courts where pickup players like the characters played by Woody Harrelson and Wesley Snipes in *White Men Can't Jump* (filmed here) take on all comers. The selection of restaurants and bars runs the gamut from cheap falafel stands and juice bars to proper restaurants.

Architecturally, Venice is often as bizarre as its boardwalk. Look no farther than Venice's north entrance, on Main St at Rose Ave, for cases in point: artist Jonathan Borofsky's 34-foot 'Ballerina Clown' on the facade of the **Venice Renaissance Building**, and four-story binoculars, the work of Claes Oldenburg and Coosje van Bruggen, posing as the front door to the Chiat/Day Inc advertising agency. The town also has scores of colorful street murals, a reminder of the preponderance of artists (some quite well-known, most struggling and bohemian) who live here. Showcases like the **LA Louver Galleries** (☎ 310-822-4955), 45 N Venice Blvd, and the

James Corcoran Gallery (☎ 310-966-1010), 1633 Electric Ave, exhibit their work.

For more information on Venice, contact the Venice **Chamber of Commerce** (☎ 310-396-7016), 583 Venice Blvd.

MARINA DEL REY (MAP 12)

Some 6000 private sailboats and motor yachts are moored in what locals call simply 'the Marina,' the largest artificial small-craft harbor in the US. Many of the Marina's single professionals live on boats; many more inhabit apartment complexes that surround the slips on streets named after idyllic Pacific isles: Bora Bora, Tahiti, Marquesas, Panay, Palawan, Bali, Mindanao and Fiji. Don't be fooled; the architecture itself – with its many high-rises and condominium complexes – is more sterile than tropical and certainly isn't visually attractive. Developed immediately south of Venice in the 1960s, this overwhelmingly young and Caucasian neighborhood now has numerous fine restaurants and hotels, including the sumptuous Ritz-Carlton Marina del Rey.

Integrated into the Marina is **Mother's Beach**, named for its placid and safe waters. It's worth coming here just to check out the cheerfully painted lifeguard station, the work of Rip Cronk; this is the first in a series of 30 such towers to be painted by local artists over the next few years.

The Marina's leading tourist site is **Fishermen's Village** (☎ 310-823-5411), 13755 Fiji Way, a hokey assemblage intended to look like a Cape Cod village. You *can* go fishing from here – book a trip with Marina del Rey Sportfishing (☎ 310-822-3625) – but most visitors settle for taking a harbor sightseeing cruise or browsing the diverse novelty and souvenir shops.

The Marina del Rey **Chamber of Commerce** (☎ 310-821-0555), 4111 Via Marina, has further information, and there's an automated information line at ☎ 310-305-9545.

Ballona Wetlands

Just south of the Marina, in an area called Playa Vista, are the last remaining wetlands in LA County. Fed by both salt and fresh water, they are home to hundreds of bird species, including the great blue heron, as well as fish and plant life. Once owned by Howard Hughes, the land has been in the hands of a major developer, Maguire Thomas Partners, since 1989. This company is responsible for constructing a new community atop the marshy lands, a project fought by environmentalists for two decades. Under a court-ordered compromise, the company was allowed to go ahead with the development, with the provision that it also keeps a large chunk of the entire area as a bird preserve.

Homes for more than 25,000 residents are in the plans, as are commercial complexes providing work to another 20,000. The most prominent resident will be Dreamworks, the entertainment company founded in 1994 by filmmaker Steven Spielberg, David Geffen of MCA (Music Corporation of America) and Jeffrey Katzenberg, formerly of Walt Disney. Environmentalists despair, but in terms of job creation and the revenue expected from another major studio, the Playa Vista project is a boon to LA.

SOUTH BAY (MAP 13)
Manhattan Beach

Manhattan Beach, 19 miles southwest of Downtown LA, is the northernmost in a series of all-American beach towns that run

Manhattan Beach Pier

DAVID PEEVERS

south from LAX to the Palos Verdes Peninsula. It's an affluent, well-educated and young community that includes many USC graduates, now firmly ensconced on the career ladder, with respectable salaries that account for the city's average annual income of $70,000.

Between the beach – jam-packed on summer days with surfers and volleyball players – and the American-as-apple-pie residential areas inland is an upscale downtown lined with boutiques and restaurants, indicating a high degree of attention to modern city planning. Most of the activity centers along Manhattan Beach Blvd and the intersecting streets of Manhattan and Highland Aves.

Manhattan Beach Blvd culminates in the 928-foot pier, which leads to a roundhouse housing the **Marine Studies Lab & Aquarium** (☎ 310-379-8117). Stocked with several tanks, this small facility is a clear winner with children, who get a kick out of getting close-up looks at moray eels, reef sharks and a 50-year-old gargantuan lobster. They also get to finger various sea creatures inhabiting a touch tank. The facility opens at 3 pm on weekdays and 10 am on weekends and closes at sunset. Admission is free, but donations are welcome.

To learn about Manhattan Beach's historical development, visit the exhibit maintained by the town's historical society (☎ 310-374-7575) at 1601 Manhattan Beach Blvd (open weekends noon to 3 pm; admission is free).

Hermosa Beach

The Hermosa Pier of Hermosa Beach, located 16 miles southwest of Downtown, is 1½ miles south from Manhattan Beach's pier. A long-standing rivalry has existed between the two beach communities. Closer to the airport and the aerospace industries, Manhattan has always been neater and more affluent, while Hermosa has been more alternative, grungy and gritty. Over the past five years, Hermosa thoroughly revamped its downtown, resulting in a pleasant pedestrian zone in the area where Pier Ave meets the beach. Dozens of funky bars and restaurants provide outdoor seating, with a few shops thrown into the mix.

DAVID PEEVERS

Hermosa Beach has an active volleyball scene.

In summer especially, Hermosa has very much the feel of a laid-back college town, with throngs of boys and girls showing off their taut, bronzed bods by wearing as little as legally possible. Both Manhattan and Hermosa have active professional volleyball scenes (16th St in Hermosa and Marine Ave in Manhattan are both good spots to see the pros bump, set and spike); tournaments take place frequently.

Similar to Manhattan, Hermosa was a sleepy village until a couple of railroad tycoons developed the land to attract business and passengers for their Los Angeles Pacific route. Since the end of WWII, Hermosa (like its South Bay neighbors) has been an enclave of well-to-do beachside residents. The Hermosa Beach Historical Society maintains a local museum below the gymnasium in the community center at 710 Pier Ave. Hours are 2 to 4 pm weekends; admission is free.

Redondo Beach

Redondo is perhaps the most intriguing of the South Bay communities. At its north end is King Harbor, a small-boat marina and fisherfolk haven. In the heart of town, at the end of Torrance Blvd, are Monstad Pier and Fisherman's Wharf, the biggest surfside pleasure complex south of Santa Monica. Joined at their seaward end, the pier and the wharf are chockablock with restaurants, bars, souvenir shops and a fishing dock. It's an oddly angular convoluted construction, typical of the multilevel interlocking concrete monstrosities built during the '70s.

Few clues survive to indicate that Redondo began as an early LA seaport, instrumental in bringing lumber and other cargo from ships to the blossoming city. The first wharf was completed in 1889, but then Redondo's dream of winning the race for biggest port in Los Angeles died in the 1910s when a series of major storms destroyed several of its wharves, and business went to the neighboring port of San Pedro.

Tourism has always played an important role in Redondo, thanks to the efforts of Henry Huntington and others who connected the South Bay towns with LA by railway. The luxurious Hotel Redondo (no longer there), a salt water plunge and several piers were among the early attractions, as was surfer dude George Freeth, hired by Huntington to delight visitors with his 'wave-walking' (see related boxed text below).

Redondo also maintains a local history museum (☎ 310-318-0684), located in a Victorian cottage at 302 Flagler Lane in Dominguez Park and open weekends 1 to 4 pm. Admission is free.

George Freeth: King of the Surfer Dudes

The Beach Boys, *Beach Blanket Bingo*, Frankie and Annette, Surfin' USA – surfing mythology and California have long been synonymous, and we may owe it all to land baron and railroad tycoon Henry Huntington's genius for promotion. Having developed Redondo Beach and brought the railroad there, Huntington planned to sell off his parcels of oceanfront property to the well-heeled. In 1907, to help lure prospective buyers to the area, he hired an Irish-Hawaiian athlete named George Freeth to perform his miracle of 'walking on the water' for visitors to Redondo. The crowds came, and Huntington sold *a lot* of real estate.

As a child in Hawaii, Freeth had seen an old painting of his mother's ancestors riding the waves and decided to revive the ancient art. When the gargantuan, traditional 16-foot hardwood boards proved too hard to handle, Freeth cut one in half, thus creating the first 'long board' – modern surfing was born. Until 1915, Freeth held the beach crowds in thrall with daily performances and eventually became the first lifeguard in Southern California. (He received a congressional medal for bravely rescuing a boatload of stranded fishermen.) Freeth fathered the surfing revolution that would eventually become an enormous industry and way of life in California. A bronze memorial to him on the Redondo Pier is frequently draped with leis from worldwide surfers who come to pay their respects.

Freeth died in the great influenza epidemic of 1919 at age 36, but the mark he left on world culture surpassed even the legacy of Huntington himself. Freeth's short sweet life was the original 'Endless Summer.' He was *awesome*, dude.

DAVID PEEVERS

LA surfers 'walking on water'

RANCHO PALOS VERDES (MAP 4)

A rocky precipice rising from the sea and separating Santa Monica Bay from San Pedro Bay, the Palos Verdes Peninsula is among the most spectacular neighborhoods in LA County. Driving along its quiet, tree-lined roads, past opulent gardens and immaculately groomed Spanish-style villas, one feels transported to the Mediterranean Riviera. Views down into the bay, where the silvery band of beach flanks a cobalt ocean, are positively otherworldly.

It should not be surprising that this is a neighborhood of affluence, further evidenced by the profusion of bridle trails. If you're lucky, you may not only see horses but also encounter a few of Palos Verdes' most graceful denizens – its resident population of peacocks. These were introduced back in the 1920s by wily real estate developers who hoped to entice future home owners. The peacocks thrived to the point where the city had most of them exiled in 1985, leaving only a few dozen to surprise visitors.

The Palos Verdes coastline is relatively unspoiled and comprises a series of coves. The only easily accessible sandy beach is Malaga Cove; Abalone Cove is an ecological reserve with large tide pools. Surfers ride the waves at Royal Palms beach, while scuba divers plow the waters at White Point.

Point Vicente Interpretive Center

This city-maintained facility (☎ 310-377-5370), 31501 Palos Verdes Drive W, is the perfect observation spot for landlubbers to scan the ocean for **gray whales**. The whales come en route from the Arctic Seas to Baja California and back between December and April. Every year, volunteers positioned here count the number of whales passing by the bluff. A small exhibit enlightens you about these amazing sea mammals and doubles as a Palos Verdes historical museum. Among the tidbits learned here is that Palos Verdes was originally an island and was only gradually linked to the mainland. The center's hours are 10 am to 5 pm daily in winter, to 7 pm in summer. Admis-

sion is $2, $1 for seniors and children ages four to 14. (There's no charge for access to the observation area.)

Wayfarer's Chapel

Located in a beautiful spot at 5755 Palos Verdes Drive S, this small chapel (☎ 310-377-1650) was designed by Lloyd Wright, son of Frank Lloyd Wright. A glass structure not unlike a greenhouse, it was built in 1949 and is canopied by a grove of trees. The fairytale-like quality of the place accounts for its appeal for weddings, some 700 of which are conducted here assembly-line style every year. The chapel is owned by the Swedenborgian Christian church, which also holds services on Sunday at 11 am.

South Coast Botanical Garden

One of the most amazing examples of land reclamation is this botanical garden (☎ 310-544-6815), 26300 Crenshaw Blvd, which started out as an open pit mine for diatomite before becoming a land fill in 1957. More than 3.5 million tons of trash landed here before the area was converted into a garden in 1961. Today, some 200,000 plants representing 2000 species, plus 200 bird species, completely conceal the fact that you are standing on a pile of trash. Bisected by a stream and anchored by a lake, the gardens are divided into about 20 sections, including the Fuchsia Garden, Succulent and Cactus Garden, Children's Garden and Flower Garden. Hours are 9 am to 5 pm daily. Admission is $5, $3 for seniors and students, $1 for children. Admission is free on the third Tuesday of the month.

SAN PEDRO (MAP 14)

About 21 miles south of Downtown LA, San Pedro is a slow-paced harbor community forming the northern fringe of the Port of Los Angeles – Worldport LA – one of the busiest ports in the world. Much of the ethnically diverse population hovers near the lower end of the economic spectrum. Not blessed with great aesthetics (its seaside location aside), trendy restaurants or high culture, San Pedro has nonetheless some pockets of charm and interest for the visitor.

The original settlers, mostly Shoshone Indians, remained the sole inhabitants until the arrival of Spanish immigrants in 1777. The Spanish allowed only two foreign ships a year to brings goods to the growing Los Angeles area, an act that only encouraged an active smuggling trade. In the 1870s, with Los Angeles seeking a deepwater harbor after the arrival of the railroad, dredging work and construction of a breakwater began at San Pedro. The town incorporated in 1888 but was annexed to LA in 1909. Five years later, after the opening of the Panama Canal, San Pedro boomed.

Downtown San Pedro centers along 6th and 7th Sts between Pacific Ave and Harbor Blvd, though there's precious little to see here. At 478 W 6th St is the 1931 **Warner Grand Theater**, a lovely movie palace with astoundingly intricate wood carvings. It's only open for special screenings; call ☎ 310-548-7672 for the current schedule.

Nearby is the San Pedro Chamber of Commerce (☎ 310-832-7272), 390 W 7th St. The staff was unfriendly and stingy with information when we went, but it's worth visiting the chamber only to pick up brochures (though naturally only services by chamber members are being touted). Hours are 9 am to 5 pm weekdays.

A good way to see San Pedro is by Electric Trolley, which shuttles from the *SS Lane Victory* along Harbor Blvd, 6th and 7th Sts to the Los Angeles Maritime Museum and Ports O'Call Village every 15 minutes Thursday to Sunday. The fare of 25¢ allows you to hop on and off as often as you wish.

Worldport LA
The Port of Los Angeles forms the western half of Terminal Island, the port area between San Pedro and Long Beach, with the eastern half taken up by the Port of Long Beach. Together, the twin ports are the third largest in the world, after Singapore and Hong Kong. Fishing is still a main activity here, though container and cargo ships abound. Fuel, coal and chemicals, machinery and food are among the most commonly transported products. The majority is destined for Asian ports, especially Japan, South Korea, Hong Kong and China. The ballet of leviathan tankers gliding slowly out to sea is an impressive sight.

Los Angeles Maritime Museum
Occupying a former ferry terminal on Berth 84 at the bottom of 6th St is the interesting Los Angeles Maritime Museum (☎ 310-548-7618). The 75,000-sq-foot facility contains more than 700 intricate ship and boat models, navigational equipment and an operating amateur radio station. The battleship section has models of the *USS Hartford*, the Civil War flagship of Admiral David Farragut and the *USS Washington*, which sank the most combat tonnage in the Pacific theater of WWII without losing a man.

Highlights of the passenger-ship section are models of the luxury steamers *Titanic* and *Lusitania*, both constructed as cutaways to expose the lavish interiors. A ramp leading upstairs has models of such historic ships as Columbus' *Pinta*, *Niña* and *Santa Maria*, Charles Darwin's *HMS Beagle*, the Pilgrims' *Mayflower* and Sir Francis Drake's *Golden Hind*. Hours are 10 am to 5 pm Tuesday to Sunday; a $1 donation is encouraged.

About 1 mile north, at Berth 94, is the **SS Lane Victory** (☎ 310-519-9545). It is one of 500 'victory' ships used during WWII to transport cargo to the Allies. Today it houses a museum, open daily 9 am to 4 pm. Admission is $3, $1 for children ages five to 15. On several summer weekends, the ship actually heads out to sea for an all-day cruise. Reservations are mandatory and tickets are $100.

Ports O'Call Village
Just south of the Maritime Museum, Ports O'Call Village is a hopeless tourist trap, supposedly evocative of the 19th-century New England seaside towns. There's plenty of predictably cutesy shops hawking overpriced trinkets, as well as ice cream parlors and restaurants. Ports O'Call is the main departure point for harbor tours offered several times daily by Spirit Cruises (☎ 310-548-8080) from Berth 77. One-hour narrated tours cost $7.50; 90-minute cruises are $9. A two-hour tour ($15) takes in the *Queen Mary* and the Navy base as it circles all of Terminal Island.

Whale-watching excursions lasting 2½ hours ($15) also leave from here December through March. If it's fish you're after, deep-sea fishing launches depart for half-day and full-day excursions around 7 am every day. Try LA Harbor Sportfishing (☎ 310-547-9916), Berth 79, which offers overnight, half-day and three-quarter-day trips.

Point Fermin Park

Landlubber whale-watchers have a great observation post at Point Fermin Park, Paseo del Mar at Gaffey St, San Pedro's southernmost cape. Occupying a clifftop due north of Santa Catalina Island – visible on clear days some 22 miles away – the park has tree-shaded lawns, sheltered pergolas, gardens and a palisade promenade. You can walk around, but cannot enter, the park's Victorian lighthouse, which dates from 1874. The lighthouse fell into disuse after WWII and is now the private residence of the park superintendent. Until the lighthouse got electricity in 1925, oil lamps provided its glow.

Angels Gate Park

A short uphill walk from Point Fermin takes you to Angels Gate Park, location of the HI hostel and the impressive **Korean Friendship Bell**, a gift from South Korea to the US on the latter's bicentennial in 1976 and fashioned after an 8th-century bronze bell. Some 12 feet high and weighing 17 metric tons, it's canopied by a pagoda-shaped belfry with a blue-tiled roof and a beamed, pillared, fanlike substructure. A small building houses a photo history of US-Korean relations from 1800 to today.

West of here is the **Fort MacArthur Military Museum** (☎ 310-548-2631), 3601 S Gaffey St. Fort MacArthur was established as a military reservation in 1888 and developed for military purposes just before WWI. It is now a residential community for personnel of the Air Force Space Division at El Segundo. Only the museum, housed in the Battery Osgood Farley, is open to the public. A defense post for enemy attacks from the sea between 1916 and 1945, it housed four batteries with 14-inch seacoast guns, which had a range of 14 miles. The museum documents

the fort's history as a defensive post. Hours are from noon to 5 pm Tuesday, Thursday and weekends. Admission is free, but donations are welcome.

Cabrillo Marine Aquarium

The lovely Cabrillo Marine Aquarium (☎ 310-548-7562) is in a Frank Gehry-designed structure at 3720 Stephen White Drive. Though it doesn't compare in size or quality to Long Beach's brand-new Aquarium of the Pacific, it is still a fun and educational place, sure to keep kids entertained. Best of all, this aquarium is free (though parking is a whopping $6.50). There are 38 salt-water tanks, displaying colorful fish and other marine life in a series of habitats that include the open ocean, kelp forests and rocky shores. Out back is a touch tank where visitors are encouraged to handle starfish, sea urchins, sea cucumbers and other denizens of the sea.

The aquarium also offers numerous educational programs geared to children of all ages and runs a 'Meet the Grunion' program (March to July). Grunion are silvery fish that spawn on sandy beaches following high tide. Females deposit thousands of eggs in the sand, which are instantly fertilized by the males and ready to hatch in two weeks, and are then swept out to sea by the next tide. Museum hours are noon to 5 pm weekdays, from 10 am weekends; closed Monday.

WILMINGTON (MAP 4)

Just north of San Pedro off the 110 Fwy is the small town of Wilmington. The 1864 Greek Revival-style home of Phineas Banning, the founding father of San Pedro's 19th-century harbor, has become the **Banning Residence Museum** (☎ 310-548-7777), 401 East M St. Tours of the restored historic mansion take in the elegant kitchen where, on 'demonstration days,' original recipes left by Banning's wife, Katherine, are re-created and served. Tours are offered hourly between 12:30 and 2:30 pm Tuesday to Thursday and weekends (also at 3:30 pm on weekends).

Only 2 blocks south is the **Drum Barracks Civil War Museum** (☎ 310-548-7509), 1052 Banning Blvd, a rare Civil War troop outpost. Also built in Greek Revival-style, it originally served as army headquarters from 1861-71. More than 7000 Union soldiers were processed through here before going east to fight in the war. The museum in the former officers' quarters displays artifacts, furniture, photographs, uniforms and a 34-star Union flag. It can be visited on guided tours only, given hourly Tuesday to Thursday between 10 am and 1 pm, weekends between 11·30 am and 3.30 pm. A $3 donation is requested.

LONG BEACH (MAP 15)

Long Beach is the southernmost community in LA County and is the county's second-largest city. Despite its size and 450,000 inhabitants, it has maintained an easy-going small-town atmosphere, reminiscent of Santa Monica until the late 1980s. The Aquarium of the Pacific, opened in June 1998, and the majestic ocean liner *Queen Mary* are main reasons for visiting. Long Beach is quickly reached from Downtown LA by the light rail Blue Line. The center of town is easily explored on foot, and there's also an excellent free shuttle bus – the Passport – whose four routes hit just about every place of interest. The AquaBus, a water taxi, shuttles hourly from 8 am to 8 pm between the aquarium and the *Queen Mary* ($1 each way).

In an effort to improve its appeal and compete with its northerly neighbors, Long Beach has been undertaking an ambitious $650 million revamping of its waterfront. Anchored by the aquarium to the west, its centerpiece is an arc-shaped harbor with docks for vessels, including whale-watching, fishing and historic vessels. In the coming years, a retail and entertainment center, linking the waterfront with the Convention Center and downtown's Pine Ave, will be taking shape as well.

Long Beach languished until the establishment of the Port of Long Beach and the discovery of oil in 1921 (some oil fields are still in operation). The Historical Society of Long Beach (☎ 562-495-1210) operates a gallery and research center at 418 Pine Ave, open Tuesday and Thursday 10 am to 3 pm, Wednesday, Friday and Saturday to 5 pm.

The nonprofit Long Beach Heritage organization (☎ 562-430-2790) conducts low-priced historical walking tours several times monthly.

The Long Beach Area **Convention & Visitors Bureau** (☎ 562-436-3645, 800-452-7829, fax 562-435-5653, www.golongbeach.org) has an office at One World Trade Center, suite 300, with weekday hours from 8·30 am to 5 pm. On weekends, there's a staffed Information Kiosk outside the Aquarium of the Pacific (same hours).

Aquarium of the Pacific

In this age of aquariums, when watery zoos are proliferating faster than rabbits on Viagra, Long Beach has fielded a contender that swims along with the best of them. It's quite wonderful to see a facility that was built so imaginatively and planned so carefully succeed so thoroughly. One of the LA area's major new attractions, the $117 million Aquarium of the Pacific (☎ 562-590-3100, www.aquariumofpacific.org), 100 Aquarium Way, should be on everyone's must-see list.

DAVID PEEVERS

See 550 species at the Aquarium of the Pacific.

Presented in a creative and informative way, the more than 10,000 fish, mammals and birds from 550 species instill a sense of wonder and awe in visitors of all ages. Sound effects, video, models and descriptive panels provide background information accessibly.

Seventeen re-created habitats and 30 smaller focus tanks represent three major littoral Pacific Rim regions. The journey kicks off in the **Great Hall of the Pacific**, dominated by a full-scale model of a blue whale, the world's largest animal. The hall ends in the titanic 30-foot tank of the Predator Exhibit – part of the **Southern California & Baja** section – whose simulated kelp forest is shared by prey and predator alike. Other aquatic denizens in this section are the frisky seals and sea lions, and gracefully drifting, otherworldly moon jellies.

Upstairs, the icy waters of the **Northern Pacific** await. This gallery is entered through a misty 'surge channel,' to the sound of waves and screeching sea birds. Puffins, murres and other diving birds give way to a large habitat featuring playful sea otters, which were once threatened with extinction. Wonderfully chilling are the giant spider crabs, whose football-sized bodies and spiny 3-foot-long arms make them look like fugitives from *Aliens*.

A completely different atmosphere prevails in the final – and most impressive – gallery, which represents the tepid waters of the **Tropical Pacific**. Particular focus is placed on the island archipelago of Palau in Micronesia (north of Australia), blessed with some of the world's most fecund and dazzling coral reefs. Fish tumbling in this environment come in a kaleidoscope of colors and include such species as angelfish, sweetlips, hawkfish, squirrelfish and several types of wrasses. Working your way through the exhibit, you 'descend' farther down the reef, encountering stunning varieties of soft and hard coral (which are animals, not plants). You will also see fragile anemones and bizarre creatures like the sea dragon, a relative of the sea horse, whose camouflage makes it look like a piece of kelp.

Laminated dive charts identifying species are available at the entrance to each section.

Several touch labs provide hands-on encounters with sea cucumbers, sea urchins, sea hares, bat rays, limpets and other underwater dwellers. Throughout the museum, there are enthusiastic volunteers on hand to answer questions. Hours are 10 am to 6 pm daily. Admission is $15, $12 for seniors, $8 for children.

Queen Mary Seaport

To casual visitors, Long Beach is best known for the passenger liner *Queen Mary* (☎ 310-435-3511), 1126 Queens Hwy, a major attraction since it was permanently moored here in 1967. The 81,237-ton liner was launched in 1934 and made 1001 crossings of the Atlantic before it was retired in 1964. One of the most luxurious of its kind, the *Queen Mary* was favored by celebrities and royalty, including Fred Astaire, Greta Garbo, Bob Hope and Marlene Dietrich. The Duke and Duchess of Windsor hold the record for most steamer trunks (72), and Winston Churchill signed the D-Day invasion papers in the 1st-class ladies' drawing room.

DAVID PEEVERS

Interior of the *Queen Mary*, Long Beach

More than 1000 feet long and 12 decks high, the *Queen Mary* was essentially divided into three sections: 3rd class in the bow (front) where the ride was the roughest, 2nd class in the stern (back) where passengers had to deal with propeller vibrations, and 1st class amidships. At $600, a 1st-class ticket cost three times as much as a 3rd-class ticket. The journey from Southampton to New York took 4½ days.

Many areas of the *Queen Mary* can be explored on a self-guided tour beginning with introductory exhibits and a short historical film with footage from the '30s. From here it's off to the engine room and the upper decks for a museum-like display of re-created state and dining rooms, as well as facilities such as the children's playroom, the gymnasium and the kitchen. A separate exhibit chronicles the ship's WWII role, when it transported 10,000 to 15,000 GIs to Europe with each journey. For a look at the 1st-class dining hall, the indoor swimming pool and other sections, you must join the Behind the Scenes Tour for an additional $7. Along the way, you'll hear amusing anecdotes and even the occasional ghost story. Part of the ship is now a pleasant hotel with 365 state rooms (see the Places to Stay chapter), elegant restaurants and lounges, a wedding chapel and gift shops.

The *Queen Mary* is open for visitors daily 10 am to 6 pm with extended summer hours. Admission is $13, $11 for seniors over 55 and military personnel, $8 for children. Parking is an additional $6.

Around the *Queen Mary*

The *Queen Mary* entrance path weaves through the **Queen's Marketplace**, a fairly tacky takeoff on 19th-century British architecture, soon to be replaced with a more tasteful setup. The huge adjacent dome-like shell once housed billionaire aviator Howard Hughes' bizarre flying boat, the *Spruce Goose*. A few years ago, the plane was sold to Oregon's Air Venture Museum and was disassembled and moved there. Today the dome is used as a Warner Bros sound stage (it was used in the making of *Batman Forever*).

The Queen has had a neighbor since June 1998, the *Scorpion* (☎ 562-435-3511), a Russian submarine whose cramped interior is open for touring. Built in 1973, it was retired in 1994. After a short introductory film, you're guided via voice-over narration by a hokey 'Russian commander' through the front torpedo room, living quarters, engine room and kitchen – all on a suffocatingly Lilliputian scale. It's hard to fathom how 78 crew members, sharing 27 bunks and two bathrooms, coexisted for months at a time. Visiting hours are the same as those of the *Queen Mary*. Admission is $10, $9 for seniors over 55 and children. Combination tickets with the *Queen Mary* are available.

Directly across Queensway Bay from the two vessels is **Shoreline Village** (☎ 310-435-2668), a shopping-and-dining complex and departure point for harbor and whale-watching cruises offered by Shoreline Village Cruises (☎ 562-495-5884), 429 Shoreline Village Drive. For deep-sea fishing expeditions – half-day to overnight – try Long Beach Sportfishing (☎ 562-432-8993), 555 Pico Ave, Long Beach.

Museums

The **Museum of Latin American Art** (☎ 562-437-1689), 628 Alamitos Ave, is one of only two facilities in the western US (the other is in Downtown LA) to showcase the works of contemporary Latin and South American artists. It's housed in a complex that integrates the historic Hippodrome Skating Rink from 1920 and the former silent-movie Balboa Studio. There's also an adjacent multipurpose entertainment and performing-arts center to get the community involved. The museum functions as the eastern anchor of the East Village Arts District, an ambitious effort at revitalizing a not-terribly-vital part of town. Hours are from 11:30 am to 7:30 pm Tuesday to Saturday, noon to 6 pm Sunday. Admission is $3.50, $2 for students and seniors, free for children under 12.

The **Long Beach Museum of Art** (☎ 562-439-2119) is housed in a 1912 Craftsman-style mansion overlooking the ocean at 2300 E Ocean Blvd. Known for its support of cutting-edge experimental artists, especially those working in video, the museum's permanent collection also has a contemporary focus. There's a small sculpture garden and a cafe. Hours are 10 am to 5 pm Wednesday to Sunday, to 8 pm Friday (free admission between 5 and 8 pm). Admission is $2, $1 for seniors and students, free for children.

NAPLES (MAP 4)

Hugging the Orange County line is the upscale residential community of Naples, which consists of a trio of islands surrounded by Alamitos Bay. The islands were reclaimed from marshland starting in 1903 by Arthur Parsons, a chronological and philosophical contemporary of Venice's Abbot Kinney. Parsons' success at community planning was more lasting than Kinney's – the **Rivo Alto Canal** still circles a network of curving lanes built up with garden-shrouded villas. It's a pleasure to stroll around the canals on waterfront walkways, although perhaps the most enchanting way to experience Naples' beauty is by water.

The boats of **Gondola Getaway** (☎ 562-433-9595), 5437 E Ocean Blvd, will cruise you à la Venice (Italy) through Naples' canals as you relax with a loaf of bread, cheese and salami (bring your own wine). The eight-boat fleet includes 30-foot authentic Venetian vessels, which have a loose oar, and the larger American boats steered with two fixed oars. Each year, Naples' gondoliers participate in the *Vogalonga* race in Venice, Italy. In fact, they beat the Italians their first time out. Gondola Getaway operates year-round daily 11 am to 11 pm; one-hour rides cost $55 per couple. Reservations are a must. (PS: Don't forget to kiss under each and every bridge.)

San Fernando Valley

One-third of the population of Los Angeles lives in what is known as simply 'the Valley,' a broad flat region of 220 sq miles that is as well-known for its earthquakes (the devastating Sylmar quake of 1971 and the Northridge tremor of 1994 both were centered here) as for its seemingly endless commercial strips and tract homes. The 1.3 million residents live in such communities as Van Nuys, Encino, Sherman Oaks and San Fernando (whose late-18th-century mission gave its name to the entire area).

Framed by mountain ranges that trap the air, the Valley is usually blanketed by a thick layer of smog and is about 20°F hotter than Westside and beach communities. Now often mocked by outsiders, living in the Valley was actually quite fashionable in the early days of Hollywood, when movie moguls including Walt Disney and John Wayne had their private homes here. Along with them came most major studios, most of which settled in and around the Burbank area. Another industry set up shop in the Valley as well: this is the capital of the adult-film industry, fed by a steady stream of wannabe actors unable to get into mainstream movies.

What the Valley lacks in cultural attractions it makes up for with vast shopping malls, a phenomenon immortalized by Frank and Moon Zappa in the song *Valley Girl*. Car culture was basically invented here, and the automobile rules supreme. Framed by four freeways, the Valley takes credit for giving birth not to just the mini-mall but also

Andrea 'researches' Gondola Getaway.

DAVID PEEVERS

to the drive-in movie theater, the drive-in bank and of course the drive-in restaurant. This is where you'll still find plenty of these '50s vestiges sporting rocket rooflines last seen in *American Graffiti*, plus one of the last places that still does car-hop service.

GLENDALE (MAP 3)

Glendale, LA County's third-largest city with a population of 180,000, is about 7 miles north of Downtown. Languishing in obscurity for centuries, Glendale finally made it onto the map in the late 19th century, when real estate holder and civic pioneer Leslie C Brand sold off the 1000 acres in the Verdugo Hills (a subrange of the San Gabriel Mountains) to settlers and convinced Henry Huntington to extend the Pacific Electric Railway from Downtown to the fledgling community. The town incorporated in 1906 and its growth catapulted from there on. Though Glendale is ethnically diverse, Armenian immigrants in particular are drawn here. Armenian has replaced Spanish as the most common non-English language in Glendale schools, and the library has a special collection on Armenian culture and history.

Glendale's central thoroughfare, Brand Blvd, is as near a middle-America Main Street as you'll find in LA County. Its highlight is the **Alex Theater**, 216 N Brand Blvd, a former movie house built in Streamline Moderne style in 1939 and restored as a fine stage venue. Nearby is the **Glendale Galleria**, Central Ave and Colorado St, a 250-store shopping mall.

Brand Library and Art Center

Brand Park, in northeast Glendale, is home to the Brand Library and Art Center (☎ 818-548-2051), 1601 W Mountain St. Housing a collection of some 50,000 books primarily on art and music, the 1904 building was originally the private mansion of the 'father of Glendale,' Leslie Brand. Inspired by the East Indian Pavilion at the 1893 Columbian Expo in Chicago, Brand had his own private phantasmagoric 'Taj Mahal' built, complete with white turrets and arches. In 1945, his widow donated it to the city of Glendale. In addition to the library, there is an art center that

runs an active schedule of painting, crafts, dance and music classes, plus a gallery and a performance hall. Hours are 1 to 9 pm Tuesday and Thursday, to 6 pm Wednesday, to 5 pm Friday and Saturday; closed holidays.

Brand Park is also home to the **Doctor's House** (☎ 818-548-2147), a Queen Anne-style home from 1880 once occupied by a quartet of doctors, which was moved here to save it from destruction and subsequently restored. Tours (Sunday between 2 and 4 pm; free) introduce you to late-19th-century medical equipment and an early 'intercom.' The park also harbors a traditional **Japanese garden** that demonstrates the link of Glendale with its Japanese sister city, Higashi-osaka; there's a teahouse called Sho-Shei-An (Teahouse of the Whispering Pines).

Forest Lawn Memorial Park – Glendale

Often cheekily called 'country club for the dead,' this humongous cemetery (☎ 818-241-4151), 1712 S Glendale Ave, is even more grandiose than its neighbor in the Hollywood Hills (see the Hollywood section). Come here to view a copy of Michelangelo's *David* and a stained-glass rendition of da Vinci's *Last Supper*. Also here are two of the world's largest paintings, *The Crucifixion* (195 x 45 feet) and *The Resurrection*.

Despite the obvious kitsch factor, it is worth a visit, if only to catch a glimpse of death culture so powerfully satirized by Evelyn Waugh's *The Loved One* (1948). It was Hubert L Eaton, a mining engineer from Missouri, who in 1917 invented the slick combination of business and death. (If you've ever gotten a call from a 'pre-need counselor,' you know what we're talking about.) The company prides itself on arranging everything for you or grandpa with just one phone call (plus a bundle of cash). Eaton's boneyards look like parks. Upright headstones are discouraged; instead there's precision landscaping and replicas of historical buildings and 'artwork.'

However one feels about this concept, Forest Lawn is a popular posthumous destination, also favored by celebrities. Most of them are literally kept under lock and guard

LA Car Culture

Detroit may have given birth to the car, but it was only after that 1000-mile cruise down Route 66 that Los Angeles added the *culture*. From hot rods to lowriders, the City of Angels has seen style and steel come together in a roaring contribution to America's artistic heritage.

It all began in the Roaring '20s, when Henry's fine Model T Fords, or 'T-buckets,' were adapted by speed demons for Los Angeles' unusually wide, straight streets. Despite the Great Depression, young people continued to modify their favorite '32 Fords, their 'little deuce coupes,' to go ever faster, tearing out seats, fenders and even removing the roofs entirely in their quest for speed. Detroit responded by building the first convertibles, but 'hot rods,' as these cut-down cruisers came to be called, remained LA's favorite example of American ingenuity.

America's booming post-WWII economy came on strong in Los Angeles, with more young people purchasing cars than ever before. Hot rodding became so popular it diversified, its practitioners splitting into two groups: the speed demons, who preferred to shoot across the salt flats of Utah in their sleek Lake Bonneville racers, reaching such dizzying speeds that their cars were made illegal on public highways, and the more urban, style-conscious cruisers, who remained partial to piling into their tamer 'street rods' for leisurely jaunts down Van Nuys Blvd and Wilshire Blvd's Miracle Mile. Showing little interest in these distinctions, newspapers simply decried the car-crazy youths as a public menace, signaling the beginning of the most mobile generation gap in history. Meanwhile, enterprising 'bad kids' Willie Parks and Jim Peterson institutionalized the craze, founding the National Hot Rod Association and *Hot Rod Magazine*, still two of the strongest automotive organizations in America.

In 1949, Los Angeles legend George Barris bought a brand-new Mercury and, with welder in hand, transformed it into a work of art. He 'chopped' the car's top for a speedy low look, raked the windshield backward and shortened the side columns. He also altered the body by welding and reshaping the Mercury's boxy nose for a sleeker profile, and stripped and filled the chrome from fender to fender for a look as smooth as silk. Calling his outrageous new car a 'custom,' Barris snared automotive artisans Gil Ayala and 'Big Daddy' Roth into his colorful camp. Custom cars were far more stylish than hot rods, with less emphasis on the engine. Their streamlined shapes and chopped tops created the illusion of speed, even as their chassis dropped so low that they scraped over speed bumps. Reshaped bodies were enhanced with luxurious interior furnishings and paint jobs featuring flames and contour-conscious murals. Barris' 'Mercs' raced through movies like *Rebel Without a Cause*, defining American cool. An entire industry of drive-through restaurants, drive-in movies and 'speed shops' made the '50s fun and California car culture a booming business.

in mausoleums. The cemetery staff is under instruction to keep celebrity-hoppers out, so you'll need ingenuity, an innocent bat of the eye or chutzpah to get inside the Great Mausoleum, where legends such as Clark Gable, Carole Lombard and Jean Harlow have made their final home. Access is easier to the Freedom Mausoleum, where you can behold the crypts of Clara Bow, Nat 'King' Cole, Gracie Allen and George Burns. Walt Disney is buried in the Court of Freedom, not far from Errol Flynn. Park hours are 9 am to 5 pm daily.

BURBANK (MAP 17)

Ever since *Rowan and Martin's Laugh-In* joked about broadcasting from 'beautiful downtown Burbank' in the late 1960s, this city has been maligned by one TV comic after another. But Burbank got the last

Detroit attempted to cater to these trends with bigger engines and bolder shapes, from the fabulously finned '57 Chevy to muscle cars – but Angelenos still found ways to improve on these. Long, low Chevrolets soon filed down thoroughfares like Whittier Blvd in East LA, sparkling with chrome veneers and glittering, translucent paint and dropped to street-scraping levels on the tiniest tires available. When police protested that these 'lowriders' were *too* low, cruisers salvaged airplane hydraulics able to lift a car to the legal height at a moment's notice. South Central youths established their own lowered look, and adapted hydraulics to make cars hop and dance, even lifting all 3500lbs of steel into gravity-defying angles. The Sunday afternoon cruise on South Central's Crenshaw Blvd is still a great spot to see the city's best rides.

Today, hot rods, customs and lowriders cruise LA's streets alongside the Lamborghinis, Rolls Royces, SUVs (sport utility vehicles) and Hummers beloved by the upper classes, as well as the 'monster trucks' and 'art cars' built by more rural Californians.

Car culture continues to grow and change. Check out the current cruisers created from Japan's best designs: the new 'pocket rockets,' Hondas and other small cars adapted for speed and style with plenty of chrome. Los Angeles' prolific gearheads won't rest as long as steel, gasoline and the wide open freeways continue to come together so seamlessly in Southern California.

Curse the freeways and smog if you must, but LA's automotive enthusiasts combine form and function like no other art form save architecture. And, when you're stuck in traffic – the quintessential LA experience – you may understand how one glimpse of a gleaming '59 Cadillac or souped-up '62 Corvette can transform your stressful situation into a moment of transcendental beauty.

Paige R Penland

laugh. It now calls itself America's entertainment center – with good reason. Walt Disney Productions, Warner Bros Studios, the National Broadcasting Company (NBC) and Columbia Pictures' television division all call Burbank home, as do several recording companies.

Located some 11 miles north of Downtown in the eastern San Fernando Valley, Burbank got its name from a New Hampshire dentist, Dr David Burbank, who came to the area in 1866. Despite growth at a glacial pace, Burbank was the first Valley city to incorporate in 1891 with just 500 residents; today it has 94,000. Besides the movie industry, the manufacturing of aircraft put butter on people's bread after Lockheed set up shop near today's Burbank Airport in the 1930s, just in time to build bombers for WWII. Dating back to roughly the same time is Burbank's **City Hall**, an Art Deco jewel built by the Works Progress Administration at the corner of Olive Ave and 3rd St.

To catch that *American Graffiti* vibe, head for **Bob's Big Boy**, 4211 Riverside Drive, on Saturday and Sunday nights for their carhop service. This classic coffeeshop from the late '40s was built in Streamline Moderne style by Wayne McAllister and is the last surviving outlet of what used to be a large chain of restaurants. Friday is 'classic car' night.

Warner Bros Studios Tour

Don't expect razzle dazzle special effects and thrilling theme rides when visiting the Warner Bros Studios (☎ 818-972-8687), 4000 Warner Blvd. Instead, you'll get a rare and realistic glimpse behind the scenes at one of Hollywood's oldest movie and TV production facilities (1998 was its 75th anniversary). The 2¼-hour tour kicks off with a 15-minute 'greatest hits' film collage followed by a visit to the Warner Bros Museum, both an archive and an altar to the stars. It's filled with costumes, letters and other paraphernalia, including James Dean's work shirt from *Giant* and the frilly hats from *My Fair Lady*.

Next up is a drive through the 110-acre backlot with its 33 sound stages where interior scenes shoot. The exact route depends on production schedules and may include a visit to Stage 24 *(Friends)*, Stage 11 *(ER)* or the 98-foot-high Stage 16, the tallest sound stage ever built. There may also be stops at technical departments such as Properties, the Garage (home of the Batmobile) and Costumes. Finally, you'll canvass several outdoor sets such as the Western-style Laramie Street *(Bonanza* and *Roots)* and the 'Jungle Set' *(Jurassic Park* and *Camelot)*. However, there is no guarantee that you'll see any stars, especially during the summer TV hiatus.

Tours run weekdays, every half-hour between 9 am and 3:30 pm in summer and every hour to 3 pm in winter ($30). They start at the visitors' center next to Gate 4 at the intersection of Hollywood Way and Olive Ave. Reservations are required; children under 8 are not allowed. Parking next to the visitors' center is free.

NBC Studios Tour

NBC Television Studios (☎ 818-840-3538), 3000 W Alameda Ave, has been an LA mainstay since 1952, producing such American TV legends as Bob Hope and Johnny Carson. Today, Jay Leno carries the torch as host of the famous *Tonight Show*. Tours usually take you behind the set of this program as well as into the Wardrobe, Makeup, Set Construction, Special Effects and Sound Effects departments. Tours last 70 minutes and leave regularly weekdays 9 am to 3 pm; they cost $7 ($3.75 for children ages five to 12). Parking is free. Make reservations in summer, as tours sell out early. For information on how to obtain tickets for a taping at NBC, see Getting into a Studio in the Entertainment chapter.

UNIVERSAL CITY (MAP 17)

Although it's a workplace for thousands and is visited by millions every year, Universal City is a city without residents – literally (the last two died some time in the 1980s). About 9 miles north of Downtown, Universal City's only purpose is being home to Universal Studios, the production company as well as the theme park, and the entertainment complex around Universal City Walk.

Universal Studios Hollywood

Universal Studios Hollywood (☎ 818-508-9600), 100 Universal City Plaza, is the world's largest movie and television studio and the county's most important theme park. The studios date to 1915, when Carl Laemmle (the founder) sold eggs to the cheering-and-jeering audiences, who paid 25¢ to watch films being made. Formal studio tours began in 1964 and have since been experienced by 90 million visitors.

A few general words of advice: You'll need to devote a full day to Universal, and to beat the crowds you should get there as early in the morning as possible. The summer months are not just the hottest but also the busiest, so be prepared for long waits in stifling heat. Bring a hat, sunblock, patience and – if cutting costs is your aim – bottled water. Overall, though, prices for sodas ($2) and snacks (less than $10) here are not nearly as extor-

Valley Secession & the Balkanization of LA

To visitors, Los Angeles is a giant metropolis that sprawls seamlessly mile after mile. Few realize that what they're looking at is actually a mosaic of 88 cities, including one called Los Angeles, that collectively make up LA County. Anger and resentment about the way the city of LA is run is so great in some communities that they are striving to secede and gain citihood of their own. Spearheading the effort is the San Fernando Valley with its 1.3 million residents. Since 1998, a group called Valley Voters Organized Towards Empowerment has been collecting the more than 140,000 signatures needed to launch a feasibility study about breaking away from LA.

If they succeed, the next step would be for the Local Agency Formation Commission to conduct a study on the viability of the new city and the impact secession would have on the remainder of LA. Based on their findings, the agency then decides on whether to place the issue on the ballot, which would put the issue to voters in the next round of elections. A majority of voters in the entire city of LA – not just in the proposed new city – would then have to approve the secession.

Already waiting in the wings are organizations in other parts of the city ready to move ahead with their own citihood petition drives if the Valley effort proves successful. Besides San Pedro and Wilmington in the South Bay, they are Westchester, Mar Vista, Playa del Rey and Venice, South Central and west Los Angeles. Planners envision a city of West LA, for instance, to have north-south boundaries from Mulholland Drive in the Santa Monica Mountains to LAX and east-west boundaries from Pacific Palisades to, and including, Hollywood.

tionate as they are at Disneyland. Beer and margaritas are served as well. Some rides, including the popular 'Back to the Future' and 'Jurassic Park,' have minimum height requirements (usually 42 or 46 inches).

Universal Studios is spread across 413 acres, the upper and lower sections connected by a quarter-mile-long escalator. To get your bearings, head straight for the **Backlot Tour**, a 45-minute part-educational, part-thrill ride behind the scenes of movie making. A tram whisks you and about 250 other visitors past the studio's maze of 35 sound stages while your guide showers you with movie trivia. You'll see where parts of *Jurassic Park* and *Apollo 13* were filmed, rumble past outdoor sets such as Courthouse Square, best known from *Back to the Future*, and the Bates Hotel featured in Hitchcock's *Psycho*. During the thrill portion of the tour you'll experience such special-effects crises as an 8.3-magnitude earthquake, a flash flood, a collapsing bridge, volcanic lava, and encounters with a hokey plastic shark and a roaring in-your-face King Kong.

Universal doesn't have Disneyland's number of rides, but this actually keeps the overwhelm quotient down, as it's usually possible to experience them all in one day. One of our favorites is **Back to the Future – The Ride**, which blasts you through time and space in a DeLorean and has you free-falling into volcanic tunnels, plunging down glacial cliffs and colliding with dinosaurs (go for a seat in the front). **The ET Adventure** is a gentle flight aboard a monorailed 'bicycle' through a charming fantasy world. **Backdraft** is a pyrotechnic walking adventure that lets you catch a glimpse at amazing special effects. The climactic conclusion has you engulfed by an inferno roaring through a chemical factory, with ruptured fuel lines and tanks exploding all around you. Top billing, though, goes to **Jurassic Park – The Ride**, a float through a prehistoric jungle past friendly herbivores before coming face to face with vicious velociraptors and a ravenous tyrannosaurus rex. The ultimate thrill is…well, let's not spoil the surprise. (Hint: You'll get wet.)

Live shows, staged several times daily, also form part of the Universal experience.

Water World features jet-ski stunts, giant fireballs and a crashing seaplane, while **Beetlejuice** is a fanciful dance and music extravaganza. Fancy quick-draws and fist fighting are at the heart of the old standby **The Wild, Wild, Wild West Stunt Show**, though we preferred learning about special effects at **The World of Cinematic**. Children howled with glee at the cute birds, pigs, dogs and cats that form the cast of the **Animal Actors Stage**, and so did we.

While walking the grounds you may run into Charlie Chaplin, Marilyn Monroe, Frankenstein or Woody Woodpecker, though it was Lucy and Ethel from *I Love Lucy* who seemed to follow us around on the day we visited.

Universal Studios is open daily (except Thanksgiving and Christmas) 8 am to 10 pm in summer, 9 am to 7 pm the rest of the year. Admission is $38, $33 for seniors over 60, $28 for kids up to 12. Unlimited annual passes are available for $69/59/54, respectively. A combined admission ticket to Universal Studios and Sea World in San Diego costs $69 for adults (including seniors) and $51 for children ages three to 11. Parking is $7.

Universal City Walk

Adjoining Universal Studios is this hugely popular artificial outdoor mall, dreamed up to provide a controlled fantasy environment

Lucy and Ethel at Universal Studios Hollywood

of shops, restaurants, cinemas and nightclubs for those too intimidated by the – largely imagined – dangers of urban reality. (It is telling that the mall opened in 1993, just one year after the Rodney King riots.) Plenty of inspiration, imagination and innovation went into the critically acclaimed design. There are lots of whimsical visual surprises, including a '57 Chevy bursting through a freeway sign and a 27-foot gorilla guarding a music-store entrance. The best time to visit is at night, when vibrant neon signs transform the promenade into a miniature Vegas-style strip. Parking is $7. For details on dining, see Places to Eat; for nightlife, see Entertainment.

NORTH HOLLYWOOD (MAP 17)

A district just west of Burbank and some 11 miles northwest of Downtown LA, North Hollywood is currently undergoing a major renaissance. Its main artery is Lankershim Blvd, which bisects the district diagonally north to south. Dubbed NoHo, it's home to a fledgling bohemian arts district centered on Lankershim and Magnolia Blvds. In the 5200 block of Lankershim is the **Academy of Television Arts & Sciences,** fronted by the distinctive Emmy statue. Close by, an arts complex with galleries, cinemas, performance space, restaurants and shops is in the works. At 3919 Lankershim is **Campo de Cahuenga**, a re-created adobe building commemorating the site where the peace treaty ending the US-Mexican War was signed in 1847. (For more on NoHo's scene, see the Places to Eat and Entertainment chapters.)

ELSEWHERE IN THE VALLEY
Japanese Garden (Map 2)

The Bureau of Sanitation came up with an inventive and pleasant way to put tax dollars to work when it built the Japanese Garden (☎ 818-756-8166), located at the Tillmann Water Reclamation Plant, 6100 Woodley Ave in Van Nuys. A serene oasis, the 6½-acre area includes Zen and tea gardens. It is entirely fed with reclaimed water. Tours ($3) are offered by reservation only, but the garden is usually open for strolling Monday to Thursday noon to 4 pm.

LA Garden Culture

Traffic and freeways? Sure. But *gardens*? Absolutely. LA's antidote to the 'overwhelm factor' has been the creation of many peaceful and exotic garden settings. The following list includes gardens throughout LA County where only your own thoughts will interrupt you.

Descanso Gardens (☎ 626-952-4400), 1418 Descanso Drive, La Cañada Flintridge. This is a year-round delight for flower lovers, with some 100,000 camellias in bloom from October through March. Lilacs and orchids are at their best in April, while roses and other annuals blossom beginning in May. Flower shows feature irises, azaleas and other varieties throughout the year. Bird lovers have identified 150 species in the gardens.

Hannah Carter Japanese Garden (☎ 310-825-4574), 10619 Bellagio Rd, Bel Air. By reservation, you can wander this garden on the edge of the UCLA campus. Built in 1961, it features a teahouse and imported vegetation.

Los Angeles State & County Arboretum (☎ 626-821-3222), 301 N Baldwin Ave, Arcadia. This arboretum re-creates many of the world's major landscapes, arranged by continent, around a spring-fed lake. That's one reason this 127-acre garden has been so popular with filmmakers – including John Huston, who filmed much of *The African Queen* (starring Humphrey Bogart and Katharine Hepburn) here.

Orcutt Ranch Horticulture Center (☎ 818-883-6641), 23600 Roscoe Blvd, Canoga Park. Huge live-oak trees, some perhaps as old as six centuries, shade a Spanish-style ranch house built in 1920. Gardening classes are offered regularly on the grounds.

Rancho Santa Ana Botanic Garden (☎ 909-625-8767), 1500 N College Ave, Claremont. This 85-acre garden displays the world's largest array of native California plants. Trails writhe through species from deserts, mountain woodlands and the coast.

Covered in greater detail elsewhere in this book are the Huntington Library, Art Collection & Botanical Gardens (San Gabriel Valley); the Japanese Garden at the Tillman Water Reclamation Plant (San Fernando Valley); the Virginia Robinson Gardens (Beverly Hills); and the South Coast Botanical Gardens (Coastal Communities).

Paramount Ranch

In the west Valley community of Agoura Hills is the Paramount Ranch (☎ 818-597-9192, ext 201), a 760-acre western movie set bought by Paramount Pictures in 1927 as a location for such movies as *The Cisco Kid* and still used today for the filming of TV's *Dr Quinn, Medicine Woman* and other projects. You can walk around the set by yourself daily from 8 am to sunset (if you're lucky, filming may take place on your visit) or join a free ranger-led one-hour tour usually offered at 9:30 am the first and third Saturday of the month. Take the 101 Fwy north from Downtown LA to the Kanan Rd exit, head south on Kanan Rd for three-quarters of mile and turn left on Cornell Way (stay to the right). Continue for about 2½ miles and look for the entrance on your right.

Mission San Fernando Rey de España

The second Spanish mission built in the LA area (after San Gabriel) – and the 17th in California – was Mission San Fernando Rey de España (☎ 818-361-0186), 15151 San

Fernando Mission Rd, Mission Hills in the northern Valley, roughly where the 405 and 118 Fwys meet. Founded in 1797, it has twice been destroyed by earthquakes (in 1818 and 1971), but each time has risen like a phoenix from the ashes with major efforts by parishioners. The highlight is the mission's 1822 convent, built with 4-foot-thick adobe walls and 21 Roman arches. The walls of the Old Mission Church are 7-feet thick. Inside the convent is an elaborate Baroque altarpiece from Spain. The museum deals with mission history and displays Native American artifacts. Peacocks strut around the grounds, which are sprinkled with statues and a 35-bell carillon. Mission hours are 9 am to 4:30 pm daily. Admission is $4, $3 for seniors and children ages seven to 15. Sunday mass in the old church is at 9 and 10:30 am.

San Gabriel Valley

The San Gabriel Valley refers to an ill-defined area northeast of Downtown LA, snuggled against the southern rim of the San Gabriel Mountains (the range that forms the northern border of the LA Basin – also see Mountains later in this chapter). Although the district derives its name from the community of San Gabriel, the cultural center of the region is Pasadena. Originally inhabited by Gabrieleño Indians, the San Gabriel Valley was claimed in 1769 by missionaries, who established Mission San Gabriel Archangel near the banks of the San Gabriel River in 1771. In the following century, land-grant ranchos were broken into smaller tracts and a series of orchard towns emerged. As population expanded, these towns grew together and today the valley has become a continuous suburban sprawl, extending more than 25 miles east from Alhambra and Pasadena in the west all the way to Claremont on the border of San Bernardino County.

PASADENA (MAP 16)

The Tournament of Roses (see The World 'Tourns' Attention to Pasadena) may have given Pasadena long-lasting fame, but it's the progressive spirit of this stately city that characterizes it today. From its impressive early-20th-century mansions to its fine art museums and culinary pleasures, Pasadena is a happening place.

Approximately a 15-minute drive northeast of Downtown, Pasadena rests in the shadow of the San Gabriel Mountains. The city was founded in 1873 by Midwestern settlers who gave it a Chippewa name meaning 'crown of the valley.' Pasadena incorporated in 1886, and before long five commuter trains a day linked it with Downtown LA. Wealthy Easterners, drawn by the temperate climes, made Pasadena a fashionable winter haunt in the late 19th century. Those who stayed permanently included Henry Huntington, whose estate – now the Huntington Library, Art Collection & Botanical Gardens – is one of LA's greatest cultural treasures.

In the early 20th century, Pasadena became a haven for writers, painters and especially architects. In 1891, Amos G Throop founded Throop University, which evolved into the California Institute of Technology. In 1940, Southern California's first freeway opened, the Arroyo Seco Parkway – since designated as the Pasadena (110) Fwy. This connected the city with Downtown LA, and ever more commuters settled in Pasadena. About 139,000 people now call the city home. The mountains are often obscured by smog, but when it's clear there are few prettier places in the LA area.

The Pasadena **Visitors Bureau** (☎ 626-795-9311, fax 626-795-9656) is at 171 S Los Robles Ave. Hours are 8 am to 5 pm weekdays, 10 am to 4 pm Saturday. A fleet of free Pasadena ARTS buses regularly shuttle people between Old Pasadena, the Pasadena Playhouse District and South Lake Ave.

Old Pasadena

Remember surf rockers Jan and Dean's 'Little Old Lady from Pasadena,' who was 'the terror of Colorado Blvd'? That was back in the '60s, but Pasadena's main street, Colorado Blvd, is still cruisin' territory for the high school and college crowd and, perhaps, an occasional little old lady.

Old Town is the heart of Pasadena, a 20-block historic district with early-20th-century buildings stretching out along Colorado Blvd between Arroyo Pkwy and Pasadena Ave. In the early 1990s, this area underwent a renaissance that lined its main streets and alleyways with restaurants and coffeehouses, upscale boutiques and bookstores, galleries and antique stores, nightclubs and cinema complexes. See the Places to Eat, Entertainment and Shopping chapters for details.

For a glimpse at Pasadena's heyday as a resort town, head 1 block south of Colorado Blvd on Raymond Ave to Green St, where you'll find an imposing Moorish and Spanish Colonial structure. Featuring a domed tower connected to the main building via a bridge, this is the complex made up of the **Hotel Green** and the **Castle Green**. Built at the end of the 19th century, they were popular lodges for vacationers arriving at the nearby **Santa Fe Railroad Station**, 222 S Raymond Ave. While the glory of the Hotel Green (entrance at 50 E Green St) seriously faded as it became a low-income and senior citizens' residence, the Castle Green was given a thorough face-lift and was converted into condominiums (closed to the public).

Adobe Buildings

Built with mud and clay bricks dried under the sun, adobe buildings are a signature of the southwestern US. Greater Los Angeles has numerous examples of Spanish-era adobe architecture, starting with the area's two missions, at San Gabriel and San Fernando. If this regional tradition is of special interest, you may want to seek out some of these other historic structures.

Andrés Pico Adobe (☎ 818-365-7810), 10940 Sepulveda Blvd, Mission Hills. Named after the military commander in Mexican LA, this house has been restored after the 1994 Northridge quake and is now home to the San Fernando Valley Historical Society. Built in 1834, it's the second-oldest house in Los Angeles and contains period furnishings. Visitors are welcome on Monday 10 am to 3 pm; free admission.

Avila Adobe This is LA's oldest house. See the Olvera St section for details.

Leonis Adobe (☎ 818-222-6511), 23537 Calabasas Rd, Calabasas. Dating from 1844, this two-story, Monterey-style ranch house has been restored to its appearance during its mid-19th-century heyday, when it was home to the colorful Don Miguel Leonis. Note the 600-year-old oak tree; there's also a bar, blacksmith shop and *horno* (adobe oven). It's open Wednesday to Sunday 1 to 4 pm; $2 admission.

Los Encinos State Historical Park (☎ 818-784-4849), 16756 Moorpark St, Encino. This park preserves a mid-19th-century stagecoach stop, including a nine-room adobe built in 1849 (it was huge by standards of the time) and a two-story limestone cottage from 1870. Both sustained earthquake damage in 1994 and can only be seen from the outside. The park is open Wednesday to Sunday 10 am to 5 pm; free admission.

Pio Pico State Historic Park (☎ 562-695-1217), 6003 Pioneer Blvd, Whittier. The adobe building here dates from 1850 and also suffered serious damage in the 1994 earthquake. It's a two-story adobe hacienda built by Don Pio Pico, the last Mexican governor of California, next to the San Gabriel River and deeded to the state in 1917. It's been the centerpiece of a 9000-acre state historic park since 1927. The park is open Wednesday to Sunday 10 am to 5 pm; free admission.

RICK GERHARTER

Castle Green was a popular lodge in the late 19th century.

Norton Simon Museum

The new Getty Center may get all the attention these days, but the Norton Simon Museum (☎ 626-449-6840), 411 W Colorado Blvd, should not be overlooked. It boasts one of the finest collections of European art, from the Renaissance to the 20th century, and an exquisite sampling of 2000 years of Asian sculpture from India and Southeast Asia. Boticelli, Cézanne, Degas, Goya, Matisse, Monet, Picasso, Raphael, Rembrandt, Renoir, Rubens, Toulouse-Lautrec and van Gogh are just a few of the big-name artists found here. Museum hours are noon to 6 pm Thursday to Sunday. Admission is $4, $2 for seniors and students, free for children under 12.

History Norton Simon (1907-1993) was a skilled entrepreneur who started out, in 1924, by investing in a bankrupt orange-juice bottling plant, eventually growing his empire into a multinational corporation that included Hunt-Wesson Foods, McCalls Corporation and Canada Dry. Simon's love for

art, evidenced by his 25 years of collecting, culminated in his reorganizing of the Pasadena Museum of Modern Art (founded in 1924) in 1974. The museum was renamed in his honor. A $5 million renovation – based on designs by Frank Gehry and begun in 1998 – is intended to improve lighting and display conditions. A high-ceiling tea house, made of glass and wood, will moor the redesigned sculptural garden. Some galleries may be closed because of the renovation.

Collection In the opinion of many an expert, Norton Simon had far better taste in art than J Paul Getty, amassing a collection superior in quality, if not in size. Indeed, rare works by history's most skilled and renowned artists are found here. Among the oldest pieces in the collection are depiction of religious figures – including a stunning *Madonna and Child* by Paolo Veneziano done in tempera and gold leaf. Veneziano presents his subjects in an oddly detached way, with the baby Jesus bearing distinct adult features. This contrasts sharply with versions of the same motif by 15th-century Italian Renaissance artists Botticelli and Raphael, who show mother and son in a soft and natural way, wrapped up in a tender embrace and with Jesus as a chubby tot.

Other highlights in the old masters galleries are the stylized double painting *Adam and Eve* (ca 1530) by the German Lucas Cranach the Elder and *The Resurrection* (1455), anchored by a strangely one-footed Jesus, by the Flemish artist Dietric Bouts.

Examples of the Baroque period include several portraits by Rembrandt, including a portrait in progress of his son Titus (1650). Also look for several works by Canaletto, an opera-set designer turned landscape artist who specialized in realistic landscapes painted with postcard-like precision.

French Impressionists are well-represented as well. Leading the pack are Edgar Degas' more than 100 pastels, drawings, oils and bronze sculptures. Degas' artistic worship of the female figure shines through brightly in his series of ballet dancers and seated nudes. Usually portrayed facing away from the viewer, their individual identities are less important than the aesthetics of their bodies and their movement. The hauntingly colored *Tahitian Woman and Boy* (1891) is a striking work by bourgeois turned-bohemian Paul Gauguin, who traded his life as a stock broker in France for that of a painter in the South Seas. Works by Pablo Picasso share gallery space with those of Matisse, Gris, Braque and Seurat. Among our personal favorites is Claude Monet's rendition of his garden at Vétheuil, a sun-splashed burst of pigment and flowers radiating happiness and beauty. A more somber style is employed by Edouard Manet in *The Ragpicker* (1865-69), showing a singular figure whose loneliness is visually enhanced by a neutral gray background.

Simon's collection of Indian, Nepalese, Thai and Cambodian sculpture will be dramatically displayed in redesigned basement galleries. Examples of Western sculpture, on view in the museum garden, include Auguste Rodin's *Burghers of Calais*, Renoir's version of his friend Rodin and abstract works by Henry Moore.

Wrigley Mansion & Gardens

South of the Norton Simon at 391 Orange Grove Blvd stands the imposing Wrigley Mansion (1914; ☎ 626-449-4100), an ornate Italian Renaissance-style villa. Once owned by chewing-gum magnate William Wrigley Jr, it now houses the headquarters of the Tournament of Roses Association. The home, with its warm wood paneling, Italian marble fireplaces and brocade wallpaper, can be toured for free February through August on Thursdays between 2 and 4 pm. At all other times only the lush gardens, ablaze with roses and camellias, are open to the public.

Rose Bowl & Arroyo Seco

Among Pasadena's grandest architectural achievements is the 98,636-seat Rose Bowl stadium (1922; ☎ 626-577-3106), 1001 Rose Bowl Drive, home of the UCLA Bruins football team. It's also the site of the Rose Bowl Game, the annual college football championship played here on New Year's Day. The second Sunday of each month, a huge flea market is held on the surrounding grounds

(see the Flea Markets boxed text in the Shopping chapter).

The Rose Bowl sits in the midst of the 61-sq-acre **Brookside Park**, a broadening of Arroyo Seco. Once an orange grove, this gorge is now a center for such recreational pursuits as hiking, biking and horseback riding. In the early 20th century, this part of Pasadena was the center of 'Arroyo Culture,' an aesthetic movement involving many of the craftsmen, artists and architects behind some of Pasadena's great homes. Dating from that period is the imposing former **Vista del Arroyo Hotel** (1903), at 125 S Grand Ave, restored in the 1980s to house the Ninth Circuit US Court of Appeals (☎ 626-441-2797). There are free docent-led tours offered on the third Friday of each month (reservations are a must).

Spanning the arroyo is the city's most infamous landmark, the **Colorado St Bridge** (1913). 'Suicide Bridge,' as it has come to be known, became the area's favorite jumping spot for those hard hit by the stock market crash in 1929 and has since remained popular among forlorn souls. The bridge recently underwent a $28 million restoration and is now open for pedestrians and auto traffic.

Art Center College of Design

Overlooking the Rose Bowl from a ridgetop is this world-renowned arts college (☎ 626-396-2200), 1700 Lida St. Founded in 1930, it runs a widely respected undergraduate program and has an international student body. Majors include advertising, film, fine art, graphic design, illustration, photography and product design. Besides a sculpture garden, it contains several public galleries with rotating shows of top-name artists and designers (as well as the usually excellent student work) in various media. Free campus tours are offered Monday to Thursday at 2 pm, Friday at 1:30 pm when school is in session. Reservations must be made at least one day prior to your visit.

Pasadena Civic Center Area

This complex along Garfield Ave, a few blocks east of Old Pasadena, contains intricately detailed structures blending Italian

Renaissance, Spanish Colonial and Beaux Arts styles. At the top end of this north-south axis is the **Public Library** (1927; ☎ 626-405-4066), 285 E Walnut St. On the southern edge stands the **Civic Auditorium** (1931; ☎ 626-449-7360), 300 E Green St, home to television's Emmy Awards ceremony. In the center, on the east side of Garfield Ave, is beautifully domed **City Hall** (1927; ☎ 626-405-4222), built around a courtyard garden and fountain. Directly east, across Euclid Ave, is Plaza Las Fuentes, a 6-acre hotel, office and restaurant complex.

Just east of this ensemble is one of Pasadena's most impressive religious structures, the **First United Methodist Church**, 500 E Colorado Blvd. This humongous Gothic Revival structure dates to 1924 and boasts some surprising architectural twists. Although its basic layout is cross-shaped, the sanctuary is actually in the form of a semi-circle. A magnificent four-manual Skinner organ, embedded in a hand-carved wooden case, looms behind the altar. There are stained-glass windows, and the ceiling has delicate fan-vaulting. The church is closed except during services, but if you ask nicely at the adjacent office, someone will gladly let you inside.

Pacific Asia Museum

With its upturned roofs, dragon motifs and serene courtyard, the Chinese-imperial-palace-style museum (☎ 626-449-2742), 46 N Los Robles Ave, is a bit of an architectural oddity. The building was commissioned in the 1920s by art collector Grace Nicholson, who inhabited her 'Chinese Treasure House' until her death in 1948. The museum, with its five-millennia compilation of both rare and

The World 'Tourns' Its Attention to Pasadena

Every year Pasadena enters the world's limelight on New Year's Day as it stages the Tournament of Roses Parade, seen locally by about 1 million spectators and beamed to millions more in some 100 countries via satellite. Conceived by the Valley Hunt Club in 1890, the event originally consisted of a parade of flower-festooned horse-and-buggies followed by young men competing in foot races and tugs-of-war.

So why 'tournament'? That name hails from a third event called the 'tourney of rings,' which is similar to a medieval knights' joust. It involved mounted horsemen equipped with 12-foot lances trying to spear three rings hung 30 feet apart while riding at top speed. Today's Rose Parade no longer includes that event, but it does feature marching bands, horses and humongous floats, all smothered in flowers and floral material. Average floats consume about 100,000 blossoms and cost $250,000 and up.

After the parade, floats can be admired close-up for two days at Victory Park, 2575 Paloma St.

Since 1902, a football game has traditionally followed the parade, later known as 'The Granddaddy of All Bowl Games.' The contest was so well received that in 1922 a 100,000-seat stadium, the Rose Bowl, was built. The New Year's Day game still matches the best Pac-10 (West Coast) university team with the best from the Big 10 (Great Lakes region).

common art and artifacts, opened in 1961. Hours are 10 am to 5 pm Wednesday to Sunday. Admission is $5, $3 for students, free for children under 12.

Collection The permanent collection consists of 17,000 objects, displayed on a rotating basis and supplemented by major touring exhibits. The museum is strongest in the field of Chinese ceramics from several dynasties. (Unlike the Western cultures, the Chinese chronicle their history not in centuries but in dynasties, with each epoch producing distinct styles, colors and shapes of ceramics.) Other exhibits include Japanese paintings and drawings by Hiroshige and Hokusai, and unusual items such as the assortment of Chinese cricket cages.

Despite their extraordinary collection, museum curators might give some thought to improving the way objects are presented. Dozens of items are normally crammed into glass cabinets, often devoid of any apparent chronological, geographical or thematic connection. Another problem is the museum assumes visitors already have some knowledge of Asian art, which may explain the paucity of informative panels.

South Lake District
Pasadena's premier financial and shopping district wraps around Lake Ave, south of Colorado Blvd about 10 blocks east of Old Pasadena. There are major department stores along this strip, but Lake Ave's distinction is its several European-style arcades. The **Burlington Arcade**, 380 S Lake Ave, is a replica of the 19th-century London original with its skylights and arches. The **Colonnade**, 350 S Lake Ave, is similarly elegant with its grand columns. Another arcade, **The Commons**, focuses on gourmet goods and imported fashions.

Kidspace
A few blocks west of the South Lake District is Kidspace (☎ 626-449-9143), 390 S El Molino Ave, a museum that will keep kids entertained in an intelligent, educational fashion. Just past the entrance are three environments that invite interaction: a super-

market, a fire station and a post office. Beyond are Eco Beach with murals, aquariums and a sandy pit, which kids explore equipped with shovels and buckets. Kidspace keeps odd hours, though you should find it open Wednesday 2 to 5 pm and weekends 12:30 to 5 pm (call ahead). Admission is $5 for adults and children, $3.50 for seniors.

California Institute of Technology (Caltech)
Twenty-six Nobel laureates and 43 winners of the National Medal of Science are faculty members or alumni of Caltech (☎ 626-395-6327, www.caltech.edu), 551 S Hill Ave, which gives you some idea why it's regarded with awe in academic circles. (Yes, Albert Einstein did sleep here.) Now one of the world's most important research centers, this diminutive university has just 800 undergraduates and 1000 graduate students. Among their recent notable projects: designing the automated gene sequencer employed in *Jurassic Park*.

Caltech actually began life in 1891 as a school of arts and crafts called Throop University, after its founder, Amos G Throop. Thanks to the instigation of astronomer George E Hale, who joined the board of trustees in 1907, the school quickly evolved into a scientific and engineering institution and was renamed California Institute of Technology in 1920.

Campus tours, conducted weekdays at 2 pm year-round (except holidays, rainy days and during winter break), include a visit to the renowned seismology laboratory. Tours leave from the visitors' center (☎ 626-395-6327), 315 S Hill Ave. Architectural campus tours are conducted on the fourth Thursday of the month at 11 am (no tours in July, August and December); they leave at 11 am from the front hall of the Athenaeum, 551 S Hill Ave. Reservations are mandatory (call the visitors' center). All tours are free.

Jet Propulsion Laboratory (JPL)
Located in La Cañada just north of Pasadena proper is the Caltech-operated JPL (Map 3; ☎ 626-354-4321), 4800 Oak Grove Drive, NASA's main center for robotic exploration of the solar system with some 5700

Famous Names of Caltech

Dozens of Caltech scientists have helped pave the way for progress in the 20th century. Earthquake studies were essentially pioneered here in the 1920s, when geologist Harry Wood invented the first seismograph. And Charles Richter, along with Beno Gutenberg, invented the Richter scale, which is still used to express the magnitude of an earthquake. Ever since, Caltech has become a clearinghouse for earthquake measurements anywhere in the world, and its scientists are usually the first to appear on TV whenever a 'shaker' rattles through California.

One of the college's most famous Nobel recipients was two-time winner Linus Pauling. His discovery of the nature of the chemical bond – how atoms link up to form molecules in both living and nonliving systems – facilitated breakthroughs both in chemical and molecular biology and in the creation of synthetic products. This netted him the Chemistry prize in 1954. He was also awarded the Nobel Peace Prize in 1962.

Another revolutionary breakthrough came in the early 1960s when physicist Murray Gell-Mann (1969 Nobel winner) detected that the smallest building blocks of matter were not protons and neutrons, but even smaller particles he named quarks. This led to new findings in subatomic physics and to greater understanding of the Big Bang. Another famous name is that of psychobiologist Roger Sperry (1981 Nobel winner), who figured out left-brain/right-brain assignations.

Many of Caltech's accomplishments have been in the field of astronomy, prompting a leading British scientist to say, 'The universe of astronomy has no center, but the universe of astronomers does.' Achievements include a first map of the sky as seen from the Northern Hemisphere in 1948; discovering countless new stars, galaxies and comets (a second survey is currently underway); and the 1964 discovery that quasars were the most powerful and distant objects, allowing astronomers a glimpse at how the universe looked long before the birth of our galaxy.

employees. Though not open to the public, JPL provides glimpses of its activities on its website at www.jpl.nasa.gov and through an annual Open House (usually in June).

JPL was an outgrowth of Caltech's Graduate Aeronautical Laboratory (GALCIT), headed by Theodore von Karman, whose experiments in the 1930s laid the scientific foundation of modern aviation and jet flight. JPL spacecraft have visited all of our solar system's planets except Pluto (the 'Pluto-Kuiper Express' is in the planning stages).

Current missions include the Cassini (orbits Saturn), the Galileo Europa (orbits Jupiter), the Mars Global Surveyor (orbits Mars) and Ulysses (flies by the sun). The most spectacular recent mission was the landing of the Mars Pathfinder on July 4, 1997.

Huntington Library, Art Collection & Botanical Gardens

Railroad tycoon Henry E Huntington named his opulent estate, built in 1910, after an Italian enclave: tiny San Marino, the world's smallest republic. Today Huntington's 207-acre manor and grounds are one of Southern California's not-to-be-missed attractions.

The Huntington Library, Art Collection & Botanical Gardens (☎ 626-405-2141, www.huntington.org), 1151 Oxford Rd, is at once a cultural center, a research institution and a wonderful place to spend a relaxing afternoon. The sprawling botanical gardens alone – with some 14,000 species of trees, shrubs, flowering and nonflowering plants – are worthy of a visit. A highlight is the Desert Garden, featuring the widest array of mature cacti and other succulents in the US. Other visitor favorites are the Japanese Garden and the Shakespearean Garden. An English tea room (reservations ☎ 626-683-8131) serves light afternoon meals.

Even more impressive is the library's collection of rare English-language books, maps and manuscripts, including a Gutenberg Bible, the Ellesmere manuscript of Chaucer's *Canterbury Tales*, Benjamin Franklin's handwritten autobiography and a double folio edition of Audubon's *Birds of America*.

The Huntington Art Gallery, in the former family mansion, boasts a collection of 18th-century British and French paintings (among them Thomas Gainsborough's *Blue Boy*). European period sculptures, porcelains and tapestries are also displayed. Nearby, the Virginia Steele Scott Gallery of American Art exhibits works from the 1730s to the 1930s, including paintings by Mary Cassatt, Edward Hopper and John Singer Sargent alongside furniture by Gustav Stickley and others.

Galleries and gardens are open Tuesday to Friday noon to 4:30 pm, Saturday and Sunday 10:30 am to 4:30 pm (except major holidays). Docent led garden tours are offered each day at 1 pm. Admission is $8.50, $7 for seniors, $5 for students, free for children under 12 (admission is free the first Thursday of each month).

Not far from the Huntington Gardens, the California Historical Society operates **El Molino Viejo** (☎ 626-449-5450), 1120 Old Mill Rd. Built in 1816 by Gabrieleño Indians for the Mission San Gabriel, 'The Old Mill'

Huntington Botanical Gardens

was the very first water-powered grist mill in Southern California. Historical exhibits include a working model of the mill. You can visit Tuesday to Sunday 1 to 4 pm; admission is free.

SAN GABRIEL (MAP 3)

The **Mission San Gabriel Archangel** (☎ 626-457-3048), 537 W Mission Drive, was the fourth in the line of 21 missions built in California. Originally founded in 1771 by Pedro Cambon and Angel Somera 4 miles south of its current location, it was forced to relocate by heavy flooding in 1791. The capped buttress design by Father Antonio Cruzado incorporates many Moorish elements inspired by the cathedral in his native Córdoba in southern Spain. The Franciscans got the local Gabrieleño workers to construct the church from stone, brick and mortar between 1791 and 1805, but already in 1804 an earthquake damaged the roof; another one in 1812 brought down the bell wall. Despite such setbacks, the mission itself was quite prosperous, reaping proceeds from the fertile land and producing soap and candles for all the other missions. It also maintained California's oldest and largest winery. The last wave of damage came during the 1987 Whittier earthquake, but the mission has since been restored.

Inside the church is a copper baptismal font and an altar made in Mexico City in 1790, plus various wooden statues of saints. The cemetery harbors, among many others, 6000 Indians who are honored with a memorial. Also on the grounds are soap and tallow vats, fireplaces, fountains and a replica of a kitchen. The museum contains Bibles, religious robes and Indian artifacts. The mission is open daily 10 am to 5:30 pm from June to September, 9 am to 4:30 pm the rest of the year. Admission is $4, $3 for seniors, $1 for children ages six to 12.

The **San Gabriel Historical Association** (☎ 626-308-3223) has an exhibition space with Indian artifacts and early photographs at 546 W Broadway (open Wednesday and weekends 1 to 4 pm; free). Nearby is the **San Gabriel Civic Auditorium** (☎ 818-308-2865), 320 S Mission Drive, a 1927 playhouse modeled after the Mission San Antonio de Padua in Monterey County. King Alfonso XIII of Spain donated coats of arms of each Spanish province for the theater's grand opening. Today it is used for concerts, stage plays and classic movies.

Mountains

SANTA MONICA MOUNTAINS (MAP 2)

Few visitors to LA realize that the metropolis actually borders wilderness in what is the world's largest urban national park, the Santa Monica Mountains National Recreation Area. Consisting of more than 150,000 acres, it's a playground cherished by LA residents. The park is often overlooked by travelers, which is a shame because it's an easily accessible sample of the rugged beauty found throughout California. Even taking a few hours for a short hike makes for a refreshing break from urban sightseeing and will increase your appreciation of the city and its natural surroundings.

The Santa Monica Mountains stretch from west of Griffith Park in Hollywood to the east of the Oxnard Plain in Ventura County. Their northern border is the 101 Fwy, while in the south, they rise dramatically above the Pacific Ocean. Several canyon roads cut through the mountains, providing easy access to trails. Outdoor activities in the park include hiking, mountain biking, horseback riding and bird watching. Nearly 600 miles of trails crisscross the area, including the popular 65-mile Backbone Trail.

The park was founded in 1978 by act of Congress with the intent to protect one of the world's last Mediterranean ecosystems (only four others still exist worldwide). Appearing relatively barren at first glance, the park actually boasts 26 ecological communities, such as oak woodlands, chaparral and coastal lagoons. More than 450 animal species, including several endangered ones, make their home here (deer, mountain lions and coyotes, for example). Hawks, falcons and eagles circle above, while rattlesnakes reside beneath the brush.

Spring, when temperatures are moderate and wildflowers are in bloom, is the most pleasant time to visit the park. Avoid midday hikes in summer (the Mercury can climb to more than 100°F), and head out in the early morning or late afternoon instead. Fall can be nice, too, though there's the threat of fire. Winter often brings rain, which may result in trail closure due to the possibility of mud slides. In general, most trails are rugged and require sturdy footwear (sneakers or light hiking shoes are OK). For longer hikes, layer your clothing, bring sunscreen, a hat and lots of water. Look out for poison oak, which has waxy, glistening leaves that cause a rash on contact.

If you get bitten by a rattlesnake (chances are slim), you will experience rapid swelling, severe pain and possible temporary paralysis. Victims rarely die, but in any case seek medical help immediately. Mountain lions are scarce in this neck of the woods, though there was a fatal attack in 1994 and frightening encounters seem to be growing in frequency. If you meet a lion, hold your ground, try to appear large by raising your arms or grabbing a stick. If the lion gets aggressive, fight back, shout and throw objects at it.

DAVID PEEVERS

Don't tread on me.

The National Park Service (NPS) maintains a visitor center (☎ 805-370-2300) at 401 W Hillcrest Drive in Thousand Oaks, in the very western San Fernando Valley. (Take the Lynn Rd exit from the 101 Fwy, head north on Lynn Rd, east on Hillcrest Drive, left on McCloud Ave, and turn at the first driveway on your right.) They dispense information and sell maps, hiking guides and books between 8 am to 5 pm weekdays, from 9 am weekends (closed major holidays).

Hiking

With 580 miles of trails from which to choose, it's impossible to describe every possible hike through the Santa Monica Mountains, but here are some of our favorites.

Santa Ynez Canyon This easy-to-moderate trail (6 miles roundtrip) leads through a lovely shaded canyon along Santa Ynez Creek and terminates at a waterfall tumbling into a rockface-enclosed pool, which makes for a nice swimming hole in summer. The easier, though less scenic, option to get onto this trail is from the Palisades Highland Trailhead. (Turn north off Sunset on Palisades Drive and turn left on Verenda de la Montura.) More ambitious hikers should start from Topanga State Park. (Turn east off Topanga Canyon Blvd onto Entrada Rd, then make two left turns to the park entrance; parking is $6.)

Sycamore Canyon Sycamore Canyon is part of Point Mugu State Park on the northern fringe of LA County, about 30 miles northwest of Santa Monica. Hiking along the canyon floor makes for a lovely, easy walk, especially enjoyable in the fall when there is falling foliage and when Monarch butterflies stop by on their southward migration. More challenging trails, such as the Overlook Trail, head into the mountainous flanks of the canyon and provide glorious views over the ocean. The trailhead is at the Big Sycamore Canyon Campground, reached via Pacific Coast Hwy (1).

Runyon Canyon Park Just a few blocks north of the Hollywood Blvd bustle is this

Escape the hustle and bustle in the Santa Monica Mountains.

largely undeveloped city park. Trails steep enough to provide a moderate workout take you to a hilltop plateau with sweeping views of the city and the Hollywood Hills. Largely ignored by tourists, the park is hugely popular with dog owners, which unfortunately requires everyone to watch their step.

The easiest trailhead is at the end of Fuller St, a side street off Franklin St. Runyon Canyon is bounded by Mulholland Drive to the north. (Street parking is available.) The ruins near the Fuller St entrance are all that's left from the estate of Irish tenor John McCormack. He had sold the estate to George Huntington II, heir to the A&P grocery-store chain, whose plan to turn it into a country club was defeated by neighbors. Errol Flynn lived in the pool house in the late '50s. The city purchased the park in 1984, but several fires have left only its foundations.

Ferndell to Griffith Observatory to Mt Hollywood Ferndell is a lovely shady glen at the southern edge of Griffith Park. Lined by ferns, alder trees, sycamores and even coastal redwoods, it leads uphill to the Lower West Observatory Trail. From the observatory, where you'll enjoy great views of the city, walk to the north end of the parking lot where the Mt Hollywood path is clearly marked. This trail, while not home to the Hollywood sign, gives you repeated views of the landmark. The moderate hike is about 5½ miles roundtrip. The Ferndell trailhead is reached by taking Ferndell Drive north off

Los Feliz Blvd. (Street parking is available.) For more hiking ideas through Griffith Park, visit the Griffith Park Ranger Station (☎ 323-665-5188), 4730 Crystal Springs Drive.

Solstice International Trail An easy 3-mile trail suitable even for families with strollers is the Solstice International Trail above Malibu, essentially a self-guided interpretive journey through Southern California flora and fauna. Pamphlets in several languages are available at the visitors' center. Solstice Canyon, which opened on summer solstice 1988, was created on the site of the former Roberts Ranch, which burned down in 1982. The path leads past the 1865 Matthew Keller House (presumed to be the oldest in Malibu) to the Fern Grotto, with its picnic area and the ranch foundations at Tropical Terrace (named for the bamboo trees, agaves and palms planted in the Roberts' garden). For the trailhead, turn inland off Pacific Coast Hwy (1) on Corral Canyon Rd; turn left to the parking lot after a quarter mile. There's a $6 parking fee.

Inspiration Loop Trail This 2-mile, easy-to-moderate hike leads through Will Rogers State Historical Park in Pacific Palisades. It begins at the west end of the tennis courts and affords superb vistas over Santa Monica Bay. It also connects with the Backbone Trail, which stretches along the mountain ridge for some 65 miles. Enter the park from Sunset Blvd (look for the signs).

Guided Hikes
Both the Angeles chapter of the Sierra Club (☎ 213-387-4287, www.edgeinternet.com /angeles/) and the National Park Service (☎ 805-370-2300, www.nps.gov/samo/) lead hundreds of guided hikes throughout the year, covering all corners of the Santa Monica Mountains. Tours range from family strolls to strenuous workouts. They take place morning, day and night, last a few hours to several days and attract a mixed bag of hiking enthusiasts from Westside families to Silver Lake grungies to Leimert Park yuppies. All hikes are open to the public and are usually free. Copies of both organizations'

quarterly events calendars are available by calling the numbers listed previously.

For educational guided tours in small groups, offered in several languages, there's Hiking in LA (☎ 818-501-1005), founded and operated by Jost Rhodius. Tours are easy to tough, lasting roughly three hours, and explore various trails in the Santa Monica Mountains. En route you'll be introduced to the region's flora and fauna, geology and history, with special emphasis on Native Americans. Fees include parking and drinks, and range from $30 to $55. There's a two-person minimum; otherwise you pay a surcharge. Rhodius also offers an excellent 4½-hour walking tour of Downtown LA ($45, including snacks, drinks and parking).

If you prefer to ramble around on your own but with more guidance than just a trail map, check out the excellent series of guides by *Los Angeles Times* columnist John McKinney. His *Day Hiker's Guide to Southern California* ($15) and *Walking Los Angeles: Adventures on the Urban Edge* ($14) each explore several dozen hikes in great detail, providing not just route descriptions but also trailhead directions and historical background. Both guides, plus four other McKinney guides, are available in bookstores.

SAN GABRIEL MOUNTAINS (MAP 1)
The mountain range to the north of urban LA contains the Angeles National Forest, another major adventure playground and getaway for stressed-out Angelenos. About 30 million visitors, mostly locals, descend upon its trails, roads and campgrounds each year. One of the nicest drives is along the Angeles Crest Highway, which winds through the forest for 65 miles and offers spectacular views over the LA Basin at many turns.

Attractions within the forest include the **Mt Wilson Observatory** (☎ 626-793-3100), atop 5710-foot Mt Wilson and built in 1903 under the direction of George E Hale, who would go on to lay the groundwork for Caltech. Also here is LA County's tallest mountain, whose official name is Mt San Antonio but is referred to as **Old Baldy** for its treeless top at an elevation of 10,080 feet. A popular ski area in winter, Old Baldy is fairly easy to climb during snowfree months.

The general information center (☎ 626-335-1251) for the entire forest is at 701 N Santa Anita Ave in Arcadia, about 20 miles east of Pasadena. It's open weekdays 8 am to 4:30 pm. The Mt Baldy Visitors' Center (☎ 909-982-2829) is on Mt Baldy Rd, the only road leading to the mountain. Open daily 8 am to 4:30 pm, this is where you can pick up trail maps and information.

Activities

The following are a few of the many activities LA has to offer. See the previous section, Mountains, for hiking information. For surfing and fishing, see Coastal Communities earlier in the chapter.

BICYCLING & IN-LINE SKATING
Although most of urban LA is not particularly inviting to cyclists or in-line skaters, the county has more than 200 miles of designated bike trails. Best of the bunch is the South Bay Bicycle Trail, a flat 22-mile paved path that follows the beach south from Santa Monica to Torrance Beach, with a detour around the yacht harbor at Marina del Rey. There are other more adventurous paths from Azusa to Long Beach (the 37-mile San Gabriel River Trail), from Commerce to Long Beach (the 20-mile Los Angeles River Path, which is probably the fastest way to get to a beach by bike from anywhere near Downtown), from Long Beach to Newport Beach (the 21-mile Oceanside Bike Path), and through Griffith Park (an 8-mile trail that passes the LA Zoo and the Gene Autry Museum). The city Department of Transportation (☎ 213-485-2265), 200 N Spring St, 12th Floor, has detailed maps.

Bike-rental places include Perry's Rentals (☎ 310-452-7609) with four outlets renting beach cruisers, tandems and in-line skates along the beach bike path in Santa Monica. Rates are $6/hour or $18/day. Skating lessons are offered on weekends. Others to try are the Venice Pier Bike Shop (☎ 310-301-4011),

Biking on Venice's Ocean Front Walk

DAV D PEEVERS

21 Washington Blvd, Venice; or Spokes N Stuff (☎ 310-306-3332) at 4175 Admiralty Way, Marina del Rey and 1700 Ocean Ave in Santa Monica (☎ 310-395-4748).

GOLF
Golfing is a popular pastime among Angelenos; it's no longer reserved for the country-club elite or the gray-haired set. Young professional males especially are drawn to the greens, and LA's many public courses are often booked. (Note that most of the 18-hole courses are located in the distant suburbs and are not covered in this book.) You'll need to buy a reservation card – available at any City of LA golf course – to book a tee time on their automated system ($15/year). Remember that golf-course hours are dependent on sunrise and sunset. The following courses are all within easy reach from central and west LA.

The Rancho Park Golf Course (Map 2; ☎ 310-838-7373), 10460 W Pico Blvd, has both a challenging 18-hole and a 9-hole course. Nicely laid out, the course is always crowded and getting a tee time as a visitor may be difficult. Fees are $17 to $22. The Harding and Wilson courses in Griffith Park (Map 8; ☎ 323-663-2555), 4730 Crystal Springs Drive, also both have 18 holes. The Harding course is more scenic and somewhat more difficult though shorter than Wilson. Greens fees are $17.50 during the week, $23 on weekends. Penmar Golf Course (Map 12; ☎ 310-396-6228), 1233 Rose Ave in Venice, is a 9-hole course that was recently overhauled and is quite busy now. It's open daily 6:30 am to 5 pm; green fees are $9 weekdays, $12 weekends.

There are two courses near LAX airport, where land is relatively cheap. Westchester Golf Course (Map 2; ☎ 310-649-9166), 6900 W Manchester Blvd just north of LAX, is an oddity because it has just 15 holes. It's short, noisy and relatively easy, but at least it's well-maintained. Hours are 5 am to 10 pm weekdays, from 4:30 am weekends. Fees are $12 to $17. The other course is Lakes at El Segundo (Map 4; ☎ 310-322-0202), 400 S Sepulveda Blvd, a 9-hole course open 6 am to 10 pm and costing $9 to $11.

HEALTH CLUBS

Angelenos' obsession with their bodies translates into a profusion of health clubs featuring the latest in exercise equipment and workout classes. New trends are usually spawned here before moving on to the rest of the country and the world (aerobics, step aerobics and kick-boxing, for example).

Many mid-range and practically all top-end hotels have their own fitness center or an agreement with a nearby club. Most outside gyms are membership-based; however, there are ways to get in. Most offer a free initial workout for nonmembers who are considering joining (you have to pretend). The downside is you will probably have to take a guided club tour and then endure the inane sales banter of commission-crazed 'counselors.' Family Fitness Centers and Bally's are clubs that operate in this way.

To avoid this hassle, go to gyms that offer day passes. If you want to pump iron with the pros, head to the legendary Gold's Gym (Map 12; ☎ 310-392-6004), 360 Hampton Drive in Venice, where you might even catch a glimpse of the next Mr Universe. This is the gym where Arnold Schwarzenegger once bulked up for the title. Day rates are $15 and include access to all equipment, classes and sauna. It's open daily till midnight.

The Power House Gym (☎ 310-914-1520), 11400 W Olympic Blvd in west LA, charges $13 a day. Another option is Bodies in Motion, which specializes in kick-boxing and boxing classes in addition to offering the usual array of workout machines and aerobics. It charges $20 a day, though you may get a discount if you're staying longer. Bodies in Motion has branches in both Santa Monica (Map 12; ☎ 310-264-0777), at 2730 Santa Monica Blvd, and Pasadena (Map 16; ☎ 626-577-2211), at 900 S Arroyo Parkway.

The latest rage in workouts is taught at the Krav Maga National Training Center (☎ 310-966-1300), 11500 Olympic Blvd in west LA. Krav Maga is a form of self-defense taught by the Israeli army and includes kicks, punches, blocks and other bold moves. Linda Shelton has adapted the formula into a tough full-body workout that strengthens, shapes, builds and increases flexibility. This club is also membership-based but will cut short-term deals for visitors as well (plan to pay $50/week).

HORSEBACK RIDING

Griffith Park is ideal territory for horseback riding. Leaving the urban sprawl behind to negotiate the hilly terrain and forested bridal trails definitely feels like entering another world. Several riding stables have set up shop on the northern periphery of the park, where the LA Equestrian Center is located as well. Circle K Riding Stables (☎ 818-843-9890), 914 Mariposa St in Burbank, rents horses for $14 for the first hour and $11 for each subsequent hour. Barbecue rides in groups of five or more include an all-you-can-eat feast for $26 total. Griffith Park Horse Rental (☎ 818-840-8401), 480 Riverside Drive, has horses for $15/hour with a two-hour maximum. The Sunday breakfast ride is $35.

In operation for more than 80 years, Sunset Ranch (☎ 323-469-5450), 3400 Beachwood Drive, offers guided hour-long rides daily. On Friday nights it offers the popular and romantic sunset ride, which takes you from below the Hollywood sign over the mountains to drinks and dinner at a Mexican cantina in Burbank, and back by moonlight ($35 plus dinner).

ICE-SKATING

With ice hockey and figure skating gaining in popularity, many people take to the rinks themselves. In LA, you can visit the state-of-the-art Culver City Ice Arena (Map 2; ☎ 310-398-5718), 4545 Sepulveda Blvd, the former training grounds of the LA Kings and now used by competitive figure skaters. Numerous classes are offered throughout the week, and the rink is open to general skating several hours daily (call for hours). Admission is $6, $5 for children under 12; skate rentals are $2.

Also try the Pasadena Ice Skating Center (Map 16; ☎ 626-578-0801), in a historic building at 310 E Green St converted from a '40s ballroom. Admission is $6, $2.50 for skates.

Another option is the ice-skating rink at the Pickwick Center (Map 17; ☎ 818-845-5300), which is located across from the LA Equestrian Center, at 1001 Riverside Drive in Burbank.

RUNNING

Joggers abound on city streets in the early morning and evening hours especially. Other favorite running places are along the beaches (such as Venice and Santa Monica) – in the sand or along paved walkways. Palisades Park atop the bluffs in Santa Monica and the green median strip along San Vicente Blvd are popular as well. Griffith Park makes for a more strenuous workout, though it also provides great city views.

TENNIS

Tennis courts are plentiful in LA, though not all are open to the public. If your budget allows, you can stay at a hotel with a private court. Other options are courts at schools, which are not always perfectly maintained but, outside of school hours, are usually empty and cost-free. The recreation departments of the various cities within LA County operate public courts and should be able to refer you to the nearest one. These are usually found in designated recreation areas, such as the Cheviot Hills Recreation Area at 2551 Motor Ave in Cheviot Hills, a neighborhood just north of Culver City. Check the phone book for the number of the City Recreation Department nearest you. Griffith Park has tennis facilities as well.

Places to Stay

Greater Los Angeles has plenty of accommodations in all price categories, although budget beds at some times of year – especially between Memorial Day (late May) and Labor Day (early September) and around the winter holidays such as Thanksgiving, Christmas and New Year's – can be as rare as a smog-free day in Pasadena.

The cheapest option is a bunk in a hostel, which usually costs $12 to $20. Hostels are communal affairs and don't offer much privacy. Most have four- to eight-bed dorms (generally, though not always, gender segregated), shared washrooms and showers, kitchens, laundry rooms and TV rooms.

Some hostels also have private rooms that cost about the same as those at motels and inexpensive hotels, about $35 to $60 per night for double occupancy. Expect accommodations in this price range to be no-frill places with basic amenities (including TV and phone), adequate to rest your head but not to hang out. You'll find them listed under the heading 'Budget' in this book.

The closer you are to the coast or to upscale neighborhoods such as Beverly Hills, the more likely you'll be staying at motels and hotels that typically run $70 to $100 per room. Spending just a little extra, from $100 to $130, generally buys more comfort and amenities, including in-room refrigerators, spas and voice mail. This spectrum of accommodations is listed as 'Mid-Range.'

LA has many luxurious properties costing $130 and up (these fall under 'Top End'). Amenities tend to be extravagant; rooms and public areas are beautifully furnished, adorned with art and fresh flowers. Often the location is central and there are special touches such as a rooftop swimming pool, tennis court or in-house massages. The sky's the limit in terms of price, and some suites and penthouses may cost several thousand dollars a night. Most of these hotels are clustered in the Downtown, West Hollywood, Beverly Hills, Bel Air, Westwood and Santa Monica areas.

Price Fluctuations

Clearly, where you want to stay in LA will dictate to a great extent how much you'll have to pay. Budget lodgings are scarce in Beverly Hills and West Hollywood but abundant in Hollywood, Downtown and Pasadena, for example. Seasonal price fluctuations also affect room rates. Summer rates – especially in the beach communities and tourist areas such as West Hollywood – may increase by 50% or more to reflect the greater demand for rooms. The same is true around major holidays such as July 4, Labor Day, Thanksgiving, Christmas and New Year's.

Hotels that cater to business travelers often charge considerably higher rates during the week, when corporate expense accounts rule, than on weekends. As a result, a fancy suite that might run you $140 Sunday through Thursday nights might cost only $85 on Friday and Saturday. In Malibu and other beach cities, however, weekend rates are jacked up for the hordes of LA refugees scurrying to the seashore after work on Friday.

Room rates also vary by type of room and even by bed size. While there are rarely different prices for single or double occupancy, it does matter whether you stay in a room with two queen-size beds or one king-size bed. The location of the room may also affect the price; larger hotels composed of several buildings may charge more for rooms in recently renovated structures. Rooms with views naturally cost more than those without. Hotels facing a noisy street may charge slightly more for quieter rooms.

Whenever possible, we have provided the range of rates a hotel may charge, though changes may occur frequently and spontaneously. Rooms get renovated, managers change and hotels are taken over by chains. Thus, the rates quoted in this book should serve merely as guidelines.

Discounts

Discounts of 10% or more off published rates are frequently available. Are you a member of the American Automobile Association (AAA) or foreign affiliate? Are you a senior citizen? (This usually means age 65 or older but can also mean 62, 60 or even 55, depending upon the hotel. Bring your AARP card – see Seniors' Cards in Facts for the Visitor.) You might also cash in on discounts for university students, military personnel and travel-industry workers. Also look out for magazines with hotel discount vouchers, often available at gas stations and tourist offices. Make it a habit to ask about discounts when booking a room.

Taxes & Tips

Your final hotel bill will swell with taxes, tips, and parking and phone-connection charges that will increase in proportion to the cost of your accommodations. The 'transient occupancy' tax on all hotel rooms in the city of Los Angeles is 14%. Percentages vary slightly in other cities, ranging from 11.85% in Pasadena to 13% in West Hollywood and 14% in Beverly Hills.

Other charges won't be a concern unless you stay in a top-end hotel, where you are expected to tip bellhops and cleaning staff, as well as restaurant servers and bartenders. While parking is generally free at budget and mid-range properties, it will run $7 to $14 or higher per day at upscale hotels, plus tips for valets. And while motels rarely charge more than 25¢ for local phone calls (often these are free), big hotels will charge you up to $1 per call. If you're calling long distance, you'll pay through the nose unless you use a credit or calling card, but they'll still hit you with that pesky connection fee.

Reservations

Where available, we have listed each accommodation's toll-free 800 or 888 telephone number in this book (also see The Chains boxed text). Note that you only use these numbers to ask for information or make a reservation; for private calls to a guest's room, use the direct hotel number and ask to be transferred. If you have trouble finding accommodations, consider using one of the free hotel-reservation services. These include the Hotel Reservations Network

(☎ 800-964-6835) and the Central Reservation Service (☎ 800-548-3311).

CAMPING

LA's campgrounds are open year-round. If you drive an RV, check whether your equipment is compatible with that of the campground. It's wise to make reservations, especially on summer weekends, when spaces are often claimed by Friday afternoon. In addition to the campgrounds mentioned here, the California Department of Parks & Recreation maintains dozens of camping facilities, often in more remote, rural locales. For information and reservations, contact ParkNet at ☎ 800-444-7275 daily from 8 am to 5 pm. For on-line reservations, log on to www.park-net.com. There's a $7.50 fee per reservation. One of its most popular sites is the kid-friendly *Leo Carrillo State Beach Campground* (☎ 805-488-5223), 9000 Pacific Coast Hwy, about 28 miles north of Santa Monica. Charging $18, it has 138 tent and RV sites, a general store, flush toilets and hot showers (for a fee).

The *Dockweiler Beach RV Park* (Map 2; ☎ 310-322-4951, 800-950-7275), 12001 Vista Del Mar in Playa del Rey, is close to LAX, making it quite a noisy, but fairly central, proposition. Catering exclusively to RVs (no tent camping), the park charges $15 to $25 in summer, $12 to $17 in winter.

Closer to town, the ocean-side *Malibu Beach RV Park* (☎ 310-456-6052, 800-622-6052, fax 310-456-2532), 25801 Pacific Coast Hwy, has 150 sites with full and partial hookups ($25 to $30), plus 52 tent spaces ($17 to $20). These rates include tax, showers and hot-tub access.

In Northridge (San Fernando Valley) is *Walnut RV Park* (☎ 800-868-2749), 19130 Nordhoff St, featuring 114 sites with full hookups ($30). To get there, take the 405 Fwy to the Nordhoff St exit and head west for 4½ miles. From the 101 Fwy, get off at Tampa Ave and drive north for 4½ miles.

HOSTELS

LA has a decent number of hostels, only a couple of which are affiliated with Hostelling International/American Youth Hostels

(HI/AYH). You will need an HI card to stay at these, or you'll have to pay a few dollars more. HI/AYH hostels expect you to rent or provide your own bedding. Dormitories are segregated by sex and curfews exist; alcohol is banned.

Reservations are advised during peak season. Get further information from HI/AYH (☎ 202-783-6161, fax 202-783-6171, hiayhserve@hiayh.org, www.hiayh.org), 733 15th St NW, suite 840, Washington, DC 20005, or use its code-based reservation service at ☎ 800-909-4776. You will need the access code for the hostel to use this service; it's available on-line, or you can obtain the code from any HI/AYH office or handbook.

Independent hostels have comparable rates to HI/AYH hostels, though usually without curfew, alcohol or smoking restrictions. Some have a few singles/doubles, sometimes with private bathrooms. Facilities may include a kitchen, laundry, notice board and TV room.

The Hostel Handbook, by Jim Williams, is a 66-page listing of US hostels (5$) and is available by writing the author at 722 St Nicholas Ave, New York, NY 10031 (make check or money order payable to the author; ☎ 212-926-7030, infohostel@aol.com). Another source is Jim de Cordova's *Back-packers Guide* ($6), a 100-page volume listing accommodations under $20 throughout the USA and Canada. It's available at some hostels, or by writing to Jim's at the Beach (☎ 310-399-4018), 17 Brooks Ave, Venice, CA 90291. The Internet Guide to Hostelling (www.hostels.com) lists hostels throughout the world.

Hollywood (Map 9)

In the immediate vicinity of Mann's Chinese Theater are two excellent hostels. The non-smoking ***Orange Drive Manor*** *(☎ 323-850-0350, fax 323-850-7474)*, 1764 N Orange Drive, offers plenty of privacy and a peaceful atmosphere. It's housed in a rambling 1920s manor, complete with creaky hardwood floors, steep staircases and high ceilings (it's not marked, so just look for the house number). Bunks in four-person dorms with adjacent showers are $20, while those with communal facilities are $11.50. Singles/doubles with shared shower are $29.50/36.50. This one's a winner – make reservations.

DAVID PEEVERS

The pool at Banana Bungalow Hollywood beckons.

A livelier option is the **Hollywood International Hostel** (☎ 323-463-0797, 800-750-6561, fax 323-463-1705), 6820 Hollywood Blvd. It has 42 dorms sleeping three to four ($12 per bunk) and a few private rooms ($30). Facilities include a tiny kitchen, gym, laundry room and TV lounge, as well as free coffee and tea. The 24-hour check-in is convenient, as is its free pick-up service from LAX, Greyhound or Union Station with a stay of more than one night ($5 otherwise). This hostel attracts a rambunctious, sociable and international crowd.

International party animals love the friendly and noisy **Banana Bungalow Hollywood** (☎ 323-851-1129, 800-446-7835, fax 323-851-1569), 2775 N Cahuenga Blvd, converted from a rambling motel right in the Hollywood Hills. It's less central than the previous two, but public buses to central Hollywood and beyond stop right outside. It has 200 dormitory beds in rooms sleeping four, six or 10 ($15 to $18), each with cable TV, bathroom and lockers. Extensive amenities include a free continental breakfast, a bistro, small store, communal kitchen, Internet access, gym, laundry, swimming pool, library and car-rental agency. There are nightly movies on a large-screen TV, parties throughout the week and free shuttles to area attractions.

Santa Monica (Map 12)

Local headquarters for the Hostelling International system, **Santa Monica HI Hostel** (☎ 310-393-9913, 800-909-4776 ext 5, fax 310-393-1769), 1436 2nd St, is without a doubt one of the cleaner, better managed and most comfortable hostels we've seen. In a huge, ivy-covered brick building, a block from the Third Street Promenade and a short walk from the beach, the hostel has a huge kitchen, a lovely courtyard, an extensive library, a theater, laundry, travel store and free pick-ups from LAX. Beds are $18 to $20; private rooms are $56. Curfew is 2 am. *Do* make reservations early, especially in summer.

Venice (Map 12)

Hostel lodgings congregate in Venice, a fun beach town and a great area in which to stay,

though not as safe as Santa Monica (but comparable to Hollywood). In general, accommodations here aren't well-maintained, although there are exceptions.

Your best bet in the area – especially if you score a bunk in an ocean-facing dorm – is the **Venice Beach Cotel** (☎ 310-399-7649, fax 310-399-1930), 25 Windward Ave. As its pamphlet explains, a 'cotel is a hostel with hotel standards.' This means ready-made beds with towels and soap; free boogie board, volleyball and paddle tennis rentals; wake-up service and airport transfers ($7); a cafe/lounge with free coffee, tea and a welcome cocktail; Internet access; and 24-hour security. Most rooms have a private bath and sleep three to six. Ocean-view bunks are $17 and well worth the extra $4. Private rooms are small but have character, decent furniture and even a TV ($45.50). (No 319, with an ocean view, is a good choice.) Check-out time is a civilized 11 am. Americans with passports are welcome.

Half a block inland is **Venice Beach Hostel** (☎ 310-452-3052), a large, multistory affair at 1515 Pacific Ave. The staff is friendly and communicative, and there's a large kitchen and huge recreational area, complete with piano. Hallways and rooms are pretty sparse, though some have been brightened with murals. All rooms have their own bathrooms, and some private rooms come with kitchens. Email and Internet access is free. Dorm beds average $18; private rooms are $45 to $47, but you can do better with a motel. Check-out is 9 am. Americans are welcome but must present a driver's license or other identification.

Of all the hostels in Venice, **Jim's at the Beach** (☎ 310-399-4018), half a block from the Ocean Front Walk at 17 Brooks Ave, is the most laid-back and least restrictive. In business for 12 years, it has 45 beds and the cluttered, helter-skelter feel of a college dorm. Rooms are large and sleep four to six; one is set aside for women. Jim provides the ingredients to make your own breakfast in the communal kitchen, and sometimes throws barbecue parties. Drinking until midnight is OK, and there's no curfew. Bunks are $20 per night or $125 per week; parking is $5. International travelers are preferred, but Americans carrying a passport are fine.

Whoever recommended the **Hostel California** (☎ *310-305-0250, fax 310-305-8590*), 2221 Lincoln Blvd, in past guidebooks must have done so in 1950. The communal kitchen is small and grimy; grim decor (read: a complete lack of it) 'welcomes' you to 30-bed (!) dorms with $13 bunks, six-bed rooms for $16 ($96/week) or private doubles for $40. Some things *do* work here, though. Internet access costs $1 for 10 minutes, and there are free safe deposit boxes. Parking, bed linen and airport pick-ups (by prior arrangement) are free. There's a laundry and, like most independent hostels, it tries to make women-only rooms. The hostel is open 24 hours, but remember that you're in a none-too-savory neighborhood. This place really should spruce itself up a tad.

San Pedro (Map 14)

HI Hostel (☎ *310-831-8109*), 3601 S Gaffey St No 613, situated on a windy bluff overlooking the Pacific Ocean, gets the top award for scenery. The hostel recently underwent a complete overhaul, leaving each dorm and public area decorated in a different theme, from 'African jungle' to 'American jazz' to 'Native American culture.' There's a big kitchen and various game and entertainment equipment, plus a volleyball court and free mountain-bike rentals. The quiet garden has hammocks, a barbecue patio and a vegetable garden, where guests may help themselves. There is a total of 60 $12 beds in gender-segregated dorms sleeping three to five; private rooms are $29.50. Check-in and check-out is at 10:45 am, and there's a maximum stay of seven days. Make reservations at least two weeks in advance between June and September. MTA bus No 466 stops right outside at the Korean Friendship Bell (see Things to See & Do).

STUDENT ACCOMMODATIONS

A steal of a deal is offered by **Brooks College** (☎ *562-597-6611*) at 4825 E Pacific Coast Hwy in Long Beach. This arts and design college makes 300 dormitory rooms available to visitors between early June and late August. There are shared bathrooms, a linen service, cafeteria, laundry and a swimming pool. Several bus lines stop directly in front of the college for the 10-minute trip into downtown Long Beach. There's 24-hour security and gender-separated floors. Singles/doubles go for $13/24, or $16/27 with linen. A meal plan gives you five meals in the cafeteria for $20. For information and reservations, call 8 am to 5 pm weekdays and ask to be connected to Student Services.

B&Bs

In the historic West Adams district south of Downtown LA is the **Inn at 657** (Map 2; ☎ *213-741-2200*), 657 W 23rd St. Each of the five apartments – some of which sleep up to four people – has antique furniture, nice decor and a kitchen, some with a microwaves and others with stoves. Rates are $110/175 singles/doubles, including breakfast, tax and parking; each extra person pays $25.

Romantic **Channel Road Inn** (Map 12; ☎ *310-459-1920, fax 310-454-9920*), 219 W Channel Rd in Santa Monica, has 12 rooms and two suites facing the Pacific. Built in Colonial Revival style in 1910, it's set into a hillside garden and offers a library, spa and laundry as well as bicycles for riding the 22-mile South Bay Trail (free). Rooms start at $125 and top out at $250.

Draped in ivy and with nine sun-drenched rooms, the **Venice Beach House** (Map 12; ☎ *310-823-1966, fax 310-823-1842*), 15 30th Ave in Venice, is a tasteful, homey retreat. Charlie Chaplin used to stay here when it was the beach house of a local developer, and you can still dream of *City Lights* in the 'Tramp's Quarters.' Doubles with shared bath are $95; those with private facilities are $120; the two suites go for $145. Kids under five stay free, and parking is gratis.

Romantic touches abound at the **Inn at Playa del Rey** (☎ *310-574-1920, fax 310-574-9920*), 435 Culver Blvd. The office is in the middle of a busy kitchen, which produces amazing aromas, and there's an unobstructed view of the city over the Ballona Wetlands' wild grasses. Homemade breakfasts; tea, wine and hors d'oeuvres in the afternoon;

The Turret House B&B, Long Beach

and fresh cookies in the truly lovely dining and seating areas make it well worth the $125 to $175 per standard room. Suites go for $225 to $245.

Historic B&Bs with rooms under $100 are pretty rare, which makes the **Lord Mayor** *(Map 15; ☎ 562-436-0324)*, 435 Cedar Ave in Long Beach, all the more remarkable. The 1904 Edwardian house was once the home of the city's first mayor and has been meticulously restored by community preservationists Reuben and Laura Brasser. Rooms get their character from stylish antique furniture rather than frilly over-decorating; bathrooms have claw-foot tubs, and there's an ample sundeck. Rates in the main building start at $85 and crest at $125. Rooms in the adjacent, slightly less-atmospheric villas are $85/95 for singles/doubles.

Also in Long Beach is **The Turret House** *(Map 15; ☎ 562-983-9812, 888-488-7738, fax 562 437-4082)*, in a restored 1906 Queen Anne-style villa at 556 Chestnut Ave. It's a friendly place owned by a woman with a penchant for floral patterns, which cover everything from walls and carpets to pillows and furniture. Fluffy robes await in your antique armoire, the furniture is polished to a tee, and bathrooms have claw-foot tubs with lacy shower curtains. Each of the five rooms has a different theme and color scheme but none have TVs or telephones. Rates are $110 to $125.

For charm, character and centrality, the **Pasadena Hotel** *(Map 16; ☎ 626-568-8172, 800-653-8886, fax 626-793-6409)*, 76 N Fair Oaks Ave, is hard to beat. In the heart of Old Pasadena, it has 12 rooms in a restored, late-19th-century building furnished with Edwardian antiques; many of the rooms are sky lit and all have TVs. Rates are $65 to $100 for singles and $80 to $150 for doubles; some rooms have a shared bath. Parking is $5 per day.

B&B enthusiasts will find two lovely homes in South Pasadena. Each of the five rooms at **The Artists' Inn** *(Map 16; ☎ 626-799-5668, 888-799-5668, fax 626-799-3678)*, in a Victorian farmhouse at 1038 Magnolia Ave, has decor recalling various artists and periods. All have private baths and cost $105 to $130. The **Bissell House** *(Map 16; ☎ 626-441-3535, 800-441-3530)*, 201 Orange Grove Ave, is a charmingly restored 1887 Victorian villa with leaded-glass windows. Each of the three rooms has a bath with pedestal sink and claw-foot tub. Rates are $100 to $150.

HOTELS
Downtown (Map 5)
Budget Although there are no hostels in the Downtown area, there's certainly no dearth of affordable accommodations. Most low-priced properties cluster in the area around the convention center, along Wilshire Blvd west of the 110 Fwy and in Chinatown. Besides the few motels, there's also a handful of low-frills hotels in historic buildings that provide a glimpse of the area's faded 1920s grandeur. Prices quoted here may rise considerably when a big convention is in town.

The funky **Stillwell Hotel** *(☎ 213-627-1151, 800-553-4774, fax 213-622-8940)*, 838 S Grand Ave, is a recently refurbished property. Each of the 250 rooms has a private bath, TV and old-fashioned air-conditioning (starting at $39/49 singles/doubles). A restaurant and the eccentric Hank's Bar (see Entertainment) are on the premises.

Side by side 2 blocks west are the **Orchid Hotel** *(☎ 213-624-5855, fax 213-624-8740)*, 819 S Flower St, and the **Milner Hotel** *(☎ 213-627-6981, 800-827-0411, fax 213-623-9751)*, 813 S Flower St. The Orchid is dirt-cheap with 63 rooms costing $30/35 ($137/162 per week). It's quite Spartan and not for those with exacting standards of cleanliness (while inspecting a room, we saw a cockroach skating in the tub). A step up in comfort, the Milner has a multilingual staff and 177 functionally furnished, smallish rooms for $40 to $65, including a full breakfast.

A few blocks farther west, the *Motel de Ville* (☎ 213-624-8474), 1123 W 7th St, has 62 plain but clean rooms for $35 to $45. There's a small coffee shop and an outdoor swimming pool – though it's not especially well-maintained. If traffic noise bothers you, ask for a room in the back. Next door, the *City Center Motel* (☎ 213-628-7141, 800-816-6889, fax 213-629-1064), 1135 W 7th St, charges slightly more, and also has family rooms for four priced at $70. Amenities include refrigerators, air-conditioning and a continental breakfast. Student discounts are available.

Mid-Range Easily our favorite Downtown hotel in this range is the *Hotel Figueroa* (☎ 213-627-8971, 800-421-9092, fax 213-689-0305), 939 S Figueroa St. The lobby of this 1927 classic evokes an oversized hacienda with such design flourishes as colored tiles, muralled doors, wrought-iron chandeliers and beamed ceilings. There's a poolside restaurant with good-value prix-fixe dinners, a coffee shop and a stylish bar upstairs. The spacious rooms have a pastel color scheme, all amenities and a price tag beginning at $88/98 singles/doubles. This place fills up quickly, so call ahead.

If the Hotel Figueroa is full, try next door at the *In Town Hotel* (☎ 213-628-2222, 800-457-8520, fax 213-687-0566), 913 S Figueroa St, which has considerably less charm but 170 decent rooms priced from $60/72 singles/doubles. It also offers a fairly shabby coffee shop and cocktail lounge.

One of the best deals Downtown is the family-run *Best Western Dragon Gate Inn* (☎ 213-617-3077, 800-282-9999, fax 213-680-3753), in the heart of Chinatown at 818 N Hill St. The large-scale renovation, which added a central atrium, should be complete in 1999. Rooms are large and pleasantly furnished. Atrium shops include an English-speaking herbalist and acupuncturist, and the Hill Street Café, selling hand-rolled cigars

The Spanish-style Hotel Figueroa

from a walk-in humidor. (According to gossip, courtesy of affable Dragon Gate owner Peter Kwong, his humidor is often a stop for police officers from the station across the street before they head out to olfactorily challenging murder scenes.) Rates are $69 to $100. Rooms at the Kwong family's much-plainer property, the *Royal Pagoda Motel* (☎ 213-223-3381) at 995 N Broadway, cost a mere $42 to $59.

The *Kawada Hotel* (☎ 213-621-4455, 800-752-9232, fax 213-687-4455), 200 S Hill St, has Japanese ownership, European appeal and room rates of $89 to $119. Extra amenities include VCRs (video rentals in the lobby) and refrigerators; some rooms have luxurious kitchenettes. The Epicentre restaurant, on the ground floor, is quite good.

Guests are charmed by Little Tokyo's *Miyako Inn* (☎ 213-617-2000, 800-228-6596, fax 213-617-2700), 328 E 1st St. Many of the 174 rooms of this 11-story hotel are Japanese-style, with tatami mats, shoji screens and low beds. This hotel has a restaurant, health club and karaoke lounge. Rates are $89 to $112.

On the edge of Chinatown, near Olvera St and Union Station, the four-story *Metro Plaza Hotel* (☎ 213-680-0200, 800-223-2223, fax 213-620-0200), 711 N Main St, is noted more for convenience than for character. Rooms have refrigerators and microwaves. Parking is free. The hotel's 80 rooms are $59/75 singles/doubles.

Recently renovated, the *Best Western Mayfair Hotel* (☎ 213-484-9789, 800-528-1234, fax 213-484-2769), 1256 W 7th St just west of Downtown, was a luxury hotel when built in 1928 and maintains a touch of faded elegance in its sky lit lobby. The Orchid Restaurant serves a popular buffet lunch, and there's also a lounge, fitness center and rooftop sundeck. Comfortable rooms range from $105 to $130, including covered parking.

The *Los Angeles Athletic Club Hotel* (☎ 213-625-2211, 800-421-8777, fax 213-689-1194), 431 W 7th St, has 72 warmly furnished rooms and suites with all the trappings, including terry robes. Rates of $120 to $150 also buy access to the posh in-house athletic club, complete with a 25-yard, sky-lit swimming pool, a gym, and racquetball and squash courts. Suites are $195.

The Holiday Inn chain is represented twice in this area with the *Holiday Inn Downtown* (☎ 213-628-5242, 800-465-4329, fax 213-628-1201), 750 Garland Ave, and the *Holiday Inn City Center* (☎ 213-748-1291, 800-465-4329, fax 213-748-6028), 1020 S Figueroa St, both popular with the convention crowd. Parking is free, and rooms feature coffeemakers, irons and hair dryers. Rates range from $119 to $139 for standard rooms and $135 to $159 for suites.

Top End Featured in nearly as many movies as City Hall, the five glass cylinders of the *Westin Bonaventure Hotel* (☎ 213-624-1000, 800-228-3000, fax 213-612-4800), 404 S Figueroa St, tower 35 stories above LA. With 1199 guest rooms and 157 suites, 20 restaurants, five bars, 40 retail stores, a swimming pool and a fitness deck the size of a football field, this hotel is definitely one of

LA's landmarks. Room rates range from $159 to $179, while suites start at $200.

New Otani (☎ 213-629-1200, 800-421-8795, fax 213-253-9269), anchors Little Tokyo at 120 S Los Angeles St. Catering largely to a business clientele, the Otani's public areas are an awkward stab at integrating East and West, and rooms are more functional than stylish. Pleasant touches include a half-acre Japanese garden and several top-quality restaurants. Standard rooms go for $165 to $305 and suites start at $475, though specials are frequent. Worth a splurge is the 'Japanese Experience' package at $599 per couple. It includes a night in an authentic Japanese suite with tatami mats, dinner at the signature restaurant and a miraculous shiatsu massage from tiny masseuses with hands of steel.

Hugging the western edge of Pershing Square is Downtown LA's poshest hotel, *The Regal Biltmore* (☎ 213-624-1011, 800-245-8673, fax 213-612-1545), 506 S Grand Ave. Built in 1923, this landmark hotel has the feel of a European palace and has hosted a galaxy of US presidents, celebrities and dignitaries. Rates for its 629 rooms are $205 to $250, with suites starting at $450 (also see the Los Angeles Architecture chapter).

Across the street is the *Wyndham Checkers Hotel* (☎ 213-624-0000, 800-996-3426, fax 213-626-9906), 535 S Grand Ave, its intricate stone facade dating from 1927. Besides an intimate lobby and sophisticated restaurant, marble bathrooms and a rooftop spa are among the elegant touches in this 1st-class,

DAVID PEEVERS

The Regal Biltmore

188-room European-style hotel. Amenities include free newspaper, shoe shine and twice-daily limo service within a 2-mile radius. Rooms are $166 to $228; suites start at $350.

Other Downtown top-end hotels are considerably more modern than the latter two. The best of them, both with more than 400 rooms and suites, are the *Hyatt Regency* (☎ 213-683-1234, 800-233-1234, fax 213-629-3230), 711 S Hope St above the Macy's Plaza shopping mall, with room rates of $119 to $239 and suites from $225, and the *Hotel Inter-Continental Los Angeles* (☎ 213-617-3300, 800-327-0200, fax 213-617-3399), 251 S Olive St atop Bunker Hill, which charges $210 to $270; suites start at $395.

Hollywood (Map 9)

Budget Not blessed with much character but certainly adequate is the *Hollywood Best Inn* (☎ 323-467-2252, fax 323-465-8316), 1822 N Cahuenga Blvd. Despite its recent face-lift, its prices are still mercifully low at $35/50 for singles/doubles. All rooms have microwaves and refrigerators.

Right behind Mann's Chinese Theater is the recently spiffed up *Liberty Hotel* (☎ 323-962-1788), 1770 Orchid Ave. Each of the 21 rooms is large and bright, has a private bath and costs $40/45 singles/doubles. There's a communal kitchen, though rooms with kitchens cost just an additional $5. Coffee and parking are free, and a laundry facility is right on the premises.

Also central is the family-friendly *Highland Gardens Hotel* (☎ 323-850-0535, 800-404-5472, fax 323-850-1712), 7047 Franklin Ave. Comfortable rooms and suites wrap around a leafy, quiet courtyard and go for $60/65. Its suites of one, two and three bedrooms with kitchens go for $75/90/120, respectively ($90/110/175 in summer). The hotel is associated with a bit of Hollywood trivia: Janis Joplin overdosed in room 105 on October 3, 1970.

You can't miss the garish Las Vegas-style sign of the *Saharan Motor Hotel* (☎ 323-874-6700, fax 323-874-5163), at 7212 Sunset Blvd. Rooms here have some sense of style and are a good deal at $55 to $65. The location (near a couple of strip clubs) isn't the most savory, though, so don't plan on walking around at night. If it's full, you'll find plenty more budget accommodations costing the same or less just east of here, including the attractive *Dunes Sunset Motel* (☎ 323-467-5171, 800-443-8637), at 5625 Sunset Blvd.

Mid-Range Easily the best value for your money in central Hollywood is the *Magic Hotel* (☎ 323-851-0800, 800-741-4915, fax 323-851-4926), 7025 Franklin Ave, whose large suites sleep up to four people. All have kitchens and modern decor; rates are $69 for singles and $85 to $125 for doubles (winter rates are slightly lower). As a bonus, the hotel can get you reservations for the Magic Castle, a private dinner club normally closed to the public that features (what else?) the talents of top-flight magicians (it is not cheap, but it's definitely memorable).

On a quiet side street near Mann's Chinese Theater is the *Orchid Suites Hotel* (☎ 323-874-9678, 800-537-3052, fax 323-467-7649), 1753 N Orchid Ave. Don't let the shabby lobby deter you: each of the 36 small apartments is nicely appointed and has a kitchen; some also have balconies. Covered parking is free, and there's an outdoor swimming pool. Its rates range from $75 to $109 and can drop as low as $59 to $89 in winter.

Two doors down, another option in this range is the *Hollywood Celebrity Hotel* (☎ 323-850-6464, 800-222-7017, fax 323-850-7667), at 1775 N Orchid Ave, in a stylish, if slightly neglected, Art Deco building. Each of the 40 rooms is spacious and quiet and costs around $80. As a special touch, the free continental breakfast is delivered to your room.

The *Hollywood Metropolitan Hotel* (☎ 323-962-5800, 800-962-5800, fax 323-466-0646), 5825 Sunset Blvd, is a contemporary obelisk near the 101 Fwy on the less-savory eastern side of Hollywood. The flamboyant Art Deco lobby sports a library and an aquarium; there is also a restaurant with a view and free parking. The 90 rooms cost $99, suites $129, including breakfast.

Top End To experience those bygone days of glamour and glory, consider checking in at the *Hollywood Roosevelt Hotel* (☎ 323-466-7000, 800-950-7667, fax 323-462-8056), 7000 Hollywood Blvd, within view of Mann's Chinese Theater. This 1927 Spanish Revival-style hotel was the site of the first Academy Awards ceremonies in 1929, and its Cinegrill Lounge was a favorite hangout for scribes such as Hemingway and Fitzgerald. Rooms cost $109 to $159; suites start at $299.

West Hollywood (Map 10)

Mid-Range The *Holloway Motel* (☎ 323-654-2454), 8465 Santa Monica Blvd, can get a bit noisy in its central location, but it's a friendly if basic place with cable TV, voice mail and a free continental breakfast. Room rates include city tax and are $70 Sunday to Thursday and $80 on Friday and Saturday.

Good value is what you get at the *Park Sunset Hotel* (☎ 323-654-6470, 800-821-3660, fax 323-654-5918), 8462 Sunset Blvd on the Sunset Strip, near the House of Blues. Contemporary rooms are none too large, but some have superb views of the urban sprawl below. Doubles are $84 to $94, and two-room suites with kitchens go for $149 to $169.

The *Sunset Plaza Hotel* (☎ 323-654-0750, 800-421-3652, fax 323-650-6146), 8400 Sunset Blvd, attracts a mixed crowd of families and couples with its high-energy, cosmopolitan flair and reasonable prices. There are 88 nicely decorated and spacious rooms, some with full kitchens, that come with a free continental breakfast buffet. A nice sundeck offers vistas of the city. Rates start at a reasonable $119.

Le Rêve Hotel de Luxe (☎ 310-854-1114, 800-835-7997, fax 310-657-2623), 8822 Cynthia St, is a charming collection of 80 French-countryside-style suites. With heavy floral accents, most rooms come with private balconies, fireplaces, kitchenettes and refrigerators. The views of LA from the rooftop garden and pool area are superb. Services include a coin-operated laundry and 24-hour fax service. It's a good hub for exploring the nearby Sunset Strip and Melrose Ave. Suites, single or double occupancy, start at a reasonable $129 and top out at $205.

Also in the European mode is the *Beverly Plaza Hotel* (☎ 323-658-6600, 800-624-6835, fax 323-653-3464), 8384 W 3rd St at La Cienega Blvd, a trendy six-story boutique hotel with 98 rooms located near the Beverly Center. Special touches include nightly bed turn-down service, free taxi rides within a 5-mile radius, a gourmet coffee bar, a fitness center, spa facilities and the popular restaurant Cava, which serves Spanish food (see Places to Eat). The large, lovingly appointed rooms are priced from $121 to $198.

The *Ramada West Hollywood* (☎ 310-652-6400, 800-272-6232, fax 310-652-2135) is in the heart of 'Boys' Town' at 8585 Santa Monica Blvd. The Art Deco-style lobby is reasonably nice, but the rooms are rather small, though some are equipped with hair dryers, coffeemakers and refrigerators. There is also a heated swimming pool. Prices are comparatively steep – standard rooms go for $149, while small suites are $169.

Top End *Le Parc Hotel de Luxe* (☎ 310-855-8888, 800-578-4837, fax 310-659-7812), on quiet, tree-shaded 733 N West Knoll Drive,

DAVID PEEVERS

Lobby of the Hollywood Roosevelt Hotel

Gay Accommodations

By law, no hotel may turn away gay couples, though some may pretend to be full or frown upon homosexual guests. Any hotel located in West Hollywood is probably gay-friendly, so also check the accommodations listed in that section.

Properties catering predominantly to a gay and/or lesbian clientele include the **Grove Guest House** (*☎ 323-876-8887, 888-524-7683, fax 323-876-3170*), 1325 N Orange Grove Ave in West Hollywood. This tall-ceiling, spacious villa, which sits behind a main house, has a living room, dining room and private kitchen. It's surrounded by a lush yard with an orange tree as well as a pool and spa. Rates start at $150.

Gay men should check out the **San Vicente Inn-Resort** (*☎ 310-854-6915, fax 310-289-5929*), 845 N San Vicente Blvd, also in West Hollywood. It has large suites and cottages – with stylish contemporary furnishings – overlooking a tropical garden. There is a heated swimming pool and clothing-optional sun patio, where bronzed beauties lounge. Free continental breakfast is served on the patio. Rates are $59 to $179 single occupancy, $79 to $199 double.

In Beverly Hills is the newly named **Renaissance Beverly Hills** (*☎ 310-277-2800, 800-421-3212, fax 310-203-9537*). From its perch at 1224 S Beverwil Drive, it overlooks the city, and some of the large rooms have private balconies. Furnishings are contemporary and include fireplaces; a swimming pool and gym are on the premises. Rates are $204 for standard singles, $234 for upper-floor rooms with continental breakfast and hors d'ouevres, and $395 to $600 for suites.

has 154 suites turned into homey and stylish digs after a recent renovation. Most have kitchenettes or wet bars as well as gas fireplaces and balconies. The athletically inclined can do laps in the swimming pool or hit some balls on the tennis court, which are both on the roof. There's also a gym and private trainers. As a special touch, complimentary limousine service will whisk you anywhere within a 3-mile radius. Suites start at $175.

Time at **Le Montrose** (*☎ 310-855-1115, 800-776-0666, fax 310-657-9192*), 900 Hammond St, seems to move a bit slower than in the rest of LA. This cozy hideaway boasts a $2 million art collection and 120 large suites with sunken living rooms and fireplaces; some have kitchenettes and private balconies. Views of the city from the rooftop swimming pool, framed by private cabanas, are breathtaking. Bicycles to scoot around West Hollywood are included in the room rates, from $175 to $475.

One of the classiest establishments in town is **The Argyle** (*☎ 323-654-7100, 800-225-2637, fax 323-654-9287*), 8358 Sunset Blvd, in a gorgeously restored, sleek Art Deco tower from 1931. The hotel's exterior is impressive, and its interior charms include an undulated steel and brass staircase that leads to furnishings copied from major museum collections. Its 20 rooms and 42 one-bedroom, terrace and penthouse suites start at $195 and crest at $1200.

Get ready for French-flavored indulgence at the **Château Marmont** (*☎ 323-656-1010, 800-242-8328, fax 323-655-5311*), 8221 Sunset Blvd, modeled after a Norman castle. Its whimsical charm, gorgeous gardens, special services (including complimentary cellular phones and newspapers) and legendary discretion make it a favorite with celebrities. Rooms are $195; suites run $250 to $1400.

Like the gates to heaven, two giant doors – but no marquee – announce your arrival at the **Mondrian Hotel** (*☎ 323-650-8999,*

800-525-8029, fax 323-650-5215), at 8440 Sunset Blvd, LA's ultimate place for celeb sightings. Despite its bland exterior, the place breathes exclusivity and sophistication served with a gallon of attitude – it's just soooo LA. Part of the empire of fine hotels owned by '70s disco tycoon and Studio 54 magnate, Ian Schrager, the Mondrian boasts decor of melodramatic minimalism that juxtaposes harsh geometry with playful lighting effects. 'Basics,' such as a 24-hour gym and gourmet restaurants, are supplemented by a yoga studio, private physical trainers and afternoon tea. The Sky Bar is legendary (see Entertainment). Expect to shell out $240 or more for a better-than-standard room and up to $2600 for a suite.

The **Sunset Marquis Hotel & Villas** *(☎ 310-657-1333, 800-858-9758, fax 310-652-5300)*, 1200 N Alta Loma Rd, is a discreet retreat and a favorite among record-industry players (it has a $600,000 recording studio on the premises). It's also noted for its rolling lawns, koi pond and tropical gardens. Suites range from $260 to $320; villas are $600 to $1200.

Mid-City

Budget One reasonable option in this area is the smallish **Bevonshire Lodge Motel** *(Map 10; ☎ 323-936-6154)*, at 7575 Beverly Blvd, with decor that hasn't changed much since Nixon was president. It charges just $39/45 singles/doubles for air-conditioned rooms with TV, and there is even a small swimming pool.

Those looking for an excellent value will like the friendly **Park Plaza Lodge** *(Map 10; ☎ 323-931-1501, fax 323-931-5863)*, 6001 W 3rd St, within walking distance of the Farmers' Market in the Fairfax District. Large rooms have antique-style furniture, refrigerators and air-conditioning, and cost $50/55.

The 1924 **Chancellor Hotel** *(Map 2; ☎ 213-383-1183, 800-446-4442)*, at 3191 W 7th St, has a sizable population of long-term residents, including international students and senior citizens. Housed in a lovely, turreted grayish-white building, it has a huge lobby and communal area, including a cafeteria where breakfast and dinner are served.

Rooms are clean, with adequate comforts and private baths, and cost $49/54 (including meals). Steep discounts for monthly stays are available.

The **Dunes Wilshire Motor Hotel** *(Map 10; ☎ 323-938-3616, 800-452-3863)* is an older property at 4300 Wilshire Blvd, with a swimming pool and laundry. Adequate rooms go for $53/62; kitchenettes are available (with a surcharge) by request.

Mid-Range Those wanting to stay in a truly exceptional historical landmark – shown in TV shows, commercials and such films as *Bugsy* and *The Bodyguard* – should check into **Park Plaza** *(Map 5; ☎ 213-384-5281, fax 213-480-1928)*, 607 S Park View St, which charges $50 to $90 per room, including continental breakfast. It's an Art Deco marvel with a monumental lobby of cathedralesque dimensions, from which a sweeping staircase leads to two grand ballrooms with giant chandeliers, coffered and painted ceilings and Gobelin-style tapestries. The catch? It's in bad need of renovation, which is just what it may be getting by the time you're reading this, so check ahead. Also, it's located adjacent to MacArthur Park, a hangout for the homeless and druggies – not the safest neighborhood.

The vintage **Wilshire Royale Howard Johnson Plaza** *(Map 5; ☎ 213-387-5311, 800-421-8072, fax 213-380-8174)*, 2619 Wilshire Blvd, is pleasant and has lots of character. Rooms in this Art Deco hotel are being gradually upgraded, but until the renovation is complete, rates of $129/149 from April through September and $109/129 the rest of the year are a tad too high.

Farther west, in Koreatown, is the **Best Western Mid-Wilshire Plaza Hotel** *(Map 2; ☎ 213-385-4444, 800-528-1234, fax 213-380-5413)*, 603 S New Hampshire Ave. The location is not too fashionable, but $60/85 buys a large, friendly room with standard amenities, including a refrigerator. Covered parking is included.

Slightly off the beaten track, the **Oxford Palace Hotel** *(Map 2; ☎ 213-389-8000, 800-532-7887, fax 213-389-8500)*, 745 S Oxford Ave, is a handsome boutique hotel with 77 rooms and nine suites. Six blocks south of

Wilshire in Koreatown, it charges $69 to $100 for singles and $74 to $110 for doubles. Rooms have refrigerators, VCRs, in-room movies and other amenities.

Top End The *Four Seasons Hotel (Map 10; ☎ 310-273-2222, fax 310-859-3824)*, 300 S Doheny Drive, is one of those exceptional hotels that dazzle with class, not glitz. A natural color scheme, tasteful art and sculptures, and smart furniture bring to mind the sophistication of time-tested European hotels. Attention to detail is impeccable – even the restaurant bathrooms have fresh flowers and plush towels. Rates run from $295 to $385 for rooms and from $450 for suites, which are almost worth a splurge.

Beverly Hills & Bel Air (Map 11)
Mid-Range Moderately priced options are hard to find in this stronghold of opulence and wealth. A good choice is the contemporary *Crescent Hotel (☎ 310-247-0505, 800-451-1566, fax 310-247-9053)*, 403 N Crescent Drive, 3 blocks east of Rodeo Drive. Smallish rooms cost $80 to $95, and one-bedroom suites sleeping up to four are $115 to $135 for two, $10 more for each extra person. Weekly rates start at $330.

The *Carlyle Inn (☎ 310-275-4445, 800-322-7595, 800-3227-5953, fax 310-859-0496)*, 1119 S Robertson Blvd, is a 24-room and eight-suite boutique hotel on the edge of Beverly Hills. Service is superb, and rates of $120 to $130 include a breakfast buffet, afternoon tea and cocktails. It offers free shuttle service within a 5-mile radius.

A small gem in this diamond-studded part of town is the cozy *Beverly Hills Inn (☎ 310-278-0303, 800-463-4466, fax 310-278-1728)*, 125 S Spalding Drive, which makes you part of the glitter world without robbing your bank account. Extra amenities include voice mail, a sauna and health center, free parking, a buffet breakfast and newspaper. Rates are $130 to $180.

Top End At the *Hotel Bel Air (☎ 310-472-1211, 800-648-4097)*, 701 Stone Canyon Rd, the emphasis is on privacy; Tom Hanks and Joan Collins are among the celebs who have

NIK WHEELER

In the early Hollywood days, the Beverly Hills Hotel was a party pad for the stars.

enjoyed the hotel's secluded bungalows, fountain courtyards and 11-acre gardens. In such a peaceful place, it's hard to imagine you're still in LA. Visit, if only to stroll the grounds or have a drink. If you want to stay, be prepared to drop $240 to $310 per room. (Also see Places to Eat.)

No other hotel dwells in legend like the *Beverly Hills Hotel (☎ 310-887-2887, 800-283-8885, fax 310-281-2905)*, 9641 Sunset Blvd. Its design, gardens and desserts have been perennially featured in the finest magazines. A $100 million face-lift in the early 1990s – courtesy of its current owner, the Sultan of Brunei – restored faded splendor to this venerable château. 'Standard' rooms start at a budget-busting $295, suites at $655, and bungalows top out at a downright ridiculous $3350. (Also see Things to See & Do.)

The contemporary *Hotel Nikko (☎ 310-247-0400, 800-645-5687, fax 310-246-2165)*, 65 S La Cienega Blvd, pulls in LA's power elite. Businesspeople on the fast track can appreciate its state-of-the-art business center, video-conferencing center and knowledgeable staff. The sculptural effect of the entranceway is echoed throughout the lobby, restaurants and 300 largish and quiet rooms. Suites are remarkable compositions of granite, shoji screens and natural lighting. Deluxe rooms hover near the $300 mark; suites run from $345 to a numbing $1800.

For a bit of Old World flair, check into the **Regent Beverly Wilshire** (☎ *310-275-5200, 800-451-4354, fax 310-274-2851, www.rih .com*), 9500 Wilshire Blvd. This bastion of Italian Renaissance style has anchored Rodeo Drive since the 1920s. Yes, it's the hotel from which Julia Roberts first stumbled, then sashayed, in *Pretty Woman*. Luxury is taken very seriously, with many of the 285 rooms featuring not one, but two bathrooms. Rates start at $265 for standard doubles, leap to $495 for the smallest suite and zoom to $4500 for the top suite. But hey, children under 16 stay free, and cribs are furnished gratis. To experience the grandeur without becoming a major stockholder, treat yourself to afternoon tea, served in the Lobby Lounge.

Westwood & Century City (Map 11)

Mid-Range There is absolutely nothing fancy about the **Westwood Inn** (☎ *310-474-4262*), 10820 Wilshire Blvd, but the people who run it try to make you feel welcome. The standard rooms go for $70; those with kitchenettes are $80. Local calls and a continental breakfast are free, as is the seventh night you stay.

The **Royal Palace** (☎ *310-208-6677, 800-631-0100, fax 310-824-3732*), 1051 Tiverton Ave, is no palace, but its standard rooms are reasonably priced at $66/72 for singles/doubles. Assets include free parking (a rare commodity in Westwood), breakfast and cable TV. It's a 2-block walk to UCLA.

Hilgard House (☎ *310-208-3945, 800-826-3934, fax 310-208-1972*), 927 Hilgard Ave, is a delightful boutique hotel with 47 rooms at the southern edge of the UCLA campus. All the rooms in this three-story brick building have antique-style furnishings, refrigerators and ice-makers, and many have spas. Room rates start at $109; suites are $169 to $239.

The **Hotel del Capri** (☎ *310-474-3511, 800-444-6835, fax 310-470-9999*), 10587 Wilshire Blvd, is a charmer. Its 36 rooms and 45 suites in four stories surround a terrace and swimming pool. More than half of the rooms have kitchens; a continental breakfast is delivered to your door; parking is free. Rates run $90 to $110 for rooms, $115 to $235 for suites.

In what used to be an apartment building, the **Century Wilshire Hotel** (☎ *310-474-4506, 800-421-7223, fax 310-474-2535*), 10776 Wilshire Blvd, has preserved a homey feel. Standard singles/doubles go for $100/125. There's a large swimming pool. Stays of a week or more are steeply discounted.

Top End The 295 rooms of the **Doubletree Hotel** (☎ *310-475-8711, 800-472-8556, fax 310-475-5220*), 10740 Wilshire Blvd, have the usual range of amenities. Staying here also gives you free unlimited access to its lovely sauna, Jacuzzi and fitness center. Rooms are $185 ($135 on weekends), and parking and shuttle service to UCLA are free.

The classy **Westwood Marquis Hotel** (☎ *310-208-8765, 800-421-2317, fax 310-824-0355*), 930 Hilgard Ave, is within walking distance of UCLA. The property is bathed in a sea of flowers and trees, and public areas and rooms ooze sophistication and Old World style. Amenities include refrigerators, voice mail and free transportation in the vicinity. Rates in this all-suite property run $260 to $700.

Presidents of countries and corporations have stayed at the **Century Plaza Hotel** (☎ *310-277-2000, 800-937-8461, fax 310-551-3355*), 2025 Avenue of the Stars. Within walking distance to the Shubert Theatre and Century City shopping mall, this hotel is sumptuously pleasant despite its size and cubic exterior. Rooms are spacious and appointed with wonderfully frivolous knickknacks; many have nice views from private balconies. Rates vary widely but start at around $200, though special weekend and promotional rates are frequent.

LAX Area (Map 2)

Budget Apart from the inexpensive chain hotels (see The Chains boxed text), you'll find numerous other affordable accommodations near the airport. Most offer free shuttle service to and from LAX. The small *Vista Motel* (☎ *310-390-2014*), 4900 S Sepulveda Blvd in Culver City, has 22 decent-size rooms from $37 to $52. Another good choice is the *Skyways Airport Hotel* (☎ *310-670-2900, 800-336-0025*), 9250 Airport Blvd, which has 69 rooms, some with kitchenettes and in-room spas, costing $40 to $60; suites are $60 to $90. Parking is free. The *Sunburst Motel* (☎ *310-398-7523*), 3900 Sepulveda Blvd in

Culver City, has standard rooms for $59 and small suites that go for $89.

Mid-Range Again, check the chain hotels. You can also try *Continental Plaza Hotel* (☎ *310-645-4600, 800-529-4683, fax 310-645-7489*), 9750 Airport Blvd. The 570 run-of-the-mill rooms have refrigerators and in-room movies and start at $85; suites start at $125.

A pleasant, resort-style property is the 770-room *Furama Hotel* (☎ *310-670-8111, 800-225-8126, fax 310-337-1883*), 8601 Lincoln Blvd, formerly the Airport Marina Hotel. It's right across from a recreation park with access to tennis courts, a golf course and a driving range. On the premises are a swimming pool, bowling alley and supermarket. Shuttle service to the airport and Marina del Rey is free. Rates range from $99 to $119.

The *Hampton Inn* (☎ *310-337-1000, 800-426-7866, 310-645-6925*), 10300 La Cienega Blvd in Inglewood, has 148 rooms and is near the Great Western Forum, playground of the LA Lakers and LA Kings. Rates of $69 to $95 include a continental breakfast, newspaper and free local phone calls.

The stylish, recently renovated *Wyndham LAX* (☎ *310-670-9000, 800-996-3426, fax 310-670-8110*), 6225 W Century Blvd, caters to demanding business travelers, offering a wide range of services, including car rental, laundry, currency exchange and in-room movies. It has an Olympic-size pool. Rates for standard rooms are a good value, starting at $109 and topping out at $169; suites are $300 to $425. Another option in this category is the *Westin Los Angeles Airport* (☎ *310-216-5858, 800-228-3000, fax 310-645-8053*), 5400 W Century Blvd, with rooms for $109 to $149 and suites starting at $275.

Top End The 15-story *Crowne Plaza LA Airport* (☎ *310-642-7500, 800-255-7606, fax 310-417-3608*), 5985 W Century Blvd, is your typical corporate hotel, big on efficiency and service, but low on atmosphere. The 611 rooms have amenities such as hair dryers and irons. The staff is unusually adept in anticipating the needs of clients, offering free airport pick-up and drop-off. Rooms cost $129 to $159; suites are $350 to $750.

The Chains

Many national hotel chains are heavily represented in greater Los Angeles. Hotels owned, managed or franchised by national chains must keep certain standards of quality, including maintenance and cleanliness; the label means you know what you're getting.

Budget

Days Inn	☎ 800-325-2525
Econo Lodge	☎ 800-446-6900
Motel 6	☎ 800-466-8356
Super 8 Motel	☎ 800-800-8000
Travelodge	☎ 800-255-3050
Vagabond Inn	☎ 800-522-1555

Mid-Range

Best Western	☎ 800-528-1234
Comfort Inn	☎ 800-228-5150
Howard Johnson	☎ 800-654-2000
Radisson	☎ 800-333-3333
Quality Inn	☎ 800-228-5151
Ramada Inn	☎ 800-272-6232

Top End

Doubletree	☎ 800-222-8733
Hilton	☎ 800-445-8667
Holiday Inn	☎ 800-465-4329
Hyatt	☎ 800-228-9000
Marriott	☎ 800-228-9290
Sheraton	☎ 800-325-3535

Biggest of the big, with similar facilities and services, is the 1200-room *Los Angeles Airport Hilton & Towers* (☎ 310-410-4000, 800-445-8667, 310-410-6250), 5711 W Century Blvd, with room rates from $119 and suites from $225. The *Los Angeles Airport Marriott* (☎ 310-641-5700, 800-228-9290, fax 310-337-5358), 5855 W Century Blvd, weighs in with 1100 rooms and rates of $129 to $169; suites are $189 to $750.

Other massive properties include the *Sheraton Gateway LA Airport Hotel* (☎ 310-642-1111, 800-325-3535, fax 310-410-1852), 6101 W Century Blvd, with 727 rooms at $145 to $175 and 83 suites starting at $250. The *Renaissance Los Angeles Hotel* (☎ 310-337-2800, 800-568-3571, fax 310-337-2008), 9620 Airport Blvd, features public areas and 557 rooms that have a comparative dash of personality. Rooms cost $150 to $190; suites crest at $900.

Malibu (Map 2)

Most accommodations in Malibu lie on the Pacific Coast Hwy and are easy to spot.

Although budget stays in Malibu are hard to come by, try the funky *Topanga Ranch Motel* (☎ 310-456-5486), still fairly close to Santa Monica at 18711 Pacific Coast Hwy, with 30 trim white cottages across the highway from the beach, going for $60 to $80. Another option in this price range is the *Malibu Riviera Motel* (☎ 310-457-9503), 28920 Pacific Coast Hwy, which has managed to keep prices at $70 during the week and $80 on weekends.

Casa Malibu Inn (☎ 310-456-2219, 800-831-0858, fax 310-456-5418), at 22752 Pacific Coast Hwy, is a lovely property overlooking a private beach. Some of the 21 rooms have private decks, fireplaces and kitchenettes, all starting at $99 and topping out at $199. Be sure to make reservations at least a few days ahead.

The *Malibu Country Inn* (☎ 310-457-9622), at 6506 Westward Beach Rd, offers a quiet retreat 7 miles north of the Malibu town center, off Pacific Coast Hwy. There are just 15 rooms here, five of them two-bedroom family suites, plus a restaurant and a small swimming pool. Rooms cost $125

Sunday to Thursday and $165 on Friday and Saturday; rooms with a Jacuzzi are $175/190.

The *Malibu Beach Inn* (☎ 310-456-6444, 800-462-5428, fax 310-456-1499), 22878 Pacific Coast Hwy, is a breezy ocean-side hideaway right on a tranquil swimming beach near the Malibu Pier. The decor is hacienda-style, and the patio area makes a lovely breakfast setting. Rooms with partial ocean views cost from $149 to $190; rooms with private outdoor Jacuzzis and suites go for $219 to $275. Rates include a continental breakfast.

Santa Monica (Map 12)

Budget Inexpensive lodgings have been rare ever since Santa Monica was catapulted onto the trendiness bandwagon. Best bets include a few chain motels, such as the *Comfort Inn* (☎ 310-828-5517), 2815 Santa Monica Blvd, and the *Days Inn* (☎ 310-829-6333), 3007 Santa Monica Blvd, about a 10-minute drive inland. There are also a couple of independently owned motels in the same general area. If you want to stay by the beach, the monetarily challenged may have to settle for the Santa Monica HI Hostel (see Hostels earlier in this chapter).

Mid-Range By far the best bet in this price category is the *Sea Shore Motel* (☎ 310-392-2787, fax 310-392-5167), 2637 Main St, which is ingenuously named, given that it's a few hundred yards from the beach. A good value, well-run and with *a lot* of European influences, the motel is owned by a German family (the Frau who serves up the food in the adjoining cafe/restaurant is actually named Brunhilde!), and you'll meet a lot of European travelers here. They serve a hearty German-style breakfast – if you wish – consisting of cold cuts, cheese and baked rolls, for around $5. Standard rooms are $65, and suites sleeping up to four are $95. Ask for special deals when checking in.

Just a block inland, *Hotel Carmel* (☎ 310-451-2469, 800-445-8695, fax 310-393-4180), 201 Broadway, has a lobby with pink ceiling rafters and newly renovated rooms, some with ocean views, for between $90 and $169. The location, a few steps from the ocean and

Santa Monica nightlife, is the best thing about the bare-bones **Ocean Lodge** (☎ 310-451-4146 ext 500, fax 310-393-9621), at 1667 Ocean Ave. Some threadbare rooms go for $110; suites sleeping four or five cost $140 to $160. Prices dip some time after October, so call and barter.

An excellent choice and a value for the money is the charming **Belle Bleu Inn by the Sea** (☎ 310-393-2363, fax 310-393-1063), 1670 Ocean Ave, a property with lots of character in the shadow of the giant Loews Santa Monica Hotel. For $115 to $225 you get a suite with a kitchen or kitchenette, polished wooden floors and great beaches just a few hundred steps away. Most of the 26 rooms have patios for enjoying the breeze, and parking is free.

The **Hotel Shangri-La** (☎ 310-394-2791, 800-345-7829, fax 310-451-3351), a swank 1939 Art Deco building at 1301 Ocean Ave, has long been the sentimental favorite of such celebs as Diane Keaton, Bill Murray and Gene Hackman, who cherish the Golden Age ambience and privacy. There is no swimming pool or restaurant, but rooms – outfitted with retro-style furniture, and some with kitchenettes – start at a very reasonable $130. An oceanfront suite with two bedrooms, a huge living room and a 50-foot terrace goes for $470. Rates include a continental breakfast and afternoon tea.

Less character but an equally good location are offered by the **Best Western Ocean View Hotel** (☎ 310-458-4888, 800-452-4888, fax 310-458-0848), at 1447 Ocean Ave. It's a standard sort of affair, where smallish rooms are $99 to $149 in winter and ratchet up to $139 to $219 during the summer. Those with an ocean view have petite verandas.

Top End At the lower end in this price spectrum is the **Four Points by Sheraton Santa Monica** (☎ 310-399-9344, 800-495-7760, fax 310-399-3322), 530 W Pico Blvd, an attractive 309-room property (formerly the Bay View Plaza), suitable for both families and business travelers. A major renovation has sheathed the spacious rooms and public areas in a contemporary, pleasing color scheme. This hotel is in a good location,

3 blocks from the beach and Santa Monica Pier, and offers easy access to the 10 Fwy. Standard rooms with partial ocean views are $165; rooms with full views are $185.

More upscale is the other Sheraton property in town, the **Miramar Sheraton Hotel** (☎ 319-576-7777, 800-325-3535, fax 310-458-7912), 101 Wilshire Blvd. The mansion of former senator and founder of Santa Monica, John Jones, was once at this site. Opened as a hotel in 1889 and thoroughly renovated to the tune of $33 million in 1994, the Miramar has 270 guest rooms and 32 bungalows set among semitropical gardens. Popular with celebrities and politicians, its room rates start at $140, $300 for bungalows.

The 84-room **Georgian Hotel** (☎ 310-395-9945, 800-538-8147, fax 310-451-3374, georgian@earthlink.net), at 1415 Ocean Ave, has been designated a Historic Hotel of America. With its blue geometric facade, it's an eye-catching Art Deco landmark with

NIK WHEELER

Santa Monica's Georgian Hotel

decor so Great Gatsby-esque that a straw boater wouldn't feel out of place. In the '20s, the speakeasy restaurant was favorite turf of Bugsy Siegel, Clark Gable, Carole Lombard, 'Fatty' Arbuckle and other legends. Try to stay in an ocean-side room for fantastic views over the famous palm trees towering above the Santa Monica Palisades. Special touches include in-room coffeemakers and free newspapers. Rooms range from $185 to $315.

Loews Santa Monica Beach Hotel (☎ 310-458-6700, 800-235-6397, fax 310-458-2813), 1700 Ocean Ave, has interior grandeur and a commanding perch right above the Pacific Ocean. Its light-flooded, galleried, five-story glass atrium provides an airy welcome. Each of the 350 rooms and suites blends rattan and wicker furnishings with a subdued palette of colors. Dining options include the refined Lavande (see Places to Eat). To help work it all off, there's a Pritikin fitness center, plus Jacuzzis and saunas. Rates run $250 to $450 for rooms, $575 to $2500 for suites.

Nearby is *Shutters on the Beach* (☎ 310-458-0030, 800-334-9000, fax 310-458-4589), 1 Pico Blvd, the only Santa Monica hotel that can claim to be practically built into the sand. It has an elegant Cape Cod appearance, two pricey and acclaimed restaurants and lots of original artwork by such notables as Roy Lichtenstein and David Hockney. Cameras are firmly discouraged here, as Shutters is frequently the nest of very high-profile lovebirds. Some rooms feature fireplaces, private Jacuzzis and a homey feel, with complimentary books, magazines, videos and even waterproof shower radios. Expect rates for 'regular' rooms to start at $325, and around $500 for ocean-view rooms. Suites run $750 to $2000.

For a special treat, ensconce yourself in the serenity of *Hotel Oceana* (☎ 310-393-0486, 800-777-0758, fax 310-458-1182), 849 Ocean Ave at the foot of Montana Ave. This all-suite luxury boutique hotel is undergoing extensive remodeling, and rooms will cost more than their current prices, which start at $295 for a one-bedroom suite with ocean view and $495 for the two-bed ver-

sion. But the Italianate swimming pool area and tastefully colorful and quiet rooms – featuring refrigerators loaded with gourmet pizzas – will appeal to the well-heeled. Think sooooothing…

Venice & Marina del Rey (Map 12)

Budget Close to the shore, the *Jolly Roger Hotel* (☎ 310-822-2904, 800-822-2904), 2904 Washington Blvd in Marina del Rey, is definitely hip to international travelers. Basic rooms with large bathrooms are a great value at $62/72 singles/doubles. More budget minded? Ask to stay in the motel section for just $49 to $59. Parking is free, and buses to the beach leave from outside the hotel.

Mid-Range One of the best bargains in LA is the *Cadillac Hotel* (☎ 310-399-8876, fax 310-399-4536), 8 Dudley Ave, right on Ocean Front Walk. It's a graceful 1930s Art Deco landmark, featuring rooms with ocean views, color TVs, safes, phones and private baths. There's also a gym and sauna, rooftop sundeck and coin laundry. Each of the 30 private rooms costs $69; bunks in four-person dorms are $20. The suite, with a view from Malibu to Catalina Island, costs $110.

Ramada Limited (☎ 310-821-5086, 800-272-6232, fax 310-821-6167), 3130 Washington Blvd, was previously the Marina Hotel. The new owners have done a complete renovation and seriously slicked up the place. Rooms have refrigerators and hair dryers, and there's an outdoor Jacuzzi. *Definitely* ask for special deals, as its rates of $69 (up to $129 for suites) change with the season and are negotiable.

The *Foghorn Harbor Inn* (☎ 310-823-4626, fax 310-578-1964), 4140 Via Marina in Marina del Rey, has some good things going for it. Best of all, it's right on Mother's Beach, a small inlet favored by parents with splashing kids. The price structure for its smallish, plain rooms is all over the place – between $79 to $149 – so bargain with them.

The *Marina International Hotel & Bungalows* (☎ 310-301-2000, 800-529-2525, fax 310-301-6687), at 4200 Admiralty Way, has 110 largish rooms decked out in a subdued peach color scheme for around $130, plus 25 courtyard bungalows topping out at $250. There's an LAX shuttle service, a restaurant, bar and spa.

Top End The *Marina Pacific Hotel* (☎ 310-452-1111, 800-421-8151, fax 310-452-5479), 1697 Pacific Ave, offers a quiet island of civilization in freaky Venice. Large, newly renovated rooms are decked out in natural colors, and many have partial-ocean-view balconies. Suites are spacious and have a full kitchen and fireplace. Rooms start at $140, with suites at $195 and up.

If you're going to spend big, it might as well be at the classy *Ritz-Carlton Marina del Rey* (☎ 310-823-1700, 800-241-3333, fax 310-823-2403), at 4375 Admiralty Way. This lavish property comes with its own marina and charter yachts, as well as lighted tennis courts, a swimming pool and spa. The 294 palatial rooms of the 12-story hotel start at $280, with deluxe units cresting at $345 and suites at $2200.

South Bay (Map 13)

Budget Motels charging $40 or less per room abound along the Pacific Coast Hwy, which barrels through all the South Bay communities. Not all are in the best of shape, though. The best of the bunch is the *Moonlite Inn* (☎ 310-540-4058), at 625 S Pacific Coast Hwy in Redondo Beach, which is within walking distance of the beach and decent restaurants. There's a coin-operated laundry next door.

Mid-Range In Manhattan Beach, you'll find the motel-like *Sea View Inn* (☎ 310-545-1504, fax 310-545-4052), 3400 Highland Ave, a mere 300 feet from the shore. Rooms, some with ocean views, have standard modern furnishings, and there's a courtyard and swimming pool. It's about a 15-minute walk to Manhattan Blvd restaurants and nightlife. Regular rooms are $90, and much larger ones cost $125; rates go down to $80/110 in the off-season. Bicycles for scooting around town or along the South Bay Trail are available at no charge. There's a two-night minimum on weekends.

Hermosa Beach has a few terrific choices for those wanting to be close to the ocean, sand and nightlife. The basic *Grandview Motor Hotel* (☎ 310-374-8981, fax 310-374-8983), 55 14th St, is a quiet property half a block from the beach, with a 2nd-floor lobby (ring the bell to enter) and friendly service. Rooms are $75/95 singles/doubles; those with ocean views go for $90/105; parking is free.

The *Sea Sprite Motel* (☎ 310-376-6933, fax 310-376-4107), 1016 Strand, puts you as close to the sand as you can get. It's popular with the college crowd and may get a bit noisy. Standard rooms are $90 ($540/week), which buys an ocean view and a kitchenette with microwave and refrigerator; larger units are $115 ($690/week). Also ask about its studios and beach cottages.

Adjacent to Redondo Beach's entertaining King Harbor pier area is the sprawling *Best Western Sunrise Hotel* (☎ 310-376-0746, 800-334-7384, fax 310-376-7384), 400 N Harbor Drive. The rooms have cheerful decor, a desk, a refrigerator, two phones and a coffeemaker. There is also a good-size swimming pool. Room prices range from $85 to $104.

Another Redondo option is *Hotel Hermosa* (☎ 310-318-6000), 2515 Pacific Coast Hwy, unfortunately right at the noisy intersection with Artesia Blvd (ocean-facing rooms are quieter). It has 80 rooms, a swimming pool and a laundry. Standard rates are $79, but you'll pay $109 for an ocean view with balcony, and up to $139 for a kitchen, loft or whirlpool unit with ocean view.

With its lace curtains, dark oak trimmings, thick carpets and stately atmosphere, *Barnabey's Hotel* (☎ 310-545-8466, 800-552-5285, fax 310-545-8621), 3501 Sepulveda Blvd at Rosecrans in Manhattan Beach, tries very hard to emulate the casual elegance of European country inns. Though homey, much of the frilly decor seems a cross between a Louisiana whorehouse and a British manor. Rooms are nice, large and well-appointed. There's a lovely patio for afternoon tea, a pub and great restaurant (Auberge, see Places to Eat). Rates range from $119 to $139 and include a big breakfast buffet.

The exterior may not be much to look at, but *Palos Verdes Inn* (☎ 310-316-4211,

800-421-9241, fax 310-316-4863), at 1700 S Pacific Coast Hwy in Redondo Beach, actually has plenty of assets. Besides a location 3 blocks from the beach, there are comfortable rooms and free bicycle rentals. There's also a glass-encased pool with retractable roof, for swimming in all climates. The restaurant, Chez Mélange, is one of the area's finest (see Places to Eat). The inn's 110 rooms start at $110/120; many have ocean views.

Top End The South Bay's ticket to oceanside elegance is the ***Portofino Hotel & Yacht Club*** *(☎ 310-379-8481, 800-468-4292, fax 310-372-7329)*, at 260 Portofino Way in Redondo Beach. Occupying the peninsula that separates the King Harbor marina from the Pacific Ocean, this neat property offers the gamut of amenities, beginning with the oceanfront lobby accented by fresh flowers and a fireplace. Rates start at $175/185 for marina views and $205/215 for ocean-view rooms.

San Pedro & Long Beach (Maps 14 & 15)

The ***Pacific Inn*** *(☎ 310-514-1247, fax 310-831-5538)*, 516 W 38th St, is a nicely appointed hotel in San Pedro. Each of the 24 decent-size rooms is comfortable and tastefully furnished. There are also family suites with kitchens. Rates are $55/69, though the proprietors assure us there's flexibility for stays longer than one night.

A central, if somewhat noisy, location and low room rates make the ***Beach Inn Motel*** *(☎ 562-437-3464, fax 562-436-4541)*, 823 E 3rd St, appealing. Expect clean, no-frills rooms, but with $40 rates, who's to complain? Try here only if the ***Inn of Long Beach*** *(☎ 562-435-3791, 800-230-7500, fax 562-436-7510)*, 185 Atlantic Ave at Broadway, is fully booked. Costing only slightly more, this very friendly establishment was recently spiffed up. Rooms have cable TV and VCRs (with free video rental) and face a central courtyard with swimming pool and Jacuzzi. Rates are $55/65 singles/doubles and include a continental breakfast.

If you've ever longed to experience the atmosphere of a classic ocean liner, the ***Hotel Queen Mary*** *(☎ 562-435-3511)*, 1126 Queens Hwy, offers you a chance. The original (refurbished) 1st-class staterooms of this permanently moored liner are cramped, to be sure, and portholes don't provide a lot of light, but the mood of Art Deco afloat is unmatched. Small interior rooms start at $80; better ones run $120 to $160.

Burbank, Universal City & Studio City (Map 17)

Mid-Range The ***Safari Inn*** *(☎ 818-845-8586, 800-782-4373, fax 818-845-0054)*, 1911 W Olive Ave in Burbank, has so much character it's been used as a movie set. The motel has a bar, swimming pool and spa. Its 103 rooms cost from $64 to $84, and some of the pricier ones have small kitchens. Prices may go up after completion of a planned renovation.

The ***Holiday Lodge*** *(☎ 818-843-1121)*, 3901 Riverside Drive, also in Burbank, has friendly service and tastefully appointed, fairly quiet rooms (some with extra-large tubs) costing $64 to $74. ***Burbank Inn & Suites*** *(☎/fax 818-842-1114)*, 180 W Alameda Ave, has 34 rooms and 17 minisuites just west of the I-5 for $70/80 singles/doubles.

Within walking distance to Universal Studios, just off the busy Ventura (101) Fwy, is the flower-festooned ***Universal City Inn*** *(☎ 818-760-8737, fax 818-762-5159)*, 10730 Ventura Blvd in Studio City, which is an excellent value. Most of the 37 rooms are modern, large and air-conditioned, costing $60/80.

A handsome garden with waterfalls and a swan pond is the centerpiece of the ***Sportsmen's Lodge*** *(Map 2; ☎ 818-769-4700, 800-821-8511, fax 213-877-3898)*, 12825 Ventura Blvd in Studio City. Simulating a British country estate, it sports a clubby restaurant, pub, huge swimming pool and spa. All 193 rooms have private patios and are priced at $105 to $133, with suites from $165 to $180.

Old World charm coupled with a full range of amenities is what you'll find at ***The Annabelle*** *(☎ 818-845-7800, 800-782-4373)*, 2011 W Olive Ave in Burbank, which bills itself as a *petit hôtel de luxe*. Recently renovated, it offers rooms ranging from $120 to $164, depending on the size and season. If you want predictable comforts, check in at the 490-room *Holiday Inn (☎ 818-841-4770, 800-465-4329, fax 818-566-7886)*, at 150 E Angeleno Ave, also in Burbank. It has an impressive lobby and rooms starting at $129.

Top End The *Burbank Airport Hilton & Convention Center (☎ 818-843-6000, 800-445-8667, fax 818-842-9720)*, 2500 Hollywood Way, is convenient to this regional airport. The nine-story hotel has 500 rooms, a restaurant, bar, two swimming pools, a sauna and fitness center. Rates are $139/149, though they usually go up when a convention is in town.

On the Universal Studios lot is the 21-story *Sheraton Universal Hotel (☎ 818-980-1212, 800-325-3535, fax 818-509-0605)*, 333 Universal Terrace Pkwy. This typical chain hotel includes in-room movies, a Jacuzzi, coffeemaker and morning newspaper among its amenities, plus transportation to the theme park. A huge lobby gives access to 417 rooms priced at $180 to $250.

The Sheraton's 24-story, steel-and-glass neighbor is the monolithic *Universal City Hilton & Towers (☎ 818-506-2500, 800-445-8667)*, 555 Universal Terrace Pkwy. It has another 446 rooms at $135 to $200, all with views of the San Fernando Valley, and the standard Hilton amenities.

Elsewhere in San Fernando Valley

Budget The *Chariot Inn Motel (Map 3; ☎ 818-507-9774, fax 818-507-9774)*, 1118 E Colorado St in Glendale, offers free continental breakfast, refrigerators and movies in its 31 spacious rooms, priced at $42 to $52 for singles, $50 to $60 for doubles.

Warner Gardens Motel (☎ 818-992-4426, fax 818-704-1062), 21706 Ventura Blvd in Woodland Hills, has 42 rooms with refrigerators and microwaves from $46 to $54 and suites costing $54 to $65. Rates include a continental breakfast, and there's a coffee shop and spa on the premises.

Mid-Range At the west end of San Fernando Valley, the *Hyatt Westlake Plaza Hotel (☎ 805-497-9991, 800-233-1234, fax 805-379-9392)*, 880 S Westlake Blvd, West-

lake Village, is a five-story conference center with charm. The 194 rooms go for $89 to $170. Amenities include a spa and in-room movies.

The *Best Western Golden Key Motor Hotel (Map 3; ☎ 818-247-0111, fax 818-545-9393)*, 123 W Colorado St in Glendale, has 55 pleasant rooms with microwaves, refrigerators and VCRs. There's also a swimming pool and spa. Rates average $119 to $139.

Top End Glendale's handsome 19-story *Red Lion Hotel (Map 3; ☎ 818-956-5466, fax 818-956-5490)*, 100 W Glen Oaks Blvd, has earned a good reputation with business travelers for its services and facilities, including free shuttles to Burbank Airport. Views from the 19th-floor bar are truly panoramic. For relaxation, there's an outdoor swimming pool, sauna, spa and fitness center. All 348 rooms have refrigerators and start at $214 on weekdays, $139 on weekends.

Pasadena (Map 16)

Budget Pasadena's 'motel row' is along E Colorado Blvd between Lake Ave and Rosemead Blvd. There are literally dozens of budget-priced motels along this strip, some in better shape than others, including such chain properties as Best Western, Comfort Inn, Econo Lodge, Holiday Inn, Ramada and Travelodge. Several independent motels (especially those clustered between Sunnyslope and Eastern Aves) advertise rooms for just $25 a night, and these are popular with transients and low-income people.

The Ritz-Carlton Huntington Hotel was featured in the film *Beverly Hills Ninja.*

A much better choice is the friendly **Westway Inn** (*☎ 626-304-9678, fax 626-449-3493*), 1599 E Colorado Blvd, a nice property across from Pasadena City College. Each of the 61 modern rooms has a refrigerator, coffeemaker and hair dryer, and there's even a small swimming pool and spa. Room rates are $53 to $59 and start at $79 for suites with private Jacuzzis.

Next door is the **Saga Motor Hotel** (*☎ 626-795-0431, 800-793-7242, fax 626-792-0559*), 1633 E Colorado Blvd, a spacious, nicely landscaped and well-kept three-story inn. It offers free continental breakfast as well as a pleasant swimming pool and spa area. There are 69 recently remodeled rooms, priced from $56 to $75.

A bit farther east is the **Best Western Colorado Inn** (*☎ 626-793-9339, fax 626-568-2731*), 2156 E Colorado Blvd, an older property with a peanut-size swimming pool. Rooms are standard-size, but bathrooms are quite large. Rooms cost $58 to $71, including continental breakfast.

Mid-Range The **Pasadena Holiday Inn** (*☎ 626-449-4000, 800-457-7940, fax 626-584-1390*), at 303 E Cordova St, is centrally located between Pasadena's civic auditorium, the convention center and a major shopping mall. The five-story hotel has a swimming pool, two tennis courts and 320 rooms at $129 to $144.

Top End The 12-story **Pasadena Hilton** (*☎ 626-577-1000, 800-445-8667, fax 626-584-3148*), 150 S Los Robles Ave, makes tasteful use of marble and skylights, and rooms are warmly furnished in dark wood. Amenities include a fitness center and swimming pool.

Rates are $120 to $205 for a large room with view. Weekend specials may get you a rate of $109.

The **Ritz-Carlton Huntington Hotel** (*☎ 626-568-3900, 800-241-3333, fax 626-568-1842*), 1401 S Oak Knoll Ave, is a sumptuous hostelry surrounded by a magnificent 23-acre garden. Built in Mission-style in 1907, it was fully upgraded following serious earthquake damage. Special touches include the covered picture bridge and California's first Olympic-size swimming pool. Rates for its 383 rooms start at $165 and climb to $500.

Pasadena's other top property is the **Doubletree Hotel** (*☎ 626-792-2727, 800-222-8733, fax 626-795-7669*), 191 N Los Robles Ave, a modern 12-story, 360-room hotel connected to the City Hall complex through a fountain-laden Mediterranean courtyard. Rates range from $179 to $299; on weekends, some rooms go for $120.

LONG-TERM ACCOMMODATIONS

Hotels often have attractive rates for stays of a week or longer. Your best bet, however, is to scan the newspapers: The *LA Times* has sections for apartment and room rentals in its classified supplement. We also suggest you select the neighborhood in which you want to live and pick up one of the free local papers usually found in retail stores (especially bookstores), restaurants and bars. Also check out the universities. UCLA, for instance, has a Community Rental Housing Office (*☎ 310-825-4491*), which finds people who will be vacating their house or apartment for a limited time and puts them in touch with those in need of accommodations for that period.

Places to Eat

Folks in San Francisco may disagree, but the fact remains: Los Angeles is the culinary capital of the US West Coast. Some would even argue, with reason, that it represents the cutting edge of cuisine in the Western Hemisphere. Why? The number one reason, perhaps, is the willingness to experiment. As a cosmopolitan crossroads, LA attracts people from around the world, and with them their food. Creative chefs (many of them, such as Wolfgang Puck, now celebrities in their own right) take bits and pieces from different traditions and combine them in ways that would have been unimaginable in an earlier day. There are restaurants, for example, espousing the gastronomic glory of California Thai, Chinese Italian, Kosher Mexican and Australian American.

Innovative cuisine is most commonly found in upscale districts such as West Hollywood, Beverly Hills, Santa Monica, Pasadena and Downtown LA. Mexican, Chinese, Japanese and other cuisines abound throughout the city, though the best places are usually the various ethnic districts such as Little Tokyo, Chinatown and East LA, a primarily Mexican American neighborhood. Italian and French restaurants are popular everywhere. And, there are enough hamburger joints, cafes and hole-in-the-wall diners to suit every pocketbook.

You can order sample menus from dozens of restaurants – casual to upscale – by fax through the Restaurant Connection, a free service at ☎ 800-774-3663.

Local Etiquette

Although dining is a casual affair in LA, you should still dress appropriately. That definitely means shoes and shirt; a jacket is appropriate for men at many upscale restaurants. If in doubt, call ahead and ask about the dress code. Classic dinner time is 8 pm, so if you're heading for a popular eatery – especially on a Friday or Saturday night – make a reservation. For the more popular restaurants, you should call days or even weeks ahead. It's customary to wait by the entrance until the host or hostess seats you; only in very casual places may you choose a table yourself.

Most restaurants count on several seatings per night, so the expectation is that you'll leave soon after you've finished your meal. In less expensive restaurants, the waitperson usually brings you the bill automatically; better establishments will present it only after you've requested it (though to hustle you along, they might come by your table every two minutes asking if you'd like to order anything else). Smoking is prohibited in all restaurants.

If you're a serious foodie, keep your eyes open for LA restaurant guides written by Merrill Shindler or Paul Wallach, two noted local food critics.

Cost

If you don't insist on lavish, sit-down meals, you need not spend a lot of money on food. Besides the ubiquitous fast food chains, there are plenty of simple hole-in-the-wall eateries, Mexican taco stands, hot dog vendors and the like, where you can fill up – and eat well – for just a couple of dollars.

If you want a more substantial hot meal, lunch is usually cheaper than dinner. Chinese and Thai restaurants in particular often offer special three-course bargain lunches under $5. Going out for dinner can also be affordable – even at fancier restaurants – as long as you stick to one main course and a single nonalcoholic beverage.

Restaurants are notorious for huge markups on beer, wine and even bottled water. If you're concerned about money, stick with LA tap water; it may not taste as good but it is perfectly safe to drink. If you want alcohol, order beer or wine by the glass and avoid expensive cocktails.

All restaurant meals are subject to California's 8.25% state sales tax. You are expected to tip a minimum of 15% on your food-and-drink bill (doubling the tax amounts to a fair 17% tip). Many restaurants also charge $3.50 or so for valet parking, not counting the dollar or two you should tip the valet when your car is returned. Thus, a moderately priced $35 dinner for two (not including $20 for wine) will actually run you about $50.

In this book, we have divided restaurants into three price categories: 'Budget' places are those where average entrees cost less than $10; those listed under 'Middle' charge between $10 and $20 per entree, while the ones listed under 'Top End' are just that, with entrees costing $20 and up.

Unless noted otherwise, restaurants mentioned in this chapter are open daily for lunch and dinner. Because LA eateries are in the habit of changing their hours frequently, we advise you to confirm them before heading out.

DOWNTOWN (MAP 5)
Budget
A dream come true for the cash-strapped – and a terrific place to sop up Downtown LA's motley mélange of ethnicities, languages

---

Restaurant Report Cards

Who would have thought dining out could be a health hazard? That's exactly what reporters of a local TV channel found during an undercover investigation in late 1997. They unveiled ghastly conditions even at some of the finest and most popular restaurants around town. Which is why you'll now find a letter grade of A, B or C posted near the door of most LA restaurants.

The grading cards are the result of a vigorous campaign by the Department of Health Services – begun in early 1998 – which rewards restaurants in compliance with its regulations and shames those that are not into cleaning up their act. Issued after routine inspections, the cards are based on a scale of 1 to 100, with an A awarded for scores between 90 to 100 points, a B for 80 to 89 points and a C for 70 to 79 points. Restaurants that fall below 70 points receive only a score card (not displayed). Those that fall below 60 more than twice within a year will be threatened with closure. Getting a perfect score is quite difficult; points are deducted for inadequate storage, using the same cleaning sponge for different counters and having insufficient lighting.

Apparently, restaurants with a low grade did feel the sting and are now in greater compliance with the regulations. In October 1998, some 64% received an A grade (as opposed to 40% a year earlier), 25% received a B (up from 12%) and only 4% fell below a C grade (down from 22%).

Displaying the letter grade is mandatory only in the city of Los Angeles. Restaurants in independent cities such as Beverly Hills and West Hollywood are also issued the cards but are not required to display them (of course, those with an A rating are proud to affix the card prominently). All scores are listed on the department's website at www.dhs.co.la.ca.us.

and cuisines – is the **Grand Central Market** on Broadway. Eating here is super-casual; simply choose an eatery and sidle up to the counter where you may rub elbows with mustachioed Mexicans, chirpy Korean housewives or three-piece-suited lawyers. Choices are numerous, but these are some of our favorites.

For fresh fish and seafood, head to **Maria's Pescado Frito** in the central aisle. Best bets are generously filled fish tacos ($1.25) and the tostadas topped with tangy ceviche ($2), a marinated fish and seafood salad. In the right aisle, **Sarita's Pupuseria** serves mouthwatering Salvadoran food including pupusas – pastries filled with cheese, pork or beans that cost a mere $1.50. In the central aisle, beneath the garish neon sign is **Roast to Go**, in business since 1952. Its tacos ($1.50) and burritos ($3) are truly delicious. Safe choices include chicken, lamb, fish or carnitas (fried and shredded beef), while adventurous types can pick from such *muy auténtico* fillings as hog maw, brains, guts and blood sausage. For huge bowls of soup – hot, steamy and delicious – check out **China Cafe** on the upper level toward the market's Hill St exit. Almost nothing on the menu costs more than $3. The market closes at 6 pm.

A popular haunt of *LA Times* reporters and Civic Center bureaucrats is **The City Pier** (☎ 213-617-2489), 333 S Spring St, where less than $6 buys sandwiches bulging with rock shrimp, crawfish or catfish. Seating is nicest

beneath umbrellas on the patio. It's open weekdays only from 10:30 am to 3:30 pm.

In the flat-iron building at the junction of Main and Spring Sts, 840 S Spring St, is **Angelique Cafe** (☎ 213-623-8698), where you can indulge in delicious French food at prices that are a veritable steal. Chef Bruno has his way with sandwiches, casseroles, salads and various hot dishes listed on a menu that tops off at $8.25. He also makes superb pâté, affordable here but served at premium prices in swank Westside establishments. It is open 7 am to 4 pm Monday to Saturday.

Whether **Philippe's The Original** (☎ 213-628-3781) is really the 'home of the French Dip sandwich' (as they claim) is beside the point. The fact is, eating at this legendary establishment at 1001 N Alameda St, in business since 1908, is a memorable experience. Some of the city's best chefs regularly join the throngs at the long service counter, where retro-clad 'carvers' prepare juicy roast beef sandwiches for dipping into fragrant juice from the roasting pan. To show you're not a novice, order a side of coleslaw or potato salad and a surprisingly decent glass of red wine. Coffee is just 9¢ (no misprint). Then find a seat at the long communal tables parked on the sawdust-covered floor and chow down. It's open daily 6 am to 10 pm (cash only).

A bit north of central Downtown, in a seedy section of Echo Park, is **Barragan's** (☎ 213-250-4256), 1538 Sunset Blvd, a Mexican restaurant with a fine reputation and a well-priced menu. The chicken enchiladas ($3.85) are your best bet, though the cocido soup, a flavorful broth with a lot of vegetables, is worth trying. Barragan's has its own parking lot across the street – use it.

For large bowls of udon – thick noodles swimming in an aromatic broth along with anything from egg to beef to shrimp and bamboo shoots – check out Little Tokyo's **Suehiro** (☎ 213-626-9132), 337 E 1st St. Other delicious Japanese delicacies, all at budget prices, include sukiyaki (a stew-like dish), tempura (shrimp or vegetables lightly deep-fried) and several combination plates. It's open till 3 am (Sunday till 1 am), so this place draws a lot of red-eyed night owls.

Roast to Go in Grand Central Market

Mid-Range

For juicy burgers amid Downtown's high-rises, the beer garden of the **Bonaventure Brewing Company** (☎ 213-236-0802), 404 S Figueroa St, is a great choice. Its half-pounder is a carnivore's dream and comes with applewood smoked bacon and Vermont cheddar ($8.95). It goes down well with their home-brewed amber ale. Other dishes can be too creative for their own good, so stick with the basics. It also offers a great 'happy hour' (see the boxed text in the Entertainment chapter). It's closed Sunday.

Dining in a train station usually has about the same appeal as a picnic next to a sewage pipe. The arrival of **Traxx** (☎ 213-625-1999) inside the historic Union Station, though, signals that good food and railway stations are not mutually exclusive. Chef Tara Thomas gets creative with the ahi tuna napoleon, and also produces dependable favorites such as crab cakes for crowds of Downtown suits and accidental travelers. Lunch is served weekdays, dinner nightly; it's closed Sunday.

The 24-hour **Original Pantry Cafe** (☎ 213-972-9279) has occupied a corner spot at Figueroa and 9th Sts for about 75 years and is currently owned by LA Mayor Richard Riordan. The city's movers and shakers are among the loyal customers who regularly crowd around the Formica tables to consume gigantic omelets, steaks and fries, pork chops and other such artery-clogging fare. Its famous sourdough bread, though, is preservative free.

A much better choice is the 'South of the Border' food of **La Golondrina** (☎ 213-628-4349), one of LA's oldest Mexican restaurants (1924). Its prime location on Olvera St translates into entrees costing two or three dollars more than Mexican restaurants elsewhere in LA, but at least the food and atmosphere are fairly authentic. The kitchen especially excels at less touristy fare such as shrimp with tangy green tomatillo sauce and pork simmered with cactus.

Little Tokyo is the obvious place for fresh sushi and **Frying Fish Sushi** (☎ 213-680-0567), in the central square of Japanese Village Plaza, has some of the best prices and quality. Sushi servings, sitting on plates colored to correspond with the price, buzz by you on a conveyor belt installed in the oval bar; you just pick up the ones you want. Your final tab is calculated by adding up the plates. The 'Tres Amigos' roll (tuna, yellowtail and salmon) is among the best anywhere.

In the same complex, near the 1st St entrance, is **Oomasa** (☎ 213-623-9048), which has comfy booths and a bar, plus carved wood boards for decoration. It's a touch more expensive. Other sushi bars with good reputations include **Hama Sushi** (☎ 213-680-3453), at 355 E 2nd St, and **Komasa** (☎ 213-680-1792) next door at 351 E 2nd St.

Be prepared to wait in line to sit at the bar of **Shabu Shabu House** (☎ 213-680-3890), also in the Japanese Village Plaza at 127 E 2nd St. Shabu Shabu is sort of a Japanese 'fondue,' which involves briefly dipping wafer-thin slices of beef and vegetables into a simmering broth. In the end, the remaining broth, now thick with flavor, is spooned up. Regular-size plates are $8 at lunch and $11 for dinner; big ones cost $9.60/13.60. The restaurant is closed Monday.

Top End

The Oviatt building, a former men's clothing store, is a glamorous landmark with a restaurant to match. **Cicada** (☎ 323-655-5559), 617 S Olive St, moved into the cathedral-like space in early 1998 and quickly garnered 'best restaurant' status among Downtown corporate types. The fine food served here is of an upscale Italian stripe and is a tad overpriced. A sweeping double staircase leads to the classy upstairs piano lounge.

For some of LA's most pleasant outdoor dining head to **Café Pinot** (☎ 213-239-6500), 700 W 5th St, set in the quirky Maguire Gardens at the Central Library. Part of the steadily expanding restaurant empire of German master chef Joachim Splichal and his wife, Christine, Pinot whips up sophisticated French-Californian cuisine. The menu is seasonal, although their rotisserie chicken is an ever-popular staple and the desserts are positively decadent. Free shuttle service to the Music Center makes this a popular pretheater supper spot (make reservations

DAVID PEEVERS

Café Pinot in Maguire Gardens is an enjoyable outdoor dining spot.

sometimes of gourmet quality – the seafood often comes straight from the tank. Most of these are also dim sum parlors. Literally meaning 'touching your heart a little at a time' in Cantonese, dim sum involves selecting bite-sized portions of various dishes from carts maneuvered around the dining room by waitresses. It's usually available from 9 am to 3 pm. The other type of restaurant is a casual eatery, where you can chow down on chow mein, jumbo shrimp or Mongolian beef at rock-bottom prices.

Among the best places in the formal category are *Ocean Seafood* (☎ 213-687-3088), 757 N Hill St, a large, upstairs Hong Kong-style place; *Empress Pavilion* (☎ 213-617-9898) on the 3rd floor of Bamboo Plaza, 988 N Hill St; and the slightly less expensive *Golden Dragon* (☎ 213-626-2039), at 960 N Broadway.

Simpler restaurants abound, but these are among the best: *Full House* (☎ 213-617-8382), 963 N Hill St; *Hong Kong Harbor* (☎ 213-617-2983), 845 N Broadway; *Sam Woo* (☎ 213-680-7836), at 727 N Broadway; and *Hop Woo* (☎ 213-617-3038), at 855 N Broadway.

several days ahead). Lunch is served weekdays; enjoy dinner daily except Sunday.

Also worth a visit is Splichal's other Downtown bistro, the more casual *Patinette* (☎ 213-626-1178), 250 S Grand Ave, at the Museum of Contemporary Art. Hours are consistent with those of the museum: Lunch is served from Tuesday to Sunday, dinner on Thursday night only (until 8 pm).

The *Water Grill* (☎ 213-891-0900), 544 S Grand Ave, draws kudos for its impeccably fresh gourmet seafood and fish. The 'Fruits of the Sea' platter gives you a sampling from the oyster bar, while Maine lobster stuffed with king crab is $24 per pound. There's also salmon, tuna, swordfish, sea bass and other fishy friends from Pacific and Atlantic waters. Lunch is served weekdays, dinner nightly.

CHINATOWN (MAP 5)

Chinatown restaurants are divided into two basic categories. At the more formal banquet-hall-type places where the menu is stylish –

EAST LA (MAP 3)

You won't find many sushi bars or fancy Italian restaurants here, but East LA offers some of the best Mexican food around. One restaurant that draws a huge following is *El Tepeyac Cafe* (☎ 323-268-1960), 812 N Evergreen Ave. Try the burritos; they come smothered in cheese and bulging with anything from machaca (shredded beef) to chorizo (spicy sausage) to scrambled eggs and pork. It's a small, simple place, anchored by a heavy bar and framed by mirrored walls festooned with Christmas lights. The restaurant is closed on Tuesday.

For an 'excursion' to Mexico, head to *El Mercado*, 3425 E 1st St, where two restaurants, *El Tarasco* and *El Gallo*, do culinary battle on the cavernous mezzanine level. In terms of food, decor and the quality of the serenading mariachis, the two are practically identical, though El Gallo seems to have a livelier vibe. The locals tell us that everything on the menu is excellent, but we personally favor the ricas botanas, plates piled high with fresh seafood – shrimp, calamari…and more shrimp – and appetizingly served with cocktail sauce. The small (chica) plate is enough for two ($24).

LEIMERT PARK (MAP 7)

Banish any worries about love handles or clogged arteries when eating at *Phillip's House of Barbecue* (☎ 323-292-7613), 4307 Leimert Blvd. A local institution, this smoky, innocuous hole in the wall serves some of the city's best pork and beef ribs. Go easy on the hot sauce unless you're auditioning as a fire-eater. Sandwich-size portions range from $4.50 to $6.25, while dinner-size meals are $6.75 to $11. Its hours are erratic, so call ahead.

The classy *Elephant Walk* (☎ 323-299-1765), 4336 Degnan Blvd, is tastefully furnished with antiques and originals by local artists, and has tables topped with crisp linen cloths and candles. Seafood dominates the menu with selections such as the Nairobi blackened catfish and the Tanzania salmon filet. It's open for dinner only, closed Monday.

Mural outside an East LA butcher shop

HOLLYWOOD
Central Hollywood (Map 9)

Budget Across from Mann's Chinese Theater, *Hamburger Hamlet* (☎ 323-467-6106), 6914 Hollywood Blvd, is perfect for grabbing a quick, casual bite of burger, sandwich, salad or pasta, costing $6 to $10 an entree. It is part of a chain with branches across town. If you like it, check the Yellow Pages for other locations.

Have you ever noticed how yucky words always sound so much nicer in French? How would you like to eat at a place called the Garbage Pail? Not so good. But how about 'La Poubelle'? The food at *La Poubelle* (☎ 323-465-0807), 5907 Franklin Ave, is simple but considerably better than what the name may suggest. The decor, though, does look put together from the reject bin, but that's just part of the charm – we guess. It's open daily for dinner only. On the same block is *Birds* (☎ 323-465-0175), 5925 Franklin Ave, a coffee shop with great marinated chicken sent through the rotisserie for that light and crispy tan. The chicken comes with a choice of tasty dipping sauces, bread and a side dish. Sandwiches, salads, burgers and more – most of them bird-based – are available as well.

Those with a hankering for fish and chips or a ploughman's lunch should head to the *Cat & Fiddle Pub* (☎ 323-468-3800), 6530 Sunset Blvd. The service is friendly, if none too swift. Lunch on the patio is especially pleasant. At night, the place vibrates with rock music, often drawing an audience of eccentric musicians (see Entertainment).

Along Sunset and Hollywood Blvds, just east of the 101 Fwy, is the heart of LA's Thai community, the best place to come for authentic pad thai noodles and tom ka gai soup. *Jitlada* (☎ 323-667-9809), 5233 Sunset Blvd, tucked away in a tacky mini-mall, serves tasty Thai in a dimmed, living-room-like environment. The choices are bewildering, but the staff is happy to make a recommendation. Jitlada is closed Monday.

Another option is the *LA Food Court* (☎ 323-993-9000), on the 2nd floor of Thailand Plaza, a development at 5321 Hollywood Blvd. (Silom, an Asian supermarket, is on the 1st floor.) The hangar-sized, cafeteria-style place only gets hopping at dinnertime, especially on Friday and Saturday nights when a Thai Elvis takes the stage. It's open until 2 am Sunday to Thursday, until 4 am Friday and Saturday.

Mid-Range Hollywood's oldest Italian restaurant (1949) is the still-lively *Original Miceli* (☎ 323-466-3438), 1646 N Las Palmas Ave. Tables are boxed in by oak dividers carved as elaborately as choir stalls, while hundreds of empty Chianti bottles dangle from the beamed ceiling. The signature dish here is linguini pescatore, though they do fine pizza as well. The house wine is a steal at $12 a bottle. Lunch is served weekdays, dinner nightly.

Not only Cubans give *El Floridita* (☎ 323-871-0936), wedged into a mini-mall at 1253 N Vine St, an enthusiastic thumbs up for its authentic food, energetic atmosphere and vibrant live entertainment. Perennial favorites include the Cuban sandwiches made with roast pork and a dish called ropa vieja (literally, old clothing) consisting of shredded beef simmered in Creole sauce. It's a small place and reservations are advised (also see the Entertainment chapter).

Top End Currently one of LA's hottest French restaurants, *Les Deux Cafés* (☎ 323-465-0509), 1638 Las Palmas Ave, must be entered through the back via Grant's parking lot. The place draws a cool crowd heavy on brass, beauty and power (actor Bill Murray is among the investors). Preferred seating is on the secluded, ramshackle patio around a log-shaped pool and surrounded by magnolia trees, geraniums and large leafy plants. Tables inside the Craftsman-style house are less idyllic and entree prices of $20 and up outdistance the chef's skill. There's also a bar with live music, which you can reach through a narrow tunnel of industrial simplicity. It's closed Monday.

A Hollywood dinosaur since 1919, *The Musso & Frank Grill* (☎ 323-467-7788), 6667 Hollywood Blvd, was already a hit with the heroines and swashbucklers of the silent film era. Later, its vinyl booths and old-fashioned

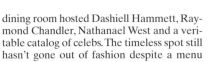

Great Celebrity Spotting

Given LA's fickle restaurant scene, what's hot with celebs today may have plunged out of favor tomorrow. The places listed below are among those that have demonstrated staying power. We can't guarantee you'll see famous faces, but this is where they are known to hang out (details within text):

Caffé Luna (Melrose/La Brea Area)
Chinois on Main (Santa Monica)
Dan Tana's (West Hollywood)
Geoffrey's (Malibu)
Georgia (Melrose/La Brea Area)
Hugo's (West Hollywood)
I Cugini (Santa Monica)
The Ivy (Beverly Center District)
KoKoMo (Fairfax District)
Les Deux Cafés (Central Hollywood)
Matsuhiha (Beverly Hills)
The Musso & Frank Grill (Central Hollywood)
Neptune's Net (Malibu)
Ocean Avenue Seafood (Santa Monica)
Orso (Beverly Center District)
Pink's Hot Dogs (Melrose/La Brea Area)
Spago (West Hollywood, Beverly Hills)

dining room hosted Dashiell Hammett, Raymond Chandler, Nathanael West and a veritable catalog of celebs. The timeless spot still hasn't gone out of fashion despite a menu that includes a politically incorrect milk-fed veal cutlet and stick-to-the-ribs fare such as steak with gravy. Service is smooth, and the martinis – made with only the best gin and vermouth – are killer. It's closed Sunday and Monday.

Journey from Tinseltown to a Thousand and One Nights simply by stepping through the doors of *Dar Maghreb* (☎ 323-876-7651), 7651 Sunset Blvd, made to look like a Moroccan palace centered around an open atrium. You'll dine here pasha-style while reclining on fluffy cushions orbiting a low wooden table. As you dig into a seven-course mouthwatering feast fit for a prince ($32) –

served family style and eaten without utensils – you may find your neck tickled by the tassel of a beautiful bellydancer. Open for dinner only.

One of our favorite places to take out-of-town friends is *Yamashiro* (☎ 323-466-5125), 1999 N Sycamore Ave, seductively perched on a southerly slope of the Hollywood Hills and overlooking the sea of glitter that is the city at night. A replica of a Japanese palace, its name suitably translates as 'castle in the hill'; movies filmed here include *Sayonara* with Marlon Brando. Do what you must to score a window table, where you'll be served by the petite, kimono-clad Japanese waitresses. The food is good, though not worth gushing about. Or just come for the view and a drink in the adjacent lounge. It's open for dinner only; closed Monday.

Serious food zealots with deep pockets shouldn't leave LA without worshipping at *Patina* (☎ 323-467-1108), 5955 Melrose Ave, the flagship restaurant of Joachim and Christine Splichal. Joachim digs deep into his seemingly bottomless culinary knowhow and creativity to create a menu that miraculously fuses Californian tastes and Germanic touches. Lunch is served Tuesday, dinner nightly.

Silver Lake & Los Feliz (Map 9)

Budget On the happening Vermont strip in Los Feliz Village, you'll find *Fred 62* (☎ 323-667-0062) at 1850 Vermont Ave, with a jazzy lime-green exterior and cool crowd that belie the updated '50s-style diner that it is. Huge plates of polyethnic sandwiches, salads, noodles and more are dished out daily around the clock to hungry hipsters on small budgets. All prices end in '62' and top out at $9.62.

An even bigger crowd flocks to *Palermo* (☎ 323-663-1178), 1858 Vermont Ave, a few doors up the street. This unpretentious neighborhood Italian eatery is as welcoming and comfortable as a hug from an old friend. Pizzas are generously topped and buried under a layer of melted cheese, and the small antipasto salad is enough – as an appetizer – for four. Occupying booths and small tables is a veritable cross-section of LA, from cops

to rockers, families to gay couples, people of all ages, classes and colors. Service is fast and super-friendly. There's usually a wait, which isn't all that bad since you'll get a complimentary glass of wine. Palermo is closed Tuesday.

Casual taco stands abound in LA, but it's hard to find one that's good and clean. *El Siete Mares*, 3145 Sunset Blvd, fits the bill with its consistently excellent – and huge – fish tacos and burritos and fresh ceviche tostadas. Nothing on the menu costs more than $5. There's free parking behind the hut and a full restaurant next door.

The Silver Lake branch of *ChaChaCha* (☎ 323-664-7723), 656 N Virgil Ave at Melrose, is a brightly pigmented eatery serving gourmet Caribbean cuisine in a lively ambience. For details, see the Long Beach section of this chapter.

Mid-Range Sunset Blvd provides myriad dining options in this price category, most of them eccentric Mexican cantinas. *El Conquistador* (☎ 323-666-5136), 3701 Sunset Blvd, is festively lit and has a bar straight out of a fishing village. Great choices include Sonorense (chicken sautéed with bacon and vegetables) and jumbo shrimp marinated in tequila sauce.

For a slice of France, head to the secluded *Cafe Stella* (☎ 323-666-0265), a friendly and popular cafe in a romantic courtyard at 3932 Sunset Blvd (look for the red star). The bistro-style menu is small and select, with the freshest offerings marked on a chalkboard. Seating spills out onto the courtyard.

Farther west is *El Chavo* (☎ 323-664-0871), 4441 Sunset Blvd, a windowless Mexican classic that's as much a visual as a culinary experience (see photo on next page). Kaleidoscopic Christmas lights, saddles and other vaquero gear beneath a ceiling festooned with fluorescent sombreros give this place superior camp value. They claim that Dolly Parton is a frequent guest and display her photograph next to the bar. Their chicken enchiladas in mole sauce are excellent. El Chavo accepts cash only.

Nearby is the *Cobalt Cantina* (☎ 323-953-9991), 4326 Sunset Blvd, a fashionable Cal-Mex restaurant that permits smoking on its

Campy El Chavo in Silver Lake

covered patio. The tapas menu features flavor bombs such as Cajun chicken spring rolls and hurricane shrimp. Interesting sandwiches and chicken dinners are among the light-fare offerings. The adjacent bar is popular among upscale gay men. Enjoy lunch weekdays, dinner nightly and their popular brunch on Sunday. There's another branch *(Map 10; ☎ 310-659-8691)* at 616 N Robertson Blvd in West Hollywood.

For a completely different ethnic experience, head to the **Red Lion Tavern** *(Map 5; ☎ 323-662-5337)*, 2366 Glendale Blvd, serving the best of German country cooking in a venerable haunt cluttered with Germanania. Beer steins, black and white glossies of old-time German movie stars and a juke box playing German songs from the '50s are part of the decor. The dirndl-dressed waitresses serve up plates of beef rouladen, schnitzel, a variety of sausages and other stick-to-the-ribs fare. The beer garden buzzes in summer (also see Entertainment).

Top End The **Dresden Restaurant** *(☎ 323-665-4294)*, 1760 N Vermont Ave, time-warps you back to the early 1960s when tall ceilings, white curvilinear booths and textured wallpaper the color of corroded metal were the *dernier cri*. The kind of place you'd expect to be teeming with the white-haired set, it's packed instead with Hollywood hipsters. Oozing Old World charm, owner Carl Ferraro pays personal attention to each guest, perhaps recommending a tender Angus beef

steak or succulent prime rib. The adjacent lounge is a popular nighttime hangout (see Entertainment).

The place to go for superior seafood and sushi in this neighborhood is **Katsu** *(☎ 323-665-1891)*, a stylish restaurant at 1972 N Hillhurst Ave. It has satisfied the sophisticated for years with lunch weekdays and dinner Monday to Saturday.

Melrose/La Brea Area (Map 10)

Budget Just off Melrose Ave, **Pink's Hot Dogs** *(☎ 323-931-4223)*, 711 La Brea Ave, is a simple stand that's been serving delicious all-beef dogs buried beneath aromatic chili and onions ($2.20) since 1939. Pink's enjoys cult status among night owls (open till 2 am weekdays, 3 am weekends), and even celebs such as Kim Basinger and Demi Moore have been seen chowing down here.

The bistro-style **A Votre Santé** *(☎ 323-857-0412)*, 345 N La Brea Ave, does all three meals fat-free, eggless, non-dairy, cholesterol-free, hormone-free – you get the idea. Sit inside or on the leafy patio. There's another branch in Venice *(Map 12; ☎ 310-314-1187)* at 1025 Abbot Kinney Blvd.

Across the walkway (immediately adjacent) is the critically acclaimed **East India Grill** *(☎ 323-936-8844)*, which has fragrant curries and tasty tandoori, though it's easy to build a full meal around its delectable

---

Dining Around the Clock

Hunger can strike travelers at any time, especially those dealing with serious time differences and jet lag. The following places are among those that serve food 24/7 (24 hours a day, seven days a week):

Beverly Hills Café (Beverly Hills)
Canter's (Fairfax District)
Fred 62 (Silver Lake & Los Feliz)
Jerry's Famous Deli (Beverly Center District)
The Kettle (South Bay)
Original Pantry Cafe (Downtown)
Van Go's Ear (Venice & Marina del Rey)

appetizers and breads. The lunch specials (around $6) are an excellent value.

Heading west on Beverly Blvd, you'll find *El Coyote* (☎ 323-939-2255), 7312 Beverly Blvd, a sprawling Mexican cantina beloved partly for its inexpensive and very basic food, but more so for its stiff margaritas, which provide a cheap buzz at just $3. The interior, featuring colored-glass lamps and large booths, is as dark as a Gothic cathedral; if you actually want to see what's on your plate, get a table in the courtyard.

On eternally hip Melrose, the Argentine grill *Lala's* (☎ 323-934-6838), 7229 Melrose Ave, has a meat-heavy menu featuring dishes that average $6. Meals are best consumed on the outdoor patio with a view of the stream of humanity flowing down Melrose.

Between Vista and Gardner is *Caffé Luna* (☎ 323-655-8647), 7463 Melrose Ave, where tables spread out in the funky and noisy dining room (the secluded, flower-festooned courtyard is preferable on a balmy night). Breakfast is served any time and the rustic Italian food is creative, delicious and plentiful. We especially like their thin-crust pizzas, and apparently so do Jennifer Aniston of *Friends* and other celebs. There's no corkage fee for the first bottle of wine you bring along. With closing times of 2 am weekdays and 4 am weekends, Luna is a popular late-night haunt.

Mid-Range An unpretentious choice for French food is *Louis XIV* (☎ 323-934-5102) at 606 La Brea Ave near the intersection with Melrose. Popular with an international crowd, here you'll feast on simple yet gourmet bistro favorites (steak au poivre, steak frites, filet mignon) enhanced by the romantic, candlelit ambience. Prices, mostly under $15, are excellent value. Dinner is available until 1 am.

A dependable Melrose favorite since 1982, *Tommy Tang's* (☎ 323-937-5733), 7313 Melrose near Fuller Ave, serves updated versions of Thai classics and also has a decent sushi bar. Favorites include the Original Tommy Duck ($14.50), though noodle and rice dishes costing around $8 are tasty as well. Sit on the outdoor deck, in the cafe-style front room or in the more formal back dining room with its booths and benches.

For a taste of Little Italy, ex-New Yorkers gravitate to *Frankie's* (☎ 323-937-2801) at 7228 Melrose Ave, an airy, uncluttered dining room complete with shiny baby grand. Traditions such as Manhattan seafood chowder, shrimp fra diablo and osso buco are all good, though lobster fiends will want to do battle with spiny creatures priced at a mere $12 per pound. At night, the place is chock-full with behind-the-scenes Industry types, most of them greeted personally by Frankie himself. Scorcese and DeNiro would dig this place.

Next door is *Georgia* (☎ 323-933-8420), 7250 Melrose Ave, which offers refined Southern soul food served in an exquisite, polished wood dining room or on the patio. Ladies in Prada and gents in Armani nibble on jerk chicken with coconut pigeon pea rice and fried chicken with okra, two quintessential offerings on the meat-heavy menu. The roster of investors includes Denzel Washington and Eddie Murphy. Dinner is served nightly.

Four blocks south and named after the seminal Mothers of Invention album, *Lumpy Gravy* (☎ 323-934-9400), 7311 Beverly Blvd, makes no bones about being inspired by Frank Zappa, dedicating its 'Zappa'd' salad to the master of musical dadaism. Industrial art constitutes the decor, highlighted by a suspended miniature U-boat and a TV-torsoed robot. A variety of Asian-tinged dishes, including 'black and blue ahi tuna,' emerge from what it calls its 'dangerous kitchen.' The Bananagasm takes the meaning of dessert to new levels of climax. Lumpy Gravy is closed Sunday.

Top End Since its opening, *Citrus* (☎ 323-857-0034), 6703 Melrose Ave, has been consistently stellar and continues to rank high among LA gourmets. The California French cuisine stems from the imagination and talent of master chef Michel Richard and his equally skillful staff. Appetizers such as the ahi tuna carpaccio with seaweed ginger sauce and entrees such as sea bass with black chanterelle crust are typical of the inventive menu. It also offers four- and five-course dinners at $55/65 and a premium wine list. Lunch is served weekdays, dinner nightly.

The fad for Southwestern food may be passé, but you wouldn't know it trying to get a reservation at the *Original Sonora Cafe* (☎ 323-857-1800), 180 S La Brea. Price tags are hefty, but the restaurant's use of supreme meats, seafood and vegetables, plus the ingenious preparation, almost justifies the cost. The tangy salsas are great, as are the wild mushroom enchiladas and duck tamales. Try lunch weekdays and dinner nightly.

Ca' Brea (☎ 323-938-2863), at 346 S La Brea, a sister property to Locanda Veneta in the Beverly Center district, offers superb Northern Italian selections in a homey, sectioned dining room. A smoking deck recently opened on the mezzanine level. Lunch is served weekdays, while dinner can be enjoyed Monday to Saturday.

Down the street is *Campanile* (☎ 323-938-1447), 624 S La Brea, which has defined 'urban rustic' cooking. Chef Mark Peel comes up with new culinary creations daily, but staples include excellent grilled meats and vegetables prepared with inspiration from the sun-drenched French and Italian Rivieras. Weekday lunches are joined by dinner Monday to Saturday and a brunch on weekends.

West Hollywood (Map 10)
Budget One of our long-time favorites for casual California cuisine is the *French Quarter Market* (☎ 323-654-0898), 7985 Santa Monica Blvd, also a popular gay hangout. We've never had a bad dish here, but we are partial to its mountains of fresh, delicious salads. Unless you're starving, splitting an appetizer and a salad between two will probably do nicely (just inform your waiter; splits are no problem here). This place is abuzz any time of day, though Sunday brunch is especially busy. Sit either on the outdoor patio facing the noisy boulevard or in the New Orleans-inspired interior with white wrought-iron balustrades and flower boxes. The surrounding shops are eccentric, to say the least.

The Abbey (☎ 310-289-8410), at 692 N Robertson Blvd, is popular with gays and lesbians, though heteros will not feel out of place here either. It has a pretty patio surrounding an Italian fountain and an outdoor bar. Best bets are the desserts, though a number of low-fat items such as salads and pastas are also worth trying. It's open 7 am to 3 am daily; breakfast is served till 2 pm.

Down-to-earth *Hugo's* (☎ 323-654-3933), 8401 Santa Monica Blvd, has sidewalk seating, healthy creations such as the tantric veggie burger and fresh pasta, and an enthusiastic entertainment-industry following. Breakfasts are especially popular and there are about 20 from which to choose. Hugo's doesn't serve dinner Monday and Tuesday. Another contender nearby is *Basix* (☎ 323-848-2460), 8333 Santa Monica Blvd at Flores St, which has an 'Ellis Island' type of a salad menu (Italian, Greek, Chinese) and interesting hand-formed pizzas grilled over fruitwood.

Mid-Range *Victor Hodd's* (☎ 323-822-9652), 7953 Santa Monica Blvd, is a stylish, grown-up place with a hushed, candlelit ambience. Its menu features mostly updated versions of classic dishes from the American South, put together with panache. One of the best bets is the Cajun-style barbecued pork loin served with Creole potato salad. To start off, you might try the duck salad. This is a fairly recent entry on LA's culinary scene, and we hope it will survive.

Most come to the *House of Blues* (☎ 323-848-5123), 8430 Sunset Blvd, for the music, but it's also a restaurant serving pretty decent Mississippi Delta food, such as gumbo, crawfish risotto and baby back ribs. Most dinner entrees cost around $14, though there's also a burger for $8. On Sunday, they do a gospel brunch with an all-you-can-eat buffet ($29, children $15) accompanied by some mighty fine singing. Seatings are at 9:30 am, noon and 2:30 pm; reservations are obligatory.

Luna Park (☎ 310-652-0611), at 665 N Robertson Blvd, offers a vibe of European sophistication in its restaurant cum nightclub cum cabaret (see the Entertainment chapter). Soft earth tones and an intimate setting are accented by original art and luxuriant drapery. The menu is Mediterranean infused with the occasional Asian flavor, such as farfalle with Thai cilantro pesto and the banana tempura dessert. The chef's special four-course tasting menu is $30, or $55 with wine. Dinner is served Tuesday to Sunday.

Top End In this day and age of chic bistros, *Dan Tana's* (☎ 310-275-9444), 9071 Santa Monica Blvd, is something of an anachronism. This is perhaps why it's been a favorite among the famous for the past couple of decades. The atmosphere here is reminiscent of some of New York's primo Italian establishments, and so is the food. It's open for dinner nightly.

L'Orangerie (☎ 310-652-9770), 903 N La Cienega Blvd, is a formal French restaurant with decor that some might consider over the top, but is incredibly romantic if you like Louis XIV-inspired pomp. The best French restaurant in LA by many critics' standards, it's an excellent place for those who truly know what good food, wine and service are about – and are able to pay for it. You can savor dinner Tuesday to Sunday.

It's impossible to write a guide to Los Angeles eateries without mentioning the original *Spago* (☎ 310-652-4025), 1114 Horn Ave, the place that launched Wolfgang Puck as a celebrity chef. Puck not only helped define 'California' cuisine, but also gave birth to the Jewish pizza (topped with lox and caviar), which has become his trademark. Fortunately, astronomical wealth and fame haven't gone to his head and the food is still good. Industry insiders love the place, and who sits where is a gauge of current power and popularity. Call at least a week, better two, in advance for a table, or come at about 10:30 pm and gawk at the crowd over dessert. Dinner is served nightly.

MID-CITY
Beverly Center District (Map 10)
Budget A prime draw among tourists is the *Hard Rock Cafe* (☎ 310-276-7605), on the ground floor of the northwest corner of the Beverly Center mall itself. Here you can dine among John Lennon's handwritten lyrics to *Help*, Buddy Holly's high school yearbook and Madonna's slinky silver dress. The food is pretty good, and portions are huge. There's another branch at Universal City Walk (☎ 818-622-7625; see description later in this chapter).

Nearby is one of the last remaining pieces of mimetic architecture in LA, the hot-dog-shaped *Tail O' the Pup* (☎ 310-652-4517), which moved to 329 N San Vicente Blvd from its original location (since 1938) on La Cienega. Once a favorite of Orson Welles', its edible, though hardly great, dogs continue to attract a loyal following of show biz folks to this day. (We'll be discreet and simply tell you that the enormous protruding hot dog and soft buns of this shack are…suggestive. Ahem.)

Tables at *Kings Road Cafe* (☎ 323-655-9044), 8361 Beverly Blvd, are almost always bustling with a predominantly young crowd,

ANDREA SCHULTE-PEEVERS

DAVID PEEVERS

LA mimetic architecture – in Mid-City (left) and La Puente (right)

Romantic Dining Spots

Leisurely, romantic dinners are integral and memorable parts of any journey. Whether you like secluded patios, flower-festooned courtyards, candlelight, quiet piano music or stunning views over the sparkling city, you'll find all or some of it at the following places (details within the text):

Bel Air Restaurant (Elsewhere on the Westside)
Bistro Garden at Coldwater (Ventura Blvd)
Ca' del Sole (North Hollywood)
Campanile (Melrose/La Brea Area)
Cicada (Downtown)
Geoffrey's (Malibu)
I Cugini (Santa Monica)
Inn of the Seventh Ray (Malibu)
The Ivy (Beverly Center District)
Le Colonial (Beverly Center District)
Les Deux Cafés (Central Hollywood)
L'Orangerie (West Hollywood)
Orso (Beverly Center District)
Patina (Central Hollywood)
Sofi (Fairfax District)
Tahiti (Fairfax District)
Yamashiro (Central Hollywood)

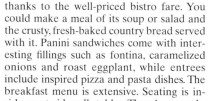

News junkies can pick up the latest tidbits from ticker-tape displays, while more relaxed types can linger over a magazine for sale at the in-house newsstand. The second, smaller branch is in Santa Monica at 530 Wilshire Blvd *(Map 12; ☎ 310-319-9100)*.

Jerry's Famous Deli (☎ 310-289-1811), 9701 Beverly Blvd, is a popular 24-hour deli with a menu as long and confusing as a Dostoyevsky novel. Offerings such as Mexican burritos and pizza may deviate from the usual deli format, but Jerry's returns to its roots with favorites such as the New York-style pastrami sandwiches served on crisp rye with potato salad. For locations of the six other branches, check the Yellow Pages.

Mini-mall restaurants are usually nothing to crow about, but *Menjin (☎ 323-782-0039)*, a casual eatery at 8393 Beverly Blvd, has come up with memorable creations revolving around the lowly noodle. They're loaded into fragrant broth, paired with seafood or Malaysian curry or served cold as a salad. Prices are very reasonable (most dishes cost $6 or less). Food is served in a clean, little-adorned space with an open kitchen. It's closed Sunday.

Mid-Range One of the best choices in this area is *Cava (☎ 323-658-8898)*, inside the Beverly Plaza Hotel (see Places to Stay) at 8384 W 3rd St, with a Spanish/Latin decor, cocktails, live music and inspired menu keeping the place abuzz. The crowd is creative, friendly and unusually animated. For tapas, be sure to try the superbly fresh ceviche served in a half coconut shell ($6.50) or the steamed mussels ($8.50). From Wednesday to Saturday, table-side master chef Octavio does his magic with hand-selected filet mignon, scallops and other delicacies ($20 and up). It's open daily 7 am to midnight.

A bit farther east is *Limbo (☎ 323-866-8258)*, 8338 W 3rd St, easily recognized by its saffron-colored facade. The vivid decor perfectly complements the Caribbean menu, which leans heavily toward fish dishes such as coconut shrimp and yam-crusted salmon. Sit beneath the tented glass ceiling in the back, the main dining room with oversized mirrors, or outdoors in a sidewalk alcove.

thanks to the well-priced bistro fare. You could make a meal of its soup or salad and the crusty, fresh-baked country bread served with it. Panini sandwiches come with interesting fillings such as fontina, caramelized onions and roast eggplant, while entrees include inspired pizza and pasta dishes. The breakfast menu is extensive. Seating is inside or at sidewalk tables. There's no corkage fee for wine brought along with you at dinnertime.

Health gurus will be in heaven at *Newsroom (☎ 310-652-4444)*, 120 N Robertson Blvd, a breezy, spacious cafe with large mirrors and a bamboo-fringed patio. Chef/owner Eddie J Caraeff uses only organic grains and produce, and exiles as much fat and sodium as possible. Everything sounds tasty, but we like the veggie burger and 'fun-filled' ravioli.

There's live music several nights a week and a happening happy hour in the raised bar area from 5 to 7 pm on weekdays. Come for lunch weekdays, dinner nightly and brunch Sunday.

With its cool tiled floor, lazy ceiling fans and rattan chairs, *Le Colonial (☎ 310-289-0660)*, 8783 Beverly Blvd, makes you feel like you've stepped onto the set of *The Year of Living Dangerously*. It's a place where the beauty is as much in the decor as it is in the faces of diners. The Vietnamese cuisine is prepared with exotic ingredients, has complex flavors and can be quite spicy. Dishes are served family-style. The dining room is pleasant, though the outside patio is more romantic on a warm evening. The lounge upstairs – with a smoking terrace – is a popular late-night spot.

Barefoot (☎ 310-276-6223), 8722 W 3rd St, in a gorgeous, ivy-covered building, has a huge bar popular for after-work socializing. The California menu is dominated by salads and creative pasta dishes priced at $8 to $12. Sit inside or on the leafy sidewalk patio.

Top End Unhurried, indulgent Italian meals are what you can expect at *Locanda Veneta (☎ 310-274-1893)*, a smallish eatery at 8638 W 3rd St. Dining takes place in a warmly decorated dining room of rustic elegance, with a Northern Italian menu that puts substance before culinary pyrotechnics. It is popular with behind-the-scene Hollywood big-wigs digging into linguine with baby lobster and clams while talking deals and dollars. Reservations are recommended. Lunch is served weekdays, dinner Monday to Saturday.

If Locanda Veneta is full, walk a few steps east to *Orso (☎ 310-274-7144)* at 8706 W 3rd St, its entrance hiding behind a discreet 6-foot wall. You might glimpse the occasional celebrity, as well as Industry wheelers and dealers, munching on affordably priced thin-crust pizza or generous pasta dishes. Ask for a table on the patio, oh-so-romantic on a warm summer night.

The powerful and the power-hungry like to 'do lunch' on the charming, flower-festooned patio of *The Ivy (☎ 310-274-8303)*, 113 N Robertson Blvd. The decor is done with laissez-faire perfection typical of the south of France, though the menu has many American touches. The Caesar salads are delicious and so are the crab cakes. Leave room for dessert; they are as sweet as the gooiest love letter. Come Sunday for brunch.

For sublime Provençal cooking, head to *Pastis (☎ 323-655-8822)*, an intimate dining room at 8114 Beverly Blvd. It's the kind of relaxed place where meals become culinary celebrations that comfortably stretch out for an entire evening. Sun-yellow walls, sensuously curved mirrors and colorful tableware combine to create an almost familial setting. The dinner-only menu changes by season but may include bouillabaisse, wild mushroom ravioli or lemon-sautéed frogs' legs.

The menu of the *Chaya Brasserie (☎ 310-859-8833)*, 8741 Alden Drive, is as tantalizing as the stylish, barrel-vaulted dining room, where special touches include large mirrors and framed Japanese prints. Executive chef Shigefumi Tachibe performs miracles with French California cuisine complimented by Asian inflections. The menu changes often but may include the rock shrimp and chicken appetizer or the Hawaiian tuna tartar. House specialties are the grilled Ji-Dori chicken dijon ($20) and roast venison ($28), available for lunch weekdays and dinner nightly.

Indochine (☎ 323-655-4777), at 8225 Beverly Blvd, is among LA's most refined and swank French Vietnamese restaurants, flaunting exceptional decor and cuisine. The owner, Jean-Marc Houmard, has cloned his hugely successful New York restaurant, re-creating the lost world of French Indochina with subdued lighting, banana leaf frescos, unhurried ceiling fans and snug green leather banquettes. Loyal patrons dine on sophisticated dishes such as nhom sath ko (spicy beef salad with lemongrass) and amok camdodgien (striped bass with coconut milk steamed in a banana leaf). Be sure to leave room for the coconut crème brûlée. Dinner is served nightly.

Fairfax District (Map 10)

At the Farmers' Market, 6333 W 3rd St, you can assemble your own picnic from all the cheese, sausage, bread and delicatessen vendors, or grab some takeout food and eat it on the central patio. Choices include pasta, hot dogs, fish & chips and burritos, though lines are usually longest at our personal favorite, the New Orleans-style **Gumbo Pot** (☎ 323-933-0358). It serves a mean jambalaya, a spicy rice dish with chicken and sausage ($6) and a more mellow seafood gumbo with shrimp and crab. Get an order of corn bread on the side – it is delicious. A good place for huge, hearty breakfasts (all around $6) is the hip, Art Deco **KoKoMo** (☎ 323-933-0733), where you belly up to a Formica counter. This place is popular with Industry types from neighboring CBS, as well as the gay crowd.

Doughboys (☎ 323-651-4202) is a bakery and cafe at 8136 W 3rd St, serving terrific breakfast all day. Unusual choices include malted cornmeal pancakes with whole blueberries and orange pieces, homemade muesli, crispy sourdough and semolina waffles.

Authentic Cafe (☎ 323-939-4626), 7605 Beverly Blvd, is similar to the Kings Road Cafe (see the previous section) but draws a more diverse clientele ranging from students to families to suits. Lunch and dinner are served daily, breakfast on weekends only.

One of the most overrated eateries in town is **Canter's** (☎ 323-651-2030), 419 N Fairfax, a vast 24-hour Kosher-style deli. Since it opened in 1948, it has sold more than 10 million matzo balls and 2 million pounds of lox, thus earning 'landmark' status by LA standards. Safe eating choices are the reuben with pastrami ($8.25), but forget about the soggy potato chips it comes with. There are also six different soups, including one called 'mishmosh,' which combines the other five into one. Canter's Kibitz Room lounge fills up after the clubs close (see Entertainment).

The enchantment of a Greek taverna can be reached through a bowling alley of a passageway that spills onto a shaded patio deck canopied by bougainvillea and leafy trees. The place is **Sofi** (☎ 323-651-0346), 8030¾ W 3rd St, and it serves all the staples, such as tsatziki, dolmades, feta and moussaka, as a combination appetizer plate. Entrees are uneven in quality, though the house specialty – succulent baby rack of lamb –

usually satisfies. The lunch crowds come in Monday to Saturday, but dinner is served nightly.

Chances are you probably won't be going to Ethiopia any time soon, so the next best thing might be to sample some of the exotic food hailing from this East African country at the mid-priced **Nyala** (☎ 323-936-5918), 1076 S Fairfax Ave. Surrounded by Ethiopian art and artifacts, you'll be noshing on wot, a spicy stew, or sharing the wondrous combination plate of beef, chicken and lamb served with several sauces. Instead of utensils, you'll be using injera, a thin bread that soaks up the juices and can be folded around meat and vegetables. African beer and honey wine are offered as libation.

If you'd rather be transported to Polynesia, venture to the magical world of **Tahiti** (☎ 323-651-1213), 7910 W 3rd St. The decor is stunning – Gauguin would have approved. The hand-painted map of the islands covering the floor, giant stylized Tahitian drums anchoring the dining area and the thatched bar are all set against the quiet gurgle of a three-tiered fountain on the narrow patio. The surroundings may well surpass the quality of the food, billed as 'world cuisine' and consisting of fish- and meat-based dishes paired with exotic sauces and vegetables. Try the sherry-sautéed chicken and spinach potstickers. Lunch is served weekdays, dinner nightly.

Koreatown (Map 2)

Thanks to its festive atmosphere and tasty food, **El Cholo** (☎ 323-734-2773), at 1121 S Western Ave, has been packing them in since 1927 and is still one of LA's favorite Mexican restaurants, despite somewhat inflated prices. Come in a group and get things started with a Fiesta Platter ($16; serves 4), a smorgasbord of taquitos, nachos, chimichangas and other lip-smacking delicacies. It all washes down well with one of their margaritas. A few years ago, El Cholo opened a second branch in Santa Monica, 1025 Wilshire Blvd *(Map 12; ☎ 310-899-1106)*.

One of the best places for Korean barbecue is **Soot Bull Jeep** (☎ 213-387-3865), 3136 W 8th St. Eating here is drama at its finest.

Order a plate of marinated meat – ribs, pork or beef – then grill it to perfection over hardwood coals right in the center of your table. Dress casually: thick smoke and flying sparks are guaranteed.

If you'd like to relive the grandeur of the 1930s, book a table at **Atlas Supper Club** (☎ 213-380-8400), 3760 Wilshire Blvd at Western Ave, a sophisticated dining and performance space where dressing up is part of the fun. Located on the ground floor of the historic Art Deco Wiltern Theater, Atlas' menu covers the United Nations of culinary tastes – from pizza to Cajun crab cakes to Asian-style scallops and *paella valenciana*. Expect to pay between $12 and $24 per entree at dinnertime Monday to Saturday, and slightly less at lunch, served weekdays (also see the Entertainment chapter).

WESTSIDE
Beverly Hills (Map 11)
Budget As far as high-concept restaurants go, **Planet Hollywood** (☎ 310-275-7828), 9560 Wilshire Blvd, does a pretty good job. The decor is eye-catching and fun, and the food's better than OK. The bar, backed by a sort of waterfall miraculously flowing skyward, is an interesting place to stop for virgin drinks or something more serious. Burgers, salads, sandwiches and pizzas all cost around $10 or less, although entrees require slightly deeper pockets.

On Beverly Hills' historic Restaurant Row is the **Beverly Hills Café** (☎ 310-652-1529), at 14 N La Cienega Blvd, a 24-hour diner founded in 1957. The menu – which comes in English, French, Spanish and Japanese – features predictable favorites such as burgers, sandwiches and salads, and more substantial meat and seafood entrees. It's nothing fancy, but it's a good unpretentious place for a quick bite.

For a make-believe flashback to the '50s, try **Ed Debevic's** (☎ 310-659-1952), up the street at 134 N La Cienega Blvd. Munch on burgers and fries while squeezed into red Naugahyde booths fitted with table-side miniature juke boxes. Tourists love this place for the prices (nothing's more than $9) and the wisecracking servers ('Good Food –

Fresh Service' is the motto here). The restaurant is usually packed.

You may not associate curry with Japan, but that's just the kind of intriguing mix you'll find at the **Curry House** (☎ 310-854-4959) a few doors north at 163 N La Cienega. Dishes such as fried shrimp curry and curry pilaf gratin come with soup or salad, and may be ordered as spicy as you can handle. The best deals are the daily lunch specials for $6.50.

Mid-Range It doesn't hurt to be the son of Harrison Ford if you want to pack 'em in, though the casual crowds at **The Farm** (☎ 310-273-5578), 439 N Beverly Drive, are also there for Benjamin Ford's creative takes on American favorites, all freshly prepared in an open kitchen. Combinations such as roast pork chop with spiced pears, roasted fennel mash and Swiss chard are served either in a noisy dining hall or on the sidewalk patio beneath lemon-colored awnings. They also do weekend brunch.

It's worth coming to **Barney Greengrass** (☎ 310-777-5877), 9570 Wilshire Blvd, the stylish deli on the top floor of the glamorous Barneys New York department store, just for a terrace table with view of the hills. As for the food, it helps if you're into fish: whitefish, sturgeon and smoked selections such as pastrami lox are available. It's open until 7 pm most nights.

In his newest restaurant, **ObaChine** (☎ 310-274-4440), 242 N Beverly Drive, star restaurateur Wolfgang Puck takes a journey through several Pacific Rim cultures to bring you such choice morsels as tea air-dried duck and his trademark grilled ahi tuna. There's also a sushi bar and two great-value happy hours (see the Entertainment chapter). You can see chefs' hats bobbing behind the counter of the huge horseshoe-shaped kitchen while seated in the colorful upstairs loft-like restaurant.

Puck's Beverly Hills' branch of **Spago** (☎ 310-385-0880) is a rambling space just around the corner at 176 N Cañon Drive. Consider yourself lucky if you can snare seating on the patio, which is anchored by two-century-old olive trees. You'll be nibbling

Wolfgang Puck: LA's culinary wunderkind

on Puck's shrimp cakes or Jewish pizza amid an adult and conservative audience that's likely to include Industry insiders. The chef's Austrian roots shine through in his wiener-schnitzel and goulash offerings. Both establishments offer lunch Monday to Saturday and dinner nightly.

The best thing about the **Stinking Rose** (☎ 310-652-7673), on Restaurant Row at 55 N La Cienega, may well be the whimsical fantasy decor that makes you feel as if you just stepped into a wizard's lair. The rambling restaurant is divided into theme sections with names including Dracula's Grotto, Garlywood and Michelangelo. Walls are covered by colorful murals, and garlic bulbs hang from the ceiling. The 40-clove garlic chicken is a typical entree (vampires beware).

Across the street is **Gaylord** (☎ 310-652-3838), at 50 N La Cienega Blvd, an elegant Indian banquet hall where the best deals are the creative set dinners of soup, various appetizers and curries, tea and coffee, priced at $18, $21 and $23. Unlike many other Indian restaurants, Gaylord has a lot of low-fat, healthily prepared choices. Buffet lunches are served weekdays, with a brunch on weekends and dinner nightly.

Top End Executive chef Elizabeth An opened the **Crustacean** (☎ 310-205-8990), 9646 Little Santa Monica Blvd at N Bedford St, as a tribute to her mother's roots in French Colonial Vietnam. An tries to recapture the slightly wicked grandeur of the era with gourmet culinary compositions and extravagant decor. The pièce de résistance in her multilevel restaurant is the sunken aquarium, where plump koi tumble lazily. Seafood reigns supreme and is often paired with elaborate sauces, here called 'emulsions.' Top honors go to the whole dungeness crab served with garlic sauce and An's 'secret spices' ($33). A glass of wine with each entree is just $4. It's closed Sunday.

In this day and age of theme restaurants, the most remarkable aspect of **Nic's** (☎ 310-550-5707), 453 N Cañon Drive, is perhaps the rather understated – indeed, unremarkable – decor, which attracts mostly sedate Beverly Hills types. In his latest offering, upscale LA restaurateur Larry Nicola has laced his menu of solid California dishes with the occasional Far Eastern touch. Sautéed oysters with spinach and walnuts are a famous appetizer (as the menu will tell you), but there's also the more traditional meatloaf with ketchup and garlic mashed potatoes. Enjoy lunch Tuesday to Saturday and dinner Monday to Saturday.

For inspired top-drawer Japanese food, there's nothing like **Matsuhisa** (☎ 310-659-9639), 129 N La Cienega, which routinely draws Madonna, Warren Beatty, Harrison Ford and other celebs. Chef Nobu Matsuhisa is as deft with the sushi knife as he is at conceiving creative seafood dishes, including broiled black cod and scallops filled with black truffles. The artistic preparation and choice ingredients are unfortunately reflected in the prices (which, incidentally, are not marked) so don't leave home without…you know what.

Elsewhere on the Westside

Budget Inside a stylish Brentwood minimall is **Taiko** (Map 12; ☎ 310-207-7782), 11677 San Vicente Blvd, a prim Japanese noodle house serving gigantic bowls of succulently flavored soba and udon, either hot or cold, plus delectable rice bowls topped with a variety of meats and vegetables. A line is guaranteed on weekends, just as it is at Taiko's sister restaurant, *Mishima (Map 12; ☎ 310-473-5297)*, in the Olympic Collection mini-mall at 11301 Olympic Blvd.

Immediately opposite Taiko, on the same floor, is the casual *California Pizza Kitchen (Map 12; ☎ 310-826-3573)*, part of a chain where it seems all the inspiration has gone into the food, since the dining room has little more charm than a school cafeteria. The pizzas are sometimes too creative for their own good, while the salads are usually quite tasty and the white corn tortilla soup is a classic. Other locations include the Beverly Center mall, Beverly Hills and Pasadena. Check the Yellow Pages or call ☎ 800-919-2273.

Some of the best Cuban food this side of Havana is served at *Versailles (Map 2; ☎ 310-558-3168)*, 10319 Venice Blvd in Culver City. The greatest item on the menu is the lip-smacking roast garlic lemon chicken, which is so tender it basically falls off the bone, accompanied by tangy black beans, rice, sweet onion and fried plantains. There is a second branch at 1415 S La Cienega Blvd *(Map 11; ☎ 310-289-0392)*.

Top End Century City's *Lunaria (Map 11; ☎ 310-282-8870)*, 10351 Santa Monica Blvd, has held forth in its unassuming locale for many years. Its decor is anything but unassuming with stylish pastel table settings, warm lighting, framed art and lush plants. The Southern French menu changes occasionally but may feature items such as the seven-hour leg of lamb ravioli or 40-garlic-clove chicken. The adjacent cocktail bar and lounge often features live jazz (see the Entertainment chapter). Lunch is served weekdays, while dinner can be had Tuesday to Saturday.

Ask anyone who's been to the restaurant *Bel Air (Map 11; ☎ 310-472-1211)*, 701 Stone Canyon Rd, at the hotel of the same name, if this is the most romantic dining spot in town. They will most likely respond with an emphatic 'yes.' Just getting there is enough to get you in the mood, sashaying along flower-festooned paths through a lush garden and

past a pond where swans preen. Impeccable service, a superb menu and out-of-this-world prices make eating here even more memorable. It's open for breakfast, lunch and dinner daily, as well as for brunch Sunday and afternoon tea Monday to Saturday.

COASTAL COMMUNITIES
Malibu (Map 2)

Neptune's Net (☎ 310-457-3095), 42505 Pacific Coast Hwy near the Ventura County line, may be nothing more than a beach shack, but people from all over LA drive here for its superbly fresh seafood at decent prices. Depending on the season, a pound of succulent shrimp, freshly cooked, will cost you about $15; crab, lobster and other fishy fare are available too. Come around sunset, when you can sit at the sturdy wooden tables, look out over the sea, peel a pile of shrimp, chow on some corn and wash it all down with a cold beer. Harley-Davidson fanatics with receding hairlines, families and Industry yuppies all love this convivial and unpretentious place.

As soon as you enter the *Saddle Peak Lodge (☎ 818-222-3888)*, 419 Cold Canyon Rd, all thoughts of urbanity are immediately banished. Rustic beyond belief, the staff of this rural oasis serve up a meaty menu of various game in an environment featuring stuffed and mounted versions of same. This is possibly the best place in LA to eat pheasant, venison and buffalo. Other choices include quail and ostrich. Its Sunday brunch is a memorable proposition, as is dinner, served Wednesday to Sunday.

Listen up: If you want to impress that hot date, take him or her to *Geoffrey's (☎ 310-457-1519)*, a sublimely romantic – and celebrity-heavy (featured in *The Player)* – restaurant clinging to an ocean bluff at 27400 Pacific Coast Hwy. Deep pockets are de rigeur for a full indulgence in delicious California cuisine, though an appetizer, a glass of champagne, the sunset and ocean waves might just do the trick. Also come for the weekend brunch.

The idyllic *Inn of the Seventh Ray (☎ 310-455-1311)*, 128 Old Topanga Canyon Rd, may well be the ultimate LA experience. The decidedly New Agey vibes at the Inn are calming yet oddly unnerving, though the drive through the mountains may have already made you more receptive to this kind of thing. The food here is karmically correct and heavy on the tofu, super-healthy and actually quite tasty. Seating is inside or on a shaded patio.

Santa Monica (Map 12)

Budget Hands-down the best shopping mall food court is *Eatz* inside Santa Monica Place on Broadway, at the southern end of the Third Street Promenade. Choices are bewildering, from Chinese stir-fries to kabobs and curries, croissants, cookies and coffee. On the left, as you enter from Broadway, is a pizza joint where minimum-wage workers slide over hot slices to a constant crowd knee-capping each other with their shopping bags. A hilarious sideshow develops whenever the lissome girls at *Hot Dog on a Stick* start thumping and pumping their next batch of lemonade in tight-fitting, clown-colored hotpants.

Quick bites of gourmet quality are a rarity, but *Wolfgang Puck Express* (☎ 310-576-4770), reached by escalator at 1315 Third Street Promenade, delivers every time with its delicious Chinese chicken salad. A whole portion is enough for two and costs $8. They also serve mouthwatering sandwiches of grilled or roasted meats and veggies, and their wood-fired pizzas are excellent. Consume it all on the terrace with a bird's-eye view of the shenanigans on the promenade below.

A huge ceramic oven that cooks burgers, bakes pizzas and grills chicken over oak flames is the trademark of *Crocodile Cafe* (☎ 310-394-4783), 101 Santa Monica Blvd, right at the western terminus of Route 66. The menu is inventive and has many low-fat and healthy options, including our favorite, the tahini chicken salad. Seating on the sidewalk terrace provides you with front-row views of spectacular ocean sunsets. There is another branch in Burbank (listed later in the chapter).

Budget spots also include the *Omelette Parlor* (☎ 310-399-7892), 2732 Main St, which has been whipping up some of the best egg dishes and breakfasts in town since they

opened during the 'Summer of Love' in 1967. Industrial-weight omelets are $6.50, and beefy deli sandwiches go for around $6. Expect a line on weekend mornings. They serve breakfast and lunch only.

Lula's (☎ 310-392-5711), nearby at 2720 Main St, has fine Mexican dining on a screened-off porch and an interior courtyard featuring a huge 'Day of the Dead' mural of skeletal jazz musicians. Inventive burritos, tacos, tostadas and more are less than $10, though the perennial favorite – duck enchiladas – rings in at $11.45. For many, the real draw are the crippling margaritas thundering forth from Tino's Tequila Cantina, named for Lula's steadfast busboy. Be afraid.

A lot less trendy but at least as good is *Laredo* (☎ 310-829-4550), 2909 Pico Blvd, for 18 years one of Santa Monica's best Mexican restaurants. Service is friendly and swift, and the menu features creative versions of traditional favorites, most under $10. There's even occasional live music.

Mid-Range Amid polished wood and polished service, munch seafood and pasta at *I Cugini* (☎ 310-451-4595), 1501 Ocean Ave. Be sure to score a table on the patio for the breeze, a lovely view of Santa Monica's famous palm trees and a good chance of seeing a star or two noshing and cutting deals. It's easy to overdose on the delicious fresh breads that arrive moments after you sit down. They go especially well with a plate of delectable antipasti, though it's worth leaving some room for the fish and pasta specialties.

Ye Olde King's Head (☎ 310-451-1402), 116 Santa Monica Blvd, is the unofficial HQ of the Westside's huge British expat community, and if you don't mind the fusty odor of 25 years worth of deep-fried fish and chips, you'll feel quite Piccadilly here. Great Brits from Churchill to the Royals to the Beatles look down on the scene from walls cluttered with ever-so-British bric-a-brac and big-game heads. Dinners are served in a series of connecting rooms well away from the dangers of the dartboard. Bangers and mash or steak and kidney pie go for around $10.50, but it's the King's fish and chips that people swear are the best in town.

Raw-fish lovers rejoice! Sushi restaurants abound in Los Angeles.

The **Border Grill** (☎ 310-451-1655), 1445 4th St, is a visual and aural cacophony that appears as though it was designed by six-year-olds – which is just what makes it so interesting. Highlights on the yuppified but delicious Mexican menu are Eulalia's Chips – served with black beans, crème fraîche and chipotle salsa – for an appetizer; for more substance try the grilled fish or the *mulitas de hongos*, Portobello mushrooms layered with guacamole, cheese, chiles and red chard. Dinner is served nightly.

Those with a voracious appetite for sushi should head for the Japanese smorgasbord at the **Light House Buffet** (☎ 310-451-2076), 201 Arizona Ave. The place is short on charm, but its all-you-can-eat buffet lets you pile it on like you're turning Japanese. At dinnertime, the staff throws in mountains of fat shrimp and crab legs to gorge on, which will make you feel like one sorry samurai. The food is a good value, with lunch costing $10 and dinner $18.

The Galley (☎ 310-452-1934), 2442 Main St, is a seafood and chop house festooned with Christmas lights and giant clam fountains burbling on the rear patio. It's been there since 1934 and looks it – with sawdust on the floor and battered maritime junk – but customers swear by its grilled swordfish ($18) and huge porterhouse steaks ($24). Owner 'Captain Ron' will be happy to treat you to the tale of how a foul-mouthed waitress first welcomed him to the restaurant.

At **Jake & Annie's** (☎ 310-452-1734), 2700 Main St, the Dust Bowl meets the Pacific. One specialty is the Oklahoma barbecued platter, though we're partial to the black linguine with rock shrimp. Ideal for the cost conscious are the three-course early-bird dinners served up between 4 and 6:30 pm. There's occasional piano music and brunch on weekends.

The **17th Street Cafe** (☎ 310-453-2771), 1610 Montana Ave, is a comfortable eatery and standard meeting place for Brentwood moms, as well as shoppers relaxing after a stroll along this trendy boutique row. We like it for its fresh, wholesome ingredients and low-fat cooking that doesn't compromise on taste. The chicken pasta is a favorite, though the balsamic grilled salmon is excellent as well. Don't be afraid to make dietary requests; in fact, they encourage it. The cafe also has breakfast weekdays and brunches weekends.

Top End For fresh seafood, one of the best places in Santa Monica is **Ocean Avenue Seafood** (☎ 310-394-5669), 1401 Ocean Ave. The oyster bar serves up some 150,000 portions a year of this slimy royalty, straight from a menu that must have been written by Jacques Cousteau. If you're fishing for celebrity sightings, chances are quite good that you'll catch a blockbusting headliner attacking a Maine lobster or slurping clam chowder. Make reservations for lunch Monday to Saturday, dinner nightly and brunch Sunday.

Great Breakfast Haunts

Enjoying a leisurely breakfast is one of life's great pleasures and only too rarely indulged in. What follows are our choices for breakfast spots that do a bit more than brew hot coffee and scramble a few eggs (all places mentioned are covered in detail under their respective area headings):

The Abbey (West Hollywood)
A Votre Santé (Melrose/La Brea Area)
Backburner Cafe (South Bay)
Beach Hut No 2 (South Bay)
Caffé Luna (Melrose/La Brea Area)
French Quarter Market (West Hollywood)
Hugo's (West Hollywood)
Kings Road Cafe (Beverly Center District)
KoKoMo (Fairfax District)
Omelette Parlor (Santa Monica)
Rose Cafe (Venice & Marina del Rey)
Sidewalk Cafe (Venice & Marina del Rey)
Uncle Bill's Pancake House (South Bay)

Hotel food isn't usually mind-blowing, but *Lavande* (☎ 310-576-3180), at the Loews at 1700 Ocean Ave, may just have the right ingredients for success: a celebrated chef, a knock-out ocean view and a menu brimming with fresh vegetables, fish and meat. Chef Alain Giraud has delved deep into his Provençal roots for such concoctions as striped bass with fennel, anise in pastis sauce and roasted salmon with onion tart. The sunsplashed terrace and pale yellow and green pottery do their part to transport you right to Aix-en-Provence. It's closed Sunday, except for brunch.

Stepping into *Röckenwagner* (☎ 310-399-6504), 2435 Main St, is like dropping into a fine country roadhouse run by old friends. Integrated into the stylish Edgemar Complex, it presents family dining – kids are not an unusual sight – in a loft-like space beneath a barrel-vaulted ceiling. A placid mural of the German countryside presides over well-spaced tables and booths where since the early '90s the fabled cuisine of owner

Hans Röckenwagner has been served up to loyal fans. Herb-crusted lamb loin and the roasted veal with shiitake mushrooms are almost worth their $21 price tab. Dinner is served nightly, along with brunch weekends.

When last we spotted them, actors Tom Cruise and Nicole Kidman were barreling out of *Chinois on Main* (☎ 310-392-9025), 2709 Main St, and into their limo. Such is the illustrious clientele at this classic Wolfgang Puck outpost that hardly an eye was batted. Since 1983, Hollywood's hungry have been nibbling on chef Makoto Tanaka's Cantonese duck and Shanghai lobster as they emerge from an open kitchen installed beneath a huge copper ventilator. Sure, it's a splurge, but you're more likely to see real stars here than during a tour of Beverly Hills that costs the same. Weekend dinner reservations are hard to come by, though with a few days' notice they can usually be clinched for lunch Wednesday to Friday and dinner weekdays.

By sheer dint of personality, the 'Terminator' himself has willed *Schatzi on Main* (☎ 310-399-4800), 3110 Main St, into some success despite – or perhaps because of – its occasional forays into Mr Schwarzenegger's native Austrian cuisine, including the Wienerschnitzel and Zwiebelröstbraten. Many come here just to taste 'the Arnold's' favorite dessert, Kaiserschmarrn – crumbled pancakes mixed with raisins, then caramelized in the oven and served with apple sauce ($9.50). On Cigar Night, the first Monday of the month, $85 buys a four-course dinner, three prime cigars and wine – plus a 90% chance of enjoying it all with Arnold himself. Come for lunch weekdays, dinner nightly and brunch weekends.

Venice & Marina del Rey (Map 12)

Budget The *Sidewalk Cafe* (☎ 310-399-5547), at 1401 Ocean Front Walk, has managed to stay true to its concept of offering lots of good, old-fashioned American fare to a steady stream of locals and tourists alike. There's almost always a line, but it moves fast and the wait is worth it. Portions are huge and can easily be shared (no split charge). Burgers are dependable, but it's the salads that lure us back. Best of the bunch is the Chinese chicken salad (here inexplicably baptized 'the Andy Warhol'), a gigantic pile of lettuce dressed in gingery, tangy sauce and topped with plenty of chicken ($9). This is the best place in Venice to dine while watching the freak show lurch along the boardwalk.

Another good option on the Boardwalk is an exotically spiced sausage from *Jody Maroni's Sausage Kingdom* (☎ 310-306-1995), at 2011 Ocean Front Walk on the southern end of the strip. Costing only $4, sausages are served hot-dog style in a crispy bun and are a satisfying repast. There is another branch on the Universal City Walk (listed later in this chapter).

Just 2 blocks from the beach is one of Venice's most enduring cafes (since 1979), the *Rose Cafe* (☎ 310-399-0711), 220 Rose Ave. Frequented by both the beefcakes working out at nearby Gold's Gym and local artists, this is a terrific place to come for a leisurely breakfast best consumed on the tree-fringed patio. Its breakfast special of a croissant, slice of brie and coffee or tea is served weekdays between 8 and 10 am for a mere $3.46. For lunch, a mouthwatering array of deli salads beckons, while more substantial entrees are available, too.

Another Venice institution is the 24-hour *Van Go's Ear* (☎ 310-396-1987), 796 Main St, in a yellow house with a rad portrait of the painter himself. Its popularity can't be explained by the quality of the food, which takes stabs at being healthy but is far from

gourmet. The place is busiest in the weekend's wee hours, when a post-clubbing crowd descends on its oversized, artsy chairs orbiting tiled tables. Replenish your energy with a 'Fruit Fuck' ($3.75), a nutritional cocktail made with psyllium husks, soy protein, wheat grass and lots of juices to make it all palatable.

Healthy Mexican food may sound like an oxymoron, but the folks at *Tortilla Grill* (☎ 310-581-9953), 1357 Abbot Kinney Blvd, have achieved the improbable, using only lean meats, fresh vegetables and no lard. The results are delicious, macho-sized burritos and tortas, all under $5, and combination plates for just a dollar more. There's a salsa bar as well as a juice bar with invigorating concoctions. A second branch is at 46 Windward Ave (☎ 310-452-5751) near the Boardwalk.

Practically next door to Tortilla Grill is *Abbot Pizza* (☎ 310-396-7334), 1407 Abbot Kinney Blvd, which some consider the best pizza place in town. Its gourmet pies come in 16-inch ($16) and 12-inch ($12.50) diameters and also by the slice ($2.50), creatively topped with choice ingredients. The Five Onion pizza with leeks, shallots, red, green and yellow onions, three cheeses and olive pesto sauce is typical. It all comes on your pick of six bagel-like crusts.

In Marina del Rey, a postage-stamp-size joint serves up some of LA's best tamales. Called *Tamara's Tamale* (☎ 310-305-7714), in Marina Plaza at 13352 W Washington Blvd, the motto here is 'hand-made, home-made, always fresh.' Concoctions include traditional chicken verde and red pork chile variations alongside such gourmet twists as pumpkin, wild mushroom and cilantro pesto costing $2.25 to $3 (items are cheaper by the dozen). It's closed Monday.

Mid-Range Laughter punctuates the lively conversations of the chic patrons at *Chaya Venice* (☎ 310-396-1179), at 110 Navy St. Hauling regulars back with a surprisingly reasonably priced Asian menu, it's short on trendiness and long on substance. If you can't decide, have the chef's daily medley, which combines salad, sushi, fish, meat and vegetables. Another good choice is the spread of

Front-row seats on Venice Beach

LEE FOSTER

antipasti, including crab cakes, sashimi, spring rolls and escargot. Lunch is served weekdays, with dinner available nightly.

Another stylish entry is *Hal's Bar & Grill* (☎ *310-396-3105)*, 1349 Abbot Kinney. The name may evoke brass and wood, but instead Hal's dining room has a cool, industrial feel with a tall exposed ceiling and Jackson Pollock-style artwork. The menu, which changes every other week, makes use of an international cast of ingredients, such as French lentils, Italian pancetta, guajillo coriander and Asian daikon paired with ahi tuna, duck breast and other fishy and meaty companions. Enjoy lunch weekdays, dinner nightly and brunch on weekends.

Top End Although not the kind of place that generates gushy reviews, *Joe's* (☎ *310-399-5811)*, 1023 Abbot Kinney Blvd, nevertheless enjoys a loyal following. The owner/chef, Joe Miller, serves up uniformly sophisticated French California food from a kitchen the size of a walk-in closet. Just about everything on the menu is bound to elicit raves, especially the slow-roasted salmon and the caramelized onion tart. Four-course *prix fixe* menus are $30 and $40. Reservations are advised. Joe's also serves a weekend brunch; it's closed Monday.

Dudley Moore and Tony Bill are the co-owners of *72 Market Street* (☎ *310-392-8720)*, at the namesake address a block from the Boardwalk. There's little in the glass, brick and mirrored decor, enlivened by some appealing artwork, to distract noshers from the food, which can best be described as updated American classics. Lunch is served weekdays, dinner nightly.

South Bay (Map 13)

Budget It's no coincidence that *The Kettle* (☎ *310-545-8511)*, at 1138 Highland Ave in Manhattan Beach, boasts the same excellent selection of fresh and sizable salads, sandwiches and burgers as West Hollywood's French Quarter Market, as they're owned by two brothers. Appearance and atmosphere at the beach branch, however, are much more family-oriented and casual. Seating at the 24-hour Kettle is American-coffee-shop style

inside, but we prefer the tables on the lovely outdoor patio, separated from the sidewalk by a curtain of exotic flowers and plants.

Hibachi (☎ *310-374-9493)*, 120 Manhattan Beach Blvd, offers fishy fare on its casual shack-like patio with orange Formica tables. The menu includes mahi mahi, salmon, swordfish and kebabs. In summer, there's a takeout window selling bowls of chili, hamburgers and hot dogs costing around $2. Next door is the *Manhattan Beach Brewing Co* (☎ *310-798-2744)*, 124 Manhattan Beach Blvd, where you can wash down simple but satisfying pub fare (burgers, salads, pizza) with one of its homemade brews.

There are a number of good Mexican eateries, all serving up combination platters for around $7 and à la carte items from $2.50. In Manhattan Beach, try *El Sombrero* (☎ *310-374-1366)*, 1005 Manhattan Ave, which has colorful decor and sidewalk tables. In Hermosa Beach, *El Gringo* (☎ *310-376-1381)*, 2620 Hermosa Ave, has Technicolor Mexican blankets for table cloths and a great rooftop terrace. The best of the bunch is *La Playita* (☎ *310-376-2148)*, at 37 14th St in Hermosa, which does delicious tacos and big burritos for under $5. La Playita is closed Monday.

For breakfast, *Uncle Bill's Pancake House* (☎ *310-545-5177)*, at 1305 Highland Ave in Manhattan Beach, has all the staples, plus creative variations such as potatoes stroganoff and the Istanbul omelet (made with *turkey*). In Hermosa, you'll find the *Backburner Cafe* (☎ *310-372-6973)*, 87 14th St at Hermosa Ave, which does buckwheat pancakes and big omelets, and the *Beach Hut No 2* (☎ *310-376-4252)*, across the street at 1342 Hermosa Ave, which has Hawaiian-style food and a surfer vibe. All these breakfast places close around 2 pm.

Finally, *Good Stuff* (☎ *310-545-4775)*, 1300 Highland Ave, has airy lifeguard-theme decor and indoor-outdoor, upstairs-downstairs seating, making it a perfect beach hangout. Less grungy than most other eateries in these beach towns, the Good Stuff serves a satisfying range of pasta and sandwiches as well as some surprisingly good Mexican choices, including fish tacos. The original beachside branch is at 1286 Strand in Hermosa Beach. Another branch in Redondo Beach is in the plans.

Choices abound on Redondo Beach's Fisherman's Wharf, though our favorite in this price range is the super-casual *Fun Fish Market*, 121 International Boardwalk, where your seafood comes from a water tank right onto your plate. During lobster season, it charges just $10 for one of these spiny fellows and always offers full meals such as whole charbroiled fish or snow crab costing the same or less. You'll find this place on the lower Level 3 across from the much pricier *Quality Seafood* (☎ 310-374-2382), at 130 International Boardwalk.

Mid-Range In Redondo Beach, *Chez Mélange* (☎ 310-540-1222), 1716 S Pacific Coast Hwy, is one hotel restaurant worth a visit. Located inside what looks like a former '50s coffee shop attached to the Palos Verdes Inn (see Places to Stay), it serves up reliably good, eclectic California French fare in an elegant, bourgeois dining room. The Cajun meatloaf, one of its signature dishes, comes with a delectable sauce and mashed potatoes. It's open for breakfast and lunch weekdays, dinner nightly and brunch Sunday.

A few steps away is *Buca di Beppo* (☎ 310-540-3246), 1670 S Pacific Coast Hwy, a recent entry in this fast expanding empire of fun eateries that look like anything but clones. Family-style portions of hearty Southern Italian pasta and pizza are nearly big enough to bend the wooden tables. Murals, framed glossies of Italian legends such as Sinatra, Loren and Lollobrigida, and gaudy paintings create a milieu that's both kitschy and fun. Don't miss the circular Pope Room, with its lazy Susan anchored by a grinning bust of Pope John Paul II. The patio is roofed by a faux pergola. The tangy sauces are made daily, as are the humongous bread loaves. Bring some friends and dig in – leftovers are guaranteed. Reservations are advised for dinner-only service. There's another branch in Pasadena (listed later in this chapter).

At Redondo's Fisherman's Wharf on the upper Pier Plaza are the old and the new *Tony's* (☎ 310-376-6223) at Nos 210 and 112, respectively, both serving seafood and meat

with typically Italian *abondanza* (abundance). For more character and a surreal '50s flashback, head for the 'old' restaurant, in business since 1952 when a shore platter, with lobster, frog legs, scallops and more, cost just $3.75. Prices have changed, but you can still enjoy the view through the panoramic windows or sit around the tabletop fireplace. (There's also a bar on top of the restaurant; see Entertainment.) Dinner is served daily, lunch on weekends only.

Top End Given the relative dearth of upscale restaurants in the South Bay, the *Auberge* (☎ 310-545-5693) at Barnabey's Hotel, 3501 Sepulveda Blvd, is a welcome island of good taste. Lunches include predictable sandwich, pasta and salad fare, but dinners, featuring specialties from Italy, France and Germany, are vastly more imaginative and interesting. Dine in private booths with subdued, almost romantic, lighting. Its opulent Sunday brunch is popular (especially for the smoked salmon, oysters and shrimp) and priced at a reasonable $24.

A hint of Paris in Redondo is what you'll find at *Le Beaujolais* (☎ 310-543-5100), 522 S Pacific Coast Hwy, which has been serving top-notch French selections since 1983. Savor intricately spiced rack of lamb or fresh halibut in an old-fashioned candlelit dining room. Sunday brunch offers the best value with entrees around $13 served with fresh orange juice, two glasses of champagne, muffins, soup or salad and vegetables. Make reservations.

San Pedro & Long Beach (Maps 14 & 15)

Budget When it comes to Mexican food, simpler is often better, and taco stands such as the sun-colored *Taco Company* (☎ 310-514-2808), on the corner of 5th and Gaffey Sts, often yield inexpensive gourmet experiences. The best bet is anything served with fish, either fried or grilled, such as the excellent fish tacos for $1.50 each and the hugely satisfying fish burritos for $3.50. Only the soupy salsa needs improvement.

ChaChaCha (☎ 562-436-3900), 762 Pacific Ave, has decor as colorful as a farmers' market fruit and vegetable display. A painted canvas shelters diners on the patio, while inside dining is among pigment-splashed walls surrounded by sculptures from Madonnas to skulls. The energetic Caribbean and Latin menu features tapas, such as black bean tamales, and various pizza and pastas. More elaborate entrees are $11 to $18. Its 'Homo Happy Hour' (their words) is a popular hangout on Tuesday evening for Long Beach's sizable gay population. There's another ChaChaCha branch in Silver Lake, located at 656 N Virgil Ave at Melrose Ave (☎ 323-664-7723).

Mid-Range Many people make the trip to San Pedro just to indulge in the authentic Greek food served at *Papadakis Taverna* (☎ 310-548-1186), 301 W 6th St. Run by John and Tom Papadakis, the restaurant was founded in 1972 after John, a former Trojan (USC's football team) linebacker, returned from his honeymoon in Greece. This family-style restaurant serves dinner only; be prepared for some sirtaki dancing, plate-breaking and other supposedly Greek customs.

Around the corner is the *Whale & Ale* (☎ 310-832-0363), 27 W 7th St, an authentic-looking brass and leather English pub with friendly service and a variety of beers on tap. The food is mediocre at best and overpriced to boot, so unless you're fond of pub grub, stick to the liquids. There's a happy hour with $3 drafts weekdays 3 to 6 pm.

One of Long Beach's top restaurants is *Mum's* (☎ 562-437-7700), right on restaurant row at 144 Pine Ave. It's elegant but, as befits a beachside town, it's anything but stuffy, and offers seating on the large sidewalk terrace or in a dining room embellished with original artwork. Most nights, live music showers diners munching on global cuisine, including low-fat wok preparations. There's also a sushi menu. Upstairs is a martini lounge, cigar and billiard room, and Club Cohiba (see Entertainment).

Down the street is *Alegria Cocina Latina* (☎ 562-436-3388), 115 Pine Ave, which has a trippy, Technicolor mosaic floor, an eccentric Art Nouveau-style bar and trompe l'oeil murals. Entrees include grilled filet mignon

in a red wine mushroom sauce, though you could make this a budget place by sticking to tapas. Stay away from its wimpy and overpriced margaritas; apparently the sangria is a better bet. Flamenco and guitar music are featured most nights.

Top End Long Beach's launch into stellar dining came with the opening of the *Sky Room* (☎ 562-983-2703), 40 S Locust Ave, a refurbished Art Deco supper club on the 15th floor of the historic Breakers building. Part of the experience is a sashay up the red carpeted stairs, where you'll be escorted to the elevators by a guy in a tuxedo and top hat. Perhaps even better than the continental food is the breathtaking 360-degree view, which extends north to LA and west to Catalina Island on haze-free nights. Leave room for Fred & Ginger, a killer crème brûlée served in a chocolate top hat. There's also dancing and live music, making it a popular place for dates and anniversaries. Dinner is served nightly, except Tuesday.

THE VALLEYS
Ventura Blvd

Mid-Range Serious carnivores will howl over the menu of *Hortobagy* (Map 17; ☎ 818-980-2273), a Hungarian restaurant at 11138 Ventura Blvd in Studio City, which features spicy sausages, thick and tangy goulash and breaded schnitzels that will bring out the Gypsy in you. It's closed Monday.

Teru Sushi (Map 2; ☎ 818-763-6201), at 11940 Ventura Blvd in Studio City, is busy, theatrical and allegedly one of the sushi bars that helped launch the unabated raw-fish-and-rice craze among non-Japanese Americans. The dishes are creatively named and prepared (for instance, a petal-shaped fish filet called 'sea flower'), and served for lunch weekdays and dinner nightly.

Spanish food without trendy touches is served at the De La Cruz family's *El Patio Andaluz* (☎ 818-999-4598), 7257 Topanga Canyon Blvd in Canoga Park in the western Valley (about 4 blocks north of Ventura Blvd). This homey, old-shoe kind of place is as inviting as the affordable menu, where a full plate of shrimp sautéed with choice vegetables and served alongside saffron rice will set you back just $10. Selections of duck, steak or chicken rarely spill over the $12 mark. It's open for lunch Monday to Saturday and dinner nightly. Come for live entertainment Friday and Sunday nights.

Top End An old favorite of Valley folks is *La Pergola (Map 2; ☎ 818-905-8402)*, 15005 Ventura Blvd in Sherman Oaks. The faithful keep coming for owner/chef Tino Pettignano's versions of Italian classics, adapted to the neurotic tastes of modern-day yuppies. The pasta here is mostly eggless, the vegetables and herbs are organically grown in a big garden out behind the restaurant, and it's all prepared with little fat and much imagination. Lunch is served weekdays and dinner nightly.

Lovely dining in the Valley means going to the *Bistro Garden at Coldwater (Map 2; ☎ 818-501-0202)*, at 12950 Ventura Blvd in Studio City, which charms with a romantic winter-garden setting and tasty variations of California staples, such as ahi tuna, salmon filet and roast lamb. Check out its menu for lunch weekdays or dinner nightly.

Burbank (Map 17)

Budget A good number of mostly low-key, rather inexpensive eateries cluster in Burbank Village along San Fernando Blvd between Olive Ave and Magnolia Blvd. Choices include *Cafe N'Orleans (☎ 818-563-3569)*, a hole-in-the-wall restaurant at 122 N San Fernando Rd, where chef Mark Antoine Foster cooks up Cajun offerings such as lip-smacking Louisiana crab cakes, jambalaya and seafood gumbo. If you can't decide, get the Big Sampler for $8. It's closed Monday.

Next door is *The Great Grill (☎ 818-567-0060)*, a mock '50s diner with decor that includes a giant vinyl record suspended from the ceiling and food that runs the predictable gamut of burgers, sandwiches, fries and salads, mostly priced under $10. Breakfast is served on weekends. Another option on this block is *Knight (☎ 818-845-4516)*, a friendly cafe with a lofty ceiling, coppertone walls and contemporary metal furniture, where you chow down on budget-priced

gyros, falafel, shish kebabs and other Middle Eastern specialties.

Chili John's (☎ 818-846-3611), 2018 Burbank Blvd, is a local institution famous for – you guessed it – chili, which unfortunately is peppered with generous dashes of hostility. It's open to 7 pm weekdays and to 4 pm on Saturday, closed Sunday and Monday. A much more friendly – and tasty – fast-food option is *Poquito Más (☎ 818-563-2252)* at 2635 W Olive Ave, part of a chain that does inexpensive ahi tuna tacos and burritos of gourmet quality. Also try the tortilla soup.

For a genuine slice of Americana, check out *Bob's Big Boy (☎ 818-843-9334)* at 4211 Riverside Drive, a classic coffee shop from the late '40s fronted by a sculpture of cheeky Bob himself. This is the oldest remaining outlet of what used to be a large chain of restaurants, built in Streamline Moderne by Wayne McAllister. Best of all, on Saturday and Sunday nights between 5 and 8 pm, its car hop service *(sans* the roller-skates) lets you catch that *American Graffiti* vibe. Fridays are classic car nights.

Bob's Big Boy, an American relic

Mid-Range Italian staples in their infinite variety are on the menu at the *Market City Cafe* (☎ 818-840-7036), 164 E Palm Ave at San Fernando Blvd. Pasta, pizza, panini and salads range from $7 to $13, though by far the best deal is the tempting all-you-can-eat antipasto bar for $8. It's best enjoyed on the nice patio. The *Crocodile Cafe* (☎ 818-843-7999), 201 N San Fernando Blvd, injects the exotic into the familiar with such concoctions as tahini chicken salad or sundried tomato and artichoke pesto pizza. There's another branch in Santa Monica (listed earlier in the chapter).

A local favorite is *Piero's Seafood House* (☎ 818-842-5150), nearby at 2825 W Olive Ave, where you dine on Italian dishes, for lunch weekdays and dinner nightly, surrounded by aquariums. Another Italian contender is *La Scala Presto* (☎ 818-846-6800), close to Warner Bros at 3821 Riverside Drive. At lunchtime, this trattoria is crawling with Industry types gobbling not-terribly-inspired Northern Italian cuisine. It's open for lunch weekdays and dinner nightly and is closed Sunday.

Universal City (Map 17)

Many restaurants on slick Universal City Walk are clones of immensely popular eateries elsewhere around the city. For a quick snack, *Jodi Maroni's* (☎ 818-622-5639) exotic sausages are your best bet. Our favorite is the Yucatán (a tantalizing combination of chicken and duck with cilantro, chiles and beer; $4), though any variety is of gourmet quality.

Camacho's Cantina (☎ 818-622-3333), in the Fountain Court, is an average Mexican restaurant with daily happy hour specials, and a budget-priced Sunday brunch with strolling mariachis ($11.25). *Marvel Mania* (☎ 877-362-7835) has a wild and wacky comic book environment where you feast on imaginatively named dishes such as 'Captain American' (a hamburger), the 'She-Hulk Salad' (a Caesar's salad) and 'Mutants' Soup' (chicken soup with X-Men pasta). Prices are reasonable (mostly under $10) here, as they are at the famous *Hard Rock Cafe* (☎ 818-622-7625), fronted by a giant electric guitar.

LEE FOSTER

A booth at Marvel Mania

Gladstone's (☎ 818-622-3485) is the place to come for superbly fresh seafood, some of which still swims around in large tanks in the back. There's an oyster bar and a salad bar. It has sandwiches from $8 to $15, though any entree is more likely to set you back $20 and up.

North Hollywood (Map 17)

There are certainly places that serve better sushi than *Tokyo Delve's* (☎ 818-766-3868), across from the Academy of Television Arts & Sciences at 5239 Lankershim Blvd. The food here is – almost – an afterthought, as it's served in a boisterous party-like atmosphere generated by insane sushi chefs who *tap dance*. There's almost always a line waiting by the roped entrance, so make reservations (dinner only), though even then instant admission is not guaranteed.

No animal is safe from appearing on the menu of *Barsac Brasserie* (☎ 818-760-7081), at 4212 Lankershim Blvd, where an open kitchen dishes out everything from scallops, snails and brains to the more mainstream lamb, veal and pork. Lively crowds of studio executives have kept this restaurant busy for years at lunch on weekdays and dinner Monday to Saturday.

One of the Valley's best restaurants is *Ca' del Sole* (☎ 818-985-4669), 4100 Cahuenga Blvd, a slice of Italy in the midst of suburbia. Curvaceous booths, panoramic windows and an airy atmosphere welcome diners who are wowed by tantalizing, flavor-intensive Northern Italian fare centered on pasta dishes (served for lunch weekdays, dinner nightly and brunch on Sunday).

Pasadena (Map 16)

Budget The *Rack Shack* (☎ 626-405-1994), 58 E Colorado Blvd, may not be much more than a bare, long and narrow corridor, but an intoxicating aroma of barbecued chicken pulls people in. Dive into the crazy Cajun chicken soaked in mystery spices and delivered with a sauce that could well take the enamel off your teeth, or play it safer with such meaty fare as beef back ribs (both $9). All meals come with two side dishes that could include green salad, baked beans, yams or rice pilaf.

For great Indian food, all prepared to order, visit *Akbar* (☎ 626-577-9916), an easy going catery at 44 N Fair Oaks Ave. Succulent tandoori staples such as chicken tikka are as good as the fragrant lamb, chicken and seafood curries. The heat of each dish is determined by a 'chili meter,' ranging from 1 to 5. Lunch specials, served till 3 pm, come with rice, nan bread, salad and lentils, and are an excellent value starting at $6.25.

La Luna Negra (☎ 626-844-4331), 44 W Green St, is a popular tapas bar with whimsically painted walls. Try the blue cheese with poached pears or the Galician scallops. Decent entrees include a variety of paellas and beef tenderloin.

A fun place to bring kids of any age is *Holoworld* (☎ 626-578-0009), a 'cosmic cafe' at 620 N Lake Ave. Dishes with names such as 'macho Martian nachos' and 'alien wings' are consumed in crazed fantasy-scapes, including the tropical Jungle Room anchored by a huge tree, the Teepee Room with desert landscape and animal skulls, and the Alien Room, featuring a mothership and galactic landscape. The complex also integrates an arcade, virtual golf and day-glo minigolf (for a few dollars more). It is open until 9 pm most weekdays and 10 pm weekends.

Mid-Range The *Twin Palms* (☎ 626-577-2567), 101 W Green St, is a casual California eatery named for a pair of palms holding court over its large canopied patio. The menu features lots of seafood prepared with the occasional French touch, such as the West Coast bouillabaisse or the prime rib served with crème fraîche and jus. The best deal is the two-course express lunch for just $6.95. There's live entertainment (cover on weekends) and a daily happy hour. Lunch is served Monday to Saturday, dinner nightly and brunch Sunday.

Great Places to Go with Kids

These restaurants are all casual and sure to be winners among the preteen crowd. All have imaginative decor, a kid-friendly menu and affordable prices:

Buca di Beppo (South Bay, Pasadena)
Good Stuff (South Bay)
Hard Rock Cafe (Beverly Center District, Universal City)
Holoworld (Pasadena)
Marvel Mania (Universal City)
Planet Hollywood (Beverly Hills)
Sidewalk Cafe (Venice & Marina del Rey)
Stinking Rose (Beverly Hills)

There's always a party at Tokyo Delve's.

LEE FOSTER

Mi Piace (☎ *626-795-3131)*, 25 E Colorado Blvd, is Italian for 'I like it,' and that's what hundreds of people crowding into this high-ceilinged restaurant seem to think. This is one of the most popular restaurants on the Colorado strip, though why, we're not sure. Since it can't be the food, which is bland and unimaginative, it must be the sidewalk tables, which provide front row center seating for see-and-be-seen types.

More authenticity and less pretentiousness are reflected on the menu at *Trattoria Farfalla* (☎ *626-564-8696)*, 43 E Colorado Blvd. The fare is mainstream Italian with minor imaginative spurts such as the fettucine with ahi tuna swimming in white wine sauce. There are other branches around town, including the one in Los Feliz at 1978 N Hillhurst (☎ 323-661-7365). Across the street is *Sorriso* (☎ *626-793-2233)*, at 46 E Colorado, another '90s restaurant – with a suspiciously similar menu – distinguished by its pretty, secluded back patio.

To escape the nouveau Italian on Colorado, we recommend heading to *Buca di Beppo* (☎ *626-792-7272)*, at 80 W Green St. Here the down-home food is garlicky, powerfully flavored and doled out in mega-portions in a vibrant and fun atmosphere. For details, see the description of the Redondo Beach branch earlier in this chapter.

Top End As soon as you step inside, you know that *Yujean Kang* (☎ *626-585-0855)*, 67 N Raymond Ave, is not your typical Chinese restaurant. The walls are copper-stained and decorated with delicate sumi paintings. Dishes are artworks, especially the duck and mushroom soup topped with a meringue and featuring a little drawing. Tea smoked duck is paired with pancakes, and prawns team up with fava beans and black and enoki mushrooms. A second branch is at 8826 Melrose Ave *(Map 10;* ☎ *310-288-0806)*.

Next door is the equally stylish *Xiomara* (☎ *626-796-2520)*, 69 N Raymond Ave, which serves world cuisine at its finest. Ceviche, foie gras, risotto, goat cheese salad and lamb shank are all comfortable neighbors on the limited menu. It's all served in a bistro ambience highlighted by a sleek marble bar, a black ceiling and large Art Deco-style mirrors. Enjoy lunch weekdays and dinner nightly.

MARKETS

Conventional supermarkets with branches all over LA include Ralphs, Lucky, Vons, Pavilions and Food 4 Less. Prices and selection are pretty much the same, though Food 4 Less is somewhat cheaper and you will have to bag your own groceries. Each has different specials every week. To qualify for discounted rates, you may have to become a 'club' member, a formality that's instantly accomplished by filling out a short form. In return, you'll be given a credit-card sized 'club card' that has to be presented at the cash register. The Sunday *LA Times* has coupons that can be clipped to help you cut costs further.

Hands-down the best food market in LA, and elsewhere in California for that matter, is Trader Joe's, which packs its barebone, warehouse-like stores with gourmet foods at discount prices. Its cheese counter is legendary, as are its wine and beer selections. It also has delicious breads, frozen foods, dairy and ready-made salads and wraps. Branches are scattered throughout LA; call ☎ 800-746-7857, punch in your hotel's zip code, and the machine will tell you where to find the nearest store.

Wild Oats is a chain of supermarkets catering to health-conscious shoppers. Higher prices translate into specialties such as organic produce, kosher food, low-fat ready-made foods and wholesome breads. Branches are becoming more common; try the one at 8611 Santa Monica Blvd (Map 10) in West Hollywood or the new one at Wilshire Blvd and 5th St in Santa Monica (Map 12).

Another contender in this category is Erewhon Natural Foods Market, 7660 Beverly Blvd in Mid-City (Map 10). It sells a bonanza of everything natural, organic and fresh to everyone from vegans to carnivores at premium prices and also stocks every vitamin and food supplement known to humankind. Instant sustenance can be had from the takeout counter or from the soup, salad or coffeebar. In-store massages are available, too.

For details on farmers' markets, see the Shopping chapter.

Entertainment

To keep your finger on what's hot in LA, your best sources of information are the Calendar section of the daily *Los Angeles Times* (especially the magazine-like Sunday supplement) and the free *LA Weekly*, published Fridays (but usually available Thursday nights) and available at many restaurants, shops and bars throughout Los Angeles.

Buying Tickets The central ticket source for concerts, sporting events, theater, musicals, etc, is Ticketmaster at ☎ 213-381-2000. Prepare for an annoying wait, overworked staff and exorbitant handling fees and charges. Tickets are charged to your credit card and either mailed to you or made available for pick-up at the will-call counter of the respective venue. Another agency selling tickets by phone is Telecharge at ☎ 800-233-3123.

Times Tix (☎ 310-659-3678) sells half-price theater tickets for same-day evening or next-day matinee shows (cash only). Tickets must be bought in person at its offices at Jerry's Famous Deli, 8701 Beverly Blvd near the Beverly Center (Map 10), and are available Thursday to Sunday from noon to 6 pm. Times Tix represents a slew of smaller theaters, as well as the Mark Taper Forum and the Odyssey Theater Ensemble. Call ahead to find out what tickets are available that day. For information on buying movie tickets, see the Cinemas section below.

Ticket Agencies For hard-to-get tickets, try several agencies; all charge hefty commissions. Check the Yellow Pages or try Union Ticket Agency (☎ 800-752-2333), 6255 Sunset Blvd, suite 702 in Hollywood; A Musical Chair (☎ 800-659-1702), 11677 San Vicente Blvd, suite 309 in Brentwood; Barry's Ticket Service (☎ 800-348-8499), 16332 Ventura Blvd in Encino; or Al Brooks Theatre Ticket Agency (☎ 213-626-5863) at 900 Wilshire Blvd, suite 104 in Downtown.

CINEMAS

Cinemas – often in the form of multiplexes with up to 20 screens – are ubiquitous in the movie capital of the world. Major chains showing mainstream first-release movies include Cineplex Odeon, Mann, United Artists, Edwards, General Cinema, Pacific Theaters and AMC. First-run films sell out early on Friday and Saturday nights, and you often have to stand in line once to buy the ticket and then again to get into the theater.

The first screening is usually around noon and the last one at about 10 pm. Shows after 6 pm cost $7.50; shows before 6 pm can be up to 50% off. To guarantee that you will get tickets, you can make advance credit card bookings by calling ☎ 213-777-3456 or ☎ 310-777-3456, or by logging on to www.movielink.com; there's no surcharge for this service.

Historic theaters include the Cinerama Dome, the El Capitan and Mann's Chinese Theater in Hollywood, the Warner Grand in San Pedro and the Orpheum Downtown. One of the largest (and with $8 tickets plus parking, the most expensive) is the 18-screen

Historic El Capitan Theater

DAVID PEEVERS

cinema on Universal City Walk. You'll find other clusters of theaters on the Third Street Promenade in Santa Monica, on Colorado Blvd in Old Pasadena and in Westwood Village.

Neighborhood Theaters

Only several of these independently run, single-screen theaters survive. Many show first-release movies on the verge of going to video, often at bargain prices. One of these is the ancient *Aero (Map 12; ☎ 310-395-4990)*, at 14th and Montana Ave in Santa Monica, where $6 buys a double bill. Another one is *Fairfax Cinema (Map 10; ☎ 323-653-3117)*, 7907 Beverly Blvd, which charges just $2.50 for any ticket, any seat, any time. In Silver Lake is the *Vista Theater (Map 9; ☎ 323-660-6639)*, 4473 Sunset Blvd, while neighboring Los Feliz has the *Los Feliz I and II (Map 9; ☎ 323-664-2169)*, at 1822 N Vermont Ave. Both have tickets for $4.50 before 6 pm.

Getting Into a Studio

To see a particular TV star while in LA, your best bet is to watch a taping of his or her show. Doing so is easy, and tickets are free – but plan well ahead. The most coveted shows, such as *Friends*, which tapes at Warner Bros, are usually booked for months. In general, the production season runs August through March, with shows on hiatus in the summer. It's best to make reservations well in advance by writing to an agency or studio listed below. Some studios also accept ticket orders by phone or via the Internet. All shows have minimum-age requirements (usually 16 or 18). Be sure to enclose a stamped and self-addressed envelope. On the day of the taping, come to the studio early to guarantee a seat, as tickets are distributed in excess of capacity.

The main distributor of studio tickets is *Audiences Unlimited (☎ 818-753-3483)*, 100 Universal City Plaza, Building 153, Universal City, CA 91608, which handles arrangements for most studios and has tickets for shows including *Friends, The Nanny, Home Improvement* and *Suddenly Susan*. It also has a walk-in office at Universal Studios and a website with schedules and ticket order forms at www.tvtickets.com. *Hollywood Group Services (☎ 310-914-3400, fax 310-914-3401, www.hollywoodgroups.com)* is another source for tickets to various shows.

Here's how to contact some of the major studios directly:

CBS Television Center (☎ 323-852-2458), 7800 Beverly Blvd, LA, CA 90036. Shows include *The Price Is Right, The Nanny* and *Just Shoot Me*. The box office opens at 6:30 am.

Paramount Guest Relations (☎ 323-956-5575 for recorded information, ☎ 323-956-1777 for tickets), 860 N Gower St, Hollywood. *Leeza* and *Frazier* are among its most popular studio-audience shows. Paramount offers limited reservations by phone or in person five days before the show taping.

NBC Tickets (☎ 818-840-3537 for recorded information, ☎ 818-840-3538 for tickets), 3000 W Alameda Ave, Burbank, CA 91523. Jay Leno's *Tonight Show* is the biggest draw and the only one handled directly by the studio box office. Tickets to NBC sitcoms are available through Audience Unlimited and Paramount (see above).

Another way to see live filming is by obtaining a 'shoot sheet.' This is a list detailing the locations where movies, TV programs, videos and commercials are being shot that day. It's available free of charge, in person, from the Film Permit Office at 7083 Hollywood Blvd near Mann's Chinese Theater. The list does not reveal which actors are involved in the shoot or whether it's an indoor or outdoor shoot.

Revival & Art Houses

New Beverly Cinema (Map 10; ☎ 323-938-4038), 7165 Beverly Blvd, specializes in reruns of obscure and mainstream classics. The *Nuart (Map 12; ☎ 310-478-6379)*, at 11272 Santa Monica Blvd in west LA, is considered one of the best art houses in town and has legendary screenings of the cult-flick *Rocky Horror Picture Show* at midnight on Saturday. Nearby is the *Royal (☎ 310-477-5581)*, 11523 Santa Monica Blvd, which specializes in arty European films. In Santa Monica is the *NuWilshire Cinema (Map 12; ☎ 310-394-8099)*, 1314 Wilshire Blvd at Euclid Ave, and the fourplex *Laemmle Theater (Map 12; ☎ 310-394-9741)*, 1332 2nd St, which both show high-brow independent US and foreign films. Classic Hollywood flics show at the Art Deco temple that is the *Warner Grand Theater (Map 14; ☎ 310-548-7672)* at 478 6th St in San Pedro.

Other Film Venues

The *LA County Museum of Art (Map 10; ☎ 323-857-6010)*, 5905 Wilshire Blvd, offers intelligent classic, obscure and arty fare in its Bing Theater ($6, $4 students). Nearby is the *Goethe Institute (Map 10; ☎ 323-525-3388)*, 5750 Wilshire Blvd, suite 100, a German cultural organization that offers occasional screenings of new and classic works by German filmmakers; you might find a Fassbinder retrospective or a Brecht series (prices vary, often free). The *UCLA Film and TV Archive (☎ 310-206-3456)* at UCLA's James Bridges Theater revives classics, often in themed presentations. The *Museum of Television and Radio (Map 11; ☎ 310-786-1000)*, at 465 N Beverly Drive, presents retrospectives as well as restored TV classics. The *American Cinemathèque (Map 9; ☎ 323-466-3456)*, a nonprofit film and video organization in the historic Egyptian Theater at 6838 Hollywood Blvd, screens independent, foreign and other non-mainstream films.

THEATER

Theater has long been a lively and integral part of LA's cultural scene. Choices range from glittery international hit musicals and plays to ensemble shows and independent

American Cinemathèque (Egyptian Theater)

fringe theater in unconventional venues. Theaters are great places to catch both the budding stars of tomorrow and to see major film and television actors return to their roots on the live stage.

Major Companies & Venues

The *Mark Taper Forum (Map 5; ☎ 213-628-2772)* at Downtown's Music Center, 135 N Grand Ave, is home to a renowned troupe that emphasizes the development of new plays and presents US and world premieres. Seating a mere 760, the Taper has more than 20,000 loyal subscribers and often sells out. Its high-caliber productions have often gone on to Broadway and then on to win Tony and Pulitzer awards (*Angels in America* and *Children of a Lesser God* among them). The Taper has a public rush for last-minute $10 tickets, starting 10 minutes before curtain.

In the same complex is the *Ahmanson Theater (Map 5; ☎ 213-972-0700)*, which seats between 1300 and 2000 for top-notch Broadway musicals and plays such as *Miss Saigon, Phantom of the Opera* or Neil Simon comedies. Another place to catch leading musical productions (such as *Sunset Blvd* and *Beauty and the Beast*) is the **Shubert Theater** *(Map 11;* ☎ *800-447-7400)*, a huge, state-of-the-art venue at 2020 Ave of the Stars in Century City. A historic venue presenting similar theatrical fare is the **Pantages Theater** *(Map 9;* ☎ *323-468-1770)*, 6233 Hollywood Blvd. The acoustics here are not the greatest, but one can't help but be charmed by this stylish Art Deco structure, especially its stunning lobby.

Small Companies & Venues

LA County's small, fringe theater scene has been thriving since organizers have been allowed to pay nonequity (nonunion) rates to actors under the Equity Waiver Program, regardless of whether they are professional or amateur. One requirement is that a theater cannot have more than 99 seats. While this usually doesn't allow performers to make a living off their acting, it gives them a chance to hone their skills, showcase their talent and act just for the love of it. To theatergoers, it means a varied menu of new plays, revival shows, experimental performances and classic productions that are often cutting edge and surprisingly good.

Downtown (Map 5) The *Los Angeles Theater Center (*☎ *213-485-1681)*, in a former bank building at 514 S Spring St, is one of the leading theater venues in Downtown. It's run by the city's Cultural Affairs Department, which rents out the four stages to performing-arts groups. *East West Players (*☎ *213-625-7000)* in the David Henry Hwang Theater of the Union Center for the Arts, at 120 N Judge John Aiso St in Little Tokyo, is the leading Asian American theater company in the US. Nearby is the Japanese American Cultural & Community Center, at 244 S San Pedro St, where the *Japan American Theater (*☎ *213-680-3700)* puts on an annual season of theater and concerts, including *kabuki, noh* and *bunraku* theater performances.

Central Hollywood (Map 9) Hollywood's 'Theater Row' stretches along Santa Monica Blvd with a series of small venues, some of them in bad shape and struggling, but often providing quality productions. Among the stand-outs is the *Actors' Gang Theatre (*☎ *323-465-0566)*, 6209 Santa Monica Blvd. The 'Gang' was founded in 1981 by a bunch of UCLA acting school graduates and presents daring and off-beat productions that have earned an LA Drama Critics' Circle Award. The Actors' Gang provokes, stimulates and amuses, making it one of the most rewarding theatrical experiences in LA.

The sophisticated **Hudson Ave Theater** *(*☎ *323-856-7012)*, 6539 Santa Monica Blvd, actually consists of a quartet of stages – plus a restaurant and a coffeehouse – each dedicated to a different type of work. You'll find a checkered schedule that may include modern stalwarts, experimental productions by ethnic playwrights and perennial crowd-pleasers like *The Odd Couple* by Neil Simon.

Theater/Theatre (☎ *888-566-8499)*, at 1713 N Cahuenga Blvd, is a 71-seat venue that makes for an intimate theatrical experience. Scheduling is eclectic and can include satirical one-person shows, ethnic drama or contemporary classics; quality tends to be high.

Nearby is **Theatre of NOTE** *(*☎ *323-856-8611)*, at 1517 N Cahuenga Blvd, which specializes in works by new playwrights, plus obscure works by classic dramatists like Bertolt Brecht's *Baal*.

In the same space since 1975 is the **Colony Studio Theater** *(*☎ *323-665-3011)*, 1944 Riverside Drive in the Silver Lake area, kept in business by a loyal following of theatergoers. The appeal lies in the quality production of both new plays and revivals of contemporary classics like the Broadway show *City of Angels*.

West Hollywood (Map 10) As LA's creative hub of art and design, West Hollywood is also rich in live theater. The 65-seat **Celebration Theater** *(*☎ *323-957-1884)*, at 7051-B Santa Monica Blvd, is among the nation's leading producers of gay and lesbian plays, winning 35 awards in 1996 alone. Its playbill includes both mainstream and provocative, cutting-edge and experimental works.

The 99-seat **Coast Playhouse** *(*☎ *323-650-8507)*, 8325 Santa Monica Blvd, is known for attracting major actors from other cities and has maintained a fine reputation for putting on quality productions.

The best time to check out the **Coronet Theater** (☎ 310-657-7177), 366 N La Cienega Blvd, is Monday nights, when the Playwrights Kitchen Ensemble (☎ 310-285-8148) holds staged readings of new plays. Besides being able to hear consistently excellent new work, you might even catch a big-shot actor as part of the reading cast. The list of luminary alumni includes Richard Dreyfuss, Peter Falk and Gwyneth Paltrow. Best of all – it's free! Show up early because the 272 seats fill quickly.

The **Tiffany Theater** (☎ 310-289-2999), in a former movie palace at 8532 Sunset Blvd, consists of two state-of-the-art, 99-seat theaters. The schedule is heavy on fine stagings of works by brilliant young writers and premiere plays that often launch the careers of both writers and actors.

Westside & Coastal Communities The Beverly Hills **Canon Theatre** (Map 11; ☎ 310-859-2830), 205 Cañon Drive, began as a movie house and got a new lease on life as a theater in the late '70s. Seating almost 400, it does primarily crowd-pleasing comedies. One phenomenal success was the production of *Love Letters* by AR Gurney, which had a galaxy of established actors from film and television taking turns at the two roles during its sold-out two-year run.

Theatre 40 (Map 11; ☎ 310-277-4221) is located at Beverly Hills High School on 241 Moreno Drive, but its thespian offerings are far from student caliber. One of LA's oldest professional companies, it was founded in 1965 and has been in its gorgeous current 99-seat space since 1974. Its annual season includes several classic and modern plays, most of them tried and true.

The **Odyssey Theater Ensemble** (Map 12; ☎ 310-477-2055), 2055 S Sepulveda Blvd in west LA, is one of LA's top small theater houses, putting on reliably excellent productions under the stewardship of Ron Sossi, who founded the company in 1969. It has three separate 99-seat theaters and does lots of daring contemporary classics, such as

Brecht's *Threepenny Opera*, Mamet's *Speed the Plow* and Ionesco's *Rhinoceros*.

In Westwood is the UCLA-operated **Geffen Playhouse** (Map 11; ☎ 310-208-5454), 10886 Le Conte Ave, a 20-year-plus venue that in 1996 was renamed after major donor David Geffen. It's a pleasant place, with a patio, fountain and nice lobby, to see high-caliber, mainstream productions.

Nestled in Topanga Canyon, in a magical natural outdoor amphitheater, is the **Will Geer Theatricum Botanicum** (Map 2; ☎ 310-455-3723), at 1419 N Topanga Canyon Blvd. Throughout the summer, its resident professional acting company performs Shakespeare and other classic playwrights. Performance quality can be pretty hippy-dippy, though it's always fun to enjoy a performance in the shaded canyon.

Comedies, musicals, dramas and even fairy tales are performed at the **Santa Monica Playhouse** (Map 12; ☎ 310-394-9779), 1211 4th St, often by noted actors. For new and avant-garde plays, head to the **Powerhouse Theater** (☎ 310-396-3680), 3116 2nd St in Santa Monica, or the **Highways Performance Space** (Map 12; ☎ 310-453-1755), 1651 18th St in Santa Monica.

The confusingly named **Civic Light Opera** (☎ 310-372-4477), in the Redondo Beach Performing Arts Center at 1935 Manhattan Beach Blvd, is the South Bay's best Broadway-style musical theater and stage play company. They also put on big-name concerts to supplement the schedule.

The Valleys The **Group Repertory Theatre** (Map 17; ☎ 818-769-7529), 10900 Burbank Blvd, has almost set a survival record with its 25-year-plus existence. It offers a wide range of shows, from experimental fare to modern classics and contemporary works, including those generated in its writers' workshop. Also in Burbank is the two-stage **Victory Theater** (☎ 818-841-5421), at 3226 W Victory Blvd. The intimate Little Victory with its 48 seats focuses on cutting-edge productions and workshops, while the 91-seat 'Big' Victory presents more mainstream fare.

For **A Noise Within** (Map 3; ☎ 818-546-1924), at 234 S Brand Blvd in Glendale, 'classical' has always equated with 'classy.' This is just what its productions of Shakespeare and his contemporaries, as well as Restoration comedies and works by Molière are. Founded by alumni of the American Conservatory Theater in San Francisco, it's housed in an interesting building that was formerly a Masonic temple.

Several small theaters have opened in the newly created North Hollywood arts district. They include *Actors Alley (Map 17;* ☎ *818-508-4200)*, 5269 Lankershim Blvd in North Hollywood, which does musicals, comedy, drama and new plays at the historical El Portal Theatre. *Actors Workout Studio (Map 17;* ☎ *818-506-3903)*, 4735 Lankershim Blvd, is a no-frills pint-sized space used for one-person shows and workshops.

One of LA's top venues is the 1924 *Pasadena Playhouse (Map 16;* ☎ *626-356-7529)*, 39 S El Molino Ave, designated the official State Theater of California in 1937. A major refurbishment in the '80s returned it to its former glory, and it has been doing box office ever since with more than 100 productions. Their quality is often so superior that plays are sent on to Broadway. Recent hits include the musical *Sisterella* and *Twilight of the Gods*.

Another Pasadena company performs at the 99-seat *Knightsbridge Theater (Map 16;* ☎ *626-440-0821)*, right in Old Pasadena at 35 S Raymond Ave, presenting a classical menu of Shakespeare, Wilde and other luminaries at budget prices. Be warned that seats are not too comfortable and the plays are rarely abridged.

Comedy Clubs

On any given night, comedy stars – some of them very famous – may be strengthening their chops in one of LA's many comedy clubs. At the very least, you'll be treated to a hilarious evening with what may well be one of next year's comic sensations: LA is where funny people come to make it big. Because most clubs are rather intimate, with a limited capacity, it's best to call ahead for a reservation. Many have a two-drink minimum in addition to the cover charge.

The West Hollywood area has the greatest concentration of comedy clubs. Best of

the bunch is the *Groundlings Theater (Map 10;* ☎ *323-934-9700)*, 7307 Melrose Ave, a repertory improv company that's tickled people's funnybones for more than 20 years. Many of its comedians go on to *Saturday Night Live*, *Mad TV* and other shows, and its alumni include Pee-Wee Herman, Jon Lovitz, Phil Hartman, Julia Sweeney and Elvira (Mistress of the Dark). The cover ranges from $12 to $17.50.

Among the legendary haunts is *The Improvisation (The Improv; Map 10;* ☎ *323-651-2583)*, 8162 Melrose Ave, which has nightly shows and features rising stars and established ones (including Drew Carey) as well as lots of Latino and African American comics. The cover is $8 to $11, plus the two-drink minimum.

The *Laugh Factory (Map 10;* ☎ *323-656-1336)*, 8001 Sunset Blvd, is a high-tech club that keeps cranking out mainstream comics and stand-up comedians. Jim Carrey, Ellen DeGeneres and Rodney Dangerfield are among those that have performed here. The owner, Jamie Masada, garners lots of PR each year at Thanksgiving: He turns the club into a soup kitchen to give the homeless a full stomach on this most American of holidays. Nightly shows are $8 to $10; there's a two-drink minimum.

The *Comedy Store (Map 10;* ☎ *323-656-6225)*, 8433 Sunset Blvd, has featured nearly every comic who has gone on to become a household name, including Roseanne and Robin Williams. Special nights devoted to ethnic groups and female comics are offered regularly. The cover ranges from free to $25; there's a two-drink minimum.

Smaller venues nearby include the *Acme Comedy Theater (Map 10;* ☎ *323-525-0202)*, 135 N La Brea Ave, for sketch and improv comedy Friday, Saturday and Sunday. The cover is $8 to $14. The *Mice Improv Comedy All-Stars (* ☎ *818-762-7547)* has a regular, free (!) gig at 10 pm on Saturday night at the West Hollywood Playhouse, 666 N Robertson Blvd. *Bang Theater (Map 10;* ☎ *323-653-6886)*, 457 N Fairfax Ave, is a pint-sized improv club that charges $5 most nights.

The *Comedy & Magic Club (Map 13;* ☎ *310-372-1193)*, at 1018 Hermosa Ave in

Hermosa Beach, has been an institution since 1978. This is where Jay Leno does weekly appearances to test out new material for the *Tonight Show*, and other big stand-up comedians like Jerry Seinfeld and George Carlin are occasional headliners. The cover usually ranges from $10 to $20; closed Monday.

Pasadena has the *Ice House (Map 16; ☎ 626-577-1894)*, 24 N Mentor Ave, which went through an earlier life as a pop and folk club before becoming one of LA's top comedy clubs. It attracts the major professional talents of today (including Dennis Miller) and the stars of tomorrow. Tickets are $2.50 to $12.50, plus a two-drink minimum; closed Monday.

Cabaret

The *Cinegrill (Map 9; ☎ 323-466-7000)*, 7000 Hollywood Blvd in the Hollywood Roosevelt Hotel, features cabaret-style acts and jazz performers, though the largish room lacks the historic feel permeating the rest of the hotel. The cover is $10 to $20, plus a two-drink minimum.

The *Gardenia Club (Map 9; ☎ 323-467-7444)*, 7066 Santa Monica Blvd in Hollywood, is an intimate, no-nonsense space where you might catch Brechtian chanteuses, jazz musicians or straight cabaret. The cover is $10, plus a two-drink minimum; closed Sunday.

Swank *Luna Park (Map 10; ☎ 310-652-0611)*, 665 N Robertson Blvd, combines a first-rate restaurant (see Places to Eat) and live-performance nightclub upstairs but also has a snug cabaret in its basement, though it's often used as a comedy and music venue as well. The cover is usually $5.

CLASSICAL MUSIC & OPERA

For highbrow music lovers, there's no finer place than the *Dorothy Chandler Pavilion (Map 5; ☎ 213-972-0700)* at the Music Center, 135 N Grand Ave in Downtown. Besides being home to three performing arts companies, its stages also host Broadway shows, the Academy Awards and other large-scale productions.

The *LA Philharmonic Orchestra (☎ 213-850-2000, www.laphil.org)* has been, since 1992, under the stewardship of Esa-Pekka

Salonen, a charismatic young Finn. He has enjoyed a loyal following despite insisting on programs that often focus on works by obscure composers, or obscure works by famous composers. The season goes from October to May; the orchestra's summer home is the Hollywood Bowl (see Outdoor Venues). It will move to the yet-to-be-built Walt Disney Concert Hall upon that venue's completion.

The city has had its own *LA Opera (☎ 213-972-8001)* since 1985. It presents a varied and high-caliber repertory of popular operas like *Carmen* and the *Barber of Seville* but also less mainstream ones like *The Flying Dutchman* and *Werther*, often managing to attract major opera singers, like Placido Domingo, as guest stars. Tickets are $25 to $137, and seniors and students rush for $20 tickets.

Los Angeles Master Chorale (☎ 213-626-0624, www.lamc.org) is a critically acclaimed 120-voice chorus. Founded in 1964, it presents stand-alone recitals and also serves as the chorus for the LA Philharmonic and the LA Opera.

Other notable classical groups include the Los Angeles Chamber Orchestra (☎ 213-622-7001), which often performs at UCLA's Royce Hall; the Hollywood Bowl Orchestra, led by John Mauceri, the resident orchestra of the Bowl; as well as the Beverly Hills Symphony (☎ 310-859-8075). The Da Camara Society (☎ 310-440-1351) is an organization dedicated to staging chamber concerts in historic venues, usually elegant early-20th-century mansions like the Doheny Mansion in the West Adams district (Map 2).

DANCE

Dance productions aren't as widely publicized as music and theater, but there remains a great deal of ballet, modern, tap, jazz, ethnic, traditional and performance art dancing in LA. Performers like Martha Graham, Alvin Ailey and Bella Lewitzky got their start here. Most dance companies do not perform in permanent venues, so check the listings in the local press. Major venues include UCLA's *Center for the Performing Arts (☎ 310-825-2101)*; the *Luckman Fine Arts Complex (Map 3; ☎ 323-343-6600)* at the California State University at Los Angeles, 5151 State

University Drive in East LA; *Highways Performance Space* (☎ 310-453-1755), 1651 18th St in Santa Monica; and *LA Contemporary Exhibitions (LACE;* ☎ 323-957-1777), 6922 Hollywood Blvd, Hollywood.

LA doesn't have its own ballet company, but touring companies like the Joffrey Ballet or the American Ballet Theater usually appear at the Music Center in Downtown. One of the oldest local dance companies is the *American Repertory Company* (☎ 213-664-0553), founded in 1969. Artistic directors Janet Eilber and Bonnie Oda Homsey have made it their mission to keep alive the legacy of early 20th-century modern dance pioneers, including Martha Graham and Isadora Duncan. Both trained and danced with the Martha Graham Company for several years.

Avaz International Dance Theatre (☎ 323-663-2829) has been dedicated to preserving the heritage of Middle Eastern dances, primarily from Iran, for more than 20 years. Artistic director Anthony Shay puts on energetic and entertaining shows with dancers clad in flashy, colorful costumes.

Like its name suggests, the *Jazz Tap Ensemble* (☎ 310-475-4412) hones the art of tap dancing, which it skillfully blends with jazz music. Performing locally, nationally, abroad and on celluloid for almost two decades, the permanent troupe – under the leadership of Lynn Dally – is often joined by top tap talent like Jimmy Slyde.

Fascinating, if slightly bizarre, are the performances of *Diavolo Dance Theatre* (☎ 818-906-3343), which practices a cutting-edge dance form called hyperdance, which sprang from the vision of Jacques Heim in 1992. It involves dancers performing in custom-built spaces by literally slamming their bodies into walls, doors or objects. Its dramatic movement is filled with physical danger and often results in bruises, sprains and even the occasional broken bone. Diavolo has been critically acclaimed internationally and has a loyal following. Another LA jewel is *Loretta Livingston & Dancers* (☎ 213-627-4684), a modern dance company led by Loretta herself, who danced with the now-retired Bella Lewitzky for 10 years. She stages innovative, avant-garde programs.

Outdoor Venues

Going to a concert at the *Hollywood Bowl* (*Map 9;* ☎ 323-850-2000), 2301 N Highland Ave, is an experience that should not be missed. The music is just one reason to spend a tepid summer night in this 1916 outdoor amphitheater. Most concertgoers start off the evening with a picnic on the park-like grounds or in the bleachers before showtime, and then relax beneath the starry skies to the sounds of Beethoven or Mozart with a glass of wine (bring your own). Carry along a pillow and blanket, as it can get a bit chilly at night. Bowl prices are the most democratic, with tickets starting at just $1 on some nights. As the summer home of the LA Philharmonic and the Hollywood Bowl Orchestra, the program is heavy on symphonic crowd-pleasers, though jazz, mariachi music and pop concerts round out the schedule.

The *John Anson Ford Theatre* (*Map 9;* ☎ 323-461-3673) is another historic outdoor venue, at 2580 E Cahuenga Blvd, not far from the Bowl. It's a comparatively intimate space, holding merely 1200, with no seat more than 96 feet from the stage. It presents a far-ranging program of music, dance and family events from May to October, including the popular 'Summer Nights at the Ford' series.

The *Greek Theater* (*Map 8;* ☎ 323-665-1927), in a natural bowl in Griffith Park at 2700 N Vermont Ave, opened in 1929 and seats more than 6000. Top rock and pop bands usually pass through here on their summer tours. A recent line-up included Tori Amos, Joe Cocker, Bonnie Raitt, Lionel Richie and Blues Traveler. Try to get seats close to the stage for better acoustics.

From July 4 to Labor Day (in early September), cheap concerts are held Sunday afternoons at the *Starlight Bowl* (*Map 2;* ☎ 818-238-5300), a 7000-seat amphitheater at 1249 Lockheed View Drive in Burbank. All musical tastes are covered, including rock, reggae, classical and big band.

CLUBS & LIVE MUSIC

LA's club scene is one of the liveliest in the country and caters to everyone's tastes and expectations, from pale-faced college-age ravers to designer-chic yuppies and ex-hippie baby boomers. No 20th-century era is off-limits these days, be it '20s jazz, '30s and '40s big band swing, '50s rockabilly, '60s rock & roll, '70s disco, '80s punk and new wave, or the techno, house, gothic, industrial, trance, etc, sounds of today. Unless mentioned otherwise, you have to be 21 or over to be admitted to any of these clubs.

One caveat: One thing constant about LA's club scene is that it changes constantly, so check the local press for up-to-date listings, or call the Club Line (☎ 323-258-2546), a free telephone service that gives you information about the hottest clubs and also has free or reduced cover passes to selected clubs.

Rock & Pop

Downtown (Map 5) Hippies to punks to grungemeisters to gothics, *Al's Bar* (☎ 213-625-9703) at 305 S Hewitt St in Downtown, has been a master of survival no matter what's been touted as the current hot trend. Dark, dank and divey, it's in the heart of Downtown LA's revitalized arts district, though the jury's still out on the artistic value of the

Al's Bar: dark, dank & divey

frantically chaotic graffiti obliterating every square inch of wall space. Drinks are cheap ($2.50 for beer or wine), bands – usually several a night – are wild and edgy, and so is the audience. There is no cover on Tuesday and Wednesday. Otherwise it's $5; Al's is closed Monday.

Silver Lake (Map 9) *The Garage* (☎ 323-662-6802), 4519 Santa Monica Blvd, in a former garage that was also once a gay cowboy bar, often looks like the headquarters of Silver Lake's self-styled grungemeisters. Come here for some unusual outfits, bands that are provocatively bizarre and wild, and wicked clubs run by drag queens with names like Vaginal Davis. Open daily; cover is free to $5.

Spaceland at Dream's (☎ 323-661-4380), 1717 Silver Lake Blvd, is the epicenter of Silver Lake's underground rock scene and the best place to catch emerging local bands (Beck and The Eels played at this venue). Put on your thrift-shop finest and join the scenesters below a ceiling festooned with satellite dishes and lamps that had former lives as motorcycle helmets. The cover is $5 to $10; Mondays are usually free.

Central Hollywood (Map 9) The huge aquarium hanging from the ceiling and whorehouse red lighting of the *Bar Deluxe* (☎ 323-469-1991), 1710 N Las Palmas Ave, should tip you off that this is not your usual club. Its musical philosophy runs the gamut from blues to punk with several, mostly local, bands on stage nightly except Sunday and Monday. The beer menu is as eclectic as the audience. The cover varies (cash only).

Dragonfly (☎ 323-466-6111), 6510 Santa Monica Blvd, is easily recognized by the giant namesake painted on the outside wall. This is a place for moshing and slam dancing. If it's not punk, then serious rock and the occasional reggae or Latin band makes it on stage here. There's a large dance floor and patio for smoking. The cover is $5 to $15.

Hollywood Athletic Club (☎ 323-962-6600), 6525 Sunset Blvd, is a gorgeous venue in a former men's gym built in 1923. There are pool tables, a huge elegant dance floor, upstairs lounges with private rooms and a restaurant. It's all decked out in rich dusky woods and soft carpets (except the dance floor, of course). Music varies, as does the cover, though it's usually from $8 to $20. (Also see Hollywood in Things to See & Do.)

Club Lingerie (☎ 323-466-8557), at 6507 Sunset Blvd, seems to have had as many incarnations as Shirley MacLaine. During its years as Red Velvet in the '60s, Sonny & Cher and the Righteous Brothers took the stage. In the '70s, when it was called Souled Out, it featured the likes of Tina Turner and Stevie Wonder. Currently, it's primarily a dance club with DJs spinning a wide mix from funk to R&B to disco to house, techno and trance. The cover is around $10.

The name **Martini Lounge** (☎ 323-467-4068), 5657 Melrose Ave, might conjure in your mind a sophisticated venue for jazz, but good ol' rock & roll is the draw here. Enter through the bar area, backed by an assemblage of stiletto-heeled shoes, and head on to the main room where bands perform on the large stage fronted by a dance floor. Oh yes, they do serve martinis. The cover is $2 to $5.

Its Liberace-style over-the-top decor is just one appeal to scenesters at **Goldfinger's Bar** (☎ 323-962-2913), 6423 Yucca St. Catering to hard-core clubbers, this raucous little joint offers live bands plus DJs on weekends, keeping the crowds grooving with a frenzied mix of funk, glam rock and techno. The cover is $3 to $5 (cash only).

They didn't waste too much on decor at the warehouse-style **Hollywood Moguls** (☎ 323-465-7449), at 1650 N Schrader Blvd, but that's just the right look for the garage and indie bands that dominate the schedule here. At least two or three bands are featured Wednesday to Saturday (doors open at 9 pm). The occasional screening or performance art gig takes place in the 99-seat theater in the back. The cover is $3 to $7; you must be over 18.

The Palace (☎ 323-467-4571), opposite Capitol Records at 1735 N Vine St, is a huge, glamorous Art Deco landmark dating to 1924. It fits about 1500 people, presents up-and-coming bands during the week and sizzles with dance tunes on the weekends.

It's open after 9 pm; cover is $10 to $12; you must be over 18. (Also see Hollywood in Things to See & Do.)

Right at the fabled intersection of Hollywood & Vine is **Jack's Sugar Shack** (☎ 323-466-7005), 1707 N Vine St, a relaxed place sure to satisfy a wide range of musical tastes, from blues to boogie. The cover ranges from free to $15 (usually around $5).

West Hollywood (Map 10) Before it was reborn as the **Key Club** (☎ 310-274-5800), 9039 Sunset Blvd, this club had a short-lived stint as Billboard Live. But it's probably the name 'Gazzarri's' that makes the location so legendary: Gazzarri's was the club that launched the Doors and the Byrds, and was one of the leading forces behind thwarting the city's attempt to close down all rock & roll clubs in the so-called 1966 Sunset Riots. Now it's an ultrachic club with galactic decor and top-notch technology, where an eclectic schedule of live acts is followed by DJ dancing. The cover ranges from $10 to $30; open Wednesday to Sunday.

Before making appearances at the major arenas, many of tomorrow's top bands play at **The Roxy** (☎ 310-276-2222), 9009 Sunset Blvd, which has hosted old-time favorites such as Neil Young and Bruce Springsteen. The cover charge varies.

For many Hollywood visitors, a visit to the place that invented go-go dancing is definitely *de rigueur*. The legendary **Whisky a Go Go** (☎ 310-652-4202) still holds court at 8901 Sunset Blvd and has seen it all over the decades. To this day, it showcases all sorts of rock & roll, from national circuit bands to upwardly hopeful locals. The cover is $10 to $15; no age minimum.

Shortly after the snug, recently remodeled **Viper Room** (☎ 310-358-1880), at 8852 Sunset Blvd, opened in 1993, 23-year-old actor River Phoenix became Hollywood's newest drug victim when he overdosed then collapsed right outside its doors. This gave the club even more name-recognition than it already had on account of its co-owner, Johnny Depp. A mobster lounge in the '40s, the Viper Room keeps its mystique with unannounced top acts (for example, Mick

Jagger has popped in on occasion) and a steady stream of rumors.

The LA branch of the **House of Blues** (☎ 323-848-5100), the largely successful chain co-owned by Dan Akroyd, is at 8430 Sunset Blvd. It features the customary faux Mississippi Delta decor, making you feel a bit like you are on location for *Midnight in the Garden of Good and Evil*. The food is Southern and only so-so, and the in-house store – à la Hard Rock Cafe – can be annoying, but the sound and the performances make up for these transgressions. Top talents of all stripes, not just the blues, go on stage here, and shows often sell out. It also has a popular Sunday Gospel brunch (see Places to Eat). The cover starts at $5 and can be $25 or higher.

Coconut Teaszer (☎ 323-654-4773) has been located at 8117 Sunset Blvd for many years now and, given its 18-and-over policy, is popular with a youngish crowd. There are up to six live acts nightly, many of them local 'talent,' with the occasional musical heavy hitter thrown in. The cover ranges from free to $12.

Doug Weston's Troubadour (☎ 310-276-6168), 9081 Santa Monica Blvd, has been an LA mainstay for more than 35 years, hosting a Who's Who in music, from Elton John to the Barenaked Ladies. The cover ranges from $5 to $20. There is no age minimum.

Club 7969 (☎ 323-654-0280), at 7969 Santa Monica Blvd, attracts the more bizarre set of LA clubbers with different theme nights any day of the week. Part of the eclectic repertory are fetish nights, drag shows, female topless dance revues, gothic balls and ladies'-only male strip shows. Their cover ranges from $6 to $10.

Fairfax District (Map 10) Skip the matzo balls but check out the late night action at the **Kibitz Room** (☎ 323-651-2030) at the 24-hour Canter's deli at 419 N Fairfax Ave. It's a compact lounge that

spills over with adrenaline- (and God knows what else) powered hipsters who've still got some energy left to burn after the clubs close. The menu includes cabaret, rock and the occasional blues jam. There is no cover.

Genghis Cohen (☎ 323-653-0640), 740 N Fairfax Ave, is a fairly mellow place that features performers nightly, many of them from the acoustic camp, delivering homegrown songs that are often surprisingly good. It also serves respectable Chinese food and cocktails with tongue-in-cheek names like 'Ori-yentl.' The cover varies; all ages are welcome.

Westside & Coastal Communities *The Mint* (Map 2; ☎ 323-954-9630), 6010 W Pico Blvd at Crescent Heights, has been dishing out live blues, rock and jazz to the faithful in a no-nonsense environment that's changed little since 1937. A recording studio in the daytime, it's also the kind of place top bands – for instance, the Rolling Stones – like to play to test out new material (they'll appear under a fictitious name to avoid getting mobbed). Recently expanded, it's also a supper club with decent food and good service. The cover is $5 to $10; all ages are welcome.

Also in west LA, at 11637 W Pico Blvd, is *The Gig (Map 12; ☎ 310-444-9870)*, a comfortable, neighborly place that's staved off the influence of trends. Fluffy sofas, a mirrored disco ball and an aquarium make for relaxed decor, attracting an audience that's similarly laid back. Featured gigs run the gamut from reggae to blues to disco. The cover is $5 to $10.

On the Santa Monica Pier is *Rusty's Surf Ranch (Map 12; ☎ 310-393-7437)*, which has nightly bands playing to a casual college crowd. The phalanx of surfboards lining walls and ceiling make this the quintessential beach club. All ages are welcome.

Emanating a distinct London vibe, *The West End (Map 12; ☎ 310-313-3293)*, 1301 5th St, also in Santa Monica, attracts lots of expat Brits and other Euro types to its lively, party-like dance nights that cover the musical spectrum from disco to '80s flashbacks, hip hop, reggae and rock. The cover ranges from free to $10.

The *Lighthouse Cafe (Map 13; ☎ 310-372-6911)*, 30 Pier Ave in Hermosa Beach, is a timeless beachside mainstay that's strong on rock and blues. Originally a Chinese restaurant, it became a major jazz venue in the '50s and '60s. There is no cover on weeknights; it's closed Monday. Redondo Beach's *Club Caprice (Map 13; ☎ 310-316-1700)*, at 1700 Pacific Coast Hwy, is the top dance club in the South Bay, with big-name live acts most weekends. The cover is usually in the $10 to $15 range, with a two-drink minimum unless you're having dinner. You must be 18 or over.

Club Cohiba (Map 15; ☎ 562-491-5220), 144 Pine Ave in Long Beach (above Mum's restaurant), is a dance club open Friday and Saturday nights. There's also a martini lounge, cigar and billiard room open nightly.

Jazz & Blues
Leimert Park (Map 7) The best place to see established and emerging jazz talent is the Leimert Park Village in the Crenshaw district. The *World Stage (323-293-2451)*, 4344 Degnan Blvd, is a no-nonsense space run by big-name local drummer Billy Higgins. There's no food or drink, just good music from some of the finest jazz musicians

around, who play low-priced concerts on Friday and Saturday. The Thursday jam session has people grooving until 2 am.

Around the corner is *Fifth Street Dick's (☎ 323-296-3970)*, 3347½ W 43rd Place, a hole-in-the-wall coffeehouse that doubles as a venue for raw and raucous jam sessions held in its rather petite loft. The crowd here is young and racially mixed. It opens daily around 5 pm; cover is charged occasionally.

Around the corner again is *Babe & Ricky's (☎ 323-295-9112)*, the oldest blues club in Los Angeles, which recently moved from Central Ave to its present location at 4339 Leimert Blvd. A slice of the American South, it has been presided over by Mama Laura (Laura Gross) for the past 34 years. Every night the darkish room, rimmed with generous burgundy booths, is home to finger-lickin' barbecue ribs and chicken and some of the most accomplished blues talent around. The cover ranges from $3 to $5.

Hollywood (Map 9) LA's leading venue, drawing big-name musicians from around the world, is *Catalina Bar & Grill (☎ 323-466-2210)*, an old-fashioned club at 1640 Cahuenga Blvd. A big poster of John Coltrane hangs on the off-pink walls next to the small stage. The cover ranges from $10 to $18, with a two-drink minimum unless you have dinner (make reservations). All ages are welcome.

Westside & Coastal Cities The elegant restaurant *Lunaria (Map 11; ☎ 310-282-8870)*, 10351 Santa Monica Blvd in Century City, has a bar/lounge area that hums with classy, subdued jazz six nights a week. There's no cover with dinner; all ages are welcome. It's easy to walk right past *Harvelle's (Map 12; ☎ 310-395-1676)*, a hole-in-the-wall blues joint at 1432 4th St in Santa Monica. Having delighted generations of music lovers since 1931, Harvelle's remains an island of trendlessness in modish Santa Monica. The cover varies, with a two-drink minimum.

In Hermosa Beach is *Cafe Boogaloo (Map 13; ☎ 310-318-2324)*, at 1238 Hermosa Ave, a warehouse-sized hall that tempers industrial simplicity with colorful artwork. It is low key and casual, with two dozen microbrews on tap. The cover varies from free (usually Sunday to Wednesday nights) to $10 for bigger-name acts.

Farther south, in Long Beach, check out the **Blue Cafe** *(Map 15;* ☎ *562-983-7111)*, 210 The Promenade, a raucous tavern with a sidewalk terrace. Live bands perform nightly and the owners are good at hauling in some pretty surprising talent. We still remember the awesome Texan slide guitar player who blew us away the night of our visit. Upstairs is a billiard room. The cover ranges from $5 to $10.

The nonprofit **Jazz Bakery** *(☎ 310-271-9039)*, in a former bakery at 3233 Helms Ave in Culver City, is an excellent venue to see major jazz artists on tour or local talent like Billy Higgins, Kenny Burrell and Branford Marsalis. The cover ranges from $10 to $25; all ages are welcome.

North Hollywood & Universal City (Map 17) BB King's Blues Club *(☎ 818-622-5464)*, 1000 Universal Center Drive on the Universal City Walk, usually bustles with tourists expecting the quality of the club to match its legendary namesake. Depending on the act, this is not always the case, though the multilevel venue has a Southern feel, reflected in the menu. If you come after 11 pm, the $7 parking fee is waived. The cover ranges from $5 to $15.

The small **Baked Potato** *(☎ 818-980-1615)*, 3787 Cahuenga Blvd in North Hollywood, has been dishing out great jazz for about three decades, served alongside a 21-varieties menu of overpriced spuds. The cover varies; all ages are welcome.

Supper Clubs
For time travel back to 1930s LA, when men were suave in their tuxedos, and women were called ladies and wore little black dresses, head to the **Atlas Supper Club** *(Map 2;* ☎ *213-380-8400)*, an Art Deco marvel in the stunning Wiltern Theater at 3760 Wilshire Blvd. Dining takes place beneath a high, midnight-blue ceiling and lamps shaped like Zorro's mark. Live entertainment ranges from Latin rock and Creole jazz to funk, salsa and R&B. Dress to the nines for this one.

The cover is $5 to $10; closed Sunday and Monday (also see Places to Eat).

El Cid *(Map 9;* ☎ *323-668-0318)*, 4212 W Sunset Blvd, is the best place in town to catch live flamenco. The rambling hillside hacienda actually began life in the 1920s as Hollywood's first sound stage for DW Griffith's movie studio. As a theater in the 1950s, it helped launch many acting careers, including Marlon Brando's. In 1961, in its third incarnation, it became a flamenco bar and restaurant – a *tablao* – which over the decades has attracted some of the finest singing and dancing talent, mostly from Spain. Three flights of stairs lead down to an intimate room with tables set up before the stage, veiled by a lipstick-red velvet curtain. There's also an outdoor patio. The cover without dinner is $9; the Dinner Show Menu costs $23. It's closed Monday and Tuesday.

In Sherman Oaks, in the San Fernando Valley, is the elegant **Moonlight Supper Club** *(Map 2;* ☎ *818-788-2000)*, at 13730 Ventura Blvd, which brings a slice of Vegas to suburbia. Various big bands serve up jazz, swing and other dance music to a slightly more mature audience. The cover is $5 to $15, plus a $10 food-and-drink minimum.

Gotham Hall *(Map 12;* ☎ *310-394-8865)*, upstairs at 1431 Third St Promenade in Santa Monica, is the kind of place that tries to be all things to all people – and is surprisingly successful at doing so. It started out primarily as a pool hall cum restaurant. The dozen or so purple felt tables are still a major draw (up to $14/hour), but more recently, a dance club, cushiony lounge, and cigar and martini bar were added to Gotham's spread.

A happening place in Long Beach is **Jillian's** *(Map 15;* ☎ *562-628-8866)*, 110 Pine Ave, a spacious hall in a converted historic bank building with a painted beamed ceiling and an elliptical bar. Food is pretty much restricted to pizza, pasta and burgers, all priced under $10. The main attraction here is the inky cavern that is **The Vault** – the bank's actual money safe that's been converted into a club. A humonguous circular steel door, crimson velvet bar stools and plump sofas adorn this space that's best suited for dedicated dancing. The cover ranges from $5 to $8.

Swing

In most other cities, the Swing Era ended in 1945, but in cutting-edge LA things are just getting started. You got me right, Daddy-O. In this town, it don't mean a thing if it ain't got that swing! We're not talking about the surviving members of the Glen Miller Orchestra; we're talking about serious swingers who can really Hi-Di-Ho and make you feel that hepcat jive. This isn't a straight retro scene, either. In typical LA fashion, anything goes in the swing revival. So what you get is a cross between big band, jazz, blues and rockabilly. Cab Calloway, Louis Jordan, Elvis Presley and Bob Wills all exert a certain amount of influence. Figure *that* one out!

LA's most sophisticated swing nightclub is the **Coconut Club** *(Map 11; ☎ 310-274-7777)*, in the Beverly Hilton Hotel at 9876 Wilshire Blvd, and there's nothing campy or false about it. This ballroom-sized venue has theatrical, yet classy, decor that makes you feel like you're in a pre-war movie. Watching sleek ladies with '40s-style hairdos and vintage dresses doing the lindy hop or jitterbug with suave zoot-suited guys is superb entertainment in itself, though the catchy tunes of the live orchestra will have you bustin' a move in no time. A small but exquisite supper menu complements a full bar. Seating is in sinuous booths or at cafe-style tables. With dishes starting at $20 plus a $20 admission, not to mention at least $8 for parking, this is not an inexpensive night out, but boy, it is definitely memorable. Admission also provides access to Chimps Cigar Lounge next door. Open Friday and Saturday after 7:30 pm.

The Derby *(Map 9; ☎ 323-663-8979)*, 4500 Los Feliz Blvd, has been LA's 'Swing Central' since 1993, proving that the revival is not just a passing fad. Discovered by a dedicated bunch of retro scenesters, the audience has gone more mainstream since the release of the movie *Swingers* (which features the Derby), when the trend caught fire. Except for absolute purists, the Derby is still a fun night out, if only to recline in curtained velvet booths, listen to some fine live music and watch dressed-up guys and dolls do their thing. PS: For those who don't know the first

DAVID PEEVERS

Swinging at The Derby

thing about swing, the Derby is the best place to learn, with free lessons Sunday to Thursday.

Almost every major club has jumped on the swing bandwagon and now offers at least one night of swing dancing. Scan the local press for current venues or check out the website www.swingset.net.

Salsa

For authentic, fiery salsa nights, head to the **Mayan Nightclub** *(Map 5; ☎ 213-746-4287)*, 1038 S Hill St in Downtown LA. The venue itself, a fantastic pre-Columbian-style ex-movie palace from 1927, is reason enough to go here. But if you're serious about salsa and meringue, this is *the* place to go Cubano and also watch some beautiful dancers in action. It is extremely dressy – definitely no jeans or sneakers. Open Friday and Saturday after 9 pm; salsa lessons start at 8 pm. The cover is $10.

Chic Westside folks who wouldn't dare go Downtown to the Mayan mix with upscale Latinos at the **Conga Room** *(Map 10; ☎ 323-549-9765)*, a lovely venue at 5364 Wilshire

Blvd in Hollywood. A roster of celebs headed by Jimmy Smits and Jennifer Lopez co-owns this super-trendy club that feels like pre-revolution Havana. It has a huge dance floor where ladies in spiky heels and nattily dressed gents writhe to the salsa beat. Top-notch bands create a sizzling atmosphere supported by the elegant decor (note the eccentric lamps, especially the rotating 'chandeliers' made from bamboo sticks above the bar). There's a tiny patio for smoking and a bustling restaurant to tank up on sustenance and rest weary feet. The club is open Thursday to Saturday; the cover is $20 most nights.

One of the most popular venues for live salsa, *El Floridita* (Map 9; ☎ 323-871-0936) is a small Cuban restaurant in a mini-mall at 1253 N Vine St (also see Places to Eat). The original Floridita in Havana was Hemingway's favorite hangout. Hollywood's Floridita has floor-to-ceiling mirrors on two facing walls, giving the place the feel of a dance studio, which is sort of what it becomes once the energetic salsa bands get the crowd going. Monday nights are legendary; other shows are Thursday to Saturday. The cover (usually $10) is waived with dinner.

La Masia (Map 10; ☎ 323-272-3502), 9077 Santa Monica Blvd, has been a West Hollywood mainstay for decades. Catering to a moneyed and mature audience, it serves Spanish fare and live salsa music courtesy of a resident duo (daily except Monday and Tuesday). The cover is $10.

DAVID PEEVERS

Conga Room salsa

Other clubs with salsa nights, usually just once a week, are the *Sportsmen's Lodge* (Map 2; ☎ 818-769-4700), 12825 Ventura Blvd in Studio City; *Cava* (Map 10; ☎ 323-658-8898), 8384 W 3rd St, a Spanish/Latin restaurant cum club in the Beverly Plaza Hotel in the Beverly Center district; and *Rudolpho's* (Map 5; ☎ 323-969-2596), at 2500 Riverside Drive, whose eclectic offerings include a 'gay salsa' night once a month.

More information on the salsa scene is at www.salsaweb.com.

Folk/Traditional Music

For decades, *McCabe's Guitar Shop* (Map 12; ☎ 310-828-4403), 3101 Pico Blvd, has been LA's primary venue for folk music. It's an intimate, some might say cluttered, room that puts you face to face with performers. Nearly everyone worth their salt in traditional music – Joni Mitchell, John Lee Hooker, Dan Hicks and the Hot Licks, and Jackson Browne among them – have made their way to this West Coast mecca of musicianship. You never know who will show up to join in on a set. It also sells the best in guitars and music books. The cover is $10 to $25; all ages are welcome.

Country & Western

Country & Western places are not abundant in LA, although a few are tucked away in suburbia, mostly in distant Valley communities. As close to the real thing as it gets is the *The Cowboy Palace Saloon* (☎ 818-341-0166), 21635 Devonshire St in Chatsworth (northwestern San Fernando Valley). A bit more central is the neighborly *Crazy Jack's* (☎ 818-845-1121), 4311 W Magnolia Blvd in Burbank. An excellent option on the Westside is the *Culver Saloon* (☎ 310-391-1519), 11513 Washington Blvd in Culver City. Usually none of these places charge cover, and most offer free dance lessons.

BARS & LOUNGES

No matter where you are in LA, you are never far from a bar. They are only open to those 21 and over, and you may be asked to show ID to enter. Besides the establishments mentioned here, many restaurants,

LA's Best Happy Hours

Traditionally, 'happy hour' is a period of time, starting in early evening, during which a bar or lounge features drinks at reduced prices. In LA, happy hour often means *food* at ridiculously low prices, and perhaps some drink deals as well. The following are some of our favorite happy hours around town.

McCormicks & Schmick, 633 W 5th St, Downtown (Map 5), and 206 N Rodeo Drive, Beverly Hills (Map 11). This serial fish house has been repeatedly voted best happy hour in LA for its dozen items, all priced at $1.95 and served weekdays 4 to 6:30 pm. Selections vary by branch but usually include quarter-pounder cheeseburgers, Caesar salad, chicken tacos, steamed black mussels and clam chowder. Drinks are full price. Until 6 pm, it also has a 1¼-pound Maine lobster for just $14.95.

Bonaventure Brewing Company, 404 S Figueroa St, Downtown (Map 5). This microbrewery has delicious brews, a nice beer garden and may well become competition to McCormicks. Besides its own cheeseburger, it has grilled barbecue pork pitas and four other yummy selections for just $1.95, served weekdays 3 to 7 pm.

ObaChine, 232 N Beverly Drive, Beverly Hills (Map 11). The downstairs bar in Puck's rainbow-Asian restaurant has two daily happy hours, a rather sleepy one from 5 to 7 pm and a more happening one from 10 pm to midnight. Sake, wine and cocktails are $3, draft beer is $2, and exquisite morsels like salmon sushi, lamb samosas and satay are just $2.95 each.

Toppers, 17th floor of the Radisson Huntley Hotel at 1111 2nd St, Santa Monica (Map 12). Our personal favorite for many years, this lively sports bar offers ocean sunsets, $4.75 baby pitchers of margaritas (ask for them 'on the rocks') and a free buffet of nachos, pizzas, hot dogs, chili and rice as well as several salads. Happy hour is 4:30 to 7:30 pm daily.

Gotham Hall, 1431 Third Street Promenade, Santa Monica (Map 12). At $1.99 each, blackened chicken, penne pasta and barbecue-chicken pizza are the types of New Orleans-style fare on the happy hour menu at this trendy, upstairs billiard hall and bar. A minimum one drink purchase is required. Happy hour is from 4 to 7 pm.

Scruffy O'Shea's, 822 Washington Blvd in Venice/Marina Del Rey (Map 12). This Irish pub is famous for its relaxed atmosphere, foamy Guinness and 'Homeric' happy hour on weekdays 4 to 7 pm (Friday to 9 pm). There's also live music and dancing nightly.

hotels and clubs also have bars that are great places to sop up the various LA vibes and observe the scene. (Check out the Places to Eat and Places to Stay chapters for more establishments.)

Downtown (Map 5) On the ground floor of the Stillwell Hotel, at 838 S Grand Ave, is ***Hank's Bar*** (☎ 213-623-7718), a classic tunnel-shaped watering hole in dungeon-like darkness, where you'll feel like you're in a Raymond Chandler novel. LA Mayor Richard Riordan used to down screwdrivers here with his friend the bar owner, Hank Holzer, who died recently.

One of Downtown's most popular sports bars is ***Grand Avenue Bar*** (☎ 213-612-1925) on the ground floor of the swank Regal Biltmore Hotel at 506 S Grand Ave. There's a free snack buffet weeknights. A more grown-up atmosphere reigns at the hotel's knockout ***Gallery Bar*** upstairs.

For drinks with an eye-popping view, ride the glass bubble elevator to the top floor of the Westin Bonaventure Hotel, 404 S Figueroa St, where you will land at the bar *Top of Five* (☎ *213-612-4743*). A nice place to start – or wind down after – an evening of theater or concerts in the Music Center is *Otto's Grill & Beer Bar* (☎ *213-972-7322*), 135 N Grand Ave. While there, admire the B&W photographs by legendary LA photographer Otto Rothschild, documenting more than six decades of LA theatrical and musical history.

Central Hollywood (Map 9) The *Formosa Cafe* (☎ *323-850-9050*), 7156 Santa Monica Blvd, is the place to go to sop up some Hollywood nostalgia. A fixture since 1939, the walls of this dimly lit, casual lounge are plastered with autographed celebrity photographs, most faded along with the fame of those pictured. Time has also worn out the carpets and the plastic booths (some are held together with duct tape), but a gritty charm has survived, especially in the section built into a 1902 Red Car (see Big Red Cars in the Getting Around chapter). Smokers will appreciate the roof deck and patio. Mai tais and martinis are beverages of choice. The food is best avoided. There's no cover.

Despite the name, you won't find lava lamps in the trendy *Lava Lounge* (☎ *323-876-6612*), in a mini-mall at 1533 N La Brea Ave (but try to find the 'lobster lamp'). A seductive tropical feel pervades this smallish place, helped along by curvaceous booths, tiny tiki lamps, bamboo and palm fronds. Open nightly after 9 pm, it has local bands doing disco, soul, swing, jazz and other sounds Sunday to Thursday nights. There's a full bar, but to get that special Maui buzz, order a Blue Hawaiian ($8). The cover charge varies but hovers around $5.

A blazing neon sign announces the presence of *The Frolic Room* (☎ *323-462-5890*), 6245 Hollywood Blvd, in the dark heart of Hollywood. Vice still rules here, with everyone jostling up to the heavy bar and downing a few stiff ones while blatantly ignoring the smoking ban. Drinks are cheap, and there's a cool jukebox and a wall of Hirschfeld-style caricatures of Hollywood legends. The Frolic Room is open daily, noon to…whenever.

Silver Lake (Map 9) Stepping into *Akbar* (☎ *323-665-6810*), 4356 W Sunset Blvd in Silver Lake, is not so much like walking into a scene from *A Thousand and One Nights* – despite the Moorish arches behind the bar – as it is like stepping into a bat cave. The place is so dark, it'll take a minute or so for your eyes to adjust and focus on the dangling cylindrical wicker lamps and couches in the back. The crowd ranges from college age to 30-somethings who, judging by the steady hum, seem to have a lot to say to each other. Smoking is permitted.

Nearby is *Tiki Ti* (☎ *323-669-9381*), 4427 Sunset Blvd, serving only tropical drinks to show-biz folks, blue-collar types and Silver Lake trendoids. The owner, Rae, has held court over this garage-sized bar since 1961. Barely over 5 feet tall, he's almost hard to spot behind the bar's wild collection of nautical kitsch and junk that gives the place a wonderfully surreal ambience. Rae has a wickedly generous elbow when tilting the rum and vodka, the fundamental elements of his secret mixtures, such as Rae's Mistake and the Vicious Virgin. Credit cards are not accepted. And – damn the torpedoes! – smoking is permitted.

An institution since the post-WWII era, the *Dresden Room* (☎ *323-665-4294*), 1760 N Vermont Ave, made a comeback after being featured in the 1997 movie *Swingers*. The campy singing duo Marty & Elaine has 'owned' this lounge since 1981, and still pack in an intergenerational crowd of the newly and eternally hip, who hunker at tiny tables

Frolic in the heart of Hollywood.

beneath mobile-like wrought-iron lamps. There is no cover charge.

West Hollywood (Map 10) The entrance to celebrity heaven is via the plain white gate of *The Sky Bar* (☎ 323-848-6025), at the Mondrian Hotel at 8440 Sunset Blvd. Plain lettering – and a line of people to Timbuktu – announces that you have arrived. But you haven't truly 'arrived' unless you've made it onto its super-exclusive guest list. Should you be famous, pretty – or maybe just plain lucky – enough to get inside, you'll be likely to rub shoulders with the headliners of blockbuster movies and coliseum-filling bands.

One place to miss – despite legendary status (Janis Joplin partied here the night before she overdosed) – is the divey *Barney's Beanery* (☎ 323-654-2287), 8447 Santa Monica Blvd. They serve 300 or more varieties of beer by the pint and hostility by the gallon. A sign saying 'No Faggots Allowed' hung above the bar until the owners were forced to take it down in the late 1980s.

Westside & Coastal Communities West of Culver Blvd is where you'll find authentic Americana bars. *Outlaws* (☎ 310-822-4040), 230 Culver Blvd in Playa del Rey, is a grubbin' and guzzlin' joint that would not look out of place in the Black Hills of the Dakotas. Oddly, it's one of the few cowboy bars we've ever seen with a full library. Ya got yer steaks, yer seafood and yer barbecue chicken, all for between $10 to $15, and there's a fine little bar where you can hunker down and listen in on the barmaid's tales of love gone wrong.

Across the street is the *Harbor Room* (☎ 310-821-6550), 195 Culver Blvd, which – legitimately – calls itself the 'smallest bar in LA County.' When the local publicans gather here to drown their sorrows, you'll be lucky to elbow your way in. The crowd is friendly, crusty and as real as they get, and it's been that way since 'some time in the '50s,' according to imperfect local recollection.

Of the South Bay beach cities, Hermosa Beach clearly has the wildest, craziest party atmosphere. Its oceanfront walk – the Strand – and the adjacent Pier Plaza are

flanked by raucous *bodegas*, where collegeage babes in neon bikinis and dudes in oversized trunks guzzle beer from plastic cups and scream at each other over blaring MTV. Things quiet down a bit during the week and in the winter, but in the hot season everyone seems to be partying like it's 1999.

Taking the honors for loudest decor, not to mention noise level, is *Aloha Sharkeez* (*Map 13;* ☎ 310-374-7823), 52 Pier Ave, a tacky tiki bar festooned with palm fronds, plastic flower leis and other Hawaiian kitsch. The objective is to get drunk as fast as possible, which is why mysterious concoctions like Lava Flow and Blue Voodoo come in 48oz pitchers ($14) and 80oz buckets ($22). As for food, you might want to try one of the pu pu snacks, though it might be better to stick with the fish tacos. Above all else, 'hang loose.' (There's another Sharkeez branch at 3801 Highland Ave in Manhattan Beach, ☎ 310-545-6563.)

Another hard-core drinking place is the charmingly named *Poopdeck (Map 13;* ☎ 310-376-3223), 1272 Strand, a sweaty and smelly bar with cheap beer; you'll feel like you're crashing a frat party. It's one of Hermosa's most revered boozing institutions. For a more 'civilized' ambience, head over to *Sangria (Map 13;* ☎ 310-376-4412), 68 Pier Ave, which has a nice large outdoor patio, a big dance floor and a sensible menu of tapas, ceviche and crab cakes.

Bars abound in Redondo Beach's Fisherman's Wharf amusement area, where you'll find the funky *Naja's Place* (lower Level 3; Map 13), a rock & roll bar and club with live bands and a small dance floor. The huge beer selection is definitely the biggest draw among the rather rough crowd. For cocktails, head to the flying-saucer-shaped glasshouse called *Tony's Bar (Map 13;* ☎ 310-376-6223), 210 on the Pier Plaza level, which has landed right atop the 'old Tony's' restaurant (see Places to Eat). The bar and tables in this establishment haven't changed since a young Elvis topped the charts.

Cigar Lounges
Aside from bulging biceps and pecs, another Schwarzenegger contribution to American

culture is the current vogue for cigar smoking. When 'The Arnold' became associated with gargantuan stogies, it wasn't long until the Chuck Norrises and Jim Belushis of the world began puffing as well. Nicotine use was suddenly hip, and it didn't require the use of steroids. Cigar lounges and clubs began springing up – accompanied by the sins of martinis and decidedly 'men only' unspoken codes. All this coincided with the recent restrictions on public smoking in California,

which has stirred an anti-nonsmoking backlash of sorts. Of particular interest to cigar smokers is a new crop of 'cigar lounges,' where men *and* women congregate to smoke stogies and share gossip in voices turning raspy. Many of them are private 'members only' affairs, but the following are tobacco dens for anyone.

Billing itself as a 'cigar sanctuary,' the **Big Easy** (☎ *310-234-3279*), 1922 Westwood Blvd near UCLA, eschews political correctness

Rolling in Stogies

As a fashion statement, Churchillian logs may – or may not – be here to stay. But at *La Plata* (*Map 5;* ☎ *213-747-8561*), LA's only handmade cigar 'factory,' they've been rolling up these decidedly Freudian smokes for over 50 years. Once largely the secret of tinhorns and tycoons, La Plata (1026 Grand Ave in Downtown) has never been considered part of any mere fad,

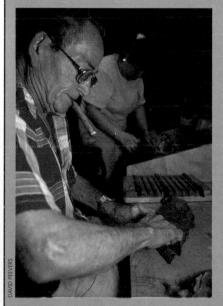

though they've been known to custom-roll their finest products for use in major Hollywood films. But to smoke a La Plata – or to watch one being rolled by hand in the diminutive back room – is to steep yourself in tradition, craftsmanship and tobacconist lore.

Owner Victor Migenes Jr holds to the same traditions and standards as his father did before him, and one of their Cuban-born rollers has been in the trade – developing the 'touch' – for half a century. When you heft a La Plata Hercules, a peppery robusto affair that draws as smoothly as a warm wind off the Cuban hills, you're quite possibly being treated to the best smoke you'll find this side of Havana.

The tobaccos are primarily Dominican and Ecuadorian, and up to nine kinds of leaf may find their way into your smoke. But if you want to get a real education in cigarese, try to get yourself locked into La Plata's humidor for 10 minutes or so with Migenes or the hilarious sales manager, Julie Ross, and ask for their insight. There, drenched in aroma that immediately makes you want to go off and fight in the hills, you will hear true connoisseurs speak about cigars in a way that can only be voiced when there are feelings of deep love.

as a haven for mostly male yuppies, connoisseurs and college students. Voluptuous nudes grace poster-size calendar sheets from the '40s. The walk-in humidor holds a selection of choice cigars, best enjoyed while reclining on their cozy, vampire-red sofas. There's a second, smaller outfit at 12604 Ventura Blvd in Studio City *(Map 2;* ☎ *818-762-3279)*.

Beverly Hills has a fine puffing establishment: *Overstreet's Wine Bar (Map 11;* ☎ *310-278-0347)*, 9713 Little Santa Monica Blvd, is a throwback to the days of British sportsmen's clubs. Jackets are required in one of its three rooms.

In Santa Monica you'll find *Lone Wolf Cigar Lounge (Map 12;* ☎ *310-458-5441)*, 223-B Broadway, which takes its name from a character played by actor Chuck Norris, who owns the place with Jim Belushi. It's all oak and leather – read: all *man* – and the testosterone poseurs flock here to preen behind panoramic windows and pretend they don't see the world gawking at their pretense. They have a damned good humidor though, where you can score a vintage 1993 Maca nudo for 25 bucks. Advice? Buy, then walk out onto Third Street Promenade to smoke your prestigious stogy. Norris and Belushi also own *Chimps Cigar Club*, an equally swank establishment in the Beverly Hilton Hotel.

Fancy a cigar to go along with a manicure, massage or haircut? Head for *Duke's Barber Shop (Map 13;* ☎ *310-792-3853)*, 1630 Pacific Coast Hwy in Redondo Beach, definitely a lounge with a twist – and a loyal following. Claiming to be the 'world's largest barber shop' (and they might be right), Duke's has antique chrome chairs, a select humidor, good attitude, free pool tables and beer. Oh, and if you just had your nails done, just coming in for a smoke is fine.

PUBS & MICROBREWERIES

Hollywood pubs are popular with musicians of all stripes, as well as expat Brits. They include the *Cat & Fiddle Pub (Map 9;* ☎ *323-468-3800)*, at 6530 Sunset Blvd, a sprawling affair with several rooms plus a large patio. Other places to try are the half-pint-sized *Coach & Horses (Map 9;* ☎ *323-876-6900)*, 7617 Sunset Blvd, which attracts a pretty rough crowd, and the more civilized *Coronet Pub (Map 10;* ☎ *310-659-4583)*, at 370 N La Cienega Blvd, popular with patrons of the nearby Coronet Theater.

For imported German brews on tap, head to the *Red Lion Tavern (Map 5;* ☎ *323-662-5337)*, 2366 Glendale Blvd in Silver Lake. Choices include the popular pilsners Warsteiner and Dortmunder, and the Spaten Weissbier from Munich, all served by dirndl-clad waitresses. You may find yourself sharing the bar or table with Germans, downtown attorneys, Silver Lake grungemeisters and air-conditioning repairmen.

With its large English and Irish expat population, Santa Monica's pub scene is the best and most authentic. Irish entries are the loud *Red Setter (Map 12;* ☎ *310-449-1811)*, 2615 Wilshire Blvd; *O'Brien's (Map 12;* ☎ *310-829-5303)*, Wilshire and 23rd (there's another branch at 2941 Main St; *Map 12;* ☎ *310-396-4725)*; and *St Stephen's Green (Map 12;* ☎ *310-393-6611)*, 1026 Wilshire Blvd, a feel-good place that looks like it's been around since St Patrick drove out the snakes, but in fact only opened in 1998.

Possibly the best English pub this side of the Thames is *Ye Olde King's Head (Map 12;* ☎ *310-451-1402)*, 116 Santa Monica Blvd, where the lager flows profusely, and Cockney and Queen's English mix easily in a way they never would back home (also see Places to Eat).

Farther south in Venice/Marina del Rey is *Scruffy O'Shea's (Map 12;* ☎ *310-821-0833)*, 822 Washington Blvd, where a boisterous college jock crowd gets down to live bands playing reggae, rock, salsa, swing and Irish seven days a week.

In the South Bay is the *Manhattan Beach Brewing Co (Map 13;* ☎ *310-798-2744)*, 124 Manhattan Beach Blvd, also frequented by the college set, bellied up to the bar set against a row of steel brewing vats lined up like organ pipes (also see Places to Eat).

San Pedro has the *Whale & Ale (Map 14;* ☎ *310-832-0363)*, a more sedate affair at 27 W 7th St. Looking like an old-time country-style English inn, complete with brass and leather, it has friendly service and a decent selection of lagers and German-style beers

Choose from 250 types of beer at the Yard House in Long Beach.

(also see Places to Eat). In Long Beach is the ***Yard House*** (*Map 15;* ☎ *562-628-0455*), 401 Shoreline Village Drive, where bartenders command an oval bar that looks like a spaceship helm. They serve some 250 beers on tap, connected to 5 miles of beer lines and 27 pumps. Serious boozers consume their brew from 'yards.'

Gordon Biersch Brewery (*Map 16;* ☎ *626-449-0052*), 41 Hugus Alley off Colorado Blvd in Pasadena, is a beer hall and beer garden in Pasadena. It is also a microbrewery working with original German recipes, churning out respectable, smooth-tasting brews, including a crisp pilsner, the slightly sweet Märzen and the full-bodied Dunkles.

COFFEEHOUSES

The days when coffee in LA meant little more than chocolate-colored water are a thing of the past. Major chains like Seattle-based Starbucks have insured that you'll never have to walk more than a couple of blocks for a jolt of java. Major competitor franchises include the Coffee Bean & Tea Leaf, Seattle's Best Coffee and Dietrich's, all of which serve up coffee concoctions from latte to cappuccino to iced mocha to machiato to – God help us! For more ambience, connoisseurs flock to the following caffeine haunts.

Hollywood (Map 9) Much more than your regular java joint, ***Highland Grounds*** (☎ *323-466-1507*), 742 N Highland Ave, is one of LA's oldest coffeehouses. They have a menu with simple but superb food and even a liquor license, which helps draw people in. Seating for their varied entertainment, offered almost nightly ($2 cover), is inside on the balcony or on their outdoor patio.

Walk into the ***Bourgeois Pig*** (☎ *323-962-6366*), 5931 Franklin Ave, and you'll soon lose any sense of whether it's day or night. Red plastic covers the large window, creating a perpetual netherworld dimmed even further by gold-colored fixtures and black carpeting. With its backroom pool tables, it looks more like a bar and the ambience feels rather anonymous and trendy. (Perhaps it's because of the spooky vibes filtering in from the Scientology Celebrity Center across the street.)

West Hollywood & Mid-City (Map 10) The ceiling of ***Insomnia Cafe*** (☎ *323-931-4943*), 7286 Beverly Blvd, is as tall as its opening hours are long. In the wee hours of the night, on weekends in particular, the space fills up with a flock of night owls in desperate need of stimuli. Hunker down at dark wooden tables or, better yet, try to grab the coveted cushiony sofas neatly tucked away in a private alcove.

DAVID PEEVERS

Caress a cuppa.

Doughboys *(☎ 323-651-4202)* is a cafe and bakery at 8136 W 3rd St, where you can order yummy breakfasts all day (see Places to Eat). ***Urth Caffe*** *(☎ 310-659-0628)*, 8565 Melrose Ave, specializes in organic coffee and tea served alongside a good selection of wholesome baked goods and desserts. New Agers especially love this place.

Santa Monica & Venice (Map 12) The

sunset-colored walls of ***Anastasia's Asylum*** *(☎ 310-394-7113)*, 1028 Wilshire Blvd in Santa Monica, draw an eclectic crowd of screenwriters with laptops, grannies with groceries, working stiffs and bohemians. They all seem to feel at home on the velvet couches and sidewalk cafe tables. The coffee is strong and the piles of baked treats are good and reasonably priced: lemon bars, monster cookies and generous sandwiches. There are also free performances almost nightly.

Near Main St in Santa Monica is the ***Novel Cafe*** *(☎ 310-396-8566)*, 212 Pier Ave. This bookstore cum cafe has crowds of

bohemians spilling out onto the sidewalk – sipping java, reading or practicing their foreign language skills. This is a great place to connect with the literary crowd (yes, LA *does* have one).

Venice has the ***Abbot's Habit*** *(☎ 310-399-1171)*, a corner coffee shop at 1401 Abbot Kinney Blvd serving hot latte by the gallon alongside scones, muffins and sticky caramel buns. It also has healthy, freshly prepared sandwiches and a small salad bar with ingredients sold by the pound ($4.50).

The Valleys *The Kindness of Strangers* *(Map 17; ☎ 818-752-9566)*, 4378 Lankershim Blvd in North Hollywood (NoHo), is a snug storefront space that has sofas and tables for lounging and free entertainment most nights (closed Monday). Grab a book from their cluttered shelf and kick back with an ice-blended mocha. Also in NoHo is the ***Hot House Cafe*** *(☎ 818-506-7058)*, 12123 Riverside Drive, a hip parlor that jolts customers into consciousness with a variety of coffee drinks, as well as some bravely spiced chili and other cafe fare. It offers free entertainment nightly.

Tucked away in an alley in Pasadena is ***Equator Coffeehouse*** *(Map 16; ☎ 626-564-8656)*, 22 Mills Place, which serves its high-octane brews in a historic carriage repair shop that gets a homey touch from colorful plump armchairs. A stylized globe adorned with twinkling Christmas lights forms the centerpiece of this relaxed place.

GAY & LESBIAN VENUES

West Hollywood (WeHo) is the heart of LA's gay and lesbian scene, and the action in bars, restaurants and clubs clustered along Santa Monica Blvd is happening every day and night of the week. Most places cater largely to male homosexuals, though some venues also welcome lesbians and mixed audiences.

Beauty reigns supreme in 'Boys' Town' and the intimidation factor can be high unless you're buff, bronzed and styled. Silver Lake is cruising heaven for the Levi's and leather crowd and also boasts a range of gay and lesbian Latino bars. The beach towns have more relaxed, neighborly scenes, while venues in the San Fernando Valley are altogether more mundane and mainstream gay. For updates and specifics about the various scenes, check out the gay and lesbian magazines available for free in bars, restaurants and gay-friendly establishments (see Facts for the Visitor).

Dance Clubs

The largest dance club for a mixed crowd in WeHo is the smart *Axis (Map 10; ☎ 310-659-0471)*, housed in a former factory at 652 N LaPeer Drive, featuring several bars, video games and a lounge. In the back of the building, through a different entrance, is the *Love Lounge (☎ 310-659-0471)*, 657 N Robertson Blvd, which has a different theme every night ('80s, Asian and drag, for example). Both are open to ages 18 and over. One night a week, each venue hosts the 'Girl Bar,' a hot club for lesbians.

Reportedly the oldest lesbian bar and party venue in WeHo is *The Palms (Map 10; ☎ 310-652-6188)*, 8572 Santa Monica Blvd. The schedule changes constantly and may include karaoke, live bands, theme parties and salsa nights. *Klub Banshee (Map 10; ☎ 310-288-1601)* is a lesbian night club held on Monday in a diminutive space above the Benvenuto Cafe, 8512 Santa Monica Blvd.

Clubs to check out in Hollywood proper include the huge *Arena (Map 9; ☎ 323-462-1291)*, 6655 Santa Monica Blvd, housed in a former ice factory, and the adjacent *Circus Disco*. Both have gay-only nights. Another one to try is *Probe (Map 9; ☎ 323-461-8301)*, 836 N Highland Ave, a cool place to wind down until 4 am. Saturdays have been dedicated gay nights since 1978.

Bars

In West Hollywood, *Micky's (Map 10; ☎ 310-657-1176)*, 8857 Santa Monica Blvd, is a posing and cruising joint particularly popular among younger gays and often has an electric party atmosphere. Attitude reigns supreme here and also at the *Rage (Map 10; ☎ 310-652-7055)*, 8911 Santa Monica Blvd. Less pretentious types might prefer *Mother Lode (Map 10; ☎ 310-659-9700)*, 8944 Santa Monica Blvd, a neighborly bar with gold-

rush inspired decor. Check out its cocktail hour specials and Sunday beer parties.

Revolver (Map 10; ☎ 310-659-8851), 8851 Santa Monica Blvd, is a stylish video bar with music, film and comedy clips playing continuously. *Spike (Map 9; ☎ 323-656-9343)*, 7746 Santa Monica Blvd, is a cruising joint favored by 30-something jeans-and-leather guys shooting pool or chatting over the pinball machine; it's closed Sunday. More mature men gravitate toward *Trunks (Map 10; ☎ 310-652-1015)*, a sociable sports bar at 8809 Santa Monica Blvd.

In Silver Lake, gay bars are concentrated along Hyperion Ave and include the Levi's-and-leather *Cuffs (Map 9; ☎ 323-660-2649)*, at 1941 Hyperion and the slightly seedy *Hyperion (Map 9; ☎ 323-660-1503)*, at 2810 Hyperion. *Faultline (Map 9; ☎ 323-660-0889)*, 4216 Melrose Ave, is for fetish, uniform, leather and blue-collar scenes; stock up at their on-premise leather store. *Gauntlet II (Map 9; ☎ 323-669-9472)*, at 4219 Santa Monica Blvd, is a sexy pick-up joint for the tattoo and leather set.

In Venice, check out the divey *Roosterfish (Map 12; ☎ 310-392-2123)*, 1301 Abbot Kinney Blvd, where a mixed crowd congregates over pool tables and pinball machines. *Babylon (☎ 310-371-7859)*, 2105 Artesia Blvd in Redondo Beach, caters to gay surfers and has beerbust, karaoke and go-go dancer nights.

Lesbians are welcome at *Rumors (☎ 818-506-9651)*, 10622 Magnolia Blvd in North Hollywood, which bills itself an alternative-lifestyle bar and offers dancing, darts, karaoke and other entertainment nightly.

Coffeehouses

In West Hollywood you'll find the *WeHo Lounge (Map 10; ☎ 310-659-6180)*, 8861 Santa Monica Blvd, an easy-going java joint with sofas, sidewalk seating and an integrated AIDS Health Care Foundation's 'Treatment Equals Life' education program. It offers free HIV testing and information. *City Bean (☎ 323-848-8500)*, 8457 Santa Monica Blvd, is not exclusively gay but is noted for micro-roasting its 25 bean varieties while dishing out pretty good desserts.

Little Frida's *(Map 10; ☎ 310-854-5421)*, 8730 Santa Monica Blvd, is an art-filled place with a Southwestern flair, despite being wedged into a small mini-mall. Named after painter Frida Kahlo, it's popular with stylish lesbians, though everyone's welcome.

SPECTATOR SPORTS

Los Angeles has an on-again, off-again love affair with its sports teams – the action heats up when they're winning, but drops off the radar when a team is merely mortal – much like love affairs in general in LA. Its professional football teams have so stunk up the joint that the Raiders beat a retreat to Oakland and the Rams headed to St Louis, leaving the country's second-largest city without a professional football team (though this may have changed by the time you're reading this, as negotiations are underway to rectify this embarrassing situation). Still, there are teams with power, pride and traditions, which – when they are playing at the top of their game – are well worth the price of admission.

Baseball

Even though the Dodgers make their home in the land of celluloid heroes, you won't find any of the players making music videos or dating Madonna. Baseball is a game far removed from self-deluding images of grandeur and show-biz hype. By all accounts, the history of baseball in LA *is* the Dodgers, at least ever since they moved here from Brooklyn in 1958. (The name 'Dodgers,' by the way,

is an abbreviation of 'Trolley Dodgers' and refers to the trolley tracks crisscrossing the area surrounding their ball field in the team's early days during the 1890s.)

The move to LA came about because Walter O'Malley, president and chief stockholder of the team since 1950, felt his team needed to play on a new and improved field. When Brooklyn balked at spending the money, O'Malley shocked the world of sports by moving his team to LA, essentially inventing the mobile professional sports franchise.

LA welcomed them with open arms and the promise to build the state-of-the-art Dodger Stadium. The team responded by producing a string of legends that included Duke Snider, Jackie Robinson, Roy Campanella, Pee Wee Reese, Gil Hodges, Don Drysdale, Sandy Koufax, Tommy Davis, Frank Howard, Fernando Valenzuela and Orel Hershiser. Walter Alston, manager since 1954, guided the team through 23 seasons, 2042 wins, four world championships and seven National League pennants. The O'Malley family maintained ownership until selling out to publishing tycoon Rupert Murdoch in 1998.

Dodger Stadium *(Map 5; ☎ 323-224-1400 for information, ☎ 323-224-1500 for tickets, www.dodgers.com)* is at 1000 Elysian Park Ave, just north of Downtown LA. Tickets, usually available at the box office on game day, start at $6 for seats in the nosebleed section and better ones costing just $8 to $12; children are half price. Regular season is from April to October.

Basketball

Los Angeles Lakers The LA Lakers have been a consistent basketball dynasty with the best winning percentage of any sports team, after the New York Yankees and the Boston Celtics. The Lakers came to LA from Minneapolis in 1960, and with players like Jerry West, Wilt Chamberlain, Kareem Abdul-Jabbar and Magic Johnson, the team pretty much set the standard for excitement in the 'round-ball' game.

It was a non-sports episode, though, that brought the Lakers to the attention of the

DAVID R FRAZIER

Dodger Stadium

Los Angeles Clippers LA's second – and secondary – men's basketball team is the LA Clippers (☎ 213-745-0400), who play at the LA Sports Arena, in Exposition Park at 3939 S Figueroa St. Tickets range from $10 to $50 and are available from ☎ 213-745-0500.

Los Angeles Sparks The LA Sparks is the city's women's basketball team, which did incredibly well in the 1997-98 season. Like the Lakers, their home is the Great Western Forum (Map 2; 310-419-3865 for tickets and schedules), though they too will eventually move to the Staples Center. Tickets range from $7.50 to $24.

UCLA UCLA's basketball team, the Bruins, is one of the best college teams in the US. They have racked up 11 men's basketball championships, and during the 1971-74 seasons went an astonishing 88 games without defeat. UCLA has appeared on the cover of *Sports Illustrated* 91 times, represented by the likes of Kareem Abdul-Jabbar, who after starring for the Bruins went on to become the only man to win six MVP Awards in the NBA. The team plays at Pauley Pavilion on the UCLA campus (Map 11). Call ☎ 310-825-2106 for tickets.

Magic Johnson: LA Lakers superstar

world. When Earvin 'Magic' Johnson announced to the world that he tested positive for HIV, it was a turning point, both for athletes and the fans who watch them play. It was an act of courage for an athlete of Magic Johnson's stature to make such an admission.

For the '96 season, the Lakers acquired another superstar in Shaquille O'Neil, who during '97/'98 was a close second in scoring to Michael Jordan of the Chicago Bulls. As the Lakers continue to pack the Forum (Jack Nicholson has a special courtside seat), the jury is still out on whether this new team is 'dynasty' material.

The Lakers play at the ***Great Western Forum*** *(Map 2; ☎ 310-419-3865 for tickets and schedules)*, 3900 W Manchester Blvd in Inglewood, but will move to the Staples Center in Downtown upon its completion. Tickets range from $10 to $130.

Football
Both of LA's professional football teams – the Rams and the Raiders – picked up and moved in early 1995. In the meantime, USC (☎ 213-740-2311) and UCLA (☎ 310-825-2106) compete in the Pacific 10 (Pac-10) Conference for the right to play in Pasadena's Rose Bowl game on January 1. The Bruins football team was the first to win a post-season football bowl game seven years in a row. In the 1998 season, its quarterback,

Cade McNown, came close to winning the coveted Heisman Trophy, which was eventually snatched by Ricky Waters.

Soccer

It may be a cold day in hell before Major League Soccer catches fire in this country, but that's not stopping the Los Angeles Galaxy (☎ 310-445-1260) from putting on an impressive show since their 1995 launch. By winning 12 consecutive games their first year out, they announced that they would be a team to be reckoned with.

The team's greatest asset is its incredibly loyal fans, some 26,000 of whom regularly descend on the Rose Bowl on game day. Since the stadium holds nearly 100,000, getting tickets is usually no problem. They cost $10, $15 and $17 and are sold either at the stadium or by calling ☎ 888-657-5425. The Rose Bowl is at 1001 Rose Bowl Drive in Pasadena (Map 16).

Horse Racing

Horse racing enthusiasts consider *Santa Anita Racetrack (Map 3; ☎ 626-574-7223, www.santaanita.com)*, 285 W Huntington Drive in Arcadia east of Pasadena, to be one of the best tracks in America. The smaller Oak Tree Meeting takes place in October and November, while the thoroughbred season runs from Christmas through April. Admission is $5 (free to those under 18 if accompanied by an adult).

The other track is *Hollywood Park Race Track (Map 2; ☎ 310-419-1500, www.hollywoodpark.com)*, 1050 S Prairie St, just south of the Great Western Forum in Inglewood. Live racing season is from April to July, while the Fall Meeting is from November to December. There's also a casino next door where you can play cards, bingo and satellite thoroughbred wagering. Admission is $6 (free to those under 18) and includes parking and program.

Shopping

WHERE TO SHOP

Most Angelenos do their serious shopping in multistory malls, some with upwards of 200 stores in a single building. But when they want to take a less frantic approach to shopping, locals head for a handful of streets where the people-watching is as much fun as the window browsing.

Shopping Districts

There are two places to come for 21st-century funk. One is the section on **Melrose Ave** between La Brea and Fairfax Aves, with its concentration of quirky and hip boutiques (also see the Things to See & Do chapter). The other is **Ocean Front Walk** along Venice Beach. Especially on weekend afternoons, ambulatory vendors display their wares on the ocean side of this beachfront promenade; permanent shops and cafes line the city side. Need a silk Italian tie or a velvet hat to rival the Mad Hatter's? A bronze dancing Shiva icon or a bronze cowbell from Switzerland? A spiked leather hat for your dog or a spiked

Third Street Promenade

leather bikini for your sister (or vice versa)? Whatever it is, this is where you'll find it.

In Beverly Hills, **Rodeo Drive** is known the world over for its up-up-upscale designer boutiques and jewelry stores, art galleries and antique shops. Start at the Two Rodeo Drive complex on Wilshire Blvd opposite the Regent Beverly Wilshire Hotel; from there, follow Rodeo north 3 blocks. Also check out shops on the side street.

Santa Monica's **Third Street Promenade** is a pedestrian mall anchored by the Frank Gehry-designed Santa Monica Place mall on Broadway, heading 3 blocks north to Wilshire Blvd. Street musicians and other buskers, not to mention Hollywood entertainment scouts, keep this strip busy day and night. This is where you'll find a Disney store, mainstream fashions at Gap and Banana Republic, novelties and casual clothing at Urban Outfitters, funky fashions at NaNa and much more. Other good shopping streets in Santa Monica are **Main St** for young designer fashions

Fun and funky Melrose Ave

293

and antiques, and **Montana Ave** for gift shops, children's clothing, furniture and elegant women's wear.

Gentrified **Colorado Blvd in Old Pasadena** has plenty of bookstores, boutiques, houseware and specialty stores. Highlights include Sur La Table cookware, Restoration home furnishings, Crate & Barrel home accessories and a huge Barnes & Noble bookstore. Also in Pasadena is **South Lake Ave**, notable for its Londonesque shopping arcades.

Silver Lake and Los Feliz have a flurry of funky clubwear stores as well as thrift and vintage clothing shops. Check out **Los Feliz Village** along Vermont Ave as well as the 3000 and 4000 blocks of Sunset Blvd.

West Hollywood is LA's center for design, with furniture and accessory stores abundant along **Robertson Blvd**. Also check out **La Brea Blvd** in Hollywood.

Visitors intent on ethnic souvenirs should head for Downtown LA. **Broadway, Olvera St** and **El Mercado** in East LA are places to find Mexican hand-crafted leather and hand-woven clothing as well as children's toys and

piñatas. **Chinatown** has many shops selling imported porcelain, furniture and silk clothing, as well as chopsticks and soapstone Buddhas. Little Tokyo's main shopping center is the **Japanese Village Plaza**, a 40-shop pedestrian lane that winds between 1st and 2nd Sts. Look for imported kimonos and books, but especially toys and crafts, from origami art to fine spun pottery. For African art – masks, sculptures, paintings and crafts – head to Degnan Ave in **Leimert Village** in the Crenshaw District.

Fanciful **Universal City Walk** in Universal City has about 40 shops, restaurants and entertainment venues. Check out Adobe Road, which sells American Indian crafts; the Nature Company, where a walk through a simulated rain forest inspires purchase of eco-sensitive gifts; or Things From Another World, for science-fiction lovers.

Fashion District

Also known as the Garment District, this 56-block area in the southern section of Downtown is the epicenter of LA's clothing manufacturing. It is framed by Broadway, Wall St, 7th St and Pico Blvd, and is on the DASH minibus route (see Getting Around). Shopping here can net you extraordinary deals, but it helps to know some of the area's special rules.

Shops with displays saying 'Wholesale Only' or 'Mayoreo' are off-limits to retail shoppers. Leave your credit cards at home because most vendors will only accept cash. It's okay to haggle over the price, though don't expect to get more than 10 or 20% off. There are usually no refunds or exchanges, so choose carefully and make sure the item is in good condition (many items sold here are 'seconds,' meaning they're slightly flawed). As many stores have no dressing rooms, wear something conducive to trying on clothes behind a rack of clothing. Men can wear tight shorts and a T-shirt; for women, tight leggings or wide flowing skirts are good choices.

There are several distinct areas within the Fashion District. The **Cooper Building**, a former warehouse at 9th and Los Angeles Sts, has six floors of outlet stores, mostly for women, and is a good choice for those seek-

DAVID PEEVERS

Día de los Muertos art on Olvera St

Shopping Malls

Nothing defines shopping in LA more than the mall, a Southern California invention resulting from reliance on the car. Much more than a place to shop, malls define and reflect the culture of vanity and commercialism so prevalent here. The mall is a home away from home, a safe haven where meeting friends and having cappuccino is as much part of the itinerary as browsing the sales racks at Bloomingdale's. Movies have been made about this phenomenon, including *Scenes from a Mall* and *Mall Rats*, while Frank and Moon Zappa's song *Valley Girl* was inspired by the Sherman Oaks Galleria. (In a bizarre twist, this prototypical mall was forced to close in 1999 for lack of customers; it is being converted into a business center.) Be that as it may, LA malls are surprisingly different and are actually fun and convenient places to shop.

The unique architecture of Seventh Street Market Place (Map 5; ☎ 213-955-7150), 735 S Figueroa St in Downtown, is at least as eye-catching as the window displays of its 50 stores. Descending three floors beneath street level, it's built around a circular atrium and is open to the sky. A profusion of flowers, iron grillwork stairs and a bird-cage elevator are among the creative flourishes. Robinsons-May and Bullock's are the anchoring department stores. Its hours are 10 am to 7 pm weekdays, to 6 pm Saturday; some stores are also open noon to 5 pm Sunday.

The Beverly Center (Map 10; ☎ 310-854-0070), 8500 Beverly Blvd at La Cienega, is the mall where you're most likely to spot a celebrity trying on shoes at Charles David or buying a skimpy dress at Betsey Johnson. Those not born to shop might find this huge place a bit overwhelming; there are about 160 upscale shops (anchored by Bloomingdale's and Macy's), a Warner Bros Studio store and about 25 men's clothing stores. The food court is quite a disappointment, though the 13 cinemas on the 8th floor are not. The first five levels of this bunker-like building are reserved for parking; stores are on floors six to eight. Hours are 10 am to 9 pm weekdays, to 8 pm Saturday, 11 am to 6 pm Sunday.

Flanked by glass and concrete stalagmites of offices, the Century City Shopping Center

Universal City Walk

ing a more traditional shopping experience. Selections often include brand-name clothing.

Those with a knack for haggling should head to **Santee Alley**, just east of Santee St between Olympic Blvd and 12th St, an outdoor bazaar where mostly Middle Eastern entrepreneurs hawk designer knockoffs at rock-bottom prices. Prepare yourself for rude comments if you don't buy.

Menswear stores are concentrated along Los Angeles St north of the Cooper Building, between 7th and 9th Sts. Along Wall St, between 8th St and Olympic Blvd, are fabric shops, children's clothing stores and stores for full-figured women.

To get oriented, take a free guided bus tour, departing at 10 am, 11 am and noon on the last Saturday of every month from the California Mart on Olympic Blvd between Main and Los Angeles Sts. Call ☎ 213-488-1153 for a reservation. (For more information on the Fashion District, see Things to See & Do.)

Santa Monica Place

ture, music and household stores, as well as a branch of the wonderful KCET Public Broadcasting's Store of Knowledge. The space itself, designed by Frank Gehry, is imaginative and pleasant, while the food court, Eatz, is definitely the best around. Hours are 10 am to 9 pm weekdays, to 10 pm Saturday, 10 am to 6 pm Sunday.

The following are also major malls:

Macy's Plaza (Map 5; ☎ 213-624-2891) 7th and Flower Sts in Downtown. There are 30 boutiques, anchored by Macy's, open weekdays to 6:30 pm.

Fox Hills Mall (Map 2; ☎ 310-390-7833) 294 Fox Hills Mall in Culver City. Features 140 shops, anchored by Macy's, Robinsons-May and JC Penney. Open weekdays 10 am to 9 pm, Saturday to 7 pm, Sunday 11 am to 6 pm.

Fashion Square Mall (Map 2; ☎ 818-783-0550) 14006 Riverside Drive in Sherman Oaks in the San Fernando Valley. There are 135 stores, anchored by Bloomingdale's and Macy's, with the same hours as Fox Hills Mall.

Glendale Galleria (Map 3; ☎ 818-240-9481) 2148 Glendale Galleria. This mall has 260 stores, anchored by Macy's, Robinsons-May, JC Penney, Nordstrom and Mervyn's. Open weekdays 10 am to 9 pm, Saturday to 7 pm, Sunday 11 am to 6 pm.

& Marketplace (Map 11; ☎ 310-553-5300), 10250 Santa Monica Blvd, is a pleasant outdoor mall. The roughly 140 stores here are elegant but still affordable and largely mainstream. The big department stores here are Bloomingdale's and Macy's. There's a 14-screen cinema complex and an excellent food court. It's open weekdays 10 am to 9 pm, Saturday to 6 pm, Sunday 11 am to 6 pm.

Although the designers did well in conceiving the pretty, glass-covered Westside Pavilion (Map 2; ☎ 310-474-6255), 10800 W Pico Blvd in Westwood, parking is a nightmare of impacted entranceways and tightly spiraling ramps. Once inside, it's a pleasure to browse through the 160 indoor and outdoor shops, including the upscale Nordstrom and the more down-to-earth Robinsons-May department stores. There's also a cinema fourplex and a supermarket. Hours are 10 am to 9 pm weekdays, to 8 pm Saturday, 11 am to 6 pm Sunday.

Though not overwhelmingly large, Santa Monica Place (Map 12; ☎ 310-394-5451) is one of the most popular malls in the LA area. Anchored by Robinsons-May and Macy's, it houses a full range of retail clothing, furni-

Outlet Malls

Outlet malls, where famous and mainstream chain stores purportedly sell off their stock at reduced prices, have become all the rage with many visitors. While bargains here are possible, it's worth noting that items are often damaged, irregular or leftover from the previous season, rejected from regular department stores. That lime-green shirt that was so fashionable last year may get you ticketed by the fashion police this summer. Service in these stores is also kept to a minimum; there are generally fewer employees, dressing rooms and mirrors.

The only outlet mall in LA County is Citadel Factory Stores (Map 3; ☎ 213-888-1220) at 5675 E Telegraph Rd (right off the I-5 Washington exit), 9 miles south of Downtown. A planned expansion is supposed to add 35 stores to what is a relatively small complex with shops by Corning Revere, London Fog and Eddie Bauer. Hours are 10 am to 8 pm daily, to 6 pm Sunday.

With more than 200 stores spread over 131 acres, Ontario Mills (☎ 909-484-8300), 4557 One Mills Circle in Ontario, about a 40-minute drive east of Downtown LA, is the Godzilla of California's outlet malls. Headliners include Saks Fifth Avenue, Guess?, Ann Taylor and Warner Bros Studio. Besides a food court with 13 eateries, the mall also integrates an entertainment complex featuring the American Wilderness Experience, which re-creates a variety of California ecosystems, including a redwood forest, the desert and Yosemite Valley. There's also a 30-screen movie theater as well as an UltraScreen Theatre, with a six-story screen and 30-speaker sound system. It's open to 10 pm Sunday to Thursday, to midnight Friday and Saturday.

Farmers' Markets

LA's best-known open-air market is the Farmers' Market, 6333 W 3rd St in the Fairfax District (Map 10). There are some 150

Flea Markets

Flea markets or swap meets: Call them what you will, the LA area has plenty. Nourished by a remarkably diverse population with some equally eclectic tastes, these massive gatherings can make for the best bargain shopping around. Whether you're hunting for a '57 Chevy hubcap or a Hopalong Cassidy pocket knife, you'll seldom find it for a better price. Arrive early, bring a bag and lots of small bills, wear those walking shoes and get ready to haggle.

Burbank Monthly Antique Market (☎ 310-455-2886) Main St and Riverside Drive. Happens the fourth Sunday of the month, 8 am to 3 pm. Admission is $3.

Long Beach Outdoor Antique & Collectible Market (☎ 213-655-5703) Veteran's Memorial Stadium, Conant St between Lakewood Blvd and Clark Ave. Takes place the third Sunday of the month, 8 am to 3 pm. Over 800 antique dealers sell here.

Melrose Trading Post (Map 10; ☎ 323-932-8155) Fairfax High School parking lot, 7850 Melrose Ave at Fairfax Ave. Happens every Sunday, 9 am to 5 pm. There are about 120 vendors of hip and bizarre collectibles.

Pasadena City College Flea Market (☎ 626-585-7906) 1570 E Colorado Blvd. Takes place the first Sunday of the month, 8 am to 3 pm. There are over 400 vendors; admission and parking are free. This is the best flea market for music.

The Roadium (☎ 213-321-3709) 2500 Redondo Beach Blvd, Torrance. Happens daily from 7 am to 4 pm. Admission is 50¢, except Wednesday when the week's treasures arrive and the price soars to an *exorbitant* $1.25 (75¢ for seniors). There are about 475 vendors; on Mondays, the focus is on antiques.

Rose Bowl Flea Market (☎ 213-560-7469) 1001 Rose Bowl Drive. Happens the second Sunday of the month, 6 am to 4:30 pm. The largest in the land, this flea market has over 1500 vendors who descend upon Pasadena's scenic Arroyo Seco. Admission is $15 before 7:30 am, $10 until 9 am, $5 after.

Santa Monica Outdoor Antique & Collectible Market (☎ 213-933-2511) Airport Ave off Bundy Ave. Happens the fourth Sunday of the month, 6 am to 3 pm. Possibly the poshest of the lot, with Victorian to Postmodern wares and tasty food besides. Another version of this market is at Santa Monica High School at 4th St and Pico Blvd on the first Sunday of the month. Admission is $4 ($5 between 6 and 8 am).

shops and stalls here, some selling fresh produce or an international selection of hot and cold foods, but many more hawking craft and gift items, from T-shirts to oil paintings. It's definitely touristy but worth a stop.

The Grand Central Market, 317 S Broadway (Map 5), has been a Downtown LA fixture since 1917. You won't find many gift items here, but it's one of the best places in LA to buy fresh fruit and vegetables, meat and seafood, hand-tossed tortillas and homemade Chinese noodles. For details on this and the Farmers' Market, see the Things to See & Do chapter.

California is famous for its super-fresh produce, and vendors at weekly farmers' markets in neighborhoods throughout the city offer the best in quality, choice and price. Come here to stock up on groceries or just to put together a beach picnic. As with anywhere else around the world, markets are also great places to catch a glimpse of local life and are fun to browse in, even without buying. Here's a selection:

Hollywood – Ivar Ave between Sunset and Hollywood Blvds (Sunday 8:30 am to 1 pm)

West Hollywood – Plummer Park at 7377 Santa Monica Blvd (Monday 9 am to 2 pm)

Beverly Hills – 200 block of Cañon Drive north of Wilshire (Sunday 9 am to 1 pm)

Culver City – 9300 Culver City Blvd (Tuesday from 3 to 7 pm)

Santa Monica – Arizona and 2nd Sts (Wednesday 9:30 am to 3 pm and Saturday 9:30 am to 2 pm), and Pico and Cloverfield Blvds (Saturday 8:30 am to 1 pm), and Ocean Park Blvd and Main St (Sunday 9 am to noon)

Venice – Venice Blvd and Venice Way (Friday from 7 to 11 am)

Hermosa – 13th St and Hermosa Ave (Friday noon to 4 pm)

Long Beach – 3rd St and Broadway on the Promenade North (Friday 10 am to 4 pm)

Glendale – 100 N Brand Blvd (Thursday 9:30 am to 1:30 pm)

Burbank – 3rd St and Orange Grove Ave (Saturday 8 am to 1 pm)

Pasadena – Villa Park Community Center at 363 East Villa St (Tuesday 9:30 am to 1:30 pm), and Victory Park between Altadena Drive and Sierra Madre at Paloma St (Saturday 8:30 am to 1 pm)

Gourmet & Ethnic Markets

Gourmet Coffee Warehouse (Map 12; ☎ 310-392-6479) is a funky, barn-like store at 671 Rose Ave in Venice, dedicated to the cult of the bean. Wholesale prices, freshness and about 40 varieties (including blends and organic varieties) account for this place's popularity. Everything's roasted in a back room every three days and stored in old-

Grand Central Market

fashioned, self-service wooden bins. Several varieties are available for tastings. It also sells fine tea and accessories.

Aficionados of Thai cuisine will find their every need catered to at Silom Supermarket (Map 9) in Thai Plaza at 5321 Hollywood Blvd. Besides every conceivable noodle, condiment and sauce, it also has a good selection of fresh and exotic produce.

For Japanese ingredients, there's no bigger market than Yaohan (☎ 310-398-2113), 3760 Centinela Ave in Culver City, which has different types of tofu, enoki mushrooms, entire shelves of sake and everything you'd need to make sushi, shabu shabu, tempura or any other Japanese dish. The downside is most products are described in Japanese only, and the staff has only limited English skills. It's best to ask other shoppers for help. Another branch is Downtown in Little Tokyo's Yaohan Plaza.

Art Galleries

Consult the Calendar section of the *LA Times* for information on galleries and openings. Also check out the free magazine *Arts Scene* (☎ 213-482-4724, artscene@artscenecal.com), available at shops and restaurants around LA, or visit its website at www.artscene.com.

Hollywood (Map 10)

Jan Baum Gallery (☎ 323-932-0170) 170 S La Brea Ave. Represents international contemporary art, primitive art and art by emerging LA artists. Open Tuesday to Saturday 10 am to 5:30 pm.

Jack Rutberg Fine Arts Gallery (☎ 323-938-5222) 357 N La Brea Ave. A top gallery representing modern and contemporary paintings, drawings, prints and sculptures by such masters as Chagall, Kollwitz, Picasso, Warhol and Manet. Open Tuesday to Friday 10 am to 6 pm, Saturday to 5 pm.

Iturralde Gallery (☎ 323-937-4267) 154 N La Brea Ave. Features contemporary Latin American masters and new talent, including works by Rufino Tamayo, Julio Antonio and Ernesto Pujol. Open Tuesday to Friday 10 am to 5 pm, Saturday from 11 am.

Fahey-Klein Gallery (☎ 323-934-2250) 148 N La Brea Ave. One of America's foremost photography galleries, with often provocative shows of vintage and contemporary images, represent-

ing Robert Doisneau, Allen Ginsberg, Robert Mapplethorpe and Herb Ritts among many others. Open Tuesday to Saturday 10 am to 6 pm.

Paul Kopeikin Gallery (☎ 323-937-0765) 138 N La Brea Ave. Practically next door to Fahey-Klein, this gallery also shows fine-art photography, especially California Pictorialism and Modernism by lesser-known artists. Open Tuesday to Saturday 11 am to 5:30 pm.

West Hollywood (Map 10)

Herbert Palmer Gallery (☎ 310-278-6407) 9003 Melrose Ave. Features modern and contemporary masters such as MC Escher, Claes Oldenburg, Man Ray and Lipschitz. Open Tuesday to Friday 10 am to 6 pm, Saturday 11 am to 5 pm.

Tobey C Moss Gallery (☎ 323-933-5523) 7321 Beverly Blvd. A leading gallery with fine prints, drawings, paintings and sculptures. Specializing in California Modernism, abstract art and Post-Surrealism. Open Thursday to Saturday 11 am to 4 pm.

Tasende Gallery (☎ 310-276-8686) 8808 Melrose Ave. Has contemporary drawings, paintings and sculptures by modern masters such as José Luis Cuevas, Giacomo Manzù and Andrés Nagel. Open Tuesday to Friday 10 am to 6 pm, Saturday 11 am to 5 pm.

Daniel Saxon Gallery (☎ 310-657-6033) 552 Norwich Drive. Located across from the Pacific Design Center, this gallery represents leading Chicano artists working in the media of glass, painting, print and sculpture. Open Tuesday to Friday 11 am to 5 pm, Saturday noon to 4 pm.

Westside

Ernie Wolfe Gallery (Map 12; ☎ 310-473-1645) 1653 Sawtelle Blvd in west LA. Has large-scale traditional sculptures from Africa, including granary ladders and house posts, as well as tribal furniture and contemporary paintings and sculptures from Kenya, Ivory Coast, Ghana and Mali. Call for hours.

Leslie Sacks Fine Art (Map 12; ☎ 310-820-9448) 11640 San Vicente Blvd in Brentwood. Has a superb collection of modern and contemporary masters, as well as Impressionist, German Expressionist and African art. Open Tuesday to Saturday 10 am to 6 pm.

Pace Wildenstein (Map 11; ☎ 310-205-5522) 9540 Wilshire Blvd in Beverly Hills. Features paintings, sculptures, drawings and photographs by international contemporary artists. Open Tuesday to Friday 10 am to 5:30 pm, Saturday 10 am to 4 pm.

Gagosian Gallery (Map 11; ☎ 310-271-9400) 456 N Camden Drive in Beverly Hills. Represents top US names in contemporary painting and sculpture, including Richard Serra, Ed Ruscha and Maya Lin. Open Tuesday to Saturday from 10 am to 5:30 pm.

Christie's (Map 11; ☎ 310-385-2600) 356 N Camden Drive, and *Sotheby's* (Map 11; ☎ 310-274-0340) 9665 Wilshire Blvd. Both are located in Beverly Hills and are LA's top auction houses.

Latin American Masters (Map 11; ☎ 310-271-4847) 264 N Beverly Drive. Represents big names in Latin American art, including Diego Rivera, Rufino Tamayo and Armando Morales. Open Tuesday to Saturday 11 am to 6 pm.

Santa Monica & Venice (Map 12)
The first three galleries listed are at Bergamot Station, 2525 Michigan Ave in Santa Monica. For more on this unique cluster of galleries, shops and museums, see Santa Monica in the Things to See & Do chapter.

Patricia Correia Gallery (☎ 310-264-1760) features paintings and sculptures by emerging LA artists. Hours are 10 am to 6 pm Tuesday to Friday, from 11 am Saturday.

Sherry Frumkin Gallery (☎ 310-453-1850) has paintings and sculptures by new LA talent. Hours are 10:30 am to 5:30 pm Tuesday to Saturday.

Bobbie Greenfield Gallery (☎ 310-264-0640) features contemporary-master prints, drawings and multiples. Among well-known artists featured are Christo, David Hockney, Roy Lichtenstein and Jasper Johns. Open Tuesday to Friday 10 am to 5 pm, Saturday from 11 am.

LA Louver Gallery (☎ 310-822-4955) 45 N Venice Blvd in Venice. Has contemporary American and European art, including works by Wallace Berman, Tony Berlant, David Hockney, and Edward and Nancy Kienholz. Open Tuesday to Saturday 10 am to 5 pm.

Thrift Shops
These shops are stores usually operated by charities, such as Goodwill, Junior League and the Salvation Army, which sell off donated used clothing, housewares, books, furniture and other items, often at ridiculously low prices. Most of the proceeds go back to the charity.

If you've spilled red wine on the only pair of shorts you brought in your backpack or weren't prepared for that sudden dinner invitation, you're bound to find amazing bargains for just a tiny fraction of what you'd pay in department stores. Designer items and brand-name clothing are especially abundant at stores in fashion-conscious neighborhoods such as Beverly Hills and Santa Monica, where – in some circles – wearing the same dress twice is considered gauche. A derivation of the thrift shop is the vintage clothing store; see the Attire section later in this chapter.

Garage Sales
As you're driving through LA's neighborhoods on Friday and Saturday, you'll probably notice signs attached to traffic signals and telephone poles announcing a 'Moving Sale,' 'Estate Sale,' 'Multi-Family Sale' or 'Garage Sale,' along with an address and the date. Whatever they're called, these sales are an LA institution, and serious bargain hunters will hit the streets early for the best finds. For those holding the sale, it's a way to clean out closets and make a buck on the side. For treasure hunters, garage sales can yield everything from vintage earrings to furniture at rock-bottom prices. Haggling, of course, is just part of the fun.

WHAT TO BUY
Books
Book Soup (Map 10; ☎ 310-659-3110), 8818 Sunset Blvd in West Hollywood, draws students, celebrities and other browsers to its eclectic assortment of books, including a large gay and lesbian section. The extensive reading and book-signing schedule attracts big-name authors, and an enormous newsstand has publications from around the world. It's open until midnight daily.

Skylight Bookshop (Map 9; ☎ 323-660-1175), 1818 N Vermont Ave in Los Feliz Village, is a small bookstore with a huge ficus tree growing right through the center. Besides a good selection of titles about LA and a large gay and lesbian section, it has an esoteric magazine rack with glossies such as *Bizarre Magazine* and *Punk Planet*. It features author readings several times weekly. Hours are 10 am to 10 pm daily.

Dutton's (☎ 310-476-6263), 11975 San Vicente Blvd in Brentwood, caters to a well-read and educated clientele. Owner Doug Dutton specializes in the humanities, with large selections of history, philosophy and poetry. The store itself is rambling and cluttered, but service is tops. Authors on book tours stop by regularly, and there's even a small area to imbibe some java. There's a second branch (☎ 818-769-3866) at 5146 Laurel Canyon Blvd in North Hollywood. Both are open until 9 pm weekdays, until 6 pm weekends.

The Midnight Special Bookstore (Map 12; ☎ 310-393-2923), 1318 Third Street Promenade in Santa Monica, owes its name to an old blues song about a train passing a prison at the stroke of midnight. If its headlight shone through the prison bars onto one of the inmates, he would be the next to be set free. The store makes no bones about its political leanings, reflected in its huge selection of books by minority writers, feminists and radical authors. Open daily till 10:30 pm, it features frequent readings and community events.

Small World Books (Map 12; ☎ 310-399-2360), 1407 Ocean Front Walk in Venice, is chock-full of literary criticism, fiction and poetry, much of it from small presses. It also has plenty of foreign-language novels catering to the flocks of tourists wandering in off the Boardwalk. Its Mystery Annex (as in mystery books) is legendary. The store is open daily to 8 pm.

A literary vibe permeates Pasadena, which boasts Southern California's oldest (since 1894) bookstore, Vroman's (Map 16; ☎ 626-449-5320), 695 E Colorado Blvd. Book signings, author readings, a newsletter, a coffee bar and a huge selection of printed matter make this a favorite among LA literati. It's open 9 am to 9 pm weekdays, until 7 pm Saturday, 10 am to 7 pm Sunday.

Specialty Heritage Bookshop (Map 10; ☎ 310-659-3674), in a turreted building at

Midnight Special Bookstore

8540 Melrose Ave in West Hollywood, offers a vast assortment of rare books, including many first editions and manuscripts; it also does book binding. Its autograph gallery showcases the writings of Hemingway and others. This shop is closed Sunday.

Nearby is the Bodhi Tree Bookstore (Map 10; ☎ 310-659-1733, 800-825-9798), 8585 Melrose Ave. This tranquil business sells esoterica and works on astrology, occult, spirituality and other New Age subjects to a clientele that includes Shirley MacLaine. It's open daily 10 am to 11 pm, while the used-book annex, located behind the main building, is open until 7 pm.

Also close by is Sports Books (Map 10; ☎ 323-651-2334), 8302 Melrose Ave, filling shelf after shelf with just what its name says, from angling to soccer. Its collection includes rare and out-of-print books, both new and used, and periodicals, including issues of *Sports Illustrated* going back to 1954. Sports celebrities often drop in for signings. It's closed Sunday and Monday.

Give someone a good meal and make them a gourmet for a day; give someone a good cookbook and make them a gourmet for life. This ought to be the motto of the Cooks Library (Map 10; ☎ 323-655-3141), 8373 W 3rd St near the Beverly Center, a diminutive store stocking every conceivable cookbook ever published, featuring recipes from American apple pie to Zambian zebra steaks. It's open Monday 1 to 5 pm, Tuesday to Saturday 11 am to 6 pm.

New Mastodon Books & Fine Art (Map 10; ☎ 323-525-1948), 5820 Wilshire Blvd, suite 101, in the Miracle Mile District, is operated by the affable and knowledgeable Hans Jürgen Schacht. It specializes in literature, coffee-table books, biographies and other material by German and German-American authors, and has German-language newspapers and magazines. It's open 11 am to 6 pm, Saturday to 5 pm, and closed Sunday and Monday.

Spacious, well-lit and well-organized, Hennessy & Ingalls (☎ 310-458-9074), 1254 Third Street Promenade in Santa Monica, reflects its specialization in interior design, art and architecture. Open daily to 6 pm, it has materials on all the visual arts, including graphic design and landscape architecture.

If it's movie memorabilia, old magazines, posters, scripts and stills you're after, one place to try is Movie World (Map 17; ☎ 818-845-1563) at 212 N San Fernando Blvd in Burbank. The store is crammed to the rafters and is absolutely chaotic, with much material stored in cardboard boxes and metal filing cabinets. Two other excellent sources for this kind of thing are right in the heart of Hollywood: Larry Edmunds Bookshop (Map 9; ☎ 323-463-3273), 6644 Hollywood Blvd, and the Collectors Book Store (Map 9; ☎ 323-467-3296), 1708 N Vine St.

Publications, books, CD-ROMs, posters, maps and other materials published by the US government are for sale at the United States Government Bookstore (Map 5; ☎ 213-239-9844), on the C Level of the ARCO Plaza mall at 505 S Flower St.

Used You'll find many rare and cherished tomes at Book City (Map 9; ☎ 323-466-2525), 6627 Hollywood Blvd, which claims to stock more than 200,000 volumes. It's open to 10 pm Monday to Thursday, to 9 pm Friday and Saturday, to 8 pm Sunday. A second branch, open until 9 pm daily (Map 17; ☎ 818-848-4417), is in Burbank at 308 N San Fernando Blvd, specializing in art, cinema, movie scripts and celebrity autographs.

The mother of all bookstores has to be Acres of Books (Map 15; ☎ 562-437-6980), at 240 Long Beach Blvd in Long Beach. It takes time, patience and a hunter's instinct to unearth gems from this labyrinth. The staff, however, is knowledgeable and friendly and will happily help you find what you need from the densely packed shelves.

If you want a recipe for Waldorf salad from the 1950s, you'll probably find one at Cookbooks (Map 17; ☎ 818-848-4630), 321 N San Fernando Blvd in Burbank. It also has fiction, books on the history of food, and culinary magazines. Cookbooks is open weekdays to 7 pm, Friday and Saturday to 10 pm.

Favored by students, the House of Fiction (☎ 626-449-9861), 663 E Colorado Blvd in Pasadena, is open until 9 pm, Sunday to 5 pm.

Travel Thomas Bros Maps (Map 5; ☎ 213-627-4018), 521 W 6th St, has been Downtown for 28 years and sells some of the most thorough and accurate city maps available. Beneath a huge globe dangling from the 20-foot ceiling are shelves with any city, county, regional, US and world map you can imagine. Bestsellers are the laminated maps you can write on and erase later. Along the back wall is a decent selection of travel books. It's open weekdays only, 9:30 am to 5:30 pm.

Small but excellent is Traveler's Bookcase (Map 10; ☎ 323-655-0575), 8375 W 3rd St near the Beverly Center. Every inch of wallspace in this diminutive store is swathed with guides, dictionaries, fiction, atlases and a decent selection of maps. It's open daily to 6 pm, Sunday to 5 pm.

California Map & Travel (Map 12; ☎ 310-396-6277), 3312 Pico Blvd in Santa Monica, has a stunning assortment of topographical, hiking, biking and driving maps from around the world. Check out its selection of travel books, globes and accessories. Slide shows take place almost weekly. It is open weekdays 8:30 am to 6 pm, Saturday 9 am to 5 pm and Sunday noon to 5 pm.

Distant Lands Bookstore (Map 16; ☎ 626-449-3220), 56 S Raymond Ave in Pasadena, is one of the city's best bookstores for guidebooks and travel-related fiction. Salespeople will bend over backwards to help you, and conveniently there's a Council Travel branch inside. Distant Lands' calendar includes frequent author signings and slide shows. It's open Tuesday to Thursday 10:30 am to 7 pm, Friday and Saturday to 9 pm and Sunday and Monday 11 am to 6 pm.

Two more options are Nations (☎ 310-318-9915), 501 Pier Ave in Hermosa Beach, and Geographia Map & Travel Store (☎ 818-848-1414), 4000 Riverside Drive in Burbank.

Gay & Lesbian See Resources & Information in the Gay & Lesbian Travelers section of Facts for the Visitor.

Sports & Outdoor Equipment

One of the best shops for all-around outdoor needs is REI (Recreational Equipment Incorporated; ☎ 310-538-2429, www.rei.com), which has a warehouse-size inventory at 405 W Torrance Blvd, right where the 110 and 405 Fwys meet. The knowledgeable staff sells everything from wool socks to stoves, and rents tents, skis, stoves, bikes, kayaks and more. Another outfitter, smaller but with a more central Westside location, is Adventure 16 (☎ 310-473-4574) at 11161 W Pico Blvd.

Two good places to buy surfing gear, from wet suits to long boards, are the funky Z-Jay Boarding House (Map 12; ☎ 310-392-5646), 2619 Main St in Santa Monica, and Becker Sport (☎ 310-456-7155), 23755 W Malibu Rd in Malibu.

Surfboard art in Santa Monica

The trademark swoosh of Nike products is everywhere at huge Niketown (Map 11; ☎ 310-275-9998), 9560 Wilshire Blvd, an emporium of sneakers, sweats and sporting equipment in Beverly Hills. You can't miss the 'shoe elevators,' which suck sneakers out of inventory and spit them out to the salespeople. They also have a running club, open to everyone, on Thursday from 6:30 to 8 pm, led by an instructor who can provide tips on improving your speed and endurance.

Beginners and pros head to Roger Dunn Golf Shop, a foursome of megastores stocking every sort of golfing equipment imaginable by such makers as Lynx, Etonic, Armour, Nike and Odyssey. Check out the branches at 4744 Lankershim Blvd in North Hollywood (Map 17; ☎ 818-763-3622) and 9970 Santa Monica Blvd in Century City (☎ 310-556-0914), or call for other locations.

Music

Dedicated listeners are almost obligated to stop by Tower Records (Map 10; ☎ 310-657-7300), 8801 W Sunset Blvd on the Sunset Strip, which claims to be the world's largest music store. Check the Yellow Pages for other branches around the city. A good source for independent labels – including its own, of course – is Rhino Records (Map 11; ☎ 310-474-8685), 1720 Westwood Blvd in west LA. Founded in the early 1970s, Rhino began as a store and then became a label, launching performers such as Phranc and Billy Vera and the Beaters.

More esoteric tunes – especially of the gothic and industrial variety – are in store at Vinyl Fetish (☎ 323-660-4500), 1750 N Vermont Ave in Los Feliz Village. Though it specializes in 33⅓-rpm albums, it also has CDs and a smallish 45-rpm section. Prices are reasonable. There's a second branch (Map 10; ☎ 323-935-1300) at 7305 Melrose Ave. Both are open daily noon to 8 pm.

For used CDs and records, there are few sources better than Rockaway Records (Map 5; ☎ 323-664-3232), 2395 Glendale Blvd. This warehouse-size place is packed with titles, many of them recent releases, usually priced at $7.99. There's even a good selection of classical music, 45s, laser discs, videos and music memorabilia. There's a different sale every Saturday after 7 pm. Hours are 10 am to 9:30 pm daily. Smaller, but still a good source for used CDs, is Penny Lane (Map 16; ☎ 626-564-0161), 16 Colorado Blvd in Old Pasadena. Both stores have similar prices and listening stations, and both will buy CDs. Penny Lane is open daily 10 am to midnight.

Jewelry
LA's historic Jewelry District is Downtown on South Hill St between 6th and 7th Sts. Prices for watches, gold, silver or gemstones are 40 to 70% less than elsewhere in the city. Much of the merchandise sold here, however, comes from the Middle or Far East and is not always the best in terms of quality – buyer beware. Places to try are the St Vincent Jewelry Center (☎ 213-629-2124), 650 S Hill St, or the Fox Jewelry Plaza, 608 S Hill St, each with dozens of outlets.

You're guaranteed superior quality at any of the shops on Rodeo Drive in Beverly Hills, where you can buy upscale and one-of-a-kind baubles. For those of us who failed to triple our income during the '90s, even a pair of tiny diamond stud earrings remains elusive at $4000. Others might actually find something to buy at Tiffany (Map 11; ☎ 310-273-8880), at 210 N Rodeo Drive; Van Cleef & Arpels (Map 11; ☎ 310-276-1161), 300 N Rodeo Drive; or Cartier (Map 11; ☎ 310-275-4272), with two outlets at 220 and 370 Rodeo Drive.

Budgets of all sizes will find something affordable at Maya (Map 10; ☎ 323-655-2708), 7452 Melrose Ave. This eclectic store stocks a huge selection of funky silver jewelry – including toe rings, waist chains and ear curls – sold alongside an equally impressive collection of East Asian masks, African fertility figures and other carved items.

Handmade, classy silver jewelry is for sale at Tantau Smith (Map 12; ☎ 310-392-9878), 1353 Abbot Kinney Blvd in Venice. Nicely displayed in glass vitrines are plenty of imaginative necklaces, rings, bracelets and other adornments, many incorporating semi-precious stones. Cotton clothing, candles, picture frames and other home accessories round out the selection.

Antiques
Major antique venues in the LA area include the Santa Monica Antique Market (Map 12; ☎ 310-314-4899), 1607 Lincoln Blvd, with more than 150 dealers and 20,000 sq feet of display space. The Antique Guild (Map 2; ☎ 310-838-3131), in the former Helms Bakery, 3231 Helms Ave in Culver City, covers 2 acres. Antiquarius (Map 10;

For silver jewelry, check out Maya on Melrose Ave.

☎ 310-274-2363), 8840 Beverly Blvd, features 40 shops near West Hollywood's Pacific Design Center. Off the Wall (Map 10; ☎ 323-930-1185), 7325 Melrose Ave, specializes in 'antiques and weird stuff' (see Melrose Ave in Things to See & Do for more details).

LA's flea and antique markets, held every Sunday in various locales, are other good sources for antiques and collectibles (see the Flea Markets boxed text for details).

Attire

Mainstream The obvious places to look for mainstream clothing are the malls (see Where to Shop, earlier in the chapter). Besides department stores such as Robinsons-May and Macy's, you're likely to find the ubiquitous Gap, Miller's Outpost (good for Levi's), The Limited, Express, Benetton and countless others. Listed here are some of the more interesting independent stores selling wearable young designer fashions and accessories, often at much better prices than those found in the malls.

If you want to wear fashions that won't make it to the malls for a few months, head to Fred Segal (Map 10; ☎ 323-651-4129), 8100 Melrose Ave, the place for mostly wearable cutting-edge fashions. Cameron Diaz, Helen Hunt and a host of other celebrities pop in here from time to time, which should suggest that bargains are rare. A second branch (Map 12; ☎ 310-395-7565) is at 500 Broadway in Santa Monica.

DNA (Map 12; ☎ 310-399-0341), 411 Rose Ave in Venice, is a tiny store run by a group of British women and is jam-packed with quality garb with a stylish European flair.

A long-time favorite is Sacks SFO (Map 10; ☎ 323-939-3993), 652 N La Brea Ave at Melrose, which stocks lots of the current men's and women's fashions – from trendy clubwear to flowery dresses – at 40 to 80% off usual retail prices. There are six more branches in LA, so call this store or check the Yellow Pages for other locations.

For more mature customers, Loehmann's (Map 10; ☎ 310-659-0674), 333 S La Cienega Blvd, has rack after rack of snazzy discounted designer labels, especially dresses, suits, silk blouses and other career gear for

Versace on Rodeo Drive

DAVID PEEVERS

women. There's also a smaller men's section. For beaded gowns, little black dresses and other evening wear, visit the back room.

Designer Designer duds galore can be found anywhere in Beverly Hills, where Chanel, Dior, Armani, Gucci, Hermès, Prada and Tommy Hilfiger are among those holding forth on Rodeo Drive and adjacent streets. Clothes by young designers are found on Melrose Ave, Montana Ave in Santa Monica and on Sunset Plaza, 8589-8720 Sunset Blvd, a strip of exclusive shops.

Celebrity Duds Fancy those pants worn by George Clooney on *ER* or the skimpy evening dress Heather Locklear seduced someone in on *Melrose Place*? Head for It's a Wrap (Map 17; ☎ 818-567-7366), at 3315 W Magnolia Ave in Burbank, where movie and television-set wardrobes – most of them designer labels – that were previously worn by stars are being sold to the public at discounted prices. Tags tell you who wore what when, so you'll know what to brag about.

Another place to try is Star Wares (Map 12; ☎ 310-399-0224), 2817 Main St in Santa Monica, though it's more pricey and deals primarily in collectors' items.

The Sick, the Bizarre & the Twisted

There's no final frontier to your shopping experience in LA. Anything goes, and apparently anything sells, as our list of the more bizarre boutiques in town shows.

Amok/Koma Bookstore (Map 9; ☎ 323-665-0956), 1764 N Vermont Ave. You may not want to visit on a full stomach. Besides various tomes on bomb-building and other subjects dear to a Unabomber's heart, you'll also find books on interrogation, torture and execution techniques, twisted sex practices and taboos of every stripe. Illustrated tomes like *Blood Art* and crime-scene photographs of twisted murders will not be everyone's choice for coffee-table books. But you might get a kick out of some bad literature, courtesy of Nazi bad guy Joseph Goebbels' semi-autobiographical novel, *Michael*. Horrors in used books, records, CDs and videos are for sale as well. It's open daily noon to 8 pm.

Panpipes Magickal Marketplace (Map 9; ☎ 323-462-7078), 1641 Cahuenga Blvd in Hollywood. LA's oldest occult supply shop (since 1961), this place is comfy and ideal for stocking up on your basic powdered lizard, crystal balls ($200), Ouija boards ($24.95) and magical potions (from $3.25). Owner and modern-day alchemist George Hiram Derby, who sports pentagram tattoos and jewelry, is trained in voodoo, pagan crafts and other ritualistic and spiritual fields – even Catholicism. He will mix up more than 6500 wet and 4600 dry metaphysical blends to help you solve problems relating to love, money, sex or whatever you desire. Ingredients, kept in neatly stacked glass vials, can be as common as essential oils and as rare as mummy dust – and you *don't* want to know what the latter costs. Hours are 10 am to 7 pm Monday to Saturday.

Necromance (Map 10; ☎ 323-934-8684), 7220 Melrose Ave. Here you'll find a stock of dog skulls, mounted deer heads and insects – even human finger bones – that make midnight digging obsolete. A mouse in formaldehyde for your mantelpiece? Don't be surprised at the store owner's ghostly makeup and she won't be surprised when you purchase magazines picturing death-row inmates. Hours are noon to 7 pm, Sunday from 1 pm.

Mondo Video a Go-Go (☎ 323-953-8896), 1718 N Vermont Ave in Hollywood. Our pick for weirdest LA emporium is this cluttered video store, operated by a giggly couple right out of the Twilight Zone. Among the most 'normal' selections are music videos by Heino, a blind German singer with platinum wig. Also available are crude videos showing violent neo-Nazis in action, though the Bad Taste award definitely goes to the Lustful Midgets porn section. It's open until about 10 pm.

Skeletons in the Closet (☎ 323-343-0760), 1104 N Mission Rd. This is a gift shop operated by the LA County Coroner's Office. In 1993, someone had the brilliant idea of raising money for the city's Youthful Drunk Driving Program by selling personalized toe-tags. From there the assortment grew to include beach towels, baseball hats, refrigerator magnets and more, adorned with the outlines of dead bodies, plus other fun items like playing cards with skeletal motifs and mugs featuring the department's mascot, Sherlock Bones. It's open weekdays 8 am to 4:30 pm (closed noon to 1 pm).

Vintage Visit Jet Rag (Map 10; ☎ 323-939-0528), 825 N La Brea, just for the unusual window decorations: missiles crashing into the storefront and animal-skeleton mannequins are not exactly everyday adornments. This warehouse-size store has high-quality clothing and accessories. Rare finds for just $1 can be had every Thursday and Sunday, when bales of used clothing are opened and dozens of thrift-loving hipsters descend upon the heaps to forage for treasure. It's open Monday to Saturday 11:30 am to 7:30 pm, Sunday 11 am to 6 pm. The beautifully decorated Golyester (Map 10; ☎ 323-931-1339), 136 S La Brea, has immaculate couture fashions, many from the '30s and '40s, as well as antique textiles, linens, laces and accessories. We once found a perfect pair of harem slippers here.

Melrose Ave also has its fair share of vintage clothing shops. Among the best is Wasteland (Map 10; ☎ 323-653-3028), 7428 Melrose, which has a neat facade and sells both vintage and contemporary fashions as well as furniture and accessories. They buy, sell and trade. At 7474 Melrose is Slow (Map 10; ☎ 323-655-3725), with two floors in an industrial-type warehouse. Most items are in good condition, even those on the $5 sales rack in the back. The sentimental favorite is Aardvark (Map 10; ☎ 323-655-6769) at 7579 Melrose, which we found overpriced; it has a second branch at 85 Market St in Venice.

Pull My Daisy (Map 9; ☎ 323-663-0608), 3908 Sunset Blvd, is crammed with vintage goodies useful for the office or for your next period costume party. In the mix are 1940s pumps, '50s sunglasses and '60s corsets, as are some pretty unusual gift items, including pens that look like syringes.

Western Wear The urban cowboy craze of the '80s may be passé, but a timeless Wild West feel nonetheless survives in California outside the big cities. A visit to King's Western Wear (☎ 818-761-1162), 11450 Ventura Blvd in the San Fernando Valley, will provide you with all the necessary accessories. So get yourself some snakeskin boots, a felt hat and a workman's shirt and head into the sunset, pardner.

For a pair of well-worn cowboy boots made from exotic animals back when it wasn't illegal (we hope), head to Kowboyz (Map 10; ☎ 323-653-6444) at 8050 Beverly Blvd. It's run by Brad Hammond, a former rock & roll manager who turned boots salesman when his collection outgrew his closet space. More than 2000 pairs are crammed onto floor-to-ceiling shelves, and may include several unique – but definitely politically incorrect – varieties, such as hippopotamus, elephant and turtle.

Lingerie & Erotica

On Hollywood Blvd between Schrader and Wilcox Aves is a cluster of semi-naughty stores, where exotic dancers, actors, ladies of the night and the merely adventurous get their nocturnal niceties. Get a kick out of 6-inch-heel, over-the-knee black vinyl boots, glow-in-the-dark platform shoes and oversized pumps for men at the strip's shoe stores. Among the best of these places is Nikki's of Hollywood (Map 9; ☎ 323-461-8208), 6500 Hollywood Blvd.

Nearby is Playmates (Map 9; ☎ 323-464-7636), 6438 Hollywood Blvd, easily recognized by its provocative window displays.

Lace and vinyl at Playmates

This jazzy store stocks everything a girl with lots of imagination might need, including leopard-patterned robes, fluffy feather boas, latex bustiers, tasseled pasties, and lace, satin and – ouch! – vinyl thongs. Check out the basement for deals. For the less professional, there's an excellent selection of decidedly wearable swimwear and lingerie at much better prices than what's sold at the famous Frederick's of Hollywood (Map 9; ☎ 323-466-8506), just west at 6608 Hollywood Blvd.

The Pleasure Chest (Map 10; ☎ 323-650-1022), 7733 Santa Monica Blvd, is a large sexual-hardware store catering to every conceivable fantasy, nice to naughty. Handcuffs, dildos and lubricants are the most mainstream items sold here; our editors wouldn't want us to write about the more exotic 'tools' and other objects on display here.

Dreamdresser (Map 10; ☎ 323-848-3480), 8444 Santa Monica Blvd, is similar, with lots of wearable vinyl and rubber gadgets as well as spiky anythings and very friendly service. Finally, there's Trashy Lingerie (Map 10; ☎ 310-652-4543), at 402 N La Cienega Blvd, which has custom-made corsets and anything else imaginable made from leather, vinyl and lace, made by local artists.

Specialties

Fancy having a hairdo à la Marilyn? Looking for angel wings? Or how about some werewolf hands? Hollywood Toys & Costumes (Map 9; ☎ 323-464-4444), 6600 Hollywood Blvd, has been in business since 1950 and has a huge assortment of costumes, wigs, feathers, hats and other accessories to fulfill any fantasy. Right by the entrance is a sunken monster pit covered with glass and flanked by rows of campy masks. Giant

plastic spiders can be had for less than $5, and those wigs – from realistic brunette to crazed pink – start at $40.

Women tired of the same old hairdo, but short on time and money for a foray to the hair salon, will love Flora Designs (Map 11; ☎ 310-888-7778), 312 N Beverly Drive. The small store in Beverly Hills is crammed with hair accessories, many of them handmade. The Persian store owner is only too happy to demonstrate his own creations.

Books on werewolves, mermaid cocktail sticks and inflatable plastic chairs make great birthday gifts – for someone. These and many more novelties bordering on the absurd are what's in store at the appropriately named Wacko (Map 9; ☎ 323-663-0122), 4633 Hollywood Blvd in Silver Lake. Pretend you came here for the art in the integrated La Luz de Jesus gallery (☎ 323-666-7667), and then go delve into this goofy universe of weirdness and bad taste.

The hearts of serious train aficionados will skip a beat when entering Allied Model Trains (☎ 310-313-9353), 4411 S Sepulveda Blvd in Culver City, a gargantuan repository of any make, model and choo-choo accessory coveted by collectors and hobbyists. Everyone else will delight at the many scale-model landscapes, which include a Bavarian village and an Old West town, navigated by fleets of buzzing miniature trains.

In the day and age of chain video superstores, Eddie Brandt's Saturday Matinee (Map 17; ☎ 818-506-7722), 5006 Vineland Ave in North Hollywood, is a survivor, largely because of its incredibly 'eclectic' selection: From samurai sex movies to episodes of *Ozzie & Harriet* and *Fawlty Towers*, you'll find it here.

Excursions

In the previous chapters, we focused on LA County, but there are many points of interest just a short hop from Los Angeles. This chapter covers Southern California's major theme parks, followed by some popular overnight destinations, including Santa Catalina Island and Santa Barbara. For more getaways close to LA, check out Lonely Planet's *California & Nevada*.

DISNEYLAND

For first-time visitors to LA, the *de rigeur* trip to Disneyland (☎ 714-781-4565, 213-626-8605 ext 4565, www.disneyland.com) is as important as visiting the Eiffel Tower in Paris. And, probably, much more fun.

When Walt Disney trotted out his famous mouse in 1928, it was the beginning of a commercial bonanza that's been relentlessly refined ever since. Fueled by the dreams of children worldwide, Disney has become a legend of corporate success – and excess – in virtually every field it has entered: movies, TV, publishing, music and merchandise. You'll see many of Disney's classic visions reflected here. But, after a day in the 'happiest place on earth' – braving crowds, standing in long lines in the stinging Southland sun, and trying to ignore the feeling that you're being manipulated (and you are) – you may well flee back to your hotel room, pour yourself a beer and watch the sun set, feeling the desperate need for reality.

So what remains of the charming dream that originally launched Disneyland in 1955? The twofold answer is very much, and very little. The original Disneyland was successful because it understood its purpose well: Cater to the imagination of kids, and the parents will foot the bill. But over the years, children have become more adult while adults have become more childlike. Disney has adapted completely. The gentle rides of yore have given way to spectacular thrills catering to over-stimulated children with cyberspace expectations. And, the parents don't come

along just to hold their tots by the hand. They scream right along with them.

Some charm remains in Disneyland – the 'Pirates of the Caribbean,' the 'Haunted House' and the perennial favorite of the under-3-feet-tall set, 'It's a Small World.' But you'd better be prepared for some major manhandling and manipulation. The shiny, happy 'cast members' grin to the point of rictus. There are few places to sit down other than in a restaurant. And during the summer months, the park is jammed, and the waiting lines – up to three hours for some rides – will eventually take their toll on all but the hopelessly good-natured.

Of course, Disney doesn't want you to do so, but you can save time and money by sneaking in your own sandwiches and drinks. The best advice we can give is to pace yourself and don't push to the point of exhaustion and family feuds. Hey – you're in Disneyland! So make the most of it.

Orientation

You enter Disneyland on **Main Street USA**, a cheery re-creation of small-town America circa 1900, with myriad shops such as the Candy Emporium. Resist the temptation to buy overpriced peanuts, but stop to have your picture taken with Mickey and Minnie, or any of the other Disney characters that usually hang around here. Plunge on into the seven Disney 'lands' centered around 'Sleeping Beauty's Castle,' which was inspired by Germany's Neuschwanstein palace.

Main Street ends in the Central Plaza. Immediately on your right is **Tomorrowland**, the high-tech showpiece of the park, where lines tend to be longest. On the 'Star Tours' ride, you're clamped into a 'StarSpeeder' vehicle, piloted by a dysfunctional android, for a wild and bumpy ride through deep space. 'Space Mountain' hurtles you into complete darkness at frightening speed, and you *will* scream long and loud. It's hard to recommend this one for anyone under 12.

And the latest ride in this Wagnerian paean to space travel is the journey to 'Imagination and Beyond' on the new Rocket Rods XPR. You blast off on a four-minute breakneck journey, making it the longest and fastest of all the Disney rides. We didn't try this one because of the 2½-hour line on the day of our visit, but those disembarking reported happiness, of all things. 'Honey, I Shrunk the Audience' was also drawing huge crowds, all anticipating the experience of becoming subminiature and being threatened by insects.

Our personal favorite section is **Adventureland**, to the left of Central Plaza. The highlight is the 'Indiana Jones Adventure,' definitely a not-to-be-missed jungle hoot. While you're waiting in line, you'll pass by a jungle office filled with ancient tomes, a vintage radio and exotic treasures that will have you smelling Harrison Ford in the air; such is the genius of Disney designers. Enormous Humvee-type vehicles lurch off for encounters with pyrotechnic, near-death experiences in re-creations of themes and stunts from the Indiana Jones movie trilogy.

Little ones will love climbing the stairways of the nearby 'Swiss Family Treehouse' and imagining what arboreal life would be like. Also here is the 'Jungle Cruise,' a mellow expedition through tropical rainforests, featuring encounters with roaring hippopotami and jungle denizens.

Just beyond is **New Orleans Square**, where charming offerings include the 'Haunted House.' Here, you will be beguiled by the hokey 'Vincent Price School of Horror' frights and sights. It's low-tech but creepy, and some of the phantasms and sounds will stay in your mind. Also here is the subterranean cruise through the tawdry land of 'Pirates of the Caribbean.' Sail past buccaneers' skeletons perched atop their mounds of booty and hilariously made-up pirates who loot, plunder and pillage while the villages burn. It's great stuff, created from the imagination that built the Disney myth.

Next up, **Frontierland** harkens back to the rip-roarin' Old West, when cowboys made their own kind of law and order. This is a fairly low-key area of the park, and even small children will emerge unshaken after a ride on the 'Big Thunder Mountain Railroad' roller coaster. Another family favorite here is a churning trip up-river on the 'Mark Twain Riverboat,' a realistic stern-wheeler.

In the park's center, **Fantasyland** can be approached through Sleeping Beauty's Castle. It's filled with the characters and experiences of classic children's stories. Here you'll find Dumbo the Elephant, Peter Pan and some quaint rides straight out of *Alice in Wonderland*. The amazing 'It's a Small World' ride floats past hundreds of animatronic children representing the world's cultures, brought together by the Disney theme song. Children are enthralled by this musical voyage, but be warned: Days after you've finished picking Disney popcorn out of your teeth, this song will still be batting around in your head. (The only sure antidote is listening to the entire collection of Led Zeppelin.) Another classic ride is the 'Matterhorn Bobsled,' a roller coaster that's certainly gentle by today's standards but fun nonetheless.

At the northern section of the park is **Mickey's Toon Town**, another favorite with the elementary-school set. This is where Mickey and Minnie make their home (separate ones, of course – this *is* Disney), Donald keeps his boat, Goofy has a 'Bounce House,' Chip 'n Dale have a 'Treehouse' and Roger Rabbit invites you to a 'Car Toon Spin.'

Information

Opening hours for Disneyland are highly arbitrary and depend on the marketing department's projected attendance numbers. In the off-season, you might expect the park to be open 10 am to 8 pm Monday to Thursday, to 10 pm Friday, to midnight Saturday, to 9 pm Sunday. During summer, weekday hours are often 8 am to 10 pm, to 10 pm or midnight on weekends.

One-, two- and three-day passes to the park cost $38/68/95 for adults and $28/51/75 for children. Parking is $8. There's a baby-care center, currency-exchange stations, banks and a kennel for your pet. Four-hour guided tours are offered for $52/40, which includes admission.

Lines are the longest during summer and around major holidays. In general, visiting midweek is better than Friday, Saturday or Sunday, and arriving early in the day is best. Also keep in mind that many rides have minimum age and height requirements, so avoid tantrums by preparing the kids.

Places to Stay

Although Anaheim gets the biggest chunk of its business from Disneyland tourism, it is also a popular year-round convention destination, and room rates shift accordingly.

The clean and friendly HI *Fullerton Hacienda Hostel* (☎ 714-738-3721, fax 714-738-0925), 1700 N Harbor Blvd, is the cheapest lodging option, with 20 beds in three dorms costing $11 to $13 each. Bus No 47 runs to the hostel from the Greyhound station; from the Anaheim Amtrak station, take bus No 41. Bus No 43A to/from Disneyland stops out front.

Cheap hotels that are within walking distance of Disneyland include the *Samoa Motel* (☎ 714-776-2815), 425 W Katella, which has island decor and ancient but large rooms costing $30 to $40. The *Village Inn Motel* (☎ 714-774-2460), 1750 S Harbor Blvd, has similar prices.

The area surrounding Disneyland teems with reasonably priced accommodations; all the major chains (Motel 6, Travelodge, Econo Lodge, etc) are represented. Rooms here are reliably clean, have basic amenities and cost $60 or less, sometimes even with continental breakfast. Most offer shuttle service to Disneyland. Prices may be slightly higher between May and October.

Those willing and able to spend slightly more should check out the *Castle Inn & Suites* (☎ 714-774-8111, 800-227-8530, fax 714-956-4736), 1734 S Harbor Blvd, which has a pool, spa, free parking and rooms from $60 to 90. Another good bet with similar prices is the *Candy Cane Inn* (☎ 714-774-5284, 800-345-7057, fax 714-772-5462), across the street at 1747 S Harbor Blvd.

The *Disneyland Hotel* (☎ 714-778-6600, fax 714-956-6597), at 1150 W Cerritos Ave, and the nearby *Disneyland Pacific Hotel* (☎ 714-999-0990, fax 714-776-5763), 1717 S West St, are connected to the park by monorail. On some days, hotel guests get to enter the park 1½ hours before the general public. One-night stays cost $175 to $275, though multiple-night packages might save some money (call ☎ 800-523-9000).

A dependable giant both in reputation and size (1580 rooms) is the recently renovated *Anaheim Hilton & Towers* (☎ 714-750-4321, fax 714-740-4460), 777 Convention Way, where the rooms cost from $165/185 singles/doubles.

Places to Eat

Within Disneyland, the nicest restaurant is the *Blue Bayou* (next to the 'Pirates of the Caribbean'), which specializes in good fried chicken and sandwiches that don't cost an arm and a leg. The healthiest and spiciest meals – grilled chicken, marinated steak and skewered vegetables (mostly around $5) – are at the *Bengal Barbecue* in Adventureland. Otherwise, you'll find mostly burgers, fries, ice cream and buckets of popcorn.

Outside the park, pickings are slim when it comes to anything other than hotel or chain restaurants. *Tony Roma* (☎ 714-520-0200), at 1640 S Harbor Blvd, has good ribs, chicken, beans and onion rings, plus large salads and desserts; lunch is mostly under $10, dinner under $20. *IHOP* (☎ 714-635-0933), 1560 S Harbor Blvd, is open 24 hours and has a good kids' menu plus the usual hash-house staples. Inside the Disneyland Pacific Hotel, the *PCH Grill* (☎ 714-999-0990) serves California eclectic cuisine and makes an artful presentation of its food, although it's rather pricey. *Hop City Steakhouse* (☎ 714-978-3700), 1939 S State College Blvd, serves angus steaks from $15 and offers fine, live blues most nights.

Getting There & Away

Disneyland is located at 1313 Harbor Blvd in Anaheim, about 50 miles south of Downtown LA. Take the Disneyland exit off I-5 and follow the copious signs.

The Greyhound bus station (☎ 714-999-1246) is at 100 W Winston Rd. Buses to/from LA depart several times daily and cost $8 one way. The Airport Bus (☎ 800-772-5299) runs between LAX and Anaheim hotels every half hour; tickets are $14, $22 roundtrip.

All San Diego-bound Amtrak trains stop at Anaheim's Amtrak station on the grounds of the Edison International Field of Anaheim Stadium. A one-way ticket from LA's Union Station is $7.

Another alternative is booking yourself on a tour (see Organized Tours in the Facts for the Visitor chapter).

KNOTT'S BERRY FARM

Just 4 miles northwest of Disneyland, off the I-5, Knott's Berry Farm (☎ 714-220-5200) is often overlooked and is therefore much less crowded. It's a kinder, gentler place, and the crush and desperation of Disneyland is noticeably lacking. In fact, many Southern Californians prefer a voyage to Knott's over subjecting themselves to Mouse-mania.

The park opened in 1932, when Mr Knott's boysenberries (a blackberry-raspberry hybrid) and Mrs Knott's fried-chicken dinners attracted crowds of local farm hands. Mr Knott built an imitation ghost town to keep them entertained, eventually hiring local carnival rides and charging admission. Mrs Knott kept frying the chicken, but the rides and Old West buildings became the main attraction.

The park continues its Old West theme with staged gun fights, gold-panning demonstrations and steam-train rides. Knott's also acknowledges pre-gold-rush history with Aztec dancers and a California Missions exhibit – there's even mariachi music in Fiesta Village.

Roller coaster highlights include 'Montezuma's Revenge,' which makes a loop as high as a three-story building and then does it again backwards; the 'Corkscrew,' which has a triple upside-down loop; and the six-loop 'Boomerang.' The newest scream on the block is the 'Windjammer,' a tandem-style roller coaster race where you perform side-by-side vertical loops and six-story drops that have even the most macho screaming.

'GhostRider' recently debuted as one of the longest wooden coasters anywhere and takes passengers on a 4530-foot track – 118 feet tall at its highest point – dropping you 108 feet with a G-force of 3.14. 'Supreme Scream' lets you fall 254 feet at 50 mph with a G-force of 4, bouncing back upward with a G-force of -1.5 – all in about 45 seconds.

For a slightly tamer adventure, 'Big Foot Rapids' sloshes down a faux whitewater river, leaving you absolutely soaked. 'Camp Snoopy' is a kiddy wonderland. (Peanuts characters – Snoopy, Charlie Brown, Lucy, Linus – are the park's equivalent to Mickey Mouse and Donald Duck.)

If you pace your day, you might have enough energy left to enjoy the Edison International Electric Nights multimedia/laser/pyrotechnics show. It is accompanied by wild water effects, and the 'ooohs' and 'aaahs' are justified by this high-tech but old-timey show.

Throughout the month of October, Knott's hosts what is possibly Southern California's best and scariest Halloween party. Professional performers in costume haunt the park, special rides and attractions are put up for the occasion, and lights around the park are dimmed or turned off.

Information

The park is open daily except Christmas. Hours are 9 am to midnight from late May to September; the rest of the year hours are 10 am to 6 pm weekdays, to 10 pm Saturday, to 7 pm Sunday. Admission is $36, $26 for children and seniors over 60. After 4 pm, admission plummets to $16.95 for all. Parking is $7.

Getting There & Away

Knott's Berry Farm is at 8039 Beach Blvd, south of I-5 and the 91 Fwy in the city of

Spinning sombreros at Knott's Berry Farm

JIM CORWIN

Buena Park, about 40 miles south of Downtown LA. Take the Beach Blvd exit from the I-5, 91, 22 or 405 Fwys. Amtrak's Fullerton Station (☎ 714-992-0530), on the LA-San Diego route, is connected to the park by bus No 99 ($1). MTA bus No 460 connects the park to Downtown LA.

SIX FLAGS MAGIC MOUNTAIN

For roller coaster lovers and thrill freaks, no other California theme park compares to Six Flags Magic Mountain (☎ 805-255-4111, 818-367-5965), 26101 Magic Mountain Pkwy in Valencia, about 30 miles north of Downtown LA. Velocity is king here, which is why you'll have to deal with so many roving, raucous, hormone-crazed teens, though they're normally just a minor irritation. (But should they get unruly, rest assured that security in this 'Time-Warner Entertainment Company' is quite capable, thank you, of calming the kids down.)

You can go up, down, fast and inside out in more ways at Magic Mountain than anywhere else this side of the Challenger Space Shuttle. There are 11 coasters among more than 100 rides, shows and attractions in the 260-acre park. The latest addition is 'Riddler's Revenge,' purportedly the world's tallest and fastest stand-up roller coaster, which hurtles you along at 65 mph through vertical loops, barrel rolls and a drop of 146 feet. Somewhere in all this, you'll experience a G-force of 4.2, close to the point where combat pilots begin to black out.

'Batman: The Ride' serves up high-speed loops and corkscrews with a 0-gravity spin. 'Superman: The Escape' blasts you from 0 to 100 mph in seven seconds and then gives you 6½ seconds of weightlessness while you fall back to earth. 'Flashback' has six spiral hairpin drops, and 'Viper' falls 188 feet into a double-boomerang turn that puts you upside down, which can be most unpleasant if you're not ready for it. 'Colossus' takes you along nearly 2 miles of track in classic wooden-coaster tradition.

Other rides include 'Tidal Wave,' where you boat over a 50-foot waterfall. Purists will want to pay homage to 'Revolution,' the first 360-degree looping steel roller coaster ever

made. Tamer activities include a 1912 carousel, a Western stage and stunt show, and Bugs Bunny World for the toddlers.

Information

Magic Mountain is open daily from early May to mid-September at 10 am, only weekends and holidays the rest of the year (closed Christmas). Closing hours vary. Admission includes all rides and attractions, and is $36, $20 for seniors over 55, $18 for children (under 4 feet tall), free for children under two. Parking is $7.

Getting There & Away

From Downtown LA, take I-5 north about 30 miles and exit at Magic Mountain Pkwy. Getting here by public transport is cumbersome but not impossible. From Downtown LA, take the Metrolink train to the Santa Clarita station, then catch bus No 10 or 20 (every half hour) to the park. Organized tours are also widely available through LA-area hotels.

HURRICANE HARBOR

Hurricane Harbor (☎ 805-255-4527, 818-367-5965), also off Magic Mountain Parkway, is a tropical-jungle-theme water park adjacent to Six Flags Magic Mountain. It gives children large and small the chance to frolic all day and get soaking wet. The park includes 22 slides splashing into awaiting pools, such as 'Black Snake Summit,' a 75-foot speed slide; 'Bamboo Racer,' where you go down head first on one of six racing slides; and 'Lizard Lagoon,' which has speed slides plus water basketball and volleyball. There are also fanciful lagoons and wave pools. A note of caution: The sunlight in Southern California is fierce and *anyone* planning to romp outdoors should wear heavy sunscreen.

The park opens at 10 am daily between May 30 to September 7 and weekends only between May 16 and 25 and September 12 and 27. Closing hours vary. Admission is $19, $12 for children under 4 feet and seniors, free for kids under two. There is a special two-park deal of $50 for both Magic Mountain and Hurricane Harbor, but it's almost impossible to do both in a single day.

Air Combat USA: The Ultimate Thrill Ride

Plunk down $795 and get ready for a life-changing experience. You'll drive to the Air Combat USA (☎ 800-522-7590) offices at Fullerton airport, about 30 miles southeast of Downtown LA, and meet with some of the top military pilots in the world. One of them will be your classroom instructor and another will be your copilot in a high-performance Marchetti aircraft, outfitted with an infrared video 'machine gun.' After a morning theory session, *you* will fly off, alongside an opponent in another plane, for your first experience of air combat. And you had best believe it's the real thing: Nothing on the ground will ever prepare you for what's about to happen in the sky.

You'll fly your aircraft to a 'combat' area over the Pacific Ocean and engage in a series of six dogfights, where you'll try to get the upper hand on your opponent, the 'bandit': Line him up in your gunsights and shoot him out of the sky. You will fly at 250 mph and experience vertical climbs, dives, snap rolls and loops. You will fly your aircraft upside down – the world spinning around your head – and roar like an animal when the G-forces threaten to tear off your helmet. You will curse when a plume of smoke pours from beneath your fuselage (meaning you've been killed) and shout for joy when you've got that other sucker in the cross-hairs of your gunsights. And it'll all be there for you to view on the video that was made of your entire flight, complete with all the grunts, groans and victory screams.

Bungee jumping, whitewater river rafting, high-speed racecar driving – forget 'em! There is no on-the-edge experience that remotely compares with this; that is, until you try the same thing in an F-16.

David Peevers

MALIBU SPEED ZONE

Despite the name, this amusement park (☎ 888-662-5428) is a long way from Malibu, at 17871 Castleton St in the City of Industry, in the eastern San Gabriel Valley. Take the 60 Fwy east from Downtown and exit at Azusa to check out this very-LA concept in entertainment.

Geared primarily toward adults, this theme park offers competitive speed auto racing in scaled-down speed demons reaching a maximum of 70 mph. Get in the driver's seat and go wheel to wheel with up to 28 other drivers at a time. There are four classes of racing vehicles, including 300hp dragsters and Indy cars.

Normal hours for adults over 18 (those 18 and under are asked to leave at 9 pm) are 11 am to midnight Sunday to Thursday, until 2 am Friday and Saturday, though it's best to confirm ahead. There is no admission, but each attraction has a separate fee, from $3 per lap in the 'Indy 500' to $10 for 'slick track' road-style racing. Miniature golf, video games and a sports bar round out the list of attractions. You must have a valid driver's license and be over 5 feet tall for some vehicle classes, but anyone can race on the turbo track and some other raceways.

GLEN IVY HOT SPRINGS

At the foot of the Santa Ana Mountains, about an hour and a half southeast of Los Angeles, is this lovely bathing complex with 15 pools and spas filled with naturally heated mineral water. It's all surrounded by 10 acres of landscaped grounds profuse with bougainvillea, eucalyptus and palm trees. Spend a relaxing day wallowing in the hot pools, take an aqua aerobics class, treat yourself to a massage, or swim some laps in a larger swimming pool.

The best part here, though, is the red-clay mud pool. Like some prehistoric animal wandering into the tar pits, you first soak yourself in muck. Then, apply what amounts to a full-body mask by grabbing a chunk of clay and smearing it all over your body before lounging in the sun until it's baked into your skin. Whether this treatment truly has therapeutic effects is debatable, but it's certainly fun. Bring an old swim suit, though, as the clay does stain a little.

The spa is located at 25000 Glen Ivy Rd in Corona and is open daily 10 am to 6 pm from March 1 to October 31, to 5 pm the rest of the year. Admission is $19.50 Monday to Thursday and $25 on weekends. Children under two get in free. From LA, take the 10 Fwy east to the 15 Fwy south; exit at Temescal

Tricky Dick & Gipper Libraries

Within easy reach from LA are two of the country's presidential libraries, honoring the lives of Richard Nixon and Ronald Reagan. No matter what your political leanings, you're likely to find these libraries surprisingly fascinating.

Visit the **Richard Nixon Library & Birthplace** (☎ 714-993-3393), 18001 Yorba Linda Blvd in Yorba Linda, Orange County. You can watch a film called *Never Give Up: Richard Nixon in the Arena*, listen to carefully edited White House tapes from the Watergate era, see the pistol given to Nixon by Elvis Presley and view the telephone used to communicate with Apollo 11 astronauts on the moon. There's also a re-creation of the Lincoln Sitting Room, Nixon's favorite White House room. The museum's brochure emphasizes that this is the only presidential library built without using taxpayers' money – at a cost of $21 million. Don't miss the gift shop. Hours are 10 am to 5 pm daily (Sunday from 11 am). Admission is $5.95, $3.95 for seniors over 62, $2 for children ages eight to 11, free to children under eight. To get there, take I-5 south to the 91 Fwy; head east on 91, then north on the 57 Fwy, and then exit east on Yorba Linda Blvd and continue straight to the museum.

The **Ronald Reagan Presidential Library & Museum** (☎ 800-410-8354), 40 Presidential Drive, is in Simi Valley in Ventura County and contains books and interactive computers where you can study the 'Reagan Revolution.' You can follow Reagan's career from his early days in radio and acting to his stints as president of the Screen Actors Guild and Governor of California. The museum features a re-creation of the White House's Oval Office and the Cabinet Room, Reagan family memorabilia, gifts from heads of state and an actual (disarmed) nuclear cruise missile. Reflecting Reagan's passion during the Cold War is a graffiti-covered slice of the Berlin Wall. The museum is open daily (except major holidays) 10 am to 5 pm. Admission is $4, $2 for seniors, free for children under 16. To get there, take the 405 Fwy north to the 118 Fwy west; exit at Madera Rd South, turn right on Madera and continue straight for 3 miles to Presidential Drive.

Canyon Rd, turn right and drive 1 mile to Glen Ivy Rd, turn right and go to the end.

SANTA CATALINA ISLAND

Santa Catalina – called Catalina locally – is one of the largest of the Channel Islands, a chain of semi-submerged mountains that rise from the floor of the Pacific between Santa Barbara and San Diego. It's a 'deer park' for the privileged and protected, to be sure. But it's also, literally, a breath of fresh air for impacted Angelenos. We know a medical student who rented a room there – far from pagers – to study for exams, and a screen-writer whose writer's block dissolved after a week in Avalon, the island's only town.

'Discovered' by Juan Rodriguez Cabrillo in 1542, the island was relatively untouched until 1811, when the native seafaring Indians were tragically resettled on the mainland. Most of the island has since been privately owned. Catalina was purchased in 1919 by chewing-gum magnate William Wrigley Jr (1861-1932), who built a mansion and a casino. He also briefly made Catalina the spring training headquarters for his major-league baseball team, the Chicago Cubs.

Even after the Mediterranean-flavored port town of Avalon began attracting tourists in the 1930s, Catalina's interior and most of its coastline remained largely undeveloped. In conjunction with LA County, the non-profit Santa Catalina Island Conservancy (☎ 310-510-1421) was able to buy 86% of the 8-x-21-mile island from the Wrigley family in 1975, assuring its preservation free of future development.

The island has a unique ecosystem, with 400 plant species, including eight endemic ones, more than 100 types of birds, and numerous animals such as deer, goats, boar and foxes. There are also several hundred wild American bison descended from those brought to Catalina in 1925 for the filming of Zane Grey's *The Vanishing American*.

Catalina's main tourist season is June to September, when prices are steepest, especially on weekends. Rates plunge for mid-week travel and during the off-season, though some activities may not be available during those times.

Avalon's Green Pier on Santa Catalina Island

DAVID PEEVERS

Avalon

Most of Catalina's 3000 permanent residents (the population quadruples during the summer tourist season) live in tiny Avalon, on the southeast shore. Most hotels and shops are lined up along the shorefront, Crescent Ave, and its side streets. The Catalina Visitors Bureau (☎ 310-510-1520, www.catalina.com) has a booth – open daily – on the central pleasure pier, known as Green Pier, with maps, brochures and tour information.

Avalon, whose name comes from Arthurian legend, is a quintessential seaside resort town with a sweep of small hotels and restaurants facing Avalon Bay. Catalina's most noticeable landmark is the white, circular, Spanish Moderne-style Casino (☎ 310-510-2500), 1 Casino Way, built for Wrigley in 1929. This is no gambling joint: The top-floor grand ballroom once featured dancing to the big-band tunes of Benny Goodman, Glenn Miller and other such legends; beneath is a gorgeous 1184-seat Art Deco theater with an organ and murals of underwater scenes.

Visit during nightly first-run movie screenings, or join a 40-minute tour ($8.50). Also here is the Catalina Island Museum (☎ 310-510-2414), which explores 7000 years of island history (open daily 10:30 am to 4 pm; $1.50 admission).

The Wrigley Memorial and Botanical Garden (☎ 310-510-2288), 1400 Avalon Canyon Rd, is about 1½ miles inland from Avalon Bay. A spiral staircase climbs the 130-foot tower of the memorial, built in 1934 of blue flagstone and decorative glazed tile to honor Wrigley. Surrounding it is the 38-acre garden with its impressive cacti groves, succulents and samples of the eight Catalina endemic species. The best time to visit is during wildflower season around February and March. It's open daily 8 am to 5 pm; admission is $1.

Two Harbors

Besides Avalon, the only development on Santa Catalina is Two Harbors, which occupies an isthmus near the island's northeastern end. There's a beachfront campground, picnic area, dive shop, general store, restaurant and saloon, and the hilltop *Banning House Lodge* (☎ 310-510-0244), an 11-room B&B dating from 1910. In the summer, you can reach this remote and pretty area by Coastal Shuttle boat from Avalon ($13, 45 minutes) and directly from San Pedro ($36, 90 minutes). It's also served by the Safari Shuttle Bus (see Getting Around).

Activities

Tours The easiest way to see Catalina is on an organized tour, offered by several operators including Santa Catalina Discovery Tours (☎ 310-510-8687) and Catalina Adventure Tours (☎ 310-510-2888). Options include exploration of the protected island interior (from $17) and of Catalina's rich underwater gardens aboard a glass-bottom boat ($9). There are also scenic tours of Avalon, harbor cruises and night cruises. Jeep Eco-Tours (☎ 310-510-2595 ext 0) offers two-hour journeys on the island's back roads for $65.

Water Sports Those with a love of water sports – above and below sea level – will find plenty to do on Catalina. Most outfitters have

set up shop on Avalon's Green Pier, where you can gather information, rent equipment and book tours.

Swimmers can take to the water from the small beach next to the pier, though a better option is the club-like Descanso Beach just beyond the Casino. It's privately owned, and there's a $1.50 admission, but it's also one of the few US beaches where alcohol is allowed.

Snorkelers should head to Lovers' Cove, on the southeastern end of Avalon Bay, which is hard to beat for sheer wildlife density and variety. Highlights include the sunset-colored, luminescent garibaldi (the official California state fish) and the occasional horn or leopard shark. Snorkeling gear is available for rent for $5 to $7/hour or $10 to $12/day from a number of outfitters set up at the cove and also on the pier. Scuba divers will want to head to the spectacular Underwater Park, right at the Casino. California Divers Supply (☎ 310-510-0330) rents equipment and operates guided dive tours from $65, including all gear.

All you need is a sense of adventure and a fat wallet to feel like you are in a Beatles' song – aboard a yellow submarine in an octopus' garden. You and one other person will

DAVID PEEVERS

Cruise underwater in a bubble sub.

be seated in a Plexiglas-bubble sub attached to a lemon-colored 'sleigh,' navigated by a diver who also acts as a guide. During the 30-minute tour ($200), the guide points out the amazing diversity of underwater life – moray eels to barracudas to garibaldi – via two-way radio. You may even get to pilot the submarine yourself. For more information, call ☎ 877-232-6262.

Kayak rentals (no experience necessary) are available from Descanso Beach Ocean Sports (☎ 310-510-1226) at Descanso Beach. Single kayaks cost $10/hour; double kayaks are $18/hour. Guided tours start at $34. Joe's Rent-A-Boat on the Green Pier (☎ 310-510-0455) rents kayaks as well as small boats, a good way to get away from Avalon and discover the secluded beaches hidden along the rugged coastline. Rates start at $25/hour for a 14-foot utility boat, also good for fishing excursions.

Places to Stay

Camp in Avalon at **Hermit Gulch Campground** (☎ 310-510-8368), in beautiful Avalon Canyon. Bring your own tent and you pay $7.50 per person per night. Those without either a tent or camping equipment can rent it all here. Rates start at $10 for a two-person tent; actual teepees cost $20. It's a 1½-mile hike or a ride aboard the Island Hopper bus (see Getting Around) to get to the campground from Avalon. For information on campgrounds in the island's rugged interior, call ☎ 888-510-7979 or check the website www.catalina.com/twoharbors/.

Hostel La Vista (☎ 310-510-0603), at 145 Marilla Ave, is a privately run affair offering bare-bones accommodations at $15 a head between June and October.

Catalina's hotels depend heavily on summer business, and rates vary widely between seasons. In general, rates go up during weekends year-round, and there's often a two-night minimum stay.

One of the best values, **Hermosa Hotel** (☎ 310-510-1010, 888-592-1313), 131 Metropole St, has cottages costing just $30 in winter and up to $85 in peak season. Family-style accommodations are what you'll find at the contemporary **Seaport Village Inn**

(☎ 310-510-0344, 800-222-8254). Be sure to get a room with a view of the bay, priced between $100 and $150.

Among Catalina's B&Bs, the **Old Turner Inn** (☎ 310-510-2236) is one of the nicest, with rooms between $90 and $150. For a real retreat, hole up at the 1929 **Zane Grey Pueblo Hotel** (☎ 310-510-0966), 199 Chimes Tower Rd. A quiet 17-room inn, the Zane Grey was formerly the pueblo adobe home of its namesake, the prolific American Western writer. Rooms have no phones and cost $75 to $145 during peak season and $65 to $90 at other times.

Top of the line is the stuffily stylish and luxurious **Inn on Mt Ada** (☎ 310-510-2030), 398 Wrigley Rd, in the historic Wrigley mansion, with superb views of the bay. Its six rooms are priced at $250 to $505 in winter and $350 to $630 in summer. Rates include three meals daily and a golf cart, the main means of getting around on this largely car-free island.

Places to Eat

In keeping with its upscale accommodations, Avalon's restaurants are similarly pricey. Good restaurants along waterfront Crescent Ave include **Ristorante Villa Portofino** (☎ 310-510-0508) for top-end Italian; **The Channel House** (☎ 310-510-1617) for upscale seafood and continental cuisine; **Cafe Prego** for pasta; and the **Blue Parrot** for casual fare like salads and burgers. **Topless Tacos** has inexpensive Mexican food.

Huge and satisfying breakfasts are served at the slightly eccentric **Pancake Cottage**, just off Crescent Ave at 118 Catalina St. A bit off the beaten path is the **Casino Dock Cafe**, en route to the Casino, a good place for simple fare and drinks.

Getting There & Away

Cruise boats headed for Avalon depart regularly from Long Beach (Catalina Express Port at the Queen Mary) and San Pedro (Catalina Sea & Air Terminal, Berth 95) as well as from Redondo Beach and Newport Beach (Orange County).

The fastest are operated by Catalina Channel Express (☎ 310-519-1212), from

Long Beach and San Pedro, and Catalina Flyer (☎ 714-673-5245) with daily departures from Newport Beach (both cost $36 round-trip and take 75 minutes). Cheaper is Catalina Cruises (☎ 800-228-2546) with 1¾-hour service for $25 roundtrip, from Long Beach, San Pedro and Redondo Beach. Fifteen-minute helicopter rides aboard Island Express (☎ 310-510-2525) from San Pedro and Long Beach cost $66/121 one way/roundtrip.

Getting Around

Only 10-year Catalina residents are allowed to have cars on the island. Bicycles and golf carts can be rented for travel around Avalon, but if you plan on going beyond the square-mile city limits, you'll need to buy a $50 permit (ask at the visitors bureau). The Island Hopper bus provides public transportation around Avalon for $1 per ride. For trips into the interior, including the airport, Little Harbor, Two Harbors and the Hermit Gulch Campground, take the Safari Shuttle Bus. In summer, the Coastal Shuttle boat operates between Avalon and Two Harbors ($13, 45 minutes).

LAGUNA BEACH

Laguna Beach is proof that there's more to Orange County than Disneyland and shopping at the giant South Coast Plaza and Fashion Island malls. About 60 miles south of Los Angeles, this gorgeous Riviera-like stretch of seaside is defined by secluded beaches, low cliffs, glassy waves, waterfront parks, eucalyptus-covered hillsides and a host of art galleries and boutiques. Home to several renowned arts festivals (see the related boxed text), as well as the highly regarded Laguna Playhouse, the city draws artists, culture lovers and art collectors from all over the world. Laguna's population of 23,000 swells with tourists on summer weekends, but away from the 'Village' (the central business district) and Main Beach (where the Village meets the shore), there is plenty of uncrowded sand and water.

History

Laguna's earliest inhabitants, the Ute-Aztecas and Shoshone tribes, called the area 'Lagonas' because of two freshwater lagoons in what is now Laguna Canyon. The name held until 1904, when it was changed to Laguna. At roughly the same time, San Francisco artist Norman St Claire came to Laguna to paint watercolors of the surf, cliffs and hills. His enthusiasm drew other artists, who, influenced by French Impressionism, were known as the *plein air* (outdoors) school. The Laguna Beach Art Association, the precursor to the Laguna Art Museum, was founded in 1918. By the late '20s, more than half of the town's 300 residents were artists.

The 1920s and '30s brought the most lasting development to Laguna. In 1926, the Pacific Coast Hwy (1) was opened between Newport Beach and Dana Point, allowing Laguna three access routes. Mary Pickford, Douglas Fairbanks, Mickey Rooney and Bette Davis vacationed here regularly and in 1932 helped establish the Laguna Playhouse (still in operation) and the Festival of the Arts, still the town's biggest attraction.

Orientation

Though Laguna stretches for about 7 miles along Pacific Coast Hwy, the shops, restaurants and bars are concentrated in the Village, along Broadway, Ocean, and Forest Sts and their intersections with Pacific Coast Hwy (all within a quarter-mile). Across Pacific Coast Hwy from the Village, Main Beach offers the most public beach access. Just four miles south, the separate community of Laguna Niguel is home to the fancy Ritz-Carlton Hotel and Salt Creek Beach, a favorite with local surfers.

Information

The Laguna Beach Visitors Bureau (☎ 949-497-9229, 800-877-1115, fax 949-376-0558, www.lagunabeachinfo.org), 1 block off Pacific Coast Hwy at 252 Broadway, has information of all kinds and will make walk-in lodging reservations for free. Hours are 9 am to 5 pm weekdays, to 4 pm Saturday, 10 am to 3 pm Sunday (July and August only). The free weekly *Coastline News*, available here and around town, lists local news and events.

Parking is a perpetual problem. If you're spending the night, leave your car at the

Lovely Laguna Niguel

LEE FOSTER

hotel and take the bus (see Getting Around). Parking lots in the Village charge $6 or more and fill up quickly in summer.

Laguna Art Museum

The showplace for the Laguna Art Association, this museum (☎ 949-494-8971), 307 Cliff Drive, has three levels of exhibit space and an interesting gift shop. Changing exhibits usually feature one or two California artists, while the museum's permanent collection consists primarily of works by early Laguna artists, California landscapes and vintage photographs. Its hours are 11 am to 5 pm (closed Monday), with free guided tours at 2 pm (except Thursday and Friday). Admission is $5, $4 for seniors and students, free for children.

Beaches

Laguna Beach has 30 public beaches and coves, and most are accessible by stairs off Pacific Coast Hwy; just look for the Beach Access signs. Main Beach fronts the Village and has volleyball and basketball courts, a wooden boardwalk and colorful tile benches. This is the best place for swimming, as the water is calm, rocks are absent and lifeguards are on duty year-round. At the north end of this beach, a path heads up the bluff (past Las Brisas restaurant) to Heisler Park, a long, skinny stretch of grass accented by hibiscus, roses and bougainvillea. Several sets of stairs lead down to the sand, including those at the north end of the park, descending to Diver's Cove, a deep protected cove popular with guess who. On the north end of town, Crescent Bay is the best beach for body surfing, with big hollow waves. Parking is difficult; try the bluffs atop the beach.

About 1 mile south of the Village is one of Laguna's less crowded beaches, Victoria Beach. Besides volleyball courts, its main attraction is the 'La Tour' landmark from 1926, a Rapunzel-tower-like structure that provides private beach access from the house above. Everyone else has to take the stairs down Victoria Drive; there's limited parking on Pacific Coast Hwy. A bit farther south is Aliso Creek Beach, which is popular with surfers; there's also a fishing pier. Parking is fairly plentiful.

Places to Stay

Accommodations get booked far in advance for summer months, when prices are hiked up by about 20%. Options include the ***Hotel Laguna*** (☎ 949-494-1151, 800-524-2927), right on the beach at 425 S Coast Highway, featuring a pool, spa, sun terrace and a private beach club. A continental breakfast is delivered to the rooms, which cost $100 to $185 ($20 less September to April).

One good spot for families is ***Vacation Village*** (☎ 949-494-8566, 800-843-6895), south of the Village at 647 S Coast Hwy. It has 130 units, about half of them with kitchens, plus a pool and spa. Rates start at $80 in summer, $70 in the off-season; a sun-deck suite with an ocean view is $288.

Romantics should try to score one of the 11 rooms at ***Eiler's Inn*** (☎ 949-494-3004), a

Laguna Arts Festivals

Laguna Beach's landmark event is the **Festival of the Arts**, a seven-week, juried exhibit of 160 artists whose work varies from paintings to hand-crafted furniture to scrimshaw. Begun in 1933 by local artists who needed to drum up buyers for their work, the festival now attracts patrons and tourists from all over the world and offers such added attractions as the Junior Art Gallery featuring children's art, free daily workshops conducted by artists, and live entertainment. The grounds are open daily from July through August, 10 am to 11:30 pm; season admission is $5, $3 for seniors and students.

The most unique aspect of the fair, and a tremendous experience that will leave you rubbing your eyes in disbelief, is the **Pageant of the Masters**, where human models are blended seamlessly into re-creations of famous paintings. This also began in 1933 as a sideshow to the main festival. Tickets ($10 to $50) need to be ordered weeks in advance, though you can often pick up last-minute cancellation tickets at the gate. Nightly performances begin at 8:30 pm. For information call ☎ 714-494-1145; for tickets call ☎ 800-487-3378.

In the 1960s, Laguna Beach artists who did not make the juried exhibition started their own festival to take advantage of the art-seekers passing through town. They set up directly across from the festival (935 Laguna Cyn Rd, half a mile from the Village), mocking its formal atmosphere by scattering sawdust on the ground. Local journalist Dick Nall coined the name **Sawdust Festival**, which, now juried itself, it has remained ever since. Many people actually enjoy this festival more, as the arts and crafts are utilitarian and quite affordable. Hours are 10 am to 10 pm. Season admission is $6; day passes for seniors are $4; children get in for $1.

A third art festival, the **Art-A-Fair Festival** (☎ 949-494-4514), runs simultaneously and is a nationally juried show focused on watercolors, pastels and oil paintings, though photography, jewelry, ceramics and other arts and crafts are displayed as well. Its grounds are at 777 Laguna Cyn Rd, and it's open daily to 9 or 10 pm. Admission is $3.50/2.50, free to children under 12. Buses (75¢) shuttle continuously from 10 am to midnight between the festivals and the Village.

B&B just a few steps from the heart of the Village and the beach at 741 S Coast Hwy. Antique furniture, Art Nouveau lamps, lots of fluffy pillows and flowery wallpaper are just some of the idyllic touches. Rooms wrap around a central fountain courtyard, where wine and cheese are served nightly; breakfasts are memorable. There's also an ocean-view sundeck. Prices are $120 to $195 in summer ($85 to $160 October to May).

One of Laguna's most elegant establishments is the **Surf and Sand** (☎ 949-497-4477, 800-524-8621), at 1555 S Coast Hwy. Recently renovated, it sports a natural color scheme commensurate with its name. Luxurious rooms have all the trappings, including some with ocean views. The Splashes restaurant serves classy California cuisine right next to the private beach. Rates range from $215 to $375.

If you're going to splurge, your first choice should be the **Inn at Laguna** (☎ 949-497-9722, 800-544-4479), dreamily perched atop the cliff between Main Beach and Heisler Park at 211 N Coast Hwy. Spacious rooms are appointed with French blinds, lots of special amenities like a selection of books and CDs, and bathrobes. A lavish breakfast is delivered to your room, and the Las Brisas restaurant is immediately next door. Rates range from $139 to $429 in peak season, about $40 less the rest of the year.

The flashiest hotel in the area is the **Ritz-Carlton Laguna Niguel** (☎ 949-240-2000, 800-241-3333), west of Pacific Coast Hwy via Ritz-Carlton Drive. The Ritz offers lap-of-luxury accommodation in an opulent setting. There are two pools, a full spa, tennis courts, terraced paths to the beach (which happens to be a great surfing spot), a library and smoking lounge, and several restaurants. Rooms start at $235, 10 times that much for a deluxe suite. The most affordable experience here is a drink in the Lobby Lounge, a grand place to watch the sunset.

Places to Eat

Surfers, the budget-conscious and those wanting a late-night snack flock to **Taco Loco**, a sidewalk cafe at 640 S Coast Hwy, with a taco bar (from $1.50) as well as quesadillas, nachos and vegetarian choices, all under $5.

A Laguna institution with one of the best views, **Las Brisas** (☎ 949-497-5434), next to the Laguna Art Museum at 361 Cliff Drive, serves Mexican seafood dishes ($20) in the dining room and appetizers and soft tacos ($7) on the patio bar. It also has a great breakfast buffet with an omelet chef whisking up your favorites. The **Cottage Restaurant** (☎ 949-494-3023), across the street, is equally popular in the morning. Assets here are the big rustic tables, free newspapers and lip-smacking cranberry orange pancakes ($2.85).

A local favorite is **Dizz's As Is** (☎ 949-494-5250), in a wood-shingled 1920s house with Art Deco interior at 2794 S Coast Hwy. The continental menu, served for dinner only, changes daily but focuses on seafood and fowl. Complete dinners include paté, soup or salad and sourdough bread, and range from $16 to $27. It's closed Monday.

The **White House** (☎ 949-494-8088), 340 S Coast Hwy, serves contemporary food and after dark turns into a bar and nightclub, often with live music. More entertainment is provided by Laguna's two microbrewery pubs, the **Laguna Beach Brewing Company**, 422 S Coast Hwy, and the **Ocean Ave Brewing Company**, 237 Ocean Ave. Both have indoor and outdoor seating.

Getting There & Away

To reach Laguna from the 405 Fwy, take Laguna Canyon Rd (Hwy 133) west; this passes the Festival of the Arts site and takes you right to the Village and beaches.

Traveling to or from Laguna by public transportation is difficult. Laguna is served by the Orange County Connection bus system (☎ 949-978-8855), which also includes Huntington Beach, Newport Beach, Fashion Island and South Coast Plaza. At South Coast Plaza, you can change buses to Anaheim, which has a Greyhound station. Buses leave every other hour; roundtrip fares are $12 and 24-hour passes are $20.

Getting Around

Laguna Beach Transit (LBT; ☎ 949-497-0746) has its central bus depot on the 300 block of Broadway, 1 block inland from the visitors bureau, and operates three routes at hourly intervals (no service between noon and 1 pm). The Gray Line covers Laguna Canyon, North Laguna and the Top of the World viewpoint. The Blue Line heads from central Laguna into the residential areas of Bluebird Canyon and Arch Beach Heights. For visitors, the most important is the Light Blue Line, which travels to the hotels and beaches along Pacific Coast Hwy, terminating at the Ritz-Carlton Hotel. Ask for the self-guided bus tour pamphlets at the visitors bureau. Each ride is 75¢.

Several places in town rent bicycles, including Laguna Beach Cyclery (☎ 949-494-1522), 240 Thalia St, and Rainbow Bicycle Co (☎ 949-494-5806), 485 N Coast Hwy. A 24-hour rental is about $20.

BIG BEAR LAKE

The main reason to come to Big Bear Lake, framed by the San Bernardino National Forest, is for outdoor recreation. The year-round, family-friendly mountain resort is an easy and enormously popular getaway for people from LA, the deserts and San Diego. In the warmer seasons, the lake itself is the main attraction. Eight miles long and 1 mile across at its widest point, it was formed in 1888 behind a dam built to provide water to citrus growers in Redlands. It's perfect for swimming, waterskiing, sailing, fishing, jet skiing and other water sports.

In winter, downhill skiers and snowboarders are drawn here by Southern California's two largest ski areas – Bear Mountain and Snow Summit – which are taken over by mountain bikers as soon as the snow melts. Big Bear Village is the town's cutesy and touristy center, which attempts to re-create the atmosphere of the Alps.

Orientation

Getting oriented in Big Bear Lake is easy, as most of the town is sandwiched between the

Meadow in Big Bear Lake

lake's southern shore and the mountains. It is bisected by Hwy 18, here called Big Bear Blvd. Big Bear Village sits right at the center, with most of the cabins and nicer motels located along the highway to the west. East of the Village is the more commercial part of town, with a number of motels, fast-food stores and a modern shopping center. The lake's northern shore, along Hwy 38 (here North Shore Blvd), is much quieter and is the departure point for most hiking trails.

Information

The Big Bear Lake Visitors Center (☎ 800-424-4232, fax 909-866-5671, www.bigbearinfo .com) is at 630 Bartlet Rd in the Village and is open weekdays 8 am to 5 pm, weekends from 9 am. They can help you with maps, general information on lodging, restaurants and activities and will also make lodging reservations free of charge. Many motels, hotels, shops and restaurants also have racks of information leaflets.

For suggestions on hiking trails, maps and wilderness permits, visit the ranger-staffed Discovery Center (☎ 909-866-3437), on the northern shore (just look for the signs). Opened in May 1998, this wonderful facility features educational exhibits, weekly events and a friendly and knowledgeable staff. Hours are 8 am to 6 pm daily in summer, closing at 4:30 pm in winter.

The Center also sells the National Adventure Forest Pass. This controversial pilot project, authorized by Congress, means anyone visiting Southern California's forests by car must purchase a permit ($5/day or $30/year) and display it on the windshield. It's transferable and you don't need one if you're just traveling through the forest without parking your car. There's a penalty of $100 if you're caught parking without it.

Activities

Skiing With an 8000-foot ridge rising above the lake's south side, Big Bear Lake is known for its downhill skiing and snowboarding. Snow usually falls by mid-December and lasts until March or April, with snow-making machines producing supplementary powder whenever necessary. The best part about Big

DAVID PEEVERS

Bear skiing is the weather – sunshine 90% of the time, and shorts and T-shirt temperatures in spring. Very basic ski, boot and pole rentals start at $9.50/day (more for high-performance gear and discounts for week-long rentals), offered all along Hwy 18 and at ski-area lodges.

Both of Big Bear's ski mountains are off Hwy 18. **Snow Summit** (☎ 909-866-5766, www.snowsummit.com) has 12 lifts, 1200 vertical feet and $32 adult day lift tickets (less for half-day and night tickets, $45 during holidays). Tickets come with a satisfaction guarantee and may be exchanged for vouchers (within 75 minutes of issue) good for another day. **Bear Mountain** (☎ 909-585-2519, 24-hour Snow Phone 800-232-7686, www.bearmtn.com) has 11 lifts, 1665 vertical feet and $40 tickets. Its Outlaw Snowboard Park is a favorite among young hotdoggers. While Snow Summit has more terrain, Bear Mountain is liked among locals for its steep upper runs. Smaller areas, good for beginners and iffy intermediates, are **Snow Forest** (☎ 909-866-8891) and **Snow Valley** (☎ 909-867-2751), 11 miles west of Big Bear on Hwy 18.

Hiking In summer, people trade their ski boots for hiking boots and hit the forest trails. The best hiking and most accessible trailheads are on the lake's north shore, off Hwy 38.

One of the nicest trails is the Pacific Crest Trail (PCT), an easy walk along a 2400-foot ridge, 2 miles long and parallel to the highway, offering great scenery and views. A moderately difficult hike up the Cougar Crest Trail starting near the Discovery Center accesses the PCT and offers grand views of Big Bear Lake and Holcomb Valley. Popular too is the Woodland Trail, an easy 1½-mile nature trail starting at the lake's eastern end.

Mountain Biking Big Bear is hugely popular for mountain biking, and the town is the site of professional and amateur racing competitions. Most popular is the terrain atop Snow Summit, crisscrossed by 40 miles of roads and trails suitable for all levels of riders. A chairlift costing $7 per ride ($19 all day) provides easy access to the top with your bike. Tickets, guides, maps and bike rentals are available from the Mountain Bike Center (☎ 909-866-4565) at the mountain base. Rentals start at $6.50/hour or $32/day and include helmets. Popular riding areas that don't require the chairlift are Holcomb Valley, Delamar Mountain and Van Duesen Canyon off Hwy 38. Less aggressive cyclists will enjoy the gentle 2½-mile bike path along the lake's north shore.

Water Sports As its name suggests, Big Bear Lake is best experienced from the water, which provides cool respite from hot summer days. Swim Beach, just east of the Village, is the only official swimming area and is popular with families. The best swimming, however, is on the lake's far-western end, in a beautiful bay accented by islands made up of piles of boulders and the privately owned China Island. There's no access from the street, so the only way to get there is by boat or jet ski.

Jet skis (for 1 to 3 people) rent from $45/hour; speed boats (for 4 to 6) are $60/hour; pontoon boats (for 8 to 10) cost $40/hour; and sail boats (for 2; two-hour minimum) are $50/hour. North Shore Landing (☎ 909-878-4386), closest to China Island at 38573 North Shore Drive, rents them all.

The lake teems with trout, catfish, bass, carp and other fish, though catching them is not always easy. Those bent on success should sign up with the affable John Cantrell Guide Service (☎ 909-585-4017, 909-593-4309), which guarantees you'll catch a fish – or your money back. You'll need a fishing license ($9/day or $27/year), available at sporting-goods stores around town, and $40/hour for the boat. John will provide all the poles, bait, expertise – and fish.

Other Activities Guided Jeep explorations of the mountainous countryside are offered by Jeep Tours (☎ 909-878-5337), 40687 Village Drive, from mid-May to mid-October. Tours start at $37.95 for a 90-minute outing, though the most popular is the three-hour White Mountain Tour ($52.95). Another way to see the mountains is on horseback.

Guided tours are offered by several companies in town, including Rockin' K Riding Stables (☎ 909-878-4677), 731 Tulip Lane.

Alpine Slide (☎ 909-866-4626), on Big Bear Blvd just west of the Village, begins with a placid chairlift ride up Magic Mountain. This is followed by a thrilling wheeled bobsled ride that hurtles down a concrete track with you at the controls – more or less. The complex also includes a water slide, go-cart track and miniature golf. For regular 9-hole or 18-hole golfing, sign up for tee time at the Bear Mountain Golf Course (call ☎ 909-585-8002).

Places to Stay

Accommodations in Big Bear Lake run the gamut from snug B&Bs and resort cabins to lodges, hotels, campgrounds and private homes. In general, rates drop during midweek and go up on holiday weekends. The Big Bear Visitors Center (see Information) has a thorough list and makes free reservations.

Camping The most convenient campgrounds are near the lake and have picnic tables, fire rings and potable water. Popular with mountain bikers and close to town, *Pineknot Campground*, at the top of Summit Blvd, has 48 spaces for $15 (mid-May to late September). On the north shore near the Discovery Center, *Serrano* is the only campground around with showers and RV hookups. It has 132 spaces, $15 tent sites and $24 RV sites (May 1 to November 1).

Lodges & Hotels Dozens of lodgings, almost all independently owned, are strung along Big Bear Blvd, most offering standard rooms from $70. The best deals in town are the $55 to $75 rooms at *Jensen's Lakefront Lodge* (☎ 909-866-8271), half a mile west of the Village on Lakeview Drive. Rooms have that '70s look but are clean, spacious, quiet and have a view of the lake. The friendly *Honey Bear Lodge* (☎ 800-628-8714), 3 blocks from the Village at 40994 Pennsylvania Ave, has spacious rooms with TV, microwave, refrigerator and fireplace for $39/89 midweek/weekend; those with lake view are $59/109. If you also want a private Jacuzzi,

it'll cost $69/139. Rates go up during holidays. For a splurge, try the new *Northwoods Resort* (☎ 800-866-3121), at 40650 Village Drive, where standard rooms are $89 to $99 midweek and $129 to $169 on weekends.

Cabins Renting a cabin is often the most affordable option for groups of four and up. These range from small and shabby to huge and elegant, offering an array of amenities such as kitchens, fireplaces, sundecks and Jacuzzis. Prices vary accordingly, starting at $100 and going up as high as $400 a night. A good option is the *Grey Squirrel Resort* (☎ 800-381-5569), at 39372 Big Bear Blvd, which also rents beautiful private homes. *Log Cabin Resort Rentals* (☎ 800-767-0205), at 39976 Big Bear Blvd, has pretty, upscale cabins and condominiums.

Places to Eat

Breakfast and dinner are the most important meals, as lunch is usually eaten on a mountain or trail. For groceries, the *Vons* supermarket, with a deli and bakery, is located toward the east end of the lake on Hwy 38 and offers the widest choices.

For bear-sized breakfasts, head to the aptly named *Grizzly Manor Cafe*, 41268 Big Bear Blvd, a popular local hangout with twisted 'Twin Peak-ish' charm. Owner Jaymie Nordine greets most guests by name, and then retires to the steamy kitchen to produce delicious pancakes the size of catchers' mitts, plus any number of huge plates of food, all costing less than $7. It's only open till 2 pm.

The closest to gourmet you'll get in Big Bear is *Mozart's Bistro* (☎ 909-866-9497), 40701 Village Drive, which has imaginative crab cakes, juicy filets mignon, huge portions of pork ribs and other upscale hearty fare costing $13 to $25 per entree. There's plenty of fine outdoor seating here, allowing you to enjoy the good mountain air. Across the street, inside the Northwoods Resort, is *Stillwells*, which makes large, crisp salads and bulky burgers. Locals like the steaks, prime rib and seafood, all for around $20, served at the rustic *Captain's Anchorage*, 42148 Moonridge Way. In business since 1947, it serves dinner only.

Getting There & Away

From LA and Orange Counties, take the 10 Fwy east to Hwy 30 in Redlands. Follow Hwy 30 to Hwy 330 to Hwy 18. For a more scenic route, exit Orange St N in Redlands and follow the signs to Hwy 38.

Mountain Area Regional Transit Authority (MARTA; ☎ 909-584-1111) buses connect Big Bear with San Bernardino's Greyhound station three times each weekday and twice on Saturday ($5). Large groups might consider reserving the door-to-door Big Bear Shuttle (☎ 909-585-5514), which costs $150 for one person, then $10 per extra person up to 10 people. They will pick you up in any part of Los Angeles.

SANTA BARBARA

Sandwiched between the Pacific Ocean and Santa Ynez Mountains, Santa Barbara is an affluent and pretty city of 90,000, about 90 miles north of Los Angeles. Its charming red-tile roofs, white stucco walls and seaside lassitude evoke the atmosphere of a Mediterranean village. The downtown has outstanding architecture, including a masterpiece of a courthouse, as well as noteworthy art and natural-history museums. Five colleges in the area, including the University of California at Santa Barbara (UCSB), give the town a youthful vivacity and balance Santa Barbara's yachting and retirement communities.

History

Until about 200 years ago, Chumash Indians thrived in the Santa Barbara area. They watched when, in 1542, Juan Cabrillo entered the channel, put up a Spanish flag and went on his way. Sebastian Vizcaino, a cartographer for the Duke of Monterey, landed in the harbor on December 4, 1602 (the feast day of St Barbara) and literally put Santa Barbara on the map. But, being claimed and named by Spain didn't affect Santa Barbara's Chumash until the arrival of missionaries in the mid-1700s.

The padres converted the Chumash to Catholicism against their will, made them construct the mission and presidio, and taught them to wear clothes and change their traditional diet. The Chumash were soon decimated by European diseases, but today the tribe is very much alive and well.

Easterners started arriving in force with the 1849 gold rush, and by the late 1890s Santa Barbara was an established vacation spot for the rich and famous. The American Film Company, founded here in 1910, was the world's largest for about three years of its decade-long existence. Thanks to the local film commission, the entertainment industry continues to thrive in the city. Each March, independent US and international films are screened at the Santa Barbara International Film Festival.

Orientation

Downtown Santa Barbara is laid out in a square grid, the main artery of which is State St, running north-south. 'Lower' State St (south of Ortega St) has a greater concentration of bars and shady characters, while 'upper' State St (north of Ortega St) is where the nice shops and museums are. Cabrillo Blvd hugs the coastline and turns into Coast Village Rd as it enters the eastern suburb of Montecito.

Information

The Tourist Information Center (☎ 805-965-3021), at the corner of Garden St and Cabrillo Blvd, offers maps, brochures and a busy but helpful staff. Summer hours are 9 am to 5 pm daily (from 10 am on Sunday and open fewer hours in winter).

The Hot Spots Visitors Center (☎ 805-564-1637, 800-793-7666), inside a 24-hour cafe at 36 State St, is staffed from 9 am to 9 pm (Sunday to 4 pm). Both of these offices maintain a touchscreen computer for information and free hotel reservations. For the latter, you can also call Passport Reservation Service at ☎ 800-765-6255 or Coastal Escapes Accommodation at ☎ 800-292-2222.

The Red Tile Tour

This self-guided 12-block walking tour takes in all major downtown sights and historic landmarks, including the Santa Barbara County Courthouse, the Museum of Art and the Historical Museum. Pick up a free map from the Tourist Information Center or Hot Spots.

Santa Barbara County Courthouse

The 1929 courthouse (☎ 805-962-6464), 1100 Anacapa St, is one sight not to be missed. Built in Spanish-Moorish Revival style, it features hand-painted ceilings, wrought-iron chandeliers and tiles from Tunisia and Spain. You're free to explore on your own between 8:30 am and 5 pm (from 10 am on weekends) or take a free guided tour, offered at 2 pm Monday to Saturday and 10:30 am Monday, Tuesday and Friday. If you miss it, be sure to see the mural room and go up the 80-foot clock tower for panoramic shots of the city.

Santa Barbara Museum of Art

This well-regarded regional museum (☎ 805-963-4364), 1130 State St, has a varied permanent collection, with works by Monet, Matisse, Chagall, Hopper and O'Keefe, as well as Asian art and classical sculpture. A new wing added exhibit space, a cafe and a children's gallery. Hours are 11 am to 5 pm Tuesday through Saturday (to 9 pm Friday), noon to 5 pm Sunday. Admission is $5, $3 for seniors, $1.50 for students, free for children under six, free for everyone on Thursday and the first Sunday of the month.

Santa Barbara Historical Museum

Located in an adobe complex at 136 E De La Guerra St, this educational museum (☎ 805-966-1601) has an exhaustive collection of Santa Barbara memorabilia, including antique furniture and an intricately carved coffer that belonged to Padre Junípero Serra. Guided tours run Wednesday and weekends at 1:30 pm. Hours are 10 am to 5 pm Tuesday through Saturday, from noon on Sunday; admission is free.

Mission Santa Barbara

Called the Queen of the Missions, Mission Santa Barbara (☎ 805-682-4713), 2201 Laguna St, sits on a majestic plot half a mile north of downtown. The mission was established on December 4, 1786 as the 10th California mission. Three adobe structures preceded the current stone one, built in 1820, with a main facade integrating Neoclassical-style columns. Today, the mission still functions as a Franciscan friary as well as a parish church and museum. Among Chumash wall decorations, the gardens in the courtyard are peaceful. Behind the mission is an extensive cemetery with 4000 Chumash graves and the elaborate mausoleums of early European settlers. It's open daily 9 am to 5 pm; admission is $3, free for children.

Museum of Natural History

Visit this museum (☎ 805-682-4711), 2 blocks north of the mission at 2559 Puesta del Sol Rd, if only to see its beautiful architecture and landscaping. Highlights include an extensive Chumash exhibit and the entire skeleton of a blue whale, though other exhibits are quite mediocre. There's also a planetarium. Hours are 9 am to 5 pm (Sunday from 10 am). Admission is $5, $3 for children, free on the last Sunday of the month.

Santa Barbara Botanic Garden

A mile north of the Museum of Natural History, at 1212 Mission Canyon Rd, this 65-acre botanical garden (☎ 805-682-4726) is devoted to California's native flora. There are 5½ miles of trails meandering through cacti, redwoods, wildflowers, and past the old mission dam, built by Chumash Indians to irrigate the mission's fields. Guided tours are offered daily (except Wednesday) at 2 pm and also at 10:30 am on Thursday and Sunday. Garden hours vary by season but are roughly 9 am to sunset. Admission is $3, $1 for children.

Santa Barbara Zoological Garden

The zoo (☎ 805-962-5339), 500 Niños Drive, has gorgeous gardens as well as 700 animals from around the world, including big cats, monkeys, elephants and giraffes. The 100-year-old vegetation was once part of a palatial estate. Hours are 10 am to 5 pm daily. Admission is $6.

Just west of the zoo at 1400 E Cabrillo Blvd, the free **Andree Clark Bird Refuge** consists of a lagoon, gardens and a path from which to observe nesting freshwater birds. Admission is free.

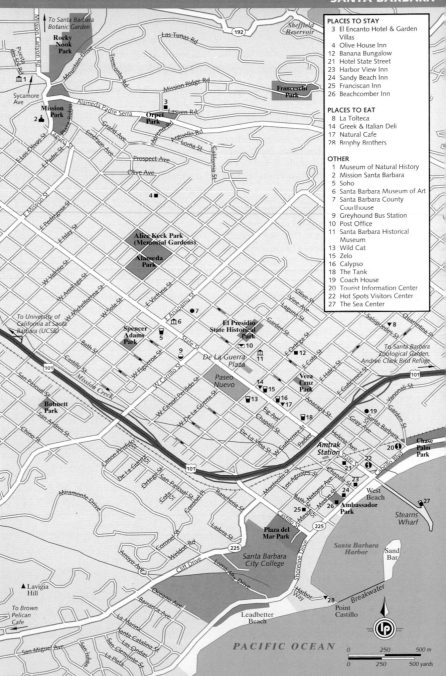

SANTA BARBARA

PLACES TO STAY
3 El Encanto Hotel & Garden
   Villas
4 Olive House Inn
12 Banana Bungalow
21 Hotel State Street
23 Harbor View Inn
24 Sandy Beach Inn
25 Franciscan Inn
26 Beachcomber Inn

PLACES TO EAT
8 La Tolteca
14 Greek & Italian Deli
17 Natural Cafe
28 Brophy Brothers

OTHER
1 Museum of Natural History
2 Mission Santa Barbara
5 Soho
6 Santa Barbara Museum of Art
7 Santa Barbara County
   Courthouse
9 Greyhound Bus Station
10 Post Office
11 Santa Barbara Historical
   Museum
13 Wild Cat
15 Zelo
16 Calypso
18 The Tank
19 Coach House
20 Tourist Information Center
22 Hot Spots Visitors Center
27 The Sea Center

Stearns Wharf

This rough wooden pier extending into the harbor from the south end of State St is a favorite place to eat seafood and watch sea lions. Built in 1872 by John Peck Stearn, it is the oldest continuously operating wharf on the West Coast. During the 1940s, it was owned by James Cagney and his two brothers.

The Sea Center (☎ 805-962-0885) features touch tanks filled with starfish and sea anemones. It's usually open daily 10 am to 5 pm (tanks noon to 4 pm). Admission is $3, $1.50 for children.

In November 1998, a major fire engulfed the pier but luckily only destroyed the outer 20%. Rebuilding began within a few months and should be completed by the time this book goes to press. Meanwhile, most restaurants and the Sea Center remain in operation.

Places to Stay

In summer, budget accommodations are practically nonexistent in Santa Barbara. Even a cheap motel room that costs just $35 in November can go for as much as $150 between mid-May and September. In general, rates go down slightly during midweek. Some hotels impose a two-night minimum stay.

Santa Barbara's only hostel is the 56-bed ***Banana Bungalow*** *(☎ 805-963-0154, 800-346-7835, fax 805-963-0184)*, 210 E Ortega St, a fairly run-down affair in a barrel-like corrugated-tin structure. There's no curfew, no lock-out, and no real chance of getting a good night's sleep when the place is full. Beds in 'semi-private' dorms sleeping eight cost $18; bunks in a large communal room are $15. In summer, there's a busy activity schedule with barbecues, hiking trips, volleyball competitions and the like. American travelers are OK for stays of up to three days.

The ***Hotel State Street*** *(☎ 805-966-6586, fax 805-962-8459)* is a good value, near the beach at 121 State St. Clean and newly renovated, it attracts Europeans and sophisticated budget travelers. Each room has a sink and towel, but bathrooms are shared. Midweek rates start at $35 but are usually in the $55 to $75 range.

Most of Santa Barbara's mid range motels are along Cabrillo Blvd, west of State St. Options include the ***Sandy Beach Inn*** *(☎ 805-963-0405)*, 122 W Cabrillo Blvd, with rooms for $95 to $165 in winter and $145 to $265 in summer. One block west is the pleasant ***Beachcomber Inn*** *(☎ 805-965-4577, fax*

The ripples of time, reflecting in the pool fronting Mission Santa Barbara

805-965-9937), 202 W Cabrillo Blvd, which has a small pool, a sundeck and 32 rooms starting at $80 but topping out at $255.

Another cluster of hotels is on Bath St just off Cabrillo Blvd. The best deal here is the delightful ***Franciscan Inn*** *(☎ 805-963-8845, fax 805-564-3295)*, 109 Bath St, which has a nice pool, spa and guest laundry and is run with efficiency and charm. Rates start at $69 in winter, leaping to $89/119 singles/ doubles in summer.

A good B&B is the ***Olive House Inn*** *(☎ 805-962-4902, 800-786-6422, fax 805-899-2754)*, in a Craftsman-style villa near the mission at 1604 Olive St. It has a terraced garden, a large sundeck and six rooms costing $110 to $180.

High-end accommodations are mostly north of downtown, in the hills, though a great choice near the beach is the ***Harbor View Inn*** *(☎ 805-963-0780, 800-755-0222, fax 805-963-7967)*, 36 W Cabrillo Blvd, with a large pool and spa and nice landscaping. Rooms start at $130 and crest at $330.

Long considered *the* hotel in Santa Barbara, ***El Encanto Hotel & Garden Villas*** *(☎ 805-687-5000, 800-346-7039, fax 805-687-3903)*, 1900 Lasuen Rd, sits on a hill above the mission with a great view of downtown and the ocean. Nestled among 10 acres of lush gardens, its secluded cottages with private patios start at $229, zooming as high as $1450.

Places to Eat

Santa Barbara's 'restaurant row' is on the 500 and 600 blocks of State St. A local institution, the ***Greek & Italian Deli***, at the corner of State and Ortega Sts, has great sandwiches, gyros, Greek salads and hot lunch specials from around $5. A couple of blocks south, the ***Natural Cafe***, 508 State St, serves Zen burgers, Buddha burritos and Yogananda lasagna for under $7.

Oceanside dining options include the reliably excellent ***Brophy Brothers*** *(☎ 805-966-4418)*, in the Santa Barbara Yacht Harbor. It's a lively restaurant and oyster bar where locals go for superb seafood; top choices include clam chowder and cioppino, served with chewy sourdough bread. Entire meals can be had for around $10.

On Arroyo Burro Beach, west of town, the ***Brown Pelican*** *(☎ 805-687-4550)* is an informal cafe with a view of the waves. Fare includes mouthwatering salads, sandwiches and seafood (the clam chowder is terrific). It's also a nice place for breakfast.

La Tolteca, in an industrial part of town at 616 E Haley St, is a 'mexicatessen' with famously authentic enchiladas and tamales, going for $1.70 to $6.

Entertainment

The best source for events listings is the free *Independent*, published on Thursday and available around town.

Santa Barbara's raging after-dark scene revolves around lower State and Ortega Sts. Most bars have happy hours and college nights, when the booze is cheap and the atmosphere rowdy. Such places include ***Calypso***, at 514 State St, and ***Zelo***, at 630 State St. ***The Tank***, 416 State St, has aquariums for decor and dancing on weekends. The ***Wild Cat***, 15 W Ortega St, is the ultimate '70s revival lounge, with a diverse crowd and good mix of music. ***Soho***, above McDonald's at 1221 State St, has live jazz nightly. Regional touring acts appear at the ***Coach House*** *(☎ 805-962-8877)*, 110 Santa Barbara St.

Getting There & Away

Santa Barbara is bisected by the 101 Fwy. For downtown, take the Garden St or Cabrillo Blvd exit. Parking on the street and in any of 10 municipal lots is free for the first 90 minutes daily and all day Sunday.

Greyhound has nine daily buses to LA for $13, and six to San Francisco for $35; round-trip fares save a few dollars each way. The Greyhound bus station, a magnet for transient types, is downtown at 33 W Carrillo St.

Three southbound Amtrak trains and one northbound train leave daily from Santa Barbara's train depot *(☎ 805-963-1015)*, 209 State St. The average fare to Los Angeles is $20, $67 to San Francisco (via Oakland).

Getting Around

To get your bearings, take the Santa Barbara Trolley *(☎ 805-965-0353)*, which makes a narrated 90-minute loop past Stearns Wharf,

A River *Roars* Through It: The Killer Kern

Can't take the stress and sheer velocity of the LA freeway system? What better cure for big-city blues than a return to the 'serenity' of nature on one of the most awesome whitewater rivers in America, the aptly nicknamed 'Killer Kern.'

When the runoff from winter snows begins in spring, part of the Kern becomes a surging monster of a river – charging through steep gorges in the Sequoia National Forest – with some of the fastest and fiercest rapids anywhere. At other times of the year, and on other sections, the passage can be enjoyed by nearly everyone. To Angelenos, the Kern has the distinct advantage of being only 150 miles north of the city, just a three-hour drive away.

Having been a guide on rivers of the Northwest myself in what seems like an earlier incarnation, I was ready to hit the water again on a tour of the Lower Kern with Whitewater Voyages (☎ 800-488-7238, fax 510-758-7238, www.whitewatervoyages .com), an outfitter with a permanent base on the river. Between April and September, this company runs one- to three-day trips on various stretches of the Kern – mild to menacing.

'Wet and wild' was definitely the norm on the Lower Kern (class III and IV) two-day run I chose. It began rather placidly on day one with a lovely float through beautiful forests and past bizarrely carved granite boulders that – when the water's high – create enormous waves and treacherous hydraulic holes. We camped on a sublime bend in the river, where – after a gourmet dinner of steak, chicken, salads and Dutch oven brownies – we slept like babes while the Kern murmured sweetly to us.

The following day, our group of four was joined by 23 other adventurers, and our armada of rafts headed into the class III and IV sections downriver. This was wild! I got to relive my former river-rat life by pulling three 'swimmers' – launched from other rafts while bumping through various cataracts – to sputtering safety. One of our boats wrapped around a boulder for half an hour and another raft popped, gimping home after a hasty patch job. There were bruises, cuts and abrasions to be sure, but the river did its work: The macho were meek, the reclusive were raucous, and the timid were tigers.

Whitewater Voyages also operates half-day and one-day trips on the Upper Kern (class III to IV) and the distinctly class V 'Thunder Run.' Those who hunger for the extreme should try the 'Forks of the Kern' run. The river drops 60 feet per mile through solid granite walls in an unending series of furious class IV and class V rapids that will all but erase your id, ego and all taints of civilization. But be warned: You have to be tough, experienced and comfortable running on the edge to go here. People *do* die – many are unprepared and/or drunken yahoos.

The two-day Lower Kern tour ranges from $236 midweek to $292 on Saturday. Half a day on the Upper Kern costs $62 to $72; one day is $98 to $128. The 'Forks of the Kern' costs $500 for two days and $620 for three days. Rates include all meals and most equipment.

David Peevers

the courthouse, the mission and Museum of Art. Tickets cost $5 and are valid all day, allowing you to get off and on. (If you get off, you'll have to wait the full 90 minutes for the next bus to arrive.)

The Downtown-Waterfront Shuttle bus runs every 10 to 15 minutes from 10:15 am to 6 pm between downtown and Stearns Wharf. A second route travels from the zoo to yacht harbor at 30-minute intervals. The fare is 25¢ per ride; transfers between routes are free.

Santa Barbara Metropolitan Transit District (MTD) buses cost $1 per ride and serve all of Santa Barbara and outlying communities.

LAS VEGAS

Las Vegas has grown in 90 years from nothing to nearly a million people. It's an exciting place for a brief visit, and if you like gambling and glitter, you'll love it – at least until your money disappears, or the incessant ding-ding-ding of slot machines and the haggard faces of down-and-out gamblers wear you out. Food and lodging are generally inexpensive, and special flight and accommodation packages are frequently available from LA (check the travel supplement in the Sunday edition of the *LA Times* or see a travel agent).

Paiute Indians and Mormon missionaries were the only settlers in this arid region until 1902, when Las Vegas became a railroad town with ice works, hotels and saloons. The Great Depression brought a collapse in mineral and crop prices, so in 1931 the state government legalized gambling and created agencies to tax it, turning an illegal activity into a revenue source and tourist attraction.

By the '50s, gambling was well-established in Las Vegas, thanks to gangsters, who bankrolled its growth, and the Hoover Dam, a New Deal project that provided the water and electricity for the burgeoning city. LA mobster Bugsy Siegel's Fabulous Flamingo pioneered the new style of casinos – big and flashy, with lavish entertainment to draw in the gamblers – which is still in vogue today.

Orientation

Las Vegas is about five hours northeast of Los Angeles by car. You enter the city on I-15, which parallels Las Vegas Blvd. Also known as the Strip, this is where all the big hotel/casinos are, so work out which cross street will bring you closest to your destination. If you want a Las Vegas overview, get off I-15 at Blue Diamond Rd (exit 33) and cruise the length of the Strip from south to north, all the way to downtown, a drive of perhaps fifteen minutes.

Downtown Las Vegas is the original town center. Its main artery, Fremont St, is now a covered pedestrian mall lined with low-key casinos and hotels, spiced up with nightly laser shows.

Information

The Las Vegas Visitor Center (☎ 702-892-7575, www.lasvegas24hours.com) is in the Convention Center at 3150 Paradise Rd. Another useful website is run by *The Insider* magazine (www.insidervlv.com).

Casinos

Most casinos are gaudy, noisy and deliberately disorienting, with no clocks or windows. The Strip's new mega-casinos also feature gimmicky themes, attention-grabbing architecture and nongambling amusements.

Casinos listed here (from north to south) are worth visiting as attractions in their own right. New casinos set to open before the new millennium are the Venetian, the Paris and the Mandalay Bay.

Except for poker, all gambling pits the player against the house, and the house always has a statistical edge. Some casinos offer introductory lessons in blackjack, roulette and craps. To enter a gambling area, you must be 18 years old.

Stratosphere (☎ 800-998-6937) – This casino/hotel has a landmark 1149-foot tower with a restaurant and two rides up top – a roller coaster ($5) and the free-fall 'Big Shot' ($6).

Circus Circus (☎ 800-634-3450) – One of the original casino-cum-theme-parks, Circus Circus offers free circus acts in the tent-like interior.

Treasure Island (☎ 800-944-7444) – The pirate ship and man-of-war in the lagoon out front stage a sea battle every 90 minutes from 4:30 pm to midnight.

Mirage (☎ 800-627-6667) – A fake volcano erupts out front every half hour. Inside are a tropical rain forest, a dolphin tank and the white tigers used in the 'Siegfried & Roy' stage show.

Caesar's Palace (☎ 800-634-6001) – You enter stylish Caesar's along a moving footpath, past classic columns and 'ancient' statues. Inside, the Forum is an imitation Roman street, with a painted sky that changes from dawn to dusk every three hours.

Bellagio (☎ 888-987-6667) – Catering to upscale tastes and fat wallets, the Bellagio offers lovely architecture and decor; a $300 million art collection of Matisse, Van Gogh and others ($10 admission); 17 restaurants; and an impressive – and free – water fountain show.

New York, New York (☎ 800-693-6763) – The hotel's facade re-creates the Manhattan skyline, with replicas of the Statue of Liberty, Empire State Building and more. The 'Manhattan Express' roller coaster ($5) is a major rush.

Excalibur (☎ 800-937-7777) – It's decorated like a medieval castle with an overworked Arthurian theme. Dinner shows feature jousting knights.

Luxor (☎ 800-288-1000) – This casino is a remarkable glass-covered pyramid with a sphinx and an imitation of Cleopatra's needle out front. Inside are Egyptian-themed rides ($5) and an IMAX movie theater ($8).

Other Attractions

There are many things to do besides gambling, and discount coupons are available for most of them. The **Wet 'n Wild** water park (☎ 702-734-0088), at 2601 Las Vegas Blvd S, looks mighty tempting on a hot day ($20). The **Imperial Palace Auto Museum** (☎ 702-731-3311), at the Imperial Palace casino, has an excellent collection of vehicles once owned by the rich and famous, from Hitler to Howard Hughes ($7). A Vegas favorite is the campy **Liberace Museum** (☎ 702-798-5595), at 1775 E Tropicana, with sequined capes, rhinestone jewelry, flashy cars and fabulous candelabra ($7).

One of the best places to sample the charms of the Southwest and escape the madness of Vegas is **Red Rock Canyon**, a dramatic valley noted for the steep red-rock escarpment, rising 3000 feet on its western edge. It's about a 25-minute drive west of Vegas on Charleston Blvd, which turns into Hwy 159. A 13-mile, one-way scenic loop starts at

the BLM visitor center (☎ 702-363-1921) near Hwy 159. The visitor center has maps and information about several short hikes in the area and is open daily 8:30 am to 4:30 pm; the scenic loop is open from 8 am to dusk. Sunset and sunrise are the best times for viewing. The park day-use fee is $5.

Places to Stay

KOA (☎ 702-451-5527), a few miles south of town at 4315 Boulder Hwy, has tent and RV sites ($24 for two people) and a swimming pool. The no-frills *Las Vegas International Hostel* (☎ 702-385-9955), in a converted apartment block at 1208 Las Vegas Blvd, is popular with international backpackers. Space in four-bed dorms is $12 to $14. Private rooms are $28. *Las Vegas Backpackers Hostel* (☎ 702-385-1150), 1322 Fremont St, is on the not-so-nice outskirts of downtown, but the facilities (including a pool) are top-notch. Dorm beds are $15; singles are $35; doubles are $45. Call for free pick-up from the Greyhound station.

The best room deals are at the big casinos midweek, when doubles are as low as $35. On a busy Friday or Saturday, the same room might be $100 or more. Deals come and go by the hour, so call before you arrive. Budget-friendly casinos include *Circus Circus* (☎ 800-634-3450), the *Stardust* (☎ 800-824-6033) and the *Riviera* (☎ 800-634-6753). Even the 'nice' casinos have packages (ie, rooms plus dinner shows and discounted meals), so call around. Some good deals on the Strip are *Caesar's Palace* (☎ 800-634-6001), the *Luxor* (☎ 800-288-1000) and the *MGM Grand* (☎ 800-929-1111). Standard rates here are $70 to $95 midweek, $125 and up on weekends.

Places to Eat

The larger casinos have multiple restaurants in all price ranges. The all-you-can-eat buffet, a Las Vegas institution, is where gluttonous gamblers pile plates with wide and heavy loads, only to return for five or six desserts. The best buffet in town is a subject of debate. Some that are commonly mentioned include the *Golden Nugget* for a $9.50 dinner, *Bally's Big Kitchen* for $12.95, and

Gambling on Luxury

On the eve of the millennium, Las Vegas is once again reinventing itself, feeding a fickle market with ever new titillation. This is nothing new for the original Sin City, which, in the Reagan-era '80s, tried to clean up its act and woo the mom, pop and kids market. The desert city became a Disneyland-like park, sprouting gigantic kiddie-themed hotels like the medieval-style Excalibur and the MGM with its Wizard of Oz decor and amusement park.

Build it and they will come, and come they did – in droves – low-rollers more interested in the $5 buffet or free pirate show than in gambling away their paychecks. But gambling is, after all, the grease that keeps the wheels spinning in Las Vegas. So in yet another turnabout, the city is shedding the family-friendly pretense and refocusing.

This time the target is grown-ups – especially the more moneyed and sophisticated kind – who have largely shunned the city in recent years. Casino mogul Steve Wynn set the tone with the opening of the 2900-room Bellagio resort in 1998, which actually prohibits access to those under 18 unless they are hotel patrons. The most expensive resort ever built ($1.6 billion plus $300 million for the art collection) seeks to emulate the splendor of a European grand hotel. The huge lagoon outside its entrance supposedly re-creates Italy's Lake Como. It is fronted by a faux Tuscan village, and the olive-and-cypress-tree-dotted swimming pool area is modeled after a Mediterranean resort. Only the art is real: Cluttering two smallish rooms are original paintings – arranged in no apparent order, theme or aesthetic approach – by Miró, Matisse, Van Gogh and other masters that would make any museum proud.

The Bellagio will be followed by a slew of other 'adult' hotels set to open before the millennium: the Venetian (with replicas of the Doge's Palace and Campanile), the Paris (with replicas of the Eiffel Tower, Arc de Triomphe and Hotel de Ville) and Mandalay Bay (with a South Seas theme).

Despite such efforts, it remains to be seen whether true high-rollers will prefer a faux Lake Como or Eiffel Tower to the real thing. Or will all this pseudo-sophistication pan out to be just another 'theme,' making Marge and Jim from Dubuque giddy with the sensation that going to Vegas is just like visiting Paris or Venice – but conveniently without those pesky French or Italians? It seems to be a gamble Vegas is willing to take.

the Palatium Buffet at **Caesar's Palace** for $14. Cheapest is the Plate of Plenty buffet at **Circus Circus**, only $3/4/5 for breakfast/lunch/dinner; you get what you pay for.

Beyond casino restaurants and buffets, **Mad Dogs & Englishmen** is a British-style pub at 515 Las Vegas Blvd, just south of downtown, serving fish and chips for about $8. **Yolie's Brazilian Steak House**, 3900 Paradise Rd, cooks outstanding grilled meats for $9 to $15. The best restaurant in town is arguably **Andre's** (☎ 702-385-5016), 401 S 6th St, with classic French cuisine, a fine wine list and predictably high prices.

Entertainment

The best source for entertainment information is the free magazine *What's On in Las Vegas*. 'Big room' casino shows can include concerts by famous artists, Broadway musicals or flashy song-and-dance shows. Tickets cost $25 to $75, more for big-name acts. 'Lounge shows' are smaller productions, in smaller venues, for smaller prices ($8 to $20). Some recommended shows are the Riviera's 'Evening at La Cage,' starring a cast of over-the-top female impersonators ($22), and the Stratosphere's classic 'Viva Las Vegas' revue ($10). Another winner is

Cirque du Soleil's 'Mystére,' at Treasure Island, featuring amazing acrobatic stunts. Unfortunately, it is expensive ($70).

For nightlife outside the casinos, check the *New Times*, a free weekly paper. A popular dance spot is ***Club Utopia*** *(☎ 702-736-3105)*, at 3765 Las Vegas Blvd S (across from the Monte Carlo), which plays techno-pop, hip-hop, alternative and Top 40 music.

Getting There & Away

The busy McCarran International Airport (☎ 702-261-5743) has direct flights to and from most LA-area airports, as well as most major US cities. Bell Trans (☎ 702-739-7990) and Gray Line (☎ 702-384-1234) provide airport shuttle service ($3.50 to $5 per person).

The Greyhound bus station (☎ 702-384-8009), downtown on Main, has regular buses to and from Los Angeles ($35). Other agencies offering bus service to Las Vegas are the USbus and the Ant (see the Getting There & Away chapter for more information).

Getting Around

Citizens Area Transport (CAT; ☎ 702-228-7433) runs local buses; bus No 301 cruises the Strip, 24 hours a day, all the way to downtown ($1.50). The Strip Trolley (☎ 702-382-1404) does a loop from the Luxor to the Stratosphere and out to the Las Vegas Hilton every 25 minutes until 2 am ($1.30).

Dozens of agencies along the Strip rent cars for $25 to $45 per day. Try Budget (☎ 702-736-1212) or Thrifty (☎ 702-896-7600).

Acknowledgements

THANKS

Many thanks to the travelers who used the last edition and wrote to us with helpful hints, useful advice and anecdotes: Caroline Bell, Stacy Benjamin, Elise Callinan, Natalie Darville, Pam Dickson, Neal Firth, Rodrigo Gouvea Rosique, C Harris, Silviu Landman, J Ferret Loophole, Claire Madden, Andreas Mahn, Frank Martini, D J Peterson, Marcia Pope, Dobromil Randa, Deborah Rogers, Sheridan Rhodes, Simon Skerrit, Allen Weekes, Alan Wong.

LONELY PLANET

Guides by Region

Lonely Planet is known worldwide for publishing practical, reliable and no-nonsense travel information in our guides and on our Web site. The Lonely Planet list covers just about every accessible part of the world. Currently there are nine series: travel guides, shoestring guides, walking guides, city guides, phrasebooks, audio packs, travel atlases, diving and snorkeling guides and travel literature.

AFRICA Africa – the South • Africa on a shoestring • Arabic (Egyptian) phrasebook • Arabic (Moroccan) phrasebook • Cairo • Cape Town • Central Africa • East Africa • Egypt • Egypt travel atlas • Ethiopian (Amharic) phrasebook • The Gambia & Senegal • Kenya • Kenya travel atlas • Malawi, Mozambique & Zambia • Morocco • North Africa • South Africa, Lesotho & Swaziland • South Africa, Lesotho & Swaziland travel atlas • Swahili phrasebook • Trekking in East Africa • Tunisia • West Africa • Zimbabwe, Botswana & Namibia • Zimbabwe, Botswana & Namibia travel atlas
Travel Literature: The Rainbird: A Central African Journey • Songs to an African Sunset: A Zimbabwean Story • Mali Blues: Traveling to an African Beat

AUSTRALIA & THE PACIFIC Australia • Australian phrasebook • Bushwalking in Australia • Bushwalking in Papua New Guinea • Fiji • Fijian phrasebook • Islands of Australia's Great Barrier Reef • Melbourne • Micronesia • New Caledonia • New South Wales & the ACT • New Zealand • Northern Territory • Outback Australia • Papua New Guinea • Papua New Guinea (Pidgin) phrasebook • Queensland • Rarotonga & the Cook Islands • Samoa • Solomon Islands • South Australia • Sydney • Tahiti & French Polynesia • Tasmania • Tonga • Tramping in New Zealand • Vanuatu • Victoria • Western Australia
Travel Literature: Islands in the Clouds • Sean & David's Long Drive

CENTRAL AMERICA & THE CARIBBEAN Bahamas and Turks & Caicos • Bermuda • Central America on a shoestring • Costa Rica • Cuba • Dominican Republic & Haiti • Eastern Caribbean • Guatemala, Belize & Yucatán: La Ruta Maya • Jamaica • Mexico • Mexico City • Panama • Puerto Rico
Travel Literature: Green Dreams: Travels in Central America

EUROPE Amsterdam • Andalucía • Austria • Baltic States phrasebook • Berlin • Britain • Central Europe • Central Europe phrasebook • Czech & Slovak Republics • Denmark • Dublin • Eastern Europe • Eastern Europe phrasebook • Edinburgh • Estonia, Latvia & Lithuania • Europe • Finland • France • French phrasebook • Germany • German phrasebook • Greece • Greek phrasebook • Hungary • Iceland, Greenland & the Faroe Islands • Ireland • Italian phrasebook • Italy • Lisbon • London • Mediterranean Europe • Mediterranean Europe phrasebook • Paris • Poland • Portugal • Portugal travel atlas • Prague • Romania & Moldova • Russia, Ukraine & Belarus • Russian phrasebook • Scandinavian & Baltic Europe • Scandinavian Europe phrasebook • Scotland • Slovenia • Spain • Spanish phrasebook • St Petersburg • Switzerland • Trekking in Spain • Ukrainian phrasebook • Vienna • Walking in Britain • Walking in Italy • Walking in Switzerland • Western Europe • Western Europe phrasebook
Travel Literature: The Olive Grove: Travels in Greece

INDIAN SUBCONTINENT Bangladesh • Bengali phrasebook • Bhutan • Delhi • Goa • Hindi/Urdu phrasebook • India • India & Bangladesh travel atlas • Indian Himalaya • Karakoram Highway • Nepal • Nepali phrasebook • Pakistan • Rajasthan • South India • Sri Lanka • Sri Lanka phrasebook • Trekking in the Indian Himalaya • Trekking in the Karakoram & Hindukush • Trekking in the Nepal Himalaya
Travel Literature: In Rajasthan • Shopping for Buddhas

LONELY PLANET

Mail Order

L onely Planet products are distributed worldwide.They are also available by mail order from Lonely Planet, so if you have difficulty finding a title please write to us. North and South American residents should write to 150 Linden St, Oakland, CA 94607, USA; European and African residents should write to 10a Spring Place, London NW5 3BH, UK; and residents of other countries to PO Box 617, Hawthorn, Victoria 3122, Australia.

ISLANDS OF THE INDIAN OCEAN Madagascar & Comoros • Maldives • Mauritius, Réunion & Seychelles

MIDDLE EAST & CENTRAL ASIA Arab Gulf States • Central Asia • Central Asia phrasebook • Iran • Israel & the Palestinian Territories • Israel & the Palestinian Territories travel atlas • Istanbul • Jerusalem • Jordan & Syria • Jordan, Syria & Lebanon travel atlas • Lebanon • Middle East on a shoestring • Turkey • Turkish phrasebook • Turkey travel atlas • Yemen
Travel Literature: The Gates of Damascus • Kingdom of the Film Stars: Journey into Jordan

NORTH AMERICA Alaska • Backpacking in Alaska • Baja California • California & Nevada • Canada • Chicago • Deep South • Florida • Hawaii • Honolulu • Los Angeles • Miami • New England USA • New Orleans • New York City • New York, New Jersey & Pennsylvania • Pacific Northwest USA • Rocky Mountain States • San Francisco • Seattle • Southwest USA • Texas • USA • USA phrasebook • Vancouver • Washington, DC & the Capital Region
Travel Literature: Drive Thru America

NORTH-EAST ASIA Beijing • Cantonese phrasebook • China • Hong Kong • Hong Kong, Macau & Guangzhou • Japan • Japanese phrasebook • Japanese audio pack • Korea • Korean phrasebook • Kyoto • Mandarin phrasebook • Mongolia • Mongolian phrasebook • North-East Asia on a shoestring • Seoul • South-West China • Taiwan • Tibet • Tibetan phrasebook • Tokyo
Travel Literature: Lost Japan

SOUTH AMERICA Argentina, Uruguay & Paraguay • Bolivia • Brazil • Brazilian phrasebook • Buenos Aires • Chile & Easter Island • Chile & Easter Island travel atlas • Colombia • Ecuador & the Galapagos Islands • Latin American Spanish phrasebook • Peru • Quechua phrasebook • Rio de Janeiro • South America on a shoestring • Trekking in the Patagonian Andes • Venezuela
Travel Literature: Full Circle: A South American Journey

SOUTH-EAST ASIA Bali & Lombok • Bangkok • Burmese phrasebook • Cambodia • Hill Tribes phrasebook • Ho Chi Minh City • Indonesia • Indonesian phrasebook • Indonesian audio pack • Jakarta • Java • Laos • Lao phrasebook • Laos travel atlas • Malay phrasebook • Malaysia, Singapore & Brunei • Myanmar (Burma) • Philippines • Pilipino (Tagalog) phrasebook • Singapore • South-East Asia on a shoestring • South-East Asia phrasebook • Thailand • Thailand's Islands & Beaches • Thailand travel atlas • Thai phrasebook • Thai audio pack • Vietnam • Vietnamese phrasebook • Vietnam travel atlas

ALSO AVAILABLE: Antarctica • Brief Encounters: Stories of Love, Sex & Travel • Chasing Rickshaws • Not the Only Planet: Travel Stories from Science Fiction • Travel with Children • Traveller's Tales

LONELY PLANET

Phrasebooks

Lonely Planet phrasebooks are packed with essential words and phrases to help travellers communicate with the locals. With color tabs for quick reference, an extensive vocabulary and use of script, these handy pocket-sized language guides cover day-to-day travel situations.

- handy pocket-sized books
- easy to understand Pronunciation chapter
- clear & comprehensive Grammar chapter
- romanization alongside script to allow ease of pronunciation
- script throughout so users can point to phrases for every situation
- full of cultural information and tips for the traveller

'...vital for a real DIY spirit and attitude in language learning'
– Backpacker

'the phrasebooks have good cultural backgrounders and offer solid advice for challenging situations in remote locations'
– San Francisco Examiner

Arabic (Egyptian) • Arabic (Moroccan) • Australian *(Australian English, Aboriginal and Torres Strait languages)* • Baltic States *(Estonian, Latvian, Lithuanian)* • Bengali • Brazilian • Burmese • Cantonese • Central Asia • Central Europe *(Czech, French, German, Hungarian, Italian, Slovak)* • Eastern Europe *(Bulgarian, Czech, Hungarian, Polish, Romanian, Slovak)* • Ethiopian (Amharic) • Fijian • French • German • Greek • Hill Tribes • Hindi/Urdu • Indonesian • Italian • Japanese • Korean • Lao • Latin American Spanish • Malay • Mandarin • Mediterranean Europe *(Albanian, Croatian, Greek, Italian, Macedonian, Maltese, Serbian, Slovene)* • Mongolian • Nepali • Papua New Guinea • Pilipino (Tagalog) • Quechua • Russian • Scandinavian Europe *(Danish, Finnish, Icelandic, Norwegian, Swedish)* • South-East Asia *(Burmese, Indonesian, Khmer, Lao, Malay, Tagalog Pilipino, Thai, Vietnamese)* • Spanish (Castilian) *(also includes Catalan, Galician and Basque)* • Sri Lanka • Swahili • Thai • Tibetan • Turkish • Ukrainian • USA *(US English, Vernacular, Native American languages, Hawaiian)* • Vietnamese • Western Europe *(Basque, Catalan, Dutch, French, German, Greek, Irish)*

Lonely Planet Journeys

JOURNEYS is a unique collection of travel writing – published by the company that understands travel better than anyone else. It is a series for anyone who has ever experienced – or dreamed of – the magical moment when they encountered a strange culture or saw a place for the first time. They are tales to read while you're planning a trip, while you're on the road or while you're in an armchair in front of a fire.

These outstanding titles explore our planet through the eyes of a diverse group of international writers. JOURNEYS books catch the spirit of a place, illuminate a culture, recount a crazy adventure or introduce a fascinating way of life. They always entertain, and always enrich the experience of travel.

FULL CIRCLE
A South American Journey
Luis Sepúlveda (translated by Chris Andrews)

'A journey without a fixed itinerary' with Chilean writer Luis Sepúlveda. Extravagant characters and extraordinary situations are memorably evoked: gauchos organising a tournament of lies, a scheming heiress on the lookout for a husband, a pilot with a corpse on board his plane ... *Full Circle* brings us the distinctive voice of one of South America's most compelling writers.

WINNER 1996 Astrolabe – Etonnants Voyageurs award for the best work of travel literature published in France.

GREEN DREAMS
Travels in Central America
Stephen Benz

On the Amazon, in Costa Rica, Honduras and on the Mayan trail from Guatemala to Mexico, Stephen Benz describes his encounters with water, mud, insects and other wildlife – and not least with the ecotourists themselves. With witty insights into modern travel, *Green Dreams* discusses the paradox of cultural and 'green' tourism.

DRIVE THRU AMERICA
Sean Condon

If you've ever wanted to drive across the USA but couldn't find the time (or afford the gas), *Drive Thru America* is perfect for you. In his search for American myths and realities – along with comfort, cable TV and good, reasonably priced coffee – Sean Condon paints a hilarious road-portrait of the USA.

'entertaining and laugh-out-loud funny'– *Alex Wilber, Travel editor, Amazon.com*

SEAN & DAVID'S LONG DRIVE
Sean Condon

Sean and David are young townies who have rarely strayed beyond city limits. One day, for no good reason, they set out to discover their homeland, and what follows is a wildly entertaining adventure that covers half of Australia.

'a hilariously detailed log of two burned out friends' – *Rolling Stone*

Index

Text

Bold indicates maps.

Bold indicates maps.

Bold indicates maps.

Bold indicates maps.

Bold indicates maps.

Boxed Text

Los Angeles Map Section

JIM CORWIN

MAP 2 WESTERN LOS ANGELES

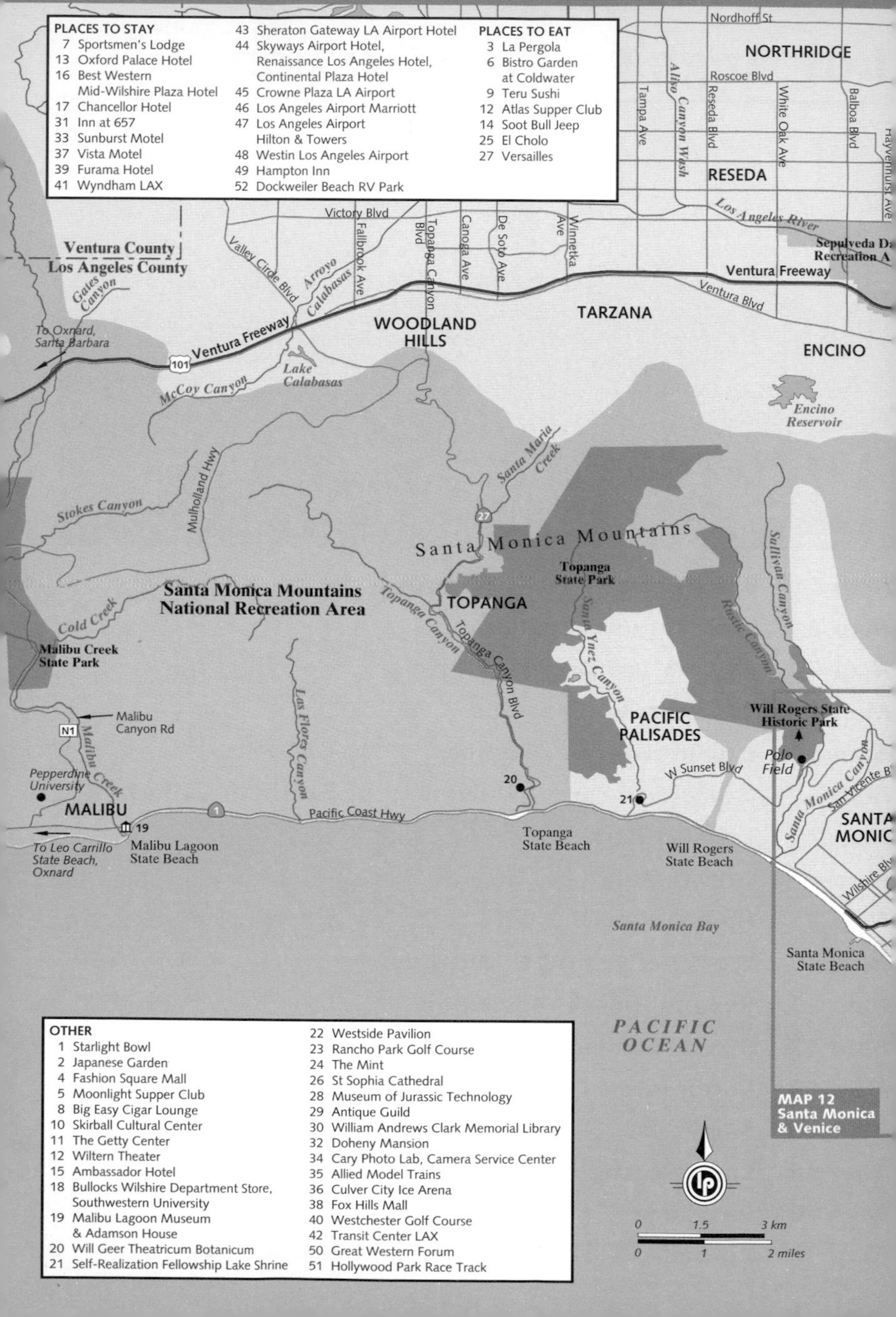

PLACES TO STAY
7 Sportsmen's Lodge
13 Oxford Palace Hotel
16 Best Western Mid-Wilshire Plaza Hotel
17 Chancellor Hotel
31 Inn at 657
33 Sunburst Motel
37 Vista Motel
39 Furama Hotel
41 Wyndham LAX
43 Sheraton Gateway LA Airport Hotel
44 Skyways Airport Hotel, Renaissance Los Angeles Hotel, Continental Plaza Hotel
45 Crowne Plaza LA Airport
46 Los Angeles Airport Marriott
47 Los Angeles Airport Hilton & Towers
48 Westin Los Angeles Airport
49 Hampton Inn
52 Dockweiler Beach RV Park
PLACES TO EAT
3 La Pergola
6 Bistro Garden at Coldwater
9 Teru Sushi
12 Atlas Supper Club
14 Soot Bull Jeep
25 El Cholo
27 Versailles
OTHER
1 Starlight Bowl
2 Japanese Garden
4 Fashion Square Mall
5 Moonlight Supper Club
8 Big Easy Cigar Lounge
10 Skirball Cultural Center
11 The Getty Center
12 Wiltern Theater
15 Ambassador Hotel
18 Bullocks Wilshire Department Store, Southwestern University
19 Malibu Lagoon Museum & Adamson House
20 Will Geer Theatricum Botanicum
21 Self-Realization Fellowship Lake Shrine
22 Westside Pavilion
23 Rancho Park Golf Course
24 The Mint
26 St Sophia Cathedral
28 Museum of Jurassic Technology
29 Antique Guild
30 William Andrews Clark Memorial Library
32 Doheny Mansion
34 Cary Photo Lab, Camera Service Center
35 Allied Model Trains
36 Culver City Ice Arena
38 Fox Hills Mall
40 Westchester Golf Course
42 Transit Center LAX
50 Great Western Forum
51 Hollywood Park Race Track
Nordhoff St
NORTHRIDGE
Roscoe Blvd
Tampa Ave
Aliso Canyon Wash
Reseda Blvd
White Oak Ave
Balboa Blvd
Hayvenhurst Ave
RESEDA
Los Angeles River
Sepulveda Dam Recreation Area
Victory Blvd
Fallbrook Ave
Topanga Canyon Blvd
Canoga Ave
De Soto Ave
Winnetka Ave
Ventura County
Los Angeles County
Gates Canyon
Valley Circle Blvd
Arroyo Calabasas
Ventura Freeway
Ventura Blvd
WOODLAND HILLS
TARZANA
ENCINO
To Oxnard, Santa Barbara
101
Lake Calabasas
McCoy Canyon
Encino Reservoir
Santa Maria Creek
Mulholland Hwy
Stokes Canyon
27
Santa Monica Mountains
Topanga State Park
Santa Monica Mountains National Recreation Area
TOPANGA
Topanga Canyon
Cold Creek
Malibu Creek State Park
Santa Ynez Canyon
Rustic Canyon
Sullivan Canyon
Las Flores Canyon
PACIFIC PALISADES
Will Rogers State Historic Park
Polo Field
Malibu Canyon Rd
N1
Malibu Creek
Pepperdine University
MALIBU
W Sunset Blvd
Santa Monica Canyon
San Vicente Blvd
20
21
1
Pacific Coast Hwy
19
To Leo Carrillo State Beach, Oxnard
Malibu Lagoon State Beach
Topanga State Beach
Will Rogers State Beach
SANTA MONICA
Wilshire Blvd
Santa Monica Bay
Santa Monica State Beach
PACIFIC OCEAN
MAP 12 Santa Monica & Venice
0 1.5 3 km
0 1 2 miles

MAP 3 EASTERN LOS ANGELES

To San Fernando, I-5

Mt Wilson Red Box Rd

Foothill Blvd

Foothill Freeway

LA CAÑADA FLINTRIDGE

Honolulu Ave

Wildwood Canyon Park

to MAP 2 Western Los Angeles

Angeles National Forest

Oak Grove Drive

Devils Gate Reservoir

W Altadena Drive

ALTADENA

Eaton Canyon Park

Eaton Canyon Reservoir

Brand Park

To Burbank

GLENDALE

W Glenoaks Blvd

Canada Blvd

Glendale Freeway

Brookside Golf Course

Scholl Canyon Golf Course

N Lincoln Ave

N Fair Oaks Ave

N Los Robles Ave

N Lake Ave

N Allen Ave

N Altadena Dr

E Sierra Madre Blvd

E Orange Grove Blvd

MAP 8 Griffith Park

E Chevy Chase Drive

E Broadway
E Colorado St

Ventura Freeway

Eagle Rock Reservoir

Rose Bowl

Brookside Park

Foothill Freeway

E Colorado Blvd

Griffith Park

Verdugo Rd

Eagle Rock Blvd

Colorado Blvd

134

Lower Arroyo Park

PASADENA

Caltech

E California Blvd

SAN MARINO

Huntington Dr

MAP 9 Hollywood

S Brand Blvd
S Central Ave

Golden State Freeway

Fletcher Drive

York Blvd

MAP 16 Pasadena

Huntington Library, Art Collection & Botanical Gardens

E Duarte Rd

San Fernando Rd

MAP 5 Downtown Los Angeles

N Figueroa St

Pasadena Freeway

Monterey Rd

W Sunset Blvd

Silver Lake Blvd

Elysian Park

Ernest E Debs Regional Park

ALHAMBRA

N Main St

N Garfield Ave

SAN GABRIEL

E Las Tunas Drive

W Mission Drive

Hollywood Freeway

Glendale Blvd

110

N Broadway

N Mission Rd

Huntington Drive

S Fremont Ave

W Mission Rd

W Valley Blvd

E Valley Blvd

To Hollywood

101

N Main St

Valley Blvd

Alhambra Ave

San Bernardino Freeway

10

Del Mar Ave

S San Gabriel Blvd

To I-405, Santa Monica

Harbor Freeway

LOS ANGELES

E 1st St

Marengo St

18

E Garvey Ave

MONTEREY PARK

S Atlantic Blvd

S Garfield Ave

Garvey Reservoir

Potrero Grande Dr

Santa Monica Freeway

E Cesar E Chavez Ave

Soto St

Cesar E Chavez Ave

Pomona Freeway

60

MAP 6 USC

E Adams Blvd

Los Angeles River

Lorena St

EAST LOS ANGELES

Whittier Blvd

E Beverly Blvd

MONTEBELLO

USC

E Jefferson Blvd

Exposition Park

E Olympic Blvd

E Washington Blvd

72

S Vermont Ave

S Main St

Avalon Blvd

S Central Ave

Compton Blvd

S Alameda St

S Santa Fe Ave

E Vernon Ave

E 37th St

25

Bandini Blvd

VERNON

26

CITY OF COMMERCE

Santa Ana Freeway

Eastern Ave

Garfield Ave

S Greenwood Ave

E Washington Blvd

Passons Blvd

PICO RIVERA

Slauson Ave

Long Beach Freeway

Pacific Blvd

Slauson Ave

Gage Ave

Rio Hondo

5

Telegraph Rd

San Gabriel River Freeway

E Century Blvd

WATTS

E 103rd St

California Blvd

Firestone Blvd

SOUTH GATE

E Florence Ave

E Florence Ave

DOWNEY

605

SANTA FE SPRINGS

Wilmington Ave

E Imperial Hwy

Martin Abbott Rd

Atlantic Ave

to MAP 4 Southern Los Angeles

710

Los Angeles River

Paramount Blvd

Lakewood Blvd

San Gabriel River

To Irvine, San Diego

Century Freeway

To I-405, LAX

105

To Long Beach

E Imperial Hwy

To I-405

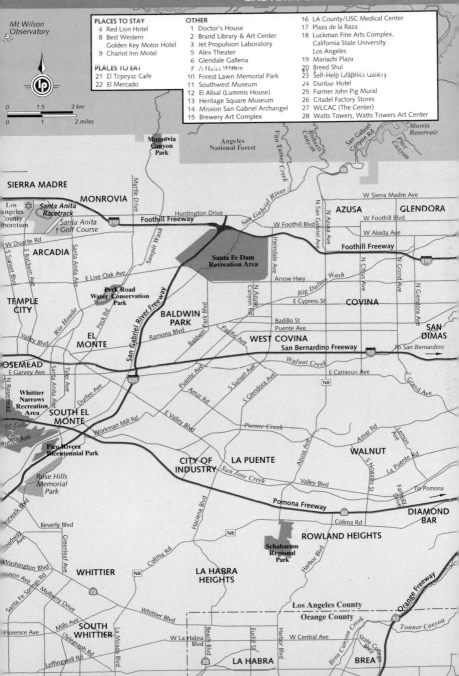

PLACES TO STAY
4 Red Lion Hotel
8 Best Western
   Golden Key Motor Hotel
9 Chariot Inn Motel

PLACES TO EAT
21 El Tepeyac Cafe
22 El Mercado

OTHER
1 Doctor's House
2 Brand Library & Art Center
3 Jet Propulsion Laboratory
5 Alex Theater
6 Glendale Galleria
7 A Noise Within
10 Forest Lawn Memorial Park
11 Southwest Museum
12 El Alisal (Lummis House)
13 Heritage Square Museum
14 Mission San Gabriel Archangel
15 Brewery Art Complex

16 LA County/USC Medical Center
17 Plaza de la Raza
18 Luckman Fine Arts Complex,
   California State University
   Los Angeles
19 Mariachi Plaza
20 Breed Shul
23 Self-Help Graphics Gallery
24 Dunbar Hotel
25 Farmer John Pig Mural
26 Citadel Factory Stores
27 WLCAC (The Center)
28 Watts Towers, Watts Towers Art Center

Mt Wilson
Observatory

0   1.5   3 km
0   1   2 miles

Angeles
National Forest

Monrovia
Canyon
Park

Morris
Reservoir

SIERRA MADRE

MONROVIA

AZUSA   GLENDORA

W Sierra Madre Ave

Los
Angeles
County
Arboretum

Santa Anita
Racetrack

Santa Anita
Golf Course

Foothill Freeway

Huntington Drive

W Foothill Blvd

W Foothill Blvd

W Alosta Ave

Foothill Freeway

W Duarte Rd

ARCADIA

TEMPLE
CITY

Santa Fe Dam
Recreation Area

E Live Oak Ave

Arrow Hwy

Big Dalton Wash

COVINA

SAN
DIMAS

Peck Road
Water Conservation
Park

BALDWIN
PARK

E Cypress St

Badillo St

Puente Ave

EL
MONTE

Ramona Blvd

WEST COVINA

San Bernardino Freeway

To San Bernardino

ROSEMEAD

E Garvey Ave

Whittier
Narrows
Recreation
Area

SOUTH EL
MONTE

Durfee Ave

Workman Mill Rd

E Valley Blvd

Walnut Creek

E Cameron Ave

Puente Creek

WALNUT

Amar Rd

La Puente Rd

Pico Rivera
Bicentennial Park

CITY OF
INDUSTRY

LA PUENTE

San Jose Creek

Valley Blvd

To Pomona

Rose Hills
Memorial
Park

Pomona Freeway

DIAMOND
BAR

Beverly Blvd

Colima Rd

ROWLAND HEIGHTS

Greenleaf Ave

Washington Blvd

WHITTIER

Schabarum
Regional
Park

Harbor Blvd

Santa Fe Springs Rd

Mulberry Drive

LA HABRA
HEIGHTS

Whittier Blvd

Los Angeles County

Orange County

Orange Freeway

Mills Ave

SOUTH
WHITTIER

Telegraph Rd

Florence Ave

Leffingwell Rd

W La Habra
Blvd

Beach Blvd

Euclid St

W Central Ave

Harbor Blvd

Brea Canyon Creek

Tonner Canyon

LA HABRA

BREA

MAP 4 SOUTHERN LOS ANGELES

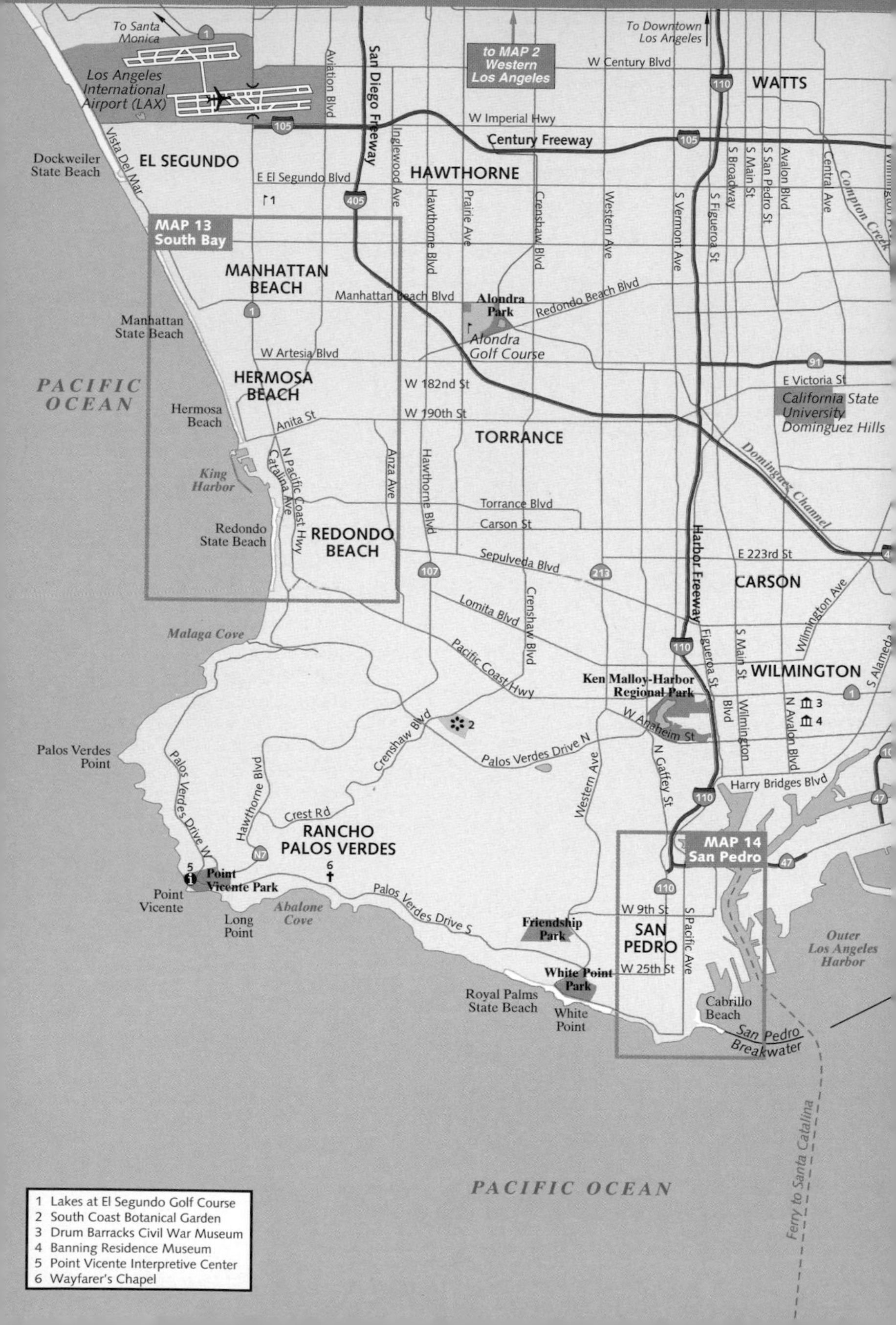

To Santa Monica

Los Angeles International Airport (LAX)

Dockweiler State Beach

EL SEGUNDO

Aviation Blvd

San Diego Freeway

to MAP 2 Western Los Angeles

To Downtown Los Angeles

W Century Blvd

110

WATTS

W Imperial Hwy

Century Freeway

E El Segundo Blvd

HAWTHORNE

S Broadway

S Vermont Ave

S Figueroa St

S Main St

S San Pedro St

Avalon Blvd

Central Ave

Compton Creek

105

105

MAP 13 South Bay

MANHATTAN BEACH

Inglewood Ave

Hawthorne Blvd

Prairie Ave

Crenshaw Blvd

Western Ave

Manhattan Beach Blvd

Manhattan State Beach

Manhattan Beach Blvd

Alondra Park

Redondo Beach Blvd

Alondra Golf Course

PACIFIC OCEAN

HERMOSA BEACH

W Artesia Blvd

W 182nd St

W 190th St

E Victoria St

91

California State University Dominguez Hills

Hermosa Beach

Anita St

N Pacific Coast Hwy

Catalina Ave

Anza Ave

Hawthorne Blvd

TORRANCE

Dominguez Channel

King Harbor

Redondo State Beach

REDONDO BEACH

Torrance Blvd

Carson St

E 223rd St

CARSON

107

213

Sepulveda Blvd

Crenshaw Blvd

Harbor Freeway

Figueroa St

S Main St

Wilmington Ave

WILMINGTON

S Alameda

Malaga Cove

Lomita Blvd

Pacific Coast Hwy

Ken Malloy-Harbor Regional Park

110

Wilmington Blvd

N Avalon Blvd

1

🏛 3
🏛 4

Crenshaw Blvd

2

Palos Verdes Drive N

W Anaheim St

Harry Bridges Blvd

47

Palos Verdes Point

Hawthorne Blvd

Western Ave

N Gaffey St

110

Palos Verdes Drive W

Crest Rd

RANCHO PALOS VERDES

N?

MAP 14 San Pedro

Palos Verdes Drive S

5 Point Vicente Park

6 ✝

110

W 9th St

SAN PEDRO

Outer Los Angeles Harbor

Point Vicente

Long Point

Abalone Cove

Friendship Park

S Pacific Ave

W 25th St

Cabrillo Beach

Royal Palms State Beach

White Point Park

White Point

San Pedro Breakwater

PACIFIC OCEAN

Ferry to Santa Catalina

1 Lakes at El Segundo Golf Course
2 South Coast Botanical Garden
3 Drum Barracks Civil War Museum
4 Banning Residence Museum
5 Point Vicente Interpretive Center
6 Wayfarer's Chapel

SOUTH GATE

DOWNEY

Florence Ave

Telegraph Rd

Mulberry Drive

to MAP 3
Eastern
Los Angeles

19

Martin Abbott Rd

Rio Hondo

Firestone Blvd

605

Carmenita Rd

Leffingwell Rd

E Imperial Hwy

710

105

5

Santa Ana Freeway

COMPTON

Rosecrans Ave

To Irvine,
San Diego

S Alameda St

Long Beach Blvd

Alondra Blvd

Lakewood Blvd

Bellflower Blvd

Studebaker Rd

Pioneer Blvd

Norwalk Blvd

Bloomfield Ave

Artesia Freeway

91

Artesia Blvd

Atlantic Ave

Orange Ave

Cherry Ave

Paramount Blvd

Downey Ave

San Gabriel River

San Gabriel River Freeway

183rd St

South St

Orangethorpe Ave

Long Beach Freeway

Los Angeles River

LAKEWOOD

Del Amo Blvd

La Palma Ave

19

Centralia St

Crescent Ave

Heartwell Park

Carson St

W Lincoln Ave

605

W Orange Ave

San Diego Freeway

Skylinks
Golf Course

Los Coyotes Diagonal

El Dorado
Park

Wardlow Rd

W Ball Rd

Cerritos Ave

Coyote Creek

Katella Ave

E Willow St

El Dorado
Park Golf
Course

LONG
BEACH

Stearns St

405

Los Alamitos Blvd

Valley View St

710

Terminal Island
Freeway

S Santa Fe Ave

MAP 15
Long Beach

E Pacific Coast Hwy

Atherton St

E Anaheim St

1

California State
University
Long Beach

22

Garden Grove Fwy

405

22

San Diego Freeway

E 7th St

Recreation
Park

Recreation
Park Golf
Course

United States
Naval Weapons Station

Bolsa Ave

E Ocean Blvd

NAPLES

Los Angeles County

Orange County

Seal Beach Blvd

Bolsa Chica Rd

Springdale St

East
Basin

West
Basin

Long Beach
Marina

Seal Beach
National Wildlife
Refuge

Warner Ave

Outer Long Beach Harbor

Seal
Beach

Middle Breakwater

Long Beach Breakwater

Anaheim
Bay

Ferry to Santa Catalina

San Pedro Bay

Sunset
County
Beach

Bolsa Chica
State Beach

To
Laguna
Beach

1

LP

Huntington
City Beach

0   1.5   3 km

0   1   2 miles

MAP 5 DOWNTOWN LOS ANGELES

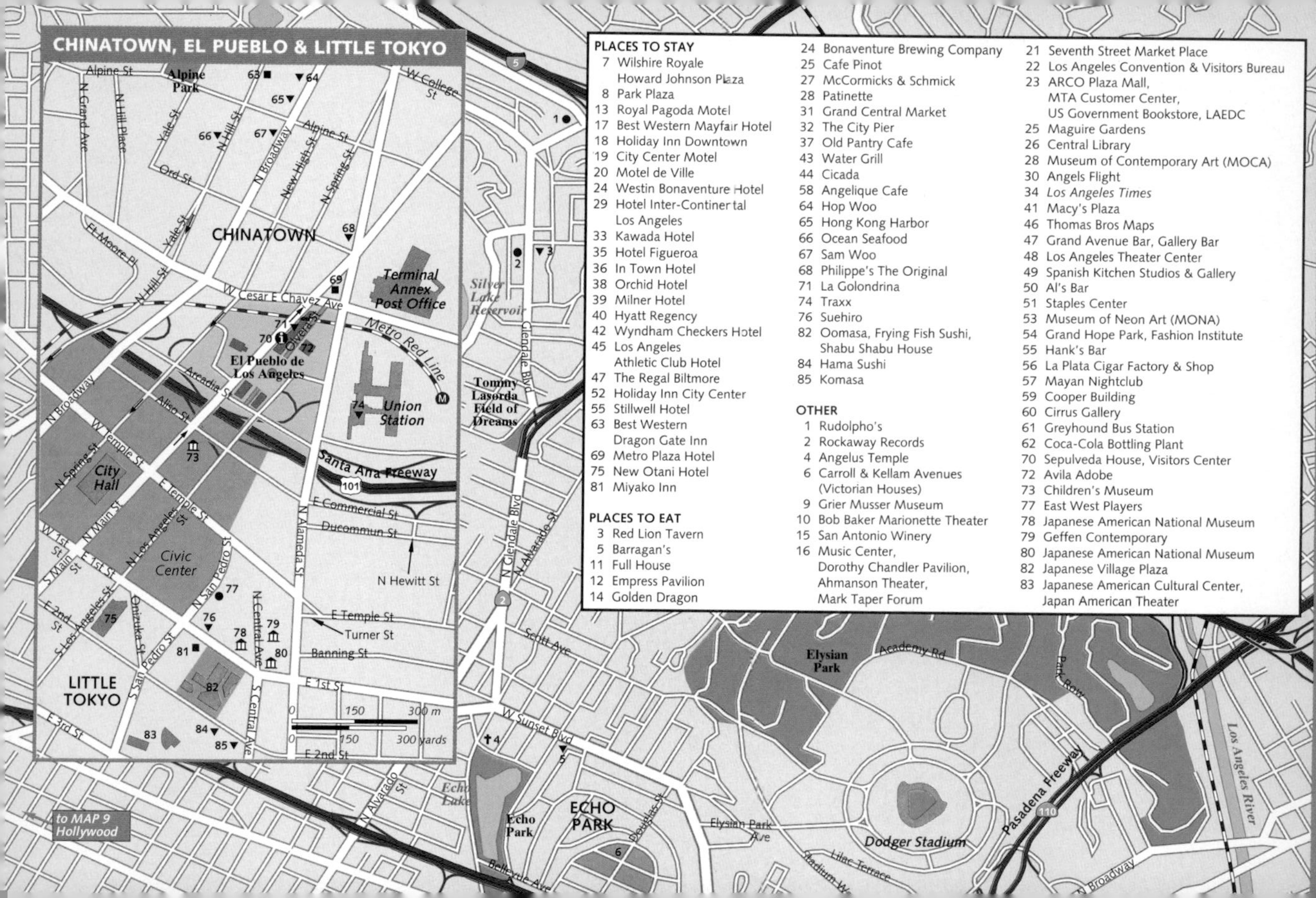

CHINATOWN, EL PUEBLO & LITTLE TOKYO

PLACES TO STAY
7 Wilshire Royale
Howard Johnson Plaza
8 Park Plaza
13 Royal Pagoda Motel
17 Best Western Mayfair Hotel
18 Holiday Inn Downtown
19 City Center Motel
20 Motel de Ville
24 Westin Bonaventure Hotel
29 Hotel Inter-Continental Los Angeles
33 Kawada Hotel
35 Hotel Figueroa
36 In Town Hotel
38 Orchid Hotel
39 Milner Hotel
40 Hyatt Regency
42 Wyndham Checkers Hotel Los Angeles
45 Athletic Club Hotel
47 The Regal Biltmore
52 Holiday Inn City Center
55 Stillwell Hotel
63 Best Western
69 Dragon Gate Inn
Metro Plaza Hotel
75 New Otani Hotel
81 Miyako Inn

PLACES TO EAT
3 Red Lion Tavern
5 Barragan's
11 Full House
12 Empress Pavilion
14 Golden Dragon
24 Bonaventure Brewing Company
25 Cafe Pinot
27 McCormick's & Schmick
28 Patinette
31 Grand Central Market
32 The City Pier
37 Old Pantry Cafe
43 Water Grill
44 Cicada
58 Angelique Cafe
64 Hop Woo
65 Hong Kong Harbor
66 Ocean Seafood
67 Sam Woo
68 Philippe's The Original
71 La Golondrina
74 Traxx
76 Suehiro
82 Oomasa, Frying Fish Sushi, Shabu Shabu House
84 Hama Sushi
85 Komasa

OTHER
1 Rudolpho's
2 Rockaway Records
4 Angelus Temple
6 Carroll & Kellam Avenues (Victorian Houses)
9 Grier Musser Museum
10 Bob Baker Marionette Theater
15 Music Center,
San Antonio Winery
16 Dorothy Chandler Pavilion,
Ahmanson Theater,
Mark Taper Forum
21 Seventh Street Market Place
22 Los Angeles Convention & Visitors Bureau
23 ARCO Plaza Mall,
MTA Customer Center,
US Government Bookstore, LAEDC
25 Maguire Gardens
26 Central Library
28 Museum of Contemporary Art (MOCA)
30 Angels Flight
34 Los Angeles Times
41 Macy's Plaza
46 Thomas Bros Maps
47 Grand Avenue Bar, Gallery Bar
48 Los Angeles Theater Center
49 Spanish Kitchen Studios & Gallery
50 Al's Bar
51 Staples Center
53 Museum of Neon Art (MONA)
54 Grand Hope Park, Fashion Institute
55 Hank's Bar
56 La Plata Cigar Factory & Shop
57 Mayan Nightclub
59 Cooper Building
60 Cirrus Gallery
61 Greyhound Bus Station
62 Coca-Cola Bottling Plant
70 Sepulveda House, Visitors Center
72 Avila Adobe
73 Children's Museum
77 East West Players
78 Japanese American National Museum
79 Geffen Contemporary
80 Japanese American National Museum
82 Japanese Village Plaza
83 Japanese American Cultural Center, Japan American Theater

MAP 6 EXPOSITION PARK & UNIVERSITY OF SOUTHERN CALIFORNIA

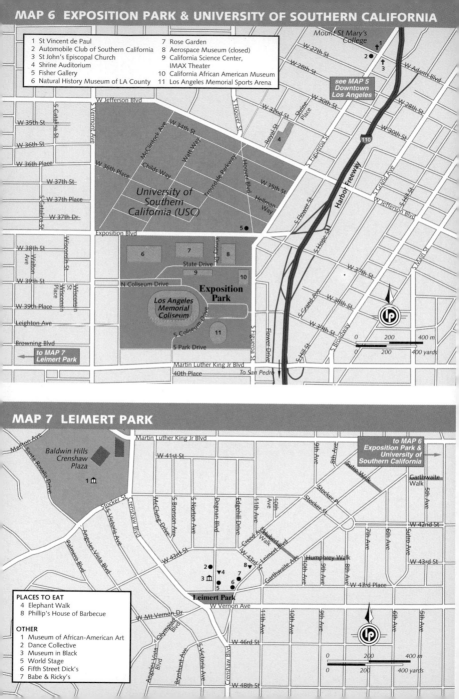

1 St Vincent de Paul
2 Automobile Club of Southern California
3 St John's Episcopal Church
4 Shrine Auditorium
5 Fisher Gallery
6 Natural History Museum of LA County
7 Rose Garden
8 Aerospace Museum (closed)
9 California Science Center, IMAX Theater
10 California African American Museum
11 Los Angeles Memorial Sports Arena

Mount St Mary's College

see MAP 5
Downtown
Los Angeles

University of Southern California (USC)

Exposition Park

Los Angeles Memorial Coliseum

to MAP 7
Leimert Park

Harbor Freeway

Martin Luther King Jr Blvd

To San Pedro

MAP 7 LEIMERT PARK

Baldwin Hills Crenshaw Plaza

to MAP 6
Exposition Park &
University of
Southern California

Leimert Park

PLACES TO EAT
4 Elephant Walk
8 Phillip's House of Barbecue

OTHER
1 Museum of African-American Art
2 Dance Collective
3 Museum in Black
5 World Stage
6 Fifth Street Dick's
7 Babe & Ricky's

to MAP 5
Downtown
Los Angeles

SILVER
LAKE

LOS FELIZ

Griffith Park

Universal City

Legend

1 Travel Town Museum
2 LA Live Steamers
3 Gene Autry Western Heritage Museum
4 Griffith Park
5 Merry-Go-Round
6 Griffith Park Ranger Station
   Griffith Observatory & Planetarium
7 Greek Theater

MAP 9 HOLLYWOOD

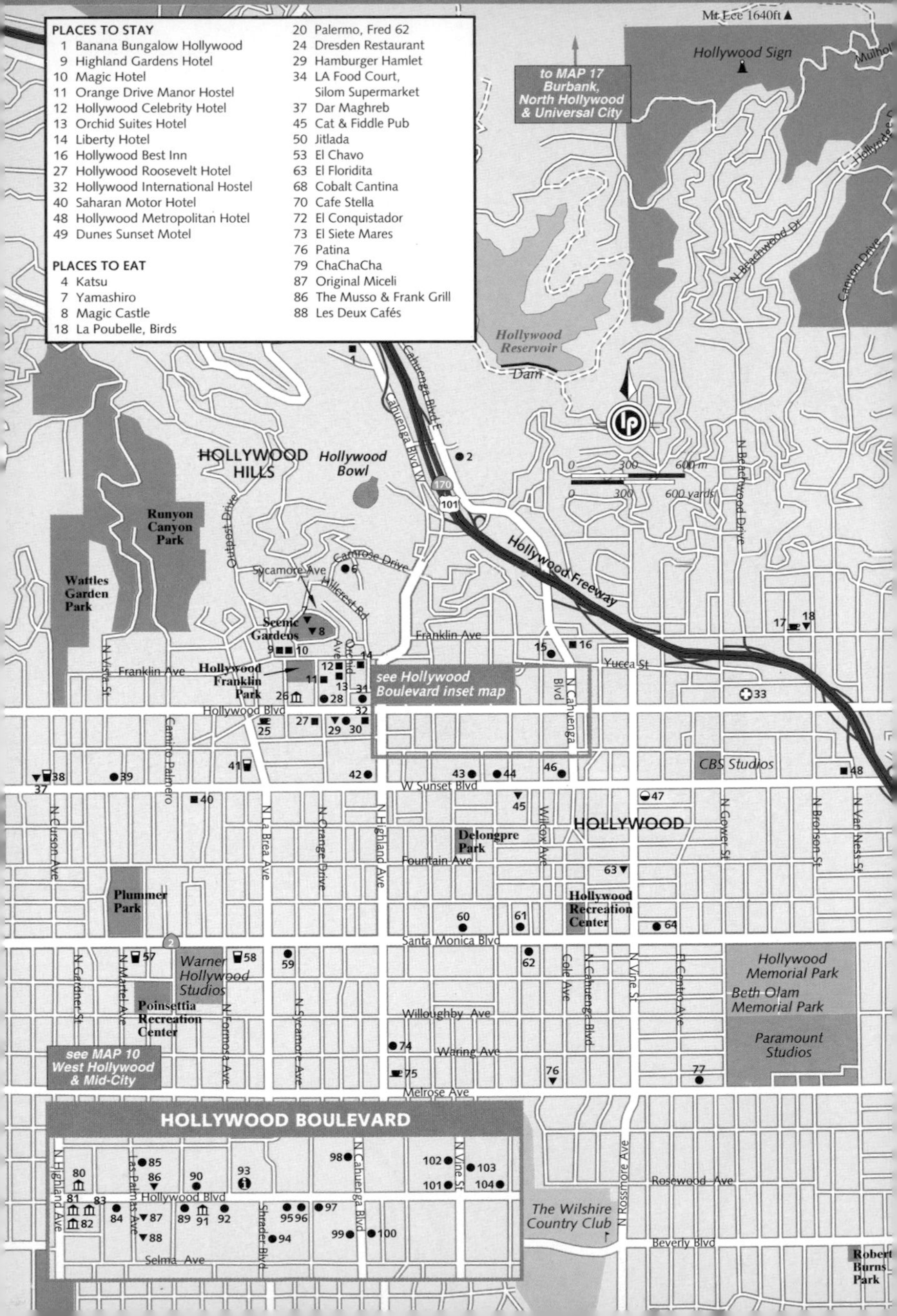

Mt Lee 1640ft ▲

Hollywood Sign

to MAP 17
Burbank,
North Hollywood
& Universal City

Hollywood
Reservoir

Dam

HOLLYWOOD
HILLS

Hollywood
Bowl

Runyon
Canyon
Park

Wattles
Garden
Park

Sycamore Ave

Camrose Drive

Scenic
Gardens

Franklin Ave

Hollywood
Franklin
Park

Hollywood Blvd

see Hollywood
Boulevard inset map

Yucca St

CBS Studios

W Sunset Blvd

HOLLYWOOD

Delongpre
Park

Fountain Ave

Hollywood
Recreation
Center

Plummer
Park

Santa Monica Blvd

Warner
Hollywood
Studios

Poinsettia
Recreation
Center

see MAP 10
West Hollywood
& Mid-City

Hollywood
Memorial Park

Beth Olam
Memorial Park

Paramount
Studios

Willoughby Ave

Waring Ave

Melrose Ave

HOLLYWOOD BOULEVARD

Hollywood Blvd

Selma Ave

The Wilshire
Country Club

Rosewood Ave

Beverly Blvd

Robert
Burns
Park

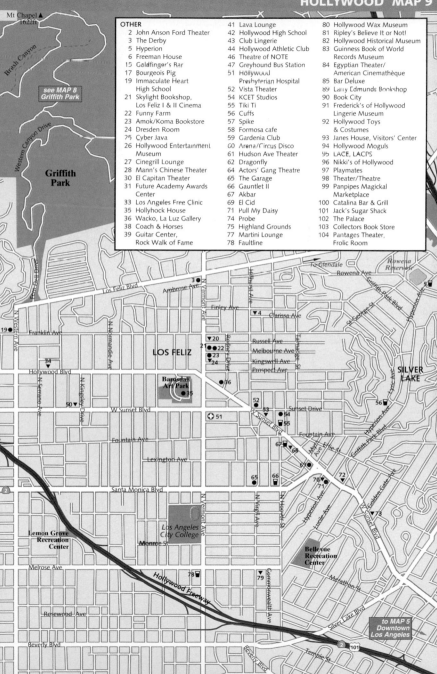

OTHER

2 John Anson Ford Theater
3 The Derby
5 Hyperion
6 Freeman House
15 Goldfinger's Bar
17 Bourgeois Pig
19 Immaculate Heart High School
21 Skylight Bookshop, Los Feliz I & II Cinema
22 Funny Farm
23 Amok/Koma Bookstore
24 Dresden Room
25 Cyber Java
26 Hollywood Entertainment Museum
27 Cinegrill Lounge
28 Mann's Chinese Theater
30 El Capitan Theater
31 Future Academy Awards Center
33 Los Angeles Free Clinic
35 Hollyhock House
36 Wacko, La Luz Gallery
38 Coach & Horses
39 Guitar Center, Rock Walk of Fame

41 Lava Lounge
42 Hollywood High School
43 Club Lingerie
44 Hollywood Athletic Club
46 Theatre of NOTE
47 Greyhound Bus Station
51 Hollywood Presbyterian Hospital
52 Vista Theater
54 KCET Studios
55 Tiki Ti
56 Cuffs
57 Spike
58 Formosa cafe
59 Gardenia Club
60 Arena/Circus Disco
61 Hudson Ave Theater
62 Dragonfly
64 Actors' Gang Theatre
65 The Garage
66 Gauntlet II
67 Akbar
69 El Cid
71 Pull My Daisy
74 Probe
75 Highland Grounds
77 Martini Lounge
78 Faultline

80 Hollywood Wax Museum
81 Ripley's Believe It or Not!
82 Hollywood Historical Museum
83 Guinness Book of World Records Museum
84 Egyptian Theater/ American Cinematheque
85 Bar Deluxe
89 Larry Edmunds Bookshop
90 Book City
91 Frederick's of Hollywood Lingerie Museum
92 Hollywood Toys & Costumes
93 Janes House, Visitors' Center
94 Hollywood Moguls
95 LACE, LACPS
96 Nikki's of Hollywood
97 Playmates
98 Theater/Theatre
99 Panpipes Magickal Marketplace
100 Catalina Bar & Grill
101 Jack's Sugar Shack
102 The Palace
103 Collectors Book Store
104 Pantages Theater, Frolic Room

MAP 10 WEST HOLLYWOOD & MID-CITY

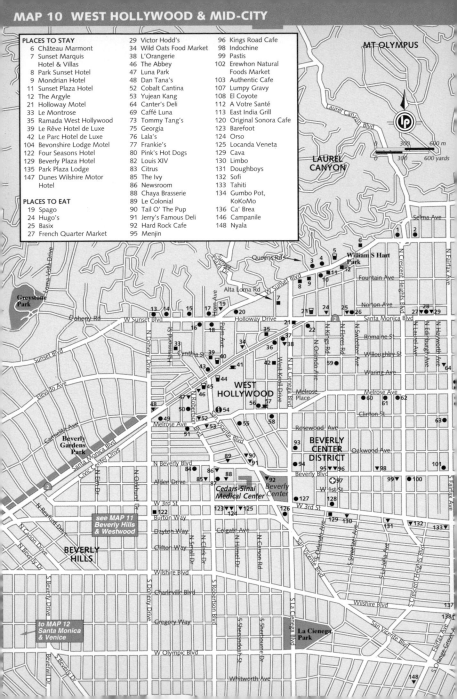

ENTERTAINMENT
- 1 Coconut Teaszer
- 2 Laugh Factory
- 3 Comedy Store
- 5 Thunder Roadhouse
- 9 Sky Bar
- 10 House of Blues
- 13 Key Club
- 14 The Roxy,
  Rainbow Bar & Grill
- 15 Whiskey a Go Go
- 16 Viper Room
- 20 Tiffany Theater
- 23 Barney's Beanery
- 26 Coast Playhouse
- 28 Club 7969
- 32 Celebration Theater
- 36 The Palms
- 37 Benvenuto Cafe,
  Klub Banshee
- 40 Trunks
- 41 Little Frida's
- 43 WeHo Lounge, Micky's,
  Revolver
- 44 Rage
- 45 Mother Lode
- 48 La Masia,
  Doug Weston's Troubadour
- 50 Love Lounge, Axis
- 57 Urth Caffe
- 61 The Improv
- 63 Bang Theater
- 64 Kibitz Room
- 65 Genghis Cohen
- 72 Groundlings Theater
- 87 Storyopolis
- 94 Coronet Theater,
  Coronet Pub
- 100 Kowboyz
- 101 Fairfax Cinema
- 109 Insomnia Cafe
- 110 New Beverly Cinema
- 115 Acme Comedy Theater
- 144 Conga Room

SHOPPING
- 17 Tower Records
- 18 Book Soup
- 22 Dreamdresser
- 31 Pleasure Chest
- 43 A Different Light Bookstore
- 49 Herbert Palmer Gallery
- 51 Tasende Gallery
- 55 Daniel Saxon Gallery
- 56 Bodhi Tree Bookstore
- 58 Heritage Bookshop
- 60 Sports Books
- 62 Fred Segal
- 66 Melrose Trading Post
- 67 Scents from Above
- 68 Aardvark
- 70 Slow, Maya Jewelry
- 71 Wasteland, Wound & Wound
- 72 Off the Wall, Vinyl Fetish
- 74 Condomania
- 78 Necromance
- 79 Jet Rag
- 81 Sacks SFO
- 84 Antiquarius
- 93 Trashy Lingerie
- 105 Every Picture Tells a Story
- 106 Tobey C Moss Gallery
- 111 Jack Rutberg Gallery
- 114 Iturralde Gallery
- 116 Fahey/Klein Gallery
- 117 Paul Kopeikin Gallery
- 118 Golyester
- 119 Jan Baum Gallery
- 126 Loehmann's
- 128 Traveler's Bookcase,
  Cooks Library
- 142 New Mastodon Books &
  Fine Art

OTHER
- 4 Hyatt Hotel
- 30 Porno Walk of Fame
- 54 Pacific Design Center,
  West Hollywood Convention
  & Visitors' Bureau
- 59 MAK Center for
  Art & Architecture at the
  Schindler House
- 66 Fairfax High School
- 97 Los Angeles Free Clinic
- 121 Samy's Camera
- 127 American Express
- 137 LACMA West
- 138 Petersen Automobile Museum
- 139 LA County Museum of Art
- 140 Carole & Barry Kaye
  Museum of Miniature Art
- 141 La Brea Tar Pits,
  Page Museum at La Brea
  Discoveries
- 143 Goethe Institute
- 145 MTA Customer Center

Runyon
Canyon
Park

Wattles
Garden
Park

Hollywood Blvd

Hawthorne Ave

N Sierra Bonita Ave

N Stanley Ave

N Curson Ave

N Gardner St

N La Brea Ave

N Orange Drive

N Mansfield Ave

Highland Ave

see MAP 9
Hollywood

W Sunset Blvd

Delongpre
Park

Fountain Ave

Plummer
Park

Santa Monica Blvd

Warner
Hollywood
Studios

Poinsettia
Recreation
Center

Willoughby Ave

N Sycamore Ave

N Citrus Ave

Melrose Ave

Clinton St

MELROSE/
LA BREA

N Fuller Ave

N Poinsettia Place

N Alta Vista Blvd

N Vista St

N Curson Ave

N Gardner St

N Stanley Ave

FAIRFAX
DISTRICT

Rosewood Ave

Oakwood Ave

The Wilshire
Country Club

Beverly Blvd

Television
City

Pan
Pacific
Park

Farmers'
Market

S Detroit St

S La Brea Ave

S Highland Ave

W 1st St

W 2nd St

W 3rd St

S Orange Drive

W 4th St

W 6th St

Hancock
Park

MIRACLE MILE
DISTRICT

HANCOCK
PARK

N Stanley Ave

N Curson Ave

Sierra Bonita Ave

N Hauser Blvd

N Masselin Ave

Wilshire Blvd

S Ridgeley Dr

S Mansfield Ave

S Lucerne Blvd

S Plymouth Blvd

Crenshaw Blvd

W 8th St

W 9th St

W Olympic Blvd

Los Angeles High
Memorial Park

MAP 11 BEVERLY HILLS & WESTWOOD

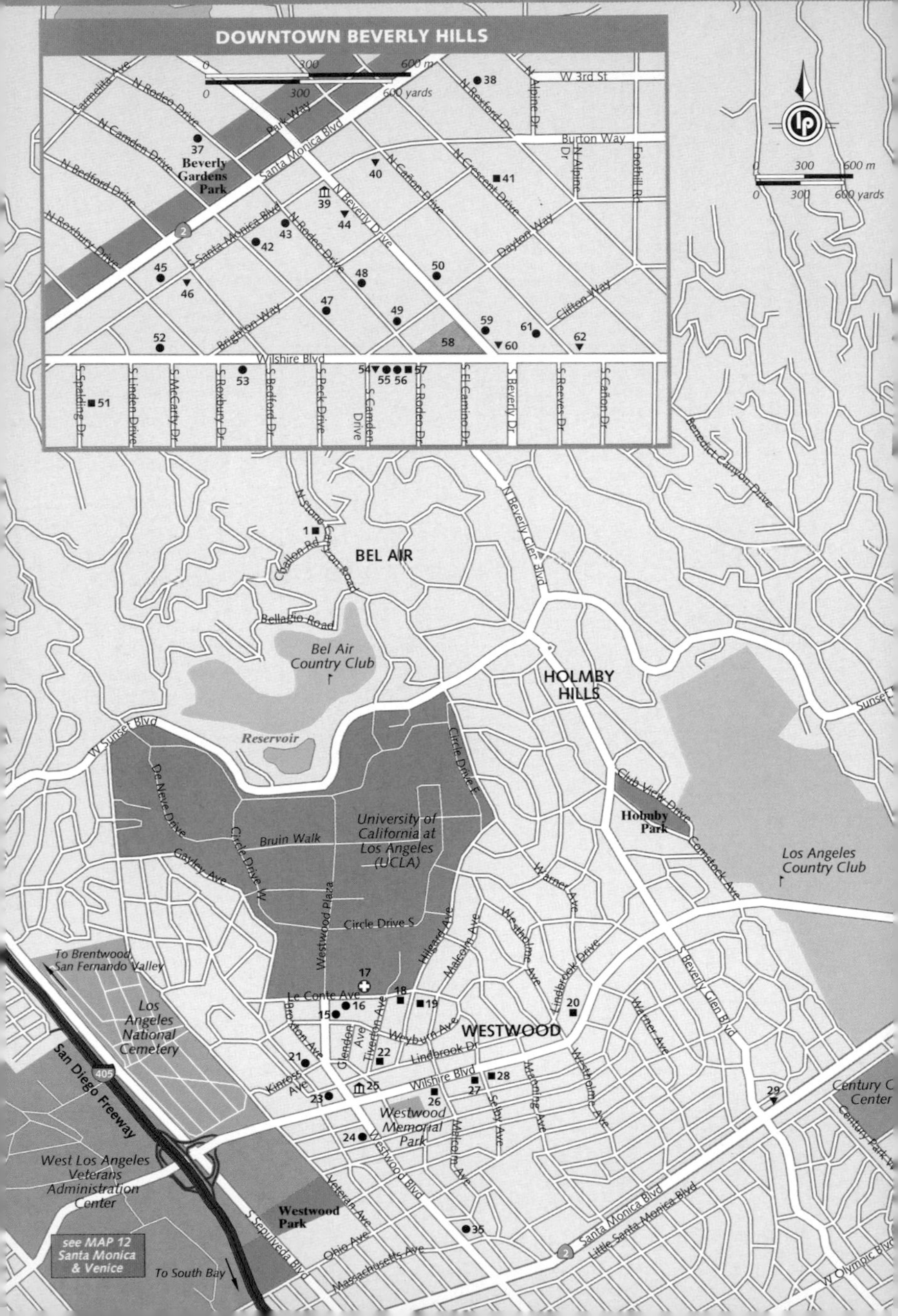

DOWNTOWN BEVERLY HILLS

W 3rd St

■ 38

W Rodeo Dr

W Santa Monica Blvd

Burton Way

N Camden Drive

N Rodeo Drive

Carmelita Ave

N Bedford Dr

37
Beverly Gardens Park

N Beverly Drive

N Canon Drive

N Crescent Drive

■ 41

▼ 40

🏛 39

N Roxbury Drive

S Santa Monica Blvd

N Bedford Drive

Dayton Way

45
46

43
42

▼ 44

N Roxbury Drive

N Rodeo Drive

48

50

Clifton Way

Brighton Way

47

49

59
61

Clifton Way

62 ▼

52

58

60 ▼

Wilshire Blvd

54 ▼ ● ● ■ 57
55 56

53

S Spalding Dr

S Linden Drive

S McCarty Drive

S Bedford Drive

S Peck Drive

S Camden Drive

S Rodeo Drive

S El Camino Dr

Beverly Dr

S Reeves Dr

S Canon Dr

■ 51

BEL AIR

1 ■

Stone Canyon Rd

N Beverly Glen Blvd

Benedict Canyon Drive

Bellagio Road

Bel Air Country Club

HOLMBY HILLS

Sunset

Reservoir

Little Drive E

Club View Drive

Holmby Park

Comstock Ave

Los Angeles Country Club

W Sunset Blvd

De Neve Drive

Circle Drive W

University of California at Los Angeles (UCLA)

Bruin Walk

Gayley Ave

Westwood Plaza

Circle Drive S

To Brentwood San Fernando Valley

Los Angeles National Cemetery

Hilgard Ave

Warner Ave

Malcolm Ave

Westholme Ave

Hilgard Ave

Beverly Glen Blvd

17

Le Conte Ave

18 ■
● 19

✚

15 ●
16 ●

Gayley Ave

Glendon Ave

Weyburn Ave

Lindbrook Dr

20 ■

WESTWOOD

Warner Ave

Wilshire Blvd

San Diego Freeway

405

21 ●

Kinross Ave

Glendon Ave

22 ■
■

29

Century C Center

23 ●

🏛 25

26
27 ■

28 ■

Westwood Memorial Park

Century Park W

24 ●

Veteran Ave

Westwood Blvd

West Los Angeles Veterans Administration Center

35 ●

Westwood Park

San Vicente Blvd

Ohio Ave

Santa Monica Blvd

Little Santa Monica Blvd

see MAP 12 Santa Monica & Venice

To South Bay

Massachusetts Ave

W Olympic B

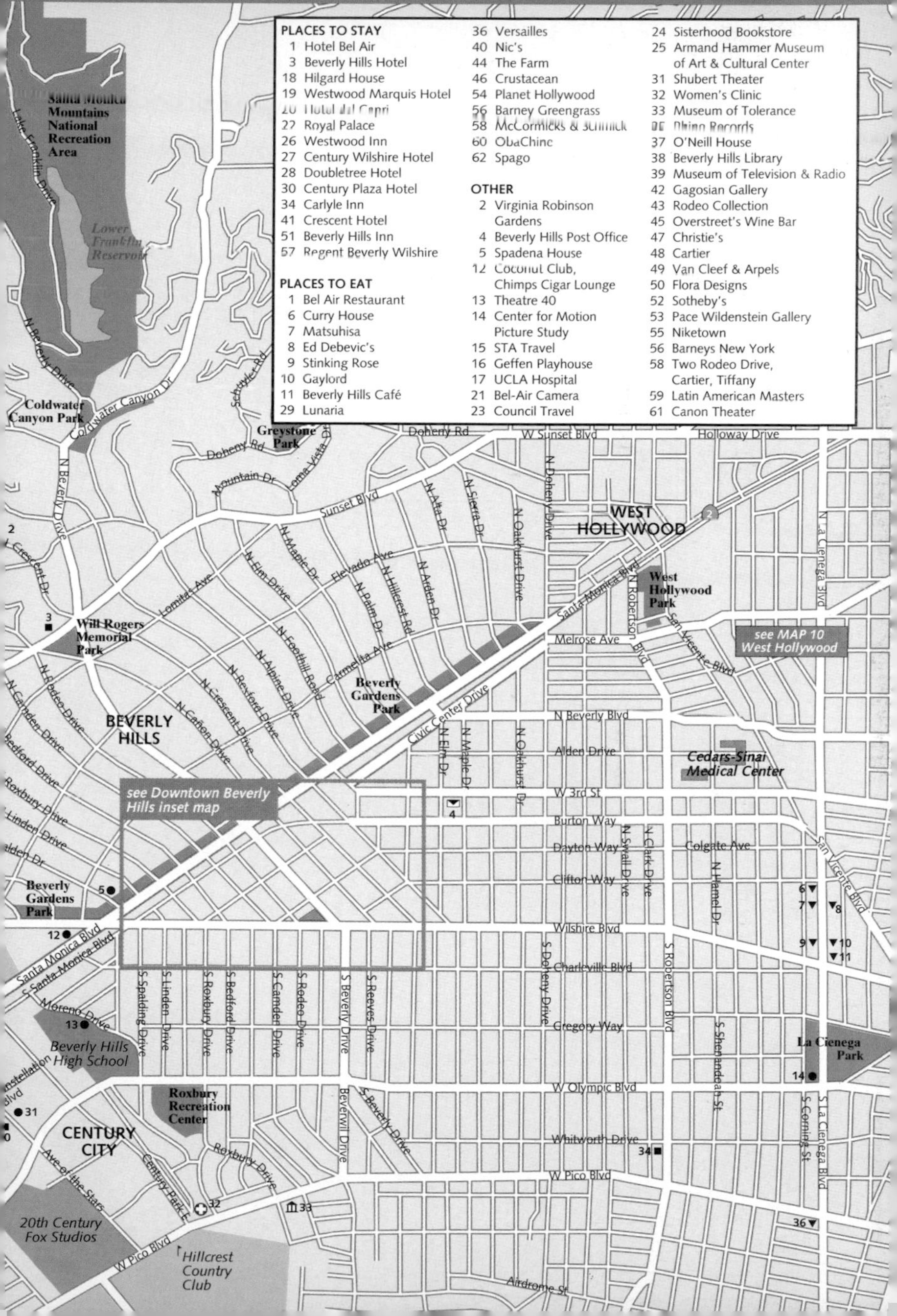
PLACES TO STAY
1 Hotel Bel Air
3 Beverly Hills Hotel
18 Hilgard House
19 Westwood Marquis Hotel
20 Hotel del Capri
22 Royal Palace
26 Westwood Inn
27 Century Wilshire Hotel
28 Doubletree Hotel
30 Century Plaza Hotel
34 Carlyle Inn
41 Crescent Hotel
51 Beverly Hills Inn
57 Regent Beverly Wilshire
PLACES TO EAT
1 Bel Air Restaurant
6 Curry House
7 Matsuhisa
8 Ed Debevic's
9 Stinking Rose
10 Gaylord
11 Beverly Hills Café
29 Lunaria
36 Versailles
40 Nic's
44 The Farm
46 Crustacean
54 Planet Hollywood
56 Barney Greengrass
58 McCormicks & Schmick
60 ObaChine
62 Spago
OTHER
2 Virginia Robinson Gardens
4 Beverly Hills Post Office
5 Spadena House
12 Coconut Club, Chimps Cigar Lounge
13 Theatre 40
14 Center for Motion Picture Study
15 STA Travel
16 Geffen Playhouse
17 UCLA Hospital
21 Bel-Air Camera
23 Council Travel
24 Sisterhood Bookstore
25 Armand Hammer Museum of Art & Cultural Center
31 Shubert Theater
32 Women's Clinic
33 Museum of Tolerance
35 Rhino Records
37 O'Neill House
38 Beverly Hills Library
39 Museum of Television & Radio
42 Gagosian Gallery
43 Rodeo Collection
45 Overstreet's Wine Bar
47 Christie's
48 Cartier
49 Van Cleef & Arpels
50 Flora Designs
52 Sotheby's
53 Pace Wildenstein Gallery
55 Niketown
56 Barneys New York
58 Two Rodeo Drive, Cartier, Tiffany
59 Latin American Masters
61 Canon Theater
Santa Monica Mountains National Recreation Area
Lower Franklin Reservoir
Coldwater Canyon Park
Greystone Park
WEST HOLLYWOOD
West Hollywood Park
see MAP 10 West Hollywood
Will Rogers Memorial Park
BEVERLY HILLS
Beverly Gardens Park
Cedars-Sinai Medical Center
see Downtown Beverly Hills inset map
Beverly Hills High School
Roxbury Recreation Center
CENTURY CITY
La Cienega Park
20th Century Fox Studios
Hillcrest Country Club
W Sunset Blvd
Santa Monica Blvd
Melrose Ave
N Beverly Blvd
Alden Drive
W 3rd St
Burton Way
Wilshire Blvd
Charleville Blvd
Gregory Way
W Olympic Blvd
Whitworth Drive
W Pico Blvd
Airdrome St

MAP 12 SANTA MONICA & VENICE

PLACES TO STAY
7 Channel Road Inn
13 Comfort Inn
16 Days Inn
32 Ocean Lodge
33 Four Points by Sheraton Santa Monica
36 Belle Bleu Inn by the Sea
37 Loews Santa Monica Beach Hotel
38 Shutters on the Beach
42 Sea Shore Motel
59 Hostel California
60 Cadillac Hotel
61 Jim's at the Beach
66 Jolly Roger Hotel
67 Ritz-Carlton Marina del Rey
68 Venice Beach House
72 Foghorn Harbor Inn
72 Marina International Hotel & Bungalows
86 Venice Beach Hostel
87 Venice Beach Cotel
88 Marina Pacific Hotel
98 Miramar Sheraton Hotel
116 Hotel Shangri-La
116 Georgian Hotel
117 Santa Monica HI Hostel
118 Hotel Carmel
121 Best Western Ocean View Hotel

PLACES TO EAT
1 California Pizza Kitchen, Taiko
5 Mishima
9 17th Street Cafe
19 El Cholo
26 Lavande
37 Edgemar Complex, Röckenwagner
40 The Galley
43 Jake & Annie's
44 Chinois on Main
45 Omelette Parlor, Lula's
54 Schatzi's on Main
55 Chaya Venice
57 Rose Cafe
65 Tamara's Tamale
74 Van Go's Ear
75 Joe's
76 A Votre Santé
78 Hal's Bar & Grill
81 Tortilla Grill
83 Abbot Pizza
84 Sidewalk Cafe
85 72 Market Street
89 Jodi Maroni's Sausage Kingdom
91 Newsroom
92 Wild Oats Food Market
100 Light House Buffet
102 Wolfgang Puck Express
107 Border Grill
109 Crocodile Cafe
110 Ocean Avenue Seafood
111 Ye Olde King's Head
113 Eatz
124 I Cugini

OTHER
2 Leslie Sacks Gallery
3 Ernie Wolfe Gallery
4 Nuart
6 Odyssey Theater Ensemble
8 Aero
10 O'Brien's
11 Red Setter
12 Bodies in Motion
15 The Gig
17 St Stephen's Green
18 Anastasia's Asylum
20 Boulevard Camera
21 NuWilshire Cinema
22 Santa Monica-UCLA Medical Center
23 A&I Photo Lab
24 Highways Performance Space
25 Bergamot Station,
27 McCabe's Guitar Shop
28 California Map & Travel
29 Santa Monica Antique Market
30 Planetarium
31 Museum of Flying
34 Pacific Park
35 Carousel, UCLA Ocean Discovery Center, Rusty's Surf Ranch
41 Z-Jay Boarding House
46 World Cafe
47 Star Wares
48 O'Brien's
49 Novel Cafe
50 Gold's Gym
51 DNA
52 Venice Family Clinic
53 Gourmet Coffee Warehouse
56 Venice Renaissance Building
58 Chat/Day Building
62 Venice Chamber of Commerce
63 Scruffy O'Shea's
70 Marina del Rey Chamber of Commerce
71 Mother's Beach
73 Fishermen's Village
77 Cyber Java
79 Tantau Smith
80 Roosterfish
82 Abbot's Habit
90 Small World Books
90 LA Louver Gallery
93 Toppers Bar
94 Santa Monica Playhouse
95 Post Office
96 The West End
97 Santa Monica Library
99 American Express
101 Midnight Special Bookstore
103 STA Travel
105 Laemmle Theater
106 Harvelle's
108 Fred Segal
112 Gotham Hall
114 Greyhound Bus Station
115 Angels Attic Museum
119 Interactive Cafe
120 Santa Monica Visitors Bureau
122 Lone Wolf Cigar Lounge
123 Camera Obscura

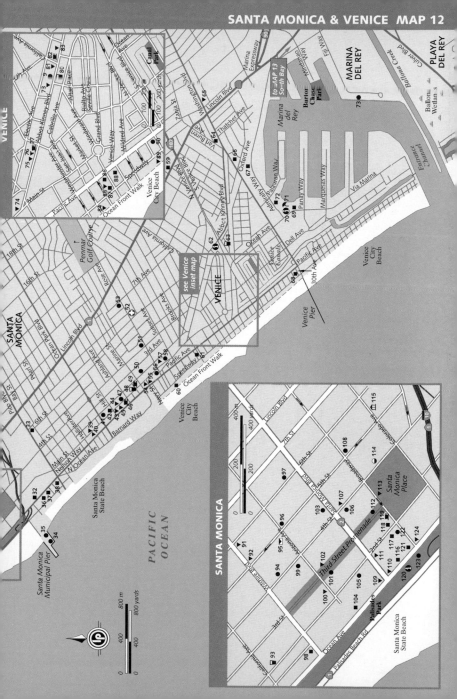

VENICE

SANTA MONICA

MARINA DEL REY

PLAYA DEL REY

Burton Chase Park

Marina del Rey

Entrance Channel

Venice City Beach

Penmar Golf Course

see Venice inset map

Venice Pier

Venice City Beach

PACIFIC OCEAN

Santa Monica State Beach

Santa Monica Municipal Pier

Santa Monica

Third Street Promenade

Santa Monica Place

Palisades Park

Santa Monica State Beach

Palisades Beach Rd

Canal Park

Ocean Front Walk

to MAP 13 So-th Bay

Ballona Creek

Ballona Wetlan s

0   400   800 m
0   400   800 yards

0   200   400 m
0   200   400 yards

0   100   200 yards
0   100   200 m

MAP 13 SOUTH BAY

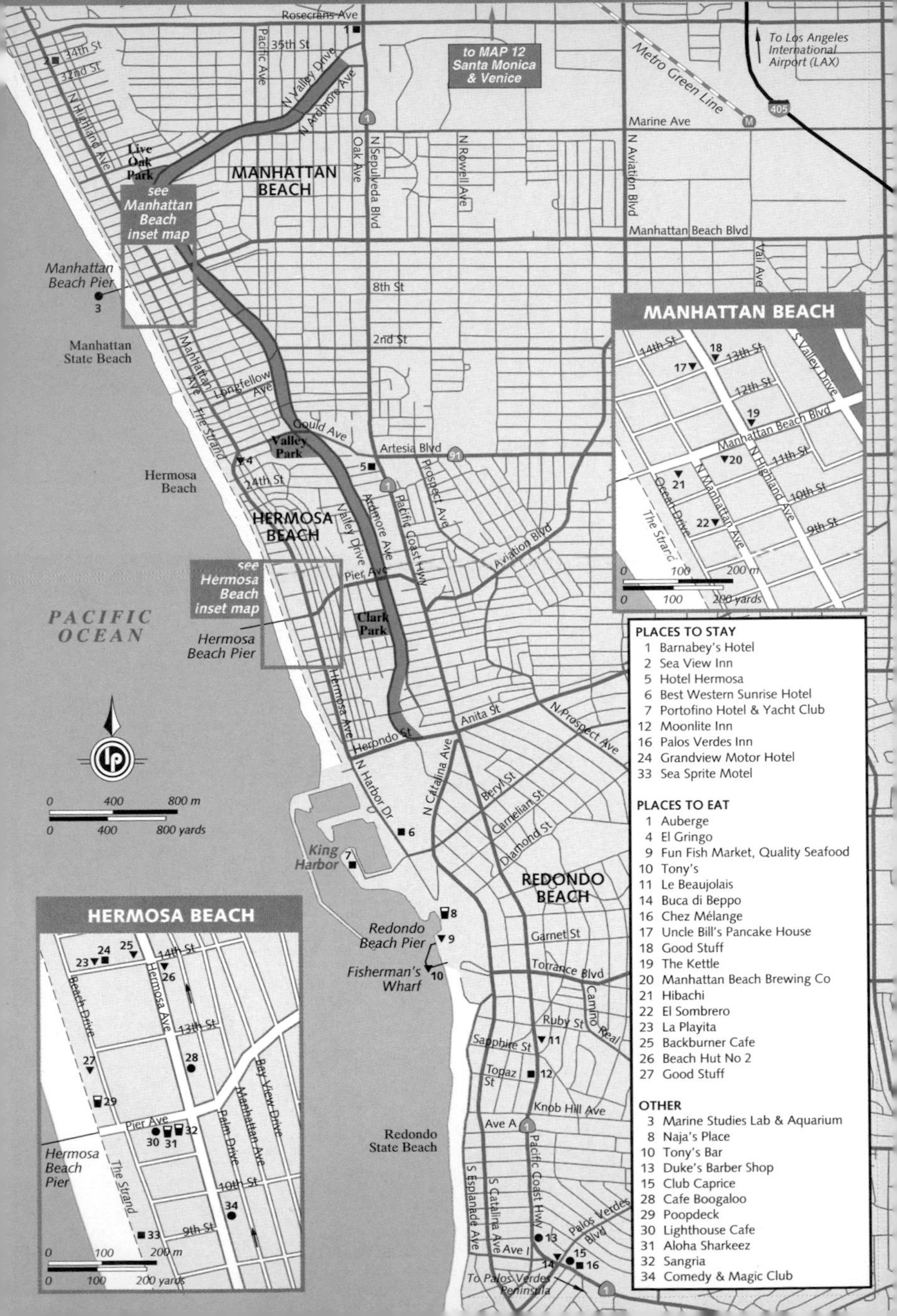

Rosecrans Ave
14th St
32nd St
35th St
Pacific Ave
N Valley Drive
N Anthony Ave
Oak Ave
N Sepulveda Blvd
N Rowell Ave
to MAP 12
Santa Monica
& Venice
Metro Green Line
To Los Angeles
International
Airport (LAX)
Marine Ave
405
M

Live Oak Park
MANHATTAN BEACH
see Manhattan Beach inset map
Manhattan Beach Blvd
8th St
2nd St

Manhattan Beach Pier
Manhattan State Beach
3

Manhattan Ave
Hermosa Ave
Longfellow Ave
Gould Ave
Artesia Blvd
Valley Park
4
5
24th St
Hermosa Beach
HERMOSA BEACH
Valley Drive
Ardmore Ave
Pacific Coast Hwy
Prospect Ave
Aviation Blvd

see Hermosa Beach inset map
Hermosa Beach Pier
Pier Ave
Clark Park
6

PACIFIC OCEAN

Hermosa Ave
Redondo St
Anita St
N Prospect Ave
N Harbor Dr
N Catalina Ave
8th St
Carnelian St
Diamond St
REDONDO BEACH

King Harbor
7
6

Redondo Beach Pier
Fisherman's Wharf
8
9
10

Garnet St
Torrance Blvd
Camino Real
Ruby St
Sapphire St
11
Topaz St
12
Knob Hill Ave
Ave A
Pacific Coast Hwy
S Esplanade Ave
S Catalina Ave / Ave I
Palos Verdes Blvd

Redondo State Beach

13
15 16
1

To Palos Verdes Peninsula

MANHATTAN BEACH (inset)
14th St
13th St
12th St
11th St
10th St
9th St
N Valley Drive
Manhattan Beach Blvd
Queens Drive
N Manhattan Ave
N Highland Ave
The Strand
17
18
19
20
21
22
0   100   200 m
0   100   200 yards

HERMOSA BEACH (inset)
14th St
13th St
Beach Drive
Hermosa Ave
Bay View Drive
Manhattan Ave
Palm Drive
Pier Ave
The Strand
10th St
9th St
Hermosa Beach Pier
23
24 25
26
27
28
29
30 31
32
33
34
0   100   200 m
0   100   200 yards

0   400   800 m
0   400   800 yards

PLACES TO STAY
1   Barnabey's Hotel
2   Sea View Inn
5   Hotel Hermosa
6   Best Western Sunrise Hotel
7   Portofino Hotel & Yacht Club
12 Moonlite Inn
16 Palos Verdes Inn
24 Grandview Motor Hotel
33 Sea Sprite Motel

PLACES TO EAT
1   Auberge
4   El Gringo
9   Fun Fish Market, Quality Seafood
10 Tony's
11 Le Beaujolais
14 Buca di Beppo
17 Uncle Bill's Pancake House
19 The Kettle
20 Manhattan Beach Brewing Co
21 Hibachi
22 El Sombrero
23 La Playita
25 Backburner Cafe
26 Beach Hut No 2
27 Good Stuff

OTHER
3   Marine Studies Lab & Aquarium
8   Naja's Place
10 Tony's Bar
13 Duke's Barber Shop
15 Club Caprice
28 Cafe Boogaloo
29 Poopdeck
30 Lighthouse Cafe
31 Aloha Sharkeez
32 Sangria
34 Comedy & Magic Club

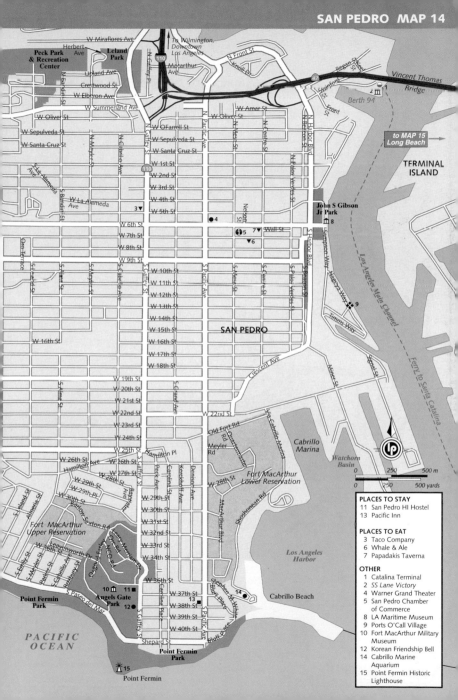

PLACES TO STAY
11 San Pedro HI Hostel
13 Pacific Inn

PLACES TO EAT
3 Taco Company
6 Whale & Ale
7 Papadakis Taverna

OTHER
1 Catalina Terminal
2 SS Lane Victory
4 Warner Grand Theater
5 San Pedro Chamber
   of Commerce
8 LA Maritime Museum
9 Ports O'Call Village
10 Fort MacArthur Military
    Museum
12 Korean Friendship Bell
14 Cabrillo Marine
    Aquarium
15 Point Fermin Historic
    Lighthouse

MAP 15 LONG BEACH

To Downtown Los Angeles

710

1 Pacific Coast Hwy

Esther St
17th St
16th St
15th St
Cowles St
14th St

16th St

15th St

1

To Brooks College

Metro Blue Line

Linden Ave

Martin Luther King Jr Ave

New York Ave

15th St

Anaheim St

De Forest Ave

Loma Vista

12th St
11th St
10th St
9th St
8th St

Magnolia Ave

Chestnut Ave

Cedar Ave

Pacific Ave

Pine Ave

Locust Ave

11th St

Long Beach Blvd

Atlantic Ave

1

Drake Park

Maine Ave

Hellman St

3

7th St

7th St

6th St
5th St
4th St
3rd St
Broadway

Daisy Ave

Golden Ave

Metro Blue Line

4

5

7

8

9

10

11

15

Long Beach Plaza

Elm Ave

Linden Ave

Elm Ave

Olive Ave

4th St

6

E 3rd St

12

13

E Appleton Ave
E Broadway
E 2nd St

N Harbor Scenic Drive

Los Angeles River

Golden Park

14

Ocean Blvd

to MAP 14 San Pedro

710

Seaside Way

Lincoln Park

16

Seaside Way

1st St

E 1st St
Bronce St

Ocean Blvd

To Long Beach Museum of Art, Gondola Getaway

Rainbow Lagoon

Shoreline Drive

San Pedro Bay

Queensway Landing

Queensway Bridge

Lagoon

Pacific Terrace Harbor

17

Shoreline Aquatic Park

Rainbow Lagoon Park

18

Shoreline Village

Downtown Long Beach Marina

East Basin

Harbor Scenic Drive

Queensway Bay

Queensway Drive

Harbor Plaza

20

19

21

22

Queens Hwy N

Queens Hwy S

Pier F

Pier G Ave N
Pier G Ave S

Pier G

Pier J Ave

Pier J

Harbor Scenic Drive

Pier J Way

Basin 6

Southeast Basin

0   250   500 m
0   250   500 yards

PLACES TO STAY
4 The Turret House
5 The Lord Mayor
6 Beach Inn Motel
13 Inn of Long Beach
21 Hotel Queen Mary

PLACES TO EAT
2 ChaChaCha
8 Alegria Cocina Latina
10 Mum's
16 Sky Room

OTHER
1 St Mary's Medical Center
3 Museum of Latin American Art
7 Greyhound Bus Station
9 Blue Cafe
10 Club Cohiba
11 Transit Terminal
12 Acres of Books
14 World Trade Center,
   Long Beach Visitors Bureau
15 Jillian's, The Vault
17 Aquarium of the Pacific
18 Yard House
19 Scorpion
20 Catalina Express Port
21 Queen Mary
22 Queen Mary Marketplace

PLACES TO STAY
5 Doubletree Hotel
9 Westway Inn
10 Saga Motor Hotel
12 Pasadena Holiday Inn
15 Pasadena Hilton
19 Best Western
    Colorado Inn
22 The Artists' Inn
24 Bissell House
25 Ritz-Carlton
    Huntington Hotel
27 Pasadena Hotel

PLACES TO EAT
1 Holoworld
29 Akbar
30 Mi Place
31 Trattoria Farfalla
32 Xiomara, Yujear Kang
33 Twin Palms
34 Jerry's Famous Deli
36 Sorriso
37 Rack Shack
40 Buca di Beppo
41 La Luna Negra

11 Vista De Arroyo Hotel,
    Court of Appeals
13 Pasadena Ice Skating Center
14 Pasadena Visitors Bureau
16 Pasadena Playhouse
17 Colonnade
18 Burlington Arcade
20 Wrigley Mansion & Gardens
21 Kidspace
23 Bodies in Motion
26 Gordon Biersch Brewery
28 Equator Coffeehouse
35 Penny Lane
39 Knightsbridge Theater
42 Distant Lands Bookstore
    Hotel Green Castle Green

OTHER
2 Norton Simon Museum
3 Public Library
4 City Hall
6 Pacific Asia Museum
7 Vroman's Bookstore
8 Ice House

DOWNTOWN PASADENA

PASADENA

SAN MARINO

see Downtown
Pasadena
inset map

Huntington Library,
Art Collection
& Botanical Gardens

California
Institute of
Technology
(Caltech)

Pasadena
City
College

Memorial
Park

Central
Park

Foothill Freeway

Pasadena Freeway

Long Beach
Freeway

Ventura Freeway

Rose
Bowl

Brookside
Park

Lower
Arroyo
Park

Arroyo Seco

**to MAP 5
Downtown
Los Angeles**

MAP 17 BURBANK, NORTH HOLLYWOOD & UNIVERSAL CITY

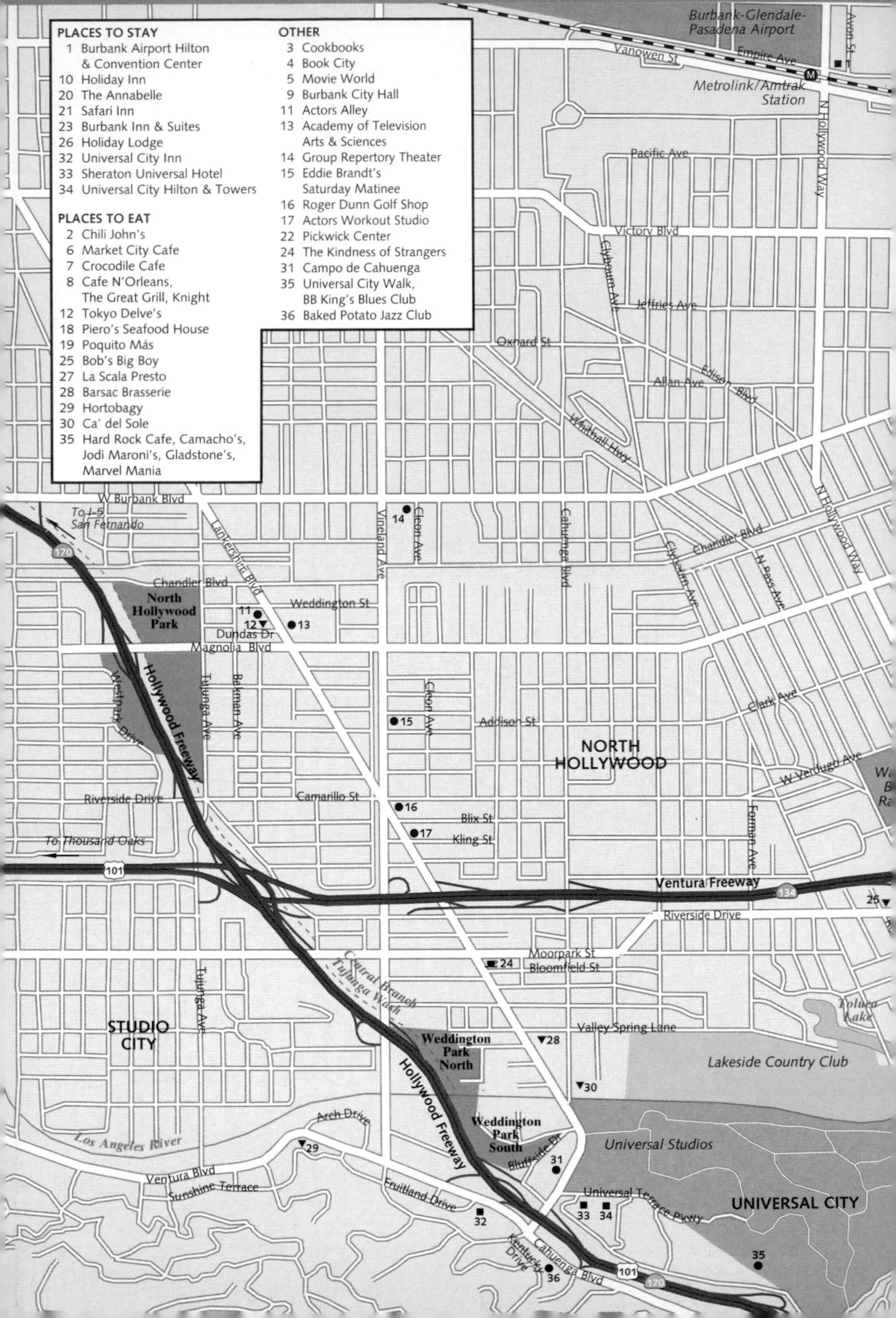

PLACES TO STAY
1 Burbank Airport Hilton
  & Convention Center
10 Holiday Inn
20 The Annabelle
21 Safari Inn
23 Burbank Inn & Suites
26 Holiday Lodge
32 Universal City Inn
33 Sheraton Universal Hotel
34 Universal City Hilton & Towers

PLACES TO EAT
2 Chili John's
6 Market City Cafe
7 Crocodile Cafe
8 Cafe N'Orleans,
  The Great Grill, Knight
12 Tokyo Delve's
18 Piero's Seafood House
19 Poquito Más
25 Bob's Big Boy
27 La Scala Presto
28 Barsac Brasserie
29 Hortobagy
30 Ca' del Sole
35 Hard Rock Cafe, Camacho's,
  Jodi Maroni's, Gladstone's,
  Marvel Mania

OTHER
3 Cookbooks
4 Book City
5 Movie World
9 Burbank City Hall
11 Actors Alley
13 Academy of Television
  Arts & Sciences
14 Group Repertory Theater
15 Eddie Brandt's
  Saturday Matinee
16 Roger Dunn Golf Shop
17 Actors Workout Studio
22 Pickwick Center
24 The Kindness of Strangers
31 Campo de Cahuenga
35 Universal City Walk,
  BB King's Blues Club
36 Baked Potato Jazz Club

Burbank-Glendale-
Pasadena Airport

Vanowen St

Empire Ave

Metrolink/Amtrak
Station

Pacific Ave

Victory Blvd

Jeffries Ave

Oxnard St

Allan Ave

W Burbank Blvd

To I-5
San Fernando

Chandler Blvd

North
Hollywood
Park

Weddington St

Dundas Dr
Magnolia Blvd

Addison St

NORTH
HOLLYWOOD

W Verdugo Ave

Camarillo St

Riverside Drive

To Thousand Oaks

Blix St
Kling St

Ventura Freeway

Riverside Drive

Moorpark St
Bloomfield St

STUDIO
CITY

Weddington
Park
North

Valley Spring Lane

Lakeside Country Club

Toluca
Lake

Arch Drive

Los Angeles River

Weddington
Park
South

Universal Studios

Ventura Blvd
Sunshine Terrace

Fruitland Drive

Universal Terrace Pkwy

UNIVERSAL CITY

Kentucky
Drive

Cahuenga Blvd

MAP LEGEND

BOUNDARIES

- ··—··—··— International
- ——·——·—— State
- ——— ——— County

HYDROGRAPHY

- Water
- Coastline
- Beach
- River, Waterfall
- Swamp, Spring

ROUTES & TRANSPORT

- Freeway
- Toll Freeway
- Primary Road
- Secondary Road
- Tertiary Road
- Unpaved Road
- Pedestrian Mall
- Trail
- Ferry Route
- Railway, Train Station
- Metrolink Line & Station

METRO LINES & STATIONS

- —Ⓜ— Red Line
- —Ⓜ— Blue Line
- —Ⓜ— Green Line

ROUTE SHIELDS

- 5 Interstate
- 101 US Highway
- 1 State Highway
- N1 County Road

AREA FEATURES

- Park, Garden
- Cemetery
- Plaza
- Golf Course

MAP SYMBOLS

☉	NATIONAL CAPITAL	✝	Airfield	⚓	Mosque
◉	State, Provincial Capital	✈	Airport	▲	Mountain
●	LARGE CITY	∴	Archaeological Site, Ruins	🏛	Museum
●	Medium City	⑤	Bank	⌂	Observatory
●	Small City	🕊	Beach	←	One-Way Street
●	Town, Village	✦	Border Crossing	♠	Park
○	Point of Interest	◡	Bus Depot, Bus Stop	▣	Parking
		⊞	Cathedral	)(	Pass
		◠	Cave	⊓	Picnic Area
		✝	Church	★	Police Station
		◣	Dive Site	⌷	Pool
		◯	Embassy	▾	Post Office
■	Place to Stay	◡	Ferry Terminal	✧	Shopping Mall
⚐	Campground	⨞	Foot Bridge	⛷	Skiing (Alpine)
⛽	RV Park	▣	Gas Station	⛸	Skiing (Nordic)
		↑	Golf Course	⛫	Stately Home
		⊕	Hospital, Clinic	▣	Tomb, Mausoleum
▼	Place to Eat	❶	Information	⚑	Trailhead
⚑	Bar (Place to Drink)	☒	Lighthouse	⫽	Windsurfing
☕	Cafe	✳	Lookout	⚘	Winery
		⛊	Monument	🐘	Zoo

Note: Not all symbols displayed above appear in this book.

LONELY PLANET OFFICES

Australia
PO Box 617, Hawthorn 3122, Victoria
☎ (03) 9819 1877 fax (03) 9819 6459
email talk2us@lonelyplanet.com.au

USA
150 Linden Street, Oakland, California 94607
☎ (510) 893 8555, TOLL FREE (800) 275 8555
fax (510) 893 8572
email info@lonelyplanet.com

UK
10A Spring Place, London NW5 3BH
☎ (0171) 428 4800 fax (0171) 428 4828
email go@lonelyplanet.co.uk

France
1 rue du Dahomey, 75011 Paris
☎ 01 55 25 33 00 fax 01 55 25 33 01
email bip@lonelyplanet.fr
3615 lonelyplanet *(1,29 F TTC/min)*

World Wide Web: www.lonelyplanet.com *or* AOL keyword: lp
Lonely Planet Images: lpi@lonelyplanet.com.au